Planet Google

Randall Stross is a professor of business at San José State University. He writes the *New York Times* column 'Digital Domain', and is the author of a number of critically acclaimed books, including *The Wizard of Menlo Park*, *eBoys*, and *The Microsoft Way*. He lives in Burlingame, California.

Also by Randall Stross

The Wizard of Menlo Park

eBoys

The Microsoft Way

Steve Jobs and the NeXT Big Thing

Bulls in the China Shop

The Stubborn Earth

Technology and Society in Twentieth-Century America (editor)

Planet Google

How One Company is Transforming our Lives

RANDALL STROSS

Atlantic Books
LONDON

First published in hardback the United States of America in 2008
by Free Press, a division of Simon & Schuster, Inc.,
1230 Avenue of the Americas,
New York, NY 10020.

First published in hardback and export and airside trade paperback
in Great Britain in 2008 by Atlantic Books,
an imprint of Grove/Atlantic Inc.

1 3 5 7 9 10 8 6 4 2

A CIP catalogue record for this book is available from
the British Library.

Hardback ISBN: 978 1 84354 980 2
Export and Airside ISBN: 978 1 84354 981 9

Printed in Great Britain

Atlantic Books
An imprint of Grove Atlantic Ltd
Ormond House
26–27 Boswell Street
London WC1N 3JZ

www.atlantic-books.co.uk

For H. Joy Stross

Contents

Planet Google

Introduction

Google began with a grand aspiration: organize the world's information. Lofty aspirations alone are not noteworthy—they are commonplace in every tiny start-up in Silicon Valley. What sets Google apart is the rapidity of its growth since its founding in 1998, growth that has, in turn, provided the company with the capital, smarts, technology, and brand to make its founders' extravagant wish to organize the world's information seem like a practical, one-item to-do list.

In the course of quickly becoming a ubiquitous presence—by 2003, a mere five years after the company's founding, the popularity of *google,* the verb, was formally recognized by the American Dialect Society—Google has undertaken initiatives to attain comprehensive control of information. It has made great progress in expanding in numerous directions, doing so well ahead of our ability to notice the details or the cumulative impact. This book explores how Google has grown up and out, how early technology choices enabled it to extend its reach without limit, how its pursuit of information of all kinds has brought it unrivaled power, and how its power affects the general interests of everyone, for better or for ill.

Google version 1.0 searched Web pages. Google 2.0 has been reaching outward beyond Web pages, omnivorously. Books, news, and videos are three of many categories of information that Google has added to its storehouses, bringing it into conflict with entire industries: book publishing, newspapers, and television entertainment.

In other industries, it has acted at times as provocateur, and at other times as a friendly ally of everyone. In the wireless industry, for example, it had sufficient cash on hand in early 2008 to indulge in a playful multibillion-dollar game with Verizon, AT&T, and other bidders in the federal government's spectrum auction. Google put $4.71 billion on the line for spectrum that it did not really want. (A Google manager later described his team's anxiety that it might win: "We kept hitting the 'refresh' button on the browser" to see if other companies had bid higher, which eventually they did.) Google also has befriended a sizable and still growing segment of the wireless industry since it decided to organize and lead a coalition of companies that will introduce new cell phone handsets based on software that Google designed.

Google's growth has not been held back by pride: when it has failed in its efforts to gain new markets that it desires, it will spend the large sums needed to acquire the companies that possess what it seeks. YouTube essentially owned the online video market, and cost Google $1.65 billion to acquire in 2006. DoubleClick essentially owned the dominating advertising network that places banner advertising on Web sites, and cost Google $3.1 billion to acquire in 2008.

As Google has expanded well beyond Web search, introducing new services developed in its own labs and absorbing market-leading companies that it acquired, the company has managed for the most part to maintain an appearance of benign innocence. Its senior executives do not speak in the militaristic language common in business—the lexicon of raw ambition, conquest, and mastery. Instead, they speak in the bland language of science and engineering, and the uplifting language of public service. The company was fortunate during its rise to acquire a patina of historical inevitability. Every age—coal, steel, oil—has a raw material that defines its historical moment. In ours it is information, and Google has become its preeminent steward.

The sense of historical predestination is illusory, however, an artifact of hindsight. Google's power derives from its financial base, which was built upon an accidental discovery, two years after the company's founding, that plain text advertisements on its search results pages produce enormous profits. Neither Larry Page nor Sergey Brin, the company's cofounders, who met as graduate students in computer science at Stanford University, predicted—nor did anyone else—that those unobtrusive ads would form the foundation of a business that within seven years would be accorded by investors a historic high valuation, in early November 2007, of $225 billion.

The ad giveth, and the ad taketh away, too. Bright future prospects for those ads drove Google's share price up to its historic peak, and when future prospects for continued growth in ad revenue dimmed, investors' interest cooled. In the last quarter of 2007, Google enjoyed 30 percent annual growth in the number of clicks on its paid ads, but the growth disappeared in early 2008. When evidence surfaced that the number of clicks in the first two months of 2008 was flat, and when dark economic clouds gathered, portending a global recession and a difficult market for ad sales for Google by mid-March 2008, investors sent Google's share price down 45 percent from its historic peak of $747. Then, when Google reported in April that its ad sales in the first quarter of 2008 had remained strong, its shares soared 20 percent in a single day.

Google's dependence upon text ads is especially remarkable given that advertising was entirely absent in the original business plans of the founders. When the Google search engine was first made available to the public, visitors noticed superior search results, but they also noticed the service was entirely free of commercial messages. Google spared them the irritating pop-ups, flashing banners, and other mutating forms of advertisements that at that time were competing in an escalating arms race for a visitor's attention on the Web.

Brin and Page were hostile to the very notion of permitting advertising on a search site. In an April 1998 academic paper prepared when they were still students, they criticized "advertising funded search engines," which they believed would be "inherently biased towards the advertisers and away from the needs of the consumers." They argued that for a search engine to remain immune from the temptation of biased results, it would have to remain "in the academic realm."

Even after Google moved from its first home, a Stanford dorm, to a rented garage off campus, Brin and Page moved cautiously in permitting advertising on their site. They decided to introduce advertisements as an experiment, restricting the format to three very short lines of text and a Web address, which were placed on the right margin of the search results page and displayed only if the advertisement was directly relevant to the search term. This was sufficiently unorthodox that even some within Google were skeptical that plain text ads would succeed in attracting attention. Marissa Mayer, a Google vice president and early employee, later recalled that a colleague leaned over at the meeting that settled on the details of the text-only advertising and predicted, "You wait, in a month, we'll be selling banners."

When Google offered the ads on a trial basis in 2000, prospective advertisers were invited to spend a modest sum to see if plain text ads, matched to the keyword phrase used in a search, would draw customers. The effectiveness of the ads was easy to measure: only if a user clicked on the ad was it deemed successful. Google's offer was risk free for advertisers: they would pay only when users clicked.

Initially, the text ads were displayed so sparingly that they went largely unnoticed. The self-imposed requirement that advertisements had to be meaningfully related to the search phrase meant that in 85 percent of all Google searches in 2000, no advertisements were shown at all because the search phrase had no relation to any commercial product or service offered by Google's advertisers. Brin said in an interview at the time that he heard Google visitors report that they never saw an advertisement. Even in 2001, the advertisements were still so unobtrusive that how Google made money remained a mystery to journalists and analysts. The founders showed no indication that they foresaw how important advertising would be to the company: Google also earned money from licensing its search engine technology to other companies, like Yahoo, and that seemed to everyone at Google to be as promising a source of revenue as any other.

As late as 2002, four years after the company's founding, Google's text advertisements seemed, at least to some informed observers, to be so insignificant that the company's ability to ever turn a profit seemed uncertain. The *New York Times* ran a story whose headline preserved the prevalent view that Google still lacked a means to make money: "Google's Toughest Search Is for a Business Model." Yuri Punj, an analyst at UBS Warburg, said, "The Internet advertising model has been shown not to work. We all know in business that free doesn't work. I think Google will realize that they have to go to some paid search capability." Indeed, Google's own Omid Kordestani, a senior vice president who oversaw sales, wondered aloud whether Google might charge for its service in the future.

Those unprepossessing text ads, however, were providing advertisers one of the most cost-effective ways of reaching desirable customers ever devised in the history of advertising. It took a while before this was noticed. Achieving a one-to-one match between an advertiser and a receptive viewer is not only feasible, but relatively easy, because the very act of submitting a search term provides precise information about what a user is currently thinking about—permitting a highly educated guess about the user's likely interest in an advertiser's product. Freed of the inefficiencies of broadcasting a message to those who may or may not happen to be in a receptive frame of mind, Google's advertisers are happy. And by setting up an auction system, in which interested advertisers bid against one another for the price they are willing to pay Google if a user clicks on their advertisements, Google is happy.

By 2002, Google's revenue passed $400 million and then grew even faster—to $1.4 billion in 2003, $6.1 billion in 2005, $16.5 billion in 2007. Net income increased apace, growing from $100 million in 2002 to $4.2 billion in 2007.

Ninety-nine percent of its revenue still is generated by those simple text ads, many of which now appear on the Web pages of affiliates, companies with whom Google has arranged to place ads and receive a share of the advertising revenue. No annoying visual gimmicks are needed. Just a handful of words, placed before the right online audience in the right frame of mind at the right time, works wonders.

As Google reached out to affiliates, it relaxed its text-only rule, permitting advertisers to use display, banner, and video ads on the non-Google sites in its affiliate network. But for years Google resisted pressure from advertisers to tamper with the plain text format on its own search results pages. The text format had been instrumental in Google's earliest growth and remained the sentimental favorite of veteran Google employees.

In early 2008, however, Google began a trial experiment that placed links to video ads on its own search results pages. It vowed it would not introduce the noise of the arcade, nor would it force any viewer to watch a video ad involuntarily. The online commercials do not roll—and Google is not paid—unless a user clicks on a plus sign that accompanies the otherwise ordinary text ad. The company said the video ads have to conform to the same principle applied when text ads are selected for placement on search results pages: all ads, of whatever format, must be directly relevant to the search. "If you search for golf clubs," Marissa Mayer explained, "you get ads for golf clubs, not a banner ad about Pepsi that you may drink on the golf course."

The best minds at Yahoo, Microsoft, and Google's smaller rivals have spent years trying to replicate Google's ad-placing formulas and all have failed to do so. Each advertisement Google places is so much more likely to attract a click and generate revenue that Yahoo in June 2006 struck an agreement with Google to outsource a portion of its own search advertising. Assuming the deal were to pass antitrust review, it was expected to generate $250 million to $450 million in increased cash flow for Yahoo in the first year of the four-year agreement, even after Yahoo shared the advertising revenue with Google. Jerry Yang, Yahoo's CEO, expressed the rather fanciful hope that "the financial benefits of better monetizing our search traffic" by relying on Google would help to strengthen Yahoo's "independent search business."

The profits generated by its ads have provided Google with ample means to add to its collection of Web pages, adding indexes of published items in a variety of formats, including news, books, scholarly journals, street maps, satellite images, corporate financial information, patents, and more. Google has also started collecting personal information about its users. If you so choose, Google stores your photos, videos, e-mail messages, calendar, word processing documents, spreadsheets, presentation slides, bookmarks to your favorite Web pages, online discussion groups, personal blog, instant messaging chats, social network messages, and stock portfolio. No category is too personal to be deemed unsuitable for Google's organizing—one's medical records can also be included, with the launch in May 2008 of Google Health. And Google's reach extends right into the home: the files that sit on your personal computer can be indexed by Google software, if you give it permission to do so.

Personal data will be collected by other software developers, which Google has invited to build applications on top of Google's infrastructure. In April 2008 when Google introduced its new program the Google App Engine, its pitch to developers highlighted three features: No assembly required. It's easy to scale. It's free to get started.

Google's expansion has been smoothed by its disarmingly anticorporate persona, the one known for its self-assigned "Don't Be Evil" mantra and the one that gives its home page over to the primary colors in its company name, lots of unused white background, and the button that asks whether one is feeling lucky. When the *New York Times* published a story in 2006 with the headline "Planet Google Wants You," it ran in the Fashion & Style section, not in business. It was a light piece on Google's popularity, not an alarm raised about Google's push for what the article called global ubiquity.

As Google has pushed outward, all has not gone smoothly. The colonization of Planet Google has taken it to places in which host governments restrict the access of citizens to Google's services. In 2006, Google had to decide whether to set up a Google site located in China that would filter out search results deemed sensitive by the Chinese government, or operate outside of China, as it had been doing, which made it easy for the Chinese government to block access to Google completely. Constructing what it called an "evil scale" to weigh which course of action was less evil, it decided to set up in China, which it viewed as a step toward the eventual goal of providing full, unfiltered access to information. Its critics saw the move as craven and "Don't Be Evil" as hollow.

Google still wears a white hat, at least in the eyes of those who see Microsoft as the Evil Empire. Google's ambition now includes persuading customers to adopt a new model for personal computing, one that directly threatens Microsoft. The company known for search already has much of the necessary infrastructure, it turns out, to perform more tasks than search, such as creating documents like those that Microsoft Office's Word, Excel, and PowerPoint applications produce. Google has begun to offer "software as a service," using its own software and storing and processing users' data on remote servers run by the company. The more that users rely upon Google's Office-like software, the less need they will have to purchase and maintain software for a desktop computer.

The computer industry has adopted a newish phrase, *cloud computing,* for this model of highly centralized computing. A user's documents will seem to float in cyberspace, accessible from anywhere with an Internet connection. The vision is not new—Sun Microsystems and a number of other computer companies had attempted a decade earlier to proselytize network computing, but the network was not ready and their marketing efforts failed. Today, the idea refurbished now as cloud computing seems feasible in all the ways it hadn't earlier. But new complications have come to the fore. Some environmental critics see the "cloud" as a gauzy euphemism for data centers that sit not on a diaphanous cloud but solidly on earth, consuming enormous amounts of scarce energy. By 2006, data centers already consumed more power in the United States than did television sets.

When Google was founded in 1998, broadband Internet connections were not in place and cloud computing simply was not possible. Google's search business certainly posed no possible threat to Microsoft's profitable Windows and Office businesses. Yet today, Google, with its multifarious interests, constitutes the most formidable challenger that Microsoft has ever faced. Google is still a much smaller company—its $16.5 billion in sales in 2007 are dwarfed by Microsoft's $51 billion. In terms of market capitalization, Google was the tenth largest U.S. company ($180 billion in June 2008) when Microsoft was the third largest ($270 billion). But Microsoft realizes which of the two is best positioned for the future, and its bid for Yahoo was widely interpreted as an expression of its fear of competing against Google alone.

For years Microsoft has tried to match Google by improving its own search and online advertising capabilities, and investing in its own nascent services in the cloud. Failing to make much headway, it decided to make its hostile bid for Yahoo. By offering a 62 percent premium on Yahoo's share price at the time of its offer in January 2008, Microsoft revealed the extent of its desperation. Michael Cusumano, a professor at MIT's Sloan School of Management, described Microsoft's bid as a pursuit of "an old-style Internet asset, in decline, and at a premium." Microsoft's merger offer was rebuffed and withdrawn in May, but it drew a fair amount of mockery, perhaps most colorfully described by Dan Lyons, in his *Secret Diary of Steve Jobs* blog: "It's like taking the two guys who finished second and third in a 100-yard dash and tying their legs together and asking for a rematch, believing that now they'll run faster."

In May 2008, Google fielded 68.3 percent of all U.S. Internet searches, up from 58.3 percent in March 2006. Second-place Yahoo's share was only 20 percent—and Microsoft's MSN Search's share was 5.9 percent.

If Google were content to prosper with Web search, and only Web search, its story would be compact. It is Google's pursuit of all information, in any form, that has made its story larger, more complicated, and more interesting. Yet it is an ambition that has remained unexamined for the most part. Google has been determined to "organize the world's information and make it universally accessible and useful" since June 1999, when the company released its first press release on the occasion of its receiving $25 million of equity financing from two venture capital firms. Until then, Google had used a modest statement of company mission that the founders had hastily put on Google's Web site at the time the site was launched: "To make it easier to find high-quality information on the web." Once the company dropped this limited aim seven months after its founding and adopted the goal of organizing all the world's information, its outsized ambition has been a matter of public record.

Google executives do understand that the further the company advances toward this ultimate goal, the more people are unsettled by the prospect that a single company controls an increasing share of precious information assets. In 2006, an unknown person at Google prepared a PowerPoint presentation that included an offhand remark in the slide's comments that Google at that point had collected only 5 percent of the information it seeks. Another slide's comments emphatically added: "We plan to . . . get all the world's information, not just some." The slides were posted on Google's corporate Web site, but apparently someone thought better of it, because they were soon removed.

Google's quest to organize all the world's information originates in the founders' engineering view of the world and their original work as graduate students in computer science. In the early 1990s, computer science was trying to come to the aid of library science, using computer technology to make the information in books searchable. Among those attracted to the intellectual challenge were Page and Brin. It was research that was based on the side of Stanford's campus that housed its School of Engineering, not its Graduate School of Business.

Page and Brin have nothing in common with the business generalists that ran IBM for decades, nor the computer hobbyists that launched the early personal computer companies. Both born in 1973, they represent more than a new generation of founders in the computer industry. Having passed through the formal programs of computer science as undergraduates at the University of Michigan and the University of Maryland, respectively, they went on to doctoral programs in computer science at Stanford. They had not completed their dissertations in 1998 when they founded Google, but their extended period of academic socialization imbued them with the optimistic notion that any problem can be solved. Design and build a suitable system, and anything can be accomplished.

They have continued to favor engineering over business. When the two young men sought a CEO with more business experience, they looked for someone of a similar persuasion. In Eric Schmidt they found that person: a seasoned industry executive (Sun

Microsystems, then Novell) who was also a computer scientist (Ph.D., University of California, Berkeley). Schmidt arrived at Google in 2001. Three years later, in 2004, on the eve of the company's initial public offering (IPO), the three men committed to working together for the next twenty years—a feat of unfathomable corporate comity for a troika, should it endure.

Google employees who sit in on meetings with the executive team see on a daily basis that these three work so closely together that their shared sense of company priorities is all but indistinguishable. They communicate their priorities in unison throughout the company so that even teams at the lowest level of the hierarchy know what principles guide their decision making and what projects will be deemed most helpful in fulfilling Google's mission.

The most visible difference distinguishing members of the trio is that Schmidt steps forward as the public spokesperson, and Brin and Page step back. Schmidt, who is eighteen years older than Brin and Page, is described in the general press as the person who supplies the "adult supervision," but it is his skill at controlling what is said publicly, saying little without appearing to do so, that is most valuable to the executive team. In describing what Google is doing, or not doing, Schmidt has a more shrewd sense of what phrasing the world outside will receive in the most positive way. When Brin was asked in 2008 about why consumers should trust Google to protect their personal data, he responded in a tone that suggested the very question was absurd: "How many people do you think had embarrassing information about them disclosed yesterday because of [using Google]? Zero. It never happens. Yet I'm sure thousands of people had their mail stolen yesterday, or identity theft." Schmidt, by contrast, regularly handles the same question calmly, without betraying irritation, acknowledging the concern about privacy and gently pointing out that Google is fully aware that its entire business relies upon maintaining the trust of its users.

Occasionally, though, Schmidt will blurt out a thought that has not passed through his internal review filter. When this happens, he sounds indistinguishable from the cofounders. One such instance was in May 2006. He was talking about Google's strategic model, which he said is "designed to scale to no boundary. We don't see today any limit to this model of continuing to grow. I'm sure there are limits, but we don't see them today. This limitless-growth model is very exciting." Exciting for Google, yes. What the prospect of growth without limit means for the public is something more complicated than a pure thrill. It's a prospect that has appeared so quickly, historically speaking, that we have not really had time to take a good look at what Google has become, let alone to consider what comes next.

It is possible that Google is currently using as many as a million computers for its operations, harnessed together to create effectively a supercomputer, the world's largest. Google will not disclose the number of computers nor say much about the data centers that house them. When Schmidt was asked in April 2007 how many data centers Google had, he replied, "I don't actually know." And then, anticipating that the answer would sound coy—how could the CEO not know such a thing?—he allowed that there were "dozens" of centers, including some of immense size. Then he added, cheerfully, "In a year or two the very large ones will be the small ones because the growth rate is such that we keep building even larger ones." He was oblivious to the possibility that such growth might strike some as ominous.

Schmidt, Page, and Brin were also slow to appreciate that Google's technical achievements would not necessarily be praised. When Google's ambitious plan to digitize entire university libraries brought upon it legal difficulties and furious criticism from book publishers and authors, the company was utterly surprised. It had viewed book scanning as a practical matter of addressing engineering issues "at scale." It had not realized that the problems on the engineering side were the easy ones; those concerning intellectual property and the law, far more difficult.

The company's allegiance to the engineers' ethos came through one day when I attended a weekly all-hands meeting at the Googleplex, the main corporate campus, in Mountain View, California. Schmidt, Page, and Brin all appear at the Friday afternoon meetings whenever they are in town. Within the company, they are not reclusive in the least. Their offices are on a busy floor, small, and in the case of Brin and Page, still shared. The TGIF gathering is a combination of official briefing, informal question-and-answer session, and party. Only a few hundred employees can pack into the atrium where the meeting is held, but live video feeds are sent to all Google offices around the world.

When I inquired about attending a TGIF, I was told that they were for employees only. Gaining admittance took a while. After five months of conversations with the company's corporate communications staff, however, I sat down with Eric Schmidt for a heart-to-heart chat (or, more accurately, knee-to-knee; the room was no bigger than a closet). There I put directly to him my wish to see more of the company than my interviews with individual employees afforded. He brought up the TGIFs before I did and suggested that I attend. He did not have to ask me twice.

On the Friday that I chose in early May 2007, Schmidt and Brin were out of town and Larry Page was the sole emcee. He led off with a set of unremarkable announcements, a short demo of a new product, and then he dove into the real business of the day, fielding employee complaints.

Of all workplaces in the world, this would seem to be the place least likely to find employee unhappiness of any kind. Every conceivable condition that might impinge on workplace productivity seems to have been attended to. The company famously provides free meals—breakfast, lunch, and dinner—that make a gourmet's heart flutter. For those who work at the Googleplex in Mountain View, a free shuttle service covering the entire Bay Area is available. Free on-site medical care is provided by two full-time doctors who are on staff. Subsidized massages are available on the premises. A company child care center is nearby and various services are provided, for a fee, right at the workplace: personal trainers, haircuts, a laundry, dry cleaning pickup, bike repairs, and car wash and oil-change services. Larry Page in 2004 had told Google's shareholders in an "Owner's Manual" to "expect us to add benefits rather than pare them down over time," and so the company had. Little wonder that Google would be named in 2007 and again in 2008 by *Fortune* magazine as the Number One Best Company to Work For.

And yet, at the Friday meeting, complaints do come in. The machines that software developers use are too slow. An internal online calendar for scheduling massages is balky. Nearby traffic lights seem mistimed, causing irksome delays in the daily commute. Google's maps for Japan lack English translations for place-names. As Page listens to each grievance, he is good-humored and patient, even when the pettiness of the grievance should embarrass the complainant. If Page agrees that the company should take action, he tries to fix the problem on the spot. When an employee complains that the legal department has decreed that every outgoing e-mail message from the sales team must include a long disclaimer in legalese, a very "un-Googley practice," Page looks out over the crowd. "Who's responsible for that?" A hand is raised. "All right. Don't do it." The audience laughs. (Whether corporate counsel will back down without a fight will be determined only later.) Page is ready to move to the next question, but he can't resist adding, "It does seem kind of ridiculous."

In the very middle of the meeting, Page fields a more hard-hitting question. It concerns Google's recent hiring of so many newly minted MBAs. "How do we insure we don't hire too many of them?" an employee asks him in an e-mail message. The question is greeted by approving applause. Page stops reading and asks for a show of hands to find out how many MBAs are present in the room. Almost no hands are raised. He tries, halfheartedly, to make the case that MBAs are "equally helpful to the world, too"—which provokes some derisive laughter. So he moves on quickly to say that he and the senior managers have taken measures to make sure that the company's high ratio of engineers to nonengineers will remain constant.

Google goes after not just the well educated, but the very well educated. Among the company's first hundred engineers, forty were Ph.D.'s. The company's emphasis on Ph.D.'s was not shared universally in the software industry. Microsoft mostly recruited computer science majors who had only a bachelor's degree; the company eschewed those with advanced degrees ("We're huge believers in hiring potential," Kristen Roby, Microsoft's director of recruiting at colleges in the United States, said in 2004). In contrast, Google sought those with the most academic training possible. A typical

Google job listing featured a three-word phrase rarely seen outside of academe: "Ph.D. a plus."

At Google, management and staff use the empiricism of science to guide their business, developing hypotheses, collecting data, revising hypotheses, and repeating the cycle. Kevin Scott, a senior software engineering manager who worked at Google, described the iterative process: "Ideas at Google do not burst forth from the heads of geniuses and then find their way unimpeded to huge audiences of receptive users. Rather ideas emerge, are torn to shreds, reformulated, torn to shreds, prototyped, torn to shreds, launched to internal users, torn to shreds, rebuilt and relaunched, torn to shreds, refined some more . . . and launched, whereupon they are torn to shreds by bloggers, journalists, and competitors."

Google has been in the enviable position of being able to afford additions to its information collections that may not produce profits, and may not even produce revenue. It is even dabbling in genomics as well as software, with an investment in 23andMe, a Silicon Valley start-up that offers individuals the ability to browse their individual genome. "Information," if interpreted as broadly as possible, encompasses many kinds of businesses, and Google has shown an eagerness to try many things.

In 2005, Schmidt explained at a public forum, "We often do things that don't make any sense from traditional norms. And we're proud of that, and we talk about that. The founders have set the mission of the company—that we work on big problems that affect people at scale that have not been solved before." That phrase *at scale*—a shortened form of *on a very, very large scale*—is heard often around campus.

Building at scale is not so much a business quest as an imperative that is dictated by Google's core search technology, the software that makes judgments about the quality of Web pages based on what other Web pages have to say about them. Its software is self-teaching. The more data it massages, the more sophisticated the software becomes. "More data is better data" is a favorite maxim of Google's engineers. Building systems at scale is the way to gather the data to create ever-smarter software.

There is no limit to the kinds of data that would help improve the software. A corollary of more-data-is-better-data is that any information not in a digital form that the software can process must be digitized. During a visit to London in May 2007, Schmidt was asked what Google might look like five years hence. He said that the total amount of information that Google possessed was still at an "early" stage. By broadening and deepening its information collections, he explained, Google will be able to provide search results better tailored to a particular user. He said the ultimate goal was to provide Google's software with enough personal detail about each of its visitors that it could provide customized answers to the questions "What shall I do tomorrow?" and "What job shall I take?"

One need not squint hard to picture a computer being able to answer such questions: it's the HAL 9000, whose omniscience made it the most disturbing and memorable character in *2001: A Space Odyssey,* the 1968 film adaptation of Arthur C. Clarke's saga. Sergey Brin told an interviewer in 2002 that HAL was "what we're striving for," with its ability to stitch together all of the information it was fed and, in Brin's words, "rationalize it." He said, "Hopefully, it would never have a bug like HAL did where he killed the occupants of the space ship."

Were Google able to endow its own supercomputer with the power of HAL—Brin had said, "I think we've made it a part of the way there"—it would command a system that is the stuff of an advertiser's dream; the more it knows about each visitor, the more precisely it can target the advertising. The better the customer response, the greater the company's profits.

Brin, Schmidt, and their Google colleagues have felt free to imagine a world in which their company will hold, in a very literal sense, all the world's information. Yet as the company proceeds, it must spend less time in dreamy ruminations about the big vision and more time on the prosaic details that, until recently, had seemed unimportant or, in the giddy rush of Google's hypergrowth, seemed to take care of themselves.

If Google's shares do not fully recover after falling steeply in early 2008, Google will no longer be able to assume that stock options for its employees will serve to ensure loyalty. Its veteran employees, having received all of their options that were granted when the strike price was extremely low, are leaving in significant numbers. It's an exodus that is natural and expected, but some of its most able talent are heading for Facebook, which indirectly competes with Google. In March 2008, Facebook hired Google's Sheryl Sandberg to be its chief operating officer; by one account, almost 10 percent of Facebook's employees were ex-Googlers.

Google's ability to pursue its most ambitious ventures depends on its continuing to have access to top technical talent, and recruiting is bound to become ever more difficult. Companies that have not yet had their own IPO and that can offer new employees both greater responsibilities and a much greater possibility of a financial windfall—like Facebook—vie with Google in the marketplace for engineers.

The company's ability to recruit the most highly qualified new employees will be diminished further should it experience a disappointing quarter and decide that the generous employee benefits that Larry Page had said in 2004 he expected to expand indefinitely would have to be pared after all. The unthinkable, a rollback of benefits, was already visible in 2008 when subsidized child care was dropped from the list of employee perquisites. Then in June 2008, Google announced that rates for new child care centers near the Googleplex would jump 70 percent (to $2,290 a month for a toddler; more for an infant). Although it also introduced at the same time a "child care scholarship program" for those for whom the rates would create a financial hardship, the very idea that an employee would have to apply for a scholarship in order to afford company-provided daycare was an unsettling reminder that Google employees belonged to one of two classes: employees who had been hired early enough to receive stock options before the IPO and were wealthy—in many cases, extremely wealthy—and employees hired since the IPO, who had the same workaday concerns about living in high-cost-of-living areas as anyone else.

Or worse, what happens to Google's golden aura when a difficult quarter or two forces its senior executives to decide that instead of hiring at a furious pace, the company must reverse course for the time being and trim its head count? There have not yet been layoffs of regular Google employees, but in March 2008, when Google completed its acquisition of DoubleClick, it did immediately terminate the employment of three hundred of DoubleClick's twelve hundred U.S. employees. This produced a headline on the Bloomberg financial news service that referred to the firings as Google's "biggest staff cuts." Even with the qualification that these involved DoubleClick employees, it was jarring to see "Google" anywhere in the vicinity of "staff cuts." But it served as a reminder that Google should not be regarded as permanently protected from encounters with the same kinds of adversity that other companies experience.

Is Google likely to be the primary beneficiary of the shift to cloud computing, or will it be supplanted by other companies, perhaps by one that has not yet been founded? Will Google's cloud be popularly embraced, as users enjoy the benefits, or is it more likely to be rejected, as fear of misuse of personal information becomes a matter of great concern? Google's future will be determined to no small degree by the view that its users hold of the company itself. Google has enjoyed mostly favorable public notice in its first ten years, but maintaining a cuddly, anticorporate image when it stands among the U.S. companies with the largest market capitalization may pose an increasingly difficult challenge.

The company that seems to be everywhere, deeply embedded in our daily lives, actually has a smallish physical presence. *Googleplex* brings to mind an architectural monstrosity the size of the Pentagon. In reality, the signature buildings are not much bigger than those of a single suburban high school. The core consists of four eccentrically ornamented two- and three-story buildings that had served previously as the home of computer manufacturer Silicon Graphics. These are arranged around a swath of shared space: young shade trees; tables protected from the almost always present sun by umbrellas in the Google colors of red, green, blue, and yellow; a grassy knoll and circular volleyball court; an outdoor garden; and "Stan," a bronze Tyrannosaurus Rex skeleton. Depending on the time of day, many or few Googlers pass among the buildings. As a group, they have one striking attribute: they are a very young workforce, even for Silicon Valley.

At the end of 2003, the last year before its IPO, Google had 1,628 permanent employees; only four years later, at the end of 2007, the number had grown tenfold, to 16,805. Given its ambition, Google could not remain small. A reminder of this came up in May 2007, before the company's annual shareholders' meeting began, when Page and Schmidt met with a small group of reporters, including me. Page was asked how he felt about seeing so many new faces on campus and watching the company grow so large. He protested that Google was not large—not when measured by what it sought to do, to provide "all the world's information to everybody in the world, and do a really good job of it." He countered, "That's just not a small company, right?"

Indeed. That is not a small company.

CHAPTER 1

Open and Closed

War, hyperinflation, breakdowns in public utility services. None of these elements of an adverse business environment have fallen into Google's path. The company has had the good fortune to enjoy a most hospitable business environment. It is not widely appreciated, however, how dependent Google is upon an environment remaining free of not only major disruptions, particular to the online world, but also other problems that would bring its business to a standstill as surely as a war would. Google needs the Internet to remain open and true to its founding spirit, without (pay) walls, without (subscription) fences, without (proprietary software) barriers, without any other impediments to the unrestricted exchange of information.

The credo that holds that "information wants to be free" has always faced an opposing school of thought: "Information is too valuable to be free." From this latter perspective, information is a commercially valuable asset, to be hoarded, not shared. Access to information is unimpeded in the open camp, and severely restricted in the closed camp. The epitome of open is "wiki" sites, which are completely open to anyone to edit, as well as read. Their opposites are social networking sites like Facebook, which permit only members to enter, limiting access to information to subsets of a member's web of friends.

Google's search engine needs access to the entire Internet, not merely the patches that remain outside the walled gardens of social networking sites. The company's very existence depends upon the advocates of an open online environment holding at bay the threat of encroachment by their opponents.

Contention between open and closed is also the defining issue roiling the world of software development. Microsoft achieved its success as a practitioner of the closed approach to software development, keeping its source code secret and using its control of the operating system to extend its reach into other sectors of the software business. It treated industry standards that belonged to no single company as competitors to Microsoft's own proprietary software. The company follows a strategy of what it calls "embrace and extend," that is, begin with industry standards but "extend" them by attaching Microsoft's own proprietary additions to them.

Microsoft's self-aggrandizement antagonized many companies and software developers in the industry, and ultimately it created a backlash, the open-source software movement, which has become a potent challenge to Microsoft's closed approach to software. Open-source software permits software developers to see all of a program's source code, something that Microsoft would never allow. The movement depends upon software developers' willingness to volunteer their time and skills, without remuneration, but hatred of Microsoft and all it stands for has provided ample motivation.

Google uses open-source software extensively for its own operations. It has not, however, placed its own proprietary search formulas into the public domain. It's a company that is attached to its own secrets and will not win any contests for corporate transparency. Still, compared to Microsoft, Google is more closely aligned to those in the industry clustered around the open model. The two companies represent not just the interests of their own firms but also the interests of two ideologically opposed camps, open and closed. It was fitting that it was Microsoft that won the privilege in late 2007 of investing in Facebook: the two companies manifest the greatest comfort with closed over open. Their alignment unites them in fighting their principal ideological rival, Google.

The social networking phenomenon attracts inordinate attention now because of its recent popularity. The World Wide Web, Google's original domain, has been a presence for so long that it has receded into the background. But as long as open and closed models contend for favorable position, the Web's founding principles remain as relevant to the present moment as ever. The Web was conceived as an alternative to closed communications systems. It was built as an open medium—open to anyone to publish or read, designed not only to make information easy to access, but also to make tracing the origins of an idea easy, as simple as clicking on a link. No geographic boundaries, no fences, nothing to impede the researcher from zipping across the Internet, link by link, to find information that was both useful and free, wherever it happened to be, anywhere in the world.

It was conceived by an academic for fellow academics, and the only place the Web existed at first was on servers that belonged to research laboratories. Tim Berners-Lee, a computer scientist who was on the staff of CERN, the European Organization for Nuclear Research, in Geneva, Switzerland, came up with the essential concepts in 1989 and built the first servers for holding Web pages in 1990. From CERN, the Web spread to other particle physics laboratories. The Web browsers at that time worked only on scientific workstations, and the Web could easily have remained what it was then, a tool used within the closed world of physicists. In 1993, however, CERN announced that its Web technologies could be used by anyone, without paying royalties. It set in motion the creation of the world's largest open network—and ultimately the creation of Google, the most valuable company to be built upon that open network.

The combination of *open* and *network* was an oxymoron in the 1990s, when commercial-grade networks were closed, by design. Cellular phone networks and cable television networks, for example, ensured quality by using a strong central authority to exert close control and restrict who and what had access to the network. In contrast, the Web lacked a central authority and also lacked built-in mechanisms for Web site publishers to collect revenue, so initially the Web appeared to be the place for academics, amateur authors, and others without interest in commercial pursuits to share information without concern about remuneration.

In its openness and radically decentralized design, the Web mirrored the design of the underlying technical standards for the Internet, the networking technologies that are used to transfer digital bits of information. But the Web was not an instant success. In June 1993, two years after it was introduced, less than one-half of 1 percent of all Internet traffic was used for Web pages—the rest of the traffic was for e-mail, file transfers, and discussions in "news groups." There were not many places on the Web to go: only 130 or so sites were in existence then. In 1994, a year after the introduction of Mosaic, the first popular Web browser, there were twenty-seven hundred sites, but Web traffic still was only 6 percent of all Internet traffic. The Web remained a curiosity.

The Web would have remained a place for academics with very specialized information needs were it not for the willingness of more and more individuals outside of academe to place information on the Web for free. Today's Google employees and shareholders should be eternally grateful to the Web's early contributors, because later demand for Google's search service came about only because so many people decided, one by one, to give information away without charge on the Web.

Before the Web, information was available online, but one had to pay dearly for access. The first generation of digital information services were commercial information providers, such as Lockheed's Dialog service, which began in the 1970s and charged high prices to business clients. The second generation of pre-Web information services were sold to consumers by American Online (AOL), CompuServe, and Prodigy. They offered customers access to their private networks, reached with a dial-up modem using the household's phone line, and information that was available only to their members.

No one in the early 1990s could have predicted that the Web would attract abundant information that was both of high quality and free. The only business model for information services that seemed practical was to build a walled garden around information and then charge users to enter the garden. Google enjoyed a huge advantage arriving when it did in the late 1990s, as a latecomer to the digital information business. It was conceived outside the walled garden and never had to pass through a painful transition, as did its forebears, replacing the core business model based on a closed network for one based on an open one.

Microsoft had the ill luck to become interested in information services later than incumbents like AOL but not late enough to grasp the competitive threat to closed networks that the Web would soon pose. Six years before Google's founding, Microsoft began planning, in 1992, to offer its own information service, which would eventually appear as MSN (Microsoft Network) in 1995. It naturally followed the closed-network model of AOL and the others. Nathan Myhrvold, Microsoft's research chief at the time, likened MSN's future role to that of a shopping mall landlord. Other companies would be invited to sell information or goods within the Microsoft Network, and Microsoft would retain 10 to 30 percent of the revenue. When the growth of the Internet loomed as a free alternative to the walled garden, he held out hope that Microsoft could still set up a toll booth outside MSN's garden by inserting Microsoft's proprietary software into all e-commerce purchases on the Internet, and exact a transaction fee of 1 or 2 percent, just as Visa or MasterCard did.

The one company that seemed to be ideally positioned to profit from the advent of the Web was Netscape Communications, whose Netscape Navigator Web browser became sensationally popular upon release in 1994. The company grew so fast that in August 1995, only eighteen months after its founding, it had one of the most successful initial public offerings for any company in the technology industry. Netscape declared itself to be the faithful guardian of "openness," the foundation of the Internet's architecture, and the company placed the internal source code for its browser into the public domain in 1998. It learned that giving away its Web browser for free was easy. Collecting revenue from paying customers, however, was far more difficult: it required offering a product that embodied intellectual property that was not freely available, and when Netscape tried to sell Web server software to corporate customers, it found that sales came slowly. It attempted, in vain, to have its proprietary additions to Web standards adopted as a new industry standard. As a chronicle of

Netscape's history summed up, Netscape was "open, but not open."

Almost every information technology company claims to be a champion of open standards—even Microsoft did so, too, touting Windows as an open platform, that is, open to any software developer who wished to create Windows applications, without having to secure Microsoft's permission and without having to share the revenue with Microsoft (in contrast to game system manufacturers likes Nintendo, which control their own closed software systems and force game developers to share revenue from game sales). When Microsoft added its own proprietary code to the industry's Internet standards, such as internal Web page tags that its Internet Explorer would recognize, but Netscape's browser would not, it euphemistically called the changes "extensions" to preserve the appearance of adhering to open standards.

When Google was founded in 1998, it did not have to fight against Microsoft's extensions, nor did it have to displace Microsoft's operating system or push back Microsoft's browser. It had the advantage of a better field position than previous Microsoft challengers had ever enjoyed—it floated above the fray. Any browser, running on any operating system, could reach Google.

Google was fortunate in another respect: the sheer mass of pages placed on the Web overwhelmed the abilities of Yahoo and others in the first generation of Web navigation and search businesses to develop search techniques that grew in sophistication as fast as the Web was growing. Their failure created the opportunity for Google.

Craig Silverstein, the first Google employee hired in 1998 by the two founders, later said that had the company been founded two years earlier, or even one year earlier, it surely would have failed. Before 1998, the Web was still small enough that almost any search method served well enough, producing a list of sites with matching Web pages that was short enough to be easy to scan in its entirety. By 1998, however, the Web was much larger and a need had arisen for a search engine that could do more than simply match the text of the search term with that of all Web pages that contained the phrase. Silverstein said it also had to "discriminate between good results and not-so-good results."

Google would have no search service to offer if Web pages were inaccessible to its "spider," the software that systematically "crawled" the Web, collecting copies of Web pages that were then indexed and analyzed, in readiness for matching when a visitor to Google later submitted a search request. (As fast as Google's software appears to perform a search, it should be remembered that when Google receives a search request, its search does not at that moment check the world's Web sites, but rather checks the copies of those sites that were collected earlier and stored on Google's servers.) When the crawling software was written in unsophisticated form, as Google's initial version was, it caused many problems for the Web sites it crawled. In some cases, where bandwidth was limited, the Google crawlers' visits resulted in a spike in traffic that the Web site could not accommodate. The software that ran the Web site would freeze, closing the site to all visitors. This did not endear Google to the sites' owners, some of whom sent Brin and Page angry e-mail messages or phoned them to convey their objections.

The upset passed. The code embedded in the Google spider was improved, which reduced the time that it spent on each site and also reduced the likelihood that it would crash the system it was visiting. At the same time, Web hosts became accustomed to the visits of automated software programs and understood spiders' visits would, in turn, make their sites visible to the search engines and could serve in the future to draw in visits by actual humans.

The Web's original designers agreed upon a piece of code Web site hosts could use to signal that a spider or any other kind of "robot" software was not welcome to visit. It was Google's very good fortune that the Web grew without Web site owners' electing to use this option to block visits by Google's spider. The relevance of Google's search results are dependent upon having access to the broadest possible range of Web pages. These provide the essential materials used in calculations that go into Google's ranking of search results, placing Web pages with the greatest presumed authority at the top of the list.

To calculate authority for any given page, Google's software looks at its database of links for the entire Web and notes which Web sites link to that page, providing, in effect, a recommendation. This provides only a beginning. The sites that provide recommendations have to be examined carefully, in order to determine whether the recommendation should be weighted heavily or lightly or disregarded entirely. The software returns to the database of links to see who recommends the recommending sites, and when those are found, to see who recommends *those* sites, and so on. The process works backwards, recursively. Checking who points to whom may seem as endless a process as going up a stairway in an Escher print, but the long chain of calculations eventually produces a distillation of relative authority for every page on the Web, which is expressed as a number, 1 to 10. It sums up whether editors at other Web sites regard any one Web page as authoritative and worthy of recommending to others. Google refers to the number as PageRank (the *Page* officially refers to Larry Page, who developed the original formula, but his surname permits the term to work nicely even if its paternity remains unknown to the reader). PageRank wasn't the first system devised to analyze the Web's structure—Cornell computer scientist Jon Kleinberg's mid-1990s work at the IBM Almaden Research Center is generally credited as a landmark in the field—but PageRank was the one that made it out of the lab first.

With its near-endless tracing of links and cross-references, PageRank relies upon a complete database of all links found on pages in the entire Web, and that in turn requires that Google's crawler be able to range freely across an open ecosystem. Google can utilize the judgments embodied in links without having to purchase rights to use them because of the open ethos of the Web. If even a small number of owners of Web sites with high PageRank scores and presumed high authority were to exclude Google's spider—demanding, perhaps, that Google share revenue earned by indexing their sites—then Google's ability to operate as it has would end.

The advent in the 1990s of an open model for publishing information on the Web did not immediately spell doom for the closed model of walled gardens. Novice users of e-mail and the Web were slow to venture out beyond the carefully manicured garden of their Internet service provider. This gave the service provider considerable leverage in negotiating deals with prospective tenants who wanted to set up shop within the proprietary network. The most sought after real estate online was screen space within the gated world of AOL, a fact that AOL exploited to the fullest in negotiations with prospective commercial tenants.

AOL was the widely acknowledged gatekeeper to online information in the place that its members found most convenient to access. The fact that the area within its garden was finite and merely a subset of what was available on the Web did not seem to bother its members. An observation that Vic Gundotra, a former Microsoft manager now at Google, made about Windows applied to AOL too: "At Microsoft, our view was that if the walled garden was big enough, it was indistinguishable from something that was open."

When AOL customers sought faster Internet service than AOL's dial-up service and switched to cable or DSL broadband service, they also began to see the limitations of AOL's information services. AOL's members began declining after 2001, falling from about 28 million membership in the United States to 9.3 million at the end of 2007. As it lost members, AOL executives realized that its wall prevented it from relying more heavily on advertising revenue to replace shrinking subscription revenue. In 2005, Michael Kelly, an ad-sales executive placed in charge of all of AOL's Web properties, complained, "My biggest problem is the walled garden. The world can't see the good stuff we do every day." AOL edged closer to the outside world when it announced a strategic alliance with Google in late 2005. The next year, AOL finally tore down its own garden wall.

The opening of AOL's closed network seemed to mark the permanent end of an era. Small vestigial gardens offering content from a single source, open to subscribers only, could be found here and there, but one by one, they, too, acknowledged the greater attractiveness of an advertising-based business model open to all visitors. The *New York Times*'s site experimented for a year with a "pay wall" that was placed around some of its columnists, and decided to remove the wall in 2007. The *Wall Street Journal*'s Web site remains the last major outpost of a gated, subscribers-only community.

At the same time, however, that the triumph of the open network model seemed complete, Facebook demonstrated that a closed network model could still work well—very well, indeed. In 2007, it grew into the second-largest social network site in the United States, with more than 42 million members by October—only MySpace, the sensation of 2006, was larger, with more than 100 million active users. For Google, Facebook's growth was somewhat worrisome. When Facebook members logged on, their online communications and activities were fenced off from outside view. The more members that Facebook signed up, and the more time that they spent within its cozy but closed confines, out of reach of Google's spider, the slower the pool of searchable information for Google to find on the open Web grew.

Google did not immediately respond to the steep climb in Facebook's membership in early 2007. Orkut, Google's own social network site, named after Orkut Büyükkökten, a Google engineer, remained on the periphery of Google's core services and priorities. The service had been launched three years before, in January 2004, and left to make its way by word-of-mouth promotion. It had become hugely popular in Brazil and in India, but not in the United States. This was not a matter of concern to Google—until May 2007, when Facebook became more than a fast-growing irritant. Overnight, it changed into a potently self-sufficient secessionist from the open Web when it invited outside software developers to create mini software applications that would run within Facebook. The company shrewdly sweetened the offer by letting the developers retain all advertising revenues that their application generated. Developers rushed to accept the offer.

In a twinkling, Facebook became a miniature Web universe—behind a wall, inaccessible to Google. As Facebook became more fully furnished with software from the outside, Facebook members had fewer reasons to ever leave the site. This development brought back to life the once-discredited notion that "if the walled garden was big enough, it was indistinguishable from something that was open."

For Google, Facebook's creation of a flourishing closed world was of much more concern than the growth of MySpace, whose walls were more porous, permitting Google's spiders to enter. Google had also struck an exclusive advertising deal with MySpace's parent, Fox Interactive Media, the year before, so it was able to profit by MySpace's growth. Facebook, however, had not struck a similar advertising deal with any search engine and had grown without building out an advertising system at the same time. To its rivals, Facebook's self-contained world was a violation of the Web's founding ethos of openness and free flow of information. Steve Rubel, an executive with Edelman, the giant public relations firm whose client list included MySpace, complained about Facebook on his blog: "Facebook gives nothing back to the broader web. A lot of stuff goes in, but nothing comes out. What happens in Facebook, stays in Facebook."

How Google should respond to the social networking phenomenon in general, and to Facebook in particular, was not clear to Google's executive troika, but they understood that the question was a pressing one. In June 2007, shortly after Facebook invited software developers in, Google appointed three executives in its applications group, Joe Kraus, Graham Spencer, and David Glazer, to organize an internal team that would provide an answer to the question, what would Google do about (in the new shorthand) "social"?

The first step was recruiting other members of the team. This did not require hiring new employees—scattered across different groups within Google were plenty of individuals who were working in one way or another on projects that could conceivably contribute to Google's social networking initiative. Kraus and his fellow team leaders could not reassign these Google employees—they had to be persuaded. This called for a "sales process," Kraus said. He had a printout of an e-mail message from the most senior executives, who bestowed their imprimatur on the "social" team. He brandished it when making the rounds of Google offices on his sales calls: "I really need your help, and your team needs to redirect because—as you see—this letter, from three levels up, says this is the project everyone should focus on." The initial response was, in many cases, a shrug. Google may appear, on the outside, to be a monolithic organization that acts with terrifying efficiency and concentrated purpose when entering new markets. On the inside, however, it is a federation of autonomous teams, staffed by feisty individuals who have no compunction about slamming the door on fellow employees and the company's top priorities.

Once a full team for the social networking initiative was signed up—and was able to secure office space, which required pushing out another group—it took up the question of whether it should try to make a success of Orkut in the United States, either retaining its name or creating a fresh brand identity and relaunching it. There was no enthusiasm for retaining the Orkut name, but there were some who believed that Google should introduce a new social network of its own. Kraus, however, was not enthusiastic. "At this point in the marketplace," he said, "do people want to join yet another social network?" He almost was convinced otherwise by another team member, who argued, "Look, social networks are one of maybe only three communications media to gather hundreds of millions of users—you have e-mail, you have instant messaging, you have social networking. How can you actually believe that you don't want to start another social network?"

Kraus's position, which eventually prevailed, was that Google should not try to persuade users to create a brand-new habit but rather should try to make all Google services more social, that is, connected to one's network of friends. Compared to starting a new social networking site, this marked a substantial shrinking of the initiative's ambitions. After a little while, the team decided it did not want to settle for modest changes to existing services. It changed course again, seizing the opportunity to make what Kraus called "the bigger play": attempting to make every site on the entire Web more social, recognizing that the way users searched for information was changing. "Information discovery is evolving," he said, "from a solitary exercise to one that involves what your friends are up to, and discovering things based on what your friends like."

Google was set up to help the solitary user find information. A socially oriented approach to search did not play to Google's traditional strengths. What Kraus and his team thought would be a wise course was to eschew anything that would appear to further Google's own proprietary interests and instead lead an industry-wide alliance to adopt standards that would make social networking data universally available to software developers for use at all Web sites. The story Google would tell itself was that this was an altruistic project, helping everyone use their social network to find the information they were seeking, even if they weren't using Google's products. If there was any self-interest at stake, Google would say only what it always said—that Google's interests were tied indirectly to the health of the Internet. Anything that induced people to spend more time on the Web is good for Google because, sooner or later, online users end up using Google's services.

Another way of viewing Google's initiative, however, was to see it as a move to try to preserve the open Web as new fences like Facebook's were erected. And still another view was that Google was acting in desperation, trying to address what it internally referred to as "the Facebook Problem" and find some means of counteracting Facebook's influence. It was remarkable that a company of Facebook's size, with only about three hundred employees, was a cause of concern at Google, with about sixteen thousand—or a bit fewer, thanks to Facebook's maddening ability to poach some senior Google engineers. In this view Google declined to promote Orkut in the United States not because it preferred a more noble cause—making the entire Web more socially aware—but because it understood it was too late for it to have a chance to compete head-to-head with Facebook.

When Facebook finally aligned with a larger partner, it was with Google's old rival Microsoft. In October 2007, Microsoft announced that it was making a $240 million investment in Facebook, which was accorded a valuation of $15 billion and reciprocally bestowed upon Microsoft the rights to serve as the exclusive intermediary selling advertising for the site to third parties. Reserving rights to sell advertising itself, Facebook prepared to unveil its own advertising system two weeks later.

The business press was filled with coverage of the Facebook-Microsoft deal, of the astounding valuation of a company with paltry revenues, and with speculation about how Facebook planned to convert its intimate knowledge of its members' lives into advertising dollars. Google decided that in the few days remaining before Facebook's next announcement it should try to reclaim some attention and make a formal public announcement of its own social initiative.

One problem: Google had little to announce, other than a name—"OpenSocial." The initiative's software standards were far from complete, and Google's efforts to assemble a roster of the most influential social networking sites as participants had not produced much. Two days before the OpenSocial announcement was to be made public, the list of participants was composed of social networking also-rans: Orkut, of course, and Bebo, Six Apart, Hi5, Friendster, LinkedIn, Ning, and some others that were not social networking sites, like Salesforce.com. Conspicuously missing were MySpace and Facebook. At the end of the week, the initiative received a badly needed injection of credibility when MySpace joined in, too. But the fact that Google had earlier that week felt it had no choice but to unveil the coalition without a major anchor tenant suggested the OpenSocial team's belief that it could not wait to try to slow Facebook's momentum.

The primary competitive weapon that Google possessed was semantic: it used *open,* and all the positive connotations associated with it, to attack Facebook at what appeared to be Facebook's most vulnerable spot, the closed nature of its software universe. It was not a hypocritical ploy. From its birth, Google had been a devotee of the creed of *open.* More than any other company, Google had depended upon unrestricted access not only to the Web, but also to the software created as open source, which it used for its search engine and other services, and to which it contributed new code. It created a free hosting site for open source projects. It hired as Google employees a number of coders who were leaders in prominent open source projects. And each year, it organized a Summer of Code, in which it paid hundreds of computer science students to work on open source projects. Google's credentials as an advocate of an open approach to software development were in good order.

When *open* was used to apply to a social networking model, however, the adjective's meaning was ambiguous. The most fundamental way that the social networking world could be opened would be by endowing all social network sites with interoperability, permitting a member's data and web of relationships that were originally collected at one site to move with the user to other sites, too—what publisher and commentator Tim O'Reilly calls "data mobility." OpenSocial had a grand-sounding name, but in its initial announcement, it spoke of no such ambition. More modestly, it would attempt to provide software developers the standards for writing mini applications designed to work within all social networking sites, making life easier for the developers by eliminating the need to customize software for each site. It was not designed to make social network data truly mobile.

When Joe Kraus was asked on the eve of his announcement of OpenSocial why Google had not yet implemented OpenSocial capabilities on its own Web properties to demonstrate the initiative's promise, he readily conceded that its absence was embarrassing. He added that his team was concerned about increased risk of privacy breaches and was moving slowly to ensure the integrity of the company's privacy protections. "Trust builds up over a very long time," he said, "and can be lost very quickly."

A week before Facebook would tell the world about its new advertising system, Kraus predicted that "because they're a start-up" Facebook would take on privacy risks that a publicly traded company like Google could not accept. He drew a surprising analogy when he offered up YouTube—by then a part of Google—as an example of a start-up that early in its history had made a critical bet that an established company would not have made. "They decided early on they didn't care about copyright issues. Huge risks," Kraus said. It turned out well for YouTube, when it was acquired for $1.65 billion, but it was the exception. For most start-ups, the assumption of large risk does not turn out so well.

The next week, on November 6, 2007, Facebook founder and CEO Mark Zuckerberg ascended a stage in New York and portentously began, "Once every hundred years media changes" and offered Facebook's new advertising systems as a once-every-hundred-years media revolution. Unlike the previous century's advertising, based on "broadcasting messages," Facebook's was based upon "getting into the conversations between people." Facebook's new Beacon program offered advertisers the opportunity to track what Facebook members did on their Web sites and automatically inform the members' friends what they had purchased. Another part of Facebook's new advertising program would match advertisements to the interests that members disclosed on their profiles. Facebook members were not asked to grant permission for Facebook to send information about their online purchases to their friends, nor were they asked whether they were comfortable having advertisers use their most personal information on their profile to guide advertisers' pitches. Zuckerberg had no sympathy: "There is no opting out of advertising."

Beacon drew the most immediate attention, and little of it was favorable. Facebook tried to explain that Beacon had been designed for the convenience of its members, who, in Zuckerberg's words, "wouldn't have to touch it for it to work." Many users did not want it to work, however. They were upset that their purchases were broadcast to their friends, whether they wanted that or not. The criticism was so intense that the company had to backpedal. Over the next few weeks, Beacon's design was changed, and changed again. At the time it was introduced, Beacon was activated automatically and reported on the purchases of all members at the forty participating sites, unless the member specifically opted out and asked that his or her purchases at a particular site be excluded. Initially, no one could opt out of all Beacon sites with a single click, but under pressure, Facebook provided an option that allowed members to opt out completely. Then Beacon became opt-in only, ensuring that only those who wished to participate would have their purchases broadcast.

Facebook executives were loath to change because they were convinced that consumers would, as one put it, "fall in love" with Beacon once they became familiar with it. After damage to Facebook's public image was widely commented upon, Zuckerberg publicly apologized for the company's handling of the controversy. But the next month, when *60 Minutes* featured Zuckerberg and Facebook, his contrition had disappeared and he was again depicting Beacon as a service that members should appreciate. He said, "I actually think that this makes it less commercial. I mean, what would you rather see, a banner ad from Bloomingdale's or that one of your friends bought a scarf?" Facebook's own sponsors, however, were not as certain as Zuckerberg that this service would be welcomed by Facebook members, and some backed out.

Google was saved from committing a blunder identical to that of Facebook because it did not possess the information about who its users' friends were. In Google's early years, when it offered just Web search and nothing more, the company was the target of criticism from some privacy advocates for permanently storing information about what users searched for. In retrospect, the alarm was premature, before Google really knew anything much about its users. Searching the Web at Google was done anonymously, so in Google's records, search terms were accompanied only by a computer's Internet address, such as 172.16.254.1, not by a person's known name.

The only circumstances in which a Google user had cause to regret conducting a search were highly unusual, such as a 2003 murder case in North Carolina in which police seized computers at the suspect's house and found that Google searches had been submitted from one of the household's computers for *neck, snap,* and *break,* and for *rigor mortis* and *body decomposition.* The victim was the suspect's wife, who had been found dead, floating in a nearby lake. (The jury found the defendant guilty after only two hours of deliberation.)

In a strange way, the murder case and run-of-the-mill advertising on Google's search pages were similar: they used what was typed into the Google search box as the next best thing to seeing what was actually on the user's mind at that moment. For advertisers, Google offered a way of making a pitch with a precision never before possible: the advertisement was displayed only when the user had indicated an interest in that topic, such as "hotels Maui." The interest might not have been present five minutes before, and it might not be present five minutes later. But at the moment that the search for "hotels Maui" was submitted, it was highly likely that the user, whoever she or he was, would be interested in hotels on Maui. That close association between what was being searched for and the user's receptivity to advertising messages that were very closely linked to the search term held true so reliably that advertisers quickly realized that advertising on Google was a very efficient way of reaching prospects.

The general public did not appreciate what Google had stumbled upon: a way to serve up highly individualized advertising to an audience of one at the best moment—when a relevant topic was on the user's mind, not later—and achieving this without having to know anything about the personal identity of the user. Age, gender, income, nationality, zip code—none of it mattered to Google's advertising engine. Google had all it needed to know—a search phrase—in order to match up the advertisement with the greatest likelihood of eliciting a response.

Google's advertisements worked so well, in fact, without access to the identity of the person conducting the search, that Google executives thought Google would be able to brush off any criticism that its service placed its users' privacy at risk. As late as 2003, Google saw itself as a search company that had no reason to collect personal information. When Urs Hölzle, a senior Google engineer, was asked at a talk about how Google safeguarded an individual's privacy, he explained that Google users did not log on to use the service, so nothing could be known about who they were. To illustrate the difference between Google and other search sites, Hölzle pointed out that Google did not offer e-mail, so user concerns about privacy were "a little bit less of an issue than, let's say, if you had an email service." Of course, within a year, Google introduced Gmail, and a host of new services followed that required a Google user to identify him- or herself. Earlier, Google had claimed it had no personal information about its users, so there was no way that information could be leaked. Now it did have that information, and it could no longer claim that a leak was an impossibility.

What turned out to cause the most trouble for Google, however, was not a leak but a deliberate decision by Google managers to apply a technical shortcut to accelerate its attempts to catch up with Facebook. Google suffered a public relations mishap in December 2007, a month after Facebook introduced Beacon, when it added a social-network-like feature to its Google Talk program, which provided instant messaging and Internet-based telephone service. Google decided to automatically define anyone who had received a call from a Google Talk user to be, ipso facto, the user's "friend." Google now began sending to these recipients items from another service, Google Reader, that were supposed to go only to people whom the user had explicitly designated as personal friends. Critics drew comparisons between this new Google feature and Facebook's Beacon (the *Motley Fool* wrote, "Everyone's following Facebook these days, even down to its missteps"). Like Facebook, Google had placed the onus on users to take action to opt out, rather than attempt to persuade users to participate through an opt-in system. Indeed, Google was so eager to create an instant social network for its users that it had made the foolish assumption that any online conversation—even with a former employer—could be treated as equivalent to induction into one's inner circle of confidants.

The lack of readiness that had been apparent at the time of the announcement of OpenSocial continued to hurt the initiative. Google had released what it called "Version 0.5," which was far from being sufficiently complete to even be called "beta." Developers who tried to build applications with the software discovered it wasn't usable. Kraus attempted to defend the OpenSocial software as merely a first version. "We didn't call it 1.0. We called it 0.5," he said. "We want our partners helping us to figure out what else it's missing and continue to develop it."

In the meantime, Facebook had put the Beacon messiness behind it and moved on to present a new challenge to Google and the OpenSocial alliance: it played the *open* card itself and annouced it was opening up the Facebook architecture, offering to license its standards for third-party software applications to other social networking sites. This move placed it in direct competition with OpenSocial as Facebook vied to have its standards adopted across the entire social networking industry. Taking a page from Microsoft's dog-eared playbook, Facebook was reclaiming the adjective *open* for its own use, even though the source code remained firmly in Facebook's hands.

The tussle between Google and Facebook over who could claim to be more open than whom was initially a matter of interest only to the digerati and software developers. But in early May 2008, MySpace and Facebook made announcements about steps that would allow their users' personal data to be used a little bit more widely than before. Then Google followed with its own announcement of the launch of Google Friend Connect, which went the furthest in opening up social networks so that users' data could be utilized elsewhere around the Web. By utilizing the programming information that Facebook had made available to software developers, Google introduced a service that would let Facebook members pull their own data out of Facebook for use elsewhere. It was a brilliant move on Google's part, putting Facebook's commitment to openness to a very public test.

Facebook failed the test. Claiming that it had to "look out for the privacy of our users," Facebook blocked Google Friend Connect from accessing Facebook data. The decision drew the ire of many commentators. TechCrunch founder Michael Arrington wrote, "How dare Facebook tell *me* that I cannot give Google access to [my] data!"

The slippery adjective *open* was used in different ways by friend and foe in another competitive battle that Google launched in November 2007 in another industry dominated by closed networks, the wireless phone business. Google announced the formation of the Open Handset Alliance, with thirty-four inaugural members, who would jointly work on the development of a new mobile phone standard, Android. The announcement sounded the theme of openness at every opportunity: "Open Software, Open Device, Open Ecosystem." Google also announced it would bid in an upcoming FCC auction of spectrum that could be used to establish a wireless network that would compete directly with the wireless incumbents.

The wireless carriers treated the Google announcements as harbingers of change and all but conceded the need to open, or at least appear to open, their networks in ways they would never have permitted earlier. The year before, Chris Sacca, a Google manager in charge of special projects, had received numerous complaints from the wireless carriers because Google had circumvented the carriers' tight controls on third-party software and directly offered customers its own software, Google Mobile Maps, for free, and without having asked the carriers' permission. Sacca had embarrassed the carriers publicly when he was speaking at Oxford University and extemporaneously told the audience in detail about the carriers' attempts to keep their wireless networks closed. He said, "They're inserting themselves in between you and an application that you want. I think that has scary, scary implications." Sacca's remarks were picked up by news media around the world and many of his Google colleagues were upset with him, fearing that the wireless carriers would exact retribution. He described his position at Google then as "in the doghouse."

Sacca discovered, however, that some Google colleagues shared his interest in breaking the hold of carriers, and a group of volunteers within Google began meeting; their work would eventually become the Open Handset Alliance. The prospect of having any impact at all on the wireless carriers still seemed remote. In the summer of 2007, Google proposed that the FCC require that users be permitted to choose their own phones to use on a new network that would be created by the winning bidder in the upcoming spectrum auction. But Verizon Wireless had immediately brushed Google's proposal aside, arguing that opening a network to phones that it did not sell itself could compromise the network's integrity. It had even resorted to claiming that use of non-Verizon phones would weaken the nation's defense, "in an era of heightened national security concerns."

Yet shortly after the Open Handset Alliance was announced, Verizon decided, in November 2007, that opening up its network to phones purchased elsewhere did not present a problem after all. In a dramatic change of its position, it announced a new "Any Apps, Any Device" slogan. By the end of 2008 it planned to permit its consumers to purchase cell phones from any store and permit them to run any software they wished. There were a couple of qualifications—Verizon would still insist that the devices meet "the minimum technical standard," which was not yet defined, and it appeared that it would treat its new "bring-your-own" customers differently from "full-service" customers. Still, its embrace of *open,* even if it turned out to be mainly rhetorical, signaled that the incumbent carriers no longer could easily defend their closed systems. Although Verizon had not agreed to join Google's Android initiative, Verizon did confer privately with Google, seeking advice about how to open its network, and Eric Schmidt declared the Verizon announcement to be "a great step forward" and used it to extol the virtues of the open network model, which creates "better services for consumers," he said, "as the Internet has demonstrated."

Google's chief executive frequently pointed to the Internet as the world's most robust working model of an open network. He readily acknowledged Google's own indebtedness to the ethos of openness that had created the foundations of Google's own success, the Internet's infrastructure, and the open source software that Google relied upon in its own operations. But Google could not claim that among information providers it best embodied the Internet's spirit of openness. That honor would more properly be conferred upon Wikipedia, which organized information in a system far more radically open than Google's—open to any contributor and to revisions by any editor.

As Wikipedia grew, its articles showed up prominently in many Google searches. A 2006 study of a thousand randomly selected topics covered by Wikipedia showed that the encyclopedia showed up either once or twice among the top ten results in 88 percent of Google searches, and in a majority of cases was placed in first, second, or third position. Google became increasingly unhappy with the fact that it was sending its users off to a site that was strictly noncommercial, open editorially but closed to advertising. Google's AdSense network, which placed advertisements on non-Google sites, could not penetrate Wikipedia, and that rankled. In December 2007, Google announced a new initiative, which invited anyone to submit to Google articles he or she had authored on any subject. The articles would be called *knols*—a neologism meaning units of knowledge. Google's Knols experiment was another instance of moving beyond indexing information hosted at other sites to hosting the information on its own site. Google's Udi Manber said that a knol was "meant to be the first thing someone who searches for this topic for the first time will want to read." This was precisely how many Wikipedia users viewed Wikipedia articles. Google hoped to lure authors with two inducements that Wikipedia did not offer: sole editorial control over the knol and the option, if the author wished, to have Google advertising placed with display of the knol, generating revenue that would be shared with the author. If Google succeeded in attracting contributors, it would be a simple matter for its knols to show up prominently in Google's search results, allowing Google to retain users that would otherwise have been directed to Wikipedia's ad-free site.

Wikipedia's very openness could turn out to be a great help to Google in building out its collection of knols. Charles Matthews, who identified himself as a Wikipedia administrator and arbitrator, pointed out that anyone could legally copy the content of a Wikipedia page, which was not protected by copyright, paste it into a new Google knol, add a simple credit, then place ads and "laugh all the way to the bank."

Google's Manber clearly anticipated that Google's knols would likely be perceived negatively by critics as a program that would increase Google's proprietary hold over information. "We do not want to build a walled garden of content," he said with an unmistakably defensive tone. "Google will not ask for any exclusivity on any of this content and will make that content available to any other search engine."

In this one case, yes, Google eschewed exclusivity and could claim a genuinely open policy. But this was not consistently the case, and left the company susceptible to the criticism that it elected to be open only when it had fallen behind a rival in a particular area. Five years earlier, in 2002, Google had begun preparations to digitally scan every book ever printed, a project so daunting that no other company had seriously considered attempting it. By 2007, Yahoo and Microsoft had begun similar projects, but Google held an enormous lead. Danny Sullivan, a veteran observer of the search business, noted in November 2007 that Google was not anything resembling open in its book-scanning project. Others had formed an Open Content Alliance to make the contents of scanned books available as widely as possible, but Google had refused to join the alliance and instead built an insurmountable "walled garden of content," forbidding other search engines from indexing the contents of its book scans. Sullivan challenged Google to show how committed it truly was to the principle of openness by joining the Open Content Alliance.

Google seemingly heard the criticism, and responded with an announcement in March 2008 that made it appear that the long wait was over: the company made available to outside software developers the programming interfaces that would enable everyone to obtain "book info where you need it, when you need it." The Google Book Search team said that it had released the interfaces because "we love books" and the company wanted to "share this love of books (and the tremendous amount of information we've accumulated about them)." The "tremendous amount of information" that Google claimed to be excited to share turned out, however, to be extremely limited. Google offered access to the information on the book's title page, the Library of Congress catalog number, and a thumbnail image of the book. But the company did not permit outside developers to gain access to the actual text of the books that it had extracted from its scans. Dan Cohen, the director of the Center for History and New Media at George Mason University, noted how little Google was providing and expressed his disappointment in a blog post entitled "Still Waiting for a Real Google Book Search [programming interface]."

For book searches, Google still occupied a position of competitive strength. For social networking, it was in a position of competitive weakness. Sullivan also called Google hypocritical for advocating that Facebook, the network with the most valuable social data about its members, open its data to OpenSocial. Sullivan asked, Why didn't Google open up its index of Web pages, which was the largest collection of any search engine, and create an Open Index Alliance, available to competitors, and let the quality of search results be differentiated by the software used to analyze a common base of information? He was not the first to present the proposal—Wikipedia founder Jimmy Wales, among others, had raised it. Sullivan said it was a matter of consistency: "If Google's going to push for those with existing advantages to open up through efforts like OpenSocial and the Open Handset Alliance, an Open Index Alliance just seems like fair play."

It was a poke, not a genuine challenge, and brought out the point that even Google was committed to an open approach only selectively, not across the board. No company was purely open, and no company was purely closed. No independent observer of the industry could dispute, however, that Google was more open than its closest rivals, and the computer industry as a whole was far more open than those it was encroaching upon, such as wireless carriers. Google's story was, in part, formed by its efforts to convince others, within the computer industry and without, that open networks were demonstrably superior to closed networks. Consumers have tended to gravitate to systems that provide more choices, and the evolution of technology was pointed in the direction of open.

Page and Brin had been fortunate to come of age when they did, when it was possible to use a wide open network of information, the Web, and use open source software as the foundation for what they would build. To make full use of the Web, they needed a lot of computing power. On this, they did not stint. They assembled a computing infrastructure that effectively permitted Google to move in many directions simultaneously, without worrying that they would run out of horsepower.

How Google went about creating capacity would turn out to be highly unconventional and strategically important. Instead of treating computer hardware as highly complex works of engineering, delicate mechanisms that, should they fail, would have devastating consequences for Google's operations, and whose manufacture should be left to companies that do nothing but manufacture computers, Google decided to assemble its own machines. This has turned out well. In the course of developing and refining expertise on the hardware side of the business, Google has acquired another competitive advantage over its rivals in Web services, providing the company with the ability to expand the range of its products at lower cost, and without becoming reliant on outside service providers. It's what makes it possible for Google to think big.

CHAPTER 2

Unlimited Capacity

Once upon a time, computers were a novelty that were put on display for their looks. In 1947, when IBM's engineers built a new 120-foot-long machine, the Selective Sequence Electronic Calculator, the company understood that a computer could dazzle the public on the basis of its appearance alone. Part mechanical and part electronic, it cost $1 million to develop and was ornamented with dials, switches, meters, and flashing indicator lights. CEO Thomas J. Watson installed it on the ground floor of IBM's world headquarters in Manhattan, providing passersby on Fifty-seventh Street with a window view. Every day hundreds of people would stop on the sidewalk to gawk at it.

The machine's impressive façade hid the fact that its designers rushed its completion. When a reporter from the *New Yorker* was given a tour with the machine's inventor, Robert R. Seeber Jr., serving as guide, the visitor peered behind a panel and noticed some wires that were not attached to anything. Seeber nodded knowingly. "Yes, it's a funny thing about those wires—nobody knows what they're doing there."

Placing its Selective Sequence Electronic Calculator in a highly visible location was a brilliant marketing stroke on IBM's part. In the popular mind, the machine's massive size and pulsing lights established what a computer was expected to look like. Strictly speaking, IBM's colossus was a single-purpose calculator, but Hollywood copied its looks whenever a movie set required something that could impersonate a computer. Today, machines incomparably more powerful and versatile than the Selective Sequence Electronic Calculator sit on our laps. Hardware no longer dazzles.

If, however, we could see all of Google's computers, arranged in a single place, we could not fail to take interest. Their sheer collective mass would be stunning. Google is a company whose founders suffered privation as graduate students—that is, they did not have enough computers to carry out their research plans. When they started their own company, they seemed determined never to suffer hunger from resource shortages again.

Google would be scalable, designed to expand its ability to search the Web just as fast as the amount of information accumulating on the Web grew. The Google founders were determined not to settle for being selective in search coverage. However large the Web would become, and whatever types of information it would encompass, Google would strive not merely to maintain the quality and speed of its search abilities, but to use expansion as a means to actively improve quality: the more information that was fed into the Google search engine, the smarter it became.

Page and Brin intuitively understood what others failed to fully appreciate: that search technology could be designed in such a way as to positively thrive when asked to organize the immensity of the entire Web. Where other search engines were overwhelmed by the growing volume of available information, unable to distinguish Web pages with the greatest likelihood of being useful, Google's PageRank system was conceived at the outset to squeeze clues about usefulness from the Web with a sophistication that no one else had attained. The more pages its search engine was fed, the more clues PageRank could extract and use in sorting Web pages for likely relevance. In this sense, Google's technology has an appetite of its own.

When Brin and Page set about organizing the world's information, they made two foundational decisions that would turn out to have ramifications not only for their company but for the broader universe of information, including the Web. The first decision was to make Google's ordering of search results entirely a matter of mathematics. Once software formulas produced search results, Google would not permit *any* human editing to refine the results. They believed that a software approach to the problem of searching the Web provided results superior to those that human editors could produce. It was also the approach that was best suited to be scalable. Even if human editors were free of biases, they could not be hired fast enough—and cheaply enough—to keep up with the addition of millions, then billions, of new Web pages.

The commitment to a hands-off, mathematical approach to evaluating the world's information required Page and Brin to make their second fundamental decision: that Google's computers would be able to scale up as fast as the Web was growing. Google would need a computing and storage system with the power and capacity to master questions that would address *all* of the world's information, more completely, and with better results, than anyone else's. Speed was an important consideration—users would not wait around to see search results that failed to appear instantaneously. Speedy delivery required speedy processing, which could be provided only by first investing in massive machine capacity. The Google founders were determined that they would not be forced by practical limits to settle for something less than their vision for *all.* This has required assembling what most likely is the largest cluster of computers in the world.

Google could have elected to rely for its computing power on the most sophisticated hardware available on the market, designed to handle the most demanding processing needs and the highest volume of Web traffic. Its rivals concentrated on the software side and let computer hardware manufacturers handle the hardware side. But scaling its operations is so deeply embedded in Google's conception of its mission, and scaling rapidly is so crucial to Google's differentiating its business from its competitors', that it decided to build its own machines, a path without precedent in the software industry. By using the same standard components that are the heart of a personal computer and building the machines itself from the start, Google has been able to add capacity cheaply, effectively, and limitlessly.

Having sufficient hardware to accommodate an ambitious project was an issue at the outset of the search engine research that Larry Page began as a Stanford graduate student, which was originally designed to "traverse the Web." He added Sergey Brin as a collaborator. The most interesting challenge for the two was indexing the *entire* Web, not just a selective portion of it. As Google's crawler collected ever more Web pages, Page's and Brin's research was hampered by the limited storage capacity of their machines. Google was run on a motley collection of machines in a dorm room. By early 1998, they had gathered 26 million Web pages, which was about half the number that the established search engines, like AltaVista, had attained two years earlier. The Stanford students desperately needed more hardware. For three years, they recalled later, they "snarfed a whole bunch of machines of all different types" by standing at the receiving dock at Stanford where packages arrived at the university. When they saw someone take delivery of twenty machines, they approached the responsible person to wangle use of a "spare" machine for their research.

To increase their search engine's capacity, the two students spent $15,000 of their own funds, spread across three credit cards, for the purchase of hard drives that could store a terabyte of data. They were intent on improving the power of their search technology, but at this point, they had no intention of starting a search engine company themselves. Rather, they wanted to license their technology to other companies, and their site google.stanford.edu served as a demo site for their technology's searching prowess. It was Yahoo cofounder and Stanford alumnus David Filo who advised the pair otherwise; he told them they should go ahead and enter the search engine business, which would serve as the best way for them to continue to develop their technology and improve their chance of being able to license it in the future.

In the meantime, a visitor to their Stanford site had to bring along some patience: the early Google search engine did not respond quickly. In early 1998, Google queries for common search terms took several seconds—sometimes ten seconds—before results were ready for display. Observers of the search engine business at the time regarded Google as a low-traffic curiosity. But even receiving only one query a second, or ten thousand a day, it used fully one-half of Stanford University's entire Internet bandwidth, a fact that brought an end to the university's welcome.

For this reason, in 1998, Brin and Page decided to move their operation off campus and accept the advice to formally found a company. Not only would the move relieve the university of carrying their network traffic, it would separate them from the nonprofit world of academe and enable them to raise money from angel investors for more hardware and additional network bandwidth. Though they were venturing into the commercial world, they struck off on a markedly different course from that taken by other young Silicon Valley entrepreneurs at the time, who were preoccupied with business buzzwords like *eyeballs* and with racing to a quick IPO. Brin and Page showed no interest in eyeballs or taking their company public; they weren't even interested in market share. They approached the business opportunity no differently than they had the research challenge: they were focused on building technology that would scale up as the Web grew, without being limited by hardware or software constraints. Mastering the entire Web interested them not because it offered the greatest likelihood of future profits, which did not seem to be the case at all in 1998, but because it was an absorbing technical challenge.

Computer science, not business, was uppermost in the founders' minds. Having tried as graduate students to pursue their research with limited machine horsepower, the two young men set off to build a company that would invest in computer resources so improvidently that the machines would always be ample for whatever task they could conceive of, no matter how ambitious. The great irony is that their shunning of conventional cost-accounting considerations, then and since, has enabled the rapid emergence of one of the most profitable businesses of the modern era.

Initially, though, their ambition of scaling up Google's search technology quickly ran into serious problems. Expanding the number of pages included in the Google index was easy enough—their crawler had by the end of 1998 brought in about 60 million Web pages. But their systems choked when trying to perform the involuted calculations required by PageRank. The crawl would take seven to ten days to complete, but constructing the index and calculating PageRanks could take weeks after that. Or even longer. A disk error or transient problem in the computer's memory would corrupt the index while it was being built but would be discovered only later. Then it would have to be rebuilt. As the size of the Web page collection grew, the difficulties in creating the index grew exponentially: once a crawl was completed, calculating PageRanks for every page dragged on beyond weeks into months.

Performance issues were also becoming painfully manifest at the Google Web site. Word was spreading that Google's searches produced more useful links than those offered up by other search engines, and Google's traffic increased rapidly from 10,000 queries a day in 1998 to 100,000 a day in 1999. Brin and Page saw, however, that the infrastructure was not scaling up to fulfill their vision. They sought help from more experienced quarters and in early 1999 met Urs Hölzle, a Stanford-trained computer scientist who had received his Ph.D. in 1995 and was on the faculty of the University of California, Santa Barbara. Hölzle spent one day a week at Stanford, where his wife was finishing her graduate program, and Brin and Page invited him to have a look at their systems.

Like most computer companies that ran busy Web sites, Google placed its machines in rented space that was specially designed for computer servers separate from its own offices. The data center provided reliable power with backup systems in case of disruption, as well as cooling systems that could handle, or at least were supposed to handle, the heat generated by the machines. Space was rented by the square foot, so tenants packed as much computing power as possible into their alloted space.

Hölzle was invited to take a look at Google's hardware, which resided in a data center in Santa Clara, about fifteen minutes away, run by Exodus Communications, the leading data center operator. Google's tiny space contained four racks, stuffed with boards using PC components, which sat within two small cages. These were enclosures built with chain-link fencing that extended from floor to ceiling and were equipped with a locked gate. The fencing permitted air to circulate and heat to dissipate and also protected the machines from mischief at the hands of the other tenants, like eBay and Hotmail, whose machines sat nearby in similar enclosures. Google's hardware was exceedingly modest.

When Brin and Page offered Hölzle a job in February 1999, he was attracted to the technical challenge of building systems that could scale. He also liked that Brin and Page were no less interested in the technical issues than he was. He was glad they were not following the herd of dot-com entrepreneurs in pursuit of a quick profit and exit, though he was mystified about how Google was going to make money. Nonetheless, he signed on.

The team agreed that the company's current index of 60 million pages was much too small. The new goal would be considerably larger: the nice round number of 1 billion pages. No one at Google, or anyone else, could measure the size of the Web at the time, and for all anyone knew the correct number of pages they should have aimed for might have been 300 million, 600 million, or 2 billion pages. "We had no idea," Hölzle said later. What they did know for certain was that were Google to succeed in finding and indexing 1 billion pages, it would far surpass the size of the largest search index, AltaVista's, which covered 150 million pages. Aiming so high so early in Google's history also shaped its institutional culture in this formative stage, implanting the expectation within Google that the company should scale its systems well in advance of its competitors.

Google's systems at the time, in 1999, were failing to keep up with 60 million pages, let alone a billion. Search requests came in slowly enough that Hölzle could watch every one scroll by on his monitor. Even processing search queries that came in a relative trickle, the servers were taking three or three and a half seconds to respond to each one. When the requests arrived in a torrent, the system was overwhelmed and the site crashed.

When Marissa Mayer, employee number 20, arrived on June 24, 1999, for her second day of work at Google, the company had about three hundred computers to handle search requests, and that day would be the first in which Google would receive search requests sent to it by its new affiliate, Netscape. Lacking a search engine of its own, Netscape worked with several search engines. Google had wanted to start off with a limited volume of queries from this new source and had directed Netscape to start off gently by sending it only one out of five search requests that came in. But Netscape forgot or ignored Google's wishes and sent Google all of its requests that day. It was too much; Google.com had to close.

That morning, Mayer stopped by the company kitchen and noticed that Larry Page was standing in a corner of the room for no clearly visible purpose. She asked Page what he was doing. "I'm hiding," he replied. "The site is down. It's all gone horribly awry." Mayer said that seeing the CEO of the company in such a state led to her estimate that Google had about a 2 percent chance of succeeding.

The core problem seemed obvious: a system cobbled together with inexpensive PC components was neither reliable enough nor powerful enough to handle the demands of thousands of queries a day. It simply could not scale. All of the major search engines and portals used commercially manufactured servers, machines engineered to serve Web pages efficiently and at high volume. Their components met the most exacting specifications, minimizing the chance of failure. By contrast, Google was using cheap, unreliable hardware.

When Hölzle surveyed Google's systems, however, he deduced that the search engine's problems with response time were not rooted in the hardware. On the contrary, he concluded that Page and Brin had done their homework well, and that using PC components was, without a question, the most cost-effective approach. The problems were in the software, which had been written on the fly in a university environment, and hadn't taken into account the flaws that would be exposed when the volume of queries went up or when a hard drive or other component failed. By rewriting all of the code, Hölzle believed, Google could gain both speed and reliability without having to forego the savings from using PC components.

After the overhaul of Google's software systems had been completed, Hölzle explained in 2003 at a Stanford computer science colloquium: "The great thing about PCs is they're easy to buy, they're cheap, they're relatively fast for how much they cost. But not the world's most reliable machines. So you have to expect them to fail." After gaining more experience, Google's engineers settled on a standard design that packed forty or eighty servers into a rack, each loaded with the equivalent processing power of a midrange desktop PC matched with a large disk drive. For about $278,000 in 2003, it could assemble a rack with 176 microprocessors, 176 gigabytes of memory, and 7 terabytes of disk space. This compared favorably to a $758,000 server sold by the manufacturer of a well-known brand, which had only eight multiprocessors, one-third the memory, and about the same amount of disk space. Google thereby learned how to obtain greater performance for far less money than its competitors were investing.

In spring 2000, Google took a step that put it ahead of many leading Web companies then, and even ahead today: it opened a second data center, on the East Coast, in addition to the original one that it had in California. This center was purposely duplicative in order to provide what engineers refer to as *redundancy,* unneeded capacity that operates in parallel and is always ready in case of system failure elsewhere. At Google, redundancy was spread not only across thousands of machines but also across the two geographically separate data centers that gave Google the ability to suffer major problems at one site or the other while providing continuous service to all of its users.

Adding a second site might seem an essential requirement for any Web company that wishes to provide uninterrupted service. And yet as late as July 2007, Craigslist, Technorati, Second Life, Yelp, LiveJournal, RedEnvelope, TypePad, and other tenants of a $125 million data center in San Francisco, 365 Main, went dark—Craigslist for eleven hours—when a power outage hit part of the city and the data center's diesel generators, which were supposed to provide a backup source of power in just such circumstances, failed.

When Google added a second data center, it not only gained protection against disaster striking the original center, but also shortened the distance that bits had to be moved. As fast as electrons travel, physical distance still affects response speed. Reducing response time by even a fraction of a second mattered to users, as Google discovered when it ran experiments to see if users noticed a difference between 0.9 seconds, on average, to render twenty-five results on a search results page compared to 0.4 seconds needed to render ten results. Users were conspicuously more likely to grow bored and leave the Google site after waiting that interminable 0.9 seconds.

To speed the transport of bits, Google realized that it could open additional data centers all over the map and do so quickly because it did not need to build its own facilities. It could lease the excess capacity available at commercial data center facilities at ridiculously inexpensive rates. In this way, the timing of Google's expansion in the early 2000s was most fortuitous: the wild funding of dot-com start-ups and the companies that provided services to them, like data centers, had come to an abrupt end in 2001, coinciding with a steep plunge in the stock market. Data centers lost their tenants and were desperate to sign new ones. Google was at the right place at the exact right time.

The company began proliferating data centers by renting more cages, then rooms, then floors of data centers, and then entire buildings. Its original landlord, Exodus, went bankrupt. So, too, did other data center owners from whom Google rented amid this artificial abundance. In 2004, in a talk Eric Schmidt gave at the Stanford Business School, he joked about Google's good fortune. While displaying a picture of a rack of servers that had wheels attached, he asked his audience, "Anybody know why the wheels are so important? To roll the racks in? No, to take them out when the data center goes bankrupt. All our data centers have gone bankrupt. Because we use so much power and we negotiate such low rates."

In fact, Google did not usually have to roll its racks out after the data center went bankrupt; instead it was able to negotiate better terms with the landlord for renting the space. All the owners asked of Google was rent sufficient to cover their costs. When it and other tenants filled in the space available for lease in 2003 and 2004, Google began to purchase the data centers at what were, in Schmidt's words, "fire-sale prices." Google also bought up cheap unused fiber capacity that had been laid by others at the most exuberant point in the giddy years of the late 1990s, using it to connect the centers into a network. This made the scattered clusters of machines work effectively as one very powerful, very capable machine. Other computer service companies, like IBM or EDS, operated more data centers than did Google, but no one else had as many machines, in as many centers, running a unified set of software applications.

Google did have to contend, though, with some problems that came with its reliance on facilities that had been built by others in a rush. Cooling was a vital function; when heat was not dissipated adequately, machines failed. Too many machines in too little space for the building's cooling system produced too much heat.

Machine rooms that are unbearably hot for computers and humans alike have been a feature of computing since the earliest days. In 1950, the UNIVAC's five thousand tubes produced enough heat that the engineers that tended it worked in their underwear. Eric Schmidt once recalled how in the 1970s, as a young programmer, he had worked on a mainframe that had to be water cooled and required elaborate plumbing.

The problem of heat dispersal has not been solved with the increase in technical sophistication of the computer industry's semiconductors; in fact, the problem in some ways is getting much worse as machines have become ever more powerful. The faster a machine runs, the more energy it consumes and the more heat it throws off. Energy consumption has increased dramatically also because so many more transistors fit onto a chip. The effect is mitigated by the fact that chips also have shrunk, so power consumption for each chip went up "only" 400 percent when performance improved twentyfold. Still, the net increases in consumption remain enormous. As early as 2005, Luiz André Barroso, a principal engineer at Google, predicted that the cost of supplying power for one of Google's servers could soon exceed the purchase price of the server. He imagined the possibility of "bizarre business models in which a power company will provide you with free hardware if you sign a long-term power contract."

Google explored energy-saving improvements in the design of the computers' power supply, which required using a more expensive component; the expense was quickly recouped with savings in energy costs. The company also looked at reducing its cooling needs and improving energy efficiency by retrofitting the data centers that it had purchased. But as Google's growing needs began to push against the capacity of its data centers, the company began preparations in 2004 for a new approach that would simultaneously ease pressure on its existing facilities and reduce its energy costs: it would build from scratch its own data center facilities for the first time and place them close to where power is generated.

The first data center to be built was at a small town, The Dalles, Oregon, about eighty-five miles east of Portland along the Columbia River and, not incidentally, home to The Dalles Dam, a 1.8 gigawatt hydropower station. The area also offered a fiber optic network that was already in place. This move opened the company up to new scrutiny. Up until February 2005, Google had been able to add data center capacity without drawing notice because its leasing contracts and real estate purchases were with private parties. The company took over existing facilities for which zoning approvals had already been obtained. But the Oregon project involved building a new facility, which required approval from local zoning authorities.

Even so, Google proceeded by stealth. The necessary blessings were obtained, the crucial arrangements with the Bonneville Power Administration were smoothed, a threat by the Bush Administration to privatize Bonneville and raise rates was quietly killed; all of the work to put the deal together was completed while officials were bound by nondisclosure agreements that Google had them sign. The land sale was publicly disclosed only after it was completed, in February 2005. Even while construction was under way, the city attorney and the city manager were bound by confidentiality agreements that they had signed at Google's insistence. Purchases and permissions for additional built-from-scratch data centers were completed in 2007 in Lenoir, North Carolina, and Goose Creek, South Carolina, each center to cost $600 million. Then two more centers were placed in Pryor, Oklahoma, and Council Bluffs, Iowa.

In each case, Google moved ahead with construction out of public view. Its stealth, combined with the tax incentives that the company received, created an image on the editorial pages of local newspapers in these areas of a sinister corporate octopus moving soundlessly, wrapping its tentacles around a small, defenseless community. Negotiations between two parties could never be truly fair if one party seemed to the other to have infinite wealth. Tommy Tomlinson, a newspaper columnist for the *Charlotte Observer,* reasoned that Google was owned by billionaires who could afford the best negotiators in the world. After listing the various tax abatements provided to Google by local and state officials that could cost more than $260 million, he wrote, “It appears our local boys got schooled like a church-leaguer guarding Michael Jordan.”

Google attempted to defend its honor and good name in North Carolina in a letter to the editor of the *Charlotte Observer.* Lloyd Taylor, Google's director of global operations, explained that Google had paid county governments millions of dollars to cover expenses and infrastructure improvements related to the project, and the tax reductions that it had been granted merely put North Carolina on par with other states. Without those concessions “to level the playing field, it would have been a better business decision for us to do our expansion elsewhere.”

Whenever state and local governments provide incentives to persuade a large corporation to place a new facility in their bailiwicks, the advocates point to the economic benefits that come with new jobs. In the case of Google's data centers, however, local advocates cannot rely on the standard arguments to defend industrial incentives: few new jobs will be generated by a $600 million Google data center. The expansion of Google's physical capacity to hold the entire universe of knowledge requires few humans to tend to the machines. Hardware systems that expected high rates of failure had redundancy built into their designs and actually needed fewer attendants than those systems that lacked redundancy and came to a halt if a component failed. In a public talk in 2005, Urs Hölzle projected on the auditorium's screen a photograph of an interior view of a Google data center—it was so dark that nothing much could be seen. He explained, “We actually do have the lights off more and more because there's nobody [in the room] and we want to save power.”

Two hundred jobs was the number that Google said it expected to create when one of its new centers was fully operational. How many of this small number would be hired locally wasn't announced. The *Charlotte Observer*'s Tomlinson pondered the mismatch between the skills that Google needed and those in the possession of the unemployed in Lenoir and concluded: “Google needs computer guys, and Lenoir has laid-off furniture workers. God bless them if they can learn how to run a server farm."

Google was going to be criticized if it failed to hire locally, and criticized if it did hire locally, poaching talent from neighboring businesses, as when Google's center at The Dalles hired an IT expert who had worked at nearby Orchardview Farms. Whether or not Google could offer examples of local talent doing well at Google's facility did not really matter in terms of the execution of the company's strategy. Though Google's local critics did their best to find a damaging argument in favor of blocking the centers, they came up short.

Data centers at dispersed sites constitute the essential postindustrial infrastructure relied upon by the information age economy, just as steam boilers and steel rails were the indispensable infrastructure for the railroad age in the nineteenth century. Google came to understand before its rivals how important centralized computing capacity would be because its founders also appreciated earlier than their rivals that the Internet was evolving into a realm of ever-deepening complexities. When Google was founded, the Web was an online reference desk, but over time, the full Internet, including services that were invisible to users as well as visible, was becoming a complete virtual world, existing in parallel to the physical one. It was becoming incomprehensibly immense, as more of life was lived online. The user's dependence upon a search engine to sort through the universe of possible destinations could only grow. Google intended to remain the one indispensable guide.

In April 2004, Eric Schmidt explained Google's overarching aim of "trying to make Google be a place where people live online." In hastening that process, Google had to make practical preparations in the physical world, in the form of adding more hard-drive platters, mounted on racks that sat securely within a heavily fortified building, and located geographically as close to users as possible to minimize response times. Google's principal competitors, Yahoo and Microsoft, have now also come to the realization that data centers are crucially important to their futures and are following Google's path, building their own centers, but they are well behind.

Google's executives do not see its current building boom as a blip that will soon subside. The company expects that we will move more information that we are accustomed to storing on computers in our offices and homes to servers in centralized locations, like Google's. It also expects us to digitize information that currently resides on paper, and this too will require building more data centers. The popularity of online video also creates demand for more centers; video creates files far larger than those holding text.

With its experience as the leader in building out its own data center infrastructure, Google now looks at the addition of a new data center as a matter of routine. Schmidt has described the process as simple: Fill a large building with servers, then plug in to the overhead power line. Repeat as necessary.

At Google, Page and Brin, the two former students, created a software company that built its own tools. By developing the ability to stamp out data centers cost-effectively in bulk, Google has the means to expand its data collection without limits, to scale its business without pausing. As fast as its business has grown, the company has never run out of capacity and been forced to hold off on the introduction of new services. Nor has the company ever been forced to cancel plans to build a new center or relocate because of local opposition. This permits the company to expand, and expand, and expand. It also provokes a growing nimbus of worry among some users and many privacy advocates as they watch the data centers multiply and wonder how Google intends to make use of all the data, so much of it personal, that it is accumulating in its digital storehouses.

Google could attempt to put the public's anxieties at ease by putting its operations on public display, even if behind a window, as IBM did in the 1940s. But Google's executives have gone to extraordinary lengths to keep the company's hardware hidden from view. The facilities are not open to tours, even to members of the press. (I requested a mere five-second poke-my-head-in-the-door glimpse and was turned down.) A Google spokesperson said that Google executives believe that their hardware expertise provides the company with a competitive advantage that would be eroded were other companies able to get a glimpse inside, even if it was through a journalist's eyes. Secrecy is the norm in any highly competitive business environment, of course, and especially so in the technology industry. But even so, Google stands out for its secrecy.

Guided by its founding mission, to organize all the world's information, Google has created storage capacity that allows it to gain control of what its users are thinking and doing in a comprehensive way that no other company has done, and to preserve those records indefinitely, without the need to clear out old records to make way for new ones. Moreover, Google differentiates its service by refining its own proprietary software formula to mine and massage the data, technology that it zealously protects from the sight of rivals. This sets up a conflict between Google's wish to operate a "black box" (completely opaque to the outside) and its users' wish for transparency.

At the very least, users would like Google to disclose what protections are in place to safeguard their privacy. It is also natural that users would be curious about the machines that hold their personal data, as well as about which employees within Google have access to that data, and about the risks that it might be leaked, stolen, or transferred, for example, to a government agency that requests it. How can users be certain that their personal information won't be put to uses to which an individual would never willingly consent? Privacy concerns extend across all Internet companies, but those concerns are greatest where personal information is gathered in the largest pool. This makes the stewardship of Google's machines a subject of public interest.

Whatever is behind a door that is intentionally kept closed will appear sinister, whether deservedly so or not. For the sake of improving its public image, it's possible that Google may relent and open its doors, at least enough to afford a peek inside. The fact that its data centers run "dark," without attendants, does not itself settle the question of whether a rogue Google employee could snoop on users' activities. But more openness would bring a measure of reassurance to users who are concerned about what happens at Google out of view. Were Google willing to open up more, it would be able to point to the absence of human intervention in the daily operations of the company. The Google model depends on automation to scale. It is software, not humans, that does the work at Google's information factory.

CHAPTER 3

The Algorithm

Anyone can call up the Google home page and summon the full power of Google's search engine without having to sign in or provide any personal information. Gender, race, age, education, occupation—all remain unknown. The search engine has only the search phrase itself to work with, along with an unhelpful Internet address of the machine that sends in the search request.

Google's skill at fielding search requests that are submitted anonymously originates in the founders' focus on extracting as much information as possible from the Web side, rather than from the user's side. An algorithm is a set of rules for solving a particular problem; it's the essential building block used in constructing complex computer software. Google's PageRank algorithm, the formula that analyzes the links that point to a Web page to discern the relative reputation of one page over another, draws on information that sits on Web pages. Google's search engine does not need to know anything about the user other than whatever can be guessed is on the user's mind when the search phrase was typed in.

Developing a core strength in searching anonymously would turn out to help Google greatly in other ways that were never anticipated at the time of its beginnings. As the online world has expanded exponentially and the amount of personal information collected online has grown apace, users have watched with queasiness as one company after another, whether accidentally or intentionally, has released information that users regard as personal and private. With each breach, privacy concerns are heightened, and users look for assurances that their personal information will not be disclosed. Fortunately for Google, its search service does not need to know who its users are in order to perform well.

Google's impersonal, mathematical approach to search also provides it with the ability to serve up advertisements that are tailored to a search, rather than to the person submitting the search request, whose identity would have to be known. In this way, Google is well positioned to compete for online ad dollars with social networking sites like Facebook, which offer advertisers the opportunity to target particular users, but only by selling access to information that users regard as personal and sensitive.

Google's advantage over social networking rivals in not needing its users' personal information to perform Web searches is mitigated, of course, by Google's expanding into many other services beyond search, in which the information that it holds is extremely personal, such as its e-mail service, Gmail. Google is aware that users may worry that its employees could snoop, at will, in the e-mail of the company's users. This problem is not unique to Google. Employees at Microsoft, Yahoo, and AOL can rummage through users' private e-mail messages, too, and these services handle a greater volume of e-mail messages than does Google. So it is a bit unfair for Google to be singled out by users of e-mail who are worried about strangers surreptitiously reading their personal messages. For its part, Google's attempts at reassuring the public have been, at best, only partially persuasive. The company says that only a small number of Google employees are permitted to access e-mail stored by Gmail, which is good. Not so reassuring, however, is the way the company has defined specific categories of users whose e-mail is placed off-limits to a Google employee: "any public figure, any employee at a particular company, or any acquaintance." Does this forbid recreational reading of e-mail messages of strangers? Is the stated punishment for violating this policy—termination—severe enough to be an effective deterrent? Has unapproved snooping ever been detected and a Google employee dismissed? Would the user whose e-mail was rifled be informed?

As much as Google protests that such concerns are unfounded, breaches at other companies create worries that extend to every company that stores users' personal data. Even though it was Facebook's employees, not Google's, who were reported in 2007 to have looked up user profiles (in one case for the purpose supposedly of examining prospective candidates for dates), or faked e-mail messages, or changed users' profile photos, Google's privacy practices have come under increasing suspicion as well.

When Google was founded, Page and Brin did not have to worry about privacy concerns. They were single-mindedly devoted to automating the process of judging Web pages. Their approach was unlike that of Yahoo, the leader in the first generation of Web guides, which relied upon human editors to maintain a hand-culled directory of Web sites. The story of how Google displaced Yahoo and gained the position of preeminence is instructive in the way Google used computer science more adroitly than much larger incumbents.

Google began with nothing more than its search engine, which performed the unglamorous work of indexing and analyzing Web pages. In 2000, the company struck a deal with Yahoo, then the far larger company, to perform Web searches for Yahoo's users. It was not a financial boon for Google, nor did it help it establish its own brand identity—Yahoo's users did not even know that Google was the wholesale supplier of search results, which were presented as if Yahoo had found them. What the deal did provide Google was something that was strategically more important than sales or brand awareness: it gave Google a high volume of search queries, which was the raw material needed to improve its search technology, with its built-in ability to turn quantitative increases in data into qualitatively improved results.

As Page and Brin's technology got "smarter" as it worked with more information, it was only natural that the two sooner or later would give thought to how they might get their hands on as much raw data, about anything and everything, as they could. How the different bodies of information would be interconnected was not regarded as the most pressing problem. Collect first, analyze later. If the information was not already in digital form, then Google would spend whatever was required to digitize it. The company's earliest experience with the Web had shown the wisdom of gathering more information than anyone else, and letting the size of the collection work in one's favor in many ways, producing a more dense collection of cross-references, contributing to the most sophisticated ranking of search results in the world.

Google understood, well before its chief rivals, Yahoo and Microsoft, noticed, that an information collection that attempts to be complete expands on a scale far beyond anything that can be curated by human editors. Just as the human mind depends upon neural connections that develop spontaneously, so, too, digital collections of information will rely on interconnections that are created by software, without human agency. Software algorithms are created by humans, but the complexity of the end products far exceeds anything that human creators could produce manually.

In building a company, Page and Brin used many different algorithms. But in a philosophical sense, the different formulas were not material: all of Google's algorithms could be said to be pieces of the Algorithm, shorthand for the software formulas that the Google founders believed were the best means to solve any given problem. Their confidence in the power of the Algorithm led them to adopt a controversial corollary: that the results produced by the Algorithm should not be edited, adjusted, or touched in any way by human intervention. The only way to scale their systems to handle all of the world's information was by automating all processes. The Algorithm could be manually adjusted and improved, but the tinkering would be with the Algorithm itself, prior to conducting a search. Were they to permit second-guessing the Algorithm and tinkering with search results after the search, such human intervention would slow the system and hobble it. At Google, achieving scale was paramount, and that required relying upon wholly automated processes.

The power of the Algorithm was not widely appreciated in the search business when Google got its start. At the time of the Yahoo-Google deal, Google seemed unlikely to pose a competitive threat to anybody. In its early years, the late 1990s and early 2000s, there was no obvious opening for Google to make its way and find acceptance as the company that would organize the world's information. Yahoo was securely entrenched as the most trusted source for all manner of sundry information and appeared to be fully capable of playing the role well. As a portal, Yahoo was the first place an Internet user would visit online, and the company offered a comprehensive array of services and information that would make its site the last site a user would need to visit. It offered e-mail, classifieds, games, news, sports, weather, stock quotes, and whatever else its curators could think of that would pull visitors in and keep them contentedly in place.

If its users felt a need to explore the Web, Yahoo provided a guide that was widely regarded as the most authoritative because it was hand edited by human editors, who carefully culled wheat from chaff and arranged the listings for Web sites into categories and subcategories. But the company's executives did not regard the consistently high quality of its Web directory to be a valuable strategic asset. The company accepted the conventional wisdom of the time that a Web search was only a minor component of a popular portal. Two out of three of Yahoo's visitors came to it for other features or services.

At Yahoo, searching the Web could involve two separate stages, though the complexity was hidden. In the first stage, after a search term was submitted, Yahoo looked among the subject categories in the Web directory that its own editors had compiled. If a search term matched any of its directory listings, the relevant directory entries were displayed. If no match turned up, then the search entered the second stage, when Yahoo sent the term out to a search engine with which it had contracted, which looked among copies of all of the pages on the Web that it had collected and indexed. The second stage was considered by almost everyone in the business to be uninteresting, a behind-the-scenes service that could be obtained from any of a number of fungible suppliers, among whom there were no clear distinctions. One seemed just as good as the next, and Yahoo changed its suppliers periodically.

In 2000, Yahoo decided to funnel stage-two searches to a new wholesale supplier: Google. For Yahoo to anoint a two-year-old firm to supply search engine services was a major achievement for then tiny Google. The quality of Google's searches was sufficiently superior that it had succeeded in standing out in a crowded field. Google came out on top among thirteen search sites covered in a 2000 study of user experiences. Still, Google obtained the Yahoo deal not because its search results were superior to incumbent Inktomi's, but because Google was hungry enough for Yahoo's endorsement that it offered Yahoo the lowest price for the service. After Inktomi lost the Yahoo contract, one of its executives sniffed, "We are not in the business of winning search at any cost."

What Yahoo failed to appreciate about Google's potential as a rival was the fact that Google, unlike Inktomi, had a "retail" presence: its own Web site, where it could attract more and more customers itself by serving up better search results. Only two years after Google made its deal to supply search results to Yahoo, Google's market share in the U.S. search business approached that of its patron. Meanwhile, globally, Google had jumped out ahead. By April 2002, Google was responsible for 47 percent of search referrals worldwide, compared to Yahoo's 21 percent. Even so, two more years would pass before Yahoo realized in 2004 that its arrangement with Google was a colossal blunder. Yahoo belatedly replaced Google's search engine on its site with its own engine in an effort to reclaim control over a function it finally understood as vital to its ongoing success. But by that time, Google had consolidated its position as Search Central.

Yahoo has not been able to come even close to catching up with Google. In May 2007, Google's share of online searches in the United States had passed 50 percent according to one survey. Yahoo had a 26 percent share and Microsoft 10 percent. Google's share continued to climb: by January 2008, Google had a 58 percent share and Yahoo had dropped to 22 percent. Rick Skrenta, the CEO of news site Topix.net, made a persuasive case that Google's actual share of searches was much higher than market research surveys showed, and had passed 70 percent even by the end of 2006. In early 2007, Skrenta confessed that his data showed that Google's market share was actually 78–80 percent, and he had rounded down to a conservative 70 percent "so as to be believable."

When Microsoft bid to acquire Yahoo in 2008, company officials offered the argument that if the two companies were to combine their engineering teams, they would be able to better compete against Google. But it was the quality of Google's engineering team, not the quantity of personnel, that best explains why Google's algorithm was able to produce better search results even when Google was a tiny company.

Both Microsoft and Yahoo were slow to appreciate the power of Google's algorithm. In the early years of Google's ascent, Yahoo was held back by its ill-fated decision to rely on human editors. In 1998, Srinija Srinivasan, who oversaw a staff of forty that maintained Yahoo's directory, said that she and her new editors would not be able to keep up with the Web's growth even if they had at their disposal "unlimited resources." Already at that early date, they no longer were attempting to do so—they had decided simply to settle for what they chose to describe as "the best of what's out there." Of course, how they could be sure they were identifying the best of such a rapidly expanding pool of data was a troubling question.

Meanwhile, Google enjoyed the benefits of relying on technology that scaled well. The more data the Algorithm crunched, the better the results. The company does not disclose how many Web pages the Algorithm processes—8 billion pages indexed was the last number it released, in 2004, before it decided not to provide updated numbers. But even by 2000, observers were raving about the apparent superiority of Google's search results compared to others. Danny Sullivan wrote in *Search Engine Report:*

> When I speak about search engines to groups and mention Google, something unusual happens to some members of the audience. They smile and nod, in the way you do when you feel like you've found a secret little getaway that no one else knows about. And each time I speak, I see more and more people smiling and nodding this way, pleased to have discovered Google.

Google also put ever greater distance between itself and its rivals by developing a more sophisticated algorithm for choosing which advertisements should be displayed on its search results page for a given search term. Google used an auction mechanism to let sponsors bid, setting the top amount that they would be willing to pay for every click. This could have been easily duplicated by any of Google's competitors. What Google added, however, was a twist that turned out to make its advertisements far more lucrative than those at any other search site: an algorithm analyzed a sponsor's history to determine the likelihood that a particular advertisement would attract clicks, and it gave the most prominent positions not necessarily to the highest bidder but to the sponsors that statistically had the most likely chance of producing the most revenue for Google, taking into account the expected number of clicks, as well as the amount paid per click. The more searches that Google was asked to perform, the more historical data it collected about the effectiveness of its ad inventory, and the more accurate its prediction model became. Thanks to Google's algorithm, which no one in the industry could duplicate, Google earned far more for each search than everyone else did.

Microsoft, burdened with the belief that no company knew more about writing software than it did, was slow to notice Google's software prowess. The notion that a company like Google, with far less experience, could develop search software that was more sophisticated than Microsoft's was inconceivable. It was embarrassing when a blogger noted in 2004 how superior Google search results were to Microsoft's. A search for "Microsoft blog" on Google led straight to the employee blogs at Microsoft. But the same search on Microsoft's own MSN service led instead to the blogs of reporters at Seattle's daily newspaper, which happened to contain frequent mention of the word "Microsoft" and confused the search engine's algorithm. This was especially embarrassing because the blogger who publicized the superiority of Google's search results was Robert Scoble, a Microsoft employee, writing on a Microsoft blog.

Microsoft's executives did not spike Scoble's remarks, but Google's commanding share of Web search rankled. The defection of Microsoft developers to Google was also upsetting. In 2004, when Mark Lucovsky, one of Microsoft's most highly decorated software developers, met with Steve Ballmer, Microsoft's CEO, to tell him that he was resigning and joining Google, Ballmer did not receive the news of the loss kindly. According to an affidavit filed later in a lawsuit involving another Microsoft employee who left to work for Google, Lucovsky recalled that when he told Ballmer of his resignation and acceptance of an offer with Google, Ballmer threw a chair across the office and vowed to "bury" Google's Eric Schmidt. In Lucovsky's presence, Ballmer also threatened—here the *San Francisco Chronicle* used strategically placed hyphens to avoid having to paraphrase Ballmer's language— "I'm going to f---ing kill Google."

When Microsoft chairman Bill Gates was asked by reporters at the 2004 World Economic Forum at Davos, Switzerland, about what he thought of Google, he was more polite than Ballmer. Gates heaped upon Google some of the highest praise he could think of—the "high level of IQ" that Google had collected reminded him of "Microsoft twenty years ago." In the search competition, he granted that "they kicked our butts," but in his view, Microsoft had done a "good job" on the most common queries that comprised 80 percent of all searches. Its mistake, he explained, was not paying attention to the more obscure topics because "that's where the quality perception is." He smiled broadly, predicting that Microsoft would soon pass Google in innovations and catch up.

Microsoft managers encouraged employees to use MSN's search engine, and also to click on its ads, rather than use Google and send money to its principal competitor. Adam Barr, a software developer at Microsoft who maintained the tartly titled blog *Proudly Serving My Corporate Masters,* wrote in 2005 that, in general, trying to "strong arm" employees to use the company's products does not solve the product's deficiencies, which are all too apparent if employees do not freely choose to use the home team's service.

Barr also did not accept the "don't send money to our competitors" argument:

> Shoot, we own like 3 iPods and an iMac, I use CorelDraw for editing, I buy books by various competitors of Microsoft Press (not to mention publishing with one). Heck, I run Firefox as my browser, although I guess that doesn't involve money. Anyway I probably make dozens of decisions every day that indirectly affect

> Microsoft's bottom line in a small way. Does [the airline that I'm making reservations on use] Microsoft for its backend servers? Does that restaurant run Windows on its cash registers? Is all the Microsoft software at my doctor's office properly licensed? Who knows. Yes, I'm an employee and shareholder of Microsoft, but I'm also a consumer and I feel free to exercise my right to dispense my money (or my eyeball impressions) as I want.

Barr was willing to accept the suggestion that employees use MSN's search if it was couched as a nudge to give it another try and see improvements. The first comment posted on his blog, however, was by another Microsoft employee, Adam Herscher, who did not see MSN's search as ready to go head-to-head with Google's. Herscher wrote, "I'd venture to say that Google's end-to-end user experience blows MSN's out of the water," and then followed with a detailed comparison. He concluded, "For what it's worth, I try to use MSN services as much as possible. But until there's parity with Google (i.e., as long as Google provides a better service), I'm going to continue to use Google—and it's probably better for Microsoft if I do."

The next year, in April 2006, Microsoft hired an outsider, Steven Berkowitz, to head its Internet division and lead the improvements that the company hoped would reverse the sliding fortunes of its search service. MSN, as the home of the enormously popular Hotmail e-mail service, had 110 million unique visitors a month and was the second-most-visited family of sites in the United States. Yet the visitors steered clear of MSN's search service. In March 2005, MSN held a paltry 16 percent of the search market, but a year later, when Berkowitz was appointed, it had slipped to 13 percent.

At the end of 2006, Berkowitz, who had been the CEO of another search service, Ask Jeeves (later rechristened Ask), spoke with candor about the quandary he faced. Counting up all users of MSN's various Web properties and services around the world produced an astounding total of 430 million people. Yet "a very small subset of them use our search," he said. "My No. 1 strategy is to keep these people from leaking."

If Google's "high level of IQ" created an algorithm that Microsoft's engineers could not yet match, then Microsoft could try something entirely new: attempt to depict the lack of a powerful algorithm as an advantage, a sign of the company's human touch. Under Berkowitz, Microsoft attempted to turn the tables and promote a new tagline in its advertising: "Algorithm, Meet Humanity." In full-page advertisements that ran in the *Wall Street Journal* and other newspapers in fall 2006, Microsoft tried to spin its deficiency this way: "Let us state the obvious. We're late to the game. We admit it. But instead of shrugging our shoulders and becoming a footnote in search history, we've decided to write a few new chapters." The ad copy depicted the Algorithm in the most negative way, as "a complicated mathematical equation" that produces results that somehow needed additional interpretation so that "we can all understand." To bolster its argument, Microsoft added to its search results some new whizzy features, like bird's-eye views of images and live traffic information, which provided "something more . . . human." The strangest part of this pitch was when Microsoft came close to making the argument that it was better equipped to compete against Google precisely because it was not encumbered with Google's "high level of IQ": the Microsoft ad boasted that its latest features improving the presentation of search results were created by "our people, some of whom didn't even pass calculus. Imagine that."

Microsoft also tried something else: it opened up its checkbook and offered to pay corporations to use its search service. Unlike the "Algorithm, Meet Humanity" advertising campaign, the "Microsoft Service Credits for Web Search" was not publicized by Microsoft. John Battelle's *Searchblog* broke the story, and as the details of how Microsoft had been reduced to paying customers to use its service were extracted, Microsoft came off looking desperately afraid of Google's algorithm. In response to a flurry of criticism in the press, Microsoft put Adam Sohn, director of global sales and marketing for Windows Live, on the line to answer reporters' questions. There was not much he could say, however, to cast Microsoft's attempts to literally buy customers in a positive light. The best thing he had to offer was this wan bromide: "There's always controversy when anyone tries something new."

Microsoft's reputation and pride were hurt, but more important, it failed to slow the steady enlargement of Google's power in many domains. In search, Google continued to expand its market share. In newer areas, such as YouTube's video, Microsoft had nothing comparable. And in Microsoft's own core software business, Google was slowly encroaching with free online services that were direct competitors of Microsoft's Outlook, Word, Excel, and related software. Microsoft did not lack cash—it had more than $21 billion burning a hole in its pocket in September 2007—but the money could not buy it a coherent strategy that could effectively match Google's multifaceted expansion. As for Steve Berkowitz, the outsider who was appointed senior vice president of Microsoft's Online Services group and charged to bring fresh ideas into the organization, his tenure did not last long; he was removed from the position less than two years after arriving.

Not only has Google trounced its rivals by its reliance on the Algorithm, but it has also achieved an extraordinary feat of corporate branding. Its name has become synonymous with searching the Web—*googling* is now a generic term. The company is now so closely associated with superior search that even when Ask, a rival with a better claim to impressive search abilities than either Yahoo or Microsoft, tried to brand itself as a Google-class competitor with its own powerful algorithm, the approach backfired.

Ask attempted to gain market share by offering the purest form of algorithmic search, and in the spring of 2007, the company launched its "The Algorithm Rocks" advertising campaign. Television commercials, billboards, and print advertisements were designed to "educate" the public so that everyone understood that "all search engines are not the same, and the algorithm they use is important." At *thealgorithm.com*, Ask gave long semicomic explanations of the "History of the Algorithm" with irreverent discursions ("It's a Good Thing Robert Frost Never Wrote an Algorithm"). Buried in its midst, all but impossible to see, was an esoteric lecture on how Ask's algorithm was developed at the same time as Google's, but on a wholly separate track, combining technology developed at two other companies, Teoma and Direct Hit.

Alex Bogusky, chief creative officer at Ask's advertising agency, Crispin, Porter + Bogusky, explained at the time of the campaign's launch that *algorithm* is "a funny word that most people do not hear every day, if at all." The advertising that Ask planned for the yearlong campaign would attempt to "inject the word into the consumer arena." Unfortunately for Ask and its agency, the word had already circulated sufficiently prior to the campaign to attach itself with strong adhesion to Google. Three months after the campaign was launched, survey results making the rounds internally at Google showed that most members of the general public who had seen Ask's "We are the algorithm" advertisements assumed that the "we" referred to Google.

The pure algorithmic approach drew a fair amount of criticism from professional observers of the search engine business. *Boing-Boing*'s Cory Doctorow argued that the algorithms that rank pages "embody the biases, hopes, beliefs, and hypotheses of the programmers who write and design them." Tim O'Reilly pointed out in 2008 that humans figure out how the algorithm works and then game the system, designing commercially oriented pages that attain high PageRank and occupy the top spots in search results. He said savvier users learn to deliberately skip to the second page of search results to avoid the spam that is predominant on the first page.

At the company's beginning, Google's founders were adamant that the Algorithm, and only the Algorithm, would determine search results. This approach faced a major challenge in 2004, when users noticed that an anti-Semitic Web site, Jewwatch.com, showed up at the top of Google's results for a search for the word *Jew*. A petition was circulated urging Google to remove the site from its results. Sergey Brin, who, like Larry Page, is himself Jewish, received many e-mail messages from friends who asked him to personally intervene. Brin said he, too, was offended by the site "but the objectivity of our rankings is one of our very important principles. We don't let our personal views—religious, political, ethical, or otherwise—affect our results."

Since then, Google's founders have not relented on sensitive political matters such as manually demoting Jewwatch. The company still maintains that the only way to keep human bias out is to let the Algorithm have the final say. Peter Norvig, Google's director of research, reiterated the point in 2006, saying Google resisted the temptation to make small adjustments when someone complained about the ordering of search results because "we think it's just a slippery slope."

Nevertheless, Google has permitted a wee bit of flexibility when the Algorithm simply fails in a small number of cases without the injection of some human intervention. For example, a search for "O'Reilly" produced results that were related to conservative political commentator Bill O'Reilly, crowding out other possible O'Reillys, such as O'Reilly Auto Parts, a Fortune 500 company. Google acknowledged the problem by creating in such special cases an exception to the Algorithm's rankings. The first page of results for "O'Reilly" is now subdivided into three bands, one for links for miscellaneous O'Reillys, one for O'Reilly Auto Parts, and one for Bill O'Reilly.

Brin and Page understood that manually inserting adjustments was an approach that could never be applied on a mass scale. They did accept, however, that humans could serve as quality-control inspectors. Google hired human evaluators to judge the relative quality of results produced by variations of algorithmic tweaks—in 2007, Google used ten thousand contractors around the world as "quality raters." But their feedback was used for making adjustments to the Algorithm itself and not with search results for a single term. Were Google to permit second-guessing the Algorithm and adjusting results by hand after the search, the system would be slowed unacceptably. At Google, achieving scale was paramount, and that required relying upon almost wholly automated processes (another small exception was its willingness to manually exclude links that users had reported were filled with spam). Yahoo's inability to scale its human-edited directory as the Web expanded showed the limitations of a system that relied upon humans. Google was determined to avoid Yahoo's mistakes and to have the ability to grow as fast as the Web.

Google's algorithms do not transfer smoothly to categories of information other than the Web, such as books and videos. The Web provides an abundance of internal data, in the form of links, that the Algorithm can utilize to make judgments about the quality of the information displayed. Will it be able to master different data that lack similar internal clues? Will Google ultimately need to modify its reliance on formulas and incorporate more human input? Will "social search"—having users' judgments about the relevance and usefulness of a Web page determine its place in the presentation of search results—be able to handle a broader range of information categories than the Algorithm can handle well? The potential of the algorithmic model in new applications, and its limitations, can be better understood by looking closely at how Google has attempted to extend its reach in new projects. In one case, when analyzing current news stories, the results have been decidedly unimpressive. In another, when translating foreign-language text into English, the Algorithm shows surprising promise.

The less promising experiment began in March 2002, when Google decided to try the Algorithm out as a replacement for human editors in sorting, clustering, and prioritizing news stories. When Google's managers prepared to introduce the service, there was some internal discussion about the wisdom of relying wholly on software to make decisions about what stories should be placed in the most visible positions on Google's news site. Jonathan Rosenberg, a Google vice president, suggested, "Throw some editors on that thing—we'll have the best news product on the web." But Larry Page vetoed the suggestion because "manual solutions don't scale."

When Google's news service was formally rolled out in September 2002, it drew upon more than four thousand news sources. In tiny print on the bottom of the news page was a whimsical note: "No humans were harmed or even used in the creation of this page." At the top of a list of frequently asked questions about Google News that the company posed and answered was this one: "Who edits the Google News homepage? One of the headlines is totally out of whack." The answer: "computer algorithms, without human intervention." Google proudly listed the absence of editors, managing editors, and executive editors. No individual decided which stories received top placement, and no political viewpoint or ideology was taken into account. Like the algorithm for Web pages, the company said, the algorithm for news stories "relies heavily on the collective judgment of web publishers to determine which sites offer the most valuable and relevant information." The company knew kinks in the Algorithm remained, so if readers saw "odd results," an e-mail address was provided to let Google engineers know, not to manually adjust results but to help to "fine-tune the algorithm."

The *Washington Post*'s media critic Howard Kurtz paraphrased Google's rationale with sarcastic humor: "Who needs reporters? Why spend money on whiny, self-centered, 401(k)-obsessed human beings when you can produce a nice news Web site with quiet, easy-to-abuse computers?" Strictly speaking, Kurtz's criticism at that time was misplaced—it was editors whose jobs were immediately threatened, not reporters. But a few years later, with the newspaper industry in dire financial straits, Google News could be blamed for contributing indirectly to the disappearance of reporters, too. By directing users to a particular news article online, Google News and similar news-aggregation sites did their part to nudge newspaper subscribers into reading news on a computer screen, not on paper, and to spending their online time browsing Google News rather than browsing the newspaper's own online home page. As print subscribers disappeared, so, too, did the advertisers that had traditionally underwritten the cost of gathering the news. Growth in online advertising on the newspapers' Web sites fell well short of offsetting the disappearance of revenue on the print side of the business, and layoffs in the newspaper business became commonplace.

The Algorithm did need fine-tuning. In one case, a corporate press release somehow reached the top of the featured stories on the business news page. In another, Google's affectless algorithm committed a major gaffe on February 1, 2003, that drew negative attention, when the space shuttle Columbia disintegrated during reentry, killing all seven of its crew members. Failing to detect the magnitude of the event, the Algorithm permitted the story to disappear from the news site's main page several times during that day.

Other anomalies showed up now and then. Google tweaked its formula and filed patents in 2005 for additions to the Algorithm that would take into account many more factors, such as the average story length from the news organization that composed the story, the number of staff members in the news bureau, the volume of visitors to the source's own Web site, the number of countries that accessed the site, and many others. The results improved, and the anomalies disappeared—almost. (A fifteen-year-old New Jersey high school student wrote a fake press release in 2006 that reported he had become Google's youngest employee, and Google News picked up the story without detecting the odor of a prank.)

In the competition for organizing the news, Google's algorithm faced off against Yahoo's human news editors, but in this case, Google did not win. Its algorithm, improvements and all, never was able to catch up with the quality of Yahoo's news site. Google News was not inferior because of the occasional bad day when the Algorithm committed a blunder that a human editor would not. Google News was inferior on its best day, never quite able to match the subtleties that guided the selections over at Yahoo News. Visitor traffic reflected the continuing difference: four years after it had launched, Google News drew only 30 percent of the traffic of Yahoo's news site, which remained the most popular news site on the Web. In this case, algorithm met humanity, and humanity won.

News, by its nature, did not show off the Algorithm's true power to gain sophistication automatically as the size of the data set grows. In the case of Web sites, webmasters endow the Algorithm that examines Web pages with additional smarts whenever they add links on their own pages to those found at other Web sites. The more pages that Google's crawler collects, the more links are gathered by the Algorithm with which to make its judgments more authoritative. When it comes to news, however, while the Algorithm can make judgments about news organizations, it cannot gather the judgments that millions of others have rendered on each news story as they read it. As a consequence, the Algorithm for news does not grow noticeably smarter as the collection of news stories scales up. And news stories are ephemeral, constantly being replenished by new ones, which leaves the Algorithm without a baseline of data to work with in observing the clicks of users, so that it could progressively sharpen its judgment.

Google News cannot serve as a showcase for the Algorithm, but mediocre results in this project have not prompted Google to question the company's founding assumptions. So robust is the Algorithm when searching Web pages that its comparative failure when applied to other tasks goes largely unnoticed by outside Google watchers. Google enjoys the luxury of running experiments like this without suffering a tarnished image if some do not turn out well.

In the case of another project that extended the Algorithm into a new area, the results were superior to expectations. This was language translation, one of the most difficult, intransigent problems ever tackled in the history of computing. In this area, Google hired a small group of researchers in early 2003 and let them have a go at what is referred to as *automatic translation* or *machine translation.* Their efforts have borne fruit. The Algorithm that they have developed is able to accomplish, at least sometimes, translations with idiomatic fluency that is a wonder to behold. It also put to good use the corpus of news stories collected by the more disappointing Google News project.

Machine translation was one of the first applications that computer pioneers envisaged in the mid–twentieth century. In 1953, Howard Aiken, of the Harvard Computation Laboratory, voiced aloud his hope to soon begin word-by-word translation from Russian into English. He thought that conveying meaning accurately would be easy, and literary polish would come as a simple matter of course when the machines became more powerful. The next year, IBM scientists and Georgetown University linguists showed off a machine that produced Russian-to-English translations—and began what would become a long tradition in the field of machine translation, of overpromising and underdelivering on the quality of the results. On the basis of only a 250-word vocabulary, the software supposedly handled politics, law, mathematics, chemistry, metallurgy, communications, and military affairs. The press, however, was asked to take this on faith.

Six years later, an IBM Mark I was translating texts—again, from Russian into English, reflecting the linguistic preoccupation in the midst of the Cold War—at a reported clip of eighteen hundred words a minute, when human translators could translate only twenty-six hundred words in an entire day. The translated text needed more than a little polishing—a passage referring to U-2 pilot Francis Gary Powers began, "It 30 years/flight. By it/its statement, it is older lieutenant air forces United States America." But optimism was in the air, and all that seemed to be missing was "syntactical rules" to supplement the word-for-word matching. The National Bureau of Standards established a "mechanical-translation group" to do research on how to add understanding of semantics and syntax to solve what was called the "water goat" problem (a reference to the phrase that frequently appeared in the English translations produced by machine of Russian engineering papers that used the phrase *hydraulic ram*).

Applied linguistics research improved the quality of machine translations, and one particular firm, Systran, which was founded in 1968 in Paris, would become the leading supplier of machine-translation services to other companies, using linguists to define sophisticated grammars. Language by language, the company added to its offerings of bidirectional translation, extending to forty language pairs by 2005. When Google wanted to provide its users with the ability to view a Web page in a different language than the original, it turned to Systran for the behind-the-scenes machine translation that would be performed dynamically upon a user's request. The quality of the translation was uneven, and at best it could convey only the gist of the meaning of the source document. Idiomatic phrasing remained elusive, but that defect seemed to be inherent to machine translation: no algorithm could replace a human translator.

Systran's rules-based technology was merely one form of machine translation, however. An alternative approach, which researchers at IBM in the 1990s had shown to be promising, was called *statistical machine translation.* Reflecting the movement away from rules-based approaches in artificial intelligence research, it was based not on linguistic rules manually drawn up by humans, but on a translation model that the software develops on its own as it is fed millions of paired documents—an original and a translation done by a human translator, such as a speech delivered in English in the Canadian Parliament and its official French translation. The software looks for patterns, comparing the words and phrases, beginning with the first sentence on the first page in Language A and its corresponding sentence in Language B. Nothing much can be deduced by comparing a single pair of documents. But compare millions of paired documents, and highly predictable patterns can be discerned, with a particular phrase in one language likely, statistically speaking, to be given a particular rendering in the target language. Statistical machine translation was the approach that Google researchers began to explore in early 2003.

Using multilingual documents prepared by the United Nations as the training corpus, Google fed its algorithm 200 billion words and let the software figure out matching patterns between pairs of languages. The results were revelatory. Without being able to read Chinese characters or Arabic script, without knowing anything at all about Chinese or Arabic morphology, semantics, or syntax, Google's English-speaking programmers came up with a self-teaching algorithm that could produce accurate, and sometimes astoundingly fluid, translations. At a briefing in May 2005, Google publicly discussed its work for the first time. To show what could be accomplished with statistical machine translation and a sufficiently large corpus of translated texts, a headline in an Arabic newspaper was displayed, then two translations in English. The first one, provided by rules-based Systran software, rendered the Arabic as "Alpine white new presence tape registered for coffee confirms Laden." The second came from Google's fledgling program, which produced a different translation: "The White House Confirmed the Existence of a New Bin Laden Tape."

Google's translation algorithm, which looked impressive at a controlled demonstration like a press conference, turned out to stand up well to independent testing. In fact, it did exceedingly well. In 2005, Google entered for the first time the annual competition for machine-translation software run by the National Institute of Standards and Technology, which drew researchers from university, corporate, and government laboratories as well as commercial software vendors. Google placed first among eleven international entrants in Arabic-to-English translation (IBM placed third and Systran seventh), and also placed first among sixteen entrants in Chinese-to-English translation (IBM placed sixth and Systran twelfth). Not a shabby showing for the rookie.

The basic statistical measure in these kinds of competitions is derived from a comparison of a translation produced by the machine against a reference translation produced by human translators that serves as the "gold standard." A score from 0 to 1 indicates how closely the machine's translation matches that of the humans—a 1 indicating a perfect match. The scoring is a straightforward counting problem and is done automatically by evaluation software, eliminating subjectivity. The same software has been used outside of competitions, too. Researchers can tweak an algorithm, feed test documents in, and instantly see whether the change results in measurable improvements in the quality of translation.

Google not only built up a translation model using bilingual parallel texts; it also used software to create a monolingual "language model" to help provide fluent rephrasing of whatever the translation model produced. The Algorithm taught itself to recognize what was the natural phrasing in English by looking for patterns in large quantities of professionally written and edited documents. Google happened to have ready access to one such collection on its servers: the stories indexed by Google News. Even though Google News users were directed to the Web sites of news organizations, Google stored copies of the stories to feed its news algorithm. Serendipitously, this repository of professionally polished text—50 billion words that Google had collected by April 2007—was a handy training corpus perfectly suited to teach the machine-translation algorithm how to render English smoothly.

When you are in the business of organizing the world's information, what is learned in one domain often finds practical application in another. If Google's statistical machine translation project benefited by the work of other departments under Google's roof, it returned the favor in various ways. The statistical techniques used to develop a monolingual language model turned out to be a convenient way of developing spell-checking software for any language, including celebrity names that appeared only recently—and all without the need to use human editors or even dictionaries: feed the Algorithm a sufficiently large quantity of published text, and the correct spelling is determined by statistical analysis of frequency of occurrence.

Progress in the research at Google was also greatly helped by the computing infrastructure that was at the disposal of the research group. A data set used by many academic researchers in the field, supplied by the Linguistic Data Consortium, contained 5.2 billion words. Google could handle much larger sets, however, such as the 2 trillion words of monolingual text that it pulled from the Web pages it had indexed. "We don't have better algorithms," Google's Peter Norvig said. "We just have more data."

To find the best translation for a single sentence, Google's algorithm searched a million possible phrase combinations. Hard drives were not a practical medium for keeping the data handy for rapid consultation; only random access memory was suitable. Vast quantities of RAM were needed—and vast quantities were what Google had on hand. Statistical machine translation was well suited for computing that was distributed across thousands of machines, and Google's data centers, though originally built for other purposes, were equipped to handle the computational load.

Having a computing infrastructure on hand that could handle computational problems of any scale gave Google's researchers an enormous advantage over others. The rapidity of their progress was reflected in Google's placing so highly in the National Institute of Standards and Technology's machine-translation competition in 2005, and then, in the 2006 competition, holding its leading position. Google again placed first, among twenty-two entrants, in overall scores for Arabic-to-English translation, and second among twenty-four entrants in Chinese-to-English (edged out by the University of Southern California's famed Information Sciences Institute).

Dimitris Sabatakakis, Systran's chairman and chief executive officer, could not grasp how statistical machine translation could produce results superior to his rules-based technology. After the 2005 competition, he had defended his rules-based approach in a manner that suggested Google, in claiming that it did not use native Chinese speakers, had somehow pulled off a sleight-of-hand trick. At Systran, "if we don't have some Chinese guys, our system may contain some enormous mistakes." He did not understand how Google, without those Chinese speakers double-checking the translation, had beat Systran so soundly in 2005, but he did not sign up for an immediate rematch: Systran disappeared from the competition in 2006. No competition was held in 2007, so whether Systran has decided permanently to avoid direct comparison with statistical machine translation is not yet clear.

Google did not claim to have the most sophisticated translation algorithms, but it did have something that the other machine-translation teams lacked: the largest body of training data. In 2007, Franz Och, the Google engineer who oversaw the company's machine-translation research, said, "There's the famous saying in the natural processing field, 'More data is better data.'" That was why Google was using those 2 trillion words of text that had been pulled from Web pages: the quality of the writing could not be vouched for, but the sheer mass of additional data led to measurable improvements in the translation algorithm.

Google's achievement in machine translation cannot be said to have paid for itself yet. One of the most perplexing aspects of Google's expansion of services is that so many of them contribute nothing, at least not directly, to the company's bottom line. So far, machine translation is a case in point. Google has not rushed to put its machine-translation capabilities into commercial use. Its machine-translation team is a part of Google Labs and is focused primarily on research. On an experimental basis, the group in 2007 supplied users of Google's Web search service with the ability to obtain English translations of text from three source languages: Arabic, Chinese, and Russian.

As far as Google's translation work has progressed, its results are far from polished and idiomatic. When Sarmad Ali, a reporter for *The Wall Street Journal* who is bilingual in English and Arabic, tried out the Arab-English online translation services of Google, Systran, and two rivals in December 2007, he produced a catalog of syntactic and semantic errors for all of them, ranging from "the merely too-literal to the laughably bad."

Speaking about the machine-translation results at a public talk earlier that year, Google's Och presented Google at its best, the organization trying to make information more universally accessible without any visible concern about its own commercial interests. If any in the audience wanted to try their own hand at building a machine-translation algorithm, he said, Google was glad to help. Working with the nonprofit Linguistics Data Consortium hosted by the University of Pennsylvania, Google had begun to supply, for the nominal cost of shipping, a set of DVDs containing the basic training data needed, listing the frequency of various word combinations, from one to five words in length (technically referred to as *pre-counted n-grams*), for a trillion words of English-language documents that Google's crawler had collected from the Web.

Statistical machine translation depends upon parallel texts for feeding the Algorithm—Och said that about 100 million words of parallel data are needed in order to build a system that produces reasonably acceptable results. This dependency upon parallel texts limits the number of language pairings available for machine translation. At present, there are not enough twin texts to create a system to go directly from Greek to Thai, for example, so a bridge language, like English, must be used in the interim. Whether machine translation will ever be able to directly translate texts in any language into any other, or whether a different approach, based on understanding linguistics and building an intermediate meta-language, will be needed, is a question that has not been answered definitively. So far, it appears that with sufficient quantities of data, impossible tasks become possible.

Google's progress, which was startling in its speed, gave reason for optimistic expectations. Its statistical machine translation offerings grew from three source languages, in the spring of 2007, to thirteen, and then to twenty-three, within a single year. The company offered not only non-English–to–English translation but also translation between any pairing of its languages, which by May 2008 were

Arabic, Bulgarian, Chinese in both simplified and traditional characters, Croatian, Czech, Danish, English, Finnish, French, German, Greek, Hindi, Italian, Korean, Japanese, Norwegian, Polish, Romanian, Russian, Spanish, Swedish, and Portuguese.

The machine-translation project illustrates the way Google is driven by the maxim "More data is better data." In the information business, completeness—both within a category of information and across categories—is crucial because ever more data makes the algorithms ever smarter, which in turn serves to increase the distance between Google's leading position and its rivals'.

Google's free phone-based information service, 1-800-GOOG-411, offers a good illustration. The service uses voice recognition software to receive queries about phone numbers for local businesses. The service does not collect a service fee, nor does it carry advertising. Google's Marissa Mayer confessed in an interview in October 2007 that she is skeptical that it will ever become a profitable business. But she is not concerned because Google offered it to collect phonemes, not profits. She said, "We need to build a great speech-to-text model that we can use for all kinds of different things, including video search." Google's speech recognition experts told her, "If you want us to build a really robust speech model, we need a lot of phonemes . . . people talking, saying things so that we can ultimately train off that." More data is better data.

Google knows that the Algorithm does not produce flawless results, but rather than view the Algorithm's inadequacies as the inherent limitations of a fully automatic process, the company views them as the result of insufficient data and still-incomplete tweaking of its inner workings. The company is determined to feed the Algorithm ever more information, which it must look ever further out to obtain. It has reached out to claim as many books as it can get hold of, as many videos as its users would like to submit, as many different kinds of maps as can be overlaid upon the earth and the sky, and as many of the documents that computer users routinely create for home, office, and school.

Some of these additions to Google's information storehouses may appear to be peripheral to its core interests in Web search and associated advertising. Some may appear to be improvident experiments. Some may appear to offer a service that is both highly popular and utterly lacking in revenue production. They may, or may not, turn out to be important to Google's future. Each one has its own story. They all, however, share a common theme: Google's zealous pursuit of new categories of information, which has not slowed or wavered, even when its public image has been damaged by controversy arising from its actions.

When each story of expansion is examined closely, the smooth façade of Google the monolith gives way, and a more complicated picture of on-the-fly decision making emerges. The official corporate culture, which places a premium on the initiative of individuals and small teams, can be seen in these stories. But there is also an unexamined confidence that the interests of Google and those of its customers are in complete alignment, and every new service is seen by Google as an advance for humankind. Some day, when the experiments have run their full course, they may be seen as the masterful fulfillment of Google's mission to organize the world's information, as farsighted vision. Or alternatively, the same stories may one day be read as accounts of misspent resources, evidence of hubris.

CHAPTER 4

Moon Shot

The Web was merely the place to start. During a talk that Larry Page and Sergey Brin jointly gave at the Commonwealth Club in San Francisco in 2001, when Google was three years old, the cofounders explained that as large as Google's index seemed to the layperson, having grown to 1.3 billion pages, the Web itself covered nothing but a fraction of information that should be encompassed. Page explained, "Right now, you can only access the stuff that's on the Internet. You can't access content that's in libraries. You can't access magazines. You can't access newspapers, in general, or old newspaper content. You can't access all the television programs that have ever been broadcast. But all these things will happen."

The digitization of traditional print media had begun long before—while a graduate student, Page himself had worked on projects funded as part of Stanford's Digital Library project—and in 2001 it was not clear whether Google would have to do anything to hurry the process along. Libraries, publishers, and broadcasters could be expected to take care of the chores of digitization and place the files on servers that were publicly accessible, and Google's crawler would index their contents just as it indexed Web pages.

One year later, however, in 2002, Page, Brin, and their Google associates decided not to wait and began to investigate undertaking on their own the digitization of the one category that, more than any other, most fully recorded humankind's understanding of the world: books. The Google algorithm excelled at comparing the presumed authority of one Web page to another, but it could not warn a user when the best information available on the Web was inferior in quality to that found off-line, between bound covers.

Digitizing books was a project that presented challenges wholly different, however, from those entailed in indexing and ranking Web pages. Converting books into digital bits involved computer science less than it did other areas of expertise, such as mechanical engineering (designing imaging equipment), diplomacy (obtaining the cooperation of the largest repositories of books, university libraries), logistics (hauling books to scanning centers and back, without mishap), and legal expertise (ensuring that the effort did not run afoul of copyright law). It also required a financial commitment unlike any the company had made before. Google set out to digitize not merely the books in a single large library, or digitize the most academically valuable books, or the most commonly used books, or the most critically acclaimed books, but instead all books, every single one of the 32 million listed in WorldCat, the union catalog encompassing twenty-five thousand libraries around the world. Every book. Period.

Marissa Mayer would later refer to Google Book Search as "our moon shot." The image is apt, at least in some ways. Digitization of all books had been a dream of many. It was widely considered too ambitious to be attainable in the short term. Similar to President John Kennedy's famous challenge in 1961 to safely land a human on the moon by the end of the decade, Google set a ten-year timetable to achieve its goal. (In September 2007, Google funded another moon shot: the $30 million Google Lunar X Prize.)

Before Google's book project began, however, the company had taken the first step in digitizing content that was not already online when it quietly began the year before to scan catalogs supplied by merchants. The catalogs were placed online and could be searched at a Google site separate from the main search site. No attempt was made to assemble the most comprehensive possible collection; merchant participation was wholly voluntary, and not many elected to participate. Google Catalogs Beta did not give Google experience in high-volume scanning.

In 2002, when Page and Mayer began talking about having

Google scan books, the two ran an experiment to see how much time scanning a book would take. The story that would be retold later on many occasions was that the two turned the pages of a three-hundred-page book, one by one, according to the cadence ticked off by a metronome. The two supposedly extracted a single, but very useful, datum from this exercise: that forty minutes would be needed to scan a three-hundred-page book. From this, they somehow believed that they could estimate the cost of scanning millions of volumes and arrived at a number that fell within the range of the imaginable.

Whether the experiment's results were treated half as seriously as the company legend claims seems dubious, at least from the perspective of the present, when Google will not divulge any details about how it captures the images of book pages. It is possible that the experiment led immediately to the conclusion that scanning bound books, which requires a mechanical arm to move back and forth, was hopelessly slow, and a decision was made to use instead a digital camera to capture a pair of facing page images in a fraction of a second. When Adam Smith, a product management director who oversees the Google Book Search project, was asked in 2007 whether Google used a scanner or a digital camera, he said, "Isn't it the same thing?"

The difference may seem slight but it could mean the difference between a project that would be too slow, and thus too costly to be feasible, and one that would not be. In 2002, when Larry Page visited his alma mater the University of Michigan and met with university officials, he told university president Mary Sue Coleman that Google would be able to scan every one of the university library's 7 million volumes in just six years—at the time, the university estimated that if it used only its own resources, the task would require a thousand years.

Google was a privately held corporation whose stock was not yet trading publicly but whose owners—the founders, the venture capital investors, the early employees—were bound together in a profit-seeking enterprise. Google executives did not view book digitization as an eleemosynary project; they were not contemplating donating funds to nonprofit organizations, like the University of Michigan, that had already begun digitizing books. Instead they were looking at the feasibility of Google performing all of the digitizing itself, and then using the digital copies for its own purposes. Even if Google Book Search did not produce immediate profits, the project would be expected, at some point, to yield a return to Google that was proportionate to the outsized investment that the company would have to make to pursue the project. The prospect of being able to search the contents of books with the ease of navigating the Web was, without doubt, an exciting one. Having a single, profit-seeking company erect the digital doorway to all the world's information that resides in books would, however, when publicly unveiled, not please all onlookers.

Google's "moon shot" differed from NASA's manned lunar landing in another respect: Google had no close competitors willing to match its spending on book search. In the 1960s, space exploration was an extension of the Cold War, and the United States and the Soviet Union were evenly matched in a number of scientific fields. In 2002 and 2003, however, when Google quietly began work on its book search project, no other company was willing to compete with it head-to-head: the investment that the project appeared to require was sufficient to scare off all others initially.

Google had the chance to jump ahead not only because of its own fiscal boldness but also because others who had tried to digitize the world's books had not gotten very far. The first significant project to take on the daunting task was Project Gutenberg, started by Michael Hart in 1971. This was so early that digitization then had nothing to do with scanners and personal computers, which had not yet appeared, but instead relied upon keyboards connected to mainframes, like the one to which Hart had access, which was owned by the Materials Research Lab at the University of Illinois. Hart sought volunteers who also had access to institutionally owned computers and had time on their hands, and would be willing to type in the complete texts of important works of literature that were in the public domain (their typing fingers restoring the old anatomical meaning of *digit* to *digitization*). The appearance of personal computers subsequently made it possible to pitch the call for volunteers broadly.

Project Gutenberg eschewed the notion of "authoritative editions," and welcomed texts that were "99.9% accurate in the eyes of the general reader." It was not well along in covering the world's literature: by 2002, the project had digitized only about 6,300 works, all of which were entirely in plain text, without an image of the original typeset pages. Project Gutenberg's goal of making printed works more widely accessible was a noble one, but one of its inherent limitations was its assumption that a reader neither needed nor wanted anything but plain text, stripped of font variations, running heads, and the subtle design features in a printed book that also inform the reading experience.

The one institution in the traditional book world that had been arguably best suited to take on the massive task of digitization of all books was the Library of Congress. By 1990, advances in scanning technology had brought digitization costs down to the point that the library began a digitization program that experimented with digitization of just about every medium but books: documents, moving images, sound recordings, photographs. The primary focus was limited to building a digital "American Memory" collection of historical materials.

The most ambitious book digitization project was begun in 2001, when Carnegie Mellon University received a $500,000 grant from the National Science Foundation for the "Million Book Project," a digitization effort that attempted to get the most books digitized for the fewest dollars by shipping them to India and China to be scanned. When U.S. libraries were asked to lend their book collections to the project for the greater good, and subject the books to the vagaries of shipment by sea in cargo containers, the libraries balked, for understandable reasons. Brewster Kahle, an Internet entrepreneur who had founded the Internet Archive in 1996, stepped forward to "prime the pump," as he phrased it, with the donation to the project of 150,000 deaccessioned books that he purchased for $50,000 from the Kansas City Public Library.

The Million Book Project raised another $2.5 million from the National Science Foundation and would eventually surpass its original target, digitizing 1.4 million books in China, India, and also

Egypt, before its termination in 2007. Most of the books were in Chinese, Indian, Arabic, French, and other languages than English, and supplied by university libraries outside the United States that were also performing the scanning. It was an experiment whose multinational model failed to pick up self-sustaining momentum.

While Google was quietly sending out fact-finding teams in 2002 to investigate the feasibility of scanning all books, Brewster Kahle was talking up the same goal, imploring the Library of Congress to digitize all 20 million of its volumes. In a talk that Kahle delivered at the library in November 2002, he lyrically described how "the idea of universal access to all human knowledge has been a dream through the ages," arguing that the ancient library of Alexandria had succeeded in gathering human knowledge in one place. Now, he said, the Library of Congress could match and exceed Alexandria, making the contents of all books universally accessible by digitizing them. Kahle was a gadfly, possessed by the idée fixe, so excited that he minimized obstacles that stood in the way of the vision's realization. He casually asserted that the entire Library of Congress's book collection could be digitized for merely $100 million. Kahle did not explain how he arrived at this back-of-the-envelope calculation, but he had to assume that the Library of Congress would happily ship off its entire collection for scanning to Hyderabad, India, the destination of the books Kahle had purchased in bulk in Kansas City.

When Google's team in 2002 looked at the experiences of prior book digitization projects, it learned that costs ranged anywhere from $10 to $100 a book, depending on many factors. If one were to use $50 as an average figure, and aim to digitize the 30 million unique book titles worldwide, the arithmetic yielded a daunting number: $1.5 billion. Google at the time was growing fast, jumping from $15 million in losses on $19 million in revenue in 2000 to profits of about $100 million on $440 million in revenue in 2002. This was heady growth. Given its size then, however, a $1.5 billion price tag on book digitization was simply too large to be financially feasible.

The company decided that it could afford to undertake the book digitization project only because Page and his associates assumed that if they applied their attention to the problem, they would be able to devise a way to obtain images of book pages at far less cost than everyone else. The approach that Carnegie Mellon's Million Book Project was using, shipping books overseas to take advantage of low labor costs, was never seriously considered. Another possible way to eliminate labor costs was to rely on robotic scanners, but what would be saved in labor costs would be dwarfed by the capital investment.

The Google solution to the problem of high costs for digitization was to sort books into two categories—those that were still in print and those that were not—and process them accordingly. If publishers were willing to assist Google, the in-print books could be digitized inexpensively. Publishers could submit the same digital files used to typeset the books electronically, though in many cases these files could not be used because many of the codes used for page elements were not standardized. In such cases, Google could digitize a bound copy of the book quickly and without incurring much expense by taking advantage of off-the-shelf technology that is called within the book trade *destructive scanning:* the book binding is chopped off and the pages shoot through a sheet feeder into a high-speed scanner. This was the easy part. Not so easy would be digitizing—nondestructively—the 90 percent of books that were no longer in print.

Google devised an approach that combined diplomacy to borrow books gratis from the leading research libraries in the West, ingenuity in devising its own speedy work-flow technology for collecting digital images of the printed pages, and low-wage temporary workers to perform the labor-intensive work of turning pages. The human touch was literally visible in some images—fingers can be seen holding the book in place.

Google did not disclose how successful it was in squeezing costs out of digitization. But Daniel Clancy, Google Book Search's project manager, told a Stanford audience in 2006 that a $1.5 billion project "is not a cost that would be acceptable." Other companies that were digitizing books spoke of a cost of ten cents a page. If Google's costs were similar, and a three-hundred-page book cost $30 to digitize, then its stated ambition of digitizing 30 million volumes suggested a total cost of the project in the general vicinity of $900 million, still a staggering sum. The costs were not likely to go down by much because this was a labor-intensive project already using the least expensive labor that the market supplies. Moore's Law, which predicts that the number of transistors that could be placed on a chip would continue to double at regular intervals and enables Google's data centers to halve costs every eighteen months or so, did not apply to the speed of human page turners. Nor did book digitization benefit from scale effects: the time required to photograph or scan each page is unaffected by the volume of books being processed in the warehouse.

Significantly, Google eschewed the easiest way of reducing its costs: by digitizing only a portion of extant books, those that would most likely prove to be of value to its users. By stating from the outset that it would digitize all books, the company neatly avoided the politically fraught task of selecting which books should be included. Misunderstanding Google's radical intention to exclude nothing, French critics suggested that a panel be set up to ensure that the best in Francophone literature was selected. Google's Clancy answered, "We shouldn't have people trying to figure out that *this* book is more valuable than *that* book. So don't spend the resources."

Google's decision to shoot for the moon meant it could not be criticized for making ill-considered selections. But it did make the company vulnerable not just to criticism, but also to lawsuits, over its inclusion of books that were still under copyright and whose copyright holders had not given Google permission to copy the works. This was an issue with which the custodians of the library of Alexandria did not have to concern themselves when organizing the ancient world's information.

Copyright law in the United States required securing from the copyright holder the right to copy, as the name itself explained. But it also provided permission-free copying of small swatches for "fair use" that used the material in a "transformative way" and that did not impinge on the commercial value of the original. Google's digitization project did not seem to fit clearly within fair use or clearly beyond it. The company would make a copy of the entire work, which seemingly would be verboten under fair use rules. Then again, Google was not proposing to make the work available to readers—the copy would be used to prepare an index of the contents. One could try to argue that the index was "transformative" and the copying done in order to prepare the index was a form of "fair use." Google would have difficulty making such an argument, however, if its users found all that they were looking for by using Google's index rather than purchasing the book.

If Google could persuade publishers that indexing their books in copyright would lead to increased sales, and enlist their blessing for the project, it would be able to move forward without worry of lawsuits. By the time it was ready to approach publishers in August 2003, however, reports had surfaced that Amazon was well ahead of Google and already was in negotiations with publishers to make nonfiction books searchable. Without knowing the details of Amazon's plans, Google invited publishers to send it all their books, either in digital or in physical form, for inclusion in its index. If the publisher was skittish, it could send just a few books, and if it was not yet ready to send full texts, then a brief excerpt from the jacket copy, or the book's introduction, or the author's biography would be acceptable. Google offered to place "Buy This Book" links to major online book retailers like Amazon, Barnes & Noble, and Books-A-Million on the book search results pages. Google would provide the links gratis and asked nothing in return if a user used a link to make a purchase.

Amazon broke the trail for Google, soothing publishers who were concerned that hosting digital copies on Amazon's servers increased the risk of piracy. In cases in which book sales were expected to decline if users could browse their pages—cookbooks, travel guides, and any reference works—the books were not considered for digitization. When Amazon publicly unveiled its new service in October 2003, it could boast that it had enlisted 190 publishers, including Simon & Schuster and Random House, and offered the full texts of 120,000 titles, a number roughly equivalent to a large, well-stocked bookstore.

A year after Amazon launched "Search Inside This Book," Google was finally ready to unveil its own foray into book indexing, which it called Google Print. Even with the additional time, Google had failed to sign up as broad a roster of participating publishers as Amazon. Random House was one of the holdouts. To publishers, Amazon was a familiar face, with a proven ability to sell books; Google was known for selling advertising on the Web but nothing else. Adam Smith, who before coming to Google had been a senior executive at Random House, was recruited, along with others with publishing experience, to help Google, as Smith would later say, "talk the talk to publishers."

At the same time that Google was speaking with publishers to secure digital copies of recently published books, it was also talking with major research libraries about digitizing portions of their collections, adding the out-of-print works to the publishers' in-print works to assemble, eventually, copies of every book ever published. As praiseworthy as Google's goal was, however, its ambitions led the company to become impatient and make a major blunder. Instead of keeping its publishers' program entirely separate from its program with libraries, and being patient with the publishers, it decided to rely on the library collections for access to current titles that it had not persuaded publishers to supply with their blessing and permission to copy. The timetable for the moon shot could not accommodate years of pokey negotiations. Google had hoped to complete its moon shot within ten years, but even that seemed unacceptably distant. Daniel Clancy would later say that ten years at Google was equivalent to fifty years at a place like IBM: "The idea that this takes ten years is not something anyone would be happy with at Google."

Google could not contain its impatience. In December 2004, Google Print was expanded—dramatically—with the announcement of agreements that Google had reached to scan books in the collections of the libraries of Harvard, Stanford, and the University of Michigan, Oxford University's Bodleian Library, and the New York Public Library. Nowhere in the announcement did Google point out that a majority of the participating libraries were not as confident as Google's attorneys were that digitizing the entirety of books that were still under copyright, without the copyright holders' permission, was protected by the fair use provision of copyright law. The Bodleian Library was willing to contribute only works published before 1900. The New York Public Library offered only fragile works that were no longer under copyright. Harvard initially limited scans to about forty thousand volumes. Stanford said it would have Google digitize "hundreds of thousands, perhaps millions, of books" from its collection but conspicuously dodged the question of whether any works under copyright would be included. Only Michigan declared that Google would be able to digitize the entire library collection, without limitation. Michigan's 7 million volumes were all Google needed to quickly secure coverage of recently published books for the moon shot.

Authors and publishers alike objected strenuously to Google's abrupt abandonment of the principle that had guided Google Print before this, which was to index works still in copyright only if the publishers granted permission. Google reacted to the criticism with an announcement that created more unfavorable publicity for Google Print: in August 2005, Google said it would suspend scanning of in-copyright books until November, by which time publishers were to have submitted a list of books still in copyright that they did not wish to have Google copy. Google declared it would then resume scanning all books that had not been explicitly excluded by the deadline.

Having a gun placed against their temples was not the best way to calm authors and publishers. Jack Romanos, who was then the CEO of Simon & Schuster, said, "There's sort of this innocent arrogance about [Google]. One minute they're pretending to be all idealistic, talking about how they're only in this to expand the world's knowledge, and the next they're telling you that you're going to do it their way or no way at all." His company and other publishers tried to negotiate a revenue-sharing arrangement with Google as a condition of granting Google permission to index books, and Google showed no interest in discussing the matter. Romanos said, "They had a holier-than-thou attitude that hasn't done them any favors."

Failing to make progress in talks with Google, the Authors Guild filed the first lawsuit in September 2005 against Google for Google

Print Library's "massive copyright infringement." The complaint mentioned in particular the University of Michigan's willingness to supply Google with copyrighted works. The next month, a group of publishers—McGraw-Hill, Pearson Education, Penguin, Simon & Schuster, and John Wiley & Sons—filed a second suit. The plaintiffs vigorously objected to the wholesale copying of entire books that were under copyright by a commercial entity without securing the consent of the copyright holders.

In their suit, the publishers pointed out that Google's publisher program and library program were essentially indistinguishable, except that in the former case, Google sought permission of the copyright holders before proceeding, and in the latter case, it did not, at least in its copying of books under copyright held by the University of Michigan. The inconsistency in Google's approach in the two programs exposed the fact that Google was perfectly capable of abiding by copyright law but had elected for its convenience not to do so. Each of the plaintiffs was, and would remain, participants in Google's Print Program for Publishers.

The publishers argued that their business depended, in part, upon ancillary revenue, such as licensing fees for granting permission for others to publish excerpts of works. In their suit, they pointed out that Google, a commercial entity, was going to display "excerpts" of scanned books in order to "increase user traffic to its site, which then enables it to increase the price it charges its advertisers." Patricia S. Schroeder, the president of the Association of American Publishers, told *New York* magazine that Google was a great search engine, which she personally loved. "But someone has to pay for the content so there's something to search for," she said. "I say to Google, 'Let's make a deal. You won't make quite as much money, but I think you'll do okay. Let's share, boys, come on, let's share! You don't have to be so greedy.'"

The litigation was embarrassing for a company whose informal motto, "Don't Be Evil," had become a well-known component of its public story. "Don't Be Evil" was an unusual corporate value—deliberately so. It originated in 1999, when Google began for the first time to add employees who were not engineers and who were hired for their business acumen. Veteran Googlers were concerned that the newcomers would pressure them to tinker with the order of search results in order to favor the company's advertising clients or build new products that only the MBAs were enthusiastic about. Amit Patel, a Google engineer who had been among the very first employees, conveyed his concern by writing in neat letters in the corner of the whiteboard in the company's only conference room, where it could be seen by Google's salespeople and their clients, "Don't Be Evil."

Several years later, when the number of employees had grown to several hundred and the human resources team was casting about for a set of corporate values, Paul Buchheit, another engineer, suggested that Patel's "Don't Be Evil" be added to the list. Buchheit, who had worked at Intel before coming to Google, was determined to avoid the bland "Strive for Excellence" mission statements typically adopted by large companies. He also wanted "something that, once you put in there, would be hard to take out." After Buchheit succeeded in having the mantra included officially, Patel spread "Don't Be Evil" on every whiteboard at the company he came across, and it became the one Google value that the public knew well, even though it was formally expressed at Google less pithily as "You can make money without doing evil" and was only one of "ten things Google has found to be true." Critics previously had said Google was failing to measure up to its declared "Don't Be Evil" philosophy when it had censored results in 2002 that pointed to an anti-Scientology Web site and when it was nominated for a "U.S. Big Brother Award" by Privacy International in 2003. A Thomas Friedman column in the *New York Times* was headlined "Is Google God?," setting Google up for being humbled. Among the most visible challenges to Google's self-defined credo for ethical business practices, however, were the two lawsuits filed by the representatives of the book world, which pointed its finger at Google and accused it of doing evil. This was a painful affront to Google's self-image.

Shortly after the second lawsuit was filed, Google dropped the tarnished project name of Google Print and adopted a new name, Google Book Search. The company said that "Google Print" had confused users who thought the service was to help users print Web pages. The official company blog post also anticipated that some observers would interpret the name change as a public relations maneuver and denied that this had been a consideration: "No, we don't think that this new name will change what some folks think about this program."

When the lawsuits charging Google with copyright violations mentioned the role played by the University of Michigan, Stanford decided that it would be prudent to permit Google to scan only books published up through 1964. Michael A. Keller, the university librarian, explained, "We're not a public institution. We don't have any state immunity from being sued ourselves." In the University of Michigan, however, Google had a stalwart partner that—with state immunity—did not flinch when the lawsuits arrived. Mary Sue Coleman, the university president, defended Google's book digitization project as "the most revolutionary enterprise I've ever experienced," a project that would provide "a massive, free directory" for publishers that they did not appreciate. She joked that publishers regarded *snippet* as "a four-letter word," but speaking for herself, "I confess I see no difference between an online snippet, a card catalog, or my standing at Borders and thumbing through a book to see if it interests me, if it contains the information I need, or if it doesn't really suit me."

The unobjectionable image of the fusty card catalog would be the one that Google and its defenders would invoke again and again. Lawrence Lessig, a professor of law at Stanford, provided a widely quoted defense of Google's book digitization: The publishers were effectively demanding, he said, "[their] permission to enable a 21st century card catalog. When in the history of man did the law require permission from an author (or publisher) for a work to be included in a card catalog?" The problem with the card catalog defense was that Google search results provided contextual snippets from the actual text, something that had not actually been seen before in the history of man—something less than the complete book, but something more than a card catalog's lean listing of author, title, publisher, and a few subject headings. Google put into place safeguards that were designed to limit a searcher from obtaining more than three snippets for one search term in a copyrighted book for which the copyright holder had not granted Google permission to copy. Still, the snippets would give Google the ability to attract more visitors, and more visitors meant increased advertising revenue and profits. So the twenty-first-century card catalog raised a new question: should Google have to share the profits with publishers and authors?

Or at the very least, should Google share access to its digital books with other search engines? The publishers in their suit pointed out that they had no objection to digitization of books and, in fact, had joined the Open Content Alliance, the digitization consortium that obtains the permission of the copyright holders and then digitizes their works, making the digital copies available to all search engines, whether they were members of the alliance or not. The initiative had begun with Brewster Kahle, of the Internet Archive, and Yahoo, in early 2005, with equipment and software donated by HP and Adobe. It was modestly funded, however. Yahoo did not disclose publicly its financial commitment but it was estimated in the $300,000–$500,000 range in the first year. The alliance was dependent upon handouts from foundations, such as a $1 million grant from the Sloan Foundation in 2006 to scan antislavery material that was held in several libraries.

The initiative was stymied also by Google's head start: Kahle said he was told by librarians at several institutions that they would permit their books to be scanned only once and they could not participate in the OCA because they were already working with Google. "We want a public library system in the digital age," Kahle said, "but what we are getting is a private library system controlled by a single corporation."

Microsoft joined the OCA in fall 2005, with a news report that it would commit to digitizing 150,000 books the next year for its newly announced Live Search Books. It limited the scope of its scanning to works that were out of copyright. Thomas Rubin, Microsoft's associate general counsel for copyright, trademark, and trade secrets, told publishers at the annual meeting of the Association of American Publishers that Google's demand that authors and publishers should notify Google if they did not want their copyrighted works to be scanned assumed that "Google is the only game in town." He noted how impractical such a demand would be if other companies around the world adopted the same policy, placing the onus on copyright owners to track down every company that was engaged in unauthorized copying. Rubin also got off a biting offhand criticism of Google when he referred to "companies that create no content of their own, and make money solely on the backs of other people's contents, [and] are raking in billions through advertising revenue and IPOs."

As a participant in the Open Content Alliance, Microsoft would not only create the two digital copies of every scanned book that Google did—one for the lending library and one for itself—but would also have to provide a third copy to the alliance, which was free to index and display the digitized book on its own Web site. By forgoing an arrangement that would give it the exclusive control that Google secured, Microsoft could only hope that the digitization project would be of sufficient benefit to users of its search service that the investment would be justified. For Microsoft, scanning books by the thousands, rather than millions, was nothing like a moon shot. Danielle Tiedt, Microsoft's general manager of MSN Search, spoke at a trade conference panel in March 2006 about Microsoft's reluctance to take on digitization, given the enormous expense, nonexclusive rights, and uncertain payoff. She said, "I would love nothing better for all of this work to already be digitized, and all I have to do is go call it and index it and make a great user experience." Imagine, she said, if Microsoft had to create every Web page in order to be able to index the page's contents for its search engine. Unfortunately for Microsoft, the contents of books were not already digitized, so Microsoft had to pick one of two choices: "Don't pick that content, or I have to put some skin in the game and actively help in the digitization process to get content in digital format so that I can deliver in what I'm trying to do."

Google's Daniel Clancy sat on the same panel as Tiedt and suggested that one alternative to private companies undertaking the digitization of books would be to have the U.S. government take on the project. "Obviously, we've spent a lot more than $1.5 billion on many things more questionable," he said, but left hanging in the air his concerns about the government "controlling" the images of the book pages.

The panel moderator, Elizabeth Lane Lawley, a professor of information technology at the Rochester Institute of Technology, suggested an entirely different approach, however, avoiding the closed, proprietary project of Google's or a costly one undertaken by the government: a decentralized, bottom-up effort depending upon individuals and libraries of any size contributing to the scanning project in the same way that individual contributors had built Wikipedia. She said, "I think we have started to buy too much into this rhetoric that it's so big that *only* something really big and scary like a corporation or The Government can do it. When in fact, we're starting to learn from these technologies that not everything has to be done in a centralized way."

Whatever might be said about alternative approaches, Google's Book Search showed that a single company, with ample funding and a willingness to defend its copy-first-delete-later policy in court, was going to move far more quickly than a loose confederation of companies like the OCA, which had scanned only 100,000 books by the end of its second year, or a grassroots movement to scan books that had not even been launched. Google signed up more university partners, a total of 28 by December 2007, including Princeton University, Cornell University, the University of Virginia, and the University of Wisconsin–Madison, as well as institutions outside the United States, including Keio University in Japan and the National Library of Catalonia. The University of California, which had first joined the OCA, then signed with Google, committing at least 2.5 million volumes to the project, giving Google sole search-engine rights to their contents. Daniel Greenstein, a University of California librarian who set up the arrangement with Google, said, "I think last month we did 3,500 books [with the OCA] . . . Google is going to do that in a day. So, what do you do?"

The Google juggernaut gained momentum over time, not penalized in the least by Google's decision to hold on to the digital copies for its own exclusive use, without permitting other search engines to index them. Microsoft decided the best course was to emulate its competitor. Just one year after joining the Open Content Alliance and extolling the virtues of sharing digital books with others, Microsoft announced that it would adopt a policy like Google's, blocking other search engines from indexing the books that Microsoft digitized. Microsoft was not willing to match Google's investments, however, and falling ever further behind in the competition to digitize books, became too discouraged to continue. After digitizing only 750,000 books, Microsoft announced in May 2008 that it was shutting down its scanning initiative.

Google's moon shot consumed enormous resources in order to get off the ground, not to mention other costs in legal challenges and unfavorable publicity. The payoff was slow in coming. In February 2006, when Clancy gave a presentation about Google Book Search at a colloquium at Stanford, he was asked, "How has what you've scanned so far changed your own personal behavior, in terms of how you use information?" Clancy was candid: "It hasn't." He had no time to do academic research, he explained, being busy with work and family. Were he working in fields like history or computer science, where material that was in the public domain was abundant, he said he would be able to report that it had made a tremendous difference.

Google's book index was stored in what was commonly referred to in the online world as a *silo,* emphasizing separateness. With the passing of a little more time, Clancy and his Google Book Search colleagues discovered that the book information that they were accumulating could be made immediately useful in new ways that let users pull information out of the silo for their own use or for sharing. In the fall of 2007, Google gave users the chance to set up a "personal collection" of book titles, which could be searched and also shared with others. A new tool gave users the chance to copy the graphic image of a favorite quotation or selected passage from books in the public domain and paste or embed the image in another Web page. And literary references to a geographic location in public domain books could be overlaid on maps provided by another Google service, Google Earth, directly connecting one silo with another.

The most important, and most conspicuous, advance for Google Book Search was its attainment of a critical mass of recently published books. Before 2007, a book search on Google was hit-or-miss, emphasis on miss. Then, suddenly, it seemed to be able to come up with most any title that was in print. The number of books that had been scanned remained small: the company said in September 2007 that it had indexed about 1 million volumes, which left it well short of the WorldCat's 32 million and nowhere near the pace that would be needed to complete the project within the eight years left to meet the original ten-year goal. And yet Google, somewhat miraculously, had achieved excellent coverage of recently published works. How had it done so?

In May 2007, it quietly made the biggest change since it had started the moon shot: it added listings for books whose text had not been indexed, using publicly available bibliographic information drawn from online library catalogs around the world. Overnight, Google Books added all books in print without waiting to scan and index them.

These books were displayed on Google's search results page with "no preview available," a new category distinguishing it from "full preview" (books in the public domain), "limited preview" (books under copyright for which Google has secured permission to show a limited number of pages in its Book Partners Program), and "snippet view" (books under copyright for which Google had not secured permission to display pages).

The entries for the "no preview" books were placeholders, but they provided far more than barebones card-catalog information: lists of references from Web pages; reviews of the book that were available online; references to the books that had been found in other books that were already indexed; and references from scholarly works indexed in Google Scholar. After it arrived at the realization that it had enormous amounts of useful information about books in other silos, including the largest one—the Web—Google could offer users a rich array of supplementary information about any given title, and it could do so without infringing on the rights of the book's copyright holders.

One has to admire the ingenuity of Google's staff, using Google's vast information assets to augment what could be known about a book beyond a bibliographic card. At the same time, one also has to wonder how foolish it had been for Google to be so impatient to build up its book collection that it had asserted a right to make digital copies of books in print without the permission of copyright holders. The two lawsuits filed against it by publishers and by the Authors Guild continued to grind on. In early 2008, the presiding U.S. District Court judge, John E. Sprizzo, set a deadline of April 2009 for submission of motions for summary judgment; trials will come still later.

Everything that Google used to create a customized Web site in 2007 for any book had also been available to it in 2004. Google's Book Search managers may have been blind to the opportunities to cross-link across different silos of information that was in the public domain because such incremental improvements lacked the stirring scale of the near impossible, the transfixing imagery of a moon shot.

With twenty-eight participating libraries, Google's Book Search collections continued to grow as the scanning proceeded, still entirely out of public view. In February 2008, the University of Michigan was the first library to reach the mark of one million books online (361, 441,145 total pages and counting). The progress was not as fast as the original moon shot's—6.5 million books in the university's collections remained to be scanned—but an end was within sight. The university expected to complete the project "early in the next decade."

The legal issues remained outstanding, but the logistical issues seemed to have been tamed. Google was well along in its endeavor to bring the entire world of published text into its digital storehouse.

CHAPTER 5

GooTube

Google's success was based on mastery of words. It was words that its crawlers pulled from Web pages, then indexed and analyzed, determining which pages were deemed the most relevant to a search. It was words between covers that its Book Search project extracted and fed into Google's hungry maw. Wherever words could be found—and digitized—the Algorithm could go to work.

Google could search, however, only words that took written form. In 2004, when Yahoo began including videos in its search results, Google could not. Its crawler completely ignored video files. Yahoo never boasted about its superiority over Google in this regard—because Yahoo itself could find only a small percentage of all the video files rapidly being loaded onto the Web by then. The problem was that most videos were invisible to Web crawlers. Even if they could be found, crawlers could not categorize their subject material because digital video files provided no exterior clues about their contents. Videos proved to be a formidable challenge for search.

How Google responded to this challenge suggests a willingness on the company's part to depart from the approaches that had served it well in developing its core strengths in searching Web pages and serving up relevant advertising. Video presented Google with an opportunity to expand from information embodied in text, which was easy to search, to forms of information that required advances in computer science in order to be understood by the Algorithm. And it also was presented with the opportunity to notice that innovation within its walls did not always keep up with innovation taking place outside. The company could have decided to stick with the tried and true, the Algorithm, and with its own talent to enter new fields, or it could have decided to scale back its ambition to organize all the world's information, deliberately excluding some categories. Instead, it decided that its mission would remain paramount, and Google would take different paths, if necessary, toward its realization. The story of how Google moved into video shows a company that was adaptable, letting go of the Algorithm and embracing, ultimately, the notion that it would have to make its first major acquisition in order to secure a significant position in the competition to organize the world's information in the form of video.

At the start, Google's executives gave no thought to the possibility that video files would require special treatment. Their attachment to automation led them to be content with whatever the Google crawler found in its travels. Video files, lacking descriptive names, were of no interest to the crawler and were ignored. Yahoo realized before Google that standard Web crawls simply would not work well for videos and came up with an innovative idea: inviting the hosts of Web sites to supply some descriptive information about videos they had posted on their sites so that a crawler could collect and use it to expand an index of online videos. In December 2004, Yahoo launched "Yahoo! Video Search Beta" to enlist the assistance of Web site hosts. "Web pages are self-describing," explained Bradley Horowitz, Yahoo's director of media search at the time of the announcement, while "a video link [is] opaque, and you don't know what's inside the video." Web hosts were invited to add a tag to video files that would provide basic information—such as title, actors, and file format—and that would be visible to all crawlers.

Some media companies did take steps to make their video offerings searchable. If one wanted to search online the contents of a particular television series, such as *Washington Week in Review,* or PBS's *NewsHour,* or *Julia Child: Lessons with the Master Chef,* one could often do so on sponsoring producers' Web sites. The sites' search technology made use of the closed-captioning transcripts prepared for the shows. One could search for the occurrence of a name or phrase mentioned in a broadcast, but that didn't do viewers much good because the sites generally didn't offer playback of the segments that were found. The search offered by ShadowTV, a fee-based service that let subscribers search many television news broadcasts, and then view selected snippets, was also based on the closed-captioning texts.

Several companies claimed to have developed voice-recognition technology for searching video, which could identify words from the audio portion of the video file, and did not have to rely on closed captioning. This promised a substantial advance in search. One of those making this claim was an intrepid start-up called Blinkx.

In December 2004, the day after Yahoo announced its Video Search Beta offering, Blinkx made a splash with its announcement of its own video search service, which included forty-two thousand hours of video clips from fifteen television channels. Visitors were promised the ability to search for a term and then be able to watch a brief video clip matched to the term.

With the back-to-back Yahoo and Blinkx announcements, video search became the topic de jour on the Web. Google was not ready. It was still preparing for the launch of its own video service, and would join the others late. Google chose not to follow Blinkx in attempting to rely on voice recognition for its video search. The voice-recognition technology turned out to be far from ready for prime time, as those who tried searches at Blinkx would soon discover. Interestingly, given Google's approach to its book search program, the company also chose not to follow Blinkx's lead regarding the posting of clips without the permission of the copyright holders. Blinkx had not made any arrangements with the media companies whose video it was making viewable, and before long, one of those companies raised concerns. When CNN was told that its clips would be available for free, the company publicly announced that it had not authorized Blinkx to use its video. Blinkx counterclaimed that under the doctrine of copyright's fair use, it could show a clip of up to thirty seconds without needing to secure permission. The likelihood of lawsuits over the impasse was noted in the press coverage.

Google did not follow Blinkx into legal difficulties over fair use, at least initially. The company blundered down a different path. Acting on the assumption that spoken words were no less useful than written ones, Google's video team investigated ways of turning video into text. It seized upon closed-captioning text for convenient searching. Closed captioning, in turn, led Google to focus on video from the major media companies, as they were the only ones that could afford the expense of preparing captioning for their programs. A television industry executive who was briefed on Google's plans said at that time, "Google's trying to bring TV to the Web the same way they're bringing books to the Web." This path would lead Google into obscurity. Videos that were accompanied by closed captioning would turn out to be an inconsequential sliver of the videos that people would want to watch online.

In December 2004, Google engineers at the Mountain View Googleplex installed racks of TV tuners in order to record television broadcasts—and the closed captioning—from ten San Francisco Bay Area stations, C-SPAN, and some other cable channels. The long-term plan for video was to set up an online video store and have users purchase rights to view videos on their PCs. When the company formally launched Google Video in late January 2005, more than a month after Yahoo Video's announcement, it had stored about two terabytes of digital videos. Google thought that was a good start.

What Google unveiled, however, was a service that was woefully behind the competition. To begin with, it did not include any videos on the Web. Google had not focused on programming its Web crawlers to spot video files that were available online, so its index of videos was restricted effectively to only those television broadcasts it had recorded. A Google video search sorted through the closed-captioning transcripts of those programs, and then listed videos that matched the search phrase. There was no link, however, that would begin playing the relevant video. Google's users had to content themselves with a still photograph taken from the matching video episode, passages in the transcript in which the search phrase appeared, and a cheerful announcement of when the next episode of that series would be aired. But as long as the episode found in the search couldn't actually be viewed, why bother searching?

Google Video could not, in short, have started with a more modest and less satisfying offering. Even so, Google's service provoked a hail of criticism from media companies. Executives at CBS and Time Warner's television unit ordered Google to back off. Larry Kramer, the head of digital media at CBS, said that Google "didn't show proper respect for us as potential partners."

The essential mistake that Google had made was assuming that videos were just another source of authoritative information, like all the text-based media that the Algorithm had learned to search through so well. What no one at Google noticed, however, was that video would be more appealing as a medium for pure, unedifying entertainment, and could be produced by anyone who owned a camcorder. The quest for professionally produced documentary or news videos, with closed-captioning transcripts, had led Google badly astray.

In the meantime, a new model for video on the Web was being born. At the same time that Google was taping television broadcasts, Jawed Karim, a twenty-five-year-old software engineer working at PayPal, was giving a good deal of thought to video and the Web. None of his thinking coincided with Google's. Karim had been a computer science major, but he had left the University of Illinois, Urbana-Champaign, before graduating to accept an offer to work in Silicon Valley, at PayPal. His résumé, which included student internships at the University of Minnesota Supercomputing Institute, the National Center for Supercomputing Applications (in Champaign), and Silicon Graphics, reflected immersion in deep computer science problems. The idea that he came up with in his free time, however, addressed a practical problem, not a theoretical one: how to make uploading and playing videos painless. It led to YouTube, the company he would cofound with two friends at PayPal, Chad Hurley and Steve Chen.

The original idea for YouTube is traceable to a moment of serendipitous discovery, in December 2004, when Karim came across a stray statistic that caught his eye. In *Wired* magazine he read an article about BitTorrent, a software technology that allows fast transfer of very large files. The trick is that it uses peer-to-peer networking. BitTorrent, for example, was the technology that enabled the viral spread of a now infamous Jon Stewart television appearance. In the fall of 2004, Stewart appeared on CNN's *Crossfire* and astringently critiqued his hosts, Paul Begala and Tucker Carlson. He called their work "partisan hackery" and singled out Carlson as "a dick." A clip posted online caromed around the Web. In a few weeks it was viewed by 2.3 million people, passed along through BitTorrent. The fact that jumped out at Karim in the *Wired* article was that the Stewart clip had been seen online by at least three times as many people as had originally watched Stewart on CNN.

The Stewart clip was not the first one to enjoy such wide circulation; the emergence of clip culture had actually begun with the sharing of the much-discussed clip of Janet Jackson's "wardrobe malfunction" during the Superbowl earlier that year. But with the clip of Stewart on *Crossfire,* the velocity of viral sharing between PCs had sped up. Soon, the diversity of types of video that people might want to share in large numbers would become clearer. Shortly after the article in *Wired* appeared, the 2004 Indian Ocean tsunami struck. CNN camera crews were not present to capture the tragedy, and it became the first large-scale disaster chronicled primarily by cell phone camcorders.

Karim perceived that viewers who attempted to watch these virally spread videos ran into all sorts of technical difficulties, and he figured that a site that made uploading and watching any video effortless would fill an unmet need.

He regarded sharing videos as the next logical step in the evolution of social networking, or what was then called the "social content space." It could be traced back to the appearance in 1999 of LiveJournal, which offered anyone space to publish personal writings. Each succeeding year brought another innovation. In 2000, HOTorNOT took off: anyone could upload a photo and anyone else could vote on that person's hotness. In 2001, Wikipedia showed the willingness of volunteers to contribute their time to an online project sharing expertise without monetary compensation. In 2002, Friendster established some of the essential elements of a social networking site, such as profile pages and access to the profiles of friends, and friends of friends. In 2003, del.icio.us popularized the sharing of favorite Web pages. Then, in 2004, Flickr combined the uploading of photos to a publicly accessible Web site allowing others to append tags with descriptive labels and comment on them—forms of sharing. Karim thought, why not create a Flickr for videos?

His friends Chen and Hurley agreed that the idea was good, but they wondered, why hasn't someone else already done this? With some investigation, they decided the answer was that they'd happened on the idea with fortuitous timing. Three crucial technological developments had only recently come about: the rapid expansion of broadband connections to the home; a significant drop in the cost of buying bandwidth, which was needed for streaming videos; and the decision by Adobe, the publisher of Flash multimedia software, to include video-playing support. Flash was being installed in most new computers, so this eliminated the problem of incompatible video-encoding formats that users often encountered when they downloaded and then attempted to play a video file.

When the three friends decided to try out their idea on venture capitalists, though, the response was tepid at best. Many didn't even bother to call them back. Others simply shrugged at their presentation. One was willing to grant that the idea seemed "cute." Undettered, Karim, Chen, and Hurley went ahead and founded YouTube in February 2005. They didn't actually need venture capitalists to get started anyway; they had considerable financial assets of their own. All three had joined PayPal in its early days and had become wealthy when eBay acquired the company in 2002.

Karim knew from the beginning that he would not stay at YouTube for long. He had completed his undergraduate degree while working and already had plans to start a full-time graduate program in computer science at Stanford the next fall. The three founders agreed to an arrangement in which Karim would not be a YouTube employee and would receive a smaller stake than the other two, formally holding only the title of adviser. (His presence tends to be omitted entirely in short versions of the company's official history, leaving the impression that Chen and Hurley were the sole founders.)

The three required only two months to develop the code and

launch the site, which they did in April 2005. The only videos they initially had to offer, however, were those that they took of one another to serve as placeholders. The historic first YouTube video was an eighteen-second segment of Karim standing in front of a pen of elephants at a zoo, explaining with a self-mocking wink how elephants have "really, really, really long trunks." This would not do, they knew. So they asked their friends to contribute videos too. Karim's e-mail to his buddies asked, "Can you help us spread the word? Since we just launched, there are no girls in it . . . YET. Can you guys upload your own videos?" They had few takers. Weeks passed, and the site drew only a smattering of submissions. What would become the fastest growing site in the history of the Web came into existence seemingly stillborn.

In May, with the spirits of the cofounders at their nadir, they captured their bleak sentiments on a video shot in the garage that served as YouTube's office. By the end of the previous week, Steve Chen said, he had become "pretty depressed" because "Dude, we have like maybe forty, fifty, sixty videos on the site." It was an appallingly small number. And the quality of what had been posted made him wince—there were few videos he'd want to watch himself.

At this point, they decided to try a desperate measure: they would run an advertisement on Craigslist in the Los Angeles area, inviting "attractive" women to upload videos of themselves. The enticement would be a payment of $100 upon submission of every ten videos. This, too, ended in failure. The advertisement drew not a single response.

YouTube desperately needed content. To attract more amateur contributors, they unveiled in June a dramatically redesigned site. When a user saw a YouTube video that he or she wished to share with friends, a single click would send an e-mail notification to as many friends as desired. This made viewers unpaid marketers, spreading the word about YouTube's offerings. The site also thoughtfully provided a little snippet of identifying code next to each video that could be copied and pasted elsewhere, making it easy to embed a YouTube video on any Web page, including those at MySpace.

Sharing word about a video became painless, and immediately the site began to draw more users. They, in turn, uploaded more videos, which then drew still more users. On a single day, the site drew fifty new videos, then sixty, and then seventy. Once every two weeks, with unfailing regularity, word about one particular video would zip around, making it a widely mentioned sensation. As the number of videos uploaded took off during the summer of 2005, these "viral" hits appeared at ever shorter intervals.

Michael Arrington, whose influential TechCrunch site covered technology start-ups, was the first to take notice of YouTube's jump in traffic and videos. In early August 2005, Arrington praised the service for fast uploads, fast playbacks, and interesting videos. He declared that his absolute favorite was *Matt Dances Around the World,* a much-viewed hit that had been uploaded only four days before. "I suspect YouTube will be quickly acquired and/or duplicated," he wrote. "We love it." That profile in TechCrunch led to coverage on Slashdot, another site widely read among the digerati. Slashdot's coverage ("YouTube—The Flickr of Video?") then brought yet another spike in YouTube's traffic.

In no time, as Arrington had predicted, YouTube's founders faced a field of competitors. Just three months after his YouTube review, when he returned to the subject to cover YouTube's competitors, he listed eight leading contenders: Castpost, ClipShack, Dailymotion, Grouper, OurMedia, Revver, Vimeo, and vSocial. When someone asked in a comment that followed Arrington's post why he had omitted Google Video, Arrington apologized for the omission ("I'm an idiot") and said, "Of course they should have been included." The fact that Google Video had slipped his mind, however, was quite telling. Google Video hardly existed.

Googlers were slow to understand that the most popular video service would not use the same approach that Google had used with Web pages, honing its software formula to determine relative trustworthiness, reputation, and relevance to a search term. YouTube's hypergrowth had nothing to do with algorithms and everything to do with the unpaid contributions of its own users: it was the users who submitted the clips, sorted out the interesting ones from the less interesting, and spread word about the best clips among friends. Viral distribution of hits took care of the marketing end, for free.

Before YouTube appeared, Google Video was slow to relinquish its attachment to professionally produced video. In April 2005, just as YouTube appeared, Google announced that it would accept videos submitted by users, of any length and size, subject to Google's review process. Unlike YouTube, however, Google made clear it was especially interested in submissions from what it referred to as "major producers"—television stations or video production houses with a thousand or more hours of video. Enlisting the owners of large collections of content would not only help seed the site quickly but also speed realization of Google's long-term plan to sell online access to videos.

At the time that Google invited users to submit videos, it was not able to make the submissions available for viewing. Jennifer Feikin, director of Google's video program, nonsensically explained the lapse by saying that Google needed to better "understand how people have authored their video" before it could learn how to search them. The Googlers appear to have thought that the company's brand commanded such loyalty that users would be willing to do almost anything to be associated with it, including contributing videos that could not be viewed.

Larry Page referred to Google's addition of video uploads as an "experiment." Indeed, Google was overtly asking video creators to help the company learn how to enter the video business. Page later described what Google did as being admittedly "weird because it was called Google Video but you couldn't actually watch any video."

Two months later, in June 2005, Google finally had a video viewer ready. Unlike YouTube's Flash-based viewer, Google's required its own separate one-time installation. At last, five months after launching its video site, Google could accept and play user-generated video. The company had not moved very far, however, from its original assumption that video would take off online when professionally produced programs were digitized. The company still clung to the idea that a closed-captioning transcript was essential for searching videos. Peter Chane, Google Video's senior product manager, said, "Once people see that if you have a transcript, you'll do better"—that is, show up in Google's search results—"more people will go back and get their stuff transcribed."

In an effort to avoid antagonizing the major media companies, Google reviewed all video uploads for possible copyright violations before they were made available to the public. Chane, however, self-deprecatingly described the company's review process as "very superficial." Videos weren't actually viewed in their entirety, just skimmed for a quick check that the contents weren't pornographic and didn't include "blatant" copyright violations.

By contrast, YouTube was inviting users to upload "any kind of personal video" as long as its running time was short. The only guidelines for contributors in its first four months were to avoid nudity and stay within a limit of 100 megabytes for any one video file. This effectively prevented users from uploading full-length television programs. A short clip of a favorite show, though, was tacitly welcomed as a form of personal expression. YouTube considered such a clip to be a "personal video."

Once YouTube was widely perceived as the one place to go for online video, which happened during the summer of 2005, the site's dominance was self-sustaining; both viewers and video creators congregated where they knew most videos, and the most viewers, were to be found. A similar phenomenon had benefited eBay, which had emerged from an even more crowded field—competing in 1997 against more than 150 online auction sites. Once eBay had edged ahead of the others in 1998, its lead quickly widened and then solidified.

YouTube's growth was vertiginous; it could be represented on a graph only with a line that angled at almost 90 degrees. Its rate of growth surpassed those of eBay, Google's Web search, Wikipedia, MySpace, Facebook, and any other prior Web site. By November, it was serving 8 terabytes of data every day. A month later, it had doubled again, to 16 terabytes, which was 3 million daily video views.

Just as Brin and Page had at first done with Web search, YouTube's founders devoted all of their attention to building a compelling service and didn't consider how it would make money. As traffic multiplied exponentially and its operational costs ballooned, the company's need for capital grew pressing. In seeking venture capital when it was growing exponentially, YouTube occupied an enviable position in which the traditional roles were reversed: venture capital firms did the pitching, and YouTube did the selecting.

YouTube's entrepreneurs Chen and Hurley (Karim had started graduate school) ended up accepting $3.5 million from Sequoia Capital, the same firm that had financed both Yahoo and Google. In landing YouTube, Sequoia would solidify its reputation as the world's shrewdest investor in Web start-ups. Sequoia did everything right. Perhaps most impressive to the YouTube founders, Sequoia was the only firm they visited that demonstrated interest in actually using the service. The day after Chen and Hurley visited at Sequoia, the partners, their assistants, and everyone in the office, it seemed, had dropped whatever else they were doing to upload and share videos.

Even drawing 3 million views a day, and growing at an unprecedented rate, YouTube was still vulnerable to being overtaken by a far more powerful competitor, such as Google. But Google missed the opportunity to exploit its size to catch up, for at least two reasons. First, YouTube grew organically out of clip culture, which required a loose interpretation of what constituted fair use of copyrighted material. Google would run into serious trouble persuading book publishers that it was attentive to their copyright concerns if it allowed the uploading of clips of television shows, or amateur videos accompanied by copyrighted sound tracks. Google was also saddled with the burden of proving that the company could move beyond a single skill: its lucrative search-based advertising business. Google Video was an opportunity to show that the company could create a new stream of revenue from a pay-to-view service. This is why Google ignored the success YouTube was having with its free service. It still planned to open an online store.

In January 2006, Google unveiled the Google Video Store at the annual Consumer Electronics Show in Las Vegas. The announcement was awkward, nothing like the kind of show Steve Jobs pulls off. One of the partners Google had brought onboard was the NBA, and former NBA star Kenny Smith was on hand. Larry Page seemed all too sincere when the script called for him to pretend not to recognize Smith. CBS's Leslie Moonves, eager to trumpet the availability of CBS programs for sale at Google's new store, said "Google not only is, but will remain, a Very Brady place."

Google remained a Very Brady place for only eighteen months, when it ignominiously closed the video store. In retrospect, it had no chance of succeeding. The pact with the NBA assumed a market demand for stale content—games were sold twenty-four hours after broadcast, as if each one were an instant classic (and the buyer lacked a recording device at home). As for the CBS programs, Google had not fared well in negotiations there, either: the Google Video Store was permitted to offer only one episode of a CBS series at a time. Apple, by contrast, had secured the right from ABC to offer an entire season of shows, such as thirty-five episodes of *Desperate Housewives* for iTunes. Google customers were further restricted to viewing the videos on a networked PC; viewing on a portable device was not an option. Unlike a purchase downloaded from iTunes, a video bought and downloaded from the Google store could be played only if the PC could obtain permission from Google's server, and the permission had to be obtained anew before each viewing. The Google Video Store was a latecomer that never came close to matching iTunes.

Meanwhile, in the spring of 2006, YouTube's growth picked up even greater speed. The 3 million daily page views in November 2005 had grown by April 2006 to an incomprehensible 100 million, a self-propelling cultural phenomenon. Growth required of YouTube's management little but attention to two matters: keeping its site operational and remembering to pay the specialized behind-the-scenes companies—content delivery networks—that maintained copies of the videos on their servers and took care of the distribution of the video streams. Sequoia and a second firm invested an additional $8 million to make sure that YouTube's bills were paid in a timely fashion.

By May, the YouTube phenomenon was affecting the strategy and thinking of every competitor. Google, too, had taken notice.

When Google's Peter Chane was interviewed by *Wired* and asked if "professionalism" in videos mattered, Chane said, "I dunno, but if you watch a video on the Web and you don't get it within a few seconds, you go to something else because it's so easy." This was an answer quite unlike what he would have given six months previously. When a reporter from the *Chicago Tribune* sat in on a meeting with Chane and his Google Video team at the Googleplex, the Googlers' frustration was evident. How could Google fail to offer a service superior to that of a tiny upstart with only sixty-some employees? "We look just like YouTube," Chane said. "We're a cleaner, more thoughtful YouTube—with less features."

YouTube had won the race against Google for content and viewers, but it had not figured out a feasible way to make money. Beginning in December 2005, YouTube began to run a few advertisements. They were displayed on its Web pages, not embedded in videos, and they were too few in number to bring in revenue of any real significance. But their presence on the site created a legal tempest. In July 2006, Robert Tur, a journalist and helicopter pilot, filed the first lawsuit against YouTube, accusing the company of profiting by the theft of copyrighted materials. A clause in the Digital Millennium Copyright Act prohibits a Web site from profiting from the display of copyrighted material, and YouTube's video collection was filled with clips that drew on copyrighted material. What had saved YouTube from legal action up until then was the absence of revenue. If YouTube was now going to advertise, that dodge would no longer work.

Tur had shot a video of the 1992 Los Angeles riots, and the footage ended up on YouTube without his authorization. YouTube's competitors, however, used this case as an opportunity to contrast YouTube's passive acceptance of infringing material with their own strict scrutiny. In August 2006, at the industry trade show Digital Hollywood, Revver's Oliver Luckett touted his company's policy of having a human editor screen every video before it was posted, which resulted in rejection of 10 to 50 percent of submissions due to the use of infringing material. He said that the copyright holders who were the victims of infringement by other sites—clearly a jab at

YouTube—were most often "the little guys," who were ignored by "the new kind of upstarts that don't respect their rights."

One of the "little guys," a woman filmmaker named Ahree Lee who had produced an experimental film for AtomFilms, was not pleased to see that her film *Me,* which consisted of a compilation of self-portraits that she took daily from 2001 to 2004, had been copied and uploaded on YouTube. AtomFilms provided its video creators a share of advertising revenue. Lee's film, which was drawing hundreds of thousands of views on AtomFilms's Web site, had the potential to produce significant income for Lee—until it was copied and uploaded to YouTube. She knew that if she filled out an online form at YouTube's site to request that the film be removed, YouTube would embark upon a lengthy process to determine whether Lee was, in fact, the copyright holder, which would take days, if not weeks. In the meantime, the brief moment when *Me* would be much discussed and viewed would have come and gone. Clip culture did not give any thought to the video creators; the culture imposed no restrictions on the instant gratification of viewers.

Lee happened to live close by YouTube's office in San Bruno, California, and she decided to present her case in person. She somehow managed to get past security and get the attention of someone who heard her out and offered to replace the full three-minute version on YouTube with an abridged one-minute version that at the end would direct viewers to AtomFilms, where viewers could generate income for Lee. A year later, the results were mixed: *Me* had been viewed about 600,000 times at AtomFilms, and more than 3.8 million times at YouTube. What portion of the YouTube views replaced AtomFilms's, and what portion of AtomFilms's visitors had been redirected from YouTube, was impossible to say. In any case, the episode offered little comfort to filmmakers who did not happen to live next door to YouTube.

One might have expected Google to join the other critics of YouTube and condemn the cavalier disregard for intellectual property rights that was found in clip culture. But Google elected to hold back, sensing an opportunity to benefit by adopting YouTube's model of hosting clips without the permission of the creators. Peter Chane was asked at a panel at Digital Hollywood what he thought about a hypothetical fan of *The Daily Show with Jon Stewart,* a regular viewer of the broadcast, who one night happened to miss the show and searched it out on an online video site. Chane said content creators were coming to the realization that posting segments of shows online was "a positive, not a negative." He reported that Google was finding more creators coming to it saying, "We *want* our clips to be online." Revver's Luckett shot back: "I don't see how Hollywood or TV Land . . . is real excited about content that they paid an exorbitant amount of money to produce and create and pay for the stars and do all that" being placed on YouTube for viewing for free. Yes, the actors on *The Daily Show* may be thrilled, because their own popularity is enhanced, but "the people that are monetizing it are probably not thrilled that the ads are stripped out and that it's floating around the Internet."

For YouTube, what the owners of *The Daily Show* thought about clips being uploaded without permission was in fact a vital unanswered question. They weren't a small independent filmmaker like Ahree Lee; *The Daily Show* was owned by media giant Viacom. Were YouTube to find itself in a legal battle with Viacom, it would not even be able to afford the legal equivalent of a slingshot. One hundred million downloads a day did not change the fact that YouTube was still a tiny start-up, just a little over a year old, with only seventy-eight employees and revenue of only about $10.6 million for the year, versus Viacom's $1.6 billion. YouTube also had yet to earn a profit.

Chen and Hurley also knew enough to admit to themselves that their legal arguments weren't likely to go very far in court. As Chen said, "I was really confident on the engineering side, the scalability side, that we could continue to grow out and be able to service the needs for the growth. But it was really more of the legal side . . . that there was just no way we could leverage or hire the resources alone." The two young men decided to approach Google and Yahoo to gauge their interest in acquiring their company.

The timing was perfect. At the very moment YouTube realized that it had made big-company enemies that it could not afford to defend itself against in court, Google realized that its homegrown

Google Video service would never be able to approach the popularity of YouTube. As soon as YouTube made itself available for acquisition, Google pounced. With a $1.65 billion bid that drew wide notice for the generosity of the valuation, Google wrapped up the acquisition quickly.

Before the deal closed, Sequoia's Roelof Botha was asked to explain why YouTube had become so much more popular than Google Video and all other competitors. Botha, whose firm had backed Google as well as YouTube, put his finger on the salient factor: YouTube, unlike Google Video, had become one of the handful of sites that many people visited daily. "At the end of the day, they take a break, have a laugh, want to be entertained." The network effect—the more videos uploaded, the more viewers and creators attracted, and then again the more videos uploaded—was critically important, creating what he described with dry understatement as "a bit of a snowball effect."

Google had recognized that the YouTube model, building a video site around entertainment and social networking, had bested its own dull model, which conceived of video as a professionally prepared information resource. But Google executives could not bear to state the obvious. When asked to comment on the YouTube acquisition, Sergey Brin said, "When I perform a search, I often find that the best answer is not necessarily a Web page. I know that sounds like heresy from Google, but in fact, if you are learning a sport, if you want to build a house, if you want to study a science, often videos are the best medium to learn about those things, to learn how to do those things." There it still was, the Google orthodoxy that it was doing nothing other than what it had always been doing, building out the world's largest reference room, and YouTube was a natural extension, purchased so that Google users could "study a science."

When the transaction was completed in October 2006, Google dropped the high-minded rationalizations and allowed YouTube to grow unimpeded, without imposing a Google master plan upon it. YouTube offices remained where they had been, in San Bruno, about twenty-five miles north of Google's Mountain View headquarters. Google's high command encouraged YouTube to carry on in the same raucous way it had, permitting users to upload almost anything they wished. A couple of initiatives to add some edifying content—such as debates among presidential candidates in the 2008 election campaigns and lectures taped from classes at the University of California, Berkeley, and other universities—did not change YouTube's essential character as the richest repository of popular culture to be found anywhere on the Internet.

Amusingly, its overwhelming lead in online video has not brought Google a new profitable way to "organize the world's information." For all its smarts and size, Google has not made much progress in answering the same vexing question that flummoxed YouTube two years earlier, when it was still a very small, very new, and very inexperienced company, which was, how does one make money from online video? Everything that Google has learned about matching relevant advertisements to users who are searching for something specific on the Web is all but useless in the different world of short video entertainment. And prospective advertisers are skittish about placing advertisements into an automated system that could match their brand with user-submitted videos that are tasteless, profane, or worse. Google is trying to gain users' acceptance of commercials that run as an overlay on top of selected videos, but the efforts have yet to produce revenue that is significant enough to warrant disclosure. An analyst with the Yankee Group said in March 2008 that he would be surprised if YouTube managed to take in $20 million in all of 2007. Yet it was spending about $1 million a day to pay for bandwidth. In April 2008, when Eric Schmidt was asked how Google planned to earn a profit from YouTube, he said that the answer continued to elude the company but it was now deemed "our highest priority this year."

As YouTube's traffic continues to expand, and Google adds still more features—introducing higher-resolution video in March 2008 and new software tools that will make it easier for Web site editors to utilize YouTube videos on their own sites, a program that Google calls YouTube Everywhere—its costs seem likely to increase faster than advertising revenue, at least in the short term.

No other Google venture has entailed an investment as large as this; no other venture brings in so much traffic for so little revenue.

It may well turn out to have been a shrewd bet. But its video assets have brought Google rather far away from its roots as a disinterested party that sent users elsewhere on the Web as speedily as possible, and have pulled it into the entertainment business, where it seeks to keep users happily engrossed with the video diversions that it stores on its own servers. If YouTube really holds an essential part of "the world's information," then so, too, does any media company. As long as Google keeps YouTube, there is no reason why it could not also acquire the *New York Times* or other media properties.

YouTube's motley collection of diversions stands so far outside of Google's original conception of information that what seems least likely is its present status as the company's sole major entertainment division, and one that continues to be a costly work in progress. Either Google will make additional investments in media properties, and deal with criticism that in doing so it is creating conflicts of interest with its core business in Web search, where it is ostensibly a neutral adjudicator of quality, or it will decide that it does not want to be in the entertainment business after all and shed YouTube. The course it adopts will probably be decided not by internal etymological discussions about the meaning of *information* but by scrutinizing the profit/loss statements for the YouTube division—and by estimating the enhanced value to the Google brand from YouTube's astonishing volume of traffic.

YouTube is an anomaly, a venture that raises questions about Google's commitment to the original interpretation of its charter. Other experiments have served to expand dramatically the range of Google's information offerings, too, but have done so in a way that reinforces Google's role as the neutral reference librarian. These have been smooth, natural extensions of Google's strength in organizing disorderly masses of data. Perhaps the one service that shows Google's innovative work in information organization at its best is the one that has added a spatial dimension to everyday information seeking. By integrating geographic information with nongeographic information, conveniently, ingeniously, even entertainingly, Google allows users to see the world in ways never possible before.

CHAPTER 6

Small World, After All

In 2004, Sergey Brin came across a very small company whose online service accomplished very big things: one could use it to travel, virtually speaking, anywhere on earth, with satellite imagery used to provide a visually riveting experience. He was eager to share his discovery of this technical marvel with fellow members of Google's executive team. He interrupted a routine meeting with a demonstration that got everyone's attention. With his laptop computer, he "flew" from a high altitude down to the house of every executive in the room.

It was a feat that required the manipulation of enormous quantities of digital data. Some forms of information can be stored compactly, some not. Web pages composed of text take little space. In 1998, the year of Google's founding, the entire World Wide Web could be stored on hard drives that fit within a dorm room. Such compact storage was possible only because most of the Web's information consisted of text. But were one to think about information about the real world, the information that covers the earth's 57,300,000 square miles of land, considerably more disk space and computing power would be required. Collections of satellite images of the earth constitute one of the bulkiest collections in the entire digital universe—these are measured not in gigabytes or in terabytes, but in petabytes, or millions of gigabytes.

With Brin's demonstration of effortless virtual flight anywhere—using just a laptop—he showed his Google colleagues that technology had evolved sufficiently to make it possible for the general public, using ordinary hardware, to enjoy access to the database of photographs that had only recently been limited to the defense establishment. Still, it was a novelty, a little bit of science and a little bit of entertainment, and nothing more. Brin would convince the others that the imagery of the earth, when integrated with other information in Google's storehouses, could be used for a more ambitious purpose that would reorient the starting point for information searches, literally and figuratively. Instead of beginning with a text phrase, a user could begin with a place. The globe itself could become the organizing structure for information—the idea that would lead to the release of a new product, Google Earth.

The possibility of using geography to organize the world's information was contemplated only because photographic images enlivened maps in new ways, making them nigh irresistible. Satellites equipped to take photographs of the earth were first launched by the U.S. government in the 1950s, and civilian access to the images was limited. But in the 1990s, the U.S. government relaxed its controls and began to permit private companies to launch satellites designed expressly to gather high-resolution digital images of the earth for commercial purposes.

Technically, it seemed easier to send satellites aloft than it was to work with the massive digital files that they sent back down to earth. The images could be used most conveniently if they could be stitched together in a seamless way, creating on a computer screen a virtual globe that a user could navigate by pointing a mouse in any direction. In the late 1990s, there was only one place in the world with the computing resources that were necessary: the basement of the Pentagon, with a machine room outfitted with the biggest beasts in graphics supercomputing, made by Silicon Graphics, the company that had made a name as supplier of the machines used in Hollywood for digital special effects in *The Terminator* and *Jurassic Park.*

In just a few years, however, a virtual globe constructed with satellite images could be displayed not just at the Pentagon, but on any PC connected to the Internet. In Google's hands, the satellite images of the earth would be integrated with overlays of city streets, geotagged photographs and videos, local business listings, and hundreds of other categories of information, many of which were formerly not thought of as geographic in nature but that could be tied in some way to place. Literary biography, for example, can be expressed in a geographic dimension. A "Jane Austen layer" can be superimposed on the earth, showing the places Austen lived or visited, the actual places that appear in her writing, and the places used in the film adaptations of her books.

The geographic possibilities were not limited to just one planet. Images of the moon, Mars, and constellations filled in a panoramic view of the entire cosmos. Google could provide its users with ready access to the remotest corner of the universe because of the founders' original fixation on building unlimited computing capacity. All of its geographic services were handled by the same ever-growing supercomputer designed originally for storing copies of Web pages.

Google has made the earth seem like a single cozy place. But in so doing, it has also made our own presence more visible, whether we wish that or not. We have begun to realize, belatedly, that distance serves to protect our anonymity and privacy. Within the small virtual world, where anyone can see every place and, as photographs are melded with maps, every earthbound resident becomes increasingly visible to more and more people, an individual's sense of privacy dissolves as fast as the earth seems to shrink.

The technology that Google used to shrink the globe was not produced originally by Google's own engineers. As was the case with YouTube, here, too, a tiny start-up jumped far ahead of the much bulkier, slower-moving Google. The service that the general public would later come to know as Google Earth was pioneered by Keyhole, a small start-up company located in Google's backyard.

Keyhole's founders foresaw that finding ways to give the public convenient access to satellite images of the earth would lead to a myriad of uses of the images. In this regard, they were extremely prescient. They were not at all sure about how to go about making a business out of such possibilities, however. What Keyhole planned was a subscription-based online service that would provide consumers with the ability to use a PC to fly around a three-dimensional virtual earth, using actual satellite images instead of the machine-generated geometric shapes of computer games. But when Keyhole was founded in 2000, the world was not yet prepared to look at itself as it actually appears in real images.

Viewing a single detailed image of the earth was one thing; viewing a seamless mosaic of images was quite another, and still required the processing power of a supercomputer. Keyhole's engineers came from companies in business lines that were serious (scientific visual simulation) and fun (computer gaming). They sensed that an opportunity would eventually open up for companies that offered the general public online access to a globe composed of satellite images. Customers' own personal computers, outfitted with 3D graphics cards and speedier Internet connections, would be able to handle the massive amounts of geo-spatial data entailed.

Preparations for greeting the future opportunity had to be timed well, though. If you start early enough, as Keyhole did, you do not have competition. Start too early, however, and you risk exhausting your start-up capital before the conditions for the new market are in place. Keyhole came very close to going under. Google's (and YouTube's) history excepted, most Silicon Valley start-ups do not execute perfect timing—and perish. Keyhole was fortunate to squeak by.

In 2000, most home Internet users relied on dial-up modems that were only about 1/60 the speed of a cable modem connection today. Moving the satellite images, which were stored as large files, from the centralized server to a user's PC posed a seemingly insurmountable obstacle. Keyhole's founding goal was to find ways to give the user the sensation of being able to fly anywhere on earth, without periodically encountering a frozen image on the computer screen while new data needed for display was downloaded.

By January 2001, Keyhole had put into place the necessary pieces for realizing its grand vision. It designed software that displayed one image while simultaneously fetching adjacent images that could be displayed next, allowing the user to move smoothly in any direction. The company struck a deal to have its software distributed by Excite@Home, a new company funded by Kleiner Perkins that was going to provide fast broadband connections to everyone. And it secured $4.6 million in first-round financing from Sony Broadband Entertainment. With the funds, it expanded its staff to twenty-five and readied its product for the mass market, spending to be in a position to hit the milestones it needed to reach in order to receive the second round of financing.

By the spring of 2001, however, the dot-com boom had gone bust and the Valley became a very inhospitable place for fledgling companies. Keyhole's CEO, John Hanke, would later describe the time as "our generational equivalent of the stock market crash of the 1920s." Excite@Home went out of business, and Sony shut down its venture capital arm. Keyhole lost both the mass distribution and the follow-on financing it had been counting on. No replacements were to be had. The plan to offer Keyhole's service to the consumer market had to be shelved.

Desperate for revenue, Keyhole rented some booth space at a trade show for commercial real estate brokers in June 2001 in Dallas. Visitors to the booth were able to fly wherever they wanted—from Dallas to Los Angeles, to Phoenix, to Miami, *click click click*—and were probably the first civilians outside of the Pentagon and Keyhole's offices to experience seamless virtual flying with real satellite images. Jim Young, the executive in charge of the show, was immediately smitten and told the attendees that Keyhole's software would transform the industry. Sales to the commercial real estate business saved Keyhole from extinction. With brokers willing to pay $1,000 a year for a subscription, and invest in a brawny $3,000 PC that could handle the graphics processing, Keyhole was able to eke out an existence and continue looking for ways to find a bigger market.

The news business offered one promising opportunity. CNN was keen to use Keyhole's software, called EarthViewer, for zooming down to wherever the moment's news stories were breaking. On the verge of CNN's signing a high nine-digit deal with Keyhole, however, budget cuts were ordered. CNN revoked the offer and instead offered Keyhole a take-it-or-leave-it arrangement in which CNN would receive permission to use Keyhole's software, and in exchange

CNN would pay a token fee and display "earthviewer.com" in a corner of the screen. Hanke was not inclined to agree—he was staring at a $300,000 revenue shortfall and an upcoming payroll that could not be met—but in the end he accepted.

In March 2003 in the opening "shock and awe" of the Iraq war, CNN's EarthViewer simulation of bombing missions over Baghdad, including dramatic swoops down to street level, brought Keyhole's software to the attention of millions of CNN viewers. Keyhole had a tiny customer base at the time, and when the exposure on CNN brought many curious visitors to its Web site, the servers could not handle the load and the site went down. The promotional plug on CNN brought not only the curious but also paying customers, enabling the company to drop the price of a Keyhole Pro subscription to $400 annually.

Keyhole benefited from the hard times prevailing in Silicon Valley in two respects. It didn't have to worry about competing start-ups, the bane of any new company in the Valley. After the crash, new companies that would have crowded into Keyhole's niche could not obtain financing. Keyhole also did not have to worry that it would lose its top engineers to other companies in the Valley dangling tempting packages of stock options. Few companies could go public between 2001 and 2003, so its engineers were not tempted to quit their jobs and chase after seemingly better opportunities that would come with an imminent IPO.

By 2004, however, venture capital firms had cleaned up their portfolios and were starting to look at deals again. Keyhole had made it through the bleak years by relying primarily on sales to real estate professionals, government agencies, and engineering firms. The time had arrived for it to dust off its original plans and try to sell its service to consumers, providing anyone with the ability to circumnavigate a virtual globe.

Hanke visited venture capital firms, found interest, and quickly received an offer for a sizable investment. It was just then, in May 2004, in the midst of finalizing the details of the deal, that Keyhole was invited by Google, its neighbor just six blocks away, to pay a friendly visit and make a presentation. Keyhole did not see why

Google was interested, and its first question was, what do satellite images have to do with Web search? The answer was: Think big. Think of geography as more than road maps and driving directions, like MapQuest. Think of geography as a window upon all information. Think of the earth itself as an organizing device for all categories of information, and satellite images as the way to pull users into a geographic framework. Think of how a user interested in, say, the history of Iraq could virtually fly down into Baghdad, where street-level images would lead to historical documents. The way the Googlers saw the possibilities, satellite images could have everything to do with Web search and any other kind of information search as well.

Google hadn't gone public yet and little was known on the outside about whether the company was doing well or was improvidently spending a dwindling pile of cash on its gourmet cafeterias and other frivolities, reminiscent of Valley spending at its most reckless, circa 1999. Hanke and his colleagues had heard rumors about Google but friends who were working there were secretive. He later recalled, "It was like peeking over the fence of your rich neighbor's house: what's really going on over there?" Now the Keyhole team found themselves on the other side of the fence, in a Google conference room. They faced six Googlers, a mix of business-development people and long-haired male engineers, and were surprised that the Googlers knew all about Keyhole and its software. Was this good, an indication that Google might be interested in acquiring the company? Or did it mean that Google was planning to offer a similar service of its own, which for Keyhole would be catastrophic? The Keyhole team could not read the faces of the Google representatives.

The next day Google called to say it was interested in acquiring the company.

Keyhole had previously tried to sell its technology to Web portals, like Yahoo, that were already using MapQuest and seemed most likely to be receptive to Keyhole's proposal to offer satellite imagery as complementary to road maps. Google did not disclose that it had formed a small group, what would eventually be called Google Maps, to develop its own maps and directions service that would be similar to MapQuest. But in Google's grand conception, maps would serve a larger purpose as one of several related components, along with satellite images and geographic information, to "organize the world's information."

On its own, Keyhole had never even conceived of anything so ambitious. Nor had any of the other companies Keyhole had approached spoken of geography as a universal information tool in such a radically unorthodox way. Hanke recalled, "This was not just a breath of fresh air—it was a *blast*! We thought, they are either delusional or they're visionary."

Another consideration in weighing Google's offer was the likelihood that Google would be able to popularize Keyhole's service much faster than Keyhole itself could. This alone was a powerful inducement to strike a deal. In Silicon Valley, most engineers work on projects that will never be completed—this holds true at large companies as well as small. If engineers are lucky enough to witness the rare day when the product is completed and launched, they will, in the overwhelming majority of cases, witness the product's failure in the marketplace. Hanke said, "Engineers live in fear of pouring their heart and soul into a project for two years, and then having it basically go on a hard drive and never see the light of day, certainly never see satisfied users, and never hear anyone say, 'Hey, that's an amazing program that you've written.'" Having Google express an interest in their work brought everyone at Keyhole closer to realization of the dream that not just thousands of people, but possibly, maybe, if the possibility could be imagined without jinxing it, *millions* of people would use it someday.

The Google offer was a mix of cash and stock. Whether the stock would really be worth much at any point was an open question. But when Google disclosed to Keyhole its current income statement, worries on that score were removed. What the public could not yet see was that Google's Web search advertising was making a nice profit. Keyhole agreed to be acquired, and over a weekend, the company moved into an empty Google building. Also installed on the floor was the Google team that was working on Google Maps, whose core had come from another recent acquisition, Where2 LLC. No formal organization chart brought the Google Maps and Keyhole teams together. The plan was simple: put engineers with similar interests in the vicinity of one another and let them figure out who would like to work with whom. This reflected the preference of the senior triumvirate to use a light touch in creating formal hierarchies at the lower levels and permit teams to organize themselves as much as possible.

Google Maps was well along in development when Google's acquisition of Keyhole was completed in October 2004. When Maps was released in February 2005, the Keyhole technology was not yet integrated with Google's. The principal innovation that Google Maps offered in its very first incarnation was providing users the ability to use a mouse to drag the map in any direction, which brought into view adjacent areas without needing to redraw the entire page, creating an illusion that the computer had maps of the entire world at the ready—it accomplished this by downloading only the data needed to extend the map that was being displayed. It showed streets and driving directions, but did not yet offer an option to display a satellite image as an underlying layer beneath the street grid.

Keyhole would provide the satellite imagery for Google Maps. But Maps was designed to display a single square of roads, and was not designed for high-speed travel. Although one could move in any direction, it was not much faster than walking by foot. It did not permit one to fly around the globe the way Keyhole's own software permitted. Technical limitations of Web browsers like Internet Explorer or Firefox made it impossible to provide smooth navigation of high-resolution images. Google wanted to offer users the same breathtaking three-dimensional flight that Keyhole had offered: Keyhole promised in 2004 that "you can fly through 12+ Terabytes of Earth imagery and data—spinning, rotating, tilting and zooming—think magic carpet ride." But users had to first install the specialized EarthViewer software that Keyhole had developed, which Google renamed Google Earth. This irksome extra step presented a marketing challenge to Google: its users, who were accustomed to using its other services without being asked to install additional software, had to be persuaded to go to the trouble of downloading the Google Earth software to their computers before they could take a test flight.

To encourage users to give it a try, Google decided to make Google Earth available for free, without a subscription fee, at least for home and personal use. Nor did it rush to collect a payoff immediately by placing advertising for local businesses on the images—advertisements would begin to show up only six months after its release. Google, no less than the Keyhole team, was giddy about bringing to a mass audience this new way of accessing information; as work proceeded prior to the launch, business considerations were not uppermost in their minds.

The Keyhole database that Google acquired was not all that Google hoped for. As a start-up, Keyhole had limited resources and had decided to focus on buying the images most likely to be of interest to its customers, who happened to be in the United States. Its coverage of the rest of the globe's surface was skimpy. This would not do for Google, which took considerable pride in the global reach of its business. Brin, who was born in Moscow and emigrated to the United States with his family at the age of six, was the one who most insistently pushed the Keyhole team to think outside U.S. borders. How could Google release a product called Google Earth that had only scanty coverage of most of the world? The staff set to work acquiring a globe-spanning collection of satellite images.

As the preparations for the release of Google Earth were under way, Google Maps did its part to draw more users to Google. That was accomplished by clever individuals outside of Google who wrote code so that data from outside of Google could automatically be superimposed upon a Google map, creating new uses for maps and giving users new ways to think geographically. Google made this possible when it permitted its users to pull map data from Google's servers to create their own hybrid mixes of maps and data, which were handled by their own Web servers. The new creations were called *mashups.*

The first Google Maps mashup was devised by Paul Rademacher, a software developer at DreamWorks Animation. He perceived that housing ads on Craigslist could be linked to a Google map and wrote code that showed each listing as a push pin in the appropriate place on a map. The Web site he set up, HousingMaps, immediately drew thousands of grateful Craigslist apartment hunters. Google noticed, and added features that made developing mashups easier. Its first step: Google hired Rademacher.

When Google Maps were enhanced by mashups, they were capable of showing much more than streets. Mashups mapped fast food restaurants in San Francisco and other cities; lowest gas prices in New York State and other places; crime reports for Chicago and other cities; and news stories in the day's *New York Times* or other news outlets. These and thousands of other mashup sites served as an introductory version of a geographic interface to other information that had not been originally organized by geographic references.

When Google Earth was released in June 2005, its database of satellite images had been filled out and made truly global. Anyone who took the trouble to install the software could zoom to any destination on the globe, but the one place that most users wanted to see first was their own home. (Brin had anticipated that this would be the case when he had given each of his colleagues a quick visit to their homes, one by one, when he had provided them with a demonstration of Keyhole's software the year before.) Not everyone was impressed by Google Earth. Barry Diller, CEO of IAC/InterActiveCorp, whose holdings included Google competitor Ask Jeeves, scoffed, "After you've seen your house and all those other buildings that look like toothpicks from that height, what do you do?"

To begin with, one could indulge in armchair tourism, and go anywhere—reaching Timbuktu, Mali, took a traveler in North America about three seconds, the same time it took for the computer to zoom up, zip over, and then zoom down to any other spot. Eric Schmidt recounted in public talks how he had fulfilled a lifelong ambition—to visit Everest—from the comfort of his office. Web sites like Virtual Globetrotting, Google Earth Hacks, and Google Sightseeing popped up, displaying the most interesting satellite images that users had stumbled upon (the tagline for the latter site was "Why Bother Seeing the World For Real?"). Virtual tourism was highly diverting, but it didn't fully answer Diller's challenge.

Enthusiasts showed the way, building their own layers of information, annotations, photographs, and mashups on top of Google

Earth. Google would eventually even give users some latitude to correct the locations of houses and businesses and add new places. User contributions gave the service a distinctly noncommercial feel. Yet when users wanted to find goods or services in a particular place, Google Earth was ready to supply local business listings, which gave its users a second reason to rely upon it. Users could see exactly where they needed to go to find whatever it was they sought, and could do so staying within the familiar mini world of Google Earth.

Google sought to minimize irritating its users with requests to fill out many boxes on a screen when they wanted to see local businesses placed on a satellite image. Thanks to its work on algorithms in other parts of Google's business, Google Earth software was able to pull apart a phrase like "cheap hotels NYC" and distinguish which part referred to a place and which part described what was sought, and then place upon an aerial view of New York an overlay of inexpensive hotels.

Finding local businesses this way was as easy as using the yellow pages, but initially the public simply shrugged. Not everyone wanted to take the time to download the Google Earth software onto his or her computer. If one wished to use Google Earth simply to find nearby businesses, one did not get a chance to experience the sensation of flying, and Google Maps served perfectly well for finding a local plumber or nail salon.

Yet Google Earth, with its capacity to incorporate the creative additions of enthusiastic volunteers who were excited about the technical capabilities of the software, grew and grew. Before long, hundreds of thousands of different answers to Diller's question spontaneously bubbled up. Humanitarian uses of Google Earth made front-page headlines. When Hurricane Katrina struck, the service helped the Coast Guard rescue victims by comparing images before and after the flooding, revealing the places where housing had been inundated. Its images elsewhere dramatized the effects of clear-cut logging in the Amazon rain forest in Brazil, and it provided the U.S. Holocaust Memorial Museum the means to visually bring home the ravages of genocide in Darfur.

Google Earth gave users the feeling that physical distance did not matter, that everyone on earth was one's neighbor, close at hand. It vanquished the very distinction between the familiar and the unknown; all places could be known, or at least felt as if they could be known, when they, too, could be visited and brought rapidly into focus as the user experienced the sensation of flying halfway around the globe, descending from a high altitude until reaching a hovering point near the ground, all accomplished in a couple of seconds. In 2007, John Hanke said in an interview:

> The ability of people to connect from the very local to the earth as a whole then back to their own, very local place, is a really powerful way to make these connections that might otherwise be remote and abstract. We're inclined to think of events as happening "out there somewhere"—"somewhere else"—and I think there's something in the experience of flying with this continuous motion from a place that you know and the familiar details of your town or city or community to this remote area, where you can also see recognizable human details, you make that connection. Historically, with *National Geographic,* you have this beautiful map, and then you have this beautiful picture, or this disturbing picture, and it's up to you to make this connection between yourself and a shape on the map. That's a pretty hard thing to do and is very different from starting out and just continuously flying in, and then the details resolve as you're coming down in this continuous zoom. It's not just the dot on a map.

American astronaut Bill Anders's photos of the earth, taken in 1968 during the Apollo 8 mission, had vividly shown earth's inhabitants how small a place the planet seemed when framed against the void. Now, Google Earth made the planet seem even smaller, a place where we are all virtual neighbors, separated by only a few mouse clicks. Robert M. Samborski, executive director of the Geospatial Information and Technology Association, a trade organization, said in 2006, only a year after the release of Google Maps and Google Earth, that "Google's done more to raise the awareness of using maps than the industry's been able to do in the past twenty-five years."

Google Earth also drew attention for its utility in less serious pursuits. Oddities turned up among its images. The Badlands Guardian, for example, a natural geologic formation near Alberta, Canada, was often visited by online aviators. It resembles a human head, wearing Native American headdress—and also appears to be naturally adorned with iPod-like earbuds that hang down—on a scale that makes the figures on Mount Rushmore look like miniatures. One could also pay an overhead visit to the Arizona farmer who carved a giant portrait of Oprah Winfrey across ten acres of cropland, or to the forty-year-old barracks complex at a U.S. Navy base near San Diego that, from an aerial view, resembled a swastika.

Sky in Google Earth, introduced in 2007, allows viewers to look upward and travel to individual stars (100 million) and distant galaxies (200 million). Attention could also be redirected back down to earth to a more familiar group of stars, found in Hollywood and its vicinity. Fans with no official connection to Google added home listings for Tom Cruise, Halle Berry, George Clooney, Angelina Jolie, and other film notables. Software that could be used for such breathtakingly disparate purposes, high and low—with the power to send a traveler either to the farthest edge of the known universe or to hover above Jim Carrey's estate—makes anywhere and everywhere appear accessible. The natural corollary, which was not fully appreciated at first, was that soon every nonfamous person in the universe will be accessible to everyone else.

Shortly after John Hanke joined Google, he began to hear the first rumblings of the general public's uneasiness about satellite images breaching the privacy of individuals. Hanke attempted to allay concerns by explaining that the satellite images that Google used were generally six to twelve months old. Users could not swoop down and spy on a neighbor's back yard in real time. Nor was the resolution of the photographs sufficient to permit a Google user to pick out any meaningful details. He added reassuringly: "It's not like you are going to be able to read a license plate on a car or see what an individual was doing when a particular image was taken."

Strictly speaking, Hanke was correct: the resolution of the commercially available satellite imagery at that time was insufficient to portray clearly objects that were smaller than two feet. The resolution was improving rapidly, however. Aerial images—that is, those taken at very high resolution by airplanes at much lower altitudes than satellites—would increasingly be Google's source of images for densely populated places. Only a year later, in 2006, the first sighting of seminude sunbathers visible in images snapped by an aerial camera excited much commentary on blogs around the world. The human figures are just barely discernible atop a house in the Netherlands; they drew attention not because they are distinct enough to be prurient but because the image graphically conveyed just how far aerial imaging technology had advanced. Surely the woman who was basking in the sun topless, facedown on the deck of her own house, did not realize that she was publicly visible—from far, far above.

Aerial photography would not seem to be all that intrusive, not when compared to what soon arrived: cameras mounted at street level. Just as Hanke was trying to reassure the public, a Google competitor launched by Amazon, called A9, dispatched camera crews to drive along the streets of ten major cities and snap photos of the storefronts of every business, with the ambition of eventually including every business in the country. Soon after, Microsoft announced, in December 2005, the availability in beta form of what it called "bird's-eye imagery" for cities covering about 25 percent of the U.S. population. The birdie, which was a low-flying aircraft, took pictures at a 45 degree angle, which made the landscape much easier to recognize and provided far more useful information than images taken from directly above cityscape objects.

These initiatives were logical extensions of the same project that Keyhole had begun and that Google was putting its own considerable weight behind, combining the specificity of a photograph with the abstraction of a map. Satellite images were the easiest way to get started and cover large swatches of the earth quickly. But the project had a logic of its own: the closer to the ground and the more detailed the images, the more useful they would be to users. A year after Google Earth's introduction, Google was well along in upgrading its medium-resolution images, which represented 15 meters per pixel, with high-resolution ones at 70 centimeters per pixel that covered about one-third of the global population and provided sufficient detail to pick out cars and houses. Images with still finer resolution, of 10 centimeters per pixel, would follow. So, too, would a fully featured flight simulator, tucked into a new software release without announcement—Google seemed almost embarrassed by the technical riches that it was able to incorporate into Google Earth.

The problem was that there was no natural way of determining that 15-meters-per-pixel resolution was socially acceptable but 10-centimeters-per-pixel resolution was overly invasive. Nor was there any law or code that decreed shots taken from above were acceptable but street-level views were not. If you were in the mapping business, you would seek out as many images, in as high a resolution as you could, from whatever vantage point provided the most visual information.

Neither Google nor its rivals had any choice: in the information business, an imperative is at work, pressing for more, more, more. Right from the start, with its insistence on indexing all Web sites, not just a good selection, Google had appreciated the need for completeness. In its Book Search program, it showed a willingness to take on the most daunting of logistical challenges. With such new services as Google Earth and Google Maps, Google tried to offer products that were more comprehensive than its competitors, but its rivals were in close pursuit. In the heat of this competition, no company was willing to pause and ask whether it had gone too far, breaching individuals' reasonable expectations of personal privacy.

Google's introduction of Street View to Google Maps in May 2007 was inevitable, not only because of Google's own history and increased competition, but also because the combination of street-level photographs with street maps was so natural a pairing. In fact this combination was so natural that it had been discovered a full century before, in the early days of automobiles. In 1907 Rand McNally published *Photo-Auto Maps,* which used photographs of streets and landmarks, with an overlay of helpful arrows, to show drivers a recommended route.

Inevitable as Google Maps's Street View was, if considered in the long view of events, its introduction was not universally well received. Initially, only streets in San Francisco, New York, Las Vegas, Miami, and Denver were available for viewing, but this was sufficient to produce many complaints about breached privacy. Mary Kalin-Casey, who wrote to the popular tech blog *BoingBoing,* received wide attention as an early "victim"—her complaint was that her cat was plainly visible in the Street View image that included the exterior of her living room window. Kalin-Casey wrote, "I'm all for mapping, but this feature literally gives me the shakes."

Wired magazine's blog invited readers to submit the most interesting "urban street sightings" found among Google Maps's Street View images. Among the entries that readers voted as favorites were several photographs of young women in bathing suits lying on the grass ("Stanford coeds enjoying the sun"); a woman in a car whose door was open as she prepared to step out, and though her face could not be seen, a portion of her underwear could ("I think I see a thong!"); and a man apparently climbing up the front of a locked security gate ("Break-in in progress").

Just as with the reaction to Book Search, Google was taken aback by the negative publicity Street View generated. After all, its cameras saw nothing more than what anyone who was driving down the same streets at the same time would have seen. The company had taken one precaution: it had anticipated the need to protect the identities of anyone in the vicinity of domestic violence shelters and had removed images of the shelters. Other than that, Google had proceeded on the reasonable assumption that it need not treat public space as if it were private.

What neither Google nor its critics realized was that our anonymity while walking about in public space in the predigital age was protected not by law but by the crude state of technology—we felt invisible only because cameras were not in place to capture our images. Similarly, what had once been a paper trail of our unwanted encounters with the legal system remained invisible, practically speaking, because it sat in folders in the courthouse, requiring that a curious citizen expend energy and time in order to examine it. Placing those records online, where they could be easily accessed by anyone, from any PC connected to the Internet, accomplished what street-view images also did: things that were always a part of public space were rendered easy to see for the first time.

As always, Google was preoccupied with its quest to improve the technology for gathering information and serving it up to viewers in useful ways. Its engineers had done exactly what they were supposed to do. They had built software that melded street maps and photographic images and devised ways to improve existing technology. In the case of four of the first five cities covered by Street View, Google had relied on images collected by another company, Immersive Media, which had invented a "geoimmersive" video camera that resembled a ball, with eleven lenses distributed around its surface. When mounted upon the roof of a car or van, it recorded a spherical video, continuously tagged with GPS data, that when played back could provide a 360-degree view from any spot. Not wholly satisfied with Immersive Media's images, however, Google had also tried out its own equipment for San Francisco's streets, which produced similar 360-degree views with the added improvement of extremely high resolution. The difference in quality was striking. When Lance Ulanoff, an editor at *PC Magazine,* attempted to sharpen with the help of Photoshop the somewhat blurry face of a woman that Google Street View had captured on the streets of New York, he found that the resolution was simply too poor. But in San Francisco's Street View images he could easily read license plates—and also see in sharp detail the man who had become infamous on the Internet because he happened to be standing in front of a strip club when the Google camera car happened by.

Legally speaking, Google was absolutely correct to argue, as Peter Fleischer, the company's global privacy counsel, did, that "in the U.S., there's a long and noble tradition of 'public spaces,' where people don't have the same expectations of privacy as they do in their homes. This tradition helps protect journalists, for example." Practically speaking, however, Google had to back down in the face of heated criticism. About ten days after the product was launched, the company began to remove images when an individual discovered his or her face in the Street View image and asked Google to remove it.

Tellingly, Google accommodated these requests without publicly announcing that it was doing so. Schmidt, Page, and Brin still hoped to preserve the general principle that individuals did not enjoy a right to privacy when standing in public space. A few months later, however, Google retreated further, acknowledging that it would remove any image that contained a person's face or license number, regardless of who submitted the request. Having conceded the point that the faces that incidentally appear in the images have no bearing on the usefulness of its street views, it was just a matter of time before Google attempted to automate the process of removing facial detail. In May 2008, the company began to test software that automatically blurred faces on its New York images.

Google did not rush to introduce Street View for Google Maps outside of the United States. Without precedents established elsewhere by other companies for street views, Google anticipated an international outcry about invasions of privacy. Satellite photos had already led to much grief for Google. When Google Earth was introduced, the governments of South Korea, Thailand, and Russia complained about images in which military facilities and government buildings were clearly in view. A Russian security analyst acidly said, "Terrorists don't need to reconnoiter their target. Now an American company is working for them." Google retorted that whether it displayed the images or not, it could not stop their circulation online because they originated from other sources, but this line of argument did not appease the governments that were upset.

When the RAND Corporation looked in 2004 at the availability of geo-spatial information, including satellite images, that would "help terrorists and other hostile forces mount attacks in the U.S.," it concluded that less than 1 percent of geo-spatial information that was made publicly available on federal Web sites and databases was not readily available elsewhere. Federal, state, and local government officials, apparently unaware of the fact that satellite images that Google Earth used were supplied to Google by other companies and widely distributed, did not hesitate in ordering Google to remove from Google Earth whatever images they deemed compromising to national security. Vice President Dick Cheney's residence at the U.S. Naval Observatory in Washington, the U.S. Capitol, and the

U.S. Military Academy at West Point were declared off-limits. The zeal of some officials extended also to protecting prying eyes from seeing overhead views of an amusement park in Rye, New York, a sewage treatment plant in Yonkers, and the site of dearest importance to our national security, the headquarters of PepsiCo, in Purchase. The futility of these measures was revealed in many instances when the images that were removed from Google were discovered on other sites. For example, a nuclear power plant in Ohio that was blacked out on Google Maps was available in clear detail on Microsoft's maps. Massachusetts officials, who tried to obscure the locations of state facilities in images they supplied to Google, were left looking foolish when Microsoft and Yahoo obtained undoctored images of the same state facilities from commercial sources.

Nonetheless, it was Google that was depicted as acting irresponsibly. One cartoon showed a barber offering a customer not just a mirror but also a PDA to use to examine the just-completed haircut: "Would you like to see the top on Google Earth?" This was harmless fun, but more serious criticisms were leveled. In June 2007, in the wake of arrests related to a plot to blow up fuel tanks at Kennedy International Airport, Thomas P. DiNapoli, New York's state comptroller, held a press conference and criticized online mapping services, naming Google Earth in particular, for providing "too much information" that "might compromise counterterrorism efforts." The suspects had used Google Earth to obtain an aerial view of the airport, but how this provided "too much information" was not clear—the *New York Times* accompanied its news story of the plot with an aerial photograph showing in crystalline detail the same fuel tanks at JFK. Still, the temptation to demonize Google was irresistible. Assemblyman Michael N. Gianaris chimed in: "In light of the use of Google Earth in the JFK plot, we must ensure these programs are not used as blueprints for an attack on our country."

Hearing such alarms, Americans naturally would feel a tug of worry about national security vulnerabilities. In such circumstances, we all too readily forget the bedrock democratic principle that American librarians have always understood and protected: access to information must never be subject to government control. Classified military secrets are the only permissible exception. Censoring images shown by Google Earth is no more effective than censoring book acquisitions at the local public library: the information originates elsewhere and will circulate no matter what symbolic action may be taken at one particular place to block its distribution.

The abundance of information that is now available online was brought home to Google's own Eric Schmidt in 2005, a few months after Google Maps was released. When Elinor Mills, a reporter for CNET News, decided to explore a story about Google and threats to personal privacy, she devised an interesting exercise: she gave herself thirty minutes to see what personal information could be discovered about Eric Schmidt using Google.

Schmidt's net worth, his political fund-raising activities, and his hobbies were readily found. Mills wrote, "That such detailed personal information is so readily available on public Web sites makes most people uncomfortable." Schmidt lashed out wildly, not at the public Web sites on which his personal information resided, but at the messenger that delivered the news. CNET was informed that Google was unhappy with the use of Schmidt's "private information" in its story and as punishment Google as a matter of company policy would not respond to any questions or requests submitted by CNET reporters for one year.

Ridicule was heaped upon Schmidt from various quarters. The *Register* derided his "hissy fit"; hadn't Schmidt promised publicly to build "a Google that knows more about you"? A *New York Times* headline sardonically read, "Google Anything So Long As It's Not Google."

Schmidt, of all people, should have understood that CNET, like Google, cannot control what information is placed on the Web sites of other organizations. His bizarre reaction overshadowed Mills's original story, which had been quite discreet, in fact, in not putting in the story Schmidt's home address, which she also found online. If she had wanted to, she could have used Google Maps to give her readers handy directions to Schmidt's home doorstep.

In speeding the democratization of technology and information, Google had made the world a smaller, more intimate place. But in a small world, its wealthiest residents feel more vulnerable to unseen threats. This had not been anticipated by Schmidt or anyone in the Google conference room when Brin had used Keyhole's software to "fly" to the houses of the others.

After two months passed and Schmidt had regained his composure, Google quietly restored a normal working relationship with CNET. Schmidt never released a public mea culpa. But by dropping the sanctions against the news organization, he belatedly showed his understanding that he had undermined Google's most basic message, which is that users will find online, with Google's assistance, whatever information they need. The company has helped to bring a high-resolution view of the entire globe within reach of our itchy fingertips, but if anyone believes the drawbacks outweigh the benefits, blame cannot be assigned to any one company. The world is experienced as smaller because computer technology now makes it possible for it to seem so, and that technology does not come with an "undo" button.

Google Maps's Street View created unease not just because images of identifiable people were being collected but because it was Google that was doing the collecting, the company that seemed to be collecting more and more information about everything. Had another company, say MapQuest, introduced Street View, a company that wasn't attempting to "organize the world's information" and didn't possess information other than road maps, directions, and traffic conditions, it seems unlikely that Street View would have excited the same reaction.

Before long, we are likely to look back upon Street View or the first-generation mashup as crude experiments. We will come to rely upon mashups that combine not two but many disparate sources of information—restaurants, menus, professional reviews, customer reviews, health department inspection reports, the presence of friends in the vicinity, one-click reservations—overlaid onto a single map, updated continuously. And we will become accustomed to having access to all of this information, seamlessly integrated together, anywhere we happen to be, on any Internet-connected device, on any screen, tiny as well as large.

The Google vision is of a multidimensional mashing together of all information, integrated in novel ways yet instantly accessible from a centralized computing "cloud." The geo-spatial dimension is one addition, and the personal dimension is another, including the very personal. Beginning with its users' e-mail, Google has taken steps to incorporate into its storehouses the digital documents that users regard as the most sensitive ones they possess. One by one, it has added new categories of information that it offers to store on its servers: word processing documents, spreadsheets, calendars, and other personal and office documents. Central storage provides convenience, to be sure, but it also creates a tension between greater convenience and diminished privacy, or at least worries about diminished privacy. When a single company is determined to organize the world's information, including one's very own personal information, will the service be welcomed more than feared?

Just as Google discovered when it introduced Google Maps and Google Earth, making our world seem smaller also serves to make us feel more vulnerable to unwanted attention from others. Putting our most personal information on the same servers that hold publicly accessible information triggers anxieties that Google's reassurances about privacy protections can never completely quell. The anxieties are less about measurable risks than about inchoate concerns. We are only too happy to avail ourselves of greatly improved access to information about others, but then, oblivious to our inconsistency, we object to others having greater access to information about ourselves. The more control we gain of information, thanks to Google, the more we also experience a nagging worry about loss of control of information most dear to us.

CHAPTER 7

A Personal Matter

Google began in the information business, but the hardware and software it developed to handle the world's information turned out to be able to do more, much more. Without planning to do so, Google has embarked on its most audacious initiative to date, offering to replace the basic software that runs on individual computers with software services that run on its own machines. Customers will send the data or documents to the "cloud," and Google will take care of everything else. Software as a Service, as it is called, promises to perform just as ably on a centralized server as the software that we place on our own machines. Eventually.

Software as a Service offers other tantalizing collateral benefits: much lower costs; elimination of upgrade hassles and virus-infection headaches; and the ability to leave laptop computers at home and rely instead on much simpler devices for portable computing, like Internet-connected cell phones, which do not need much processing power because software performs the necessary work on the centralized server.

A shift from local computing, using software that is installed on the PC, to cloud-based Software as a Service, using software that runs on a centralized server, represents a threat to two of Microsoft's core businesses: its Windows operating system franchise and its Office applications suite. Software as a Service renders the kind of operating system used on a customer's end irrelevant: it could be a Mac system, Linux, or something other than a PC entirely, such as new kinds of ultracompact tablet computers that will be Internet connected, what chip manufacturer Qualcomm calls "pocketable computing." Nor will customers have reason to purchase new copies of Office if they can create Office-like documents using software that runs on someone else's computer and is available for much less cost. In 2008, Google further encroached upon Microsoft when it began providing Google Docs users the ability to work on documents even when they lack an Internet connection, such as on a plane. Google engineer Philip Tucker described it as "bringing the cloud with you." When the connection is restored, the work that was done off-line is automatically sent back up to the cloud.

Google's interest in expanding beyond a role of merely providing information to one of providing software services for a wide gamut of purposes has become visible not as a clearly announced vision but in bits and pieces. Google has not declared itself to be a strategic competitor with Microsoft and it seems to have taken pains to downplay the competitive threat that its Software as a Service poses to Microsoft's businesses. When Eric Schmidt was chief executive at Novell, he repeatedly warned that it would be foolish for any company that challenged Microsoft to "moon the giant." Google was reluctant to develop a Web-based e-mail program partly because many Googlers believed that doing so would, in the words of one Google engineer, "incite Microsoft to destroy Google."

Google's Software as a Service offerings have been introduced without the benefit of decent marketing—beginning with Google Apps for Your Domain and evolving into today's simpler Google Apps. Among the applications are an online word processor that it acquired in 2006, originally called Writely, and an online spreadsheet that Google developed internally. In October 2006, the company rechristened the two as Google Docs & Spreadsheets. Determined not to be copying its rival, Google stubbornly refuses to use the name that would be most natural: Google Office.

One by one, Google has added online versions of Microsoft software that users were accustomed to using on their desktop. Google Calendar was released in beta mode in 2006. A PowerPoint-like presentations module for Google Apps arrived in 2007. As Google expands its portfolio of services, its servers host categories of personal information that extend well beyond the functions of Microsoft Office: online purchase histories (Google Checkout), instant messaging (Google Talk), blogging (Blogger), social networking (Orkut), and recordings of phone conversations (GrandCentral). Eric Schmidt predicted that only a few, specialized applications, like high-end graphics processing, would stay on desktop computers, while 90 percent of the computing for which we use desktop PCs today would be handled in the cloud, on remote servers like Google's.

The first step that Google took in the direction of building Software as a Service was to offer its own e-mail service, Gmail. Adding e-mail marked a significant departure from its original single-minded focus on Web search. When Sergey Brin was interviewed by the Stanford student newspaper in April 2000, he said that Google was deliberately following a different path from Yahoo, which offered a complete set of information services that were intended to keep users from having any reason to go to another Web site: "All we do is search," he said proudly. The year before, Larry Page had said, "I won't say we won't add services, but we wouldn't put free email on our site unless we thought we could do a much better job." In those earliest years, Google was supplying search services on a wholesale basis to Yahoo, and it hoped to supply search to other portals, all of which had their own e-mail services. By deliberately sticking to search only, he said, Google minimized "the competition we have with people we might work with."

Google's focus on search led it inexorably to e-mail, however. Internet users spent far more time working with e-mail every day than they did carrying out Web searches, and e-mail messages were as difficult to search as the Web had been before the arrival of search engines. Important messages were mixed with unimportant, and when the accumulation of messages grew beyond a certain point, it was difficult to find a particular message easily. Sorting messages into folders was helpful but required a maddening investment of time. Many users did not bother, with the result that many messages a user would have liked to save fell victim to mass purging when the in-box became full. It's not surprising that Google, the company with the all-encompassing mission of organizing the world's information, would feel compelled, sooner or later, to have a go at organizing e-mail, too.

Google's e-mail project began in modest fashion. Paul Buchheit, Google employee number 23 who had coined "Don't Be Evil," was asked in 2002 if he would be interested in starting work on an e-mail product. He had experience working on another e-mail project before joining Google and was delighted to be asked: he was the much-vexed recipient of five hundred messages a day and wanted to have a better way to search his messages. A colleague, Sanjeev Singh, joined him on a part-time basis, but it took a while before the rest of a small team was assembled. When Brian Rakowski, an engineer freshly graduated from Stanford, was told he would be assigned as associate product manager to Google's e-mail project, he was taken aback. E-mail? What did e-mail have to do with working on search algorithms?

The answer was simple: Brin and Page had come to view e-mail as an unsolved search problem. A move into e-mail now seemed natural to them, but they did have to persuade other Googlers. "Look," they said to skeptics, "the information in e-mail is at least as important as some random Web page. The fact that you can't find an e-mail that you want is ridiculous."

Once the newly hired Rakowski adjusted to the idea that Google was planning to provide an e-mail service, he plunged in happily. He had spent his share of fruitless hours attempting to retrieve particular messages that refused to appear, and he realized a user could find any message in a trice if Google's search engine could be applied to the problem. Most veteran Google engineers were more resistant to the idea. Their main concerns were that e-mail would be a distraction, diluting the company's focus on its core strength, Web search, and that it would be costly, requiring more hard drives to store messages and attachments. Who would be willing to pay for it?

The e-mail service that would become Gmail would indeed be costly. Rakowski was asked to prepare financial projections that showed scenarios of all kinds, but Gmail promised to be a money loser under even the sunniest assumptions. Page's and Brin's support of the project wasn't unconditional. The team had to pass periodic executive reviews. It would have to figure out how to make a profit from the service, and it would have to demonstrate that the payoff was large enough to risk alienating Google's two largest partners at the time, Yahoo and AOL, both of whom had enormously popular e-mail services. The Gmail team got by with candor: we admit we don't know at this point how we're going to make money, but as we learned from our experience with Web search, if we provide the public with something useful, we'll eventually figure out a way to make the service profitable.

Buchheit and Marissa Mayer shared an office and often discussed business models. Later, Mayer recalled telling Buchheit, "Look, this is easy. We're going to give them small mailboxes for free, and up-sell them into larger mailboxes. That's what everybody does." Buchheit counterproposed placing advertisements on Gmail. "Paul, Paul, Paul," Mayer replied.

> Ads are never going to work! Either we run banner ads, and they're not going to be targeted, and people will develop blind spots, and they'll fail in terms of effectiveness, and, we're not going to get money, and annoy our users. Or, we're going to target the ads at their email, which is just going to be creepy and weird. People are going to think there's people here reading their emails and picking out the ads—it's going to be terrible.

The two went back and forth, with Mayer returning again and again to her prediction that the ads would be either "irrelevant" or "cause a lot of privacy concerns." The highest priority, she felt, was to fix the problems that afflicted their prototype so that it could perform the basic functions of sending and receiving messages. About 3 A.M., the time the two customarily brought their work days to a close, Mayer prepared to go home but Buchheit stayed behind. Her parting words to him were, "So, Paul, we agreed, we're not exploring the whole ad thing right now?" He said he agreed.

But in an empty building in the wee hours of the morning, no one was around who could deny his having a little fun with the e-mail prototype, which was sufficiently functional that he, Mayer, and four other Google employees were relying upon it, including Brin and Page. Buchheit downloaded semantic analysis software from the Internet that could analyze any block of text, identifying the grammatical function of every word in every sentence, and then figure out the sentence's meaning and distill the meaning into a few keywords. He hooked it up to the ad database that Google used for Web search results, which was designed to match a given keyword with particular advertisements. Then he connected the advertising code to the e-mail program so that it automatically served up ads based on the content of each individual e-mail message. By 7 A.M. he had the satisfaction of seeing a functioning ad system running, and he went home.

When Mayer came into the office around 9 A.M. and logged into her e-mail, she saw the ads and was irked. She weighed calling Buchheit immediately to have him restore the system before Brin and Page saw the ads, as she knew they "sometimes have weird views about privacy and what's creepy, and what's not." Brin, in particular, had been outspoken about his belief that attempting to target ads based on what users were reading, rather than what they were actively searching for, would never work effectively, and the ads would be perceived as an aggravating distraction. She decided to let Buchheit sleep for another hour before ordering him to return to the office and take the ad function out. But before long, she noticed that a few ads that accompanied her e-mail seemed reasonably useful. In one message, in which a friend had invited her to go hiking, an ad for hiking boots appeared. In another, mention was made of Al Gore's upcoming visit to the company, and the ad server displayed ads for books related to Gore. She decided to let the experiment run a bit longer, and was glad she did. When Brin and Page rolled in and saw the ads, they were delighted. Seeing how well even a rudimentary prototype of an ad-matching service worked convinced Brin that he had been wrong to dismiss it.

Buchheit's improvised use of semantic analysis demonstrated that algorithms could do a satisfactory job of selecting advertisements to accompany any given text that was displayed online. This late-night experiment became the basis of Google's second-most-important advertising program, AdSense. Google offers Web site owners the opportunity to run advertisements on their Web sites that are supplied by Google's network of advertisers. For participating Web sites, Google's software crawls the site, performs semantic analysis on the text on each page, and then automatically selects ads that are displayed on the right hand side of the page, matched to the meaning of the text. It calls this "contextual advertising." Site owners and Google split the proceeds when visitors click on the ads.

When the Gmail team stumbled across the opportunity to use semantic analysis software to serve ads matched to any text, even text on other Web sites, Google moved quickly to introduce the service. AdSense was launched in March 2003, a year before Gmail was ready.

Mayer had been concerned that users would perceive advertising that was closely matched to the contents of their e-mail as "creepy," and that was an issue that would surface as soon as the product was publicly released. But in the near term, the team became preoccupied with other, more technical issues in getting the service up and running. The hardware and software infrastructure that Google had built for Web search was not well suited for hosting e-mail. File systems that had been designed to be updated occasionally, when Google's Web crawler noticed a change at a Web site, had to be redesigned so that they could be updated continuously. This necessitated significant changes in Google's back-end software systems.

Google also had to learn to treat data that it was collecting with greater care. The inexpensive hardware it relied upon was expected to fail, and the company expected that some of the information its crawlers had captured would occasionally be lost before the system had made backup copies. Those data losses were inconsequential as long as the service being offered was merely Web search because the lost information, before long, would be captured by the crawlers again. A lost e-mail message, however, was not replaceable. Google's e-mail system would receive only one copy, and it would land on a machine whose components could not be relied upon. Google had to redesign its system to be truly fail-safe.

Google could have resorted to buying the special hardware used by the leading Web e-mail providers for solving this problem. Google's engineers did consider this option, but the company's grand vision for its e-mail service made that impractical for economic reasons. At the time, Yahoo provided its e-mail users with 4 megabytes of storage. Google, however, was preparing to offer 250 times more—1 gigabyte—to each user for free, providing what was seen at the time as sufficient space to permanently store all e-mail messages that an individual ever received. It would have been exorbitantly expensive for Google to use the hardware that others were using, which had the most reliable—and most expensive—components available. The only way Google could execute its plan would be to work with the same inexpensive hardware it used for Web search and develop new software systems that would ensure e-mails would not be lost.

By early spring 2004, work had progressed sufficiently that a date for launching the service could be penciled in. Brin weighed in with the suggestion that it be introduced on April 1. After all, April Fool's pranks were a treasured tradition at Google. What better joke could be arranged for the day, Brin said, than to introduce a real product in such a way that the public would not know whether it was to be taken seriously or laughed off as a prank?

The press announcement of the "preview release" of Gmail mixed the serious and the comical. The headline said that Google had created "search-based Webmail," a transparent attempt to make the expansion of Google's Web search business seem a natural one. It explained that search was the number two online activity and e-mail was number one, and appended a strange comment from Brin and Page: "'Heck, Yeah,' Say Google Founders." The inspiration for the project was attributed to a Google user who "kvetched" about wasting time trying to find messages and having to constantly "delete e-mail like crazy" to stay under the 4-megabyte limit imposed by a Google competitor. With 1 gigabyte of storage, Google offered its users a way "to be able to hold onto their mail forever."

Predictably enough, the announcement was received with puzzlement. Was Google serious? The "Heck, Yeah" suggested not. The promise that users would be able to hold onto e-mail "forever" also seemed like a joke. Who could possibly afford to offer a free service that made promises that extended to "forever"? The fact that Gmail was not available initially to anyone but a tiny group of invitees meant that most of the curious could not sign up and see for themselves, which further stoked skepticism. While some news publishers, such as the Associated Press and Reuters, treated the announcement seriously, others treated it as a publicity stunt. At *Slashdot*, one person chortled that mainstream news organizations had fallen for a joke that would "go down in history as one of the biggest pranks ever pulled." The confusion led the British news site *The Inquirer* to call the announcement "Google's April 1 Cock-Up."

The fuss was a boon in free advertising for Gmail. But the public's initial reaction was wary, just as it tended to be whenever Google announced an expansion of its information collections. Some initial Gmail users were spooked by the feeling that Google was "reading" private e-mail in order to match ads. There was also some grumbling about Gmail's decision not to offer a delete button. By forcing users to work their way through cumbersome menus in order to delete a message, Gmail encouraged users to simply ignore and retain their unwanted e-mail. The two problems, of Google's reading e-mail and retaining e-mail, seemed connected in a sinister way, as if Google was intentionally trying to probe as much of its users' private lives as it could for commercial purposes.

Whether a delete button should be provided was a question that had been debated at length by the Gmail team. Buchheit was a dogged advocate of no delete button and his arguments had prevailed. Users would be best served, he said, by a design that made retention of e-mail the easiest course. He wanted to save users the burden of "cognitive overhead" as they pondered whether to save or delete messages. With Google search available within the Gmail system, users would eventually realize, he believed, that it was best to just archive everything.

To Gmail's first-generation users, however, e-mail was highly personal, the most personal information that an individual processed on her or his computer in a day. They didn't want to be told how they should manage their messages, and they were demonstrative about their feelings. Jen Fitzpatrick, a senior engineer at Google, later said that every member of the Gmail team had stories to tell about "their family, their friends, random strangers they would meet at parties when they would tell them they worked on Gmail—the common refrain was, 'I want a delete button. Don't you get it? I want a delete button.'" In January 2006, almost two years after Gmail's introduction, a delete button was added.

The other problem, the concern that Gmail's ads were encroaching on users' privacy, was not so easily solved. Googlers had convinced themselves that Gmail users would see advertisements as helpful. In their 2004 *Playboy* interview, the two Google founders were grilled about Gmail. Yes, Page admitted, the matching of ads to the content of messages "seems a little spooky at first," but Brin emphasized that the only alternative would be intrusive "big glaring videos" that would appear before a message appeared, so "it's a pretty obvious choice."

The Googlers were flummoxed when Gmail's first users were uncomfortable about Google's deciphering the meaning of their e-mail messages. It did not seem fair that Google was criticized for this—after all, the other Web e-mail services also used software to scan the contents of messages, looking for viruses and spam. All e-mail messages could be said to be scanned, too, whenever a user performed a search. Brin tried to call attention to the fact that scanning was "automated—no one is looking, so I don't think it's a privacy issue." But the fact that Google introduced ads that were linked to the contents of the e-mail messages seemed to make the difference. Yahoo Mail and Microsoft's Hotmail were getting a free pass on their automated scans simply because their systems ran banner ads, as most Web sites did, oblivious to the contents of the rest of the Web page.

The attack on Gmail that most frightened Google was mounted in the California Senate, where Liz Figueroa, a Democratic state senator, sponsored a bill placing limits on the information gleaned from "scanning" of e-mail messages that could be shared with third parties. Figueroa said that her legislation "guarantees that our most private communications will remain just that—private." The California State Senate passed the bill, but it died after being sent to the state Assembly.

One could argue that Google should have anticipated the public's distrust of its plans for Gmail, with its centralized, permanent storage of personal data. Microsoft had tried years before to move users' personal data from scattered places into a centralized repository in the cloud. The spectacularly unsuccessful outcome of Microsoft's efforts should have provided cautionary lessons for all who followed.

In 2001, three years before Gmail was introduced, Microsoft had launched its own centralized data storage service, My Services, which would include, in due time, an address book, personal calendar, word-processing documents, and e-mail. Its users would retain full control over who would have access to their information, which was supposed to make My Services "user-centric." The first offering would be Passport, a service that would permit a user to use a single log-in name and a single password at all Web sites that signed up to participate and work with Passport's master repository of log-in information. Microsoft planned to show how convenient the service was by introducing Passport first to Hotmail.

The company thought its plans for a new family of information services would be heaped with praise. But the project, all too aptly named HailStorm, was instead assailed. The unfortunate name made for an inauspicious beginning. Mark Lucovsky, the senior Microsoft engineer on the project, had been responsible for assigning a temporary name while the project was in development. He chose HailStorm for fun, knowing that it would aggravate Microsoft's marketing group, which would come up with the final name. The Microsoft marketers dithered, however, and when the day of introduction arrived, no replacement name had been agreed upon, so, by default, HailStorm it was.

The service drew nothing but derision. Microsoft was a company that had failed to secure the public's confidence that it could handle sensitive personal data. In the previous twelve months, Microsoft had issued twelve security-related software updates for its Internet Explorer, trying to address gaping vulnerabilities. It had also suffered the recent embarrassment of an intruder breaking into its own internal corporate network. In order to address the breach, the company was forced to block all external access for a while, even preventing forty thousand of its off-campus employees from using its own network.

Perhaps the biggest obstacle to Passport's winning acceptance was the public's unease about a system that made all of one's personal data, including credit card information that Microsoft offered to manage as an "electronic wallet," accessible with a single password. Having one's personal information scattered in various places seemed to many people to be a sensible form of protection from identity theft, a problem that had become impossible to ignore. Earlier that year, a Brooklyn restaurant worker had been charged with successful online theft of the identities of Oprah Winfrey, Steven Spielberg, and Martha Stewart.

When HailStorm was introduced, a coalition of privacy groups mobilized and formally complained to the Federal Trade Commission about "Microsoft's ability to track, profile, and monitor" users of its Passport service. Microsoft had no allies in this fight, and HailStorm was dead on arrival. When Microsoft was unable to sign up a single company willing to work with it on the project, the company quietly dropped it.

Google's executive leaders were determined to succeed precisely where Microsoft failed. The introduction of Gmail drew criticism, but nothing like the public outcry about HailStorm, because Google had merely introduced e-mail alone, not a comprehensive plan that would encompass the centralization of all personal documents. The criticism of Gmail soon faded, the bill in the California legislature was never passed, and Google was able to proceed.

Google learned from its Gmail launch. Brian Rakowski enumerated the mistakes that Google had committed: the company had not prebriefed journalists and had not conferred in advance with the leading privacy advocates, like the Electronic Frontier Foundation and the Electronic Privacy Information Center. The proper sequence, he said, was to first "get their opinions and figure out if you're doing something wrong."

In looking back, Rakowski marveled at the public's focus on the scanning for matching ads, while ignoring much more serious privacy issues, such as the increased risk that e-mail on centralized servers could easily be subpoenaed or personal information in e-mail messages could be shared with advertisers. "Nobody was talking about those privacy issues and the few things we were doing to protect users' privacy," he said. Rather than talking about the inherent "downside" to storing your e-mail on a server "that you don't control," users were worried about the matching of ads to content by a nonhuman device. How many times would Google have to field the same question from users—"Is Google reading my email?"—and answer with, "Google is NOT reading your email"?

Brad Templeton, the chairman of the Electronic Frontier Foundation and a sometime consultant to Google, agreed that the matched advertisements were not a substantive problem, and called the concern about Gmail "silly and a bit paranoid." But he conceded that the widespread fear of computerized scanning of e-mail, however irrational, could not be dismissed: "It is not only important to have your privacy; it is important that you believe you have your privacy," he pointed out. The mere suspicion of being monitored "changes your behavior and you become less free as an individual."

Templeton might not have found the advertising problematic, but he did have other concerns about Gmail and Google's privacy policies. The Electronic Communications Privacy Act (ECPA), which treated e-mail as a private means of communication, like a phone call, required that police obtain a wiretap warrant in order to read it. Once an e-mail message was stored centrally, however, it would no longer be considered as private communication, but rather as data in a database, and would not be protected by the act. Not only that, but Google's privacy policy allowed the company to look at—or even release to a law enforcement agency—a user's e-mail in circumstances that would never be permitted were the company to gain access, theoretically, to its customers' postal mail. This was true not just of Google, but also of its competitors, like Yahoo and Microsoft, which were also combining Web-hosted e-mail with Web search. Templeton was concerned about a "troubling risk" that e-mail would become a target for government surveillance. He noted, "When our papers are at home, mass surveillance of them simply doesn't scale. It's too expensive. Online, it scales well."

Google stood apart from its rivals in its success in adding many other categories of personal information to its centralized collections. As individuals spent more and more time online, records of what they did and what they thought were created automatically, and Google happily offered to serve as the single home for all of it. If a single user were to fully utilize all of Google's services, the amount of sensitive personal information that would end up residing on Google's servers exceeded what Microsoft had envisioned for HailStorm. Yet as Google expanded, it did not face a firestorm of protest about what it was storing after the initial fuss about Gmail passed.

Google's ability to proceed unimpeded, without drawing public ire, is partly explained by the fact that Google's newest personal information services were dwarfed by much more successful offerings from its competitors. Google Checkout, a service that stored a user's credit card number, to be quickly tapped when shopping online, was unable to take much market share away from eBay's PayPal, another online payment system. Google's Orkut was an extremely popular networking site in some places in the world, but not in the United States. Even Gmail, the service that had gained the highest visibility of any of Google's newer offerings, was in a distant fourth place among Web-hosted e-mail providers three years after its introduction.

Google's expansion was also helped by the cultural shift toward much freer public display of personal information on the social networking sites. Intimate disclosure became routine on MySpace and Facebook, and reached its natural apotheosis at newer live video sites, such as Justin.tv, where everyone was invited to "lifecast"—treating one's daily life as entertainment suited for broadcast—to the world via the Internet, unedited, twenty-four hours a day, seven days a week. Even if the number of lifecasters remained small, and their average age skewed young, their mere existence was a leading indicator of the spreading acceptance of private lives being made public.

John Battelle, an entrepreneurial publisher and longtime observer of Google, who in 2005 had written a book about the company, *The Search,* was one of the few who raised concerns that Google users were granting a single organization control over too much data. In

June 2007, Battelle said in a blog post that he had reached what he called his "Google saturation point," and was no longer willing to "let too much of my online life run through any one control point, regardless of who it is." He decided deliberately not to use Google Calendar and Google Spreadsheets for some business planning because he didn't want Google to have access to information about his publishing business. What exactly "Google" would do with the information—he self-mockingly put the company's name within quotation marks, making fun of his own implied notion that the corporation would act as if it were a person—he did not say, and attributed his concern to "some primal lizard brain fear of giving too much control of my data to one source."

Google's Matt Cutts saw Battelle's post and added his own comments, which were supposed to be reassuring: "Given Google's strict privacy policies, I wouldn't worry about something like using Google Calendar or Gmail." Cutts said he would make inquiries within Google and try to get a colleague to talk at length about the policies that the company had in place to protect personal data. But "Don't worry" was not much of a response. Battelle revisited Google's terms of service that its users must accept and found language that was anything but reassuring to a business that was competing in any way against Google: "By submitting, posting or displaying the content you give Google a perpetual, irrevocable, worldwide, royalty-free, and non-exclusive license to reproduce, adapt, modify, translate, publish, publicly perform, publicly display and distribute any Content which you submit, post or display on or through, the Services." Google also reserved the right to "use personal information for auditing, research and analysis to operate and improve Google technologies and services."

Yet the chief concern now expressed by Google's users wasn't that someone at Google might take a peek at their personal data; it was that Google might be sloppy and not take good care of their data. In February 2007, Larry Dignan, a columnist for *ZDNet,* addressed this concern. "Will You Trust Google with Your Data?" he asked, and answered, "No." Speaking as a businessperson, he reasoned that if Google were to lose a company's data, it might not treat the incident with due seriousness because Google disclaimed any liability for damages beyond the subscription fee—this amounted to no liability if the service was offered for free. Dignan said he spoke as someone who had watched hosted data disappear permanently and had learned the importance of selecting a "data keeper" carefully. He suggested that corporate data would be safer in the hands of a software company like Salesforce.com, whose entire business was Software as a Service and whose very existence depended upon maintaining a sterling reputation for reliability.

As large and seemingly successful a company as Google appeared to be, it remained an unknown to those who ran the information technology departments in large companies and government organizations. Its dominance in the world of Web search did not impress technologists, whose concerns centered on Google's ability to have its Google Apps running and available to its customers 99.9 percent of the time, as it promised. They also wanted to see convincing evidence that Google's systems could handle the increased load of Google Apps without accidental data losses.

Google's strategic vision, of moving all computer users to the cloud, would remain unrealized unless it devised a way to gain the trust of customers. It needed lots of customers to show that Google Apps scaled—but until it could demonstrate that the new service scaled, corporate customers would not be willing to sign up. The only way it could win over customers, at least initially, would be by giving the software away for free, and yet do so in a way that did not undermine its ability to charge customers later. Google Apps managers realized that college and university campuses were the ideal place to give Google Apps services away, with student populations that would be large enough to demonstrate that the service scaled well. Google Apps Education Edition would be offered to campuses without charge and free of advertising, which gave it the opportunity to extend the Google brand without being accused of seeking immediate financial gain. A Google Apps Premier Edition would be sold on a subscription basis to corporations, which would be charged $50 annually for each user.

In October 2006, Arizona State University was the first major campus to roll out Google Apps Education Edition for its sixty-five thousand students. In the year that followed, many other universities tested the service, but adoptions by entire institutions came slowly.

In the meantime, Google experienced for the first time the problem that the Gmail team members had lain awake at night worrying about when they had first conceived of putting Gmail on Google's unreliable hardware: permanent loss of all Gmail messages for a handful of its users. The possibility had been anticipated and safeguards were supposed to make sure that it could not ever possibly happen. But in December 2006, some Gmail users began posting an incredible story: they had logged on to their accounts and found that everything—in-box mail, sent messages, contacts—had disappeared.

The story was followed closely at *TechCrunch,* but Google was fortunate that it did not receive wide coverage in the print media. The company sent *TechCrunch* a note that acknowledged that "a small number of our users—around 60" had lost all of their e-mail messages, but it did not explain what had gone awry. It offered only bland corporate-speak—"We know how important Gmail is to our users"—and vague claims about "extensive safeguards" that guaranteed that "this is a small and isolated incident."

The incident did not have major repercussions, but only because prospective customers were not interested enough in Google Apps to bother to notice. Progress selling the Premier Edition to corporate customers came even more slowly than giving away the Education Edition to higher education. In the first quarter of 2007, Google collected only $37 million from sales of software licenses, less than 1 percent of its quarterly revenue, and much less than 1 percent of the $4.8 billion in revenues that Microsoft's business division, which included Microsoft Office, reported for the quarter. Nevertheless, Microsoft treated Google Apps as a potent threat to the core of its existing business, and would not permit Google to use giveaways to higher education uncontested. Significantly, Microsoft decided to battle Google online, and offer Web-based e-mail and chat to colleges and universities for free. It was not fully comparable to Google's package:

Microsoft's lacked online word processing and spreadsheet capabilities and also lacked a calendar. But Microsoft's entry provided campuses with a real choice: free e-mail and a suite of software equivalent to Office from Google, or free e-mail software from Microsoft, in a new program that Microsoft gave the awful name of Windows Live@Edu—not as bad as HailStorm but bad enough to be an embarrassment.

With its long history of working with campuses, Microsoft had an insider's advantage over Google. It also could compete effectively with Google without matching the various Office-like applications that Google provided because campus administrators were interested in e-mail and not much else. Students had always paid for their own software applications like Office; whether they continued to do so, or were spared doing so by adopting Google's online Software as a Service, was not a concern of the administrators. Microsoft quickly signed up campuses in fifteen countries that were willing to try the service.

One notable trophy gained in the spring of 2007 was the University of Pennsylvania, whose School of Arts and Sciences, and also its business school, Wharton, concluded a long evaluation process for adopting a new e-mail system that had begun a year before—and culminated with the selection of Microsoft over Google. One of the criteria that university officials used when looking at the competing offerings was the companies' commitment to protecting the privacy of student information. Both Google and Microsoft scored poorly; both conceded that they might turn over to government officials information such as users' search histories or browsing patterns, if the government requested. A student advisory board recommended that Penn adopt Google Apps, but negotiations with Google foundered. Microsoft then walked off with the prize.

In April 2007, Google and Microsoft had the opportunity to make their pitch for Web-hosted e-mail to the country's largest university system, the California State University, which had 417,000 students spread across twenty-three campuses. The university's information technology managers (with one outsider: me) gathered in a hotel meeting room in Los Angeles to hear Jeff Keltner, representing

Google, and Walter Harp, representing Microsoft, do their best to sell to a tough crowd that arrived without showing signs of being ready to embrace Web-based e-mail systems for their campuses. Keltner and Harp were both in their thirties, both had graduated from Stanford, and both realized that before they could compete against each other, they had to first convince their audience that hosted e-mail, managed on servers beyond the campus, offered compelling benefits to their institutions. (Yahoo had also been invited to participate and had agreed to send a representative, but at the last minute canceled.)

Google's Keltner had the opportunity to speak first. Google, he said, viewed its free Google Apps, with its special ad-free version of Gmail for students, as a way of "giving something back" to universities. University information technology departments had become burdened managing their own e-mail systems, based on Microsoft's Exchange Server or similar software. These were expensive to maintain and back up, susceptible to viruses, and prone to fail. Only by historical accident had universities ended up in the e-mail business. He said, "For almost none of you is running a scalable, reliable, redundant, secure infrastructure to run massively parallel collaboration activities really a core process." Let Google handle it—and you can return to the educational technology that you know best how to provide.

Keltner reassured the administrators that the e-mail, documents, and other data managed by Google Apps would be absolutely safe because data was copied to at least three servers, creating multiple backup copies. He did not mention the problem of lost Gmail a few months earlier, and the administrators had apparently not heard of the incident. He was about to continue with his spiel when I raised my hand and asked him, How was it possible for Google's backup systems to have failed the previous December, resulting in the loss of everything that the sixty Gmail users had stored?

"Good question," Keltner said, whose normally fast-paced delivery slowed as he paused and gathered his thoughts. "We haven't talked a lot, publicly, about what exactly happened in December." He stalled for time with more flattery: "Very astute observation." He granted that e-mail had been lost for about sixty users, which was "literally about one in a million," and it was the sort of loss that happens everywhere in the computer world. It was "not a failure of any hardware, it was a failure of the brain." Regrettably, somebody at Google "hit the delete button when they shouldn't have hit delete."

Microsoft's Walter Harp did not talk about Microsoft Exchange and the benefits of using campus-based computing resources to handle e-mail. Instead he emphasized Microsoft's experience handling Web-based e-mail, which far exceeded that of Google's. Not only did MSN Hotmail have 233 million users worldwide compared to Gmail's 62 million, but also Microsoft had experience hosting corporate e-mail for Qwest, Verizon, and telecommunication giants around the world. "We don't make it into the press all the time," he said. "We're not a shiny new object. For some people, we're 'the Evil Empire.' The point being is, we're quietly doing quite well."

The administrators in the room were most concerned with the inherent problem of hosted services: messages and documents are irretrievable when systems go down. Earlier that week, BlackBerry service had failed globally and many BlackBerry users could not get their e-mail for fourteen hours. Someone in the audience asked the two representatives, "If things do fail at Microsoft or Google mail, are we failing with the rest of the world, or are we just failing in the education environment?" The two companies gave similar answers: their education customers were not segregated. As Harp explained, "There's strength in numbers here because you are failing with the rest of the world." Google's Keltner added, "The answer from us is much the same. If you're down, somebody at the Googleplex is down. That sets off a lot of alarms."

The representatives for Google and Microsoft had their sharpest exchange when Microsoft was asked about extending its education program to faculty and staff members, as well as students, as Google had done. Web-based software would be a "letdown," Harp said, for "a high-intensity productivity worker." If he himself were forced to use either Google's or Microsoft's Web-based calendar service, "I'd be pretty upset about it."

This offered the chance for Google's Keltner to pounce. Everything that Google was offering to campuses was used by Googlers themselves. He said, "This is where my e-mail is—it's a Gmail account. It's where my calendar is. All of our corporate calendar is Google Calendar. We absolutely believe this is ready for the enterprise." An old expression in the software industry, "eating your own dog food," embodied the notion that a company should never offer software that it wasn't willing to rely upon itself. In the 1980s and 1990s, Microsoft upheld and practiced "eating your own dog food," but for Web-hosted services, clearly it was Google, not Microsoft, that was committed to using its own products for its own internal needs.

Harp was not an automation, spouting the official party line of Microsoft. In fact, he was refreshingly candid and left the best impression when he declined to criticize Google for matching ads to e-mail contents in the regular version of Gmail. I asked him whether Microsoft scanned the contents of Hotmail messages and he answered, yes, the e-mail is scanned to prepare an index for the user's searching, but was not scanned for the purpose of selling advertisements. Then he said, "Honestly? My personal opinion is I don't have a problem with that myself. I think it's neat—we can do a lot of cool stuff with that." For example, he said, the software could detect a FedEx tracking number in an e-mail message and then automatically show the user where the package was. This was merely a hypothetical use, he said, and the company had no plans to use scanning to add services.

Still, unvoiced concern about scanning seemed to linger. Google's Keltner knew from his own experience that the very word *scanning* was encumbered with negative connotations. Three years after Gmail's introduction, Keltner felt compelled to explain, once again, that scanning of e-mail was a necessity. Scanning simply meant that a machine read the contents of messages, which it had to do in order to detect spam or viruses. Talking about the topic of scanning upset him to the point that he almost lost his composure: "Anybody who says they don't scan your e-mail—point-blank, they're lying."

The day of presentations to California State University representatives ended anticlimactically: the administrators dispersed and no campus followed up with an immediate decision to use Google Apps. The next fall, Google could point to the University of Phoenix as its largest partner in education—250,000 accounts for students, faculty, and staff. But it still had too few customers to be willing to talk about the aggregate number of student accounts other than to say that it was in "the hundreds of thousands." Microsoft, however, happily provided specifics, claiming six million active accounts used by students, faculty, and alumni within three years of the 2005 introduction of Windows Live@Edu.

As time passed after the Google-versus-Microsoft meeting in Los Angeles in April 2007, Jeff Keltner's instinct that Google's competitors and critics would continue to dwell on the scanning issue turned out to be well justified. Microsoft's Walter Harp had taken the high road, refusing to use scanning to give Microsoft an advantage over Google. But Harp's ultimate boss, Steve Ballmer, did not have scruples about misstating what the competition did. In October 2007, he casually dropped a remark at a conference in the United Kingdom that was a new variation on the old falsehood, and one that was far more sinister than anything that had come before: at Google, Ballmer said, "they read your mail and we don't." The audience murmured and laughed nervously, and Ballmer paused for a moment to let the commotion subside. He resumed, "That's just a factual statement. It's not even meant to be pejorative."

Ballmer had it exactly wrong: his was not a factual statement and he most certainly meant it in a pejorative way. In fact, software analyzed the contents of each e-mail message at Microsoft's MSN Hotmail, just as Harp had explained, even though Microsoft did not do as much with the information extracted from the scan as it could have. More egregious than Ballmer's pretending that e-mail hosted by his own company was never scrutinized was his use of the pronoun *they* as the ones who "read" the e-mail at Google. Without a clarifying antecedent, the *they* left the impression that it was humans that were doing the reading of Gmail messages. With a seemingly offhand remark, consisting of just those seven words—"they read your mail and we don't"—Ballmer conjured the most frightening images that could be imagined and attached them to Google.

What was perhaps most interesting about Ballmer's comment was that he felt the need to strike out at Google, a company that had not won over significant numbers of customers for the software that competed against Microsoft's. Ballmer was not concerned about Google's inroads to date into Microsoft's core software businesses, but he was unmistakably concerned with Google's ability in the future to make cloud computing into a popular replacement for Microsoft's desktop software.

Microsoft understands that in the long term, local computing on desktop machines and in-house e-mail servers will be replaced by cloud computing. As can be seen in its marketing of Web-based e-mail to higher education customers, it has abandoned any hope of being able to sell the merits of software that is sold in packages when facing competition from the cloud. It is trying to reinvent itself as a Software as a Service company itself, ready to greet the future.

Microsoft's on-off-on bids for Yahoo in 2008 were an expression of the company's rather desperate wish to better meet the competitive challenge posed by Google by moving the place of battle from Microsoft's home ground, office applications, to Google's home ground, Web search and advertising. In May, when lack of agreement between the two companies about Yahoo's valuation led Microsoft to withdraw its offer, Microsoft changed tactics, but no one doubted that its most pressing strategic challenge remained Google. As Microsoft devotes more attention—and more of its treasury—to its online businesses, no major software company will remain to defend the notion that personal data should remain physically close to the individual and scattered among different media and devices. Centralization of data seems inexorable, and as it proceeds, the concerns about protecting individual privacy seem likely to diminish.

A parallel might be drawn to the transition in America's cities in the 1880s, when the generation of electrical power, based on alternating current, was centralized in large power plants, where electricity could be produced at much less cost, replacing the earliest, small plants, based on direct current, that were located on the premises of hotels, office buildings, and the homes of wealthy individuals. Centralization of power generation brought the need to transport electricity considerable distances, and electrocution became a risk for passersby as well as for electricians, as power lines filled the cityscape. Critics sounded alarms about the dangers, but the advantages of inexpensive electricity were too great to be ignored, even though accidental electrocutions were a frequent occurrence. Centralized power generation became so well accepted that later generations of Americans were not aware that the local mode of power generation had preceded it. In the same way, centralized computing may become ubiquitous, despite occasional data losses—the computer age's equivalent of accidental electrocutions—and later generations will not realize that there ever was a time when data was not stored at a centralized location in the cloud.

The technical advantages of moving to the cloud are clear, but the transition will be slowed by legal considerations that large corporations must weigh before they unplug their in-house servers. Unlike individuals and universities providing students with e-mail accounts, a corporation must, by law, preserve and manage every e-mail message and every internal document, maintaining absolute confidence in its ability to protect confidentiality and yet be able to retrieve whatever materials a judge may demand in the future. Compliance with the law is manageable when one uses one's own servers; relying instead entirely on Google Apps in the cloud has yet to be tried, let alone sanctioned.

In May 2008, David Berlind, an *InformationWeek* blogger, told his readership of corporate IT administrators, "Yes, It's Time to Destroy Your E-Mail Servers. What App Is Next?" Based on his experience administering Gmail for his organization, he listed many reasons why Gmail was ready to replace the Microsoft and IBM e-mail systems used within large enterprises. Or, he grudgingly added, Gmail was almost ready—the "beta" label that was still attached to the Gmail logo was a sign that the provider was not fully confident in the reliability and maturity of the service.

Google could take its time working on Gmail, preparing for the day when it could comfortably remove the "beta" qualifier. University students would supply a flow of customers who could stress test the system and also help to test out the other Google Apps that were a cloud-based alternative to Microsoft Office. Strategically speaking, Google was in a most desirable position, a company that was old enough—and large enough—to be ready to benefit more than anyone else whenever the shift to the cloud gathered momentum. But it was not so old and so large that it had a legacy terrestrial business, supplying software to organizations in-house, that would disappear. Google could greet the future in the cloud as its own.

CHAPTER 8

Algorithm, Meet Humanity

Most of corporate America develops new products stealthily. Many ideas will be tested out of public view, most will be found wanting in some significant way, and few will actually emerge from the lab. The experiments that end in failure remain unknown, the company's private business.

Google is not so reticent, however. It, too, has many projects under way that will never see light. But the company is far more willing than its counterparts to do much of its experimentation out in the open, in the marketplace. Instead of convening focus groups to gather initial impressions from prospective customers before a product's introduction, Google goes ahead and releases the product, affixing the "beta" label to warn users that the product lacks important features, and turns the general public into its focus group.

Google's reputation has not suffered. On the contrary, the company enjoys a public image that associates its brand with experimentation and innovation. Google does not have to release fully finished products; the public credits it as an inspirational achiever for merely trying out new things at a frenetic pace that its rivals cannot match. But the public's attachment to Google's culture of innovation celebrates the birth of new Google products and neglects the need for incremental improvement of older ones. Googlers themselves worry, at times, that the company has moved too fast to attend properly to making its newest offerings truly great ones. At one of Google's Friday meetings that I attended in 2007, a young woman asked Larry Page a pointed question: "We seem to be introducing a lot of products like the docs, spreadsheets, and presenting, and so on. If we're introducing those kinds of products, don't you think that they should offer more than what's already existing out there? And should we sort of complete packages? Because they seem to be, still, sort of rudimentary and not fully formed." She wondered if they were purposely designed without essential features in order to make it easier for skittish users to try the software. Her voice trailed off midsentence.

"I think that's a fair criticism," Page said. The question that Google has always wrestled with when readying new services is whether to wait until each is fully baked. It has been company policy to release products before they were polished, in order to get early feedback. If they were released in an overly buggy state, however, users would simply walk away. Page said that all of the products that she had mentioned were experiencing rapid growth, which suggested that they were fulfilling unmet needs, whatever their current shortcomings.

The rapid growth in Google Apps that he offered as exculpation began with a baseline of zero; any growth at all would appear rapid. He left important questions unanswered: How might Google's brand be tarnished by its offering Google Apps that were incomplete? Was its pursuit of personal information a strategic distraction, impeding its ability to stay ahead of the pack in search and catch up with the leaders in social networking? Was its internal culture, which lavished rewards and praise on those who conceived entirely new projects, leaving too few people to do the less glamorous work of incremental improvements needed for second, third, or fourth versions of its products?

The little-known Google Answers service is an example of a promising experiment that suffered from neglect. In 2002, Google offered users the opportunity to pose questions that would be answered by Google Answers Researchers, independent contractors who had been screened and certified by Google employees as "experts at locating hard-to-find information on the Web." The service charged customers a fee for each question answered, a radical departure from the advertising-based revenue model Google was using for its core search service. The amount a customer paid varied—customers determined for themselves the amount they were willing to pay when they submitted their questions. Google did not attempt to guarantee an answer in all cases: only if the amount offered for an answer was sufficiently high to attract the interest of one of Google's contractors would an answer be supplied.

Google retained one quarter of the fee collected by Google Answers, and the contractor received the remainder. This also was a curious departure for Google because the service did not rely on sophisticated algorithms but rather on human researchers. It was a service that would not scale, at least not quickly, in the hypothetical case that its customer base grew quickly.

Once Google unveiled the service, Google's managers gave it little thought. Despite its failing to attract customers, no one at Google bothered to tinker with the format or considered rethinking the business model. In 2005, three years after Google Answers was launched, Yahoo saw the opportunity created by Google's neglect and unveiled its own service, Yahoo Answers. It was a noncommercial service: anyone could submit a question, for free, and anyone who wished could supply an answer, though no compensation was paid. The lack of remuneration was not a problem, however. Yahoo's volunteer researchers competed for the approbation of users, who rated the quality of the answers.

Within a year, Yahoo Answers was pulling in about 14 million users monthly and had built up a database of more than 60 million answers, which were made available to all of its users. Despite Google's three-year head start, Yahoo had raced far ahead of Google. In late 2006, Google decided to pull the plug on its own Answers. Closing the business was momentarily embarrassing but not a significant blow to Google's overall revenue growth. But it did reveal a weakness at Google: the company did not know how to go about tapping the knowledge of strangers whose collective contributions were defining a new generation of online services, Web 2.0. The success of Yahoo Answers came about because Yahoo enlisted the contributions of users who enjoyed the online company of others and regarded the group's voluntary association as a community. Yahoo understood before Google how important virtual online communities were to many people.

Not only did Google fail to give consistent attention to products after they had been released, it also neglected work on bringing its disparate collections of new types of information—such as books, scholarly journals, maps, videos—together so that a single search could rummage through all of its new information silos, in addition to its database of Web pages.

Users could, of course, go to the various Google sites and do separate searches, but the sites had been developed separately, in haste, before Google could figure out how to make all of them accessible in a single search. Even when Google had only a few collections of information other than Web pages, its product managers understood that without "universal search," users were not likely to go to the trouble of searching here and there to find all of the information that Google had to offer. Either they would not think to look anywhere but on Google's home page, or they would find visiting the various sites too time-consuming. In 2001, David Bailey, a young Google engineer, did a few mockups of sample screens to show what integrated search results might look like—"Britney Spears" was called upon to illustrate how news and images could be tapped in addition to Web pages—but universal search was left on a list of desiderata.

Between 2001 and 2006, several other Google engineers briefly took on universal search as a project. But they lost interest before making progress. In Google's internal culture, engineers decide what projects are of greatest personal interest. Without champions, ideas for worthy projects sit on a shelf and gather dust. Universal search was one of those. In 2006, Bailey returned to it with what he called an "inner fire" to see the project through. It took about a year for him and his team to build the code that allowed a single search to extend to more than one silo.

The universal search algorithm had to determine whether the other kinds of information were of equally high quality as the top Web page results, which entailed developing more sophisticated software than that used for Web pages alone. The greater the variety of material, the greater the possibility that the software would make erroneous deductions. A search for "Kentucky Fried Chicken" on the Web would lead to the restaurant chain, but when the same search phrase was submitted to Google Maps, would the Algorithm know that this was not a request only for restaurants located in Kentucky? The software should be smart enough to sense that when a search term like "Wichita tornado" was submitted, what the searcher most wanted to see was not perfect matches on Web pages, which had been crawled weeks before, but rather news stories about a tornado that had just hit Wichita a few minutes earlier (a crucial clue that the news angle was most important would be the fact that in the previous five minutes more people had searched for that phrase than had done so in the entire year). In May 2007, Google was ready to announce a limited version of Universal Search.

The search results that users now saw were changed only subtly—only a few non-Web items were added to the first page of search results. Google moved with deliberate slowness, not wanting to introduce ill-chosen items that would hurt the company's reputation for trustworthy search results. For all of its innovation in new areas of information, Google remained deeply conservative in its attachment to the same basic methods that it had used for Web search since the time of its founding, and it was extremely reluctant to adopt new methodologies.

While Google clung tightly to its faith that analyzing links was the best way to sort the quality of Web pages, start-ups saw an opportunity to move beyond link analysis and develop software that organized online information by what it could understand of its actual meaning, moving well beyond word matching. Tim Berners-Lee, the inventor of the World Wide Web, has proselytized for the creation of a successor to the Web, "the Semantic Web," in which Web pages would contain code that would facilitate machine understanding of the contents of each page. His vision, which would require tremendous work on the part of every Web site editor, may never be realized. But in the meantime, new companies are springing up, like Powerset, Metaweb, and Radar Networks, to improvise new techniques for searching information on the basis of meaning extracted by software, even without the help of embedded code. In May 2008, Powerset made its first public appearance, initially searching only Wikipedia, not the entire Web. As a demonstration of proof of concept, it was quite successful; only two months later, Microsoft announced it would acquire the company. Google's dominance in the search business has not scared off entrepreneurs and venture capitalist backers. Between 2004 and 2006, no less than $350 million was invested in new companies that planned to pursue some aspect of Internet search.

Some of the challengers are attempting to write a superior search algorithm. But others have abandoned altogether the quest for a better algorithm, and look to an entirely different source for improved search results. They have turned to the approach that Yahoo used, pre-Google, at the very beginning of Web search: humans.

No one ever doubted the ability of humans to distinguish good Web pages from bad. The problem was that the Web had grown faster than Yahoo had been able to add editors to keep its Web directory current. This created the perfect opportunity for Google to supply an automated method of evaluating the quality of pages. The difference between 1997, the last year of the pre-Google era, and 2007 was that ten years later no one in the search business was trying to do as Yahoo had done, hire as many experts as needed to organize the Web. Instead every other search start-up, it seemed, was attempting to do as Wikipedia had done, harness the contributions of volunteers. A new phrase was coined—*social search*—to refer to this new category of search service, which relied not upon an engine powered by algorithms but upon the collective judgments of the group. Anyone willing to recommend Web sites that matched a particular search phrase was invited to do so. Squidoo, Sproose, and NosyJoe prepared search results based on the assumed wisdom of crowds; another little start-up, Bessed, welcomed submissions from anyone but reviewed them before making them available.

In December 2006 Jimmy Wales, the founder of Wikipedia, announced plans to introduce a search service modeled after Wikipedia, to directly compete with Google. In many cases, he said, Google "produces nothing but spam and useless crap." The spam he referred to was Web pages that used deceptive means to pull in unwitting visitors who generated revenue for the Web site, which was paid by advertisers based on the number of visitors that viewed the site's advertisements, willing or not. The most basic task of a search engine is to make a qualitative decision, he said, determining, "This page is good, this page sucks." Algorithmic search has to make a guess, using roundabout means. A human can tell with just a glance. He was confident that he could enlist a network of contributors to make those judgments, just as he had done with Wikipedia.

Mahalo, another challenger to Google, was started in 2007 and received funding from Sequoia Capital. Mahalo claimed—extravagantly—that it was "the world's first human-powered search engine." Its founder, Jason Calacanis, shared Wales's disgust with search results served up on Google that were infected with spam. He too emphasized that a human editor could produce spam-free results. Mahalo began with about thirty editors. Rather than attempting to match the comprehensiveness of Google's search index, Calacanis chose instead to have his staff prepare results for the search phrases that were most frequently submitted to Google. They began by winnowing Google's top search results to create spam-free lists of what they judged to be the best Web links by topic. Within a few months they had prepared results for five thousand terms. Soon they were also vetting submissions from users, who were paid $10 to $15 per topic for results pages that were accepted.

When Mahalo served up a list of links, a visitor benefited from what Calacanis described as "basically your own personal research assistant doing 4–10 hours of research on your search query." A hand-built Mahalo page organized links under subthemes that speeded scanning. The page on global warming, for example, had clusters of links under recent news stories, background articles, science and data, groups advocating action, groups arguing against, and other headings, including climate change humor, with videos that included online snippets of Stephen Colbert, Will Ferrell, *South Park,* and *The Simpsons.* Each link required only a single line, so the Mahalo global warming page easily accommodated eighty-five handpicked sites, far more than the fifteen that Google serves up on its usual first page of results.

Mahalo was able to ride on top of Google's algorithms: when Google made improvements, Mahalo contributors and editors, who used Google searches to compose their list of choice selections, benefited, too. Calacanis described Mahalo as a melding of human capabilities with those of the machine: "John Henry and the steam hammer versus the steam hammer alone."

Googlers were irked, however, by Calacanis's comparison of Google's search engine to the steam hammer, cold, mechanical, devoid of the human touch. As social search became more and more visible in 2007, the company's emissaries tried to humanize the Algorithm. In June, Marissa Mayer was in Paris for the company's European Press Day and did her best to place a human face on Google's core technologies. The opportunity appeared when she was asked by a British reporter why Google often prominently featured links to Wikipedia articles, without checking on the reliability of the information to be found in them. She began her answer along the old groove, stressing the value of the objectivity of an automated selection process. "Rather than trying to make individualized judgments about particular sources, like Wikipedia," she said, "we rely on automated methods, like along PageRank." She took pains, though, to point out that Web site editors made the crucial choices, in placing links to the sites that they valued most, sending the signals that Google's search engine processed. Wikipedia placed highly only because "people like the content." In her rendering, the Google algorithm was a populist instrument of the people.

Little Mahalo was hardly of a size that would make Google tremble. Yet Google did take seriously the competitive threat posed by a combination of machine algorithm and human intelligence, especially if deployed by a large rival. For an article I was preparing in June 2007 about Mahalo, I interviewed Matt Cutts, the head of Google's Web spam team, to obtain Google's official response to Mahalo's reliance on human editors. Cutts had nothing disparaging to say about Mahalo; he emphasized Google's own interest in considering new approaches to search, too. "I don't think we're ideologically bound to only computers, only algorithms," he said. The company had already taken the trouble to remove all references to "automatic ranking" in every one of its own Google help pages.

The editorial changes cleared the way for experimenting later that year with a search page that allowed its users to vote on search results, just as Digg's users vote on news stories.

Cutts shared extended thoughts on the subject in a post on his personal blog titled "The Role of Humans in Google Search." After noting that all opinions that would follow were his own, not Google's, he said that his view was that Google was perfectly amenable to social search, personalized search, or any means of "using human feedback to improve search quality." He noted that he had publicly expressed the same points the previous fall, welcoming more human input into search at Google, with the reservation that attention had to be paid to "potential abuse by bad actors," a problem he confronted daily in his battles with Web spam. He also mentioned that Larry Page had publicly expressed Google's willingness to consider alternatives to the Algorithm. Page had appeared in the midst of Jason Calacanis and a small group of fellow conferees at Foo Camp, an informal techie conference, and had remarked—in Calacanis's paraphrasing—that search engines were best for finding information, but when it came to organizing information, "Wikipedia found a better way."

Cutts, Mayer, Page—all were roving ambassadors for Google, telling the public that Google was not a frozen monolith. Indeed, the company was detaching from the Algorithm, becoming more flexible and attentive to the wisdom of the crowd, albeit slowly. Credible rumors of its interest in acquiring Digg, the social news site, swirled in 2007 and again in 2008. The notion that Google would permit users to determine the placement of items on a page was beginning to seem not just possible but likely. Still, the Algorithm remained Google's area of greatest competence.

Software, which could analyze text with ease, did not perform as well, however, when applied to the task of closely analyzing video. In 2007, after its YouTube acquisition, Google was slow to develop an algorithm for defining a video's "fingerprint," a pattern that would serve as a unique identifier. Without video fingerprints, Google would not be able to reliably automate the identification and removal of copyrighted material in videos that were uploaded to YouTube. In January 2007, Eric Schmidt pointed to Google's development work on audio and video fingerprinting as evidence of how "very concerned" the company was about respecting copyright ownership, and said that the fingerprinting technology that it was developing was "in various stages of being rolled out."

Even as it was promising the imminent release of a technical solution to the problem of copyright infringement, Google was also arguing that it did not need to release anything, that it was in full compliance with the Digital Millennium Copyright Act. The law did not require it to block the uploading of videos that infringed copyright, only that it remove videos whenever copyright holders brought to its attention instances of copyright violations. Google did not show any sympathy to copyright holders, like Viacom, that had to assign a team of employees to pore through YouTube videos, looking for unauthorized clips, sending "takedown" requests to YouTube, then repeating the same cycle endlessly as the clips reappeared almost as soon as YouTube removed them. In February 2007, Viacom submitted to YouTube a batch of more than a hundred thousand takedown requests.

At this point, Google could have made a conciliatory gesture, saying: We see the problem—it's admittedly a serious one. We have our best technical team at work on video fingerprinting, which has long been one of the most difficult standing problems in computer science. We are hopeful that we'll have technology ready soon. Instead, Google chose a more combative course, complying with Viacom's takedown requests but gratuitously adding derision, characterizing the requests as evidence that Viacom executives were too dense to understand that YouTube's hosting of their clips drew new audiences to Viacom's television programs and ultimately served Viacom's interests, too.

Viacom did not buy Google's argument. The expected lawsuit arrived in March 2007, when Viacom went to court seeking "at least" $1 billion in damages from YouTube and Google for copyright infringement. The suit argued that YouTube actively monitored uploads and removed pornographic videos, but declined to do the same for Viacom's copyrighted programs. Viacom did not take Google to task for failing to deliver the video fingerprinting technology that it had promised; instead it pointed out that Google had not even bothered to automate a simple comparison of the text in the tags that users appended to videos, or in the searches that users submitted, with a database of show titles and the names of characters of television shows and movies. Viacom asked not for perfection, but simply "exercising care," which it said "is not a Herculean task."

Google responded to the lawsuit by retreating to its interpretation of the law, which was that copyright owners did all the monitoring and Google's sole responsibility was to respond to the requests of the copyright owners. Eric Schmidt characterized the lawsuit as a form of "business negotiation" in the media industry, where, he said, one could be expected to be "sued to death."

By poking fun at Viacom's lawsuit as a negotiating stunt, Schmidt directed attention away from Google's failure to introduce software that would automatically identify and remove material that infringed copyright. A few months later, he announced at the National Association of Broadcasters meeting in Las Vegas that Google was "very close" to turning on a new service, Claim Your Content, that would "somewhat automate" the submission of requests to remove copyright-infringing videos. The new technology, he said, "is not a filtering system." Rather it was software that would come into play after the video was uploaded, looking for unauthorized copies of videos protected by copyright and deleting them if the copyright owner directed Google to do so.

Months passed, and no sign of Claim Your Content appeared. The National Legal and Policy Center, a conservative public-interest group based in Washington, D.C., made Google's lax policing of copyright infringers on YouTube and Google Video an issue of public interest and uncovered embarrassing data: random spot checks identified over three hundred full-length copyrighted movies that were available on Google Video. Google Video also ran advertisements placed by video-pirate Web sites such as MillionMoviesDownload.com. Other video Web sites had introduced video filtering technologies, but not Google. Ken Boehm, the center's cofounder, wrote Senator Patrick J. Leahy expressing puzzlement that "a company that has been largely successful in its endeavors to 'organize the world's information and make it universally accessible and useful' has apparently been unable to implement a working filtering technology to identify copyrighted content in a timely fashion."

Philippe Dauman, Viacom's CEO, sounded the same theme in October 2007, when Google finally released what it had decided to call the YouTube Video Identification Beta—six months after the company had said it was very close to releasing it. The timing was also curious because it came just two days before a consortium of content providers and Internet companies—including, besides Viacom, Walt Disney, Microsoft, NBC Universal, CBS, Fox, MySpace, and Dailymotion—announced an industry-wide copyright-protection initiative in which Google had chosen not to participate. Dauman dryly remarked, "Google is a very high quality company [with] a lot of very, very smart people. They can do things very quickly when they want to. I guess they haven't wanted to until this point." Whether Google could have moved more quickly or not, the company could hardly be surprised that its vaunted expertise in developing the most successful algorithms in the search industry would naturally lead to the expectation that it could produce industry-leading algorithms in other areas, were it genuinely interested in doing so.

The criticism that Google was deliberately holding back video fingerprinting technology seems unfounded. The evidence suggests the opposite: Google seems to have released its own video identification technology hastily, as if its executives could not stand to be embarrassed by another day of delay. YouTube was able to test the new software for only one week prior to its release, using videos supplied by only one partner. The system had found a grand total of only eighteen pirated clips on all of YouTube during the week's scouring. Shortly before Google's hasty announcement, Eric Schmidt attempted to lower the industry's expectations, saying that a system that would identify copyrighted clips with 100 percent accuracy was impossible. He suggested that reaching a target of 80 percent or 90 percent accuracy would be the best that could be hoped for.

Google claimed that its software could accurately detect an exact copy of a long clip that had not been altered. But an algorithm for matching could be thrown off by changes to the copy; the shorter the clip, the greater the difficulty in detecting a match. Even if a clip could be identified, the software could not make judgments about whether the clip was being used in a way that would fall under what copyright permitted as fair use.

Google's software required the active cooperation of the entire entertainment industry. It was designed to compare YouTube clips with a master library of all television shows and films, which Google announced it would set up and maintain on its own servers. In order for owners of copyrighted material to be able to enjoy protection, however, they had to supply Google with a copy of all works for which protection was sought. For large media companies, with deep vaults filled with programs, the requirement meant placing its most precious intellectual property into the care of Google—and by doing so, setting a precedent that would then require that they do the same thing, turning over digital copies of their entire libraries, again and again, to every Web site that hosted videos. In its haste to announce the availability of the new tool, Google could claim only that Walt Disney, Time Warner, and CBS were experimenting with the technology, but tellingly none of the three was willing to state its willingness to turn over all of their content to Google.

A more practical alternative would be the creation of an independent video repository to be used by all video Web sites, not just Google, for checking copyright status. Like most young, precociously successful companies, Google had grown too fast to bother learning how to cooperate with competitors on matters of industry-wide concern. When Google undertook book scanning, it had similarly ignored the pleas of others to join with partners to create a centralized repository. With video, Google proposed to create, once again, its own storehouse, but its plan imposed prohibitive costs and risks upon the prospective content providers.

For all of the progress that had been made in pattern recognition work in computer science, computers simply were not yet smart enough to screen video content for potential problems. YouTube was able to identify pornography and graphic violence, not because it relied on sophisticated algorithms but because it used the unpaid labor of volunteers: its users were invited to flag videos, alerting YouTube to clips that contained sexual or violent content. Once alerted, YouTube would confirm the problem and then remove the video. As YouTube cofounder Steve Chen gratefully said, "Nothing beats our community flagging." That method could not be used, however, for policing copyright problems: "We all know pornography and violence when we see them. But copyright status can only be determined by the copyright holder." Chen, however, was conveniently ignoring the presence of entire categories of material found on YouTube—beginning with thousands of clips of *The Daily Show with Jon Stewart*—whose use was notoriously unauthorized and impossible to miss.

YouTube could have adopted other means of screening for copyright problems, approaches that were labor-intensive and expensive, at least compared to free. YouTube competitor Revver was paying humans to check every single video upload for infringement, as well as for pornography and hate speech. For its punctiliousness, Revver was rewarded with obscurity in the marketplace. Carefree YouTube, meanwhile, continued to grow faster than any other online video site. By March 2008, Google/YouTube's share of online video watching was 38 percent, almost ten times the 4 percent share of second-place Fox Interactive. (Revver had such a small share of video viewing that it lacked sufficient share to make the list of top ten video sites.)

In April 2008, one year after Schmidt's appearance at the National Association of Broadcasters meeting at which he had announced Google's video filtering service, it was impossible for neutral observers to notice a drop in the number of unauthorized clips from televisions shows and series. One could find, for example, scenes from every one of the last five movies that received the Academy Award for Best Picture. The 10-minute limit on clips prevented one from viewing a full-length feature film such as *The Departed,* but the entire movie was available to anyone willing to watch it in twelve 10-minute clips.

When asked about the ongoing problems, Google always politely avowed its concern for copyright protection, but in practice the company did not seem much concerned. The Viacom lawsuit moved slowly and seemed so remote as not to even register as an irritant. In the meantime, YouTube continued to grow and grow. By spring 2008, 85 million U.S. viewers watched 4.3 billion videos on YouTube in a single month, about 50 per viewer. according to the Internet research firm comScore. Even while online video viewing grew, YouTube continued to gain share of the overall video market, as video contributors sought the one place in which the largest possible audience could be reached, and the growth in the number of clips that were uploaded at YouTube brought still more viewers. How Google should go about converting those billions of videos shown each month into a profitable business line was a question it could not answer, but its core business, serving up advertisements based upon text, paid all tuition costs while the company learned about this and the other unfamiliar businesses it was entering.

Conclusion

Google's ascendance has been accompanied by Microsoft's decline. No computer company has ever been able to enjoy pre-eminence that spans two successive technological eras. IBM in the mainframe era could not head off the ascent of Digital Equipment Corporation in the minicomputer era, which, in turn, could not head off the ascent of Microsoft in the personal computer era. Fully aware of this history, Bill Gates and his associates nonetheless hoped that, by dint of unceasing vigilance and wise management, Microsoft would become the first to succeed in maintaining its position of leadership into whatever era would succeed the one defined by the PC.

When the Internet spread from research labs and universities and seeped into the commercial world, the first challenger that gave Microsoft a fright was Netscape, which was undercapitalized and easily batted away. Subsequently, Google succeeded in pushing Microsoft into a defensive crouch.

Google could easily have lost the opportunity for dominance to another company, one born earlier in the Internet era: Yahoo was a more likely candidate, having had a considerable head start in growth by the time Google was founded. By relying on a labor-intensive approach to organizing the Web, though, Yahoo failed to keep up with the growth of the new medium and lost its early lead to the little company with which it had contracted to handle Web search queries.

Google was able to grow as fast as the Web itself because it relied upon hardware and software technology that was designed to scale up fast and inexpensively. It was able to acquire a market capitalization that exceeded all other Internet companies because it chanced upon text ads linked to the keywords of a search phrase, ads that turned out to be a highly efficient means for advertisers to reach prospective buyers. By 2007 it was able to acquire sufficient stature to successfully launch two industry-wide coalitions: OpenSocial, for social networks, and the Open Handset Alliance, for cell phones. Both initiatives in their first six months gathered many partners and seemed likely to dramatically reshape their respective industries. Considerable achievements all.

Along the way, however, Google was unable to lay claim to attracting the largest number of U.S. visitors to its Web sites. In its early years, when it functioned only as a site that referred its users elsewhere, Google took pride in its ability to speedily direct its visitors to the best site on the Web for whatever it was they were searching for. Later, as it added categories of information that it stored, it became a destination site itself. But in the meantime, Google's Internet predecessors—Yahoo, MSN, and AOL—had established comprehensive Web portal offerings designed to supply many kinds of information. They had also developed enormously popular e-mail services that long predated Gmail. Consequently, Google's competitors attracted more U.S. visitors to their sites in any given month than did Google.

Yet in April 2008, Google passed a milestone in its history when the number of visitors to its U.S. sites exceeded that of all competitors. Among the overall U.S. Internet audience of 190.7 million unique visitors—that is, disregarding multiple visits to a site by one person—Google drew 141 million visitors, edging past Yahoo, Microsoft, and AOL. It attained the number one position partly due to an increase in the volume of search requests, but also partly due to the continuing rapid growth of traffic headed to YouTube.

Converting that YouTube traffic into profits proved a problem resistant to solution. Even though by March 2008 YouTube was serving those 4.3 billion videos a month in the United States alone, Google had yet to report revenue of any material size from its operation. Google's other attempts to move beyond Web search similarly lacked an appreciable return on investment, at least in the near term. Each continued to do well in acquiring content—Columbia University in December 2007 became the twenty-eighth library to join Google Book Search, a second dozen cities in February 2008 acquired street views in Google Maps; the *New York Times* in April 2008 added a new layer to Google Earth. Each contributed to the Google aura of commanding the best information, regardless of type. But none individually could be declared a clear financial success (or failure) for Google.

Collectively, Google's multiplying services constitute a set of assets that no other Internet company has the means—strategical, technical, financial—to match. The intangible value to Google of having so many kinds of information under a single roof cannot be calculated precisely, but it's likely that all Google properties share a halo effect. Each appeals to more users simply because of its Google identity and the way the very multiplicity of services conveys authority. Visitors to one site are also more likely to use another Google site because of the irresistible convenience of staying within the Google family of services. Circumstantial evidence suggests that the non-Web services have strengthened the Google brand for Web search. Google's share of Web searches in the United States increased to almost 68.3 percent in May 2008 from 58.3 percent in March 2006. During the same period, Microsoft's share dropped to 5.9 percent from 13.1 percent. The quality of Google Web searches, compared with Microsoft searches, did not improve that dramatically; if anything, the qualitative gap narrowed. But Google has succeeded in strengthening the association in users' minds between Web searches and the Google brand, to the detriment of Microsoft, Yahoo, and its other search-engine competitors.

Eric Schmidt is fond of saying that Google users are merely "one click away" from leaving, as Google does not lock its users in. "One click away" may have applied in Google's early years, but as time has passed and Google has become a one-stop destination for information, and a one-stop destination to some for Software as a Service, its users have made an investment in their Google accounts that cannot be abandoned casually with a click.

All in all, Google has yet to stumble badly in undertaking new initiatives. But it has been mocked for failing to create a second profitable business in addition to search-related advertising. Microsoft's CEO Steve Ballmer likes to deride Google as a "one-trick pony." Microsoft, he says, is a two-trick pony—software for desktop computing and software for servers—that is trying to add a third and fourth trick to its repertoire. Ballmer hardly stands in a good position to criticize Google, however. Since becoming Microsoft's CEO in 2000, his company has continued to flounder in its efforts to build up its online services. In May 2008, the company's market capitalization remained $300 *billion* less than it had been when it reached its historic peak in 1999. The last year that its online services unit posted a profit was fiscal year 2005, and its online losses grew in each successive year, reaching $745 million in 2007. Losses in the first three quarters of 2008 indicated that the year's total will far surpass that suffered the year previously.

Google has no such worries about mounting losses. It has managed to generously fund its various online experiments while at the same time posting ever-growing profits. Its fiscal year is slightly different from Microsoft's, but for rough comparison, place Microsoft's losses in its online services segment against Google's $1.5 billion in profits in fiscal year 2005, $3 billion in 2006, and $4.2 billion in 2007. Google's growth has been so remarkable that Henry Blodget of *Silicon Alley Insider* predicted in May 2008 that by May of the following year, Google's search business will be both larger and more profitable than Microsoft Windows, which he described as "the most profitable and legendary monopoly in history."

Google's financial results have given its shareholders no reason to complain about imprudent outlays on YouTube or Google Book Search. In any case, Google's executive leadership does not have to contend with restive shareholders. The company has a dual-class voting structure. Brin, Page, and Schmidt control almost 40 percent of the voting power, which effectively gives these three control of the company. Public shareholders show no sign of dissatisfaction with the broadest possible interpretation of the company's mission to organize the world's information, nor with the speculative initiatives to expand beyond Web search. Page gave due warning in 2004 about their intentions in the company prospectus on the eve of its IPO: "In our opinion," he explained, "outside pressures too often tempt companies to sacrifice long-term opportunities to meet quarterly market expectations." Google would pursue its long-term interests and would not "shy away from high-risk, high-reward projects because of short-term earnings pressure." Anticipating that shareholders might become antsy if the company's "bets" do not quickly show a positive outcome, Page wrote: "We will have the fortitude to do this. We would request that our shareholders take the long-term view."

The company's fortitude has not yet been put to a genuine test, in which its core advertising business encounters serious turbulence and slips, or one of its very big bets turns into a very big failure. If, under adverse circumstances, Google reaffirms its commitment to organizing the world's information and does not scale back its ambition, then it will pass another milestone.

In 2005—when Google ran into legal difficulties by recording television programs for Google Video without obtaining the permission of television producers; when the Association of American University Presses had warned Google that its plan to digitize books would violate copyright law; and when Google was sued for Google News's unauthorized use of short excerpts from news articles and thumbnail-size photographs—it seemed that Google's attempts to do more than search the Web would be stymied on all sides. When Eric Schmidt was interviewed at what seemed to be a trying time for Google, he smoothly acknowledged the complications and conveyed the sense that Google was working hard with the aggrieved parties to resolve all outstanding issues. This was all predictably soothing.

And then Schmidt said something that was rather surprising: he gave an estimate of how much time Google would need to organize all of the world's information—"It will take, current estimate, 300 years." The combination of many centuries and crisp precision made the number seem whimsical, outlandishly distant. This is a company that likes not just to think big, but to think bigger than anyone else—"300 years" was showing off, wasn't it?

It turned out to be neither a joke nor a boast. It was merely a dispassionate calculation. The year before, Craig Silverstein, the company's director of technology, who had been the first employee hired by Brin and Page, also used three hundred years as an estimate, in his case as the upper end of a range of years, 200–300, that would be needed before an intelligent computer would be able to "understand emotions and other nonfactual information" and be able to do as well as today's human reference librarians.

In 2005, when Eric Schmidt referred to a three-hundred-year timeline, he was speaking not about artificial intelligence in a search engine, but about the amount of time that would be required for his company to organize the world's information. He mentioned the three hundred years a second time, a few months later, when addressing a convention of advertisers. In his talk, he explained that he spoke not as a person with a marketing background but only as a computer scientist. He said that only about "two or three percent" of all information in the world that could be indexed and searched had been converted into a form that made indexing and searching possible. Predicting the progress of digitization was a matter of simple calculation. "We did a math exercise," he explained, when asked to project how long it would take Google to fulfill the company's mission. "And the answer was 300 years."

Google's first ten years of organizing the world's information has taken it a considerable distance. It may not need 290 years to complete its mission.

Notes

Introduction

1 **American Dialect Society:** Society members designated *google* as the second-most-important word or phrase in the society's 2002 Words of the Year competition (it was runner-up to *weapons of mass destruction*). American Dialect Society, "2002 Words of the Year," 13 January 2003, http://www.americandialect.org/index.php/amerdial/2002_words_of_t he_y/. *Google* became a draft entry in the *Oxford English Dictionary* in 2006. "Dictionaries: The June Issue of the Oxford English Dictionary Newsletter Is Now Online; Google as a Verb Now in Oxford English Dictionary," *ResourceShelf*, 29 June 2006, http://www.resourceshelf.com/2006/06/29/dictionaries-the-june-issue-of-the-oxford-english-dictionary-newsletter-is-now-online-google-as-a-verb-now-in-oxford-english-dictionary/.

2 **multibillion-dollar game:** "An Auction That Google Was Content to Lose," *New York Times*, 4 April 2008, http://www.nytimes.com/2008/04/04/technology/04auction.html. Richard Whitt and Joseph Faber, "Cone of Silence (Finally) Lifts on the Spectrum Auction," *Official Google Blog*, 3 April 2008, http://googleblog.blogspot.com/2008/04/cone-of-silence-finally-lifts-on.html.

2 **spend the large sums:** Google also happily spends small sums, too, acquiring smaller companies. These transactions often involve an acquisition price that falls below the size that Google is required to disclose to its shareholders. In one especially busy two-month period in mid-2007, Google acquired seven companies: (1) GrandCentral Communications, a Web-based service for managing phones and messages that can, for example, have an incoming call ring a home number and cell phone number simultaneously; (2) FeedBurner, an advertising network for blogs and RSS feeds; (3) Postini, which provides security-related services for corporate e-mail, a capability that would make Google's e-mail more competitive with Microsoft's corporate e-mail systems; (4) Image America, which makes very-high-resolution cameras used in aerial photography, such as those used to gather images of the devastation in New

Orleans following hurricane Katrina (Stephen Chau, "Imaging America," *Google Lat Long Blog*, 20 July 2007, http://google-latlong.blogspot.com/2007/07/imaging-america.html); (5) Panoramio, which links photos to precise geographic locations; (6) Zenter, which provides software for creating online slide presentations, giving Google's online software package, which already had the equivalent of Microsoft Word and Excel, the missing third component: a PowerPoint equivalent (Sam Schillace, "More Sharing," *The Official Google Blog*, 19 June 2007, http://googleblog.blogspot.com/2007/06/more-sharing.html), (7) PeakStream, which writes software for improving computer performance.

3 **visitors noticed:** Randall Stross, "How Google Tamed Ads on the Wild, Wild Web," *New York Times*, 20 November 2005, http://www.nytimes.com/2005/11/20/business/yourmoney/20digi.html.

3 **Brin and Page were hostile to the very notion:** Sergey Brin and Larry Page, "The Anatomy of a Large-Scale Hypertextual Web Search Engine," April 1998, http://infolab.stanford.edu/~backrub/google.html. The authors probably had in mind Open Text as a cautionary example of what could happen if a search engine's search results were tainted by outside considerations. Open Text had introduced in 1996 a pay-for-placement experiment, permitting advertisers to be listed at the top of search results. In 1998, GoTo, later renamed Overture (and eventually acquired by Yahoo), also offered pay-for-placement to the highest bidder. Danny Sullivan, "Go To Sells Positions," *Search Engine Watch*, 3 March 1998, http://searchenginewatch.com/showPage.html?page=2165971. For a detailed account of GoTo's brief brush with success, prior to Google's, see John Battelle, *The Search: How Google and Its Rivals Rewrote the Rules of Business and Transformed Our Culture* (New York: Penguin, 2005), 95–121.

4 **Marissa Mayer, a Google Vice President:** Stross, "How Google Tamed Ads."

4 **Brin said in an interview:** "Search Us, Says Google," *Technology Review*, November/December 2000.

4 **founders showed:** Sergey Brin and Larry Page, "The Future of the Internet," Commonwealth Club of California, 21 March 2001, http://commonwealthclub.org/archive/01/01–03google-speech.html; Q&A: http://commonwealthclub.org/archive/01/01–03google-qa.html. When Eric Schmidt arrived at Google in 2001 and he was shown the ads, which were producing revenue of about $20 million a year, he said, incredulously, "You have got to be kidding. People actually click on this stuff?" Eric Schmidt, "Technology Is Making Marketing Accountable," transcript of speech delivered to the Association of National Advertisers, 8 October 2005, http://www.google.com/press/podium/ana.html.

5 **As late as 2002:** "Google's Toughest Search Is for a Business Model," *New York Times*, 8 April 2002.

5 **Yuri Punj:** "Google May Charge for Internet Search," *Telegraph.co.uk*, 10 April 2002, http://www.telegraph.co.uk/digitallife/main.jhtml?xml=/connected/2002/10/04/ecngoog.xml.

5 **Achieving a one-to-one match:** "Google's Targeted Keyword Ad Program Shows Strong Momentum with Advertisers," Google press release, 16 August 2000, http://www.google.com/press/pressrel/pressrelease31.html; John Battelle, "Titans Column: Omid Kordestani," *Searchblog*, 26 October 2005, http://battellemedia.com/archives/001974.php.

6 **Google began a trial experiment:** Saul Hansell, "Google Tests Video Ads on Search Results Pages," *New York Times Bits* blog, 14 February 2008, http://bits.blogs.nytimes.com/2008/02/14/google-tests-video-ads-on-search-results-pages/.

6 **Yahoo in June 2006:** "Yahoo! to Strengthen Competitive Position in Online Advertising Through Non-Exclusive Agreement with Google," Yahoo press release, 12 June 2008, http://yhoo.client.shareholder.com/releasedetail.cfm?&releaseID=316450. Financial terms were not disclosed by either company. Also see Google's announcement: "Google Announces Non-Exclusive Advertising Services Agreement with Yahoo in U. S. and Canada," Google press release, 12 June 2008, http://www.google.com/intl/en/press/pressrel/20080612_yahoo.html.

6 **Jerry Yang:** Jerry Yang, "Our Google Deal," *Yodel Anecdotal,* 12 June 2008, http://ycorpblog.com/2008/06/12/our-google-deal/.

7 **In April 2008:** "Google App Engine," a part of Google Code, http://code.google.com/appengine/.

7 ***New York Times* published:** "Planet Google Wants You," *New York Times*, 15 October 2006, http://www.nytimes.com/2006/10/15/fashion/15google.html.

7 **Google site located in China:** Andrew McLaughlin, "Google in China," *Official Google Blog*, 27 January 2006, http://googleblog.blogspot.com/2006/01/google-in-china.html; "Google CEO On Censoring: 'We Did An Evil Scale,'" *Infoworld*, 27 January 2006, http://www.infoworld.com/article/06/01/27/74874_HNgoogleceocensoring_1.html.

8 **Some environmental critics:** Ginger Strand, "Keyword: Evil," *Harper's Magazine*, March 2008, http://harpers.org/media/slideshow/annot/2008-03/index.html.

8 **market capitalization:** Ranking based on closing prices on 13 June 2008. For current rankings, see the online chart "Large Caps," maintained by the Online Investor, http://www.theonlineinvestor .com/large_caps/.

9 **Michael Cusumano:** Randall Stross, "Maybe Microsoft Should Stalk Different Prey," *New York Times*, 24 February 2008, http://www.nytimes.com/2008/02/24/business/24digi.html.

9 **Dan Lyons:** "Monkey Boy's Three-Legged Race," *The Secret Diary of Steve*

Jobs, 2 February 2008, http://fakesteve.blogspot.com/2008/02/ballmer-im-completely-out-of-ideas.html.

9 **In May 2008:** "Google Receives 68 Percent of U.S. Searches in May 2008," Hitwise press release, 10 June 2008, http://www.hitwise.com/press-center/hitwiseHS2004/leader-record-growth.php.

9 **organize the world's information:** "Google Receives $25 Million in Equity Funding," Google press release, 7 June 1999, http://web.archive.org/web/20000309205910/http://google.com/pressrel/pressrelease1.html. In an e-mail message to the author on 4 April 2008, Craig Silverstein, the first Google employee that Page and Brin hired, said that after checking the company's files, it appeared that this was the first time that the "organize the world's information" mission statement had been placed on Google's Web site.

9 **modest statement of company mission:** A sample page containing the first mission statement, saved by the Internet Archive's Wayback Machine, an online archive of Web pages, in a crawl done on 11 November 1998, is preserved at http://web.archive.org/web/19990221202430/www.google.com/company.html.

10 **In 2006, an unknown person:** Google Analyst Day comments in PPT file, preserved by Paul Kedrosky before Google removed the file from its site. *Infectious Greed* blog, 2 March 2006, http://paul.kedrosky.com/archives/002797.html#c44483, slides 8 and 20. Kedrosky was the executive director of the William J. von Liebig Center for Entrepreneurialism and Technology Advancement at the University of California, San Diego.

11 **the three men committed:** "Google Wins Again," *Fortune*, 29 January 2008, http://money.cnn.com/2008/01/18/news/companies/google.fortune/index.htm.

11 **see on a daily basis:** Chris Sacca, "Channeling Decision-Makers," *What Is Left?* blog, http://www.whatisleft.org/lookie_here/2008/02/for-reasons-i-w.html.

11 **When Brin was asked:** Ken Auletta, "The Search Party," *New Yorker*, 14 January 2008, http://www.newyorker.com/reporting/2008/01/14/080114fa_fact_auletta.

11 **Google's strategic model:** Eric Schmidt, Press Day, 10 May 2006, http://google.client.shareholder.com/Visitors/event/build2/MediaPresentation.cfm?MediaID=20263.

12 **a million computers:** The possibility that Google had 1 million machines, running Linux, was mentioned as early as May 2006, in a speech delivered by publisher Tim O'Reilly: "My Commencement Speech at SIMS," *O'Reilly Radar*, 14 May 2006, http://radar.oreilly.com/archives/upcoming_appearances/index.html.

12 **in April 2007:** "Text of Wired's Interview with Google CEO Eric Schmidt," interviewed by Fred Vogelstein, *Wired*, interview conducted 23 March 2007, posted 9 April 2007, available only online at http://www.wired.com/techbiz/people/news/2007/04/mag_schmidt_trans.

13 **The company famously provides:** For a list of what Google refers to as "benefits . . . beyond the basics," see http://www.google.com/support/jobs/bin/static.py?page=benefits.html#bbb. Eric Schmidt is quoted on the page: "The goal is to strip away everything that gets in our employees' way." For an estimate of the cost of Google-provided meals, see Vasanth Sridharan, "Google's Ginormous Free Food Budget: $7,530 Per Googler, $72 Million A Year," *Silicon Alley Insider*, 23 April 2008, http://www.alleyinsider.com/2008/4/googles_ginormous_food_budget_ 7530_per_google_r. Sridharan's figure was not based on any hard data provided by Google; it assumed that Google's employees in Mountain View and New York ate two meals a day at the company's cafeteria and that the two meals, combined, cost the company about $30. Another estimate of the cost that was mentioned in the same article placed the daily cost at $15, not $30.

13 **Larry Page:** "Letter from the Founders: 'An Owner's Manual' for Google's Shareholders," 2004, http://investor.google.com/ipo_letter.html.

13 **Number One Best Company:** "100 Best Companies to Work For," *Fortune*, 21 January 2008, http://features.blogs.fortune.cnn.com/2008/01/21/100-best-companies-to-work-for/.

14 **emphasis on Ph.D.'s:** Brin and Page, "The Future of the Internet"; Randall Stross, "What Is Google's Secret Weapon? An Army of Ph.D.'s," *New York Times*, 6 June 2004.

15 **Kevin Scott:** "Google—Working at Google—The Faces at Google/Fast Company," *FriendFeed*, 18 February 2008, http://friendfeed.com/kevinscott. Scott was prompted to offer his thoughts after seeing Fast Company's "The Faces and Voices of Google," http://www.fastcompany.com/magazine/123/google.html, which he referred to as one of similar "unreservedly positive fluff pieces [that] really aren't doing the company a service." Scott himself had left Google.

15 **23andMe:** Google invested $3.9 million. In its filing of a form 8-K with the U.S. Securities and Exchange Commission (http://sec.gov/Archives/edgar/data/1288776/000119312507120640/d8k.htm), the company disclosed that Anne Wojcicki, a cofounder of 23andMe, was married to Sergey Brin, Google's president and a cofounder. (They were married just a few weeks earlier.) This first round of financing for 23andMe, which included Genentech's participation, was used partially to repay $2.6 million in interim debt financing that Brin had provided to 23andMe. The personal relationship between Brin and Wojcicki made Google's investment in her company suspect in the eyes of many bloggers. But Kevin Kelleher, a commentator at GigaOM, provided a clear-eyed evaluation of the transaction, arguing that "I haven't yet found a company that gives Google a better entry into a genomics-for-consumers startup." See "Google, Sergey and 23andMe: Why It All Makes Sense," *GigaOM*, 24 May 2007, http://gigaom.com/2007/05/24/google-sergey-and-23andme-why-it-all-makes-sense/.

15 **In 2005, Schmidt explained:** Eric Schmidt, Donald Graham, James Fallows, moderator, "Proprietary Information in the Age of Search," Zeitgeist '05, the Google Partner Forum, 27 October 2005, http://www.google.com/press/podium/eric.html.

16 **Schmidt was asked:** "Google's Goal: To Organize Your Daily Life," *Financial Times*, 23 May 2007, http://www.ft.com/cms/s/df7d8850-08ca-11dc-b11e-000b5df10621.html.

16 **Sergey Brin told:** Spencer Michels, "The Search Engine That Could," *NewsHour with Jim Lehrer* transcript, 29 November 2002, http://www.pbs.org/newshour/bb/business/july-dec02/google_11-29.html.

16 **the more it knows about each visitor:** Schmidt also defended the continuing expansion of the company's information storehouse on humanitarian grounds, stating in a podcast interview with the *Economist* in 2007 that giving the public access to "far more information than they can ever handle" was a very good thing: "More information crowds out bad ideas, bad governments, bad behavior." Before finishing, he had managed also to claim that increased access to information made the world faster growing, more profitable, and safer. "*Economist* Podcast Interview with Eric Schmidt," *Economist: The World in 2007*, n.d., http://media.economist.com/media/audio/world-in-2007/The_future_of_the_internet.mp3.

17 **10 percent of Facebook's employees:** Justin Smith, "10% of Facebook Employees Came from Google," *Inside Facebook*, 27 March 2008, http://www.insidefacebook.com/2008/03/27/facebooks-dna-is-10-google/. Smith identified forty-one employees who had worked at Google, listing them by name.

17 **June 2008:** Owen Thomas, "Google's Daycare Debacle: The Kinderplex Memos," *Valleywag*, 16 June 2008, http://valleywag.com/5016952/googles-daycare-debacle-the-kinderplex-memos; Thomas, "Google Daycare Now a Luxury for Larry and Sergey's Inner Circle," *Valleywag*, 13 June 2008, http://valleywag.com/5016355/google-daycare-now-a-luxury-for-larry-and-sergeys-inner-circle.

17 **Bloomberg financial news service:** "Google Trims DoubleClick Jobs in Biggest Staff Cuts," *Bloomberg*, 2 April 2008, http://www.bloomberg.com/apps/news?pid=newsarchive&sid=aHPI8hip9Zr8.

19 **few Googlers:** Today, Google employees refer to themselves as "Googlers," but it's amusing to note how usage has changed: in 1999, Michael Moritz, one of the venture capitalists who invested in Google, spoke of Google's possessing "the power to turn Internet users everywhere into devoted and lifelong Googlers." See "Google Receives $25 Million in Equity Funding."

19 **At the end of 2003:** Google Financial Tables, 2003, http://investor.google.com/fin_data2003.html, and 2007, http://investor.google.com/fin_data.html.

1. Open and Closed

23 **CERN announced:** CERN European Organization for Nuclear Research, "Statement Concerning CERN W3 Software Release into Public Domain," 30 April 1993, http://tenyears-www.web.cern.ch/tenyears-www/Declaration/Page1.html (for reproduction of first page of the two-page statement) and ~/Page2.html (for second page). "CERN" is the organization's most recognizable name, but the "C" may cause puzzlement when placed against its full English name: "European Organization for Nuclear Research." The acronym CERN was created by a predecessor organization, the French Conseil Européen pour la Recherche Nucléaire, or European Council for Nuclear Research. When the council was replaced in 1954 by the European Organization for Nuclear Research, "CERN" was retained.

24 **In June 1993:** Matthew Gray collected statistics about the Internet's traffic while an undergraduate and graduate student at MIT. See his page on the Web's growth at the MIT Web site: "Web Growth Summary," http://www.mit.edu/people/mkgray/net/web-growth-summary.html. In 1993, almost half of all Internet traffic was for file transfers, about 10 percent was for discussion groups (called, rather confusingly, "news groups"), about 7 percent was used for e-mail. Postscript: Gray joined Google in early 2007 and one month after joining, he posted on Google's Book Search blog an entry that began, "I love data. That was no small factor in my decision to join Google." Matthew Gray, "Earth Viewed from Books," *Inside Google Book Search*, 12 March 2007, http://booksearch.blogspot.com/2007/03/earth-viewed-from-books.html.

25 **Microsoft began planning:** Randall Stross, *The Microsoft Way: The Real Story of How the Company Outsmarts Its Competition* (Reading, MA: Addison-Wesley, 1996), 161–65. Ken Auletta wrote in 1997 that "Myhrvold and Microsoft [were infuriated] that the Internet was free. They saw it as a flower-child culture that disdained profits and copyrights—and Microsoft." Auletta, "The Microsoft Provocateur," *New Yorker*, 12 May 1997, http://www.kenauletta.com/themicrosoftprovocateur.html.

25 **Netscape Communications:** At the time of its founding in April 1994, the company was named Mosaic Communications Corporation and the beta version of its browser was Mosaic Netscape. The company was forced to change its name and branding because of objections raised by the National Center for Supercomputing Applications, which had developed the Mosaic browser and sought to protect its trademark.

25 **Netscape declared itself:** Michael A. Cusumano and David B. Yoffie, *Competing on Internet Time: Lessons from Netscape and Its Battle with Microsoft* (New York: Free Press, 1998), 132–40. Cusumano and Yoffie offer a multifaceted analysis of Netscape's strategic and tactical missteps and apply the phrase *open, but not open* to Netscape.

26 **called the changes "extensions":** Perhaps the person who has written about extensions most trenchantly is a strategic consultant-turned-entrepreneur, Charles H. Ferguson, whose company, Vermeer Technologies, deliberately created extensions to standard HTML for proprietary advantage in its software for Web site creators, FrontPage. Microsoft purchased Ferguson's company in 1996. See Ferguson's memoir, *High Stakes, No Prisoners: A Winner's Tale of Greed and Glory in the Internet Wars* (New York: Times Books, 1999).

26 **had the company been founded two years earlier:** "Searchology@Google," press briefings, Google headquarters, Mountain View, CA, 16 May 2007, http://google.client.shareholder.com/visitors/event/build2/mediapresentation.cfm?MediaID=25550.

27 **This did not endear Google:** Sergey Brin and Larry Page, "The Anatomy of a Large-Scale Hypertextual Web Search Engine," April 1998, http://infolab.stanford.edu/~backrub/google.html.

27 **a piece of code:** The code is the Robots Exclusion Protocol, which was adopted as a standard in 1994. In its simplest form, two lines of text will keep all search engines that honor the protocol away from the site: *User-agent: *; Disallow.* See Martin Koster, "A Standard for Robot Exclusion," n.d., http://www.robotstxt.org/orig.html.

28 **demanding, perhaps, that Google share:** Mike Masnick, "AP: The News Gatekeeper Is Dead! Long Live the News Gatekeeper!" *Techdirt*, 2 November 2007, http://www.techdirt.com/articles/20071102/025323.shtml. Also see Tim Lee's follow-up post, "Search Engines Should Ignore Bossy Publishers," *Techdirt*, 6 December 2007, http://www.techdirt.com/articles/20071202/161208.shtml, which looks at an Automated Content Access Protocol proposed by a new consortium of Web publishers. Among the Frequently Asked Questions on ACAP's Web site is this: "Isn't this all about money?" The reply begins, "No, but no one would deny that it is partly about money." See "ACAP Frequently Asked Questions," http://www.the-acap.org/faqs.php, accessed 15 December 2007.

29 **AOL exploited:** In 2000, AOL had 24 million members, which was about 45 percent of all online users. Any company that wanted to advertise or sell its wares to AOL members had to be prepared to accept extortionate terms imposed by AOL gatekeepers. CUC International, the discount shopping service, agreed to pay AOL $50 million and a share of revenues. Barnes & Noble agreed to pay $40 million to be AOL's "exclusive" bookseller. Music retailer N2K signed a three-year $18 million deal, which included an up-front payment of $12 million, even though it had generated only $11 million in the previous year. AOL's appetite grew and grew. For new companies, AOL demanded a significant share of equity in the company, in addition to payments for access to AOL's customers. AOL acquired a reputation for being the most arrogant negotiator in the country. An executive at a start-up said that AOL had demanded a 30 percent stake in her company, "and then for good

measure, they tell us, 'These are our terms. You have 24 hours to respond, and if you don't, screw you, we'll go to your competitor.'" See Gary Rivlin, "AOL's Rough Riders," *Industry Standard*, 30 October 2000, http://www.thestandard.com/article/0,1902,19461,00.html.

29 **Vic Gundotra:** Vic Gundotra, interview, Mountain View, 18 December 2007. Gundotra worked at Microsoft for fifteen years.

29 **began declining after 2001:** AOL, Inc., "AOL Membership Surpasses 28 Million," press release, 8 March 2001; "Time Warner Inc. Reports Results for 2007 Full Year and Fourth Quarter," press release, 6 February 2008, http://biz.yahoo.com/bw/080206/20080206005597.html.

29 **In 2005, Michael Kelly:** "Free Internet Site: A Portal to AOL's Future?" *New York Times*, 3 June 2005, http://www.nytimes.com/2005/06/03/technology/03aol.html.

29 **strategic alliance:** In addition to an advertising pact, the alliance included Google's purchase of a 5 percent equity stake in AOL for $1 billion. Time Warner Inc., "Time Warner's AOL and Google to Expand Strategic Alliance," press release, 20 December 2005, http://www.timewarner.com/corp/newsroom/pr/0,20812,1142800,00.html.

29 **AOL finally tore down:** Time Warner, "Time Warner Announces That AOL Will Offer Its Software, E-Mail and Many Other Products for Free to Broadband Users," press release, 2 August 2006, http://www.timewarner.com/corp/newsroom/pr/0,20812,1222063,00.html. Only weeks before AOL's announcement, however, the company maintained tight control of the exits to its garden, instructing its customer service representatives to attempt to prevent members who called to cancel their memberships from successfully doing so. For an account of one customer's ordeal, which was recorded and broadly disseminated, see Randall Stross, "AOL Said, 'If You Leave Me I'll Do Something Crazy,'" *New York Times*, 2 July 2006, http://www.nytimes.com/2006/07/02/business/yourmoney/02digi.html.

29 ***Wall Street Journal's*** **Web site:** Rupert Murdoch, the *Journal*'s new owner, had initially indicated after the acquisition that he believed that removing the pay wall would greatly expand the site's audience and boost its Web advertising revenue. He directed that more material be placed on the part of the Web site that was freely available, but was persuaded to stop short of eliminating the subscription model entirely. See "Wall Street Journal Web Site to Remain Subscription-Based," *Wall Street Journal*, 24 January 2008, http://online.wsj.com/public/article/SB120119406286813757.html.

30 **42 million members:** "Microsoft to Pay $240 Million for Stake in Facebook," *New York Times*, 25 October 2007, http://www.nytimes.com/2007/10/25/technology/24cnd-facebook.html.

31 **exclusive advertising deal:** Google Inc., "Fox Interactive Media Enters into Landmark Agreement with Google Inc.," press release, 7 August 2006, http://investor.google.com/releases/20060807.html. The agreement obligated

Google to guarantee minimum revenue share payments of $900 million for the agreement's term, which would run through the second quarter of 2010.

31 **Steve Rubel:** "Walled Gardens and the Lesson for Social Networks," *Micro Persuasion* blog, 28 June 2007, http://www.micropersuasion.com/2007/06/walled-gardens-.html.

31 **appointed three executives:** Joe Kraus and Graham Spencer had joined Google less than a year previously, when Google had acquired JotSpot, a company that made wiki software for group collaboration. Kraus and Graham's business experience on the Web stretched back to 1993, when they had cofounded Excite, a search-engine pioneer that predated Google. Kraus was also an investor in, and active member of, LinkedIn, a social network for professionals.

31 **Kraus said:** This account draws from an interview with Kraus, 4 January 2008, in Mountain View.

33 **Facebook's maddening ability:** Nick Gonzalez, "Facebook Stealing Googlers at an Alarming Rate," *TechCrunch*, 21 November 2007, http://www.techcrunch.com/2007/11/21/facebook-stealing-googlers-at-an-alarming-rate/.

33 **Microsoft announced:** "Facebook and Microsoft Expand Strategic Alliance," Facebook press release, 24 October 2007, http://www.facebook.com/press/releases.php?p=8084.

34 **in the few days remaining:** Joe Kraus had set the date for the announcement for November 5, long before Facebook set the date for its announcement on November 6. As the date approached, Kraus's team moved the date for its announcement up by four days—it would say, unconvincingly, that it was for reasons unrelated to Facebook—which gave it more time to command headlines before Facebook stole attention back.

34 **injection of credibility:** Randall Stross, "Why Google Turned into a Social Butterfly," *New York Times*, 4 November 2007, http://www.nytimes.com/2007/11/04/technology/04digi.html.

34 **open source:** Google's search engine utilized the Linux kernel, GCC, Python, and Samba. Chris DiBona, "Three Summers of Open Source," *Official Google Blog*, 15 March 2007, http://googleblog.blogspot.com/2007/03/three-summers-of-open-source.html.

34 **free hosting site:** The site was code.google.com.

34 **a number of coders:** Among the ranks of Google employees were Andrew Morton (Linux), Greg Stein (Apache), Jeremy Allison (Sambra), and Ben Goodger (Firefox). "Google's Secret Weapon," *Redmondmag.com*, January 2008, http://redmondmag.com/features/article.asp?editorialsid=2395. Google poured tens of millions of dollars into the Mozilla Foundation, underwriting the open-source development of Firefox and Thunderbird, but this was not pure altruism; Google, in essence, purchased favorable placement as the default search engine that came with Firefox. In June 2008, Danny Sullivan pointed out that Google had fought hard to pressure Microsoft to

make sure that no single search engine provider was the default in Internet Explorer 7, and had succeeded in that campaign. But Google had turned around and arranged for favorable placement for itself in Mozilla's Firefox browser. Sullivan asked Google to stop making the user's initial search choice and ensure that "any provisions of the secret contract between you and Firefox are altered to allow for the consumer choice you're so happy to espouse should happen in Internet Explorer." Danny Sullivan, "Hey Firefox—Let Us Pick Our Own Search Engine!" *Search Engine Land,* 6 June 2008, http://searchengine land.com/080606-103041.php.

35 **Tim O'Reilly:** When O'Reilly was able to see what OpenSocial offered, he was greatly disappointed to discover that it was not so open after all, and would not provide a user with the ability to move and manage a set of friend lists from one social network to another. Tim O'Reilly, "OpenSocial: It's The Data, Stupid," *O'Reilly Radar*, 7 November 2007, http://radar.oreilly.com/archives/2007/11/opensocial_social_mashups.html. Mark Cuban proposed that his personal information be made portable not by using a new set of standards, OpenSocial's, but by having Facebook, where they currently resided, make them available for export, if the member wished to do so. Cuban wrote, "I don't want to have to publish and maintain a database for every application I want to use or happen to use. Nor do I want to have to maintain multiple social network accounts to make this information available. . . . [Google's OpenSocial is] too late . . . if Facebook opens their API [Application Programming Interface, i.e., programming standards] up further and allows for its use outside the Facebook.com domain." Mark Cuban, "An Open Facebook API vs. Google OpenSocial," *Blog Maverick*, 4 November 2007, http://www.blogmaverick.com/2007/11/04/an-open-facebook-api-vs-google-opensocial/.

35 **A week before Facebook:** Joe Kraus, phone interview, 29 October 2007.

35 **Facebook founder and CEO:** Erick Schonfeld, "Liveblogging Facebook Advertising Announcement (Social Ads + Beacon + Insights)," *TechCrunch*, 6 November 2007, http://www.techcrunch.com/2007/11/06/liveblogging-facebook-advertising-announcement/. Schonfeld was taking notes and publishing without benefit of a tape recorder; Zuckerberg's phrasing may not have been transcribed exactly.

36 **Zuckerberg had no sympathy:** "Official: Facebook Poised to 'Take Over the World,'" *Daily Brief* blog, Portfolio.com, 7 November 2007, http://www.portfolio.com/views/blogs/daily-brief/2007/11/07/official-facebook-poised-to-take-over-the-world.

36 **design was changed:** Christopher Caldwell, "Intimate Shopping," *New York Times Magazine*, 23 December 2007, http://www.nytimes.com/2007/12/23/magazine/23wwln-lede-t.html.Caldwell dryly remarked: "We used to live in a world where if someone secretly followed you from store to store, recording your purchases, it would be considered impolite and even weird."

36 **they were convinced:** Louise Story, "The Evolution of Facebook's Beacon," *Bits (New York Times* blog), 29 November 2007, http://bits.blogs.nytimes.com/2007/11/29/the-evolution-of-facebooks-beacon/.

36 **Zuckerberg publicly apologized:** Mark Zuckerberg, "Thoughts on Beacon," *Facebook Blog*, 5 December 2007, http://blog.facebook.com/blog.php?post=7584397130.

36 ***60 Minutes* featured Zuckerberg:** Kara Swisher, "Facebook: The Entire '60 Minutes' Segment," *Boomtown*, 14 January 2008, http://kara.allthingsd.com/20080114/facebook-the-entire-60-minutes-segment/.

37 **own sponsors:** Coca-Cola decided to take what it called a "wait-and-see" attitude before proceeding with its participation. Louise Story, "Coke Is Holding Off on Sipping Facebook's Beacon," *Bits (New York Times* blog), 30 November 2007, http://bits.blogs.nytimes.com/2007/11/30/coke-is-holding-off-on-sipping-facebooks-beacon/. Overstock.com also suspended its participation. See "Facebook Revamps Beacon Program Amid Protests," *Online Media Daily*, 30 November 2007, http://publications.mediapost.com/index.cfm?fuseaction=Articles. showArticleHomePage&art_aid=71880, and Erick Schonfeld, "More Facebook Advertisers Bail from Beacon, Plus, New Concerns," *TechCrunch*, 3 December 2007, http://www.techcrunch.com/2007/12/03/ more-facebook-advertisers-bail-from-beacon-plus-new-concerns/.

37 **a computer's Internet address:** Google stored a small file, called a "cookie," on a user's computer when a search was conducted, which allowed it to keep track of a succession of searches, even though the searches were conducted anonymously.

37 **a 2003 murder case:** "Petrick Googled 'Neck,' 'Snap,' Among Other Words, Prosecutor Says," WRAL.com, 10 November 2005, http://www.wral.com/news/local/story/121729/; "Petrick Prosecutors to Reopen Case with New Computer Evidence," WRAL.com, 28 November 2005, http://www.wral.com/news/local/story/122105/. The defendant Robert Petrick, who represented himself at his trial, did extract from the prosecution's computer expert the admission that all that could be said with certainty was that the searches had been conducted on the computer, but not who was on the computer at the time. See "Prosecution: Computers Map Out Petrick's Plan to Kill Wife," WRAL.com, 10 December 2005, http://www.wral.com/news/local/story/121815/.

37 **defendant guilty:** "Robert Petrick Found Guilty in Wife's 2003 Death," WRAL.com, 29 November 2005, http://www.wral.com/news/local/story/122121/.

38 **Urs Hölzle:** Urs Hölzle, "Finding Needles in a Terabyte Haystack," talk delivered to Stanford EE380 Computer Systems Colloquium, 14 May 2003, http://stanford-online.stanford.edu/courses/ee380/030514-ee380-100.asx.

39 **automatically define:** Eric Eldon, "Dear Google Reader: Use OpenSocial to Figure Out Who My Friends Are," *VentureBeat*, 27 December 2007, http://venturebeat.com/2007/12/27/dear-google-reader-use-open-social-to-figure-out-who-my-friends-are/.

39 ***Motley Fool:*** Rick Aristotle Munarriz, "Google Comes Face to Facebook," *Motley Fool: Investing*, 28 December 2007, http://www.fool.com/investing/general/2007/12/28/google-comes-face-to-facebook.aspx.

39 **foolish assumption:** Miguel Helft, "Google Thinks It Knows Your Friends," *Bits (New York Times* blog), 26 December 2007, http://bits.blogs.nytimes.com/2007/12/26/google-thinks-it-knows-your-friends/.

39 **Developers who tried:** Erick Schonfeld, "OpenSocial Still 'Not Open For Business,'" *TechCrunch*, 6 December 2007; Caroline McCarthy, "Google: Don't Give Up on OpenSocial," News.com, *The Social*, 13 December 2007, http://www.news.com/8301-13577_3-9833723-36.html.

39 **played the *open* card:** Ami Vora, "Opening Up Facebook Platform Architecture," *Facebook Developers* (blog), 13 December 2007, http://developers.facebook.com/news.php?blog=1&story=60.

40 **MySpace and Facebook made announcements:** Michael Arrington, "My Space Embraces DataPortability, Partners With Yahoo, Ebay and Twitter, *TechCrunch*, 8 May 2008, http://www.techcrunch.com/2008/05/08/myspace-embraces-data-portability-partners-with-yahoo-ebay-and-twitter/; Dave Morin, "Announcing Facebook Connect," *Facebook Developers*, 9 May 2008, http://developers.facebook.com/news.php?blog=1&story=108.

40 **Google Friend Connect:** Mussie Shore, "A Friend-Connected Web," *Official Google Blog*, 12 May 2008, http://googleblog.blogspot.com/2008/05/friend-connected-web.html.

40 **Facebook blocked:** Charlie Cheever, "Thoughts on Privacy," *Facebook Developers*, 15 May 2008, http://developers.facebook.com/news.php?blog=1&story=111.

40 **Michael Arrington wrote:** Michael Arrington, "Data Portability: It's the New Walled Garden," *TechCrunch,* 16 May 2008, http://www.techcrunch.com/2008/05/16/data-portability-its-the-new-walled-garden/. For a close and skeptical analysis of Facebook's claims to be protecting its members' privacy, also see Steve Gillmor, "Facebook's Glass Jaw," *TechCrunch*, 17 May 2008, http://www.techcrunch.com/2008/05/17/facebooks-glass-jaw/. Facebook's "walled garden" seemed to be of declining interest to software developers. See Vasanth Sridharan, "Google's OpenSocial Is Killing Facebook App Buzz," *Silicon Alley Insider*, 14 May 2008, http://www.alleyinsider.com/2008/5/developers_googles_opensocial_killing_facebook_app_buzz.

40 **Google announced:** "Industry Leaders Announce Open Platform for Mobile Devices," Google press release, 5 November 2007, http://www.google.com/intl/en/press/pressrel/20071105_mobile_open.html.

40 **Chris Sacca:** "Google: Mobile Operators Want to Block Our Apps," ZDNet.co.uk, 24 November 2006, http://news.zdnet.co.uk/communications/0,1000000085,39284850,00.htm.

41 **Google colleagues were upset:** Chris Sacca, "The Difference a Year Can Make," WhatIsLeft.org, 28 November 2007, http://www.whatisleft.org/. Sacca resigned from Google in December 2007; John Battelle, "A Brief Interview with Chris Sacca," *Searchblog*, 18 December 2007, http://battellemedia.com/archives/004157.php.

41 **In the summer of 2007:** Randall Stross, "When Mobile Phones Aren't Truly Mobile," *New York Times*, 22 July 2007, http://www.nytimes.com/2007/07/22/business/yourmoney/22digi.html.

41 **Verizon decided:** "Verizon Wireless to Introduce 'Any Apps, Any Device' Option for Customers in 2008," Verizon Wireless press release, 27 November 2007, http://news.vzw.com/news/2007/11/pr2007-11-27.html.

42 **Verizon did confer privately:** Russ Mitchell, "Search Mission, *Conde Nast Portfolio*, April 2008, http://www.portfolio.com/executives/features/2008/03/14/Google-CEO-Eric-Schmidt-Interview.

42 **Eric Schmidt declared:** "Verizon to Open Cell Network to Others' Phones," *Wall Street Journal*, 28 November 2007.

42 **Wikipedia:** Wikipedia always had a small number of topics—in June 2006, they numbered eighty-two—that were closed to public editing because of repeated vandalism or interminable editorial disputes. Another small group of topics were placed into "semiprotected" status, which were open to editing only by people who had been registered at the site for at least four days. See "Growing Wikipedia Refines Its 'Anyone Can Edit' Policy," *New York Times*, 17 June 2006, http://www.nytimes.com/2006/06/17/technology/ 17wiki.html.

42 **A 2006 study:** Jure Cuhalev, "Ranking of Wikipedia Articles on Search Engines for Searches About Its Own Articles," paper, http://www.kiberpipa.org/~gandalf/blog-files/wikistatus/wikistatus.pdf. Cuhalev provides a summary of his findings on his blog: "Seeing Lots of Wikipedia In Your Google Searches?" *Jure Cuhalev: In Pursuit Of the Idea*, 13 October 2006, http://www.jurecuhalev.com/blog/2006/10/13/seeing-lots-of-wikipedia-in-your-google-searches/.

42 **could not penetrate Wikipedia:** It should be remembered that the original Internet spirit, the one that goes back to the Internet's beginning in the defense establishment and in academe in the 1970s, was noncommercial. Commercial use of the Internet was expressly forbidden, until external pressure for change led in 1985 to the creation of the dot-com suffix. Wikipedia, which is overseen by a not-for-profit foundation, is a far better exemplar of the Internet's founding ethos than is Google.

42 **In December 2007:** Udi Manber, "Encouraging People to Contribute Knowledge," *Official Google Blog*, 13 December 2007, http://googleblog.blogspot.com/2007/12/encouraging-people-to-contribute.html.

43 **Charles Matthews:** See Matthews's post among the comments posted after Nicholas Carr's post, "Google Knol Takes Aim at Wikipedia," *Rough Type*, 13 December 2007, http://www.roughtype.com/archives/2007/12/google_knol_tak.php.

43 **Manber clearly anticipated:** Udi Manber, "Encouraging People to Contribute Knowledge."

43 **Danny Sullivan:** "Google: As Open as It Wants to Be (i.e., When It's Convenient)," *Search Engine Land*, 6 November 2007, http://searchengineland.com/071106-102435.php.

44 **an announcement in March 2008:** Frances Haugen and Matthew Gray, "Book Info Where You Need It, When You Need It," *Official Google Blog*, 13 March 2008, http://googleblog.blogspot.com/2008/03/book-info-where-you-need-it-when-you.html; Bethany Poole, "Preview Books Anywhere with the New Google Book Search API," *Inside Google Book Search*, 13 March 2008, http://booksearch.blogspot.com/2008/03/preview-books-anywhere-with-new-google.html.

44 **Dan Cohen:** Dan Cohen, "Still Waiting for a Real Google Book Search API," 31 March 2008, *Dan Cohen* [blog], http://googleblog.blogspot.com/2008/03/book-info-where-you-need-it-when-you.html.

45 **no company was purely closed:** In January 2008, Facebook joined an industry organization, the DataPortability Workgroup, created to establish standards facilitating the sharing of content among social networks. Becoming a member, however, did not signal the company's commitment to sharing its users' data with others, only that it wished to be present at the discussions of the topic. Scott Gilbertson, "Google and Facebook to Join the Data Portability Debate," *Wired Blog Network: Compiler*, 9 January 2008, http://blog.wired.com/monkeybites/2008/01/google-and-face.html; Duncan Riley, "Facebook, Google and Plaxo Join the DataPortability Workgroup," *TechCrunch*, 8 January 2008, http://www.techcrunch.com/2008/01/08/this-day-will-be-remembered-facebook-google-and-plaxo-join-the-dataportability-workgroup/. Tim Faulkner, in *Valleywag*'s characteristically tart voice, described the announcement as "about as historic as the intake of oxygen. The beauty of working groups is that they rarely change anything other than public perception." See "Facebook and Google Join Data-Swapping Group, Change Nothing," *Valleywag*, 8 January 2008, http://valleywag.com/342340/facebook-and-google-join-data+swapping-group-change-nothing.

2. Unlimited Capacity

47 **In 1947:** Thomas J. Watson, *Father Son & Co.: My Life at IBM and Beyond* (New York: Bantam Books, 1990), 190–91.

47 **When a reporter:** "Never Stumped," *New Yorker*, 4 March 1950, 21.

47 **Hollywood copied its looks:** Kevin Maney, *The Maverick and His Machine: Thomas Watson, Sr., and the Making of IBM* (Hoboken, NJ: John Wiley & Sons, 2003), 345–46. Placing the company's new machine on very public display was a brilliant stroke of marketing on Watson's part, but it fell well short of redeeming Watson's disastrous decision to turn away John Mauchly and J. Presper Eckert, the inventors of the pathbreaking ENIAC computer, because Watson was put off by Mauchly's "loud socks."

49 **without precedent:** Google's rivals may wonder whether they should follow Google's path. In the meantime, they attempt in public to make a virtue out of their own decision to stick with just the software side of the business. In 2006, Kevin Timmons, a vice president at Yahoo, took a swipe at Google when he observed: "At some point you have to ask yourself what is your core business. Are you going to design your own router, or are you going to build the world's most popular Web site?" Google's answer has been consistent: it will do both. "A Search Engine That's Becoming an Inventor," *New York Times*, 3 July 2006, http://www.nytimes.com/2006/07/03/technology/03google.html.

49 **Larry Page began:** Philipp Lenssen, "Before Google There Was Backrub," *Google Blogoscoped*, 28 December 2007, http://blogoscoped.com/archive/2007-12-28-n47.html. For a ten-year tour of Google.com's home page, see Lenssen's "Google.com 1997–2007," *Google Blogoscoped*, originally posted 21 April 2006 but subsequently updated, http://blogoscoped.com/archive/2006-04-21-n63.html.

50 **gathered 26 million:** The 26 million Web pages, with software tricks, could be squeezed down to 53 gigabytes.

50 **established search engines:** Danny Sullivan, "How Big Are Search Engines?" *Search Engine Report*, 13 June 1997, http://searchenginewatch.com/showPage.html?page=2165301. Sullivan noted that "hardware limitations"—not only in hard drive storage capacity but also in processing power required to sort through the collected material—had kept the major search engines from expanding their coverage in the previous year. All were reporting the same number of pages, 25 to 50 million, that they had been reporting a year earlier.

50 **For three years:** "Search Us, Says Google," *Technology Review*, November/December 2000.

50 **$15,000 of their own funds:** "Search Us, Says Google"; Google Inc., "Google Milestones: The Search for a Buyer," http://www.google.com/intl/en/corporate/history.html.

50 **In early 1998, Google queries:** Sergey Brin and Larry Page, "The Anatomy of a Large-Scale Hypertextual Web Search Engine," April 1998, http://infolab.stanford.edu/~backrub/google.html.

50 **one query a second:** J. Bradford DeLong, "Google and Larry Page," *Semi-Daily Journal* (blog), 14 February 2003, http://www.j-bradford-delong.net/movable_type/2003_archives/000032.html.

51 **found a company:** Urs Hölzle, "How I Learned to Love Terabytes," talk at CERN Computing Colloquium, 7 July 2005. Brin and Page looked closely at prices and performance specs and discovered that by buying the same central processing units and same components as 100 million PC buyers, they were able to purchase thirty times the computing power that could be purchased for the same investment in high-performance servers. Brin's adviser, while encouraging him to start a company with the Google technology, assured him that he could return to complete his Ph.D. if the company didn't succeed. Brin said, "There was relatively little downside to trying." See Sergey Brin, talk as guest lecturer in the University of California, Berkeley, course "Search Engines, Technology, Society, and Business," 3 October 2005, http://video.google.com/videoplay?docid=7137075178977335350&q=sergey+brin%27.

52 **Performance issues:** This and the following account of improvements is based largely on an interview with Urs Hölzle, Mountain View, CA, 24 July 2007.

52 **received his Ph.D.:** Hölzle's dissertation title was "Adaptive Optimization for Self: Reconciling High Performance with Exploratory Programming."

52 **like eBay and Hotmail:** "The Lost Google Tapes: Interview with Larry Page, Part 3," podcast released 30 December 2006, *PodVentureZone*, January 2000, podcast from www.podventurezone.com.

53 **offered Hölzle a job:** Fifty years after IBM's rejection of John Machly on the basis of his "loud socks," socks again entered the history of computing, this time, however, as a footnote: Hölzle included in his official company biography a bit of color: that he is renowned for his "red socks," a predilection that did not bar his eligibility for his position at Google.

53 **largest search index:** Danny Sullivan, "Search Engine Sizes," *Search Engine Watch*, 28 January 2005, http://searchenginewatch.com/showPage.html?page=2156481. Sullivan reviews the history of the competition among search engines. See especially the section "Search Engine Size War I: December 1997–June 1999."

53 **When Marissa Mayer:** Julian Guthrie, "Googirl," *San Francisco*, March 2008 (the title for the online version was changed to "The Adventures of Marissa"), http://www.sanfranmag.com/story/adventures-marissa. *Valleywag* took great pleasure in noting upon the article's first appearance that the magazine editors apparently had failed to Google the word *googirl* and discover a most unflattering, raunchy noun in the Urban Dictionary. Melissa Gira Grant, "Marissa Mayer Not Really That Kinky," *Valleywag*, 28 February 2008, http://valleywag.com/361923/marissa-mayer-not-really-that-kinky. *Valleywag* then also took pleasure observing the magazine hurriedly replacing the original title for an innocuous one. Owen Thomas, " 'Googirl' Article Vanishes from Web," *Valleywag*, 28 February 2008, http://valleywag.com/362143/googirl-article-vanishes-from-web.

54 **Stanford computer science colloquium:** Urs Hölzle, "Finding Needles in a Terabyte Haystack," talk delivered to Stanford EE380 Computer Systems Colloquium, 14 May 2003, http://stanford-online.stanford.edu/courses/ee380/030514-ee380-100.asx. Google's software engineers built a special file system that broke a file into smaller chunks—*shards* was the technical term—and then spread multiple copies of the chunks over many machines. If the hard drive on any given machine failed and all of the bits on it were lost, it was a matter of no consequence: identical copies of those bits were readily available on other machines. Rather than purchase commercial disk drives that were built to be fault tolerant but were five to ten times as expensive as the ordinary, off-the-shelf hard drives that PCs are equipped with, Google wrote its own software to handle disk failures in inexpensive hard drives without missing a beat.

54 **settled on a standard design:** Luiz Andre Barroso, Jeffrey Dean, and Urs Hölzle, "Web Search for a Planet: The Google Cluster Architecture," *IEEE Micro*, March/April 2003. Hölzle believed that relying on unreliable hardware was preferable for a reason that had nothing to do with favorable economics—hardware that was likely to fail enforced discipline on software engineers, who knew they had to plan in advance how to handle failure "in a graceful manner." Purchasing the most expensive hardware available did not eliminate the need to plan for component failure: all hardware will fail. Even components certified as "five-9's" reliable (99.999 percent of the time) would experience failure somewhere every day in a sufficiently large collection of such machines. Programmers who assumed that hardware never fails are inclined to grow lazy, in Hölzle's view, and when a part fails, "it'll be a bad outcome." See Hölzle, "Finding Needles."

55 **Craigslist, Technorati, Second Life:** "Generator Failures Caused 365 Main Outage," *Data Center Knowledge*, 24 July 2007, http://www.datacenterknowledge.com/archives/2007/Jul/24/generator_failures_caused_365_main_outage.html; "Eleven Empty Hours for Craiglist Users," *Bits*, 25 July 2007, http://bits.blogs.nytimes.com/2007/07/25/eleven-empty-hours-for-craiglist-users/.

55 **Reducing response time:** Account based on notes taken of Marissa Mayer's presentation at a Google Scalability Conference by Dare Obasanjo, a Microsoft program manager. *Dare Obasanajo aka Carnage4Life*, 25 June 2007, http://www.25hoursaday.com/weblog/2007/06/26/GoogleScalabilityConferenceTripReportScalingGoogleForEveryUser.aspx. In its experiments, Google researchers sought to learn whether it should continue to display as a default ten search results on a page, the number Google had picked only because that was the number AltaVista had used, or instead display twenty search results on a page, as Yahoo did, which took a little bit longer to show. Google researchers tried a variety of different numbers of search results to display at one time and tracked what users did after seeing the first page.

56 **Eric Schmidt:** Eric Schmidt, Last Lectures Series talk, Graduate School of Business, Stanford, 13 April 2004, http://www.gsb.stanford.edu/multimedia/Lectures/LastLecture/schmidt.ram.

56 **in Schmidt's words:** Eric Schmidt interview at Bear Stearns 20th Annual Media Conference, 6 March 2007, http://www.youtube.com/watch?v=9HM-ZO21NwA.

57 **UNIVAC's five thousand tubes:** Kevin Maney, *The Maverick and His Machine*, 399. *Fortune* showed its readers in 1949 a picture of engineers surrounded by electric fans. The caption added that "it has been estimated that to operate a computer as complex as the human brain would require all the power of Niagara Falls to cool its millions of electronic tubes." See "Mechanical Brains," *Fortune*, May 1949, 110.

57 **Eric Schmidt once recalled:** Eric Schmidt, keynote at Roads to Innovation conference, Graduate School of Business, Stanford University, 14 November 2006, http://www.executivetalks.com/.

57 **As early as 2005:** Luiz Andre Barroso, "The Price of Performance," *ACM Queue* 3.7 (September 2005). With computer equipment's power consumption seeming to spiral out of control, Barroso worried about the impact on "the overall health of the planet," an issue that had never come up in the earlier years of computing history.

57 **design of the computers' power supply:** Urs Hölzle, "How I Learned to Love Terabytes." The standard power supply is 68 percent efficient, the more expensive one, 90 percent efficient.

58 **work to put the deal together:** "Port Deal with Google to Create Jobs," *The Dalles Chronicle*, 16 February 2005, http://www.gorgebusiness.com/2005/google.htm; Ginger Strand, "Keyword: Evil," *Harper's Magazine*, March 2008, http://harpers.org/media/slideshow/annot/2008-03/index.html.

58 **the city attorney:** "Hiding in Plain Sight, Google Seeks an Expansion of Power," *New York Times*, 14 June 2006, http://www.nytimes.com/2006/07/03/technology/03google.html.

58 **cost $600 million:** "Google Building Data Centres at a Quick Pace," *Computerworld*, 16 April 2007, http://computerworld.co.nz/news.nsf/news/C923353259FC2FDDCC2572BB001462F5.

58 **Pryor:** Sanders Mitchell, an administrator for the MidAmerica Industrial Park where Google's data center was to be located, said that his park used power from the nearby Grand River Dam Authority and offered rates that Google officials said were comparable to those they would pay in Oregon. See "Google," *Byte and Switch*, 4 June 2007, http://www.byteandswitch.com/document.asp?doc_id=123302.

58 **Council Bluffs:** The Council Bluffs area does not have a hydropower plant. The MidAmerican Energy Company, which will supply electricity to Google's center, had a newly expanded coal-fired plant in the city. It would not discuss with a Reuters reporter its arrangements with Google, however, citing its con-

fidentiality agreement with Google. See "Google to Build $600 Million Data Center in Iowa," *Reuters*, 19 June 2007, http://www.reuters.com/article/idUSN1916606420070619.

58 **Tommy Tomlinson:** Tommy Tomlinson, "Were We Googled or Gouged?" *Charlotte Observer*, 11 February 2007, http://www.charlotte.com/mld/observer/news/local/16674221.htm.

59 **Lloyd Taylor:** Lloyd Taylor, "Letter: Why Google Did What It Did," *Charlotte Observer*, 8 February 2007, http://www.charlotte.com/mld/observer/news/opinion/16649216.htm. Taylor ended up confirming the very criticism that large companies encourage states to participate in a "race to the bottom," each encouraged to match or outdo the lowest bid among the others.

59 **In a public talk:** Hölzle, "How I Learned To Love Terabytes."

59 **Two hundred jobs:** John Foley, "Google's Data Center Strategy Revealed . . . at the Rotary Club," *InformationWeek's Google Weblog*, 30 November 2007, http://www.informationweek.com/blog/main/archives/2007/11/googles_data_ce.html.

59 ***Charlotte Observer*'s Tomlinson:** Tomlinson, "Were We Googled or Gouged?"

60 **hired an IT expert:** "Inside the World of Google The Dalles," *The Dalles Chronicle*, 5 August 2007, http://www.thedalleschronicle.com/news/2007/08/news08-05-07-02.shtml.

60 **In April 2004:** Schmidt, Last Lectures Series talk.

61 **Schmidt has described:** Schmidt interview at Bear Stearns.

3. The Algorithm

64 **The company says that only a small number:** Matt Cutts's comment, 20 February 2008, http://battellemedia.com/archives/003744.php#comment_128693, to a post John Battelle had made seven months previously: "Just Asking," *Searchblog*, 19 June 2007, http://battellemedia.com/archives/003744.php. Cutts apologized for taking a long time to send in Google's official response to Battelle's inquiry about the company's privacy policies. Cutts said that he had sought and received a response from his company's officials, but that it had sat unnoticed in his e-mail inbox for more than six months.

65 **Facebook's employees:** Owen Thomas, "Why Facebook Employees Are Profiling Users," *Valleywag*, 29 October 2007, http://valleywag.com/tech/your-privacy-is-an-illusion/why-facebook-employees-are-profiling-users-316469.php. Thomas wrote, "What happens when you put twentysomethings in charge of a company with vast amounts of private information? Sheer madcap chaos, of course."

66 **unlikely to pose a competitive threat:** Chris Sherman, "Google Announces Largest Index," *Search Engine Report*, 5 July 2000, http://searchenginewatch.com/showPage.html?page=2162751.

67 **conventional wisdom of the time:** Danny Sullivan, "Microsoft's MSN Search to Build Crawler-Based Search Engine," *Search Engine Watch*, 1 July 2003, http://searchenginewatch.com/showPage.html?page=2230291.

67 **Two out of three of Yahoo's visitors:** "With Goto.com's Search Engine, the Highest Bidder Shall Be Ranked First," *New York Times*, 16 March 1998. Yahoo was the most popular site, however, for conducting Web searches. Danny Sullivan, "Lycos Transforms into Directory," *Search Engine Report*, 4 May 1999, http://searchenginewatch.com/showPage.html?page=2167171.

67 **Yahoo changed its suppliers:** Yahoo contracted with, successively, Open Text, AltaVista, and Inktomi.

67 **a major achievement:** Danny Sullivan, "Yahoo Partners with Google," *Search Engine Report*, 5 July 2000, http://searchenginewatch.com/showPage.html?page=2162831.

68 **in a crowded field:** Sullivan, "Yahoo Partners with Google"; Sullivan, "NPD Search and Portal Site Study," *Search Engine Report*, 6 July 2000, http://searchenginewatch.com/showPage.html?page=2162791. Ninety-seven percent of 33,000 respondents reported that they found at Google what they were looking for every time or most of the time.

68 **Google was hungry enough:** Danny Sullivan, "Good for Google Does Not Equal Bad for Inktomi," *Search Engine Report*, 5 July 2000, http://searchenginewatch.com/showPage.html?page=2162771.

68 **By April 2002:** "Google Is the Most Popular Search Engine on the Web According to OneStat.com," OneStat.com press release, 15 April 2002, http://www.onestat.com/html/aboutus_pressbox3.html.

68 **its own engine:** When Yahoo switched to its own search engine, it did not have to build one from scratch: it had technology from no fewer than three search-engine companies that it had acquired—Inktomi, AltaVista, and AlltheWeb.

68 **In May 2007:** "comScore Releases June U.S. Search Engine Rankings," comScore press release, 16 July 2007, http://www.comscore.com/press/release.asp?press=1525.

68 **by January 2008:** "comScore Releases January 2008 U.S. Search Engine Rankings," comScore press release, 21 January 2008, http://www.comscore.com/press/release.asp?press=2068. Microsoft's share was 9.8 percent.

68 **Rich Skrenta:** Rich Skrenta, "Google's True Search Market Share Is 70 percent," *Skrentablog*, 19 December 2006, http://www.skrenta.com/2006/12/googles_true_search_market_sha.html.

68 **In early 2007, Skrenta confessed:** Rich Skrenta, "Winner-Take-All: Google and the Third Age of Computing," *Skrentablog*, 1 January 2007, http://www.skrenta.com/2007/01/winnertakeall_google_and_the_t.html.

68 **company officials offered:** "Microsoft Proposes Acquisition of Yahoo! Conference Call," transcript, 1 February 2008, http://www.microsoft.com/presspass/press/2008/feb08/02-01Transcript.mspx.

69 **settle for what they chose:** Danny Sullivan, "Yahoo: Delays Expected," *Search Engine Report*, 3 September 1997, http://searchenginewatch.com/showPage.html?page=2165541.

69 **8 billion pages indexed:** Google Inc., "Google Milestones," http://www.google.com/corporate/history.html.

69 **When I speak about search:** Sullivan, "Yahoo Partners with Google."

70 **a blogger noted in 2004:** Robert Scoble, "Just a Little Search Comparison," *Scobleizer*, 28 November 2004, http://radio.weblogs.com/0001011/2004/11/28.html#a8764. Scoble left Microsoft in 2006.

70 **the defection of Microsoft developers:** "Move to Google Said to Upset Ballmer," *San Francisco Chronicle*, 3 September 2005. The case in which the affidavit was filed involved Kai-fu Lee, who had been vice president of Microsoft's Interactive Services Division. Microsoft sued Lee and Google in July 2005 for allegedly violating the noncompete clause in Lee's employment contract. The suit was settled in December 2005 with a private agreement among the parties. See "Microsoft Settles with Google over Executive Hire," *News.com*, 22 December 2005, http://news.cnet.com/Microsoft+settles+with+Google+over+executive+hire/2100-1014_3-6006342.html.

71 **Microsoft chairman Bill Gates:** Tony Perkins, "Gates on Google," reprint of 2004 post, *AlwaysOn*, 3 February 2004, http://tuneinturnon.goingon.com/permalink/post/706.

71 **managers encouraged employees:** Adam Barr, "Using Our Own Products," *Proudly Serving My Corporate Masters* (blog), 6 October 2005, http://www.proudlyserving.com/archives/2005/10/using_our_own_p.html. In 2000, Barr published an account of ten years of experience at Microsoft: *Proudly Serving My Corporate Masters: What I Learned in Ten Years as a Microsoft Programmer* (Writers Club Press, 2000). According to his blog, Barr was still proudly serving in June 2008.

72 **The first comment posted:** Adam Herscher comment, posted 7 October, 2005, http://www.proudlyserving.com/archives/2005/10/using_our_own_p.html. Herscher left Microsoft to start a new company in June 2007. Adam Herscher, "Leaving Microsoft," *The Road Less Traveled*, 25 June 2007, http://adamjh.blogspot.com/.

72 **Microsoft hired an outsider:** "Chief of Ask Jeeves to Lead Microsoft's Internet Unit," *New York Times*, 22 April 2006, http://www.nytimes.com/2006/04/22/technology/22msn.html.

72 **At the end of 2006:** "Looking for a Gambit to Win at Google's Game," *New York Times*, 9 December 2006, http://www.nytimes.com/2006/12/09/technology/09msn.html.

73 **attempt to depict:** "Why on Earth Does the World Need Another Search Engine," Microsoft advertisement, *Wall Street Journal*, 27 October 2006.

73 ***Searchblog* broke the story:** John Battelle, "Microsoft Deal for Large Customers: Use Live Search, Get Free MSFT Products," *Searchblog*, 15 March 2007, http://battellemedia.com/archives/003447.php.

73 **Adam Sohn:** Randall Stross, "If at First You Don't Succeed, Write a Check," *New York Times*, 1 April 2007, http://www.nytimes.com/2007/04/01/business/yourmoney/01digi.html. Microsoft sought thirty companies with five thousand or more PCs that would "earn" $2 to $10 per employee annually in credits for Microsoft products based on the number of searches performed using MSN's search service. The year before, Yahoo had explored what appeared to be a rewards program for its search service, and had surveyed Yahoo mail customers about what reward would be sufficiently enticing to be worth designating Yahoo as their primary search engine. Free music downloads? Netflix discount? Frequent flier miles? But after the survey was completed, Yahoo decided not to start the program.

74 **removed from the position:** "Microsoft Reassigns Several Top Executives," *New York Times*, 15 February 2008, http://www.nytimes.com/2008/02/15/technology/15soft.html. Berkowitz had joined Microsoft in April 2006; his position was eliminated in February 2008, at which time Microsoft said he was expected to leave the company in August.

74 **in the spring of 2007:** "Ask.com Debuts 'The Algorithm' Brand Advertising Campaign," Ask press release, 3 May 2007, http://www.irconnect.com/ask/pages/news_releases.html?d=120812.

75 **Cory Doctorow:** "Wiki-Inspired 'Transparent' Search-Engine," *BoingBoing*, 1 January 2008, http://www.boingboing.net/2008/01/01/wikiinspired-transpa.html.

75 **Tim O'Reilly pointed out:** Tim O'Reilly, "Human vs. Machine: The Great Challenge of Our Time," *O'Reilly Radar*, 4 January 2008, http://radar.oreilly.com/archives/2008/01/human_vs_machine_google_wallstreet.html. O'Reilly cited the comments of Eric Blossom, who had posted comments on an earlier *O'Reilly Radar* post, "Trading for Their Own Account," on 28 December 2007, http://radar.oreilly.com/archives/2007/12/google_knol_trading_own_account.html.

75 **is himself Jewish:** For a profile of Brin prepared for an independent Jewish magazine, see Mark Malseed, "The Story of Sergey Brin," *Moment*, February 2007, http://www.momentmag.com/Exclusive/2007/2007-02/200702-BrinFeature.html.

75 **he, too, was offended:** "Google Says Anti-Semitic Site Offends, but to Stay," *Reuters News*, 13 April 2004. The primary reason Jewwatch.com turned out to rank at the top of the results for *Jew* or *Jews* was the hate groups' predilection for using *Jew* where everyone else used the adjective *Jewish* or other nouns, like *Judaism*. The site's high placement also benefited by the way the

Google formula favored sites that were in place for a long time—Jewwatch had been started in 1997—and by inbound links from other sites. The Anti-Defamation League could have been expected to call for Google to take action but the organization was persuaded that it was best that Google not interfere with the workings of its own system. It issued a letter that supported Google's use of an algorithm to determine results: "The ranking of Jewwatch and other hate sites is in no way due to a conscious choice by Google, but solely is a result of this automated system of ranking." Anti-Defamation League, "Google Search Ranking of Hate Sites Not Intentional," press release, 22 April 2004, http://www.adl.org.rumors/google_search_rumors.asp. Without giving any ground on the central question of whether it should in certain instances hand-edit results, Google executives held to their position that the algorithm should have the final say. The only concession the company made was to place on the search results page for the term *Jew* an additional link, labeled "Offensive Search Results," which provided users a full explanation of the linguistic quirk that produced high placements of hate sites on the results page for the search term *Jew* and of the company's policy to remove only sites that "we are legally compelled to remove or those maliciously attempting to manipulate our results." It closed with an apology for "the upsetting nature of the experience." Sergey Brin to Abraham H. Forman, 21 April 2004, http://www.adl.org/internet/google_letter.asp; Google, "An Explanation of Our Search Results," http://www.google.com/explanation.html. When a search for *Jew* was submitted at Google on 16 June 2008, the Jewwatch.com site appeared third, following Wikipedia entries for *Jew* and for *Judaism.*

76 **Peter Norvig:** Comments made at "The Ethics and Politics of Search Engines," panel discussion at the Markkula Center for Applied Ethics, Santa Clara University, 27 February 2006, http://www.scu.edu/ethics/publications/submitted/search-engine-panel.html.

76 **creating in such special cases:** O'Reilly, "Human vs. Machine." Peter Norvig disclosed the existence of these special cases that are "a small percentage of Google pages."

76 **human evaluators:** Marissa Mayer mentioned that Google had "10,000 human evaluators" at a Google Scalability Conference in 2007, as reported by Microsoft blogger Dare Obasanjo, *Dare Obasanjo aka Carnage4Life*, 25 June 2007, http://www.25hoursaday.com/weblog/2007/06/26/GoogleScalabilityConferenceTripReportScalingGoogleForEveryUser.aspx. Peter Norvig also publicly described how contractors identified spam and other sites for Google to avoid when presenting search results. See "Q&A: Peter Norvig," *Technology Review*, January/February 2008, http://www.technologyreview.com/Infotech/19868/.

76 **manually exclude links:** Saul Hansell, "Google: There's Nobody in Our Black Box. Yet." *Bits* (*New York Times* blog), 19 December 2007, http://bits.blogs.nytimes.com/2007/12/19/google-theres-nobody-in-our-black-box

-yet/. Hansell said that Google's Matt Cutts "would not go so far as to say Google never uses this sort of distributed workforce to help flesh out parts of its formulas," and allowed that human reports of Web spam were used to clean up Google's index. But Cutts said that "Google vastly prefers a fully automated way to solve a problem."

77 **in March 2002:** The company officially launched—that is, officially announced its beta version of—Google News in September 2002, but the site had appeared months earlier. The Wayback Machine first crawled news.google.com on 25 March 2002. See http://web.archive.org/web/*/http://news.google.com.

77 **Jonathan Rosenberg:** Jonathan Rosenberg, remarks at Google Press Day, 10 May 2006, http://www.google.com/press/pressday.html.

77 **"No humans were harmed":** Jonathan Dube, "Novel Approach to News," *Web Tips/Poynteronline*, 27 September 2002, http://www.poynter.org/column.asp?id=32&aid=7127.

77 **questions about Google News:** "Google News Search," included in the Wayback Machine's crawl that was completed on 1 November 2002, http://web.archive.org/web/20021013214112/news.google.com/help/about_news_search.html. An earlier version of the information page had used slightly different wording, referring to selections made by "computer algorithms, based on how and where the stories appear elsewhere on the web." See the version collected in the crawl completed on 22 September 2002, http://web.archive.org/web/20021013214112/news.google.com/help/about_news_search.html.

78 **media critic Howard Kurtz:** "Robotic Journalism: Google Introduces Human-Less News," *Washington Post*, 30 September 2002. Kurtz acutely observed another reason why Google's news site referrals would likely hurt news organizations financially. Even though Google's links sent readers to the online sources of the stories it listed, Kurtz noted that "it is less lucrative for news outlets to draw readers for a single story than those who come in through the 'front door' because they're exposed to fewer ads."

78 **corporate press release:** "This Is Google News: Press Releases," CBS.Marketwatch.com, 18 December 2002, http://www.marketwatch.com/News/Story/Story.aspx?guid=%7B27C5CF0B-BB3D-411F-8341-1BAA5BAB138C%7D&source=blq%Fyhoo&dist=yhoo&siteid=yhoo.

78 **on February 1, 2003:** Staci D. Kramer, "Shuttle Disaster Coverage Mixed, but Strong Overall," *Online Journalism Review*, 3 February 2003, http://www.ojr.org/ojr/kramer/1044260857.php.

79 **filed patents in 2005:** Barry Fox, "Google Searches for Quality Not Quantity," *New Scientist*, 30 April 2005, http://www.newscientist.com/article.ns?id=mg18624975.900.

79 **New Jersey high school student:** Jim Hedger, "Google News Credibility Foiled by 15-Year-Old," *Stepforth SEO News Blog*, 13 March 2006,

http://news.stepforth.com/blog/2006/03/google-news-credibility-foiled-by-15.php; "Google News Dumps Partner After Prank Item Appears," News.com, 20 March 2006, http://news.com.com/Google+News+dumps+partner+after+prank+item+appears/2100-1025_3-6051690.html.

79 **four years after it had launched:** Bill Tancer, "Google, Yahoo! and MSN: Property Size-Up," *Hitwise Intelligence*, 19 May 2006, http://weblogs.hitwise.com/bill-tancer/2006/05/google_yahoo_and_msn_property.html. For the week ending 13 May 2006, Yahoo News drew 6.3 percent of all Internet visits to news sites, compared to Google News's 1.9 percent.

80 **In 1953, Howard Aiken:** "Will Machines Replace the Human Brain?" *American Mercury*, January 1953, 55. Faster machines were also expected to help in the textual analysis and assembly of a concordance of the Dead Sea Scrolls. Father Roberto Busa, who was attached to Rome's Gregorian University and was overseeing the textual analysis of the complete works of Saint Thomas Aquinas, was quoted in *Time*: "I am praying to God for ever faster, ever more accurate machines." See "Sacred Electronics," *Time*, 31 December 1956, 48.

80 **The next year, IBM scientists:** "Electronic Translator," *Time*, 18 January 1954, 82; "Bilingual Machine," *Newsweek*, 18 January 1954, 83.

81 **Six years later:** "Machines Are This Smart," *Newsweek*, 24 October 1960, 86–87.

81 **extending to forty language pairs:** "Fancy Math Takes On *Je Ne Sais Quoi*," *Christian Science Monitor*, 2 June 2005, http://www.csmonitor.com/2005/0602/p13s02-stct.htm.

82 **At a briefing in May 2005:** "Fancy Math Takes On *Je Ne Sais Quoi*," *Christian Science Monitor*. A prepared demonstration that produced a good translation of one headline, even if impressively idiomatic, could have been nothing more than a parlor trick. When IBM in 1954 had given reporters a demonstration of its Russian-to-English translation software, a sentence in Russian had been typed in and, voilà, the "mechanical brain," with its 250-word vocabulary, had produced "We transmit thoughts by means of speech." A scholar affiliated with Georgetown University, Leon Dostert, predicted at the time that machine translation could well be "an accomplished fact" within five, perhaps even three, years. "Electronic Translator," *Time*.

82 **In 2005:** National Institute of Standards and Technology, "NIST 2005 Machine Translation Evaluation Official Results," 1 August 2005, http://www.nist.gov/speech/tests/mt/doc/mt05eval_official_results_release_20050801_v3.html.

84 **"We don't have":** Norvig was quoted in Tim O'Reilly, "Why Google Is Offering 411 Service," *O'Reilly Radar*, 13 April 2007, http://radar.oreilly.com/archives/2007/04/why_google_is_o.html.

84 **Dimitris Sabatakakis:** Gary Stix, "The Elusive Goal of Machine Translation," *Scientific American*, March 2006, 95.

85 **in 2006:** "NIST 2006 Machine Translation Evaluation Official Results," 1 November 2006, http://www.nist.gov/speech/tests/mt/doc/mt06eval_official_results.html.

85 **Franz Och, the Google engineer:** Franz Och, "Challenges in Machine Translation," talk to International Macintosh Users Group, Apple headquarters, Cupertino, CA, 19 April 2007.

85 **supplied users:** Users could not fully see what Google's machine-translation algorithm was capable of because the version used in "production" on Google's public Web site was not permitted to tie up machines for an hour working on the translation of a single sentence as the researchers' own version could.

85 **When Sarmad Ali:** "With Online Services, Foreign Texts Can Get Lost in Translation," *Wall Street Journal*, 20 December 2007, http://ptech.allthingsd.com/20071220/with-online-services-foreign-texts-can-get-lost-in-translation/.

86 **at a public talk earlier that year:** Och, "Challenges in Machine Translation." The world outside of Google and outside of the machine-translation research community does not seem particularly interested in this work. The audience for Och's talk was so small that no auditorium was needed: everyone who was interested in the subject of Google's "Challenges in Machine Translation" fit around a square of tables in a side conference room.

86 **a set of DVDs:** The data, which were released in September 2006, took up about 24 gigabytes of compressed text files, required six DVDs, and cost $150 to purchasers who were not members of the Linguistics Data Consortium. See the LDS's catalog entry for "Web 1T 5-gram Version 1," http://www.ldc.upenn.edu/Catalog/CatalogEntry.jsp?catalogId=LDC2006T13.

86 **translate texts in any language:** Eric Schmidt ventured some thoughts on the subject in 2007: "What happens when the million books in Arabic that have never been translated into any language other than Arabic are translated into English? What happens when all the English texts that have never been translated into Arabic are translated into Arabic?" He did not predict the imminent arrival of peace and harmony, nor did he predict a melding of languages into a universally shared one ("the fans of Esperanto might fight me on this"). See Schmidt interview at Bear Stearns 20th Annual Media Conference, 6 March 2007, http://www.youtube.com/watch?v=9HM-ZO21NwA.

86 **by May 2008:** Jeff Chin, "Google Translate Adds 10 New Languages," *Official Google Blog*, 15 May 2008, http://googleblog.blogspot.com/2008/05/google-translate-adds-10-new-languages.html; "Google Translate FAQ," http://www.google.com/intl/en/help/faq_translation.html.

87 **Marissa Mayer:** "Google Wants Your Phonemes," *Infoworld*, 23 October 2007, http://www.infoworld.com/article/07/10/23/Google-wants-your-phonemes_1.html. Tim O'Reilly pointed out that Eckart Walther of Yahoo had told him that speech recognition software had advanced significantly

when automated speech recognition had been used for directory assistance calls and enormous amounts of data—millions of voices and accents—could be captured. Tim O'Reilly, "Why Google Is Offering 411 Service," *O'Reilly Radar*.

87 **More data is better data:** As time passed and Google's information silos grew ever bigger and its algorithms smarter, the opportunities for dramatic improvements diminished steeply. Google's machine-translation team discovered that the law of diminishing returns severely restricted the pace of progress. Doubling the size of the monolingual training data was now improving the quality index (that 0 to 1 scale) by only 0.5 percent. If Google could double the number of pairs of texts in two languages like those prepared by the European Union or the United Nations—what was referred to in the field as "parallel data"—the 100 percent increase in the volume of training data would improve the scores by only about 2.5 percent.

4. Moon Shot

89 **Page explained:** Sergey Brin and Larry Page, "The Future of the Internet," Commonwealth Club of California, 21 March 2001, http://commonwealthclub.org/archive/01/01-03google-speech.html; Q&A: http://commonwealthclub.org/archive/01/01-03google-qa.html.

90 **"our moon shot":** Jeffrey Toobin, "Google's Moon Shot," *New Yorker*, 5 February 2007, http://www.newyorker.com/reporting/2007/02/05/070205fa_fact_toobin.

90 **Google Lunar X Prize:** "Google Sponsors Lunar X Prize to Create a Space Race for a New Generation," press release, 13 September 2007, http://www.googlelunarxprize.org/lunar/press-release/google-sponsors-lunar-x-prize-to-create-a-space-race-for-a-new-generation.

90 **high-volume scanning:** The engineering challenges posed in scanning books were of standing interest to Larry Page. In 2005 he said that eight years earlier he had been curious to learn how fast the speediest available scanners could scan and had visited a local electronics store to investigate. There he had discovered that all of the scanners provided information about the resolution of their scans, but none disclosed their scanning speeds. Recalling the experience later, he said he did not want a scanner that provided 2,400-dots-per-inch resolution, which was sufficiently sensitive to record "dust on your paper." What he wanted was a machine that could scan pages quickly. None made such a claim because "they were all really, really, really slow." "Continuous Innovation," Zeitgeist '05: The Google Partner Forum, 26 October 2005, http://www.google.com/press/podium/brin.html.

91 **ran an experiment:** Google, "History of Google Book Search," Google Book Search: News & Views, n.d., http://books.google.com/googlebooks/

newsviews/history.html. Another example of the tale being told is in Craig Silverstein's talk at the University of North Carolina at Chapel Hill, "Google's Vision for the 21st Century", 26 October 2006, http://www.hsl.unc.edu/google/Videos.cfm (specific video segment: "Google Books/Google Scholar").

91 **Adam Smith:** Smith was asked the question by this book's author during an interview in Mountain View, 19 September 2007. Smith's corporate biography described his position as "Product Management Director at Google with product development responsibility for Content products including Google Book Search, Google Scholar, and Google News Archives."

91 **when Larry Page visited:** Mary Sue Coleman, "Google, the Khmer Rouge and the Public Good," 6 February 2006, http://www.umich.edu/pres/speeches/060206google-print.html.

92 **started by Michael Hart:** Michael Hart, "Gutenberg: The History and Philosophy of Project Gutenberg," [1992?], http://www.gutenberg.org/wiki/Gutenberg:The_History_and_Philosophy_of_Project_Gutenberg_by_Michael_Hart.

93 **eschewed the notion:** Hart, "Gutenberg."

93 **about 6,300 works:** *Project Gutenberg Weekly Newsletter*, 6 November 2002, http://www.pg-news.org/nl_archives/2002/pgweekly_2002_11_06.txt.

93 **the library began:** Library of Congress American Memory, "Mission and History," n.d., http://memory.loc.gov/ammem/about/index.html. In 1994, the National Digital Library Program began with $13 million in donations from the private sector, and with congressional funds that added $15 million over five years and another $45 million in private sponsors between 1994 and 2000. Private foundations were willing to fund pilot programs for digitization of important historical materials, which, in some cases, did include books. The University of Michigan and Cornell University received funding from the Andrew W. Mellon Foundation, for example, to begin a project in 1995 on "Making of America," which entailed digitizing about 1,600 books and ten journals from a narrow swath of time in U.S. history—1850 to 1877. Neither foundation nor the universities, however, contemplated a moon shot, digitizing all books.

93 **$500,000 grant:** National Science Foundation, ITR/IM: The Million Book Project, award abstract #0113878, 21 August 2001, http://www.nsf.gov/awardsearch/showAward.do?AwardNumber=0113878.

93 **stepped forward:** Brewster Kahle, "Public Access to Digital Materials," talk at the Library of Congress, Washington, D.C., 20 November 2002, http://www.loc.gov/rr/program/lectures/video/kahle-press.ram.

93 **another $2.5 million:** Carnegie Mellon Libraries, "Frequently Asked Questions About the Million Book Project," revised 9 April 2007, http://www.library.cmu.edu/Libraries/MBP_FAQ.html.

94 **Kahle was talking up:** Kahle, "Public Access to Digital Materials." Four years after his 2002 talk at the Library of Congress, Kahle described the

opportunity to make all the world's information universally accessible: "This is our chance to one up the Greeks!" Quoted in Kevin Kelly, "Scan This Book!" *New York Times Magazine*, 14 May 2006, http://www.nytimes.com/2006/05/14/magazine/14publishing.html.

94 **When Google's team:** Daniel Clancy, "Google Book Search," talk delivered to Stanford EE380 Computer Systems Colloquium, 15 February 2006, http://stanford-online.stanford.edu/courses/ee380/060215-ee380-250.asx.

95 **The Google solution:** Adam Smith, interview, Mountain View, CA, 19 September 2007.

95 **The human touch:** For two instances of plainly visible fingers, see Duncan Riley, "Google Books Adds Hand Scans," *TechCrunch*, 6 December 2007, http://www.techcrunch.com/2007/12/06/google-books-adds-hand-scans/; Dan Cohen, "Google Fingers," *Dan Cohen* (blog), 26 June 2006, http://www.dancohen.org/2006/06/26/google-fingers/.

95 **Google did not disclose:** Clancy, "Google Book Search."

95 **Other companies:** Microsoft representative Danielle Tiedt put the digitization cost per page as ten cents. "Book Digitization and the Revenge of the Librarians Episode," panel discussion at SXSW Interactive Conference, Austin, TX, 11 March 2006, http://www.podcastdirectory.com/podshows/327406.

96 **Clancy answered:** Clancy, "Google Book Search."

96 **still under copyright:** Earlier book digitization projects had skirted copyright problems by working only with historical works long out of copyright, like "Making of America" and Project Gutenberg. The Million Book Project encountered copyright issues from the moment of its inception. India and China, the two countries most active in the actual scanning for the Million Book Project, passed laws that, in the project's description, "effectively circumvent the need to acquire permission from the copyright owner to digitize copyrighted works." See Carnegie Mellon Libraries, "Frequently Asked Questions About the Million Book Project."

97 **reports had surfaced:** "Amazon Plan Would Allow Searching Texts of Many Books," *New York Times*, 21 July 2003.

97 **Google invited:** Chris Sherman, "Google Introduces Book Searches," *Search Engine Watch*, 17 December 2003, http://searchenginewatch.com/showPage.html?page=3290351.

97 **soothing publishers:** "Publishers Grudgingly Cooperate with Amazon Database Effort," *Publishers Weekly*, 15 September 2003.

97 **When Amazon publicly unveiled:** Gary Price, "Amazon Debuts New Book Search Tool," *Search Engine Watch*, 27 October 2003, http://searchenginewatch.com/showPage .html?page=3098831.

98 **Google Print:** Google began to integrate references to books as early as December 2003, but was unwilling to comment on how many book excerpts were available or even how long the "experiment" would last. See "Google

Experiment Provides Internet with Book Excerpts," *New York Times*, 18 December 2003. The official launch of Google Print came at the Frankfurt Book Fair in October 2004. "History of Google Book Search," http://books.google.com/googlebooks/newsviews/history.html. The following publishers had joined at the time of the official launch: Blackwell, Cambridge University Press, the University of Chicago Press, Houghton Mifflin, Hyperion, McGraw-Hill, Oxford University Press, Pearson, Penguin, Perseus, Princeton University Press, Springer, Taylor & Francis, Thomson Delmar, and Warner Books.

98 **Adam Smith:** Adam Smith, interview, Mountain View, CA, 19 September 2007.

98 **Daniel Clancy would later say:** Clancy, "Google Book Search."

98 **In December 2004:** "Google Checks Out Library Books," Google press release, 14 December 2004, http://www.google.com/press/pressrel/print_library.html.

98 **the participating libraries:** "Google Is Adding Major Libraries to Its Database," *New York Times*, 14 December 2004. The *Times* article said that Stanford was, like Michigan, making nearly all of its library collections available, but this was not the case. See Stanford's press release, "Stanford and Google to Make Library Books Available Online," Stanford News Service press release, 14 December 2004, http://news-service.stanford.edu/pr/2004/pr-google-011205.html.

99 **Jack Romanos:** John Heilemann, "Googlephobia," *New York*, 5 December 2005.

99 **Authors Guild:** "Authors Guild Sues Google, Citing 'Massive Copyright Infringement,'" Authors Guild press release, 20 September 2005, http://www.authorsguild.org/news/sues_google_citing.htm. In addition to the Authors Guild itself, three guild members were the nominal plaintiffs: Daniel Hoffman, Betty Miles, and Herbert Mitgang. For the complaint, see http://fl1.findlaw.com/news.findlaw.com/hdocs/docs/google/aggoog92005cmp.pdf.

100 **a group of publishers:** The McGraw-Hill Companies Inc., Pearson Education, Inc., Penguin Group (USA) Inc., Simon & Schuster, Inc., and John Wiley & Sons, Inc. v. Google Inc., complaint filed in United States District Court, Southern District of New York, 19 October 2005, http://www.publishers.org/press/pdf/40%20McGraw-Hill%20v.%20Google.pdf., 3.

100 **Patricia S. Schroeder:** Heilemann, "Googlephobia."

100 **originated in 1999:** "Don't Be Evil or Don't Lose Value?" *Sydney Morning Herald*, 15 April 2008, http://www.smh.com.au/news/biztech/dont-be-evil/2008/04/15/1208025168177.html.

101 **Patel spread:** Jessica Livingston, *Founders at Work: Stories of Startups' Early Days* (Berkeley, CA: Apress, 2007), 169–70. Buchheit said that "I believe that [the meeting] was sometime in early 2000," but in John Battelle's account, his sources said it took place on 19 July 2001. See Battelle, *The Search*, 138.

101 **"ten things:** Google Web site, "Corporate Information: Our Philosophy," http://www.google.com/intl/en/corporate/tenthings.html.

101 **Critics previously had said:** Danny Sullivan, "14 'Is Google Evil?' Tipping Points Since 2001," *Search Engine Land*, 1 January 2007, http://searchengineland.com/070101-215524.php. One of Sullivan's fourteen "tipping points" was a January 2003 article in *Wired* magazine: "Google vs. Evil," http://www.wired.com/wired/archive/11.01/google_pr.html.

101 **A Thomas Friedman column:** Thomas Friedman, "Is Google God?" *New York Times*, 29 June 2003. Friedman did not refer to Google's "Don't Be Evil" motto; he discussed the company's growing international traffic as an example of how "the world is getting more integrated."

101 **Google dropped:** Jen Grant, "Judging Book Search by Its Cover," *Official Google Blog*, 17 November 2005, http://googleblog.blogspot.com/2005/11/judging-book-search-by-its-cover.html.

102 **When the lawsuits:** Toobin, "Google's Moon Shot."

102 **Mary Sue Coleman:** Coleman, "Google, the Khmer Rouge and the Public Good."

102 **Lawrence Lessig:** Lawrence Lessig, "Four Anti-Google Book Search Fallacies—All In One, Single Essay," *Lessig Blog*, 13 March 2007, http://www.lessig.org/blog/archives/003731.shtml. Another law professor, Columbia's Timothy Wu, offered another argument in defense of Google Print: that it was part of the broader shift from "the culture of authorial control" to that of "authorial exposure." Wu attempted to draw an analogy between Google's index to Web pages and to book pages: "Consider what it would mean, by analogy, if mapmakers needed the permission of landowners to create maps. . . . Imagine how terrible maps would be if you had to negotiate with every landowner in the United States to publish the Rand McNally Road Atlas." Tim Wu, "Leggo My Ego," *Slate*, 17 October 2005, http://www.slate.com/id/2128094/.

103 **three snippets:** Clancy, "Google Book Search."

103 **initiative had begun:** "In Challenge to Google, Yahoo Will Scan Books," *New York Times*, 3 October 2005, http://www.nytimes.com/2005/10/03/business/03yahoo.html.

103 **dependent upon handouts:** "Google Book-Scanning Efforts Spark Debate," *Associated Press Online*, 20 December 2006, http://www.nytimes.com/aponline/technology/AP-Digital-Library.html.

103 **The initiative was stymied:** Tim O'Reilly, "Book Search Should Work Like Web Search," *O'Reilly Radar*, 11 December 2006, http://radar.oreilly.com/archives/2006/12/book_search_sho.html. O'Reilly said that he had spoken with the American Antiquarian Society and Stanford about their willingness to lend their materials for a second scan; both organizations said that the most important rare works would have to be rescanned to attain images of archival quality, but they did say that for the present only a single scan was feasible.

103 **"We want a public library system":** "U. of California Will Provide Up to 3,000 Books a Day to Google for Scanning, Contract States," *Chronicle of Higher Education*, 25 August 2006, http://chronicle.com/free/2006/08/2006082501t.htm.

103 **Microsoft:** "Open Content Alliance Expands Rapidly; Reveals Operational Details," Information Today, 31 October 2005, http://newsbreaks.infotoday.com/nbreader.asp?ArticleID=16091.

103 **limited the scope of its scanning:** Microsoft declined to disclose the number of books that it intended to scan. In June 2006, the company announced agreements with the University of California and University of Toronto libraries, and referred to the size of the collections—34 million volumes and 15 million volumes, respectively—but did not say what percentage would be scanned. See "Microsoft to Collaborate with University of California and University of Toronto Libraries for Windows Live Book Search," Microsoft press release, 8 June 2006, http://www.microsoft.com/presspass/press/2006/jun06/06-08BookSearchPR.mspx.

103 **Thomas Rubin:** Thomas C. Rubin, remarks for the Association of American Publishers Annual Meeting, Yale Club of New York, 6 March 2007, http://www.microsoft.com/presspass/exec/trubin/03-05-07AmericanPublishers.mspx.

104 **As a participant:** "Book Digitization and the Revenge of the Librarians Episode," panel discussion at SXSW Interactive Conference, Austin, TX, 11 March 2006, http://www.podcastdirectory.com/podshows/327406.

104 **Google's Daniel Clancy:** "Book Digitization and the Revenge of the Librarians Episode."

105 **only 100,000 books:** "Google Book-Scanning Efforts Spark Debate," *Associated Press Online*, 20 December 2006, http://www.nytimes.com/aponline/technology/AP-Digital-Library.html.

105 **University of California:** "U. of California Will Provide Up to 3,000 Books a Day." For a copy of the contract between Google and the University of California, see The University of California and Google, Cooperative Agreement, August 2006, http://www.cdlib.org/news/ucgoogle_cooperative_agreement.pdf. The agreement required the university to display "Digitized by Google" on any Web page in which the university displayed any portion of its digital copy.

106 **Just one year:** "Google Book-Scanning Efforts Spark Debate," *Associated Press Online.*

106 **Microsoft was not willing:** Satya Nadella, "Book Search Winding Down," *Live Search,* 23 May 2008, http://blogs.msdn.com/livesearch/archive/2008/05/23/book-search-winding-down.aspx.

106 **In February 2006:** Clancy, "Google Book Search."

106 **Google gave users:** Adam Mathes, "Collect, Share, and Discover Books," *Inside Google Book Search*, 6 September 2007, http://booksearch

.blogspot.com/2007/08/share-and-enjoy.html; Bill Schilit and Okan Kolak, "Dive into the Meme Pool with Google Book Search," *Inside Google Book Search*, 6 September 2007, http://booksearch.blogspot.com/2007/09/dive-into-meme-pool-with-google-book.html; Brandon Badger, "Google Book Search in Google Earth," *Google Lat Long Blog*, 20 August 2007, http://google-latlong.blogspot.com/2007/08/google-book-search-in-google-earth.html. One outside commentator noted that the scarcity of scanned books that are in the public domain and provide the full text prevented the "personal library" from being anything more than "a personal card catalog." Jeffrey R. Young, "Google Allows Cutting and Pasting from Its Library of Books," *Chronicle of Higher Education: The Wired Campus*, 20 September 2007, http:// chronicle.com/wiredcampus/article/2395/google-allows-cutting-and-pasting-from-its-library-of-books.

107 **In May 2007:** Viresh Ratnakar, "Found: More Books," *Inside Google Book Search*, 17 May 2007, http://booksearch.blogspot.com/2007/05/found-more-books.html. Ratnakar's post says little about the scope of the added listings, other than to offhandedly say that now Google Book Search includes "millions of books that we know about but that aren't yet online." He also thanks "our union catalog partners worldwide for helping make this happen."

108 **John E. Sprizzo:** U.S. District Court Southern District of New York, *The Authors Guild, et al. v. Google, Inc.*, and *The McGraw-Hill Companies, Inc., et al, v. Google, Inc.*, "Amended Case Management Order Regarding Coordination and Scheduling," 29 January 2008, https://ecf.nysd.uscourts.gov/doc1/12714389563.

108 **In February 2008:** University of Michigan, "Million," http://www.lib.umich.edu/news/millionth.html; Paul Courant, "One Million Digitized Books," *Au Courant*, 2 February 2008, http://paulcourant.net/2008/02/02/one-million-digitized-books/.

5. GooTube

109 **Google could search:** In its formative early years, Google was devoted to textual information. Even when Google researchers investigated the flow of information in daily life that took the form of a stream of speech, such as when listening to television, making a phone call, or conversing with another person, what was most interesting, from a computer science perspective, was how the constituent words in the stream could be captured and analyzed. In a paper presented at the 12th International World Wide Web Conference in 2003, three Google engineers, one of whom was Sergey Brin, along with an academic colleague, examined the design of an algorithm that would analyze the closed-captioning text accompanying a live television news broadcast and then suggest, on the fly, supplemental news articles found on the Web that would be matched to what was

said every twenty seconds or so in the broadcast. Whether anyone was really interested in such a service was a question left unexamined. But the paper showed, if nothing else, the researchers' interest in finding new text sources—in this case, the closed captioning of broadcasts—that a machine could read. Monika Henzinger, Bay-Wei Chang, Brian Milch, and Sergey Brin, "Query-Free News Search," paper presented at 12th International World Wide Web Conference, 2003, http://people.csail .mit.edu/milch/papers/www2003.pdf. The paper was subsequently published in *World Wide Web: Internet and Web Information Systems* 8(2):101–26 (2005). Henzinger, Chang, and Brin were at Google; Milch was a doctoral student in the Computer Science Division at the University of California, Berkeley, who had a summer research internship at Google in 2002.

110 **Yahoo launched:** "Yahoo! Video Search Beta," *Yahoo! Search Blog*, 15 December 2004, http://www.ysearchblog.com/archives/000060.html. The code that Yahoo suggested that Web publishers provide was an RSS Enclosure tag.

110 **"Web pages are self-describing":** "Search Spotlight Pans to Video," *eWeek*, 17 December 2004, http://www.eweek.com/c/a/Enterprise-Apps/Search-Spotlight-Pans-to-Video/.

110 **If one wanted to search:** Gary Price, "Searching Television via Closed-Captioning," *Search Engine Watch*, 5 November 2004, http://blog.searchenginewatch.com/blog/041105-093901. Three companies that were credited for developing voice-recognition software were HP (Speechbot), Nexidia, and StreamSage.

111 **the day after Yahoo announced:** "TV's Future May Be Web Search Engines That Hunt for Video," *Wall Street Journal*, 16 December 2004.

111 **When CNN was told:** "TV's Future May Be Web Search Engines."

112 **A television industry executive:** "Striking Up Digital Video Search," News.com, 16 December 2004, http://news.com.com/2102-1032_3-5466491.html.

112 **ten San Francisco Bay Area stations:** Chris Sherman, "Google Debuts Video Search," *Search Engine Watch*, 25 January 2005, http://blog.searchenginewatch.com/blog/050125-000100.

112 **about two terabytes:** "Google Launches Video Search," *eWeek*, 25 January 2005, http://www.eweek.com/article2/0,1895,1743640,00.asp.

113 **Executives at CBS:** "Google Sees Content Deals as Key to Long-Term Growth," *Wall Street Journal*, 14 August 2006.

113 **Jawed Karim:** This chapter's account of YouTube's origins is based largely upon Karim's highly detailed "YouTube: From Concept to Hypergrowth," talk at Reflections/Projections conference, sponsored by the Association for Computing Machinery at the University of Illinois at Urbana-Champaign, 21 October 2006, http://www.acm.uiuc.edu/conference/2006/video/UIUC-ACM-RP06-Karim.wmv.

113 ***Wired* magazine:** Clive Thompson, "The BitTorrent Effect," *Wired*, January 2005.

115 **publisher of Flash multimedia software:** The publisher at the time was Macromedia. It was acquired by Adobe in 2005.

115 **Karim knew:** "The Gurus of YouTube," *Time*, 16 December 2006, http://www.time.com/time/magazine/article/0,9171,1570721-2,00.html. In the article Chen concedes that the story of the company's founding that he and Hurley repeated often to members of the press, the version that involves an epiphany about sharing videos that occurred at a dinner party at Chen's apartment, was related to "marketing ideas around creating a story that was very digestible." He and Hurley also reluctantly, but clearly, said that Karim did deserve the credit for the original idea for the site.

115 **His presence tends to be omitted:** The "About YouTube" page (http://www.youtube.com/t/about) on display 15 March 2008 states that the company was founded in February 2005 without naming the trio, but introducing Chen and Hurley by name as the "first members of YouTube management team" after receiving funding from Sequoia Capital. It does provide a link to another page introducing "Founders," http://www.youtube.com/t/founders, which mentions that Karim was present at the time of the company's founding but "left the company to pursue an advanced degree at Stanford."

116 **historic first YouTube video:** *Me at the Zoo,* shot by Yakov Lapitsky, uploaded 23 April 2005, http://www.youtube.com/watch?v=jNOXAC9IVRw. Also uploaded that day was a sixteen-second segment consisting of Karim rolling down a snow-covered road for a few yards: *Rolling down a Hill,* uploaded 23 April 2005, http://www.youtube.com/watch?v=nGzAI5pLbMY. For inanity in its purest form, see *Why Was Steve Late?* featuring Steve Chen and annotated by Karim as *Chad and I Wait for a Late Steve,* uploaded 27 April 2005, http://www.youtube.com/watch?v=8hKqnBiQngA.

116 **they captured:** The video was played by Karim during his October 2006 talk at the University of Illinois.

117 **Arrington praised:** Michael Arrington, "Profile—YouTube," *TechCrunch*, 8 August 2005, http://www.techcrunch.com/2005/08/08/profile-youtube/.

117 ***Matt Dances Around the World*:** Arrington's title was more descriptive than the actual one, which was simply *Man Dancing,* supplied by the short film's author: http://www.youtube.com/watch?v=PaluLFfvOEI.

117 **Slashdot:** "YouTube—The Flickr of Video?" *Slashdot*, 14 August 2005, http://slashdot.org/articles/05/08/14/1320217.shtml?tid=95&tid=129.

117 **cover YouTube's competitors:** Michael Arrington, "Comparing the Flickrs of Video," *TechCrunch*, 6 November 2005, http://www.techcrunch.com/2005/11/06/the-flickrs-of-video/.

118 **would accept videos:** Google Video Beta's Video Upload Program, first posted April 2005, https://upload.video.google.com/. This post contains a link to a second page, "Video Upload Program for Major Producers," https://services.google.com/inquiry/video, which refers to the "1,000 hours

or more of video." It is not possible to tell if the current version of this page is identical to the one posted in April 2005, however, because Google blocked the Wayback Machine's crawler from preserving pages in this directory of the company's Web site.

118 **Jennifer Feikin:** Chris Sherman, "Google Wants Your Video," *Search Engine Watch*, 13 April 2005, http://blog.searchenginewatch.com/blog/050413-163129.

118 **Larry Page:** "Google Video to Accept Public Submissions," *PC World*, 4 April 2005, http://www.pcworld.com/article/id,120284-page,1/article.html.

118 **Page later described:** Larry Page, keynote address at the 2006 International Consumer Electronics Show, 6 January 2006, http://www.google.com/intl/en/press/podium/ces2006.html.

118 **Two months later:** "DVD Jon Modifies Google Video Viewer," ZDNet.co.uk, 30 June 2005, http://news.zdnet.co.uk/software/0,1000000121,39206455,00.htm.

118 **separate one-time installation:** "Google Video Viewer," http://web.archive.org/web/20050629022820/video.google.com/video_download.html, from crawl performed on 28 June 2005.

118 **closed-captioning transcript:** Danny Sullivan, "More Q&A with Google Video Manager," *Search Engine Watch*, 27 June 2005, http://blog.searchenginewatch.com/blog/050627-125353.

119 **self deprecatingly described:** Sullivan, "More Q&A with Google Video Manager."

119 **The only guidelines:** YouTube help page (preserved at Internet Archive, crawled 1 August 2005), http://web.archive.org/web/20050724003639/ www.youtube.com/help.php. From April to 1 August 2005, YouTube's guidelines for uploading did not mention copyright considerations. The Internet Archive's Wayback Machine preserves the precise day—2 August 2005—when the guidelines were expanded to include YouTube's avowal that it "respects the rights of copyright holders and publishers and is only accepting video uploads from persons who hold all necessary rights to the uploaded material." See YouTube help page preserved at the Internet Archive, crawled 2 August 2005, http:/web.archive.org/web/20051001080750/youtube.com/ help.php.

119 **more than 150 online auction sites:** Randall Stross, *eBoys: The First Inside Account of Venture Capitalists at Work* (New York: Crown, 2000), 76.

119 **By November:** "YouTube Receives $3.5M in Funding from Sequoia Capital," YouTube press release, 7 November 2005, http://www.youtube.com/press_room_entry?entry=OPPIn7PRss.

119 **doubled again:** "YouTube Opens Internet Video to the Masses," YouTube press release, 15 December 2005, http://www.youtube.com/press_room_entry?entry=OcN9xXYar1g.

120 **Sequoia Capital:** When YouTube's cofounders knocked on Sequoia's door, they had better than even odds that Sequoia would be interested by virtue of

shared ties within clubby Silicon Valley. YouTube's Chen, Hurley, and Karim all were PayPal alumni, as was Sequoia's Botha, who had been PayPal's chief financial officer—and Sequoia had been a PayPal investor. The PayPal connection did not mean that funding would be assured, however. When a comment on Matt Marshall's *VentureBeat* blog suggested that the YouTube entrepreneurs enjoyed "a unique competitive advantage" when approaching Sequoia, Marshall pointed out that "Sequoia's not going to back you just because you knew one of their partners. But true, if you *do* know one of their partners, and they respect you and trust you, sure, you have an unfair advantage." Matt Marshall, "Q&A with Roelof Botha, the Web 2.0 Guy at Sequoia Capital," *VentureBeat*, 1 June 2006, http://venturebeat.com/2006/06/01/qa-with-roelof-botha-the-web-20-guy-at-sequoia-capital/.

121 **Larry Page:** Page, 2006 International Consumer Electronics Show.

121 **closed the video store:** Google did not issue a press release. It merely sent an e-mail message on 10 August 2007 to the store's customers, with the subject heading "Important Information About Your Google Video Account," which explained: "In an effort to improve all Google services, we will no longer offer the ability to buy or rent videos for download from Google Video, ending the DTO/DTR (download-to-own/rent) program. This change will be effective August 15, 2007." The company did not offer a refund, only a credit that could be redeemed at Google Checkout, a decision that brought upon the company even more opprobrium. A few days later, the company relented. Bindu Reddy, Google Video's product manager, wrote a humorous post on *Official Google Blog* to acknowledge, "We had made a mistake in the case of *Google Video's Download to Own/Rent Refund Policy vs. Common Sense*." See Bindu Reddy, "An Update on Google Video Feedback," *Official Google Blog*, 20 August 2007, http://googleblog.blogspot.com/2007/08/update-on-google-video-feedback.html.

121 **The pact with the NBA:** "Google Online Video Store Starts Without a Bang," *USA Today*, 19 January 2006, http://www.usatoday.com/money/industries/technology/2006-01-19-google-video_x.htm.

121 **further restricted:** Cory Doctorow, "Google Video Robs Customers of the Videos They 'Own,'" *BoingBoing*, 10 August 2007, http://www.boingboing.net/2007/08/10/google_video_robs_cu.html. Doctorow wrote that Google's video store and Amazon's Unbox store "claim to 'sell' you things, but you can never truly own the things they sell—they are your theoretical property only, liable to confiscation at any time. That's the lesson for DRM [digital rights management]: only the big motion-picture companies, search giants, and other corporate overlords get to own property. We vassals are mere tenant-farmers, with a precarious claim on our little patch of dirt."

121 **content delivery networks:** The content delivery network that appeared to be YouTube's principal distribution partner, but that never officially confirmed the relationship, was Limelight Networks. For a brief introduction to Lime-

light and its older competitor Akamai Networks, another CDN, see Michael Bazeley, "Video Is Hot, Continued: Limelight Raises $130 Million," *VentureBeat*, 25 July 2006, http://venturebeat.com/2006/07/25/video-is-hot-continued-limelight-raises-130-million/; "Limelight Readies for Spotlight," *Forbes*, 23 January 2007, http://www.forbes.com/2007/01/23/limelight-youtube-broadband-tech-intel-cx_df_0123limelight.html?partner=yahootix.

121 **additional $8 million:** "YouTube Uploads $8M in Funding," YouTube press release, 5 April 2006, http://www.youtube.com/press_room_entry?entry=jwIToyFs2Lc. The press release referred only to Sequoia and omitted the participation of Artis Capital Management, whose contribution became public knowledge in a later regulatory filing. See "Hedge Fund Scores on YouTube," *PE Week*, 9 October 2006, http://www.pewnews.com/story.asp?sectioncode=44&storycode=40625.

121 **bills were paid:** YouTube's single largest cost was paying for the bandwidth to deliver videos to its users. It apparently enjoyed a significant discount in the rate it was charged by Limelight Networks, its service provider, because of the scale of YouTube's operations, serving 200 terabytes of videos daily in April 2006. The standard charge was a penny per minute of streamed video, but YouTube was reported to pay between a tenth of a cent and half a cent per minute. See "Your Tube, Whose Dime?" *Forbes*, 28 April 2006, http://www.forbes.com/home/intelligentinfrastructure/2006/04/27/video-youtube myspace_cx_df_0428video.html.

122 **interviewed by *Wired*:** Frank Rose, "Are You Ready for Googlevision?" *Wired*, May 2006, http://www.wired.com/wired/archive/14.05/google.html.

122 **When a reporter:** "Inside a Web Giant's Manic Search for Staying Power," *Chicago Tribune*, 20 September 2006, http://www.chicagotribune.com/technology/chi-0609200122sep20,1,5465696.story.

122 **YouTube began to run:** Chad Hurley, interviewed on *Charlie Rose*, 11 August 2006.

122 **Robert Tur:** "YouTube Dances the Copyright Tango," News.com, 24 July 2006, http://news.com.com/YouTube+dances+the+copyright+tango/2100-1025_3-6097365.html.

122 **Digital Millenium Copyright Act:** Another clause in the DMCA requires Web sites to remove copyright-infringing material when it is brought to their attention, and when NBC had asked YouTube to remove *Lazy Sunday: The Chronicles of Narnia*, a hip-hop parody clip from *Saturday Night Live*, YouTube had done so—and received free national publicity in the bargain. "SNL Cult Hit Yanked from Video-Sharing Site," News.com, 17 February 2006, http://news.com.comSNL+cult+hit+yanked+from+video-sharing+site/2100-1026_3-6041031.html.

122 **Revver's Oliver Luckett:** Digital Hollywood, "Building Blocks 2006," San Jose, CA, 15 August 2006, http://www.digitalhollywood.com/%231BBlkSessions/BBTuesOne.html.

123 **Ahree Lee:** Lee's story was told by Scott Roesch, vice president at AtomFilms. Digital Hollywood, "Building Blocks 2006," San Jose, CA, 15 August 2006, http://www.digitalhollywood.com/%231BBlkSessions/BBTuesOne.html. The YouTube version is labeled *Me: Girl Takes Pic of Herself Every Day for Three Years:* http://www.youtube.com/watch?v=55YyaJIrmzo. The full version at AtomFilms is found at http://www.atomfilms.com/film/me.jsp.

123 **Chane was asked:** Digital Hollywood, http://www.digitalhollywood.com/%231BBlkSessions/ BBTuesOne.html.

124 **$10.6 million:** "Google's YouTube to Launch New Type of Ads," *San Jose Mercury News*, 21 August 2007.

124 **had yet to earn a profit:** Hurley, on *Charlie Rose*.

124 **"I was really confident on:** "Personal Journey with Steve Chen," Committee of 100's Sixteenth Annual Conference, New York, 21 April 2007, Part 4, http://www.youtube.com/watch?v=om3_nao3rZ0.

125 **Before the deal closed:** Matt Marshall, "Q&A with Roelof Botha, the Web 2.0 Guy at Sequoia Capital," *VentureBeat*, 1 June 2006, http://venturebeat.com/2006/06/01/qa-with-roelof-botha-the-web-20-guy-at-sequoia-capital/.

125 **Google executives:** "Google Q3 2006 Earnings Call Transcript," transcript of 19 October 2006 call, prepared by SeekingAlpha, http://www.seekingalpha.com/article/18858-google-q3-2006-earnings-call-transcript.

126 **how does one make money:** *Valleywag* published an unverifiable report in March 2008 that Eric Schmidt had told YouTube employees at the time of the acquisition that they need not worry about revenue but more recently told them, "Forget I said that." Owen Thomas, "Eric Schmidt Puts the Screws on YouTube," *Valleywag*, 18 March 2008, http://valleywag.com/369296/eric-schmidt-puts-the-screws-on-youtube.

126 **An analyst with the Yankee Group:** The Yankee Group analyst was Anton Denissov. "YouTube Looks for the Money Clip," *Fortune*, 25 March 2008, http://techland.blogs.fortune.cnn.com/2008/03/25/youtube-looks-for-the-money-clip/.

126 **In April 2008:** "Exclusive Interview with Google's Eric Schmidt," *CNBC*, 30 April 2008, http://www.cnbc.com/id/24387350/site/14081545.

126 **higher-resolution video:** "YouTube Videos in High Quality," *Broadcasting Ourselves* (the YouTube blog), 14 March 2008, http://www.youtube.com/blog?entry=ponKL3LTyr0.

126 **YouTube Everywhere:** "YouTube Everywhere," *Broadcasting Ourselves*, 11 March 2008, http://www.youtube.com/blog?entry=yFIR6EEySg8.

127 **acquire the *New York Times:*** In spring 2007, Eric Schmidt said Google was not interested in "businesses where we would own the content." "Google: No Plans to Exit Fast Lane," *E-Commerce Times*, 11 May 2007, http://www.ecommercetimes.com/story/57347.html. But one year later, when asked if Google might consider acquiring the *New York Times*, Schmidt allowed that "I'd never rule anything out." Without talking about the future, he looked to

the past and observed, "So far, we've stayed away from buying content." He added, "It's not our area of expertise. But the more strategic answer is that we'd be picking winners. We'd be disenfranchising a potential new entrant. Our principle is providing all the world's information." Russ Mitchell, "Search Mission," *Portfolio*, April 2008, http://www.portfolio.com/executives/features/2008/03/14/Google-CEO-Eric-Schmidt-Interview.

6. Small World, After All

129 **He was eager:** "Google Maps Is Changing the Way We See the World," *Wired*, July 2007, http://www.wired.com/techbiz/it/magazine/15-07/ff_maps.

130 **basement of the Pentagon:** This chapter draws heavily on two interviews with John Hanke, in Mountain View, CA, on 10 August and 21 August 2007. Google had no need for the Silicon Graphics computers that the Pentagon had depended upon to display satellite images. Silicon Graphics's story tangentially touched Google's for an entirely different reason: when the older computer manufacturer fell on hard times, it had to vacate its corporate headquarters in Mountain View. The new tenant—Google—turned this into the Googleplex.

131 **"Jane Austen layer":** "Jane Austen's Life & Works," *Google Earth Community*, 7 April 2006, http://bbs.keyhole.com/ubb/showthreaded.php/Cat/0/Number/411188.

131 **Keyhole's founders:** The team of founders included Mark Aubin, John Hanke, Michael Jones, Phil Keslin, and Brian McClendon, and Chikai Ohazama, who would end up at Google, and Remi Arnaud, Christopher Tanner, and Avi Bar-Zeev, who departed Keyhole before Google's acquisition.

134 **In March 2003:** "Tiny Tech Company Awes Viewers," *USA Today*, 21 March 2003.

134 **$400 annually:** "Google Earth Pro," Google information page at Keyhole.com domain, n.d. [2004?], https://registration.keyhole.com/choice_kh_initial.html.

136 **Keyhole agreed to be acquired:** "Google Acquires Keyhole Corp," Google press release, 27 October 2004, http://www.google.com/press/pressrel/keyhole.html.

137 **principal innovation:** Bret Taylor, "Mapping Your Way," *Official Google Blog*, 8 February 2005, http://googleblog.blogspot.com/2005/02/mapping-your-way.html.

137 **Keyhole promised:** "Keyhole2 Lt," Keyhole Web page (apparently predating Google's acquisition), http://www.keyhole.com/body.php?h=products&t=keyhole2LT.

138 **six months after its release:** Mike Pegg, "Google Maps Blog Buzz—BlackBerry, Google Maps Ads, DIY," *Google Maps Mania*, 16 January 2006,

http://googlemapsmania.blogspot.com/2006/01/google-maps-blog-buzz -blackberry.html; Gary Price, "Still Seeing 'Blue Pins' on Some Google Maps; Google Now Testing Paid Links in Google Earth," *Search Engine Watch*, 18 January 2006, http://blog.searchenginewatch.com/blog/060118-112211. Google began offering the advertisements without an announcement. When asked about ads that were appearing in a Google service that formerly had not carried any advertising, a Google spokesperson said, "We are currently conducting a limited test of ads in Google Earth. We do not have any other specifics to share at this time."

138 **Paul Rademacher:** "Google Maps Is Changing the Way We See the World," *Wired*, July 2007, http://www.wired.com/techbiz/it/magazine/15-07/ff _maps.

139 **fast food restaurants:** fastfoodmaps.com, http://www.fastfoodmaps.com/.

139 **lowest gas prices:** *Times Herald-Record*, "Record Gas Watch," http:// www.thrnewmedia.com/maps/gas2.html.

139 **crime reports for Chicago:** *EveryBlock Chicago,* http://chicago.every block.com/.

139 **news stories in the day's *New York Times: Mibazaar,*** http://www .mibazaar.com/worldnews/index.html.

139 **thousands of other mashup sites:** One directory to Google Maps mashups is Google Maps Mania—unaffiliated with Google: http://googlemapsmania .blogspot.com/.

139 **Barry Diller:** "The Earth Is Ready For Its Close-Up," *Newsweek*, 6 June 2005.

139 **Eric Schmidt recounted:** Google Inc. Press Day, 10 May 2006, http:// www.google.com/press/pressday.html.

140 **correct the locations:** Ramesh Balakrishnan, "It's Your World. Map It," *Google Lat Long Blog*, 18 March 2008, http://google-latlong.blogspot.com/ 2008/03/its-your-world-map-it.html.

140 **helped the Coast Guard:** "Google Annual Report 2005", 2006, http:// investor.google.com/pdf/2005_Google_AnnualReport.pdf., 2.

140 **effects of clear-cut logging:** Rebecca Moore, "Trading a Bow and Arrow for a Laptop," *Google Lat Long Blog*, 15 June 2007, http://google-latlong.blog spot.com/2007/06/trading-bow-and-arrow-for-laptop.html.

140 **U.S. Holocaust Memorial Museum:** "USHMM + Google Earth," United States Holocaust Memorial Museum Web page, http://www.ushmm.org/ googleearth/.

141 **"The ability of people":** John Hanke interview, 21 August 2007.

141 **photos of the earth:** Poet Archibald MacLeish memorably described the impact of Anders's photographs: "To see the Earth as it truly is, small and blue and beautiful in that eternal silence where it floats, is to see ourselves as riders on the Earth together, brothers on that bright loveliness in the eternal cold—brothers who know now that they are truly brothers." Quoted in

Peggy Wilhide, "New Views for a New Century," *Aerospace Technology Innovation*, July/August 2000, http://ipp.nasa.gov/innovation/Innovation_84/wnewview.html.

141 **Robert M. Samborski:** "Start-Ups Try to Plot a Complete Picture," *Washington Post*, 27 November 2006.

142 **natural geologic formation:** "In Pictures: The Strangest Sights in Google Earth," *PC World*, second image, http://www.pcworld.com/article/id,134186-page,2-c,mapping/article.html. It can also be seen at Google Maps: http://maps.google.com/maps?f=q&hl=en&q=medicine%2Bhat,%2Balberta&ie=UTF8&z=16&11=50.010083,-110.113006&spn=0.009432,0.026951&t=k&om=1%20/.

142 **Arizona farmer:** "In Pictures: The Strangest Sights in Google Earth," fifth image, http://www.pcworld.com/article/id,134186-page,5-c,mapping/article.html.

142 **forty-year-old barracks:** "Navy to Alter Swastika-Shaped Barracks," Associated Press, 26 September 2007, http://ap.google.com/article/ALeqM5i8o4u2vVJILcEt_tFMtGnH_sYJ4w. The navy said that it would spend $600,000 on landscaping and structures to alter its appearance from above. The barracks can be seen at Google Maps: http://tinyurl.com/2x659b&usg=AFQjCNHivL1I0GhIhhuskrcNs1qwFgM1g. For nineteen more Google Maps images of no less interest than the swastika-shaped barracks, see the collection assembled by Chris Silver Smith, "20 Awesome Images Found in Google Maps," *Search Engine Land*, 14 January 2008, http://searchengineland.com/080114-124703.php.

142 **Sky in Google Earth:** Lior Ron, "Sky: The Final Frontier," *Google Lat Long Blog*, 22 August 2007, http://google-latlong.blogspot.com/2007/08/sky-final-frontier.html.

142 **Hanke attempted:** "Google Lets Users Spy on Satellite Images," *Advertiser*, 8 April 2005.

142 **available satellite imagery:** FAQ, *DigitalGlobe*, accessed 20 August 2007, http://www.digitalglobe.com/press/FAQ_press.shtml.

143 **the first sighting:** "Bloggers Ogle at Google Earth's Topless Sunbathers," *Daily Mail*, 28 September 2006, http://www.dailymail.co.uk/pages/live/articles/news/news.html?in_article_id=407401&in_page_id=1770&in_a_source. A Google spokesperson gave a lighthearted comment: "Things like this do happen and people will find them for a bit of fun."

143 **A9:** "The Earth Is Ready for Its Close-Up," *Newsweek*.

143 **Microsoft announced:** "New Windows Live Local Service Delivers State-of-the-Art Advances for Web-Based Mapping and Local Search," Microsoft press release, 7 December 2005, http://www.microsoft.com/presspass/press/2005/dec05/12-07NewLiveLocalPR.mspx.

143 **A year after:** John Hanke, "Happy Birthday, Google Earth," *Official Google Blog*, 12 June 2006, http://googleblog.blogspot.com/2006/06/happy-birthday-google-earth.html.

144 **flight simulator:** Marco Gallotta, "Google Earth Flight Simulator," *Marco's Blog*, 31 August 2007, http://marco-za.blogspot.com/2007/08/google-earth-flight-simulator.html. Frank Taylor, "Google Earth Flight Simulator Tips," *Google Earth Blog* (an independent blog unaffiliated with Google), 3 September 2007, http://www.gearthblog.com/blog/archives/2007/09/ google_earth_flight.html. Visitors to Google's blog interested in finding help for using the flight simulator were directed to Taylor's post. See Gerhard Wesp, "Where Do You Want to Fly Today?" *Google Lat Long Blog*, 6 September 2007, http://google-latlong.blogspot.com/2007/09/where-do-you-want-to-fly-today.html.

144 **Rand McNally:** Lauren Weinstein noted in a People for Internet Responsibility forum the similarity of Google Street View and the Rand McNally maps. See his post on 13 August 2007, http://forums.pfir.org/main/messages/663/696.html. He provides an example of a page from a Photo-Auto Map that was for a trip from Toledo to Detroit: http://www.pfir.org/photo-auto.jpg.

145 **only streets in San Francisco:** Stephen Chau, "Introducing . . . Street View!" *Google Lat Long Blog*, 29 May 2007, http://google-latlong.blogspot.com/2007/05/introducing-street-view.html. Street views for San Diego, Los Angeles, Houston, and Orlando were added in August 2007. Chau, "More Street View Cities," *Google Lat Long Blog*, 7 August 2007, http://google-latlong.blogspot.com/2007/08/more-street-view-cities.html. San Diego images had the same high resolution as did San Francisco's.

145 **Mary Kalin-Casey:** "Google Maps Is Spying on My Cat, Says Freaked Out BB Reader," *BoingBoing*, 30 May 2007, http://www.boingboing.net/2007/05/30/google_maps_is_spyin.html. See also Xeni Jardin's follow-up post, "Google Street View: A Cavalcade of Reactions, Gag Pix, Paranoid Rants," *BoingBoing*, 5 June 2007, http://www.boingboing.net/2007/06/05/google-street-view-a.html. In April 2008, Street View again drew attention when Aaron and Christine Boring, a Pittsburgh couple, sued Google for invasion of privacy for including photographs of their home, located on a "clearly marked 'Private Road,' in Street View." "Couple Sues Google over 'Street View,'" *The Smoking Gun*, 4 April 2008, http:// www.thesmokinggun.com/archive/years/2008/0404081google1.html. Press coverage of the case led to the discovery that Google's cameras had traveled down the long, winding driveway of the home of the Borings' neighbors, Janet and George McKee: "Warning: Google Is in Your Driveway!" *The Smoking Gun*, 7 April 2008, http://www.thesmokinggun.com/archive/years/2008/0407081google1.html.

145 ***Wired* magazine's blog:** Ryan Singel, "Request for Urban Street Sightings: Submit and Vote on the Best Urban Images Captured by New Google Maps Tool," *Wired Blog Network*, 30 May 2007, http://blog.wired.com/27bstroke6/2007/05/request_for_urb.html. Another site, Streetviewr, whose tagline was "Because Seeing Is Believing," collected more than six hundred

submissions, http://streetviewr.com/. Its home page in late September 2007 indicated that submissions were no longer being accepted and the site owner was planning to bring the "experiment" to a close. Another blog that sprang up, *Google Maps Mania*, provided a guide, "6 Ways to Find Cool Google Maps Street Views," 9 June 2007, http://googlemapsmania.blogspot.com/2007/06/6-ways-to-find-cool-google-maps-street.html.

145 **it had anticipated the need:** "Google Zooms In Too Close for Some," *New York Times*, 1 June 2007, http://www.nytimes.com/2007/06/01/technology/01private.html.

146 **When Lance Ulanoff:** Lance Ulanoff, "Google Is Watching You," *PC Magazine*, 1 August 2007, http://www.pcmag.com/article2/0,1895,2165020,00.asp. In October 2007, Google added street views of six additional cities—Chicago, Pittsburgh, Philadelphia, Phoenix, Portland, and Tucson—with the "added bonus" of high-resolution images in Phoenix, Tucson, and parts of Chicago. See Stephanie Lafon, "More Street View Cities to Explore," *Google Lat Long Blog*, 11 October 2007, http://google-latlong.blogspot.com/2007/10/more-street-view-cities-to-explore.html.

146 **Peter Fleischer:** "Street View and Privacy," *Google Lat Long Blog*, 24 September 2007, http://google-latlong.blogspot.com/2007/09/street-view-and-privacy.html.

147 **In May 2008:** Andrea Frome, "Street View Revisits Manhattan," *Google Lat Long Blog*, 12 May 2008, http://google-latlong.blogspot.com/2008/05/street-view-revisits-manhattan.html. The face-blurring technology was in development for a year, but face recognition is a longstanding challenge in computer science and has yet to be fully mastered. Google's software was less than perfect in identifying faces. See Stephen Shankland, "Google Begins Blurring Faces in Street View," *News.com news blog*, 13 May 2008, http://news.cnet.com/8301-10784_3-9943140-7.html.

147 **the governments:** "Governments Tremble at Google's Bird's-Eye View," *New York Times*, 20 December 2005, http://www.nytimes.com/2005/12/20/technology/20image.html.

147 **When the RAND Corporation:** RAND Corporation, "Publicly Available Federal Geospatial Information of Little Unique Risk to Terrorists, Rand Study Says," press release, 25 March 2004, https://rand.org/news/press.04/03.25.html.

147 **government officials:** "Top Secret, in Plain View," *San Francisco Chronicle*, 18 May 2007, http://www.sfgate.com/cgi-bin/article.cgi?file=/c/a/2007/05/18/MNGR2PTFPL1.DTL.

148 **One cartoon:** *New Yorker*, 1 October 2007, 80, http://www.cartoonbank.com/item/124378.

148 **more serious criticisms:** "Google Earth Makes Some Officials Nervous," *City Room* (blog), *New York Times*, 28 June 2007, http://cityroom.blogs.nytimes.com/2007/06/28/google-earth-makes-some-officials-nervous/;

"Papers Portray Plot as More Talk Than Action," *New York Times*, 4 June 2007, http://www.nytimes.com/2007/06/04/nyregion/04plot.html.

149 **Elinor Mills:** Elinor Mills, "Google Balances Privacy, Reach," News.com, 14 July 2005, http://news.com.com/Google+balances+privacy%2C+reach/2100-1032_3-5787483.html.

149 **lashed out:** "Google's Chief Is Googled, to the Company's Displeasure," *New York Times*, 8 August 2005, http://www.nytimes.com/2005/08/08/technology/08google.html.

149 ***Register* derided:** "Google Snubs Press in Privacy Fury," *The Register*, 6 August 2007, http://www.theregister.co.uk/2005/08/06/google_privacy_snub/.

149 ***New York Times* headline:** Randall Stross, "Google Anything, So Long as It's Not Google," *New York Times*, 28 August 2005, http://www.nytimes.com/2005/08/28/technology/28digi.html.

150 **quietly restored:** Elinor Mills, "Google to Yahoo: Ours Is Bigger," News.com, 26 September 2005, http://www.news.com/Google-touts-size-of-its-search-index/2100-1038_3-5883345.html; "Google Talks to CNET Again," *The Register*, 28 September 2005, http://www.theregister.co.uk/2005/09/28/google_talks_cnet/. *The Register*'s amusing subheadline was "Sulk Cancelled."

150 **Schmidt never released:** Three years after his intemperate punishment of CNET over Elinor Mills's article, Schmidt had an opportunity to present to Mills a more cooperative, helpful demeanor. Instead he was most unhelpful, which gave Mills the opportunity to write an amusing account of her one-on-one interview with him: "My Stunted Interview with Google's Eric Schmidt," News.com, 29 February 2008, http://www.news.com/8301-10784_3-9883410-7.html.

150 **created unease:** The reach of Google's cameras was imagined by some as being ridiculously intrusive, or at least was a convenient subject for someone with a sharp sense of humor. See the Street View image of a commercial sign with letters that spelled out, as if it were a file placed on a Web site to block a search engine crawler, a four-line message for Google's camera van:

robots.txt
User-agent;
GoogleVan;
Disallow: bedroom

See "robots.txt" at "Request for Urban Street Sightings," *Wired Blog Network*, 30 May 2007, http://blog.wired.com/27bstroke6/2007/05/request_for_urb.html.

150 **excited the same reaction:** Xeni Jardin of *BoingBoing* asked a different hypothetical question: "Would we feel differently about street-level image mapping if it were done by a government agency? The FBI? CIA? NSA? DHS? Not implying that it should be, and this isn't 'backlash.' Just asking aloud."

See "Google Street View: Would It Be More/Less Evil If It Were CIA or NSA?" *BoingBoing*, 3 June 2007, http://www.boingboing.net/2007/06/03/google-street-view-w.html.

7. A Personal Matter

154 **Qualcomm calls:** "Intel Makes a Push into Pocket-Size Internet Devices," *New York Times*, 2 April 2008, http://www.nytimes.com/2008/04/02/technology/02chip.html. Intel, which introduced a family of chips that compete with Qualcomm's, has its own term for the category of devices that fall in between a laptop and a cell phone: *mobile internet devices.*

154 **providing Google Docs users:** Philip Tucker, "Bringing the Cloud with You," *Official Google Docs Blog*, 31 March 2008, http://googledocs.blogspot.com/2008/03/bringing-cloud-with-you.html.

154 **When Eric Schmidt was chief executive:** "Google Gets Ready to Rumble with Microsoft," *New York Times*, 16 December 2007, http://www.nytimes.com/2007/12/16/technology/16goog.html.

154 **acquired in 2006:** "New Beginnings," *Official Google Docs Blog*, 10 October 2006, http://googledocs.blogspot.com/2006/10/new-beginnings.html.

154 **presentations module:** Jeff Grimes, "And Now We Present . . ." *Official Google Docs Blog*, 17 September 2007, http://googledocs.blogspot.com/2007_09_01_archive.html.

155 **Eric Schmidt predicted:** "Google Gets Ready to Rumble," *New York Times*.

155 **Sergey Brin:** "Former Students Go Far with Search-Only Site," *Stanford Daily*, 12 April 2000, http://www.stanforddaily.com/article/2000/4/12/innovationGooglesOfDollarsShyFormerStudentsGoFarWithSearchonlySite; "'HailStorm' on the Horizon," Microsoft press release, 19 March 2001, http://www.microsoft.com/presspass/features/2001/mar01/03-19hailstorm .mspx.

155 **The year before, Larry Page:** Danny Sullivan, "Google Goes Forward," *Search Engine Report*, 29 June 1999, http://searchenginewatch.com/showPage.html?page=2167311.

156 **Paul Buchheit:** Jessica Livingston, *Founders at Work: Stories of Startups' Early Days* (Berkeley, CA: Apress, 2007), 162–63. When Gmail was released two years later, on 1 April 2004, Google's press release boasted that it was the result of Google's policy of providing engineers with the freedom to devote 20 percent of their workweek on a project of their own choosing. "Google Gets the Message, Launches Gmail," Google press release, 1 April 2004, http://www.google.com/press/pressrel/gmail.html. The myth that Gmail was produced by the "20 percent" policy was repeated again in 2008 when Google produced a promotional video in which Joseph O'Sullivan, a Google engineer who had worked on the Gmail team, repeated the claim; http://www.youtube.com/watch?v=KCXxFdpsus0. Philipp Lenssen's *Google*

Blogoscoped called attention to the discrepancy between O'Sullivan's claim and Buchheit's own disavowal that Gmail came from the "20 percent" policy. Buchheit wrote: "Oh no, now even Joseph is repeating the Gmail in 20% time myth! . . . It wasn't a 20% project—it was my regular project. It predates the 20% time rule, in fact (though I always had side projects anyway)." O'Sullivan subsequently hedged his statement, and Buchheit wrote in again to emphasize that "20% is important as a concept because it gives license to work on things that other people don't think are important." See Lenssen's "Google Distorting Info on 20% Time?" *Google Blogoscoped*, 24 March 2008, http://blogoscoped.com/archive/2008-03-24-n79.html.

156 **Brian Rakowski:** Much of the material concerning the early history of Gmail is based on an interview with Brian Rakowski, Mountain View, CA, 2 October 2007.

157 **Ads are never going:** "Marissa Mayer, VP of Search Products and User Experience at Google," *iinnovate*, podcast, 31 August 2007, http://iinnovate.blogspot.com/2007/08/marissa-mayer-vp-of-search-products-and.html.

159 **AdSense was launched:** "Google Builds World's Largest Advertising and Search Monetization Program," Google press release, 4 March 2003, http://www.google.com/press/pressrel/advertising.html. AdSense revenues would soon account for more than $1 billion in revenue per quarter for Google, though it should be noted that 85 percent of the gross revenue was spent on traffic-acquisition costs, most of which was the revenue share that Google split with the sites that hosted the advertisements, so Google earned only about a 15 percent margin on its AdSense business.

160 **press announcement:** "Google Gets the Message, Launches Gmail," Google Press release, 1 April 2004, http://www.google.com/press/pressrel/gmail.html.

161 **At *Slashdot*:** "Google's Gmail to Offer 1GB E-mail Storage?" *Slashdot,* 31 March 2004, http://slashdot.org/articles/04/04/01/0038200.shtml?tid=126&tid=95. See LostCluster's comments with the subject heading "Re: Wahoo."

161 **The confusion led:** "Google's April 1 Cock-Up," *The Inquirer*, 2 April 2004, http://www.theinquirer.net/en/inquirer/news/2004/04/02/googles-april-1-cock-up.

161 **intentionally trying to probe:** Google attempted to quell public concerns by issuing a clarifying statement about its privacy policies, but its attorneys made things worse when they said, "If you request that we delete your e-mail, it may remain on a backup system for a while," without making clear that Google would indeed fulfill the user's request. When Larry Page was asked in an interview about the policy statement's ambiguous language, he said, "You wouldn't want us to lose your mail, either. There's a trade-off." This only served to confirm the fears of critics. See "Google Guys," *Playboy*, September 2004, http://www.sec.gov/Archives/edgar/data/1288776/000119312504139655/ds1a.htm#toc59330_25b.

161 **Jen Fitzpatrick:** Jen Fitzpatrick, "The Science and Art of User Experience at Google," talk at Google, 7 June 2006, http://video.google.com/videoplay?docid=6459171443654125383&.

162 **In January 2006:** Aaron Whyte, "It's in the mail . . . ," *Official Google Blog*, 20 January 2006, http://googleblog.blogspot.com/2006/01/its-in-mail.html.

162 **In their 2004 *Playboy*:** "Google Guys," *Playboy.*

162 **Brin tried to call attention:** "Google Guys," *Playboy.*

162 **attack on Gmail:** "California Senate Approves Anti-Gmail Bill," News.com, 27 May 2004, http://www.news.com/California%20Senate%20approves%20anti-Gmail%20bill/2100-1028_3-5222062.html.

163 **HailStorm:** Mark Lucovsky, interview, Mountain View, CA, 29 January 2007. Looking back on HailStorm in 2007, when Lucovsky was a Google employee and was asked whether he thought another company today could fill the role of the trusted central hub, unifying all personal data, he said he thought no company would ever be trusted sufficiently to succeed. "I don't think it could be a Google," he said. "I don't think it could be a Yahoo. I don't think it could be a Microsoft. It's a really hard story to tell, to say, 'We're doing this for the good of everything.' Nobody trusts that story. I think HailStorm, to some extent, ruined it for the Web. The opportunity came and went."

163 **derision:** Randall Stross, "Trust Us (Again)," *U.S. News & World Report*, 4 June 2001.

164 **a coalition of privacy groups:** Jeff Chester, of the Center for Digital Democracy, et al., letter to Federal Trade Commission chairman Timothy Muris, 23 October 2001, http://epic.org/privacy/consumer/microsoft/ftcletter10.23.01.html. Other documents related to Microsoft Passport are available on the Electronic Privacy Information Center's Web page "Microsoft Passport Investigation Docket," http://epic.org/privacy/consumer/microsoft/passport.html.

164 **Microsoft was unable to sign up:** "Microsoft Has Quietly Shelved Its Internet 'Persona' Service," *New York Times*, 11 April 2002. At the time of HailStorm's debut a year previously, Microsoft had placed onstage representatives from American Express, eBay, Expedia, and two other, smaller companies who showed prototypes and conceptual demos, all of whom subsequently backed out. See " 'HailStorm' on the Horizon," Microsoft press release.

165 **"Is Google reading":** Gmail Help Center, "Is Google Reading My Email?": https://mail.google.com/support/bin/answer.py?answer=6599&topic=1546.

165 **Brad Templeton:** Brad Templeton, "Privacy Subtleties of GMail," essay published online, April 2004, http://www.templetons.com/brad/gmail.html.

166 **distant fourth place:** In the United States, Yahoo Mail had 54 million users; Microsoft's Hotmail, 32 million; AOL, 31 million; and Gmail, only 12 million. "Google Buys Web Security Specialist," *San Jose Mercury News*, 10 July 2007.

166 **Justin.tv:** Michael Seibel, Justin.tv's CEO, said in October 2007 that the site received 500,000 unique visitors in its first five days after its launch, 11,500 accounts were created, and 15 percent of those account holders broadcast video. E-mail correspondence with author, 9 October 2007. For a commentary about the quality of Justin.tv's programming, see Randall Stross, "A Site Warhol Would Love," *New York Times*, 14 October 2007.

166 **John Battelle:** John Battelle, "Just Asking," *Searchblog*, 19 June 2007, http://battellemedia.com/archives/003744.php. Matt Cutts's post was composed on 19 June 2007, http://battellemedia.com/archives/003744.php#comment_122000. His follow-up post was on 20 February 2008, http://battellemedia.com/archives/003744.php#comment_128693.

167 **Larry Dignan:** Larry Dignan, "Read the Fine Print of Google Office," *Between the Lines*, 22 February 2007, http://blogs.zdnet.com/BTL/?p=4537; Larry Dignan, "Will You Trust Google with Your Data?" *Between The Lines*, 23 February 2007, http://blogs.zdnet.com/BTL/?p=4544.

168 **In October 2006:** Adrian Sannier, "Like Technology from an Advanced Alien Culture", *Adrian Sannier Blog*, Arizona State University, 16 October 2006, https://uto.asu.edu/blog/2006/10/16/like-technology-from-an-advance-alien-culture%e2%80%a6/. For all parties, it was a decision that was made with public relations in mind. For Google, having ASU decide to adopt Apps permitted it to boast of an installation that was done on a large scale and quickly, within two weeks of the university's decision. For ASU, the association with Google was used to demonstrate the "agility" of ASU as it reshaped itself into what it called "the New American University." The university told its various constituents that the Google connection also "places ASU on Google's exponential technology development trajectory," which would automatically ensure that ASU would keep pace with "the leaders in the field."

169 **Google experienced for the first time:** Michael Arrington, "Gmail Disaster: Reports of Mass Email Deletions," *TechCrunch*, 28 December 2006, http://www.techcrunch.com/2006/12/28/gmail-disaster-reports-of-mass-email-deletions/.

169 **In the first quarter of 2007:** "Google Buys Web Security Specialist," *San Jose Mercury News*, 10 July 2007.

170 **One notable trophy:** "Student Privacy a Concern with Webmail Switch," *Daily Pennsylvanian*, 16 January 2007, http://media.www.dailypennsylvanian.com/media/storage/paper882/news/2007/01/16/News/Student.Privacy.A.Concern.With.Webmail.Switch- 2633726.shtml; "Officials Say Google Was the First Choice," *Daily Pennsylvanian*, 20 April 2007, http://media.www.dailypennsylvanian.com/media/storage/paper882/news/2007/04/20/News/Officials.Say.Google.Was.The.First.Choice-28 71128.shtml.

171 **without showing signs:** Not all campuses were resistant. Administrators at San Jose State University had approached Google and Microsoft about Web-hosted e-mail and decided to accept Microsoft's offer. Don Baker, a San Jose

State administrator in the university's computing services group who was a member of the selection committee, was dismayed that Google was unwilling to come to campus to make a presentation about Google Apps to the committee, even though the Googleplex was close to the university's campus. Microsoft, on the other hand, had gone out of its way to send a representative to make a presentation—and it could point to a hundred schools that were using Hotmail accounts, whereas Google could point to only a single campus that was using Google Apps. Baker said, "If it is this difficult to get the vendor's attention in order to use a product, what was their maintenance support going to be like during and after the installation?" Baker e-mail to author, 6 April 2007.

174 **an immediate decision:** San Jose State's Don Baker said in a phone interview with the author on 7 May 2008 that he was aware of four CSU campuses among the system's twenty-three that had decided to adopt Google Apps for Education. Google declined to confirm whether this tally was accurate or complete.

174 **250,000 accounts:** Brin mentioned the University of Phoenix account in passing during a quarterly earnings call. "Google Q3 2007 Earnings Call Transcript," prepared by *SeekingAlpha*, 18 October 2007, http://seekingalpha.com/article/50487-google-q3-2007-earnings-call-transcript.

174 **too few customers:** In August 2007, Google announced five schools that were adopting Google's education package: the University of North Carolina–Greensboro, Clemson University, University of Texas–San Antonio, Kennesaw State University, and Arkansas State University. But the press release did not mention total numbers, nor did the company respond to requests for the information in October 2007 and in May 2008. "Google@School—More Universities Announce Google Apps on Campus," Google press release, 16 August 2007, http://www.google.com/intl/en/press/annc/google_at_school.html.; Jeff Keltner, "One-Year Mark for Google Apps Education Edition," *Official Google Blog*, 25 October 2007, http://googleblog.blogspot.com/2007/10/one-year-mark-for-google-apps-education.html.

174 **six million active accounts:** Bruce Gabrielle, e-mail message, 12 May 2008.

174 **he casually dropped:** Ballmer was speaking at the UK Microsoft Startup Accelerator Program. See Microsoft's Lars Lindstsedt, "The Online Opportunity," *Microsoft Startup Zone: United Kingdom*, 4 October 2007, http://microsoftstartupzone.com/blogs/united_kingdom/archive/2007/10/01/the-online-opportunity.aspx. A link to a video snippet of Ballmer's remarks is available in Lindstedt's post: http://www.mydeo.com/videorequest.asp?XID=48644&CID=133678. Ballmer's remark about Gmail is found at the two-minute point in the question-and-answer segment. Also see Ed Moltzen, "Microsoft's Ballmer: Google Reads Your Mail," *The Chart* on ChannelWeb Network, 7 October 2007, http://www.crn.com/software/202300583.

175 **transition in America's cities:** Randall Stross, *The Wizard of Menlo Park: How Thomas Alva Edison Invented the Modern World* (New York: Crown Publishers, 2007), 172–81.

176 **David Berlind:** "Yes, It's Time to Destroy Your E-Mail Servers. What App Is Next?" *InformationWeek: David Berlind's Tech Radar*, 14 May 2008, http://www.informationweek.com/blog/main/archives/2008/05/get_over_it_for.html.

8. Algorithm, Meet Humanity

180 **In 2002, Google offered:** "Google Answers: Frequently Asked Questions," n.d., http://answers.google.com/answers/faq.html#who; "Latest from Google: For-Pay Search," *New York Times*, 25 April 2002.

181 **three years after Google Answers:** "Google Plans to Cancel Paid Service for Answers," *New York Times*, 30 November 2006, http://www.nytimes.com/2006/11/30/technology/30google.html; "If You Think You Have All the Right Answers, This Site Is for You," *Wall Street Journal*, 12 July 2006.

183 **Tim Berners-Lee:** Tim Berners-Lee, James Hendler, and Ora Lassila, "The Semantic Web," *Scientific American*, 17 May 2001, http://www.sciam.com/article.cfm?id=the-semantic-web.

183 **new companies are springing up:** John Markoff, "What I Meant to Say Was Semantic Web," *Bits*, 19 December 2007, http://bits.blogs.nytimes.com/2007/10/19/what-i-meant-to-say-was-semantic-web/. Cuill, another search engine whose product was in development in early 2008, was reportedly working on technology that "can index web pages significantly faster and cheaper than Google." Blekko was another search engine company in stealth mode in early 2008. See Cuill entry (last edited 20 March 2008) in CrunchBase, http://www.crunchbase.com/company/cuill, and Blekko entry (last edited 25 February 2008), http://www.crunchbase.com/company/blekko. Also see Michael Arrington, "Stealth Search Engine Blekko Gets Money from Marc Andreesen, SoftTech," *TechCrunch*, 14 May 2008, http://www.techcrunch.com/2008/05/14/stealth-search-engine-blekko-gets-money-from-marc-andreesen-softtech/.

183 **In May 2008:** Danny Sullivan, "Powerset Launches 'Understanding Engine' for Wikipedia Content," *Search Engine Land*, 12 May 2008, http://searchengineland.com/080512-000100.php; Chris Morrison, "Powerset: Don't Call Us a Search Engine," *VentureBeat*, 10 April 2008, http://venturebeat.com/2008/04/10/powerset-dont-call-us-a-search-engine/; "Powerset Joins Live Search," *Live Search*, 1 July 2008, http://blogs.msdn.com/livesearch/archive/2008/07/01/powerset-joins-live-search.aspx.

184 **Between 2004 and 2006:** "Looking for the Next Google," *New York Times*, 1 January 2007, http://www.nytimes.com/2007/01/01/technology/01search

.html. In May 2007, Don Dodge, a Microsoft executive who did not work with Microsoft's search group, published on his personal blog a post that showed why investors were so keen to enter the search business: Dodge calculated that every 1 percent of the U.S. search market would be worth about $100 million in annualized revenue, which, with certain assumptions, would lead to a market capitalization that exceeded $1 billion. See Don Dodge, "Why 1% of Search Market Share Is Worth over $1 Billion," *Don Dodge on the Next Big Thing*, 26 May 2007, http://dondodge.typepad.com/the_next_big_thing/2007/05/why_1_of_search.html. Also see Bernard Lunn, "11 Search Trends That May Disrupt Google," *ReadWriteWeb,* 16 June 2008, http://www.readwriteweb.com/archives/11_search_trends.php.

184 **Squidoo, Sproose, and NosyJoe:** Randall Stross, "The Human Touch That May Loosen Google's Grip," *New York Times,* 24 June 2007, http://www.nytimes.com/2007/06/24/business/yourmoney/24digi.html.

184 **Jimmy Wales:** "Founder of Wikipedia Plans Search Engine to Rival Google," *The Times Online*, 23 December 2006, http://technology.timesonline.co.uk/tol/news/tech_and_web/article1264117.ece. Wales was overly sanguine about how quickly the project could be launched: in December 2006 he said that the provisional launch date was the first quarter of 2007, which came and went. For a critical view of Wikipedia, see Randall Stross, "Anonymous Source Is Not the Same as Open Source," *New York Times*, 12 March 2006, http://www.nytimes.com/2006/03/12/business/yourmoney/12digi.html.

185 **Calacanis described:** Jason Calacanis, e-mail to author, 19 June 2007.

186 **"John Henry":** Stross, "The Human Touch."

186 **Marissa Mayer was in Paris:** Marissa Mayer, presentation at Google European Press Day 2007, Paris, 19 June 2007, http://www.youtube.com/watch?v=dNRE5x-V-sQ. Matt Cutts quoted an account of Mayer's answers to questions posed by journalists at the Press Day in a journalist's blog post that included an interesting exchange between Mayer and the *Guardian*'s Jemima Kiss. Kiss asked whether there was a place for human intervention in guiding Web search, like Mahalo's, expecting Mayer to say no, but she instead answered, "Up to today we have relied on automation, but I believe the future will be a blend of both, combing [*sic*] the scale of automation and human intelligence." Jemima Kiss, "Google's Press Day 2007," *Guardian Unlimited: OrganGrinder*, 19 June 2007, http://blogs.guardian.co.uk/organgrinder/2007/06/googles_press_day_2007.html. I was unable to confirm the accuracy of the account; I could not find it in the videos of the event that Google placed on YouTube.

187 **Cutts shared extended thoughts:** In his post, Cutts spared me any direct criticism and kindly referred to the article as "interesting." Among the comments that followed his post was one from Aaron Pratt that was not as gentle: "Forced myself to read that *New York Times* article and just wanted to say that human edited search engines like Mahalo suck. The article almost seemed

anti-Google as if the writer was being paid off by Mahalo. Expect many more of these types of articles in the future, everyone hates a winner." Cutts responded with a follow-up comment to Pratt's, saying that he did not think that I was "anti-Google" and regarded the basic question—will human-powered search threaten Google?—to be a fair one. He did take issue with my blurring the line he drew between spam and search engine optimization. See Matt Cutts, "The Role of Humans in Google Search," *Gadgets, Google, and SEO*, 23 June 2007, http://www.mattcutts.com/blog/the-role-of-humans-in-google-search/.

187 **expressed the same points:** John Battelle, "A Brief Interview with Google's Matt Cutts," *Searchblog*, 26 September 2006, http://battellemedia.com/archives/002917.php.

187 **Larry Page had publicly:** Jason Calacanis, "FooCamp: OpenSearch," calacanis.com, 23 June 2007, http://www.calacanis.com/2007/06/23/foocamp-opensearch/.

188 **Eric Schmidt pointed:** "Google Q4 2006 Earnings Call Transcript," prepared by SeekingAlpha, 31 January 2007, http://seekingalpha.com/article/25717-google-q4-2006-earnings-call-transcript.

188 **Viacom did not buy:** "Viacom Tells YouTube: Hands Off," *New York Times*, 3 February 2007, http://www.nytimes.com/2007/02/03/technology/03tube.html. In a tally that was by no means complete, Viacom had found 150,000 unauthorized clips of its shows on YouTube, which had been viewed 1.5 billion times. Surely, the lawsuit argued, the wide availability of that material on YouTube and the fact that YouTube had attained a $1.65 billion valuation in its short history before it was acquired were directly related: the infringing works had helped to draw the audience that propelled YouTube's growth and astounding valuation.

188 **expected lawsuit:** Viacom International Inc., Comedy Partners, Country Music Television, Inc., Paramount Pictures Corporation, and Black Entertainment Television LLC, v. You Tube Inc., YouTube, LLC, and Google, Inc., United States District Court, Southern District of New York, 13 March 2007, http://www.lessig.org/blog/archives/vvg.pdf., 1–2.

189 **Schmidt characterized:** Eric Schmidt interview at Bear Stearns 20th Annual Media Conference, 6 March 2007, http://www.youtube.com/watch?v=9HM-ZO21NwA.

189 **Schmidt directed attention away:** Google was not consistent in arguing that under the law it had no responsibility for monitoring what was uploaded. A year earlier, in early 2006, YouTube set a little-noticed precedent that it was willing to monitor uploaded videos for infringing material when it offered what it called a "producer program," which permitted uploading videos that were longer than the standard ten minutes. The videos were not made publicly available immediately. Roelof Botha, a YouTube board member, explained that when the longer videos were uploaded, "we do extra verifica-

tion, make sure copyright is actually clear." One could have asked, why go to the trouble to make sure that copyright was clear if the DCMA absolved the host video service of any and all responsibility? See Matt Marshall, "Q&A with Roelof Botha, the Web 2.0 Guy at Sequoia Capital," *VentureBeat*, 1 June 2006, http://venturebeat.com/2006/06/01/qa-with-roelof-botha-the-web-20-guy-at-sequoia-capital/.

189 **he announced:** "A Conversation with Eric Schmidt," interviewed by John Seigenthaler, National Association of Broadcasters 2007, Las Vegas, 16 April 2007, http://www.youtube.com/watch?v=gAaBVUpLJ10. Also see Schmidt's description of Claim Your Content in "Google Q1 2007 Earnings Call Transcript," 19 April 2007, prepared by SeekingAlpha, http://seekingalpha.com/article/32897-google-q1-2007-earnings-call-transcript.

189 **National Legal and Policy Center:** Ken Boehm to Patrick J. Leahy, 25 September 2007, http://www.nlpc.org/pdfs/Letter%20HSCJ.pdf.

190 **Philippe Dauman:** "Viacom Chief Jabs Google's Antipiracy Effort, Talks Up Copyright Guidelines," *Computerworld*, 18 October 2007, http://www.computerworld.com/action/article.do?command=viewArticleBasic&articleId=9043252.

190 **a consortium:** "Disney, Microsoft Lead Copyright Pact," *Wall Street Journal*, 18 October 2007, http://online.wsj.com/public/article/SB119269788721663302.html.

190 **test the new software:** "Nabbing Video Pirates: Who Needs Google?" *BusinessWeek*, 16 October 2007, http://www.businessweek.com/technology/content/oct2007/tc20071016_876447.htm.

190 **Eric Schmidt attempted:** "Google Takes Step on Video Copyrights," *New York Times*, 16 October 2007, http://www.nytimes.com/2007/10/16/business/16video.html.

191 **Google claimed:** Liz Gannes, "YouTube Finally Launches Video ID Tool," *NewTeeVee*, 15 October 2007, http://newteevee.com/2007/10/15/youtube-finally-launches-video-id-tool/.

191 **In its haste to announce:** "Nabbing Video Pirates," *BusinessWeek*.

192 **Steve Chen gratefully said:** Steve Chen, "The State of Our Video ID Tools," *The Official Google Blog*, 14 June 2007, http://googleblog.blogspot.com/2007/06/state-of-our-video-id-tools.html. In March 2008, another weakness of YouTube's vaunted "community flagging" was exposed: its operation is slow. A clip that was posted in England showing what appeared to be a young mother being gang raped by three teenage boys was watched six hundred times before being removed. When Kent Walker, Google's general counsel, was called before a parliamentary committee to explain how such a clip could have been allowed to have been posted, he said it would be "inefficient" to screen every minute of footage. "You do not have a policeman on every street corner to stop things from happening, you have policemen responding very quickly when things do happen," he said. "Google Admits YouTube Rape Video Was 'a Mistake,'" *Times*

Online, 1 April 2008, http://technology.timesonline.co.uk/tol/news/tech_and_web/article3662228.ece. The case took an unanticipated turn when the woman who had appeared to be a rape victim was subsequently arrested "on suspicion of underage sex and perverting the course of justice." "YouTube 'Rape Victim' Arrested," *Register*, 1 April 2008, http://www.theregister.co.uk/2008/04/01/alleged_youtube_rape_victim_arrested/.

192 **Revver:** Digital Hollywood, "Building Blocks 2006," San Jose, CA, 15 August 2006, http://www.digitalhollywood.com/%231BB1kSessions/BBTuesOne.html.

192 **By March 2008:** "Number of Online Videos Viewed in the U.S. Jumps 13 Percent in March to 11.5 Billion," comScore press release, 12 May 2008, http://www.comscore.com/press/release.asp?press=2223.

192 **impossible for neutral observers:** Greg Sandoval, "YouTube's Filtering Issues Still Not 'Moot,'" *News.com News Blog*, 18 April 2008, http://www.news.com/8301-10784_3-9921916-7.html.

193 **By spring 2008:** "Number of Online Videos Viewed in the U.S.," comScore press release.

Conclusion

196 **Yet in April 2008:** "comScore Media Metrix Ranks Top 50 U.S. Web Properties for April," comScore press release, 15 May 2008, http://www.comscore.com/press/release.asp?press=2229.

196 **by March 2008:** "Number of Online Videos Viewed in the U.S. Jumps 13 Percent in March to 11.5 Billion," comScore press release, 12 May 2008, http://www.comscore.com/press/release.asp?press=2223.

197 **Columbia University:** Gabriel Stricker, "Columbia University Joins the Google Book Search Library Project," *Inside Google Book Search*, 13 December 2007, http://booksearch.blogspot.com/2007/12/columbia-university-joins-google-book.html.

197 **second dozen cities:** Vaibhav Vaish, "A Dozen More Cities in Street View," *Google Lat Long Blog*, 12 February 2008, http://google-latlong.blogspot.com/2008/02/dozen-more-cities-in-street-view.html.

197 ***New York Times:*** Wei Luo, "All the News That's Fit to Print on a Map: The New York Times in Google Earth," *Google Lat Long Blog*, 7 April 2008, http://google-latlong.blogspot.com/2008/04/all-news-thats-fit-to-print-on-map-new.html.

197 **Google's share:** "Google Receives 68 Percent of U.S. Searches in May 2008," Hitwise press release, 10 June 2008, http://www.hitwise.com/press-center/hitwiseHS2004/leader-record-growth.php.

198 **Steve Ballmer likes:** Ballmer made the remarks at a talk he gave at Stanford University. "Microsoft CEO Says Google a 'One-Trick Pony,'" cbs5.com, 15

March 2007, http://cbs5.com/business/local_story_074175502.html. He returned to the "one-trick pony" characterization of Google in October, at the Web 2.0 Conference. "Ballmer: Search Like 'Precocious' Tot," *Associated Press*, 18 October 2007, http://ap.google.com/article/ALeqM5grlwt32poMtIMBrxig_ocloy2LNgD8SBRNV04. He said the two new tricks that Microsoft was trying to learn were "devices and entertainment, and advertising and the Web."

198 **Henry Blodget:** Henry Blodget, "Google Search To Surpass Size of Microsoft Windows in 2009," *Silicon Alley Insider*, 13 May 2008, http://www.alleyinsider.com/2008/5/google_to_surpass_size_of_microsoft_windows_in_2009.

199 **"outside pressures":** Larry Page, "Letter from the Founders: 'An Owner's Manual' for Google's Shareholders," 2004, http://investor.google.com/ipo_letter.html.

199 **When Eric Schmidt was interviewed:** "For Soaring Google, Next Act Won't Be as Easy as the First," *Wall Street Journal*, 30 June 2005.

200 **Craig Silverstein:** "Google's Man Behind the Curtain," News.com, 10 May 2004, http://www.news.com/2008-1024_3-5208228.html. Silverstein made the same point six weeks earlier, but instead of referring to the local reference librarian, which was clearly his intended meaning, he was quoted as saying it would be 300 years before computers were as good as "your local reference library." See "Inside the Wide World of Google," *CBS News*, 28 March 2004, http://www.cbsnews.com/stories/2004/03/25/sunday/main608672.shtml.

200 **a second time:** "Google ETA? 300 Years to Index the World's Info," News.com, 8 October 2005, http://www.news.com/Google-ETA-300-years-to-index-the-worlds-info/2100-1024_3-5891779.html; Eric Schmidt, "Technology Is Making Marketing Accountable," transcript of speech delivered to the Association of National Advertisers, 8 October 2005, http://www.google.com/press/podium/ana.html.

Acknowledgments

This book would not have been written were it not for Elizabeth Kaplan, my stalwart literary agent for almost twenty years. I began the book with a wisp of an idea and some hesitation about whether it was a feasible project. Elizabeth supplied the encouragement I needed to lace up my shoes and start, and when I ran into difficulties at the end and became wobbly, she knew exactly what I needed in order to finish.

At Google, Karen Wickre was liaison extraordinaire. She was on duty around the clock, it seemed, responding immediately to my requests with exactly the information or referrals I was looking for and adding a good dash of humor, too.

Karen worked closely with her colleagues in Google's corporate communications group, who did their part to persuade other Googlers to make themselves available. For their efforts on my behalf, I am indebted to group head David Krane, and to Sean Carlson, Erin Fors, Jason Freidenfelds, Courtney Hohne, Rachael Horwitz, Meghan Hughes, Michael Kirkland, Jon Murchinson, Megan Quinn, Oscar Shine, Gabriel Stricker, Katie Watson, and Larry Yu.

I'd like to thank the following individuals at Google for making time for interviews: David Bailey, Peter Chane, Matt Cutts, Vic Gundotra, John Hanke, Urs Hölzle, Joe Kraus, Mark Lucovsky, Franz Och, Brian Rakowski, Eric Schmidt, and Adam Smith. Craig Silverstein was helpful, too, filling in some holes in my understanding of Google's early history.

Bruce Gabrielle of Microsoft helped bring his company's portion of the story up-to-date.

In reporting that I did for various *New York Times* assignments that pertained to Google, I received the help of Marissa Mayer of Google, Jason Calacanis of Mahalo, Michael Cusumano of MIT's Sloan School of Management, Adam Jusko of Bessed, Kristen Roby of Microsoft, Michael Seibel of Justin.tv, and Allan R. Adler of the Association of American Publishers.

At San Jose State University's College of Business, William Jiang and Anne Lawrence, who served as chair and vice chair, respectively, of the Department of Organization and Management, cleared the way for the book, lightly tossing aside bureaucratic obstacles so that I could take a yearlong leave to work on the project.

Don Baker, who oversees San Jose State's computing services group, kindly allowed me to join him when fielding sales presentations by Google and Microsoft.

In 2006–2007, I was a postdoctoral fellow of Stanford Law School's Center for Internet and Society. Thanks in particular go to Lauren Gelman, who was then the center's associate director, and to the law school's librarians.

For arrangements that enabled me to hear Google executives present talks off campus, I wish to thank Roger Sherman of the International Macintosh Users Group and Dennis Wharton and Kathy Roberts of the National Association of Broadcasters.

At the Free Press, Emily Loose was an active editor who did not wait idly for me to send her the first pages; from the start, she debriefed me regularly and helped shape my research agenda. When I finally did begin to write up my discoveries, she was demanding, pushing me to make improvements after I was ready—*more than ready*—to declare the narrative complete.

Danielle Kaniper of the Free Press deftly handled sundry arrangements. Chuck Antony and Edith Lewis supplied sharp eyes as copy-editors.

Gail Hershatter, Lee Gomes, Pamela Basey, and Gary Rivlin read the manuscript with tough love and delivered the detailed criticism that I both hoped for and dreaded. Addressing their suggestions served to greatly improve the work.

Most of all, I would like to thank my wife, Ellen Stross, who supplied indispensable encouragement, perspective, and counsel on all questions. With her at my side, I am the most fortunate of authors.

Index

First published in Great Britain in 2011 by
Hodder Arnold, an imprint of Hodder Education, an Hachette UK company,
338 Euston Road, London NW1 3BH

http://www.hodderarnold.com

British Library Cataloguing in Publication Data
A catalogue record for this book is available from the British Library

Library of Congress Cataloging-in-Publication Data
A catalog record for this book is available from the Library of Congress

ISBN 978-0-340-99066-7

1 2 3 4 5 6 7 8 9 10

Commissioning Editor: Francesca Naish
Project Editor: Mischa Barrett
Production Controller: Joanna Walker
Cover Design: Helen Townson

Cover image © Photodisc/Getty Images

Typeset in 9.5 on 11.5 Formata Light Condensed by Phoenix Photosetting, Chatham, Kent
Printed and bound in India by Replika Press Pvt Limited

Bailey & Love
REVISION GUIDE

SBAs & EMQs for the MRCS PART A

VIVIAN A ELWELL MB BS, MRCS, BA (Hons), MA (Cantab)
Neurosurgery Specialist Registrar, The National Hospital for Neurology & Neurosurgery, Queen Square, London

JONATHAN M FISHMAN BM BCh (Oxon), MRCS (Eng), DOHNS (RCS Eng), BA (Hons), MA (Cantab)
ENT Specialist Registrar, The John Radcliffe Hospital, Oxford

RAJAT CHOWDHURY BM BCh (Oxon), MRCS, BSc (Hons), MSc (Lond), MA (Oxon)
Radiology Specialist Registrar, Southampton General Hospital, Southampton

All are Managing Directors of Insider Medical Ltd

SUNMAKERS

SPIRITUA FOOD for HUNGRY PEOPLE

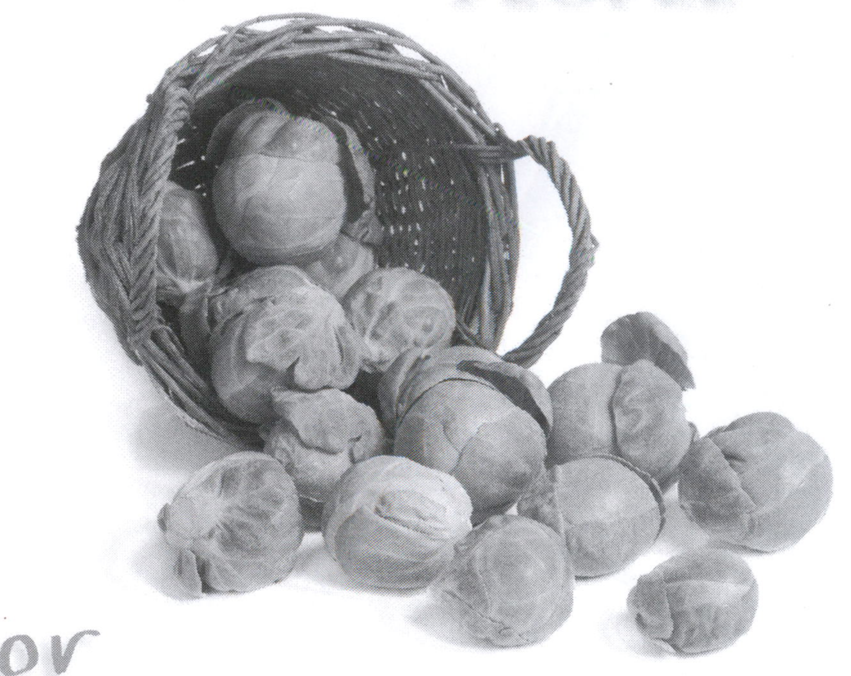

or

THE GOSPEL ACCORDING TO THE BRUSSELS SPROU

Neil Dorward and Maria Victoria Ba

IRITUAL FOOD for HUNGRY PEOPLE

SPIRITUAL FOOD for HUNGRY PEOPLE

Published by Sunmakers, a division of Eldamar Ltd,
157 Oxford Road, Cowley, Oxford, OX4 2ES, UK
www.sunmakers.co.uk
el +44(0)1865 779944

ion 1.0

08693-24-2

To the lovely Wilma

Happy reading

Bless you

Neil x

We dedicate this book to Our Lord God Almighty, for all the inspiration and help He has given us in writing this book and for His support and encouragement throughout our lives.

Neil dedicates this book to his darling daughter Katie.

Maria offers a particular dedication to the love of her life, her late husband Tony who passed away on 17th August 2011.

And finally, to her sons Tony and Jamie for their support and encouragement.

You know sometimes when you read these dedications and you wonder why your name is not there. Well guess what? It is. This book is dedicated to you … and the humble Brussels sprout.

To Wilma,

As a token of my thanks for all the encouragement.

Love & Bless you.

Maria x

ACKNOWLEDGEMENTS

Larry, Drew and Beth for editing and to all family and friends for their encouragement.

FOREWORD

It is customary in many books for a Foreword to be written by a well-known personality. That person would declare and endorse the writings in the book and give accolade to the authors.

In our case, we believe that on this occasion, our Foreword should be an encouraging word from God. And the word is:

'If God is for us, who can be against?'

This quote from St. Paul's Letter to the Romans 8:31 underscores everything we have tried to share in this book.

I know that nothing in this world can ever take us from
His love.

This is Good News because there are only 3 things in life that last; faith, hope and love and the greatest of these is love.

Contents

INTRODUCTION

"And God said, 'Behold, I have given you every plant yielding seed that is on the face of all the earth, and every tree with seed in its fruit. You shall have them for food'" – Genesis 1:29

It's the middle of February 2014 here in Kinross in Central Scotland and I still have this season's much loved Christmas vegetable in my fridge; the Brussels sprout. Don't worry, it's not the same pack bought before in December, now black and pungent; they are fresh ones. In fact I have been eating them every week since 25th December; they are good for you. The quintessential Christmas dinner vegetable is one of the world's healthiest foods. They help lower cholesterol, their fibre components aid digestion, they stabilise our white blood cell count, their glucosinolate content fight cancers and overall they have fantastic health benefits.

Ever since I was a young boy, we have been culturally conditioned to say Brussels sprouts are "yuk". I still have memories of my mum telling me as an 8-year-old child to eat my sprouts at Christmas or there will no trifle and my mum's trifle was yum; it was always decorated with crumbly Cadbury's Flake. Although to be fair to myself, when I was 8 years old I hadn't a Scooby Doo about the health benefits of eating my greens. But now at the age of 48, I eagerly await their arrival at my local Sainsbury's every Christmas because I know the benefits of eating the mini cabbage. One quick Google and you find out how amazing this little vegetable really is.

That can happen so often in life. Things we were taught when we were children, we don't fully understand the benefits until later on in life. We have to make a choice that something is good for us, don't we? If we want something to be a part of our life, we have to have a desire

for it, be that going to the gym or eating our 5-a-day. We have to make a conscious and informed decision to bring something into our lives because we know it's good for us and brings us health and wholeness. It's no different when it comes to having a healthy spiritual life.

The purpose of the book

This book wants to encourage that desire for you to have a spiritual life. It aims to show you the health benefits of having an active spiritual life and why things like Jesus, prayer, the Bible and having an active spirituality can be good for your health. We are what we eat and when we eat good things we reap the health rewards. It is the same in the spiritual life. This book will show you how to get in spiritual shape. It's a Good News book. It aims to be a straight talking book about the spiritual life without falling into the trap of speaking Christian-ese and using words that don't resonate with people anymore in 21st century Scotland.

Although the purpose of this book is not to lead people to any specific form of religion we, the authors, come from a Christian perspective and our hunger for spirituality has been found within mainstream Christianity and the teachings of the Old and New Testament. It is inevitable, therefore, that our reflections on our spiritual journey will connect with Bible stories that resonate with us.

We want to demystify words like: the Bible, 'being saved', revelation, salvation, sin and church, as for some people these are the weird cousins of the Brussels sprout like broccoli, spinach and cabbage. This book is not setting out to convince you to have a spiritual life. It is all about you and the choices you want to make to live the fullest life possible. You will choose what you want to have in your life. It's our belief and experience that the spiritual life is really good for you. 'Spiritual Food for Hungry People' will show you the incredible health

benefits of having a spiritual life and how by developing spiritual habits you will find:

- peace
- a positive mind-set
- happiness
- joy
- humility
- patience
- a sense of belonging
- a lessening of the ego
- a spirit of thanksgiving
- a capacity to overcome hardships

There is even research to suggest that people with a strong spiritual life have an 18% reduction in mortality. Giancarlo Lucchetti, lead author of the study, exploring the impact of spirituality and health in the Journal of Science and Healing (July 2011) calculates that the life-lengthening benefits of spirituality and prayer can be compared to eating a high amount of fruits and vegetables. My goodness the humble Brussels sprout is really good for you.

When we know something is good for us there can be new-found enthusiasm to embrace this knowledge, which can develop into new habits and behaviours with an overall vision of having a more fulfilling and authentic lifestyle. When we know that something as small as a Brussels sprout is good for us; we want to have more. It is the same for those who want to explore the spiritual life. When we have a greater knowledge of who God, Jesus, church and the basics of the spiritual life are, this can lead to a change of behaviour and a development of new and healthy habits.

Let me ask you this question: What have you been conditioned to believe about the spiritual life, God and religion? Are spiritual people all a bit bonkers? Do spiritual people all act and speak in a certain way? Are many of them hypocrites? Is it better not to get too enthusiastic about the spiritual life in case people talk? Would you think twice about putting a spiritual comment on your Facebook page as you think these sorts of things are best kept behind closed doors? Would you want the Prime Minister of this country to talk about prayer and the spiritual life or should they stay silent?

Barrack Obama will use the word 'pray' in some of his speeches but you won't catch many UK politicians saying words like, "We pray for the victims of …" Perhaps they have been coached by their media gurus never to use religious words in case it offends another community within our diverse multi-cultural society. Is the spiritual life a purely personal, individualistic thing or is it something we should speak more about and explore?

The BBC recently reported in an online magazine on 17th Jan 2014 that three quarters of the world population live in countries where religion is highly restricted and it further reported that hostility to religion is now at a worldwide high. Then it went on to say that when it comes to social hostility to religion, the UK is ranked as the 31st most socially hostile country in the world towards religion. This certainly seems to be backed up by my experience of conducting hundreds of funerals where people say they do not want a 'religious' funeral or one that the formal church conducts. However, the anecdotal evidence I encounter on a daily basis suggests people; at least privately, want to hear about the values of having a healthy spiritual life.

That is the intention of this book, to help you explore those areas of life that are spiritual without you feeling the spiritual life is a bit weird, like a Brussels sprout.

Healthy options

Come on, what's the worst thing that can happen if you explore the spiritual life or the healing properties of the mini cabbage? Why not explore the potential health benefits of all things that are good for us? Would you not want to journey on this earth and have all the tools you need to live a happy and healthy life? If you think the spiritual life is at least worth exploring then this book is for you. Why not journey with us and at least allow us to whet your spiritual appetite and even quench your thirst. You have nothing to lose, and if like us you have a curious mind then who knows what mysteries we might unravel in the process.

I work in a specialised field where I get an insight into what people really want from life and I can't help but conclude that the spiritual life is good for you.

Every day of my life I work with bereaved families. I work as a Funeral Celebrant in Central Scotland and after having conducted over 2500 funerals in the last 9 years and through my anecdotal research at work I know that God, religion and all things churchy have a bad name with many bereaved families; even yuckier than our beloved Christmas vegetable. Why is that?

Well, in my opinion, we haven't been taught the real health benefits of living an active spiritual life, just like an 8-year-old child who does not know why they eat their greens. We were often taught the basics as a child but then forget as an adult. But how much of our information about the spiritual life being a bit weird is mis-information? How much is based on myth, personal perception, bad life experiences and what others have told us about the spiritual life being a bit yuk?

I write funeral ceremonies for families who have lost a loved one and frequently hear families say to me, "I don't want any of that religious

stuff at my dad's funeral ... if I hear that story about God's mansions one more time..." But then, if I ask them, "Do you believe you will meet your wife/dad/son again?" Nine out of ten families tell me they believe they will meet their loved ones again. Most people in Scotland are not fully signed up atheists; most people believe in something and hold on to a bit of faith that death is not the end. We all have a spiritual life even if we do not label ourselves as being spiritual. Over the last 9 years I have spoken to a quarter of a million people at funerals and I know people have a desire for spiritual truths.

Who the book is written for

This book is written with these people in mind; the people who have their own faith and spirituality but don't necessarily go to church. Ninety-five per cent of the families that I work with have a desire for spiritual truths and this book wants to encourage as well as develop this spiritual life that exists in each and every single one of us so that it grows deeper and stronger. I admire people who have a zest for life in all its fullness and I understand this does not happen by chance. We need to have a desire, a desire to live a healthy life. The more we practise these healthy habits, the stronger and more rooted we become. We may even get so excited about living a healthy, physical, emotional, intellectual or spiritual life that we develop a proverbial six-pack in every area and become so strong that nothing will ever shake us; no depression, no illness, no personal set-backs.

Do you want that? Would you like a strong spiritual life that will sustain you, encourage you, support you and constantly remind you of just how wonderful our life on this earth is? Given my work within the funeral ministry it's a cliché to say we only get one life, so why not make the most of it? Why not access and use all the tools of happiness and health that are available to us right now instead of saying "no thanks that's a bit yuk, that's a bit weird". Spiritual health is an

integral part of that human happiness and contentment we all seek as we journey on this earth. That is what we were born for, to know life in all its fullness or as St. John once said in his Gospel, "To have life and have it to the full" (John 10:10).

This book is written for anyone who thinks, "Why on earth would I go to church or have a spiritual life?" If you have already asked yourself that question then you have just demonstrated that within you there is a spark of spirituality and you are interested to know more about God, Jesus, church, eternal life; asking does prayer work, how can I be healed of past hurts, how can I get a new positive mindset?

This is not a self-help book per se

That might sound a bit strange that this is not a self-help book. Let me clarify. Countless self-help books whether they are for diets, or helping you to become the best golfer in the world, will show you a pathway. The basic idea is follow this path, obey the rules, do everything you can do to meet the standards and you will get there. The spiritual life is slightly different. We cannot do it all by ourselves, and so in that sense this is not a self-help book. If we try to do it all by ourselves who will pick us up when we fall, when the weather is miserable, when we are not in the mood or when someone or something brings us down?

Self-help books can be inspirational and I have read and studied many of them. However, the most significant growth happens when we have a coach, a mentor, or a confidante; someone to whisper good news to us every now and again. That is self evident within the sporting world or within the world of athletics; we sometimes need a coach, we can't do it all by ourselves. Well, those who embark upon the path to a spiritual life accept that not only will they get help and support from fellow travellers on the spiritual journey, but they will get unlimited

help, support, power and Grace from a great Being; the God who lives in each and every one of us. The God who is faithful, who has His eye on us and will bring us to that place of inner happiness, self-worth and self-confidence where we are meant to be. Do you have many people in your life who give you that sort of confidence?

Confidence is like a muscle the more you use it, the stronger it gets. Self-confidence has limited potential. God confidence has unlimited possibility. Confidence is not based on you having all the resources needed to take care of yourself; confidence is based upon the truth that God is faithful. St. Paul once said to the people of Philippi, in modern day Greece in 49 AD, "I can do all things through Him who gives me strength" (Philippians 4:13). Brussels sprouts can give you physical strength but who is giving you spiritual strength and confidence?

That is what the spiritual life is going to do for you. It is going to give you confidence through God's Word, through your prayer life and by having a new mindset. A Christ-like mindset and coming into His Presence will give you a happiness the world cannot fully give. That is what the spiritual life is all about and what this book intends to show you, how to have a healthy spirituality and avoid the other options of apathy, cynicism or just 'cannae be bothered'. We want you to be bothered about your happiness and health and we want to help you find it. That is partly why we decided to write this book.

In writing this book, I think of what I do every Christmas, once I have eaten my Brussels sprouts of course. A few days after Christmas a Facebook message goes out from people I went to school with thirty years ago. The messages say something along the lines of, "Everyone is meeting up for a few drinks in The Post Office Bar in Broughty Ferry this Saturday at 7pm". We have been doing this for the past 20 years and although none of my former school friends go to church, it is interesting the amount of times we end up talking about some aspect of the spiritual life. I feel I am partly writing this book for people like

my school friends. Just ordinary every day guys who get on with their lives and experience the many trials and tribulations of life that we all have, but who on occasion, ask; 'Is this all there is? What happens when we die? Will I meet my mum again for real? How can I forgive my partner who betrayed me? I've lost my job, I have spiralling debts, and what else can I do to stay sane?'

In my observations from my funeral work, the vast majority of people still have an interest in the spiritual side of their lives by the mere fact that they ask deep and meaningful questions like that. These stirrings of the heart show that all human beings have a thirst and interest in the areas the spiritual life addresses; love, forgiveness, positive thinking, death, how to cope with the stuff life throws at us, divorce, unemployment, my reputation and what people think of me. Occasionally, as we sit in The Post Office Bar a few days after Christmas sipping a cool Stella Artois questions can move onto the church, God, prayer and the deeper things of the spiritual life. If you too want answers about the spiritual life and what it can do for you, read on.

This book offers you 'appetisers' for the spiritual life

This book wants to help and support people who see no need for church but have a spiritual life, a personal belief. Spirituality has been filtered out within so many conversations and I wonder if this is because people do not understand it, just like they may not understand the health benefits of the Brussels sprout. Perhaps we need a fresh perspective and awareness of why a spiritual life is good for you.

This book will offer you 'tasters' to get started on the spiritual life. We will explore the main areas that anyone interested in having a healthy spiritual life would want explained. There could be many

understandings of the Bible, for example, from the Bible being a mythical book of irrelevant stories to the Bible being a book that only fundamentalist people will quote. We will show you how it is an enriching guide book and storybook that can help in every human situation and best of all that it is a love story. We will need to delve into the nature of God Himself. Or is that Herself? There are many names and images of God. If this all seems confusing we will simply ask who and what God really is, how God revealed the fullness of His/Her love and where we can find God today.

Central to all your searching there is a belief that if we genuinely invite God to come into our lives, just as we might invite the gym or healthy eating into our lives there will be transformation. Some of this transformation happens through our own efforts but there will be other changes that come directly from God, call it God's gift or Grace and that is how the spiritual muscle, if you like, will grow. That is why this book carries on to say that, we can come to know Jesus Christ as a real person and have a real personal relationship with Him. This is something that the Holy Spirit of God enables us to do.

When we start this journey to the spiritual life there will be a new fire and energy in our lives. We will have a new desire to read God's Word, the Bible. We will have a new and deeper perspective on the church and see that church is not really the physical building; the church is the people. This in turn will give us a genuine desire to pray and to have a grateful heart. The spiritual life will show us another way to understand love and forgiveness and this call to have new mindsets, attitudes and behaviours. We are what we eat. If we eat healthily then over time our bodies become stronger and will withstand the man flus and the attacks that will come our way. Same with the spiritual life. We will have a new strength and power that the world cannot give. It is God's power and love living in us, sustaining us, comforting us, challenging us and allowing us to flourish. We will have a spiritual

'six-pack', maybe even a 'nine-pack'; love, joy, peace, patience, kindness, goodness, faithfulness, gentleness and self-control.

This book aims to help people feel more comfortable exploring things like God, prayer and church in a way that is simple and straightforward. People who say things like:

- Who am I now my parents are no longer alive? What is my purpose now that my children look after themselves? Is this all there is for the rest of my days?
- Are the institutional churches relevant anymore? What will prayer do for me? How do I cope with injustice, past hurts or guilt without getting a "churchy" answer?
- I read the newspapers and I am appalled by the many scandalous stories that have emerged over the year and all I can say is; "Well if this is the church you can stuff it I want to find my own pathway to the spiritual life".
- I have explored the spiritual life before and although it made me feel good for a while it did not last. How do I maintain a healthy spiritual life when I don't feel God near me anymore?

From every discussion with bereaved families, to seasonal conversations with school friends I know there is a thirst out there for the spiritual life. The problem may be that we have lost our way as adults and we need someone to help us and guide us; we need to hear more Good News about the health benefits of the spiritual life. I fully accept that many people do not want a spiritual life and do not believe in God. Lots of people seem to get by adequately without a spiritual life just as many people get by without ever going to the gym or eating their 5-a-day. The question is; what kind of life do you want? I am 48 years old I don't want adequate or just to get by. I want to access all the sources of happiness and health. It's your choice. It is entirely up

to you what you want and desire in life and who you want to have a relationship with.

As we said earlier this is not just about me, this is not just a self-help book. The spiritual life is calling us to a life where we help other people and create a better world. The Book of Ecclesiasticus reminds us that, "If we aspire to serve the Lord, prepare yourself for an ordeal" (Ecclesiasticus 2:1). The ordeal being the avoidance of human temptations to lament, to be idle, to fear, to have no faith or be lost. God wants none of these for us. He wants us to have a full and happy life, and that includes words like service, sacrifice, and giving without expecting anything in return. That is love.

Anyone who has picked up this book because it has a picture of Brussels sprouts on it and they mistakenly think it's a health book, well I have good news for you, it is a health and wealth book.

Brussels sprouts are really good for you, that is beyond scientific doubt. But so is having an active spiritual life. If you have doubts, please read on and I hope we can show you there are many health benefits to having a fulfilling spiritual life including:

- A deeper understanding of our purpose here on earth.
- A greater sense of inner peace that will help us in those moments when life hits us square in the coupon, as they say in Scotland. A lack of peace can tempt us down a path of depression and isolation.
- A focus on developing new healthy habits and focussing on behaviours which are natural to us; such as love, joy, peace, forgiveness, and humility.
- A greater tolerance and a sense of hope.
- It can help to eliminate fear from your life.

It's all about what you desire in life

I conducted a funeral in early 2014 of a 92 year old man called Tom Smith. Tom had the most incredible life; life really was an adventure for him. In his 90th year he decided to do something new; he joined Bannatyne's Gym in Dunfermline. His body was frail, his sight and hearing was very poor but he went to the gym 3 times a week. Sometimes Tom and his pals would play tricks on the Bannatyne's staff and not come out from the swimming pool when his session was up as he was having too much fun. For his 90th birthday the staff threw him a surprise party and gave him a cake and a card.

What I love about that story is the fact that a 90 year old man never stopped trying. He still had a desire in his mind to "do his exercises" and just "turn up" at the gym, with an attitude that said, "What's the worst thing that can happen if I do something positive today".

We will never get fit or have the proverbial six-pack by staying indoors, we need to "turn up" and "do the exercises". We know exercise is good for us, we know our greens are good for us. This book will show you why the spiritual life is amazingly good for us and the incredible health and wealth benefits it will bring. There is nothing to fear but everything to gain.

The Game Changer: we will be given a new Spirit

One of the central messages that God wants to teach us and one of the central messages of this book, is the idea of separation. Most people will be familiar with the Adam and Eve story in the Book of Genesis; how they ate from the tree, called the tree of knowledge. This knowledge gave them the ability and freedom to choose to either be close to God or separated from God. In many ways that is the story of the whole of the Old Testament. This tension between choosing what God wants us to do and what we in our ego and our selfishness want to do, is always there. It's how we are made; a bit weak, a bit sinful, with a propensity to think we can survive by ourselves without God and we can do everything with our own logic and strength. During these Old Testament years the physical part of us seemed to rule the day. God was close to His people but we didn't have the full inner strength we needed to have the fullness of life that God wanted us to have.

The Prophets in the Old Testament, people like Isaiah, Jeremiah, Ezekiel and Daniel called us to change our ways and our hearts and the Prophets also spoke of a time in the future when everything was going to change. "And I will give you a new heart, and I will put a new spirit in you. I will take out your stony, stubborn heart and give you a tender, responsive heart" (Ezekiel 36:26). That is what God promised us. He made a covenant or a promise and He said He would keep it and so He did when He sent His Son Jesus Christ into the world. He carried out that promise and called us to be baptised in His Spirit. If there is one single event in the world that changes everything for the human condition then it is the death and resurrection of Jesus and the gift of His Spirit. God promised that the Spirit would be poured into our hearts and become part of our DNA and now it is impossible

for us to be separated from God, unless we choose not to listen or follow Him.

That is the Good News we want to highlight in this book to anyone who wants to start the spiritual life. God's very Spirit lives in us; there is nothing to fear. That does not mean we will be spared of sorrow or challenges in life, even the top athletes have to train hard and experience failure to win the prize. The prize being a life that can never separate us from the love of God and the fullness of life He offers. That is the choice God offers us. "I came that you may have life and have it to the full" (John 10:10). A life of wealth, health and happiness.

Choose to be fed by this Good News and you will see the results: love, joy, peace, patience, kindness, goodness, faithfulness, gentleness and self-control. "Taste and see that the Lord is Good" (Psalm 34:8).

Where do we start this journey to health and wealth? In the beginning of course, which curiously is the first line in the Bible.

SPIRITUAL FOOD FOR THOUGHT

The 7 benefits of the spiritual life

When you start doing spiritual exercises like Scripture reading, praying, chanting or meditating it may soon develop into a daily practice. Over time, you feel the benefits of this daily practice. These may include the following:

1. Clarity within your life and a realisation that there is more to be grateful for in life than there is to grumble about. When you practice the habit of gratitude you will become more energised and will have greater optimism and vitality.

2. Self-awareness and awareness of others can make us more generous. A survey was conducted to find out who the happiest person in the world was and he was named as a Tibetan monk called Mattheu Ricard. When asked what the secret of his contentment was, he said it was meditating on the value of compassion and then practising it.

3. The spiritual life can raise your spirits, lift your moods and increase your joy. Most people want more of that.

4. Spiritual exercises can make you feel more grounded and rooted. Human experiences can knock some people 'over the edge', but when faced with a spiritual inner strength and calmness, we will have a balance and equilibrium that saves us from feelings of 'going under'.

5. More life fulfilling relationships. The spiritual life is connected to our self-esteem and how we relate to other people. It is often said that we mirror to the outside world what is in our inside world. So

if we are angry, lost or embittered inside, that will come out within our relationships. The spiritual life will show you how to replace negative destructive feelings with more positive ones. (Galatians 5:22-23, tells us that the fruits of the Spirit are: love, joy, peace, patience, kindness, goodness, faithfulness, gentleness and self-control) and this in turn will impact our relationships for the good.

6. The spiritual life will invite us to a simpler and humbler life. A life where you are no longer just getting by or accepting mediocrity. You will have a new outlook, a different set of priorities that stop you from getting bogged down by what the world may be telling you are the only source of happiness. Spiritual people desire self-actualisation and they know life is not all about themselves and their needs and wants.

7. Spiritual people are aware that the so called ordinary steps and daily practices build up over time to give you an inner strength no-one can take away from you. Spirituality is the search for sacred things in life that money can't buy.

CHAPTER 1

THE BIBLE AND WHAT IT REALLY MEANS

"The grass withers and the flowers fall, but the word of our God endures forever." — Isaiah 40:8

The Bible is one of the best-selling books in the world. There was a time in the past when just about every home had a family Bible, when every hotel room had a Gideon's Bible and when swearing on the Bible within a court of law was the norm. Although there is no swearing on an actual Bible anymore in Scottish courts, there is debate about the relevance of the oath which says, "I swear by Almighty God that I will tell the truth, the whole truth and nothing but the truth".

In this chapter we want to explore the truth of the Bible, its message, meaning and the relevance of the Bible to living an authentic and healthy life. We will do this by exploring what we mean when we say that the Bible is true and the importance of context. We will come to an understanding that the Bible has to be read within a specific historical and cultural context. Finally it will become clear that we will have a better understanding of the Bible and what it really means when we have some form of Bible Study or training from those who have been longer on the spiritual path.

I am fully aware that the Bible is a book that seems fairly irrelevant and has little guidance for many people's lives these days. Sometimes

this is not helped by situations where individuals abuse and misquote the Bible to justify certain personal beliefs. In February 2014 a local counsellor within the UKIP party, David Silvester was caught up in a media storm when he said that UK Government had abandoned biblical teachings and that the Government's abandonment of the Bible in part caused the floods to happen in South West England. He was mocked for using the Bible in this situation to support what is arguably a barmy belief about how floods happen. In March 2014 a religious Preacher in Manchester was awarded a £13,000 pay out from the Police after he was locked in a UK jail for 19 hours without his medication. The preacher John Craven ended up in jail because two young men approached him and asked what the Bible said about homosexuality. The preacher wasn't preaching on that subject but since he was asked, he quoted from the Bible and said gay love was a sin, however he then went on to say "whilst God hates sin, He loves the sinner." The two young men complained to a nearby Policeman saying, his views were offensive and so the Preacher was arrested and thrown into jail. This story may perpetuate the belief that the Bible is homophobic, misogynistic, irrelevant and simply out of date.

When I hear stories like these about the Bible and how it is irrelevant, homophobic, out of date or historically inaccurate I think; why do some people quote passages from the Bible out of context? I believe these well-meaning people put themselves in a position whereby the credibility of the Bible is lessened. It confuses people and can lead some to believe the Bible is an out of date book that is not worth reading. The problem here is one of context. If you read or quote the Bible out of context the truth of the message can get lost, or even watered down. So, to understand the Bible and what it really means, you have to look at context.

When I was a student at Glasgow University in the 1980s I heard a story about a fellow student citing a 15th Century University law for

failing his exam. He claimed there was a medieval University law that allowed him to have a glass of port during his exam. When he requested his glass of port during his 1989 exam he was promptly told to go away, or similar words. He left the exam hall without finishing his test paper. He failed the exam then appealed to the faculty quoting the 15th Century law and something about not having fair exam conditions. The claim against the University was thrown out and it's said the next day he was fined 15 Guineas for walking across the University courtyard without his sword and scabbard.

The point is, a 15th Century law concerning glasses of port and swords made sense at that time, but the social context had changed considerably 500 years later. So too with many of the stories from the Bible. We cannot blame fields being flooded in England in 2014 because the Government had abandoned biblical teaching. Surely the floods had something to do with unusual meteorological patterns that just so happened to drop a lot of rain in one particular part of the country.

Understanding the context

The Bible has a specific historical context and has to be understood within the social, political, economic, and spiritual context of the day. Some of the books in the Bible date from 1400 BC and others were written or re-written over a period of time between 1400 BC and the early 1st Century. People living in 1400 BC had radically different views on all kinds of things from; who makes the crops grow or how women should be treated. We cannot use our 2014 eyes to re-read such an ancient book. We have to have some understanding of the historical context in which these words were originally written.

You might want to look at the Bible like a newspaper. A newspaper has many different genres. You get factual headline news; you get

opinion stories, cartoons, poetry and fantasy. All kinds of different writing styles exist within a newspaper, same too with the Bible. Some books in the Bible report genuine historical facts and others contain historical inaccuracies. Other books are personal stories about real historical people such as, Isaiah, Jeremiah. Others are poetry like the Song of Songs. We even have 4 different versions of Jesus' life within 4 Gospels: Matthew, Mark, Luke and John. These four writers are addressing four different communities and they tell the same story in four different ways. When we read any book in the Bible it is worth remembering this point about context and who the book is written for. Once we understand this we can synthesise the message from that particular part of the Bible into our own lives.

For example, the Book of Jonah may not be historically true, but a truth will emerge and we can synthesise that truth into our own lives. One message of the book is that you may have experienced being swallowed by "a whale" and spat out. That "whale" being anything from food, people, work, apathy, cynicism that may be swallowing our lives. In other words the Book of Jonah is telling us a life truth that can help us live more authentic lives. When we understand that Jonah is not a historical figure but is allegory to being swallowed in life, then we will better understand the message of the Book of Jonah. The same is true for all the books in the Bible. The Bible is truth presented in another way. It is a spiritual truth.

In a similar vein, these ideas of context and truth help us understand the historical inaccuracies and inconsistencies in the Bible. The archaeologist Dr Francesca Stavrakopoulou has cast doubt through her work as to whether King David's kingdom, as described in the Book of Samuel, ever existed. But what is not beyond doubt is that the story of Samuel proclaims a spiritual truth. The spiritual truth being that God chooses everyone, just as he chose Samuel to stay close to him, to stay loyal to him; no matter what happens to us in life and no matter what other people think of us.

The Bible as truth

This whole idea of context and what is true in the Bible is a contentious issue even amongst Christians. There are some Christians who say every word in the Bible is true and that places like the Garden of Eden are real gardens that existed once upon a time. This may be true, some kind of gardens may have existed when the book of Genesis was written and the gardens were used to illustrate a spiritual point first and foremost rather than a geographical point. Please do not get hung up on whether a real garden existed in a specific geographical location try and read the Bible as a book that is telling us God's relationship with us. Biblical scholars tend to agree that the Garden of Eden is a story and the purpose of the story is to explain how man and woman separated themselves from God. We cannot get distracted on the idea that the Garden of Eden was a genuine garden that existed in time, although there is evidence to suggest a garden did exist. The Bible is guiding us to a spiritual and theological truth rather than the geographical truth that such a garden truly existed. We have to be careful about saying every word in the Bible is historically true. What we can say is that every word is spiritually true. The same argument can be used when Jesus said, 'if your eye causes you to sin, pluck it out' (Matthew 18:9). Ask yourself the question, what is the spiritual truth here? What is Jesus commanding us to do? Self-mutilation; surely not? If that is the case, why are there not more one-eyed Christians walking about? Jesus uses strong language here to remind us of the basic human choice between life and death, misery and happiness. Jesus is asking us what our goal and purpose in life is and that if we are serious about having a spiritual life, then we may have to face some radical choices. We may have to choose to stop doing some things and opt to have new and healthier habits in life. Are we willing to do what it will take to have a full and active spiritual life? I dare say many an

athlete asks the same question, 'Am I willing to do what is necessary to get to that final goal?'

The Bible may look like a single book but it's a collection of books; it's like a library. The word Bible literally means 'little library'. There are 66 books in the Bible, all written at different times, with different intentions, messages, purposes and literary genres. Every book tells us truths about the spiritual life. Many messages are comforting, others are challenging, but the purpose of the Bible is to help us become spiritually fit. It is like a manual or roadmap to spiritual enlightenment.

Although the Bible covers many different genres, cultures, messages and moods, what holds the Bible together is that it is an inspired book. St. Paul wrote a letter to his friend Timothy and said, "All Scripture is given by inspiration of God, and is profitable for doctrine, for reproof, for correction, for instruction in righteousness" (2 Timothy 3:16).

An inspired book

What do we mean when we say the Bible is inspired? Whenever we read the Bible, foremost in our minds should be the notion that this is a book about how much God loves us and always has. Ultimately God showed us how much He loved us and what price He was willing to pay to save us, by sending His Son Jesus from heaven. God loved us first. It is an unconditional and eternal love, we choose either to want God's love or not. The people that wrote the books of the New Testament wrote not just so that we would not forget this man Jesus, they wrote to remind us that God is a faithful God. A God who will never let us down and that He has a Divine plan to draw us into a loving union with Himself. That is His plan; to love us no matter what. It's an eternal plan and we are free to choose whether we want a spiritual life or not. God wants us to have an eternal life with Him in heaven and for us to experience as much of that Divine life as we can while we are here on earth.

This echoes what we have already said about the Bible's purpose not being a purely historical book. The Bible's main purpose is to tell us spiritual truths of God's love and to what lengths God went to save us. That is why the Bible is an inspired book. It's about how to deepen and rejoice in our relationship with God. The Bible is a guide for us to know who we are and who God is. It was written by people just like you and me who have loved, suffered, hoped, laughed and cried. It is the words of God written in our own words as a guide to help us live the full and authentic lives we are asked to live. We say the Bible is inspired because it tells us about what God has done for us.

On the night before Jesus died, a true historical figure called Pontius Pilate had a conversation with Jesus who had been beaten up and imprisoned. Jesus told Pilate the reason and purpose of why He was born. Jesus said He came to bear witness to the truth and that those who are on the side of truth will listen to His voice (Gospel of John 18:33). Then Pilate asked, "Truth, what is that?" For Christians the answer came 3 days later, very early on Easter morning when Jesus rose from the dead. Whether people believe the resurrection of Jesus to be a historical fact or not, the Bible declares this and many other things to be true, spiritually true.

Fascinating archaeological evidence

In 1947 an incredible discovery was made in the mountains surrounding the Dead Sea in Israel. Hundreds of papyrus scrolls were found in caves perfectly preserved. They were exact copies of many of the books in the Bible, mainly books from the Old Testament and can be dated back to 3 BC. What was fascinating about the Dead Sea Scrolls is that there was very little difference between these ancient texts and a modern day Bible. God's word has literally been preserved

from the first moments when it was written down. As an aside, the oldest New Testament scroll is a scrap of parchment, dating back to 130 AD. It comes from John's Gospel and the words written on the parchment are the words of Pilate "What is truth?"

Remember that poor guy at University who proclaimed that having a glass of port during an exam was the truth? It wasn't the case was it? Once the context was understood we saw where he went wrong and sometimes we need that don't we?

So far we have said that the Bible only proclaims spiritual truths of how God wanted to show His love for us and how He saved us. The Bible claims to tell the truth of who God is and what He has done for us through His Son Jesus and that is why anyone who is genuinely interested in the spiritual life will in time want to explore the messages of the Bible. If you are seriously interested in the spiritual life you will want to take that interest to the next level or at least explore what it is that is on offer. If you knew the specific cancer fighting properties of the Brussels sprouts would that not increase your interest in wanting to eat them? Although sometimes, as I have already said, we do need other people to give us this information and guide us in order to fully understand what is on offer.

We need help to understand the Bible

I guess this brings us to the question: where do we start? What should someone do were they to pick up the Bible for the first time? How should they read it? Where should they start?

We can answer that by saying it doesn't matter where you start, just begin reading it anywhere. Why not read the story of Jesus' life? The 4 Gospels of Matthew, Mark, Luke and John are an interesting place

to start. I would recommend Luke's Gospel as being the most readable. Find your favourite stories and if you struggle with certain passages seek some help and guidance. There is a lot of help out there on the Internet for example. Also there is no harm in asking for God's direct help. You will find a prayer at the end of this chapter to the Holy Spirit to help you and raise your awareness of the Book of the Bible you have decided to read. We all need help.

I remember being at High School and we read a play called 'Juno and the Paycock' by Sean O'Casey and I really did not understand the message until we got another small book, I am sure they were called Letts Notes and this gave a simplified version of the play and its message. When I read these notes the play became alive and I understood it had something to say about the tensions between living in the real world and living in a world of fantasy and daydreams and what happens when these illusions are taken away and we see the true reality of our lives. I would never have understood the meaning of that play without the help of someone else.

We sometimes need help to explore the Bible; we need guidance notes or some kind of coach to tell us what a particular book is all about. Just start somewhere and try and develop a regular habit of reading the Bible, perhaps at the same time or in the same place. In other words, turn up and do the exercises. Open the book and read. You will find your own particular characters and stories that speak to you. Being a man who is only five foot five and a half, I love the story of the 'wee' man Zacchaeus in the Gospel of Luke, chapter 19, verses 1-10. This beautiful story reminds me that sometimes we have to make an effort if we want to see Jesus. He climbed a sycamore tree to catch a glimpse of Jesus when He just so happened to be walking through his village. He had a desire and a thirst to see this man and Jesus responded to his enthusiasm and desire and had a meal in his home that night. I love too the story of two men walking down the road to Emmaus (Luke 24)

as it likewise reminds me that when I am down and dejected in life and I speak to God in prayer He will make His presence known to me.

The Bible is a very interesting library of books with fascinating characters and stories and it recalls the journey that many people have made to discover God. But more than that, the Bible will take us to a place of mystery and faith. The more we are familiar with the book, the more we read and practise, the more it will console, encourage and challenge us. Pick up a Bible, delve in, feel free to write on it and underline words you like. Once we discover stories that speak to us we will discover more about God and ourselves. Over time pages may become tatty, the cover may lose its gloss but tatty is ok. I like the phrase, 'Bibles that are falling apart are for people who aren't".

Remember it's all about context. It's all about spiritual truths. It's all about God's love for us and His covenant and promise to never let us down, for us never to be separated from Him. In order to understand the message of a particular book of the Bible we have to comprehend the context in which it was written and the community or audience the author is writing to. Remember too, if you need guidance or help reading the Bible, seek it.

The late Seve Ballesteros was a wonderful golfer and practised his sport so much he had a master level. To get to that pinnacle took a lot of hours and a lot of coaching. If you read the story of the two men journeying to Emmaus in the Gospel of Luke, chapter 24 you will see that ultimately Christ is our coach and guide.

When it comes to creating a spiritual life and building the spiritual muscle we don't need to be at a master's level straight away. Start on the putting green, enjoy the spiritual life, do something; talk with God in prayer, open the Bible, look at the healthy spiritual habits you are interested in building and the less healthy ones you want to get rid of. Do something, turn up and do the exercises and the muscle and the relationship will deepen.

Think of the Bible as a spiritual survival handbook and what it really means to you. For some people it will be a daily resource book that guides their lives and they can easily dip into for comfort and consolation. For other people it's a means of historical study and for others it is a book that brings them closer to God and gently encourages them and challenges them to live a healthier and more balanced life. Ultimately, the Bible and what it really means is a question only you can answer and rejoice in.

Some interesting facts about the Bible that you may not know:

- The middle of the Bible is Psalm 118.
- Before that there are 594 chapters.
- After that there are 594 chapters.
- Add the two together and you get 1188.
- The middle verse of the Bible is Psalm 118:8 "It is better to take refuge in the Lord than to trust in man".

That may be one of the main messages of the Bible; to make God the centre of everything we do.

SPIRITUAL FOOD FOR THOUGHT

How to start reading the Bible

1. One night, before you go to sleep tell God you want to read the Bible and ask Him to give you the motivation and desire to read His Word.

2. The next day, create a time when you have some uninterrupted peace, it could be first thing in the morning or last thing at night. Try and get into a routine of keeping that time. It may help, for example, to keep the Bible on a bedside table to give you that reminder to read before you go to sleep, just as a toothbrush is a reminder to brush your teeth.

3. Choose a book from the Bible or a chapter that interests you and pray before you start reading, for the Holy Spirit to be your teacher. You may say something like:

   Holy Spirit, reveal to me the love of God the Father and of His Son Jesus Christ as I meditate on His word. Give me a real understanding of what I need in my life and what I have to change in my life and put into practice.

   In the words of St. Peter, help me Lord to "Make every effort to add to my faith goodness; and to that goodness, knowledge; to that knowledge, self-control; and to self-control, perseverance; and to perseverance, godliness; and to godliness, mutual affection; and to mutual affection, love". (2 Peter 1:5-7) Give me confidence Lord to develop new spiritual habits so that it is no longer "I that live but Christ that lives in me" (Galatians 2:20).

I thank you that you have given me this time and that you have given me faith to read your Word. Please bring me close to you. Lead me into the truth. Open my eyes to see all that you want me to see. I trust the Holy Spirit to teach me, because Jesus said "He will teach you all things" (John 14:26).

Holy Spirit, I call upon you now to enlighten my life with your Divine life. Amen

4. Start reading. Some people who are new to the Bible start with the Gospels in the New Testament—Matthew, Mark, Luke, and John. Try to devote a minimum number of minutes to Bible reading each day, but don't be concerned about the number of verses or chapters that you cover within the allotted time.

5. When you have finished reading try and memorise a word or a phrase to take with you that day. Select a verse that means the most to you. Write it down if it helps and as your list of memorable verses grows, so will your thirst for reading the Bible grow.

CHAPTER 2

GOD AND WHO EXACTLY IS HE/SHE?

"I Am who I Am." Exodus 3:14

How many people do you know without a name? I don't think there is anyone in this world without a name, unless you are a film star called Clint Eastwood. He was in a movie called 'A Fistful of Dollars' and his name was: 'A Man Without a Name!'

In reality, when you are born unless your birth is registered it is almost as if you just don't exist. It may be that your name was chosen by your parents before you were born. For others, who cannot make up their minds, the name is chosen after they are born. I know of someone who had not named their baby for weeks and kept referring to their new-born child as 'it' or 'baby'. But 'it' and 'baby' are not 'proper' names, so they were unable to register the birth until a real name had been chosen. How ridiculous is that?

"I Am who I Am". What kind of name is this? Is this not ridiculous as well? Would you register your child with this name? What do you think the Registrar would say or think? Would he laugh? Would he think you are crazy? Without doubt, the name has a certain air of conviction, of knowing who you are, despite what others may think. But do you think in this day and age, this name would be acceptable by most? Isn't it a name that appears as if there is something missing, because it doesn't

look like it's a proper name? The surprising thing is, 'I Am who I Am' is the name God wanted everyone to know Him by.

In this chapter we want to explore God's name and who exactly God is. God knows His name, God knows our name and because He knows us intimately by name He wants us to have everything that is good for us in life. We will explore how we can have many images of God and how the fullness of God's presence was revealed in this world when His Son Jesus Christ was born. Then it will become clear that Jesus is our truest and deepest identity. We are made in the image and likeness of God and called to be Christ like in all our thoughts, behaviours and actions. People will ultimately know who God is by how we treat other people. There are countless good people in the world from all religions; Hindus, Jews, Muslims, Buddhists, Christians of all denominations, and many more good and loving people who aren't affiliated with any religion. Does God love them? Of course He does. Maybe one reason why God didn't claim a name beyond "I Am who I Am" (Exodus 3:14) is that God didn't want to be pigeon-holed as a particular gender, denomination or race. He calls us all to holiness. This again asks the question, "Who is God to you?"

The Divine Name Revealed

Let me take you back to the year 1300 BC. The Jews were slaves in Egypt and they had a leader called Moses who was to lead the Jewish people out of slavery to Israel; the land God promised them. The first five books of the Bible are traditionally ascribed to Moses and Moses was chosen to be the conduit or channel between God and the Jewish people. Let's reflect on this further:

God had given Moses his first mission. He was to go to Pharaoh to bring the sons of Israel, out of Egypt. The sons of Israel were God's people. Moses questioned God about this as he did not feel worthy to

accomplish this task, but God said to him: ‘I shall be with you.’ Moses still perplexed did not know what to do. He must have thought: ‘How on earth can I go to Pharaoh. What am I going to tell him? He’ll probably think I am crazy.’ But just to make sure that what he had heard from God was true, he repeated it and said to God: ‘I am to go, then, to the sons of Israel and say to them, “The God of your fathers has sent me to you”. But if they ask me what His name is, what on earth am I to tell them?’ And God said to Moses, ‘I Am who I Am. This’, He added ‘is what you must say to the sons of Israel: “I Am has sent me to you”. This is my name for all time; by this name I shall be invoked for all generations to come’ (Exodus 3).

Do you think this is really a proper name? So, if this is not a real name it might also mean that the person does not exist, for it would not be an acceptable name for the registration.

“I Am” is a name that does not make much sense and will not appear in the Mumsnet Top 100 Names for 2014 but actually, it shows a certain conviction on God’s part. God knows who He is. He is sure of His name. He knows He exists. The question is: ‘do you?’ If you do believe in the existence of God, what kind of image do you have of Him or her for that matter?

What’s in a name anyway? YHWH or Yahweh whichever you choose merely means - I Am.

Yahweh is the principal name in the Old Testament by which God reveals Himself and is the most sacred name of God. In the Bible the name for God is written as YHWH which is the word Yahweh without vowels.

The name Yahweh is best known from the famous “I Am” interaction with Moses, and it proves that God has always existed and will always exist. Though this is true, it is also a very basic understanding of the meaning of Yahweh. In the ancient world, names communicated

something about a person's character, so a name carried much meaning with it. God chose to reveal Himself in the name Yahweh. We should expect this name to communicate a lot about the character of God.

We know that in the Bible God also revealed Himself to us through His many other names. Here are a few examples:

El Shaddai - (Lord God Almighty)

Adonai - (Lord, Master)

Yahweh - (Lord, Jehovah)

Jehovah-Raah - (The Lord My Shepherd)

Jehovah Rapha - (The Lord That Heals)

Jehovah Shammah - (The Lord Is With You)

Jehovah Jireh - (The Lord Will Provide)

Jehovah Shalom - (The Lord Is Peace)

The reason for listing God's names above and what they mean, is basically because not many people are aware by how many names God reveals Himself to us in the Bible, and these are only a few. If you care to research there are many, many more. It is also to make you aware of how much you can trust God and how He will give you everything you need for a healthy life and the benefits the spiritual life can bring.

When we know the name of what is good for us we will not hesitate in consuming it. Health professionals tell us the names of things like broccoli and Brussels sprouts are good for us. The Bible tells us not just one name for God, but many names of God and the good things God can give us like peace, provision, healing and a shepherd to guide our lives. This book is asking whether you accept the advice and guidance of the professionals. Could you accept that God has revealed Himself through many names so that we can taste the many facets of

Himself? You may be in need of healing and this book will show you that one of the treasures the spiritual life offers is, healing of emotions, physical conditions and spiritual healing.

Perhaps this is why Psalm 9:10 says, "And those who know Your name will put their trust in You, For You, O Lord, have not forsaken those who seek You."

As we read through Scripture we can see the importance of names. God has many names and each reveals Him in a different way. God's names represent His attributes, and His nature. Therefore, it is important that we know God by His many names.

When we study these names that He reveals to us in the Bible, we will better understand who God really is. The meanings behind God's names reveal the central personality and nature of the One who bears them.

Your name, therefore, is your identity. It is who you are known by. However, some people don't like the name they have been given by their parents. Take mine, for example.

The name that is written on my birth certificate is: Maria de las Victorias Gladys Rosales. Maria de las Victorias is a Spanish abbreviated name which literally translated means: Mary of the Victories. Gladys on the other hand is from the old Welsh name Gwladus, possibly derived from Gwlad 'country'. Rosales, which is my maiden surname, means "bed of roses" in Spanish. And do you know what? It has not always been a bed of roses!

When I look back at the meaning of my name, however, I now understand why Maria de las Victorias was chosen first! It was so that I could be victorious over any weakness that might have come upon me during my life here on earth, of which there have been many. It is one of the first lessons I learnt in the spiritual life that God calls us by

our name. It doesn't matter what our name or gender is, what's important is that God has called us to have a relationship with Him. He knows us by our name. He loves us as we are.

"Do not fear, for I have redeemed you; I have called you by your name; you are mine" (Isaiah 43:1). Another favourite quote of my own is, "I have heard the Lord call my name, listen close you'll hear the same!" I used to have this as a screensaver on my computer at work and it simply touched the people who read it.

Is God male or female? What is your image of God?

Whilst we are on the subject of names and identity, I have met many people who wonder whether God is male or female. This very much depends on the image you have of God. God's image is very different for everyone.

I'll start with myself. I grew up in a very loving home with my father, my mother and my younger sister Vivienne. My mother was fun loving and great to be with. There were times, however, when due to frustration at our misbehaviour, she might raise her voice at us and even 'clip' the dishtowel on our derrières.

My father on the other hand, was quite Victorian and stern. He was very loving too, but when he wanted to discipline us, he would put on an austere look that demanded respect. I was quite a tomboy in those days; perhaps I still am and was always getting into trouble and getting punished for it. My dad never placed a hand on me, but he did chastise me by removing what I liked. I remember my father had also set very high standards that I had to meet, no matter what. Academically, he expected me always to succeed. From a very young age, I was always 'first' in class with top marks of between 90 and 100%. I do believe

this was due to my father's influence and the fact that every time I excelled in my studies, he rewarded me. That is until I reached the beginning of my teenage years when I started going downhill in more ways than one. My exam results started going from 'first' to 'second' to 'third' until I managed to come 'last' of the class. My father was not pleased and my rewards ended.

My interests were always in the arts field. I loved singing and dancing. I imagined myself growing up and becoming a singer or a dancer. Alas, no, it was not to be! My father thought better and sent me to commercial college where I attained my certificates in Business Studies. Thankfully I did well here and was able to get a very demanding and responsible job with the Government Secretariat, in Gibraltar. I must admit that had my father not taken this stance with my life, I would probably not have achieved as much as I did in later life. His counsel and wisdom has helped me time and time again, and to this day I have never looked back. Father always knows best!

You might well ask the rhetorical question, 'What has this got to do with our image of God?'

The truth is that if you grew up with an image of a strict and disciplinary father or mother, you are more likely to see God as a stern father or mother, who punishes you for every misdemeanour or single act of disobedience you ever committed. I know this not to be the case, for God is a loving Father who wants to give good things to His children.

Although this has been one of my experiences within my 67 years on this earth, as a result of many years of spiritual exercises, I have since learnt that there are many images of God that are comforting, encouraging and also bring healing.

There is the image of:

- God of surprises.
- God of healing.
- God of consolation.
- God of comfort.
- God of love.
- God of forgiveness.
- God of second chances.

Let's look a little bit deeper into who God is or might be. For millions of years men and women have looked up into the sky, and had a deep sense of wonder and awe from the galaxies and the universe out there. For me, this is something I have done for most of my life and continue to do so. In fact, I remember when my fiancé Tony and I were courting in Gibraltar; our favourite past-time was fixing our eyes deeply on the vastness of the sky and looking up at the stars. The depth of that sky transcended our understanding. We just don't know what is beyond what we can see. We just know that 'out there' exists some form of universe with many galaxies. We believe this because there is scientific evidence that tells us so.

However, it's not the purpose of this book to examine the awesomeness of how the world was created or even the fascinating subject of quantum physics. In order to give a deeper answer to the question of who God is, we simply need to look at one man, Jesus Christ. I cannot put it in a better way than the author of the Gospel of John who said, "In the beginning was the Word, and the Word was with God, and the Word was God. He was in the beginning with God. All things came into being through Him, and without Him not one thing came into being. And the Word became flesh and lived among us, and we have seen His glory, the glory as of a father's only son, full of Grace and truth" (John 1: 1-3 and 14).

Getting back to the question of who God is, can you imagine that God came to earth as a baby, by being conceived in the virgin womb of a woman called Mary, who gave birth to Him in a stable and named Him Jesus? God, Almighty and Divine, chose to become a human being so that He could communicate with us as a man, since our spiritual relationship with Him was broken and to identify Himself completely with the human race. Part of this plan was so that we should become more like Christ and have Christ like behaviours and Christ like habits. His promise is if we take on this identity we will have happiness and a wealth beyond our imagination.

I dare say there are many people who buy a twelve-month membership for Bannantye's gym and think they will never achieve the proverbial six-pack and total fitness, but by doing the exercises and turning up, that fitness can be achieved if you truly desire it. That applies as much to spiritual fitness as it does to physical fitness. By doing the spiritual exercises of prayer, reading, keeping faith, loving others and thanking God in everything we do, we will, over time become like Christ and be His presence in the world. The more we become like Christ, the more Christ's light and energy will shine in the world for people to see. As I was writing this book I saw that, with the grieving parents of James Foley who was killed by Islamic State fighters in Iraq in August 2014. The love, faith and forgiveness of his parents, John and Diane, were for me an example of Christ's presence in the world when they said they were working on forgiving the man who killed their son. God's light does shine in the world.

God as Energy

We know what it's like, don't we, when we go to the gym and we exercise? We feel a renewed strength of energy and a build-up of muscles. It's the same when we eat our vegetables isn't it? All those lovely nutrients being absorbed into our blood streams making us

stronger, healthier people with greater energy levels. God, likewise, can be understood as energy.

God has no beginning and no end; just as energy. Energy is omnipresent, just as God is. If you know how to utilise energy, you can do just about anything.

Energy cannot be seen, just like God who is invisible! Both are never seen, and both can only be felt. Scientists have faith in energy, and Christians have faith in God.

God is energy and God is also love. "And so we know and rely on the love God has for us. God is love. Whoever lives in love lives in God, and God in them" (1 John 4:16).

Love is an energy that is all around us and it's against the laws of physics and God for that energy to die. Energy simply cannot be destroyed and because God loves us, He wants us to live life to the fullest.

So God has revealed the fullness of His identity. We now know who God is, we know His Name, first it was "I Am" then God revealed Himself fully in Jesus Christ. We have seen His face. We can read His story and we can come to know Him as a real person.

Jesus is our truest identity

Within my spiritual life I now see that not only is my identity in my proper name, Maria de las Victorias Gladys Rosales, but I also have a deeper identity; a spiritual identity in Christ. I echo the words of St. Paul who once said, "It is no longer I that live, but Christ who lives in me". I say this with the utmost confidence because my parents baptised me and the tiniest spark of Divine life was ignited within my real identity. Over the subsequent 67 years of my life even though it has not always been a bed of roses and there have been times when I have

rejected or turned away from my spiritual identity, I know who I am. When I do the spiritual exercises (prayer, faith, hope, forgiveness, church), and live my life in accordance with God's plan, my true identity is even more apparent to me. I am a spiritual being. God lives in me and I live in Him (John 15).

If looking into our own identity is not enough, if the Scriptures are not enough, the prayers are not enough, we can always look at the stars and the wonder of the universe for further evidence of who God is. Does looking up into the stars not give you a sense of the Divine? If you want to understand or find God's identity there is plenty of scientific evidence out there to make us think or reflect about God's existence. What we have concluded is that the fullness of God's identity was revealed in the person of Jesus Christ and because Jesus was born as a human this now gives humans access to an even greater and deeper identity that we call the spiritual life. If you would like a spiritual shortcut to know God's identity and who He or She is, then look at Jesus Christ.

This book is a guide to getting started in the spiritual life and one of the first places to start the spiritual life is through exploration of our truest identity; who we are and what our purpose in life is. It is true that once upon a time someone went to a Registry Office and registered our names and that gave us an identity. This book invites you to explore your true identity and suggests that we can only fully understand who we are by accepting that we have a spiritual identity. And who is our spiritual identity? It's Christ. That is the ultimate purpose of our lives; to grow closer to Christ and to become like Him. God wants us to live the deepest most fulfilling life that we can achieve this side of heaven.

Life and all of existence are all about God and His great Glory. God is a glorious God. He has always been. He was glorious in eternity past, even before the very beginning of creation. So why did God create

anything? He created the vast, unfathomable universe to manifest and show off His awesome Glory. 'In the beginning, God created the heavens' (Genesis 1:1). Why? God tells us why; 'the heavens declare the Glory of God... and the firmament shows His handiwork' (Psalm 19:1).

We all have differing views and beliefs about creation and God. Some believe that the world and the universe were created by God. Others believe in the 'Big Bang' theory. My beliefs are more simplistic and lean towards a God that is all encompassing, loving and true. I believe in God the Father, the Son and the Holy Spirit. I believe in Jesus Christ His only Son, who was conceived by the Holy Spirit, and was born in a town called Bethlehem in Judea of a young virgin Jewish girl, called Mary. I believe Jesus is the Bridge that came to reconcile us back to the Father. He suffered death on a cross at the hands of Pontius Pilate. I also believe He died, was buried, descended into hell to rescue Adam, the first created man and Eve his wife and to raise up all who were sleeping from the ages and those to come. I believe, without a doubt that Jesus Christ, on the third day, rose again from the dead and ascended into heaven, where He sits at the right hand of God, the Father Almighty. I also believe in the resurrection of all who have died and that He will come again to this earth and we will have to give account of ourselves to Him and everything we have done in our lives will be exposed. 'It is to God, therefore, that each of us must give an account of Himself' (Romans 14: 10-12). 'But I tell you that everyone will have to give account on the day of Judgement for every empty word they have spoken' (Matthew 12:36).

I also believe in His church, as the Body of Christ, referred to in the Bible as His Bride, as already mentioned. I believe God forgives sins and He has paid the price for them, on our behalf. I also believe He did it all for me personally, not just for those in the world. My ultimate goal is to spend eternity with Him when I myself die and experience

completeness in Him and new life in my heavenly home. Wow, what a privilege!

We all have choices to make and it is not for me or Neil to tell you what choice you have to make in your life, or what you are to believe. I myself will take the road Jesus has prepared for me, for I'd rather believe in God and find out when I die that He doesn't exist; than not to believe in Him and find out when I die that He does exist. Why? He may not know me. Would you let a stranger into your house if you did not know them?

I say this because when I read the story of the virgins in Matthew 25: 1-13, it had a huge impact on me. The story begins:

'God's kingdom is like ten young virgins who took oil lamps and went out to greet the bridegroom. Five were foolish and five were sensible. The foolish virgins took their lamps, but they brought no oil. The sensible virgins took flasks of oil as well as their lamps. The bridegroom didn't show up when they expected Him, and they all fell asleep.

In the middle of the night someone yelled out, "He's here! The bride-groom's here! Go out and greet him!"

The ten virgins got up and got their lamps ready. The foolish virgins said to the sensible ones, "Our lamps are going out; lend us some of your oil." They answered, "There might not be enough to go around; go buy your own."

They did, but while they were out buying oil, the bridegroom arrived. When everyone who was there to greet him had gone into the wedding feast, the door was locked.

Much later, the other virgins, the foolish ones, showed up and knocked on the door, saying, "Master, we're here. Let us in." He answered, "Do I know you? I don't think I know you."

So stay alert. You have no idea when he might arrive.'

Now to some people starting on the spiritual life this might sound like an alarming story because of this real possibility that we might not get to heaven unless we know Jesus. The counterbalance to all of this is that God knows us first. Go and read Psalm 139, I bet you will be impressed by the intimacy of God's love for us. This is the first principle we need to understand within the spiritual life; God's love for us.

This chapter set out to explain who God is. I shared with you many of my own personal beliefs and these are things I have learnt and experienced within my spiritual journey on this earth. I know these to be true and we have to stay alert, just as we have to stay alert to what foods we eat; to what messages come into our minds every day. The Bible is called 'Good News' for a reason. The Good News is God's love for us is so enormous, so overwhelming that He wishes us to be with Him for eternity. God doesn't want us to have the joys of eternal life only at the end of our lives, He wants us to have them now, whilst we are on this earth and that is what this book intends to show you. We understand the Good News of God's love and who God is through prayer, faith, church, fellowship and the love that we have for our fellow human beings. You know that song, "you know that they are Christians by their love", that is what God is asking of us; to live spiritual lives.

If you want a further counterbalance to the perhaps alarming ten virgins' story, look at what Jesus says in Matthew 25 where he talks about feeding the hungry, giving drink to the thirsty, welcoming the stranger, clothing the naked and visiting the sick. This is where we live out our spiritual lives; in helping others. This is where we bear real spiritual fruit; love, joy, peace, forbearance, kindness, goodness, faithfulness, gentleness and self-control (Galatians 5:22-23).

Going to church doesn't make you any more a Christian than going to the garage makes you a car. Your beliefs don't make you a better person, your behaviour does. Your words mean nothing if your actions are the complete opposite. Having true faith in whatever it is you believe must be shown through actions; believing is only half the battle.

This then asks the question directly to you within your own spiritual lives:

Who is God to you?

- Is He your Most High God, All sufficient One, Master, Lord of Peace, the Lord who will Provide?
- Is He your Father? We must be careful not to make God into an "it" or a "thing" to which we pray. He is our Jehovah Raah, the Lord our Shepherd.
- Is He your beloved; the one you want to spend time with and get to know better?
- God knows us by our name; shouldn't we know Him by His?

How fortunate are we that Jesus Christ told us how we can know God and how to pray. He told us to pray the Our Father.

Our Father, who art in Heaven, Hallowed be Thy Name, Thy Kingdom come, Thy will be done on earth, as it is in Heaven. Give us this day our daily bread and forgive us our trespasses, as we forgive those who trespass against us and lead us not into temptation, but deliver us from evil. For Thine is the Kingdom, the power and the glory, for ever and ever. Amen.

Hallowed be Your name?

- To hallow a thing is to make it holy or to set it apart to be exalted as being worthy of absolute devotion. To hallow the name of God is to regard Him with complete devotion and loving admiration.
- God's name is of the utmost importance (Nehemiah 9:5) therefore we ought to reserve it a position of grave significance in our minds and hearts.
- We should never take His name lightly (Exodus 20:7, Leviticus 22:32) but always rejoice in it and think deeply upon its true meaning.

This chapter has been all about God's name and our beliefs, although the fundamental point at which to begin the spiritual life is not so much about our beliefs in God, but God's belief in us and what He has done for us. He showed us love in its fullest meaning. So in order to answer the question: 'Who is God?' I would suggest that the answer is, God is love. That is the goal of the spiritual life, to love God and our fellow human beings as He loves us.

Speaking of God's love and how since the beginning of time He has loved us, I'd like to share here a beautiful poem by a very dear friend of ours, Ian Young.

SPIRITUAL FOOD FOR THOUGHT

Emmanuel (God is with us)

God a foetus?
So you think it was a miracle
When Jesus arose from the tomb,
Then what do you think of the miracle
Of God in a virgin's womb ?
He came from the highest of Heaven
Where angels extol Him as Lord,
Who was there in the stable
To cut the umbilical cord?
The winds and waves obeyed Him
Were still at his behest,
He was entirely dependent
On milk from Mary's breast.
He healed the sick, He raised the dead
He enabled the lame to walk
Have you thought that Mary and Joseph
Taught the Word of God how to talk ?
Have you thought that the Author of life
No less,
To fulfil that wonderful plan
Became a foetus,
And suffered the shock of birth,
That He should be
No more
Than man.

CHAPTER 3

SO THIS GUY JESUS, WHO IS HE?

"But what about you, who do you say I am?" Luke 9:20

Now that we have explored the name of God and how God the Father revealed the fullness of His love in His Son Jesus Christ, I think we need to go deeper and find out more about this man Jesus and how He can help us within our spiritual lives. This chapter will show you that Jesus has another way of looking at life.

I guess if we go right back to the beginning of Jesus' life that takes us to His birth and Jesus being a baby.

We all know what happens when you smile at a baby; you get a smile back. It's innate, it's natural and joyful. It's like the little baby knows that you have something good for them. It's like they are saying' "Yes please I will have some more food, another cuddle and another smile". Then as they grow and develop they increasingly look up to you. For safety to cross the road, for comfort when they experience their first thunder and lightning storm, for instruction and how to do their A,B,C's. Babies look up to us, it's like we are their hero.

The purpose of this chapter is to remind us to encourage anyone who is embarking on the spiritual life to know that, they are never alone. There are people in our lives who care for us, who look up to us and

one of these is Jesus Christ. I am not going to be disingenuous and say that the spiritual life is always easy. Ask Mo Farah if his journey to winning gold medals at the 2012 London Olympics was easy. Ask any parent if raising a child is easy. I know they say the best things in life are free but Jesus isn't a thing, He is a person and like all relationships, we have to work at them. I want to show you, that while the world can teach us so many wonderful things about life and relationships Jesus took another approach. He gave a new set of commandments and a new set of be-attitudes to live by. When we live by the mindset of Jesus (Romans 12:1-2) we will have a health and happiness that the world cannot fully give.

To grow and be fully human we need teachers, educators, encouragers, heroes, people who love us and smile at us. When I interview families about their loved ones in order to write up the funeral tribute, it can often become clear that children even in their 40s and 50s still want to be like their parents. Recently I had a 45-year-old woman tell me she was still a daddy's girl and her dad was her hero. How beautiful is that? But we need people like that don't we? We need hero figures, those we can look up to, or people who, as my Professional Speaking Association friend Dave Hyner says, we can look into and learn from and be inspired by.

When I sit in the living room of a family home during one of my funeral interviews one of the questions I invariably ask of the surviving children, who are often my age is; "What has your mum/dad taught you about life?" I usually prefix this by saying, "You know that phrase 'See you, you are just like your dad' well now you are adults how are you like your dad, what has he given you, what has he taught you?" Often someone in the room points to a brother or sister and says, "She's exactly like our dad". Sometimes there are tears in the living room when a 40-something man or woman acknowledges that one of the highest compliments they can have in their life is that they are like

their mum and dad in terms of their values and virtues. We need role models; we need hero figures, people we can look up to and into.

Although there is a section on my Facebook page to list my favourite books or my favourite movies, there is no section to list my heroes or heroines. But if there were, Jesus would be one of my heroes.

Jesus was truly human

So who is this man Jesus? Well for a start He is a true historical figure, He is not a mythical character. A first century Jewish historian called Flavius Josephus wrote a book called 'Antiquities' and he makes reference to a man called Jesus who lived and did extraordinary things during His life. So Jesus was a real man, He lived in a human body and was here on earth sometime between 5 BC and 33 AD. Jesus grew up in a small village in the Galilee area of Israel called Nazareth with His mum Mary and His step dad Joseph. We know from the 4 Gospels of Matthew, Mark, Luke and John that there was a three year period of His life when He did His main work and accomplished His primary mission in life. What else do we know?

- He taught people.
- He performed miracles.
- He understood the importance of rest; getting away from it all.
- He prayed.
- He loved people.
- He had a special affection for the poor and the marginalised of the world.
- He spoke in the language of the people. He told them lots of stories and parables using everyday imagery of His era such as bread and

wine to explain what God and faith is like. Perhaps He saw His mum Mary baking bread and that is why He said faith is like the yeast that makes dough rise and gives life to bread.

- He noticed things like people's suffering and their isolation and He offered words of comfort and encouragement to them.
- He had human ups and downs; He got angry like He did in the temple when He turned over the money changers' tables.
- He had moments of loneliness as He did in the Garden of Gethsemane.
- He had lots of friends.
- He went to parties and weddings.
- He worked as a carpenter.
- He also did things many of us find hard and challenging to do. For example, he forgave people who betrayed Him, as His friend Peter did 3 times.
- He had a spirit of gratitude and thanksgiving for everything He had in His life even when He didn't want to die on the cross.
- He spoke about God being His Abba, His Father, His Daddy.
- He trusted that God His Father would look after everything for Him and all would be ok in the end. And it was.

What all of this tells me, is that Jesus fully understands what it is like to be a human being; all the joys and sorrows, the achievements and disappointments, the births and deaths. He experienced every human condition there is. Yet even as a 33 year old man, Jesus still looked up to His Father. He trusted and relied upon someone to reassure Him that all would be well; perhaps like the baby or the people I meet at my

funeral work. That sense of needing someone to look up to is a good and healthy thing to have in life.

Who do you look up to or into? Who are your role models? Who are your hero figures? Who gives you a new way of looking at life when things are not going according to plan? Who helps you have a new take, a new perspective and reignites your passion for living again? Jesus is for many people a man to admire and follow because of how He lived a full and authentic life. Would you like a new way of looking at life? If you do, come and explore the spiritual life and what it can offer.

There have been times during my 48 years on this earth when I had great enthusiasm and passion to follow this man Jesus and wanted to be like Him. But equally there have been long periods in my life when I have been zapped by apathy and a sense of 'I can't be bothered'. Before you know it I got out of the habit of wanting to be like this man. I got out of the habit of regularly speaking to this man or relying on Him. Over time the norm became; no prayer, no church, no taking on the mindset of Christ. My attitudes and habits had changed and they were no longer mirroring the Christ-like attitudes and habits I once had. During those years when I thought I did not need Jesus or prayer in my life, I was happy in my own wee world. I knew there was this spiritual life out there, I just didn't want it at this time in my life; I was ok by myself. I was working hard, I had a family and I had most things I wanted. Then in the summer of 2010 there was a crash in my personal life and the signs, the behaviours, the feelings were not good; sorrow, tears, frustration, despair, this is not fair, why me and a deep sense of loss.

Don't worry I am not going to give you a long sob story about what went wrong with my life at that time when my whole world crumbled all around me, except to say at the precise moment my world fell apart I knew the remedy. I knew what I had to do to put my life back together

again. For me it was four things:

- Being able to speak to friends who would listen to me. Thankfully I had four good friends who I called upon, a lot!
- Being able to exercise my body and keep high levels of serotonin and endorphins so that my body naturally fought these darker feelings. Swimming vigorously twice a week with a swimming buddy was enough free drugs for me!
- Being able to work and taking on a mindset of, "Hey look what I still have in life" rather than over thinking what I no longer had in life. How lucky was I to have a job and a wage!
- And the final thing that kept me sane was returning to prayer and basically asking Jesus to do something to help me. So I joined a prayer group and possibly for the first time in my life I really did know that Jesus was real and that He listens to our prayers.

If there is a common theme to these remedies it is relationships and a realisation that my mindset on life, my attitudes were not going to get me out of this mess. I needed help, I needed support, I needed friends. Then it dawned on me that one of the most loyal and loving friends I will ever need in life was there ready to once again share some of His positive, encouraging and uplifting words with me. How I needed that Good News. It's very tempting to want to stay independent in life; to believe that by ourselves we are strong and self-sufficient. "Look at me mum", I said age 5 as I flew down Lochee High Street on my tricycle, "I don't need you to hold onto my bike anymore, I can do it all by myself". I can however laugh about that day when I forgot to brake and I crashed into the dentist's wall and knocked my front teeth out.

I didn't want to crash but I learnt even at the age of 5 that there are things we can do in the future to stop that kind of thing happening again:

- Gain more confidence on a bike and have greater competence.
- Pass my cycling proficiency test.
- Learn to use the brakes when I see danger.
- Avoid cycling near dentists' walls.

I am sure my mum will confirm that I have always been an independent kind of guy. During my formative years I did my own thing, enjoyed my own company and enjoyed being independent. I would walk down to the Cubs by myself aged 7. I cycled to pick strawberries in fields 5 miles away by the age of 12. I thought nothing of jumping on my Claude Butler bike when I was 16 during the 7 weeks summer holidays and having a 10 day trip through the Cairngorms and a Youth Hostelling experience. I remember it well, me and my Sony Walkman cycling all over Scotland listening to Jon and Vangelis. Ah 1980s nostalgia..."Somehow I'll find my way home" as Jon Anderson constantly reminded me. I still need that place I can call home, that place where I know I am loved and I can hear encouraging words. Central to my home and my life is this man Jesus Christ. He keeps me sane, guides me on the right path, and gently invites me to take on a new way of thinking. He is consistent and faithful. In my 48 years Jesus Christ has never let me down.

I am not knocking independence and self-reliance. These are good and healthy things to develop as adults. In my 20s I admired a friend of mine who went backpacking all over Australia and New Zealand. But I also fully understand the value of being dependent and reliant on others, especially those whose words remind me of my purpose in life. I need people to guide, coach and encourage me so that I will get back on the bike again after the proverbial fall. I need others to rely upon, call upon, lean on and support me should there be another valley of darkness (Psalm 23) and I need to navigate my way out of it.

Who is giving you this new vision or fresh encouragement? Thankfully I have a handful of people to do that through my work, my swimming and my affiliation with a great organisation called the Professional Speaking Association. But one of the greatest encouragers in life for me is a man called Jesus of Nazareth. He's actually the number one hero figure I now look up to.

Anytime I default from being in a relationship with Jesus to being self-reliant I notice one major change, a change in attitude. This is followed by a slow but tempting pull into a world of self-pity, lack of forgiveness, cynicism, criticism, fear, apathy, guilt and depersonalisation. Anytime I have stopped listening to the words of Jesus and no longer practise His attitudes and habits my life changes big style; and not for the better.

One of the amazing things about being dependent as opposed to independent is that life is not all about me; it's more about you. I need that someone. It's one of the basic messages of the Bible, "It's not good that man should be alone". The baby, the teenager, the adult is called to have relationships of dependency. We need people to look up to. This is what Jesus is for me; He is a relationship of dependency. I have lived life without Him but if I have a choice, I would much rather live life with Him guiding me to live by His values. And what are His values? They are values of service, co-operation, and refusing to be driven by anger. Being non-judgemental; keeping faith and hope. Most importantly Jesus has shown me the value of love as being both joyful yet sacrificial with a definite promise that His love is both earthly and heavenly.

As much as Jesus is a real historical figure and did incredible things like miracles and reaching out to the marginalized of society, for me Jesus is a relationship; as real a relationship as I have with my daughter, my parents or my friends.

But how will I know Jesus is real and true?

Whilst I can read books like the Bible and know about the historical person who lived in Galilee 2000 years ago, how can I in the year 2014 know this historical figure as a real person? How do I get as real a relationship with Jesus, as real as the one I have with my daughter for example? I could smile at Katie and see her smile back at me but how will I know Jesus is real?

This is a simple but very important question. How and when will I know that Jesus is a real person? How do I develop a real relationship with Him?

Jesus is a Divine person

Well we have agreed so far that Jesus was a real historical person and for those who have faith there would be agreement that Jesus was also a Divine person; that He was the only Son of God, He was both human and Divine.

By definition a person is an individual although I like the description Archbishop Desmond Tutu used when he said, "A person is a person because he recognizes others as persons". We are all aware of man's inhumanity to man and the horrors of war when someone is deemed to be a non-person. In order to be a person, there has to be a mutual relationship and at the basic level recognition of the other being a person. It seems to be innate and natural when we are babies but over time, as adults, we can lose this recognition. We can lose this sense of relationship and the danger there is that we forget to see people as people and then lives can crash and fall all around us.

If Jesus is a human and a Divine person then as Desmond Tutu says, there has to be, at the most basic level, a recognition that in order to be a person we need to have a relationship of some sorts with them otherwise they are mythical or mere figments of our imagination like Santa Claus or the Tooth Fairy.

To know Jesus and to know whether He is real or not, we have to accept either that:

- He is just an individual and I am just an individual and no relationship is possible or,
- Jesus is a relationship because we recognise each other as individuals.

As we know from horrors like the Holocaust if there is no relationship there is a very real risk that there is no love or care for that person before us.

I heard the story of a funeral that took place in Dunfermline Crematorium. A father had died and only two people were there at the funeral, the two sons. There was no music, no words were said and no one officiated at the service. Instead the coffin was brought into the crematorium in silence and the two sons sat there in the front row and said nothing for five minutes. After five minutes the pair of them looked at each other, stood up and gave their dad the middle finger sign and walked out. I can only assume there was very little love there between the two sons and their father and very little of a relationship.

So how do I know Jesus is a relationship? How do I know He is real? I guess one answer to that question is what we mean by 'real'. What I know to be real and someone else knows to be real can be two different things, perhaps that explains that funeral story. What is real to some is illusionary to others.

The brilliant mathematician John Nash, played by Russell Crowe in the film 'A Beautiful Mind' is diagnosed with schizophrenia and his life is deeply disturbed because he believed he saw other people. To John these people were as real to him as his wife Alicia even though these people existed only in his imagination. It was only through extensive therapy and the supportive love of his family and friends that John finally realised these hallucinations were not real. In a similar vein we could ask the question, "Is Santa Claus real?"

To a child the answer is yes but as adults we develop a different understanding of what is real and we conclude Santa Claus is not a real person. However, on Christmas Day when we see the joy in children's faces when they open their presents, there is an acceptance that Santa is real at least for children.

What is consistent in all of these examples of people with delusions, children who believe in Santa and people who believe in Jesus, is that there is some kind of relationship and this is real.

The atheist and the Santa Claus argument

"Ah great; thanks Neil", says the sceptic, "you have now confirmed everything I have always thought about God and Jesus. It's all an illusion, a delusion and God and Jesus are fantasy figures that only exist in my mind much like Santa Claus. Gotcha!"

I once had a friend who, whenever we met for drinks, liked a good argument about God and why it was all a load of nonsense. I would hear arguments along the lines of; "I don't believe in God for the same reasons I don't believe in Santa Claus". I am sure these sorts of things were said partly as a joke but also to bait me into a response and for me to justify my ridiculous beliefs as God was pretty much like Santa, the Tooth Fairy and the Easter bunny; childish nonsense.

Within such conversations the arguments can be; we religious people have no direct evidence of God or Santa Claus, therefore God is not real and cannot be proved. Has anyone come back from heaven and told us it's all true? "Ok", says the atheist, "you naïve believers can come back at us and explain everything you believe because you have 'faith'. Of course no one can argue with the faith but still the rational, sane people know the God thing is all a delusion".

So how do we know Jesus? How do we know He is real? Should we take the adult rational approach or should we take the childlike approach? For the atheists a more mature adult like approach to God will show God should be rejected as God is akin to beliefs about Santa and the Tooth Fairy.

The only thing about the adult rational argument is that not every rational adult agrees with the atheist's conclusion. Who should we listen to, the adult or the child? Surely not the child? Children will believe anything you tell them, whereas when was the last time you heard of a grown up entering adulthood and they think; "Yeh, now is the right time to believe in Santa". Children don't know the cancer saving properties of the Brussels sprout. They have no real interest in eating their 5 a day; we need logic and reasoning to understand that one. Yet children trust the people who love them and why do they trust those they love? Because they have felt that love, they have heard words of love from their parents, they know because they know!

If you want an answer to the question, "How will I know that Jesus is real?" it will boil down to trust and love. Do you trust your parents and friends or do you think you can do everything alone? Do you need relationships in your life? Do you have loving people tell you good news and words of support and encouragement? We need the coach, the hero figure, someone to say; you might not fully understand this right now about these little mini cabbages, but believe me this is good for you, do you trust me? I love you and I will always give you what

you need to be fully alive because I love you. That is what parents do. Logic doesn't need to come into the equation, it's all about love and trust. Do you trust, for example, some of the words of Jesus when He tells us who He is? He once asked that very question to His closest friends, "Who do people say that I AM?" and the replies varied from John the Baptist to Elijah and then Jesus asked Peter the very same question, "Who do you say I AM?' and Peter said, "You are the Christ, the son of the living God". Jesus said "Simon son of John, you are a happy man because it was not flesh and blood that revealed this to you but my Father in heaven". No logic, it was a revelation.

No one can force you to accept love and no one can force you to trust, you have to want to do it for yourself because you believe it is good for you. It's up to you what you consume in life. Logic will only take you so far in that decision making process. The time will come when you decide either to believe or not to believe. If you choose to believe, God will give you the Grace to believe even more and like Simon Peter, one of His first followers, give you revelations and insights that will help you see life and people in a totally new way.

Logic and faith, not logic or faith

When it comes to answering the question as to who Jesus is and whether the whole God thing is real or not, logic and rationality can only take us so far. After that we either take a leap of faith or we just know. We just know what we know, just like a baby knows what a baby knows. How do we know we love someone? We can look for evidence, we can ask them, we can rationalise it but there will come a time when words run dry. You either believe someone loves you or you don't. Logic comes somewhere down the pecking order after faith and trusting something to be as you know it to be. Sometimes you even

hold on to the decision to love someone when logic says don't do it. I guess that is why love is first and foremost a free gift we either want to accept or reject. The previous chapter on the Bible reminded us that God loved us first (page 32) and we choose either to trust that love, believe in that love, or to live by ourselves without having any need for God's love in our lives.

Within this chapter we have offered logical and philosophical arguments to suggest Jesus is real and God's existence is real. We spoke about the historical evidence that Jesus really did wander round the land of Galilee and we have mentioned within the chapter on the Bible that Jesus was unique in the sense that He claimed to be God through His various "I Am" statements. Remember "I Am" was a sacred word that when translated into Hebrew read YHWH (Yahweh) and hence Jesus did declare He was God. That is one of the reasons why He was crucified, for blasphemy. We have also rationally spoken in other chapters about other things like miracles, the Dead Sea Scrolls and the power of prayer.

In short, there is ample evidence for Jesus' existence and for His love being real but sometimes during my conversations with my atheist friend it was as if this evidence was irrelevant and Jesus was akin to Santa Claus. So often the conversations would end with an acceptance of the other person's take on God and an agreement to disagree. What we had in these conversations were statements of personal belief. His belief that God does not exist and my belief that God is real. We have a difference of opinion. It comes down to a personal choice and the personal relationships we want or don't want to have. Logic and reason can only take us so far in our attempt to answer the question; Is Jesus real and how can I know this to be true? I can prove Santa is not real but whether God is real or not for you is your choice, just as eating your 5 a day, or going to the gym to get that fit body is your choice.

My experience of arguments and debates with friends over God's existence is that it spoils my enjoyment of a glass of Rioja Crianza wine. I have met people who think that my belief in miracles and God answering prayers is down to things like luck, probability and the natural order of the world. The argument being God does not cause miracles, God does not answer prayers if He did the world would not be in the mess it is in. Hence there is no all-powerful, omnipotent, all seeing God who loves me or cares for the world and who we can turn to in our time of need.

All I can say is this is not my experience of Jesus within my world, even when my world crashed around me. When I needed Jesus to come back into my life, He was there. When I needed to hear the Good News of the Bible, I heard those words and they consoled me and encouraged me to crack on with my beautiful life. To the atheist I may have recovered through,

- The happy co-incidence of having good friends who just so happened to return my telephone calls.
- The natural order of my body craving exercise.
- Thankfully having a job to keep me sane.

But none of this was God's doing so their argument goes. God is not an omnipotent puppet master controlling my life it was all down to luck, co-incidence the natural order of the world.

But this propensity to use 'luck' and 'co-incidence' or as I call it 'God-incidence', to explain away things like miracles or prayers being answered is no different than non-believing parents talking to their children about Easter Bunnies and falling back on the 'magical' argument. We need a better argument than that. During many conversations with atheists, the conversation has developed along the lines that atheists are mature, rational thinkers and anyone who

believes in God and Jesus is deluded, immature and gullible; much like a child who believes in Santa Claus.

I want the mature, logical argument to the question, "Who is Jesus? Is He real? How will I know He is real?" But who says it has to be either or; who says it has to be logic or faith? Why can't it be both logic and faith? Who says only the rational adult has the right answers to whether Jesus is real or not and the Santa-believing child is deluded? Maybe it's not either or. Maybe we need to have both the perspective of the adult and the perspective of the child in order to answer the question "Is Jesus real?"

Although to be fair to the atheist thinker who has advocated the adult only logical approach, at least they have tried to address the question, "How do I know if God or Jesus is real?" So fair play to them for at least answering the question through their own logic and reason just as a child should be commended for their willingness to believe and their open mindedness.

One major difference between an intelligent person and an intelligent person who consistently reasons well is open-mindedness. If we are not open-minded, we cannot learn in the same way. Be open to Jesus; invite Him in to your life. When we are open-minded we are humble, we are not arrogant and we are willing to learn from our mistakes. Competency in any task comes through skills, knowledge and practise and we learn a great deal from our failings and mistakes. If you cheat at Trivial Pursuit because you have memorised all the answers you won't learn very much and will simply play that game going through the motions. Who wants to live life going through the motions where everything is predictable and known? It's good and healthy to fail and it's good and healthy to have an open mind, much like the mind of a child.

Maybe that's why Jesus, when He was out talking to the people who lived in Galilee once said, "Truly, I say to you, unless you turn and

become like children, you will never enter the kingdom of heaven. Whoever humbles himself like this child is the greatest in the kingdom of heaven" (Matthew 18:3-4).

As we have already said, before a certain age, a child has a simplistic view on life, they will believe in Santa but to adults the idea of a man coming down our chimney to give us presents is nonsense. But to a child, Santa is real. If we as adults have a childlike mentality then the notion of God and Jesus being real is equally simple.

How do we bridge this gap between childlike trust and logic? There is a constant tension:

- Sure Jesus loves me and will look after my needs but I have no money right now to pay my bills.
- I have heard all the stories about Jesus having the power to heal the sick but why hasn't He healed my sick mother, why did she die?
- I know Jesus forgives our sins if we only believe, but surely He won't forgive what I once did?
- How will I know that my mum will give me my next feed?
- How will I know that I am unconditionally loved?

Adults can struggle with logic and reason but children will believe; they trust. Children don't filter beliefs through logic, reason and common sense, theology, circumstances, any of that. They just simply believe and trust.

I want to be like a child. No, I'm not going to start believing in Santa Claus again, but I am going to, on a daily basis, believe in the love and power of God and that He will answer my prayers in His way, He will heal the sick to bring people closer to Him and He will never give up on us because we have been made in His image and likeness and He loves us as we are.

What is logically fascinating about Jesus is that He claimed to be God and He encouraged us to come and have life and have it to the full. He invites us to trust like a child. Seek and you will find, knock and the door will be opened to you, what father would hand his son a snake when he asked for an egg? (Matthew 7:7-10). Jesus is the only Son of God, He is the fullness of God and because we are made in His image and likeness His purpose is that one day we will be like Him so that as St. Paul says, "It is no longer I that live but He that lives in me" (Galatians 2:20).

Anytime in the Bible Jesus uses the words "I Am" He was telling us that He was in a relationship with His Father and that He was going to help us know who God was by giving us the gift of the Holy Spirit. He said the Holy Spirit will teach us everything we need to know and the Holy Spirit will lead us to the Father. He said, "I am the light of the world, he who follows me will not walk in darkness, but will have the light of life" (John 8:12). He claimed attributes belonging only to God and promised that those who believe would have a more abundant life. Neither should we forget that when we pray we do not pray alone. We pray 'through' Jesus, we pray 'with' Jesus and we pray 'in' Jesus. The relationship is already there. Just as the human body has a desire to stay healthy and be all it can be, so the human spirit has a desire to be all it can be and that is to live and breathe the be-attitudes that Jesus lived and breathed by. Jesus Christ showed God to be gentle, loving, forgiving, humble, joyful and worthy of our trust.

Does Jesus exist? If you want to know the answer, have an open mind and an open heart. God does not force us to believe in Him, instead He has left enough evidence for us to make our own minds up and for us to respond with love or at least with, "What is the worst thing that can happen if I at least explore this man called Jesus and what He did for us?'

It is impossible for us to know Jesus exists unless He reveals Himself to us and He becomes a reality in our lives. God the Father has given

us the heart and mind to know Jesus is real. The next step is for us to have a desire and a thirst to have a relationship with God. This is no different than the desire of the body to stay healthy and eat our 5 a day.

I can't help but think here of the famous William Holeman Hunt painting from 1853 'The Light of the World' where Jesus is depicted standing at an unopened door with no handle as the door can only be opened from the other side'. "Behold, I stand at the door and knock; if any man hear My voice, and open the door, I will come in to him, and will eat with him, and he with Me" (Revelation 3:20).

Maybe when we say yes to that call to have a relationship with Jesus we too, like a child, will see that Jesus is real. Ho ho ho!

It's child's play really. To get to know Jesus as real and have a relationship with Him we could start, like a baby, with a smile. Look up to Him, look into Him, learn about Him and talk to Him like we talk to a friend. Think not so much as presents from Him as presence with Him.

SPIRITUAL FOOD FOR THOUGHT

Who is He?

When writing this poem Ian Young said: This poem came from the revelation that Jesus is God the Son, the Creator of all things and He died for me. The most amazing event in history, God experienced death! I realised I had been singing words which I either did not believe or did not register in my mind.

"Amazing love and can it be that Thou my God should die for me"
Who is He kneeling there in the garden alone?
Praying in sorrow and fear.
As He thinks of tomorrow the cross of disgrace,
And the sins of the world He must bear.

Oh my God Jesus Christ. Is it you? Is it you?
Maker of earth and of heaven
Did you come here to live and to suffer and die
That I might be saved and forgiven?

Who is He standing there with the soldiers around?
They beat Him and treat Him with scorn.
Down His back runs red blood, off His chin drips their spit,
On His head there's a crown of thorns.

Who is He hanging there with those nails in his hands?
And that gaping wide hole in His side.
The crowd gathered round Him, had mocked Him and jeered.
"If you're God - just come down" they had cried.

I stand amazed – can it be God's own Son did this for me?
Suffered, all forms of human pain,
Even death - that I should gain Eternal life.

Love beyond our deepest thought moved God to give his only Son.
You want to do something? You feel you ought?
Believe in Him - the rest is done.

Ian Young © (used with permission from the author)

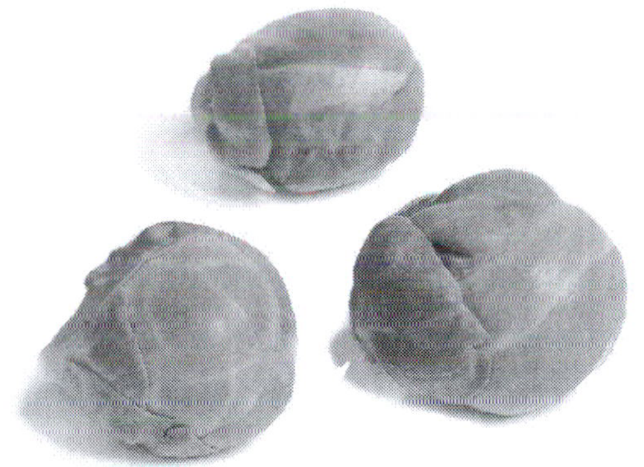

CHAPTER 4

WHO IS THE HOLY SPIRIT?

"And you also became God's people when you heard the true message, the Good News that brought you salvation. You believed in Christ, and God put His stamp of ownership on you by giving you the Holy Spirit he had promised. The Spirit is the guarantee that we shall receive what God has promised His people, and this assures us that God will give complete freedom to those who are His. Let us praise His glory!"
— Ephesians 1:13-14

I'll never forget the day when my cousin from Gibraltar came to visit me in Edinburgh in 1982. I was working at Hill Thomson, a subsidiary company of Glenlivet Distillers at the time. Sitting at my desk on a warm sunny morning I was surprised when the receptionist announced that I had a visitor from abroad. I did not expect anyone and could not think who it might be. It was with sheer delight that I opened the door to my office and embraced my cousin Pillie and her husband Joe. They had come a long way and were just as keen as I was to meet up again after such a long time.

Joe had always been concerned about my spiritual growth as a child and both he and Pillie would sometimes take me and my sister to church. He was heartbroken when years later I left the church and showed no interest in it for five years. I always believed in God and prayed but church to me became boring and monotonous, full of laws

and I always felt guilt ridden; if you were a good girl you went to heaven, but if you misbehaved hell awaited you. How wrong a theology was this? No wonder that as a child I was kinda scared of God, just as I was of Santa Claus incidentally. I remember going to bed at night at Christmas time and pulling my legs right up to my chest in case Father Christmas as we called him, touched my feet. For that matter what if God did the same? I was scared of God coming close to me too.

I knew that Joe had continued to pray for me for many years and had never given up on me and neither had God. So it was with great pleasure that I announced to him that I had gone through a spiritual experience or awakening and did not know what was happening to me as I could not stop praying. His face I remember lit up as he gleefully looked me in the eye and said, "My dear, you have been filled with the Holy Spirit". I foolishly said, "And who is that?" I had been away from the church for so long that I did not recognise who this was. When I left the church all those years ago, I just knew God the Father, God the Son and God the Holy Ghost. I did not know who this new Spirit was! Joe laughed and said, "That is what we call the third person of the Holy Trinity now". Ah at last, that made more sense to me.

So how about the Holy Trinity, how difficult is that to explain? For many this remains a mystery, but for many others who have attempted to understand the three-in-one relationship, explanations have abounded.

I remember myself 25 years ago, listening to a talk by the late Fr. Ian Pettit entitled, 'The Basic Gospel Message'. Much as I tried to understand what he was saying, I simply could not. My spirituality levels were low at the time and much as I tried, every word seemed to be going over my head. It was just too difficult to understand. I was getting frustrated at my lack of understanding and so I prayed and asked God to enlighten my mind and explain the message to me in

simpler language. He made me think of an egg with its shell, yoke and white. Three different entities contained in one. My mother who had a very good sense of humour, joked as I tried to explain it to her, "Well all I can is that you better be careful or you might end up with an omelette!" she said.

One of the simplest ways of explaining the mystery of the Trinity was reportedly given by Saint Spyridon of Trimithund at the Council of Nicaea (AD 325). According to tradition, when asked how it is that Three can simultaneously be One, Saint Spyridon responded by taking up a brick and squeezing it. From the soft clay in his hands a flame showed up while simultaneously water flowed downwards. 'As there is fire and water in this brick', said Saint Spyridon, 'in the same way there are three Persons in the one Godhead'.

On my recent trip to Bucharest in Romania, we visited a Romanian Orthodox Church. My attention was drawn to a huge icon on the outer wall of the church. Traian, our local host explained that this was indeed a painting of Saint Spyridon explaining the meaning of the Holy Trinity. In his hand you could clearly see the brick with water gushing from the bottom and a flame of fire belting up into the air from the top. I thought this was extremely interesting and it made me feel good to see that my egg analogy was not that daft after all.

In this chapter, however, we are concentrating more on the Third Person of the Holy Trinity, the Holy Spirit and the purpose is to show you that the Holy Spirit is the power and energy of our spiritual lives, a power that lives within us. The Holy Spirit is a real person who enables us to do far more than we can through our own power and efforts. Most often when you think of a third person you have an image of three people. In the worldly sense there is a phrase "two's company, but three's a crowd". Logic tells us that quite often this is true, the third person often feels like the "odd one out". In families with three children, there is always one of the children that feel left out. Not in

the case of the Holy Trinity. They are one, they cannot be separated and each one is integrated into the other; God the Father, God the Son, and God, the Holy Spirit.

The Holy Spirit is not an enigma, nor a nonentity nor an impersonal force. The Holy Spirit is a real person. The Bible teaches that He is active in our lives, a distinct person, and fully God. So the third person of the Holy Trinity is not an inanimate object. If God the Father is love, then it stands to reason that His Son and His Holy Spirit are love too.

Think about this for a second. What happens when we as human beings love? Sometimes we hurt, sometimes we experience great joy.

I believe that the Holy Spirit has feelings too. He hurts when we turn away from God and His Son Jesus Christ, and it is the Holy Spirit that cries and suffers the pain. When a sinner repents and turns to the source of all life, the joy that the Holy Spirit experiences is indescribable. We can never imagine or understand how grateful God is when we answer His call.

Understand then that the Holy Spirit is a real Person, not just a force or a presence or a power. You must recognize Him as a Person. He can speak. He is praying for you, just as Christ is praying for you. He will teach you what you need to know. He will guide you in your decisions. He tells you that you are a child of God. He will personally clean up the "rooms" of your innermost being when you let Him. You can submit to His voice or reject His voice. If you disobey His voice, He will be grieved. Respecting the Holy Spirit as a person is necessary for your relationship with Him.

The Holy Spirit is also the Comforter; the Enabler, the Strengthener, the Overcomer, the Revelator, the Supporter, the All-knowing and the Giver of Life.

There are many references in the Bible relating to the Holy Spirit and the power of the Holy Spirit. John 20:19-23 tells us that after Jesus died he appeared to His Disciples:

"On the evening of that first day of the week, when the disciples were together, with the doors locked for fear of the Jewish leaders, Jesus came and stood among them and said, "Peace be with you!" After He said this, He showed them His hands and side. The disciples were overjoyed when they saw the Lord. Again Jesus said, "Peace be with you! As the Father has sent me, I am sending you." And with that He breathed on them and said, "Receive the Holy Spirit. If you forgive anyone's sins, their sins are forgiven; if you do not forgive them, they are not forgiven."

The Power of the Holy Spirit

When Mary was asked to be the Mother of God she questioned the angel how this could be as she was a virgin and had not been with any man. The angel answered, "The Holy Spirit will come on you, and the power of the Most High will overshadow you. So the holy one to be born will be called the Son of God" (Luke 1:35).

"And now I will send the Holy Spirit, just as my Father promised. But stay here in the city until the Holy Spirit comes and fills you with power from heaven" (Luke 24:49).

In Acts 1:8 Jesus says to His disciples, "But you will receive power when the Holy Spirit comes on you; and you will be my witnesses in Jerusalem, and in all Judea and Samaria, and to the ends of the earth."

On the day of Pentecost, all were filled with the Holy Spirit. Incidentally, whilst they were waiting for the Holy Spirit in the Upper Room it is interesting to note that Mary the Mother of God and other women were there too. Acts 4:31 says, "After they prayed, the place

where they were meeting was shaken. And they were all filled with the Holy Spirit and spoke the word of God boldly."

Ponder for a moment on the power of the Holy Spirit that enables us to do far more than we can ever think of, or imagine.

How can we understand this power? Think of a huge generator or dam. If you have ever visited the dam at Loch Tummel in Pitlochry, Scotland, you will understand the concept of the power of the Holy Spirit.

How Hydropower Works

Generating hydroelectricity starts with the annual hydrologic, or water cycle, providing seasonal rain and runoff from snowpack. The runoff from rain and snow collects in lakes, streams and rivers and flows to dams downstream. The water funnels through a dam, into a power house and turns a large wheel called a turbine. The turbine turns a shaft that rotates a series of magnets past copper coils in a generator to create electricity. The water then returns to the river. From the powerhouse, transmission lines carry electricity to communities.

The sight is awesome as you sense the power of the water and the huge generators providing electricity to every household in Scotland. And like electricity you cannot see it or explain it; so it is with the Holy Spirit. Just think the power of God flows out from Him as energy to us in order that we can then deliver that energy to others.

The disciples were unable to do anything without this power. It was only when they received the Holy Spirit at Pentecost that they were able to preach with boldness and perform all the miracles Jesus did.

The power of the Holy Spirit was not only for a group of people 2,000 years ago. The promise of the Holy Spirit is for you and me and all mankind today right up to the last days. Joel 2:28-29 confirms this, "I

will pour out my Spirit on all people. Your sons and daughters will prophesy, your old men will dream dreams, your young men will see visions. Even on my servants, both men and women, I will pour out my Spirit in those days."

On the day of Pentecost, after the Apostles had been filled with the Holy Spirit they appeared to the crowds as if drunk. Acts 2:13 says, 'Some, however, made fun of them and said; "They have had too much wine."'

Peter Addresses the Crowd

Then Peter stood up with the Eleven, raised his voice and addressed the crowd: "Fellow Jews and all of you who live in Jerusalem, let me explain this to you; listen carefully to what I say. These people are not drunk, as you suppose. It's only nine in the morning! No, this is what was spoken by the prophet Joel, "I will pour out my spirit on all people" (Joel 2:28).

Too much booze makes you drunk and it becomes an addiction. I used to drink more than I should have as a teenager and also in later years. Now, since I was filled with the Holy Spirit, I am just inebriated with Him. It is like electricity buzzing through my body and God Himself has become my addiction. It is wonderful to be on a high with the Almighty, and the best thing is that it is free too.

There are many addictions in life but the Holy Spirit helps us to overcome them all, if you let Him.

The Holy Spirit, therefore, is given to us also to help us in our life's journey. He takes us through the trials and tribulations that come our way. He directs our lives when our rudders have broken and we are floating aimlessly not knowing where to go. He gives us our identity in Christ and makes us whole. The Holy Spirit is like the air that we breathe.

The Holy Spirit as Breath

Interestingly if you go to the first book in the Bible God is described as being breath.

"In the beginning God created the heavens and the earth. And the earth was without form, and void; and darkness was upon the face of the deep. And the Ruah of God moved upon the face of the waters" (Genesis 1:1-2).

In the Bible, the Hebrew term for the Spirit is ruah and the Latin translation spiritus, is "breath." We all understand that breathing is natural and innate. Yet the air we breathe cannot be seen; it is intangible, it cannot be grasped. The person who does not breathe cannot live and for believers our life, our breath, comes from God. Over time spiritual people have understood breath and life within a spiritual context.

Again it says in the book of Genesis that, "Yahweh, God fashioned man of dust from the soil. Then He breathed into his nostrils a breath of life, and thus man became a living being" (Genesis 2:7).

This passage helps me to understand the question we asked at the beginning, 'Who is the Holy Spirit?' For me the Holy Spirit is the breath of God who innately lives in me.

My young son Jamie used to laugh at his granny Reme, my mum, because every time she came to stay at my house from Gibraltar, she would talk to my plants. She was convinced that the plants grew better if you talked to them. The funny thing is that when she was back in Gibraltar, my plants went all limp and did not do as well as when she was here in Scotland talking to them. Astonishingly, every time she came back to stay, the plants would revive and the leaves would go all shiny. So I used to think that perhaps there was some truth in what she

was saying. Jamie, however, would explain that the reason the plants came to life was not because she talked to them, but it was her breath. The plants fed from the carbon dioxide coming from her breath as she talked to them and they were strengthened.

When we think of the Spirit of God, we can apply this principle to our own spirituality. We grow strong and healthy because God continually breathes on us, giving us life through His Spirit, just as He did for the first man, called Adam and as Jamie's granny did for my plants.

The Holy Spirit as Wind

Man's breath bears a relationship to a much more powerful external breath, the wind. Just as the word ruah in Hebrew means 'breath' or 'spirit', in Greek it is pneuma. This word pneuma also means wind and air.

Ask any sailor and they will tell you that the effects of the winds are impressive. The winds drive the clouds, shake the trees, sail the ships and whip up storms. And once again the analogy of the wind has been used to describe the Holy Spirit.

"The wind blows wherever it pleases; you hear the sound, but you cannot tell where it is going. That is how it is with all who are born of the Spirit" (John 3:8).

On Thursday 18th February 1999 I was invited by my dear friend the late David McFarlane, leader of the Dunkeld Catholic Charismatic Renewal to talk on God's Love; for a series of 'Life in the Spirit' Seminars that were being held in their Prayer Group in Dundee. I remember how astonished and surprised I was at this invitation since I had never stood in front of a crowd before delivering a talk. I spoke at the time how my breath had been taken away when David called me on the phone as it was so unexpected.

At this talk I also played two songs: 'Take my Breath Away' a well-known song from the Tom Cruise movie, Top Gun and 'The Wind Beneath My Wings' by Bette Midler. These tunes were motivated by my late husband's encouragement. At the time of the phone call I had turned to my husband Tony and said, "Gosh Tony, David has just taken my breath away" and it was then he suggested I made that my theme for the night. It was later when I arrived home after visiting a friend that I found a little hand-written note lying on the settee. Tony had gone to bed and was sleeping, and this is what the note said, "The Lord takes your breath away and uses it to power the wind beneath your wings so you can fly with Him! This is the Lord's wish that you fly with Him and settle like a butterfly on those that are in need of the Lord's blessings."

I was so touched by what Tony had written because there had been a time prior to this, where there was great resistance in my home every time I wanted to go to the Prayer Group or do anything related to God. Tony had been an atheist; he did not believe in God but over the years, with a lot of prayer, God changed all that and not only changed my life but also the life of my husband. He was converted and then developed a real intimacy with Our Lord. At his death years later, I can confirm this love that Tony had for Jesus, because my sister Vivienne had a vision as we were sitting around his bed in deep prayer and worshipping God. She saw an extremely bright light and Jesus appearing. Jesus went over to Tony and put his arm around his shoulders and Tony in turn put his arm around Jesus' shoulders. She saw them animatedly talking to each other and remarked at how intensely happy Tony looked. They walked off together into the Light and seconds later he breathed his last and died. Incredible as this might sound, Jesus did come to meet my husband Tony and took him to his eternal home. I know this to be the truth.

Anyway, getting back to the talk I delivered at the Prayer Group in Dundee, the wind of the Holy Spirit blew over me that night. Again, incredible as it sounds I truly heard that wind, but could not tell where it was going. What I understand is that this wind was related to His desire that I should speak about the Love of God and although I was not a preacher, nor was I a professional speaker and I normally would get tongue tied in front of a large crowd, I was given the capability to speak eloquently. That is the power of the Holy Spirit. The response was tremendous and you could have heard a pin drop when I spoke. I know for a fact that God used me that night and my words touched many people. What a privilege and honour it was.

One of my favourite birds of prey is the eagle. What a majestic bird this is. The eagle always reminds me of the wind of the Spirit. Why do I say that? Well, because eagles do not fly like other birds, they don't flap their wings, they soar. They wait on the thermal winds and soar to heights of 15,000 feet or greater. Flapping their wings would use incredible amounts of their own strength and endurance, and they would require so much more food as fuel if they didn't soar. Isaiah 40:31 reminds us that, "Those who wait on the Lord will renew their strength, they will soar on wings like eagles; they will run and not grow weary, they will walk and not faint."

The eagle is a symbol used many times in Scripture. In fact, it is mentioned 39 times throughout the Bible. We can learn some very important lessons from this majestic creation of God.

If you think about it the eagle has an aerial view of the land, when it soars. When we are in trouble and finding it hard to see a solution to our problems, it's as if God lifts us up on eagles' wings so we can see the bigger picture. But we have to let Him.

Soren Kierkegaard, the Danish philosopher, once told a story about a flock of barnyard geese in Denmark. Every Sunday the geese would

gather in the barnyard near the feeding trough. One of their number, a preaching goose, would struggle up on the top rail of the fence and exhort the geese about the glories of goosedom. He would tell them how wonderful it was to be a goose, rather than a chicken or a turkey. He would remind them of their great heritage and tell them of the marvellous possibilities in the future.

Occasionally, while he was preaching, a flock of wild geese, winging south from Sweden across the Baltic Sea on their way to sunny France, would fly overhead in a marvellous V-formation, thousands of feet in the air. When that happened, all the geese would excitedly look up and say to one another, "That's who we really are. We are not destined to spend our lives in this stinking barnyard. Our destiny is to fly."

But then the wild geese would disappear from sight, their honking echoing across the horizon. The barnyard geese would look around at their comfortable surroundings, sigh and return to the mud and filth of the barn. They never did fly!

Sadly, there are a number of people who remain in the barnyard, rather than spread their wings and learn to fly. Why remain like the barnyard geese when you can fly high and see the bigger picture?

The Holy Spirit always lifts you up out of a bad situation. The problem might not disappear, but I know for a fact that he cocoons you and lifts you out of any bad circumstance in your life so you have a different perspective and a healthier approach.

One of my favourite songs that best describes this concept of God being the wind beneath our wings is, "You Raise Me Up" by Josh Groban and sung by Westlife. The lyrics are an amazing example of how God raises us up. 'When I am down and, oh my soul, so weary; When troubles come and my heart burdened be; Then, I am still and wait here in the silence, until you come and sit awhile with me. You raise me up, so I can stand on mountains; You raise me up, to walk on

stormy seas; I am strong, when I am on your shoulders; You raise me up to more than I can be.'

What about sky diving? Have you done that before? Isn't it amazing and thrilling to be up so high? Don't you just get a better view and picture of the land from such a great height? For many though the fear of heights prevents them from ever going up high. Unless you overcome your fears and meet them head-on you will always stay close to the land or the barnyard and miss out on the great opportunity of seeing your situation with new eyes. You have to have faith and trust God. The Holy Spirit, however, can eliminate your fears, for He is the parachute that will enable you to land safely. Remember F.E.A.R. is False Evidence Appearing Real.

The Holy Spirit as Fire

On the day of Pentecost the Apostles were filled with that same kind of fear. Imagine being in that Upper Room with Mary the Mother of God, the apostles and other women. They are waiting, they are afraid. All of a sudden they heard a powerful wind from heaven the noise which filled the entire house in which they were sitting and something appeared to them that seemed like tongues of fire; these separated and came to rest on the head of each of them. They were all filled with the Holy Spirit. So the Holy Spirit can be compared to fire as well.

The Holy Spirit as Air

When we think of the Holy Spirit it is difficult to understand exactly what this means. It is like the air. We can sense it, but it is just space, we cannot touch it, it's as if there is nothing there. It must have been quite a strange feeling for the first man when he went to the moon. He looked down on earth and everything around him was space.

The Holy Spirit as All-encompassing

We are asked to love the Spirit of God and that is strange too. For those who are not used to this kind of terminology it is hard to comprehend. How on earth can you love a Spirit? How can you love something or someone that you cannot visibly see? How can you touch it with your hand? So, tell me, how can you touch the Lord, our God?

There is a song that says: 'All you have to do is give yourself to His command.' And what is His command? His command is, love me, love my brother, that's the way God says it has to be. His Spirit is made flesh in His people, so you can love the Lord now in me. It is quite easy to say that we love God the Father. After all, He's not too hard to live with day by day. But it doesn't mean much to Him if we are neglecting to love one another come what may. Have you ever felt you wanted to touch Jesus, but you never feel that you are getting through?' For me touching God is something that can be achieved by reaching out to your brother or sister who is sitting next to you.

The Holy Spirit as Life

There are people being born every day; just as there are people dying every day. It is the cycle of life. You cannot avoid it. Coming into this world and leaving it are the two things that we have no choice over. It is an inevitable occurrence. You live and then you die. It is the same for everyone; from the Queen to the Pope, from the rich to the poor, from the young to the old, no-one can escape this fact of life. Have you noticed what a joyous occasion it is when a new baby comes into a family? What a fuss everyone makes of this new addition and so it should be for a new life is a blessing from God.

A new baby can change your life; it is a new life stepping into an unknown future. It is the same for those that die. They too are stepping

into the unknown and they too are experiencing new life and are met with joy. I believe God makes a fuss of you when you are born into this life and more so, when you die and are born into eternal life.

The difference about being born into this world is that throughout our lives we have trials and temptations. Life can be hard for a lot of people. There are incurable diseases, poverty, unemployment and a lot of tears along the way. No-one escapes it. At one time or another, life can hit you hard with painful blows that never seem to end. Life can be cruel when you think of the mother whose husband has died suddenly at a tender age and she has to raise very young children on her own. Or the prognosis of an incurable disease for a young person who was once full of life and promise and future years ebb away out of his control.

What about the sick babies that are abandoned in a hospital in Bucharest, Romania? Their parents cannot cope with their children's conditions so they dump them on the nursing staff, hoping they can give them a better future. It might sound cruel but until you are faced with a similar situation you cannot understand the agony these parents go through and how their minds work in moments of extreme stress. Thankfully there are always good people who are willing to stand in the gap and help either by praying or in more practical ways.

If you look around there are always 'angels' standing at every street corner, wonderful kind and generous people. That is the world we live in but life and this world is what you make it too. It is not all doom and gloom. God's creation is beautiful if you have eyes to see. I believe that God raises our spiritual awareness so we can better understand the kind of world He envisioned. Sin took care to destroy His plan. But there is a place, another world that awaits us all where there are no more tears and no more suffering or pain. It is called heaven. If this world is beautiful, heaven is beautiful beyond our imagination. Heaven is indescribable. There is joy, there is happiness, and there is consuming love. And the best thing is it lasts for ever!

Revelation 21 says, “He will wipe away every tear from their eyes, and death shall be no more, neither shall there be mourning, nor crying, nor pain anymore, for the former things have passed away.”

Heaven is real

According to the Bible and many accounts of people who have died, gone to heaven and come back again, heaven is real. There have been many eye witnesses to prove heaven exists. It is a real place. Since my husband Tony died three years ago, I feel closer to heaven than I have ever been. It is so close that there are days when I can raise my hands and feel like I could almost touch it.

‘Does heaven exist?’ “Yes it does.” ‘How do you know for sure?’ “Because I’ve been there.” These are the words of a young Scottish Minister called Maggie Lane who drowned whilst on holiday in the Holy Land. She was declared dead and remained so for three days. During this time she was taken up to heaven and came back to earth with a message to the church. I actually met her in person at the beginning of the year and know her story to be true.

What we’ve been trying to say in this chapter is that the Holy Spirit gives us a new perspective on life and how to cope with the many eventualities that will come our way. We have spoken about the Holy Spirit raising us on eagles’ wings and allowing us to see the bigger picture. We know from our own experience of suffering and loss that it is easy to lose sight of this bigger picture, for the wind to be taken from our sails, to be overcome by the suffering we see in the world. It is precisely on these occasions, like the Josh Groban song when we are down, that the Holy Spirit breathes on us and lifts us up to new heights. We can only rejoice that the Holy Spirit is alive and is real, that He speaks to us, He breathes on us and we are comforted with the many wonderful truths of this life and the next.

When I have these experiences of knowing for example that my husband is in heaven, that there are wonderful people in Romania who care for orphans, or even that I can overcome my fears about making an inaugural speech; this only confirms the truth that my life is a spiritual life.

The spiritual life is not some woolly, vague concept. It is as real as the physical or emotional lives we all have. It is the same for everyone. We know that our bodies need oxygen. We hear the messages from the health professionals about eating our 5 a day fruit and vegetables. Likewise we need the Spirit. The Spirit is the guarantee that we shall receive what God has promised His people.

SPIRITUAL FOOD FOR THOUGHT

A prayer for spiritual awakening

Holy Spirit, come like a rushing wind and awaken me out of
my complacency, my apathy and my indifference.
Disturb me Lord, for I am too content to let things go on as they are
in my life.
Penetrate the closed gate of my heart and make me live again.
O Holy Spirit, create a mighty Christian revolution around me
And cast the fear of the unknown out of my life.
Amen.

CHAPTER 5

SIN AND HOW IT HAS A BAD NAME

"For God took the sinless Christ and poured into Him our sins. Then, in exchange, He poured God's goodness into us."
– 2 Corinthians 5:21

In early 2014 a man called Jorge Mario Bergoglio won 'Man of the Year' and millions of people had high hopes for this guy when he was elected as the new Pope. Within his first year in office he did some pretty incredible things. He denounced anyone who spoke ill of homosexuals saying; "If someone is gay and searches for the Lord and has good will, who am I to judge?" He embraced and kissed a man called Vinicio Riva, a man who is mocked in public for his grotesque facial disfigurement. He sneaked out of the Vatican to feed the homeless. He has reached out to Islam and the Protestant evangelical churches, blessing their work. He said atheists are worthy people if they do good. His best friend is a Rabbi. I am not quite sure how Pope Francis ended up with a Harley Davidson motorbike but he decided to sell his Harley and give the money to the poor.

At the same time Pope Francis was creating a new wave of optimism within the Catholic Church, the well published scandals of the Catholic Church still hit the headlines. Not just the well-known scandals; there were even some new ones. In early 2014 the Bishop of Limburg in

Germany, Franz-Peter Tebartz-van Elst had to stand down because he spent £26 Million decorating his house. Known locally as the 'Bishop of Bling' he was suspended by Pope Francis. How curious as well, that five centuries before an Augustinian Catholic priest called Martin Luther launched the Reformation in Germany. Why? Because of the excesses and abuses within the Church.

The new Pope Jorge Mario Bergoglio has certainly won many admirers and seems likable, trustworthy and honourable. He seems to be a spiritual man who has his priorities right. Although in saying that, many who were wronged by the church in the past are still waiting for restorative justice.

God loves the sinner but hates sin

I think it's pretty obvious that the sins of the church have been scandalous and have been the perfect opportunity for others to condemn the church. But the interesting thing is, when it comes to sin God does not condemn. The guilty Priests of the church who have sinned should not be let off Scot free, justice should be done and seen to be done. But within any discussion on sin, one of the first things to be said is that while people may condemn, God does not. The spiritual life is all about being healthy and whole, on right relationships so it follows that we have to know how God sees us. God does not like the sin but He always loves the sinner. There is the beautiful passage of the woman caught in adultery. Jesus spoke those words to Mary of Magdalene "Woman has no one condemned you? Neither do I, go and sin no more" (John 7: 10-11).

The purpose of this book is not to condemn or be negative; it is not to judge people or force anyone into having a spiritual life. This book aims to be a positive offering on why the spiritual life is good for us,

just as going to the gym or eating our vegetables is good for us. The evidence is there, keeping ourselves physically, emotionally, intellectually and spiritually fit makes us healthier and happier people.

So where does sin come into all of this? Surely sin is a bad thing? If we sin doesn't God write down all our transgressions in a big book and one day we will have to see God face to face and explain ourselves like some unruly child meeting the school headmaster?

Is sin a bad thing? What is sin? Has sin been given a bad name? Sin is, turning away from the source that gives life and turning towards the source that brings death.

Sin is a reality, it can harm ourselves and others; it can affect our relationships. But I contest that sin has been given a bad name and that within the context of love, sin isn't as bad as people have been led to believe. Before any believer squirms at this statement, let me explain.

So what is sin? To sin is to break or transgress the law of God. I grew up in a Catholic household and was taught my catechism, the basic beliefs. I believed sin was about acts I did or did not do. Sin was a legal imperative, it was about my actions. If I stole a yoyo from my local Post Office at the age of 8 and was caught and knew I had sinned I had to go and confess that sin to the priest. I grew up with the idea that God had laws and rules, like the 10 commandments and I better not break them or God will not be happy. Frowny face in text speak. Sin was all about the acts I did or did not do. For many years I then added to my understanding of sin as an act, things like scruples and guilt. Now sin definitely is bad. But it may have a bad name because the emphasis can sometimes be more about me and what I have done rather than what God has done to heal the sinner. Remember what we said in the introduction to this book about separation and Jesus Christ being the game changer; nothing can separate us from the love of God, not even our sin.

However, it is wrong to deny there is no such thing as sin. Sin is real and is a choice we make to take ourselves away from God. When I went to university, I encountered all kinds of thinking and philosophies, including relativism that argued there was no such thing as sin anymore.

Given the church's track record with scandals and my poor understanding of what sin was, is it any wonder sin had a bad name. But I think sin has been given a raw deal and sin has been given a bad reputation.

Sin is a choice we make to move away from God's love. When you read Chapter 6 "The Church – why bother?" you will hear something about getting the order right. To enable us to have an active and healthy spiritual life we have to get the order right. Love of God comes first; going to church comes second. Eating Brussels sprouts comes first; taste comes second. Our motivation and desire for doing anything in life has to be greater than the act itself. Hence vegetables make more sense if we know why we are eating them. We eat them for the health benefits, all the good things the mini cabbage contains and all the lovely things they do for our body (although maybe not the wind!). Church similarly makes more sense when we know why we are there. The primary reason to be in church is:

- To grow in a love relationship with the God in whose image and likeness we have been made (Psalm 139).
- To hear good news and to be comforted and challenged to live the most authentic human life we can live.
- To be reminded that we are spiritual beings and while life on earth can be a wonderful thing, one day we will have an eternal life with God.

- To belong to a community of faith and deepen our faith, deepen our spiritual muscle by doing spiritual exercises (prayer, Bible, good works, fasting, learning, and getting involved in some way).
- To see the call we have to reach out, in any way we can to the poor be they physically, emotionally, socially or spiritually poor.

Church makes more sense when we get the order right. If you are into keeping your body fit, the most important thing is the exercises not the building where the exercises take place. The primary motivator for any kind of fitness, physical or spiritual is a personal desire to deepen the spiritual or physical muscle.

In a similar vein when we ask the question "Is sin a bad thing?" we have to think what is the right order to view sin? Should we view sin first as my act? I have sinned because I stole a yoyo. Or should we view sin first and foremost from God's perspective, that God never judges, His love is always greater than our sin and although God hates sin, He loves the sinner. So to answer the question "Is sin bad?' please think in the context of; first it's God's love for us, second is the act we did or did not do. We have to get the order right or there will be total confusion, misunderstanding, apathy or even paralysis of our minds and spirits and that means there will be no growth of the spiritual muscle.

But if we have to think of God's love for us first and the act comes second, does this mean we can do anything we want and God does not mind, since He loves us? If we ask that kind of question, I think we have to ask why we would think like this. Putting aside anyone with particular eating issues or allergies, we know we are free to eat anything we want, fill our bellies with whatever foods we want. But if a middle aged Scotsman like me has a diet of pies, chips and deep fried Mars Bars and I guzzled down gallons of fizzy pop, there would be consequences. Same if I don't exercise my body. It's not healthy to

treat the physical or the same spiritual body in any way I wish just because I can. Self-indulgent choices will create unhealthy consequences so why ask self indulgent questions?

We know the laws of eating 5 a day and the laws of healthy exercise. The laws of the healthy spiritual life still have value, the Ten Commandments and universal teachings of what is wrong and sinful still have value. It's healthy to avoid greed, selfishness, discrimination, injustice and so on and have a more emotionally intelligent understanding of sin. We need to look at our attitudes, our intentions and our perceptions.

If our perception of God or the spiritual life is, "God won't mind, He loves me, I can do whatever I want" that will reflect the images and picture of God, church and sin we carry around in our hearts. My question is; are these the most accurate images of God? Do we need to re-visit our perceptions of the spiritual life just as at times we need to revisit our perceptions of healthy vegetables or doing our exercises? The spiritual life is a life that needs to develop and mature.

It's good to learn and relearn what it means to have a spiritual life. When I stole the yoyo from the Post Office as a young boy I probably went to the priest and said, "Bless me Father for I have sinned I stole a yoyo, I have also been disobedient to my parents and I said some rude words". As an 8 year old that was probably my thinking of what sin was. I am not breaking the confessional seal when I say the following, but during my 11 years as a Priest the majority of confessions I heard were at that level. This is not a criticism of anyone who goes to confession as to be honest I included myself in that group. But sometimes we need to have a fresh perspective on what sin is in order to have a healthy understanding of the spiritual life. I think we can say the following 3 things about sin.

1. Sin and unconditional love are part of the human condition

Weakness is part of the human condition. We were born with a predisposition of wanting to put ourselves first. There is a natural pull towards selfishness and individualism that takes us away from co-operation and relationships. The church has sometimes called this Original Sin. The idea being that collectively, through every human being that lives on this planet, there is more selfishness in the world than we could create just by our own selfishness. Sin or human weakness is part of our condition and this creates struggles and tensions in our lives as to what we should or should not do.

However while Original Sin is trying to drag us in one direction, there is a power and an energy moving us in the other direction and the church calls this God's Grace.

This is this side we have to work on. This is where we have our spiritual workout. We grow spiritually through our spiritual tensions, through our temptations, through our failings and weaknesses. It is precisely at these moments that we can turn to God in prayer and say, "I need your help". In order to grow the spiritual muscle we need God's Grace, we need His power to change direction and say, "I ain't sinning anymore, I am going in this direction, not that direction". That is what St. Paul had on the Road to Damascus (Acts 9:1-19), a conversion, a metanoia, a change of heart and change of direction in life. He decided he was going to rely less on his own power and more on God's Grace to help him move away from temptation and selfishness.

Again within the world of healthy eating, we are all aware within the United Kingdom, that a diet of pies, donuts and dare I default to Scottish caricature, deep fried Mars Bars, are not good for us. Sometimes these things tempt and pull us but we know they are not

good for us. Yes have an occasional one but the idea is to gradually move from that calling to another healthier and holistic calling. So we are encouraged to eat 5 portions of fruits and vegetables every day. There is constant tension and in order to rise above this tension and choose the healthy option, the spiritual life, we need:

- A positive mindset; a mindset like Jesus.
- A wider and deeper perspective of what the spiritual life is.
- Healthy habits of justice, truth, humility, joy, peace and love.

It is the presence of love, unconditional redeeming love that allows us to live with the tension. That is what God's Grace can do for us once we begin the spiritual life. We are able to live with the tensions of life in a healthier way but always turning to God's love and forgiveness when we fail. That in turn can only call us to praise God for what He has done for us. I heard an amazing story many years ago about a man who was importing tropical fish from America to the UK but when his precious cargo arrived at Heathrow Airport many of the fish had died. So he decided the next time he would put a small shark in the fish tank and guess what? The tension of having the shark in the tank resulted in more fish being alive.

Temptation, tension, struggle this is what the spiritual life is all about. The spiritual life is not some woolly concept of someone sitting blissfully in quiet contemplation of God with no worries or anxieties, no tension or strife. The struggle is part of the process of growing. Ask anyone who goes to the gym if they are always in the mood for jumping in their cars on a cold winter's night and driving to the gym. The struggle and tension is always there and sometimes we can't be bothered. So we need a deeper vision, a new mindset and a different set of motivators to get us to the gym. For many people the motivator to get there week after week after week is as simple as going to the gym with someone else. Someone who will encourage you and spur

you on. It's 5pm on a Monday night, you still have work to do, you are feeling a bit tired, a text comes in from your gym buddy, "Pick you up as usual, 7pm , hope you've had a good day". It is at the moments of tension, worry, tiredness, apathy and temptation that we need that text. Exercising our mind or spirit by ourselves is great and should be encouraged but in order to develop the healthy habits and grow the muscle, we need support, friendship and community. We need love, we need relationships and that is what Jesus Christ is.

Temptation and sin is always there but so too is love; if we want it that is. Many say they see no need for God's love and forgiveness, they are fine by themselves but again that is our choice. Love is a free gift. God no more forces His love on to us than the government forces us to eat 5 a day or a friend's text compels us to go to the gym with them. Don't get bogged down in the trials and the tensions. Don't get bogged down in the sin. After his conversion experience on the Road to Damascus, St. Paul wrote about sin and God's overwhelming love. "While sin abounds", he said, "love abounds even more" (Romans 5: 20). How do you cope with sin, failure and tension? Where do you turn with that tension, that sense of failure, that guilt? Have you ever felt you are constantly being pulled in a direction you don't really want to go down? Would you like another way? God's Grace is inviting you now to walk in His way.

Tomorrow, were I to do something more sinful than stealing a 99 pence yoyo and I go to confession, I would like to think that the words I say to the Priest are less about my actions and the laws I have broken and more about God's love and how I can grow in that love and have better loving relationships. Who knows I may say something like:

"Bless me Father for I have sinned. It's been a tough few months for me. I am noticing changes in my behaviour that I don't like. Not sure what it is, could be that I have stopped swimming. I've had several doses of man flu over the winter months, so I have hardly been

swimming. Anyway I am staying up later at night, sometimes I am hardly moving from the sofa for 3 hours and I cannot count how many hours I have wasted and I mean wasted on Facebook and eBay. That internet just drags you in! I used to read stories to my daughter before she went to bed. Because she is older now I am telling myself she doesn't need that anymore so that has gone by the wayside in the last wee while. I used to spend a lot more time with my family but over the last 6, possibly 12 months that has all changed. So I want to confess a sin of isolation, selfishness and apathy. I want you to prescribe for me a penance that will help me change my life and give more time with the people I love. I want a penance of organising a family picnic this weekend and putting a yellow sticky note on my computer. Let's do it in code, let's go for "Douche". I am going to write that word on a sticky note. If you are wondering why Douche, well my daughter and I jokingly call each other a douche if we do something silly. But from now on a Douche will mean" Don't Overdo Ur Child Has Expectations of your love" and I will know what that means".

Being aware of sin or selfishness is akin to being aware that we are not looking after our bodies or our minds. But rather than feeling guilty for not spending time with my family or taking out a gym membership and only using it 5 times in a year, let's use these new moments of awakening to make different, healthier choices. Rather than our failings making us feel guilty, let's use the tension within these choices to return home to sources of love, health and happiness.

Don't get the order wrong. Don't think of the law first; think love first. If we get the order wrong the dangers are:

- Apathy - can't be bothered to eat those healthy vegetables or go to the gym.
- Individualism - who needs other people or their advice? I will do it myself, which is fine as long as our motivation levels and our mindsets stay positive.

- No muscle growth.

Selfishness and sin will create a barrier to us knowing love because we are too tied up with ourselves. I accept, there are times when we can't be bothered; fine have a day, a week, a month off. But don't give up the healthy habits and find a friend or coach to encourage you to get up and start again, should you ever stop practicing these healthy habits.

I was speaking to a friend of mine the other day who is trying to lose weight. They have done very well by themselves but then he stopped going to the gym. Not long after that he thought it was too much hassle to bring fresh fruit to work for his lunch and joked that the local bakers had some great offers on that week. He told me that he stopped going to the gym for 2 months and the weight started to come back on again. That in turn affected his self esteem and made him feel guilty and depressed and on top of that he was giving himself a hard time for failing. All I could do was offer words of encouragement to start going to the gym again and find someone to go with, so that a real person was there supporting him.

No-one said the journey to growth is easy, but the end results are always worth it and the other options that are available (lack of motivation, depression, apathy, low self- esteem) really don't appeal to me. I need a spiritual life and want it to deepen. Sometimes it's a case of not looking too far into the future and thinking 'I will never get that six-pack', 'I will never have that relationship I want', 'I will never feel God's awesome presence in my life again'. Instead, look how far you have already come on the spiritual journey and be glad for the life you still have.

I work within the funeral ministry and have people who have given up on life. I meet people who die without really living and others who live life like they are never going to die; the 92 year old man who went

to the gym was a great example of that. We are meant to have life and have it to the full. Some people want to experience everything that is good in life; others only want to experience some of the good things. Don't miss out on the fullness of life that is available to everyone. Come and explore the spiritual life and what God can bring to you. That is not what being human is all about. "I came that they may have life and have it to the full" (John 10:10) are words attributed to Jesus but we could have equally said, 'Carpe diem', seize the day.

2. Sin is relational and has a social characteristic

Another misunderstanding of sin, again we can blame a legal take on the word sin, is that sin is only about me and what I do and sin only causes harm to me. Not true.

An unhealthy addiction to my laptop will affect my relationship with my daughter. Sin has a social context. Sin can disturb and break relationships. Just think of gossip. It's like a virus, it spreads, it infects and in this instant world of Twitter and selfies we see the power of our acts on other people. So sin asks us to think of the bigger social picture and directs us to ask questions about such things as injustice, world peace and corruption. Recently Pope Francis hit out at the Mafia in Italy more or less saying, "Boys and girls don't think that your actions on this earth won't have repercussions for the afterlife".

Self-interest is generally not a good idea especially if it creates suffering, oppression, exploitation and marginalisation of other people. Sin is not just a personal thing, it can be seen everywhere. Sin connects to education, housing, police, tax, immigration, cancellation of debt, healthcare, employment, voting and every aspect of human life. Many of the world's structures and rules are self-serving and in that sense sinful. The world banking crisis and the impact this has had on the

poor, on employment, on trust is incredible. It has had other selfish side effects like cynicism, intolerance, lack of forgiveness and scapegoating.

In March 2014, we had the privatisation of the Post Office by the U.K. Government. A select number of financial institutions and hedge funds were given priority and preferential allocation of shares on the promise that these financial institutions would not sell their shares when the Post Office moved from public to private ownership. Guarantees were given that there would be no quick profit made by these financial institutions. Guess what, many of these financial institutions sold their shares within 24 hours, they made a 38% profit on the sale price and said thank you very much. Worse still when the Conservative/Liberal Democrat coalition government of the day took professional advice of how to carry out the sale of the Post Office they took advice from the very financial institution that would get the preferential treatment. The same people who would within 24 hours sell their shares at a 38% profit. On top of that these same financial institutions were incredibly paid £13 million for their advice. I would say the sale of the Post Office and how it happened was a sinful and selfish act as certain parties broke promises and certain institutions were given preferential treatment.

Sin has a social context. Whilst we cannot always change structures we can change our personal attitudes. Would we, for example, make a false claim on our insurance policy? Would we claim whiplash if someone gently nudged our car in the supermarket car park because of the possibility of compensation from no win no fee solicitors. Would we laugh at sexist jokes? The tension and the temptation will be there. Sin has a social context but that is when we learn that some jokes are unacceptable, that some behaviours are not good for the general order of society.

3. Re-learn the health benefits of doing something.

When it comes to having a healthy understanding of the spiritual life there may come a time when we have to re-visit what things we have learnt in the past and have a reappraisal of our beliefs and mindsets.

I am asking you to think about how you understand the word sin and to see that it has been misunderstood by many and in that sense it has a bad name.

If you were asked to draw a picture of sin, what would you draw? Do we need to take on board some more knowledge and learning about what sin is and is not?

- According to the Christian tradition, all sin has been conquered by the single act of one man, Jesus Christ, dying on a cross on Good Friday and rising from the dead on Easter Sunday. We were told by Jesus that all sin and all death has now been conquered.
- Sin is damaging, it breaks relationships on a temporary basis but all sin can be forgiven by the other person who loves us.
- Some people can hold on to sin and refuse to let go of it and decide for whatever reason that they will not forgive and will stay in a place of hurt, resentment and bitterness.
- Spell out the word S-I-N, who is in the middle? I am. The ego is a very powerful force in our lives and it can deceive us and trick us into thinking that it's all about me, whereas the spiritual life is saying, "No, it's all about the other person". Get the order right, the focus right, if it's all about you.

It's good to eat vegetables, something I relearned at the age of 48 and it's good to view sin first within a context of God's love as opposed to

what I have done and again I relearned that lesson when I was in my 40's.

Remember those big black plastic discs called LPs? Who has a collection they have never listened to in years? Who has had the experience of hearing an old song and re-hearing that song in a new way? The lyrics suddenly speak to you in a new way 30 years later. When I was aged 17 I enjoyed the songs but I didn't really know that Fleetwood Mac's "Rumours" album was all about love, hurt, betrayal and forgiveness. But 30 years later after having lived many of these events and experiences that Fleetwood Mac sang about I saw and heard in a new way. Maybe it's the same with the spiritual message we heard when we were younger. Perhaps we need to revisit these messages and listen again in a new way.

In late March 2014 I was at church in Kinross and I heard a Bible reading that I have not heard for some 5 or 7 years. I always loved the story of the man born blind (John 9:1-41) and how Jesus rubbed earth/dirt and spit into the eyes of the blind man to make him see again.

When Jesus performed that miracle some of the temple (church) going people of the day objected to Jesus curing this blind man and said, "This man cannot be from God as He does not keep the Sabbath". If you were a faithful Jew in Jesus' day you kept the laws and rules. Some of the faithful Jews called Pharisees sincerely believed that because they kept the rules and Jesus (being a Jew) did not keep the rules then Jesus wasn't as holy as them. So in their eyes there was no way Jesus could have the same kind of right relationship with God as they did. The Pharisees had the same opinion about the blind man who was cured; that he was not as good and as holy as them because he was born blind. In first century Jerusalem there was a belief among the Jews that if you were born blind it was because your parents or forefathers had sinned and God was punishing the sins of your family's past with blindness. The irony of this story is that it is the Pharisees

who are blind not the blind man. They could not see who Jesus was and so they labelled him and convinced themselves they were right and everyone else was wrong. What is it they say; there is none so blind as those who refuse to see.

Revisiting this story that Sunday morning in church after many years of not attending church was very powerful because that day the words really came alive to me. What came through strongly with me as I listened is that God is not looking for an IQ approach to spiritual life like the Pharisees who thought they knew. What struck me that day is that it doesn't matter so much how many laws of the church you know or keep, how many times you go to the temple or the church what matters is your heart relationship with God. It's all about the heart. It's all about the loving relationships we have or do not have. God wants spiritual fruits not religious nuts.

In that Bible reading from the Gospel of John, Chapter 9, Jesus spoke to the blind man and more or less asked him, 'What does your heart say now that you have been healed?' The response of his heart, not his head was, 'I believe you are God. I have truly seen with my heart who you are and I know. Yes there are others who may mock my belief and tell me I am crazy.' The blind man knew that he knew. The blind man just knew; simple as. Whereas the Pharisees who also saw the miracle being performed before their very eyes could not see. Their hearts were closed, they created an IQ explanation for why this man was not the Son of God and Jesus' message being a load of nonsense. They knew what they knew, it just came from a different place and they didn't have any interest in learning anything other than what they knew whereas the blind man was open to re-learning.

Have you ever had that experience of being in love where you just know? You cannot rationalise or explain, you just know. The experience was real and actually you do not need to explain to others, your heart just knows.

No wonder sin has a bad name, and can be easily misunderstood if we close our ears and our hearts from re-learning. The Pharisees thought that sin was all about the acts they did or did not do. Whereas the blind man who was labelled a sinner (hence he was blind) was the only one who could see. The blind man said, "I don't care too much about why I am like this (blind from birth) or the (alleged) past sins of my family. All I know is that this man loved me so much He healed me".

I believe Jesus read the heart of the blind man, He could see the love in his heart and Jesus as God responded to an open heart. He also read the hearts of the Pharisees but He could do nothing for them as they were not interested in God's love, their primary interest was keeping to their understanding of God's rules on life. Their hearts were closed, their re-learning was over. To bring in the Brussels sprout analogy again; they knew eating 5 a day was nonsense, they were sticking with their own diet despite the invitation to have a slightly healthier one.

When you love someone, you would do anything for them wouldn't you? Would you not do everything and anything in your power to help them and to remind them how much you loved them? It would be awesome if, like Jesus from 2000 years ago we all had this power to heal the blind. But maybe, just maybe we do have that power to heal. To heal those we love, to heal those who have hurt us. Sometime in 2014 Pope Francis and his Jewish Rabbi friend are going to Syria to talk to both sides of the debate and hope they can convince people to have a metanoia, a change of heart and make the Syrian war end. All they want to do is talk and share love with both sides and see what happens. Through love incredible healings can happen, former enemies can be reconciled, people can forgive. There is even the moving story of Hilary Clinton visiting the UK in 2014 and the media again asked her about Monica Lewinski. Hilary Clinton spoke of how healing and liberating it was to forgive her husband.

Last year in the UK the former leader of the United Defence League Tommy Robinson quit as leader. Some claim the United Defence League is a racist anti-Muslim group. In an astounding move, Tommy Robinson then joined up a group run by Maajid Nawaz called Quilliam. Quilliam is a think tank to combat extremism. Maajid Nawaz formerly ran a hate group called Hizb ut-Tahrir, but now works to promote tolerance, peace and dialogue. Could such a move have happened without some degree of learning, respect and love? That is what the spiritual life is asking us to think about; our hearts, how we love and where do we turn to strengthen and deepen that love. How are we strengthening our spiritual muscles? We can change if we want to. Do you have a desire to change? You can have a strong healthy spiritual life if you want one. All you have to do is start the journey. Start developing new habits, behaviours and mindsets that are based on the person of Jesus Christ.

What do you think of when you picture Jessica Ennis or Mo Farrah? What do you think of people who go to the gym four or five times a week? What do we make of the latest health advice and it wasn't an April Fools when it was announced on 1st April 2014 that we should eat seven not five portions of fruit and veg a day? That's something like; one banana, one apple, one tomato, one carrot, some broccoli, some salad leaves and some grapes. In the UK in 2014 the average Brit is eating two portions, what do we make of those who eat seven?

The point is; at least do something to grow the muscle. Walk up the stairs to strengthen the body rather than using the lift. Eating one portion of vegetables a day is better than eating none. Do something; that is the point of the advice. Something is better than nothing.

Don't just eat Brussels sprouts once a year at Christmas. Start developing new habits. No-one is asking us to be obsessive. No-one wants us to feel guilty if don't eat seven a day but let's do something. Let's have some healthy physical, emotional, intellectual and spiritual

exercises. I mean what about developing a habit of thanksgiving. The aim being to become truly thankful no matter what happens in life. I say it again, no matter what happens.

What if once a week for example, before we went to sleep, we put a photograph of those we love at our bed-side table and we think gratitude. We think how lucky am I, how blessed am I just to have this day. Gratitude is one of the best spiritual exercises we can practise, to give thanks on good days and the not so good days.

Set yourself new targets to have a healthier spiritual life, to read the Bible, to believe in the power of prayer, to treat other people as Christ treated them and to accept that failing is ok, sin is even forgiven by God. It's not the sin that we committed yesterday that should determine what we will do tomorrow, it's where and to whom we turn so that we are raised up from our sin and have a new life in Christ. Nothing can separate us from Christ. We have that new life every day and that is a cause of thanksgiving and praise to God. By developing a healthy habit of thanksgiving, praise and gratitude we might not end up being Man or indeed Woman of the Year, but we will deepen our understanding of what it means to be a spiritual being and what Jesus and the spiritual life is all about.

SPIRITUAL FOOD FOR THOUGHT

Sin in your life

Sometimes fear and anxiety is the result of one's own sin and guilt. If you have committed a sin or done anything wrong, your fear and anxiety is probably God and your own conscience trying to get your attention. You need to repent, confess your sin, seek God's forgiveness, and set it right.

Psalm 50

Have mercy on me, God, in your kindness.
In your compassion blot out my offence.
O wash me more and more from my guilt.
And cleanse me from my sin.
My offences truly I know them;
My sin is always before me.
Against you, you alone, have I sinned;
What is evil in your sight I have done.
O purify me, then I shall be clean;
O wash me, I shall be whiter than snow.

CHAPTER 6

PRAYER AND DOES IT WORK?

"Prayer is a powerful thing for God is bound and tied to it. No-one can believe how powerful prayer is, or what it is able to effect." – Martin Luther

What is prayer?

In the first instance, we need to ask ourselves 'What is Prayer'? The first thing that comes to my mind is the old 'penny' Catechism of the Catholic Church. As a very young child I remember sitting in class having to memorise what appeared to me as nonsensical words that held little or no meaning. I believed them because they sounded good, but now I realise that at that age I was terribly naïve and would have believed anything. Anyway, the definition of prayer in this little red book that I kept always by my side, said: 'Prayer is the raising of one's heart and mind to God.'

Can you imagine at such a young age trying to figure out how to do that? Even in later years I still found it hard!

I would imagine that for most people prayer can be hard to understand. I prayed because I was told to pray at school and since I did not want to be put in the naughty corner, I did what I was told. I had books that taught me how to pray. It was easy as all I had to do was read the words that had already been printed for me. I prayed with my intellect. I

prayed out of habit. I prayed because I had 'head knowledge' of what I was supposed to say. Now don't get me wrong, my heart was always in the right place, it's just that I did not know the true essence of prayer. I did not know that God was my friend and I could speak to Him from my heart. I did not know that prayer is simply talking to God; a normal dialogue between two people who know each other well.

It was twenty-nine years later that I was to recognise how powerful prayer really is and how much it can change your life, "If the Son of God sets you free; you are free indeed" (John 8:36).

What I want to offer you in this chapter are my reflections on the who, what, where, why and how of prayer. I want to talk about the reality of prayer, how it heals and comforts, how it inspires and challenges, how it strengthens our faith and trust in God and even in God's power, at times, to perform miracles. Above all else I want you to know that prayer works! I know this personally to be true, as I have experienced the power of prayer in my own life and I would like to tell you about it.

All of my life I was tied and bound like a slave, to a 'set of chains' and I didn't even know it. The attraction of the world was far more appealing to me than God was. I was tied to the dependency of prescribed drugs and to repressed grief and unforgiveness. In June 1982 God broke these chains in my life and set me free.

I had turned away from God at the time and I had reached rock bottom. My relationship with my husband was breaking down. My relationship with God was zero. I didn't know God. I was self-centred; rather than God centred. I then had the most incredible experience that would not only change my life forever but also my understanding of prayer.

My mother-in-law, whom I dearly loved, became ill. A whole series of events happened during the months of her illness when she struggled to stay alive. I was struggling too as I did not realise at the time that

God was calling me to change and turn away from the life I was leading.

As the months progressed it was obvious that mum was getting worse. No-one in the family could face the impending verdict of her illness, so I took it upon myself to go to mum's doctor and ask what was wrong with her. The doctor was pleased to see me as she had tried to speak to my father-in-law but to no avail, as she felt he was in denial. She told me that mum had cancer and that she only had one week to live. The strangest feeling came over me as the doctor spoke; I sensed an inner strength and a thought telling me that she would not die within that week. How could this be? Was this a thought that was leading me also into denial, just like my father-in-law, or was this genuinely coming from a higher being, whose name I now know to be God?

My mother-in-law was a non-believer and although a very compassionate, kind and loving person, her belief did not go beyond this world. She often told me that her belief of heaven and hell was limited to this world, 'If you were happy, it was heaven, but if you were sad, it was hell', she used to say.

Soon after, fear started gripping me, as from a very young age I had been led to believe that should my mother-in-law die in a state of unbelief; her soul would be lost for eternity. I remember my distress at this prospect.

At the time my involvement with church was practically none. However, as God would have it, he put a lady from St. James's church in Kinross in my path, who at seeing my distress, suggested I went to pray for my mother-in-law at a prayer service, called a Holy Hour. She said that this kind of prayer service was very miraculous. She also informed me that the service was to take place on the Sunday of that particular week.

I knew that if the doctor's verdict was right I did not have much time as my mother-in-law only had a week to live and because I felt I had nothing to lose I attended the Holy Hour, even though I had not been to one before, and was not sure what it was all about.

On entering the church and kneeling down in front of the altar my heart was heavy. I then felt as if God Himself was speaking to me through the priest, as he led us in meditation and said, "Yes, my child, tell me what is wrong. I am your Heavenly Father who loves you, give me your worries and I will help you".

In my desperation I found myself pleading with God and asking Him to save my mother-in-law, to heal her unbelief, and to prevent her from dying in this state. It was at this point that I made a pact with God by offering Him my life, in return for her life. I had no idea where this came from and what was going to happen next. All I knew was that I was desperate and did not want her to die without knowing she had a Saviour God that loved her.

I then sensed what I could only describe as an intense inner peace rising up within me and coming all over me, a peace that I had never experienced before. When I went home my husband, who was used to my moodiness noticed the difference in me and remarked on it. I remember saying to my husband, "Don't worry, your mum is not going to die, I have given God my life in return for hers". His words: "Does that mean you are going to die?" And my reply: "No, I don't think so!"

Of course, I did not die, and neither did mum. It was peculiar, because in the past, when I was hooked on prescribed drugs, my husband had once said to me: "If I turned you upside down and shook you, you would rattle with all the drugs you have in you!" The difference this time was that God turned my life upside down instead and He shook me.

The changes in me were dramatic. I developed a real thirst for prayer and prayed for the first time from my heart. I became God centred instead of self-centred. I came off the drugs and my husband did not need to turn me upside down anymore!

My marriage was healed and my relationship with my husband took on a new meaning. I fell in love with him all over again and it was better because God was in our lives. The same thing happened to my parents-in-law.

These changes were so real that my father-in-law said to me, "I want what you've got!" As a result many members of my family turned to prayer and accepted God in their lives.

So, what did my mother-in-law think of all this? Well she had a tremendous sense of peace. She lived a full year and died in that same state of peace at St. Columba's Hospice, Edinburgh, where she recited the Our Father every day of her remaining life, with the nuns, until God called her home.

This experience of my mother-in-law's illness was the beginning of my spiritual journey and of truly knowing the power of prayer. Little did I know that shortly before she died, I would be asked to start a Prayer Group in Kinross, which is still going strong after 31 years. That is what prayer can do for you. That is how God can change you if you have a great need. He will instil in you a desire and thirst for Him and give you an active prayer life.

To think as well that it all started when I crossed the Forth Road Bridge one evening.

I was working in Edinburgh at the time and remember that I was driving home to Kinross on the motorway. I had just crossed the Forth Road Bridge and was approaching the Rosyth/Dunfermline junction, when I spotted a field with a growing crop I had not seen before. I was

curious to know what it was, and was quickly trying to read the large board on the side of the field when the words, "I am going to help you start a prayer group" cut right through my thoughts. I was puzzled and perturbed at this, as my attention and concentration at the time, was completely taken up with trying to find out what the field contained. I later found out it was oilseed rape.

However, needless to say, my mind focused on other thoughts as I drove further up the road. I thought, "I wonder if I imagined all that and if that is God speaking to me?" Within seconds, the same words cut through my mind, "I am going to help you start a prayer group."

The prayer group is another story in itself but for now I want to thank God for the many, many people whose lives have been changed through our prayers in the last 31 years. We have witnessed many healings, both emotional and physical. The one thing the prayer group has taught me is that prayer works. Just as going to the gym develops our physical muscles, so too the spiritual exercises will do something to us and will definitely work.

I know prayer has done a lot for me. What I want to show you in this chapter is what prayer can do for you. I am going to do it through a sequence of who, what, where, why, when, and how.

Who to pray to?

It might seem obvious who we pray to, namely God, but let me expand on this a bit. Prayer is just praying to God the Father. We are praising and thanking the Father for giving us His Son, Jesus Christ. This life of Christ now lives in us like a spark, like energy and that is quite joyful because every time we pray to the Father, we pray through Jesus, with Jesus, and in Jesus. Do you know what that tells me? All prayers are guaranteed to reach heaven. God listens to us. He will act in our prayers. When Jesus left this earth, He left a special gift in the hearts

of all those who believe in Him and that gift is called the Holy Spirit. It is the Holy Spirit who moves us to pray in Christ, in order that these prayers will reach our Father in heaven.

Now we know who we pray to, let's look at what prayer does.

What does prayer do?

- Prayer changes situations.
- Prayer changes us internally.

Never underestimate the power of prayer during those tough times in our lives. So talk to God in short little prayers throughout the day. Tell Him how you feel. Before you go to bed at night, say a little prayer and give all of your worries and troubles to God. He will be up all night anyway, so He won't mind. Above all, never underestimate the power of God to see you through any difficulty. Read the encouraging words of the Bible that tell you how much you are loved. Prayer should be just like talking to a friend. It should also invigorate you and animate you at every moment.

Within this book we have consistently been going on about the healthy spiritual life being like eating your 5-a-day, or going to the gym. We know that in order to get the proverbial six-pack we need things like perseverance, commitment and faith that small consistent acts and healthy habits will make a difference in the long term. If I want to swim 100 lengths by the end of this year, I would start by swimming 10 then 20 then 30 lengths and slowly build up a healthy exercise pattern. It is the same within the spiritual life. Do something. Develop healthy habits. Enjoy being 'there' and recognise the results when you see them. Like the gym we have to have some intentionality and focus, want to do the exercises, and believe the exercises will work and produce a fitness that others will recognise.

Where to pray?

You should not worry about how you pray, or where you pray. It doesn't matter whether you pray aloud, or in the silence of your heart, or on your knees, folding your hands or bowing your head. It's good to humble yourself, but it's not your posture or how long you pray for that makes it effective. What's important is that you pray consistently, or as it says in the Bible, "pray without ceasing". I think of prayer as the key of the morning and the lock of the night or like two buckets in a well, one ascending and one descending.

There are many places where we can pray. In the:

- Car
- Bath
- Shower
- Bed
- With friends
- Before big decisions

Prayer, as I have said already, is simply conversation with God. It's asking Him to meet your need or someone else's. It's praising Him and thanking Him. It's about committing things to Him and consecrating things to Him. We can pray about everything and anything. No prayer is too insignificant for God.

Why do we pray?

Sometimes when you are in pain, you may think, why bother praying, does God really care how I feel? Of course, He cares. If you think of God as your 'daddy' or your 'mummy', would you not run to Him/her so He/she can kiss it better? If you stand still you might even feel a 'hug' and His warm embrace. Try it, it works!

You may also be asking, "But how could God, an entity massive enough to create the universe, really care about the little details of my tiny life?"

The heart of the Christian message is that God cares so deeply about each one of us that He has provided a way for us to have an authentic, intimate relationship with him. Genuine, sincere prayer brings a person into a closer relationship with God. Think of it as a relationship with the one you love. When you spend time with the one you love, you get to know them better. Intimacy can only happen when you get to know someone very well. Prayer is simply spiritual communion and spiritual intimacy with God. It is only when you enter into a relationship with God that you will fully comprehend the power of prayer.

Prayer is one of the most incredible blessings of the Christian faith, for the more we believe, the more God reveals Himself.

I think some people don't pray much because they don't find it easy, or they are tired or something else is on their mind. Equally others may not fully understand how powerful prayer is. Usain Bolt came to the Commonwealth Games in Glasgow in 2014. Like any athletes preparing for a race, they will have gone through many struggles and doubts. At times their motivation levels may be low, they may be struggling with their diets and all of this will affect their energy levels and their breathing. We need focus. We need desire. The truth is, prayer

is one of the greatest privileges Christians have, but we have to desire it.

When we pray, we open the door for God to come into our problems and situations and work on them. Prayer makes us partners with God. Although we can't really change people and make them love God, He can minister to their hearts and reach them.

I also believe that prayer is easier than we think it is. It can be so much a part of our life that we don't even realize how much we pray, like breathing. Oxygen brings life to our blood, brain, heart, all our body systems and affects our chemical balance. Prayer too puts us on the right balance.

Prayer changes the one praying because in prayer, you are in the presence of God as you lay before Him your complete self in confession and dependence. There is nothing to hide when in quiet supplication we are reaching into the deepest part of ourselves and admitting our needs and failures. In so doing, our hearts are quieted and pride is stripped and we enjoy the presence of God. James 4:8 says, "Draw near to God and He will draw near to you." Prayer is the privilege of touching the heart of the Father through His Son, Jesus Christ.

Prayer brings many benefits too. The one benefit which I associate with in prayer is peace. Philippians 4:6-7 tells us to, "Be anxious for nothing, but in everything by prayer and supplication with thanksgiving let your requests be made known to God. And the peace of God, which surpasses all comprehension, shall guard your hearts and your minds in Christ Jesus," I can certainly vouch for this.

- Prayer makes you stress free. It can relax the body and the mind.
- Prayer can reduce your chances of suffering from anxiety and depression.

- Prayer makes you happier and can boost the levels of dopamine in your brain.
- Prayer speeds up post-surgical recovery and helps in the quicker healing of scars.
- Prayer makes you a better person as it reduces the level of one's ego.
- Prayer is good for your heart. It can regulate your heart beat and makes it stronger.
- And as was mentioned at the beginning of this book (page 11) incredibly, prayer helps you live longer.

What makes prayer so powerful?

The Bible tells us in James 5:16, "to pray for each other so that you may be healed." It teaches us that, "the earnest prayer of a righteous person has great power and produces wonderful results". Prayer is passionate. It's about sincerity of heart and putting your whole heart into it.

In our prayer group we have found that because our prayers are so heartfelt and are said in unison, they travel faster and are answered.

How should we pray?

- We should pray by faith, trusting God.
- We should pray consistently, trusting God.
- We should pray for others, trusting God.

We pray because we know that God hears us and He loves to be sought.

One of the chief purposes of prayer is to transform the heart of the person praying, to more closely resemble the heart of God. It is an opportunity to know God more fully, to better understand what He wants of each of us, and to establish a lifelong relationship.

Having said this, however, God also wants us to make specific, personal requests seeking his direction and provision. God wants to answer our prayers for in speaking to his disciples about prayer, Jesus said, "Ask and it will be given to you; seek and you will find; knock and the door will be opened to you. For everyone who asks receives; the one who seeks finds; and to the one who knocks, the door will be opened" (Luke 11:9-10).

God promises not to harm us. "For I know the plans I have for you… plans to prosper and not to harm you, plans to give you a hope and a future" (Jeremiah 29:11).

According to these verses, prayer is an opportunity to approach the greatest Father of all time and openly express our needs and desires and directly ask for help.

Jesus Prayed for Himself

If you think about it, even Jesus prayed to His Father asking for help. He prayed at critical times in His life. Before He chose his apostles, He needed to be sure that He was picking the right twelve people for the job, so He went up on a mountain to pray, and He prayed to God all night (Luke 6:12). Now that's perseverance! So this teaches us that sometimes we have to persevere in prayer until we see results. P.U.S.H. - Pray until something happens. It also teaches us that before we make

any important and critical decisions in life, we should pray and seek direction and spiritual wisdom.

Jesus also prayed on the Mount of Olives before His agony (Luke 22:44). "Now an angel from heaven appeared to Him, strengthening Him. And being in agony He was praying very fervently; and His sweat became like drops of blood, falling down upon the ground. When He rose from prayer, He came to the disciples and found them sleeping from sorrow."

How many times have you been in an impossible situation where you felt that there was no way out? Perhaps you had no-one to turn to? All your friends deserted you and you felt alone. What about now though, the present; is your life so difficult that you feel life is not worth living? Your situation has become so excruciating that you are almost in agony, "I can't take any more of this", you say; "When is this all going to stop?" For some it might be the recent news of a life ended in your family, through suicide, or the devastating diagnosis of an incurable cancer with the impending death sentence that follows. Or perhaps you have lost your job and don't know how you are going to manage to pay the bills. All I can say to you and I know this from 31 years of doing these spiritual exercises is that, whatever it is, Jesus associates with all of our struggles and wants to help us. He has gone before us in so many ways. He had His own struggles, but He always took them to His Father. So many times we carry burdens that could simply be lifted off our shoulders if we would only give them to God. Our Heavenly Father wants us to take our burdens to Him in Jesus' name and leave them at His feet. He cares so much for us. 1 Peter 5:7 says, "Give all your worries and cares to God, for He cares about you." This especially works at the end of the night.

Many times we try to solve our problems on our own and end up in a worse state than when we started. I sometimes say, "Lord, I give this problem to you. You are the only One who can solve this. You are the

Only One who can heal me and help me". It is also good to remind ourselves to apply in our lives what Philippians 4:6-7 tells us to do, "Don't worry about anything; instead, pray about everything. Tell God what you need, and thank Him for all He has done. Then you will experience God's peace, which exceeds anything we can understand. His peace will guard your hearts and minds as you live in Christ Jesus". Think of the positive rather than focus on the negative, be thankful for what you have in life rather than what you don't have. As Jesus prayed for Himself to cope with the times of: Why? Why? Why? So we are encouraged to pray for ourselves and to persevere like the top athlete preparing for that race. But there is more.

Jesus prays for us

Jesus not only prayed for Himself but also for His disciples at the time:

"I pray for them. I am not praying for the world, but for those you have given me, for they are yours. All I have is yours, and all you have is mine. And glory has come to me through them. I will remain in the world no longer, but they are still in the world, and I am coming to you. Holy Father, protect them by the power of your name, the name you gave me, so that they may be one as we are one... My prayer is not that you take them out of the world but that you protect them from the evil one. They are not of the world, even as I am not of it. Sanctify them by the truth; your word is truth. As you sent me into the world, I have sent them into the world. For them I sanctify myself, that they too may be truly sanctified' (John 17:6-19).

Jesus prays for all believers

"My prayer is not for them alone (meaning His disciples). I pray also for those who will believe in me through their message, that all of them may be one, Father, just as you are in me and I am in you. May they

also be in us so that the world may believe that you have sent me. I have given them the glory that you gave me, that they may be one as we are one, I in them and you in me, so that they may be brought to complete unity. Then the world will know that you sent me and have loved them even as you have loved me.

Father, I want those you have given me to be with me where I am, and to see my glory, the glory you have given me because you loved me before the creation of the world.

Righteous Father, though the world does not know you, I know you, and they know that you have sent me. I have made you known to them, and will continue to make you known in order that the love you have for me may be in them and that I myself may be in them" (John 17:20-25).

Jesus Christ prayed this prayer to the Father the night before His crucifixion. He could have spent the time praying for Himself only and been very self-centred, anticipating his own excruciating agony, but He did not do that but rather prayed for those who were His and those who believed in Him. When He did pray for Himself, it was only to accomplish what He was sent to do, so He could bless all of us. So, even when He prayed for His own glory, it was indirectly geared to us. Jesus prayed for His disciples and all believers at that time and in the years to come, and that includes us today.

Many came to Jesus for prayer. He never turned anyone away. Today nothing has changed. Many, many people come to God in their need and desperation, and He always welcomes us with open arms.

Prayer is not new. People have been praying since the beginning of time. There were many people in the Bible who prayed and had their prayers answered. Let's look first at how some of them prayed:

- Jesus's Prayer - "Father, I thank you that you have heard me. I know that you always hear me" (John 11:42).

- Jesus's Submission - "Father, if You are willing, take this cup from me; yet not My will, but Yours be done" (Luke 22:42).
- David's Prayer - "To you, O Lord, I lift up my soul. O my God, in you I trust, let me not be put to shame; let not my enemies triumph over me" (Psalm 25:1-2).
- Samson's Prayer - "O Lord God, please remember me and please strengthen me" (Judges 16:28).
- Jonah's Prayer - "I called out of my distress to the Lord, and He answered me. I cried for help from the depth of Sheol; You heard my voice" (Jonah 2:1-9).
- Thief at the Cross - "Jesus, remember me when You come into Your kingdom!" (Luke 23:42).
- Prayer of Jabez -"Oh that you would bless me and enlarge my territory! Let your hand be with me, and keep me from harm so that I will be free from pain" (1 Chronicles 4:10).

When these believers in the Bible prayed, God's power showed up. What amazes me about all these people and their prayers is that, they could well be the people of today. A total array of prayers with differing needs, just like us in this present age.

There are many examples of answered prayer in the Bible. Abraham prayed to God, and God healed Abimelech and his wife and his maids, so that they bore children (Genesis 20:17).

Hannah was a woman greatly distressed for she could not conceive, she prayed to the Lord weeping bitterly making a vow and said, "O Lord of hosts, if You will indeed look on the affliction of Your maidservant and remember me, and not forget Your maidservant, but will give Your maidservant a son, then I will give him to the LORD all the days of his life, and a razor shall never come on his head." And

Elkanah had relations with Hannah his wife, and the Lord remembered her. It came about in due time, after Hannah had conceived, that she gave birth to a son; and she named him Samuel, saying, "Because I have asked him of the LORD." She asked and she received.

Does prayer even work?

There are many today who are struggling to believe in God, never mind believing in prayer or whether it works. They are self-sufficient and don't think they need to go to anyone when they are hurting, or in trouble. Many also may well ask, "What's the point of praying if God already knows the future, orchestrates what's going to happen, and knows what we need?" Yet, billions of people all over the world practice some form of prayer. Why bother if it doesn't make a difference?

Buddhists, Christians, Hindus, Muslims, and members of many other religions share a common thread of prayer.

For instance, Buddhists believe not so much in praying to an external god but in praying to awaken their own abilities buried deep within. Muslims believe that their prayers, which are required five times a day, are a reminder of God and a calling to a greater purpose beyond themselves.

Christians, too, believe that prayer can powerfully change lives, that it should be practised regularly, and that it can help us refocus our priorities. Christianity further teaches that prayer also has the ability to dramatically affect the world and influence how God chooses to interact with humanity.

But how does that work? If God is a supreme, omnipotent being, won't He work out his purposes however He wants? It seems unlikely that our measly little prayers would affect His plans.

Many Christians would describe it like this: In mysterious but sovereign ways, God has decided to allow prayer to influence and accomplish His will. He chose prayer as the means through which to involve His followers in His plan. Prayer is one way God accomplishes His purposes in, and through, the one who prays.

You may well ask, and what about me? What if you are the one whose prayers have not been answered? Not in the way you wanted anyway. What about if you have been trying for years and years to conceive, as in the case of Hannah, and no amount of prayer has produced the baby you so much desired? I think of myself in this instance, I was expecting my third child and complications arose. There was every chance that the baby in my womb would not grow to its full stature. I prayed and prayed and prayed to God that my baby would live, and unfortunately the baby died. I was devastated as I wanted this baby so much! At first I thought I might have done something wrong and that perhaps I was being punished. I now know that these were negative thoughts promoted by the stress and anxiety I was experiencing at the time. I now know that God was not punishing me. I did not know that God loved me at the time. Today I do. Today I recognise that there was a chemical imbalance in my body that did not allow me to carry my child full term. Today I truly believe that God knew best and took my child into His loving care.

I named my child Peter. I knew he was a boy. I have also miscarried three other children whom I named Mary, Elizabeth and John. It is cathartic to name your child if you have had the misfortune of miscarriage. Thank God that today I still have my other two living sons, Tony and Jamie, who are a tremendous blessing to me.

Just because we think God does not answer our prayers in the way we would really want them to be answered and we experience some kind of 'silence' from God does not mean that the silence is indicative that the prayers are not being heard. Silence is part of the prayer experience.

Many of the greatest people of prayer describe long periods of silence and emptiness, they have even called them 'desert experiences' or 'dark night of the soul'; but because God is your friend, these are moments of great opportunities for God to draw us closer to Himself.

If listening to silence sounds like a contradiction, that's because it is. What we are suggesting is to relax and let God take over. Surrender to His Will. God knows what we need.

Building Trust

Like anything worthwhile, prayer is a process. It takes time, commitment, and discipline. Prayer is not meant to happen only in times of desperation. As I have already pointed out, it is meant to be an ongoing conversation.

That's where it gets fascinating. As someone invests in and becomes more comfortable with prayer, one of the ways in which it "works" is in the growing trust that person gains.

Prayers Answered

Praying people have reported miracles and answers to prayers that they never would have imagined and certainly couldn't have created on their own. They believe that prayer made the difference.

In our Prayer Group, we not only believe that prayer works, but we have witnessed many answers to prayer during the thirty-one years we have been praying together and interceding for the needs of others. Incidentally, do you know who our greatest intercessor is? He is Jesus Christ, who sits at the right hand of the Father and prays without ceasing interceding for all those in need.

Over a thirty-one year period, the Prayer Group have had innumerable answers to prayer, some quite remarkable.

- We were asked to pray for a badly burned boy, his face was terribly scarred and within days of our prayers his face had started healing; in fact he looked like he only had a sun-tan.
- A girl fell down the stairs and fractured the tail end of her spine with x-rays to prove. After praying through the laying on of hands she was instantly healed. What I mean by the 'laying on of hands' is that I physically laid my hands on her coccyx and prayed.
- Man turned out of his house by his wife with no hope of reconciliation. He turned to drink and was a nervous wreck. Now completely healed, his marriage restored.
- Girl involved in accident with no hope of recovery for her; healed.
- The dog of a member of our Prayer Group was run over and suffered crushed lungs. Vet said the dog would not recover and needed to be put down. The owner of the dog prayed over it during the night and it was healed by the morning.
- Woman suffering from heart trouble for years with punctured tubes leading to heart, she was healed.
- Several couples who were unable to conceive for medical reasons, we prayed and they all had healthy babies. They all asked us to stop praying after their third child was born!
- Two women diagnosed with breast cancer – both now cancer free.

We have been looking at this whole area of, 'Does prayer work?' On a more personal level I too have witnessed many remarkable answers to prayer. One of the closest to my heart was when God answered my prayers for my nephew Terrence.

When Terrence was a teenager his parents' marriage broke up and he went off the rails. He became involved with the wrong crowd and soon he was hooked on drugs. I remember one night when I was visiting

my sister in London, which is where they lived at the time, young Terrence came in at 4 o'clock in the morning. My sister had spoken about her fears for her son and at first I thought she was exaggerating; she was crying that night as she told me about her despair concerning her broken marriage and her son's drug addiction.

We had just gone to bed but a strong sense within me urged me to get up and go to Terrence's room. It was probably sympathy for my sister and anger at what her son was doing to her and to himself.

When I saw him I was shocked. He looked filthy, he was totally spaced out, he didn't have a clue where he was, or who I was for that matter. He collapsed into his bed with an eerie smirk on his face. I felt like hitting him. I was so angry, but instead God's compassion came over me. I saw my nephew as a dead soul, totally broken and wasting his young life. Christ's compassion compelled me to pray with him as he lay there in a state of drugged stupor.

A couple of days later, I got an opportunity to speak to him about what he was doing to himself. I told him how much God loved him. He then allowed me to pray with him once again. He was moved to tears and I felt that perhaps nothing much would happen.

It was later that he became involved in eastern spiritual practices that cut me to the core. I kept telling him that Jesus was the only way to the Father. In those days his head was so full of junk that he ended up offending me. My husband asked him not to speak to me in that manner again, or try to knock my faith. It was very upsetting because I had high hopes that he would have changed after the prayer ministry.

For years after that we all prayed fervently for his conversion and drug addiction. My mum constantly prayed to God and asked also for the intercession of Mary, the Mother of God. He was very close to his granny and he would often sit and listen to her, but he was still very much living in his own fantasy world.

When my mum died, I was upset as she had prayed so much for Terrence and nothing had changed. One night while feeling a little bit despondent, I came across a file where I kept all the letters people had sent me asking for prayer. I started reading a couple of letters from my sister and then experienced what I can only describe as an intense anger coming over me. I started shouting at God and giving vent to my pent up emotions about my nephew. I had made myself so miserable that I decided to check my e-mails instead. As I connected to the internet, a message was coming in that seemed to be taking a long time to get through. I got angry at this too, as my impatience that night was great. I was just about to delete it when I felt a strong sense within me preventing me from doing so. I then heard an inner voice saying, "Don't be so impatient, wait and see".

When the message finally came through, the first words I saw were, "Your prayers have been answered" and it was from my nephew Terrence, all the way from Hong Kong. I couldn't believe it. I thought someone was playing a joke on me, particularly because I had not heard from him for many years. But it was true, our prayers had been answered.

Terrence had met a flamenco guitarist, called José, who was on a concert tour in Hong Kong. This encounter was to change his life forever. After attending one of his concerts, Terrence and José became friends. José who was also on drugs, had been suffering from severe pain in his back for a number of years. He visited numerous consultants and doctors seeking respite from the pain. It was only later through prayer ministry in England that José received Jesus into his life and was healed not only of his back condition, but his drug addiction.

José returned to Hong Kong and related his story to Terrence; who was amazed at his transformation. That night they spent some time around a fire in the garden and José then told Terrence that God had sent him back to Hong Kong to visit him. This amazed Terrence as he knew that

my mum and I and people from the prayer group had been praying for him.

José prayed with Terrence that night. And this is what Terrence commented in his e-mail:

"It was quite abrupt at first as he was breaking me free from my parents, family and even myself. It was almost as if he was waking my spirit from deep within me. I felt naked and exposed to the Holy Spirit. I prayed for His company and tenderness to be within me and in my life. I cried a lot for a long time. Then I felt peace and a feeling as if I was being nurtured. There was a strong spiritual presence around me.

The next day my wife Jane came back home. We hadn't been having an easy time together due to our own individual problems which we both brought into our relationship. Our marriage was not looking promising at the time. It was almost as if an evil force was trying to destroy it. We talked for a while and then Jane agreed to let José pray over us. We were outdoors in the front garden; the fire was still lit from the night before where I had slept. When José was praying I began to cry again, more and more. I called for Jesus; I wanted Him in my life, and needed Him to be with us. At that moment, I felt and saw a bright light in the shape of a hand coming towards me. The hand appeared to open out and beckoned me to hold it. I reached out and held it. As I did this, a great peace filled my heart and I experienced deep sorrow for my previous blindness."

Terrence has never looked back since this moment and is now totally healed from his drug addiction, as is his wife. They are both committed Christians and totally in love with God. Jane's father too gave his life to Christ shortly after. Considering they are both Chinese and of a different spiritual culture, this is nothing short of a miracle. Praise God!

God did the impossible in their lives. They are now fully restored and live very happily in the knowledge that they have a God that loves

them and cares for them. In July 2012 they were further blessed with a beautiful baby girl, after waiting for seven years to conceive. Is God good or what?

Terrence's gratitude shows in the note I received from him shortly after his story was published in our 25th Anniversary Prayer Group booklet, 5 years ago. "I thank my Auntie Marie, my granny Reme, Pat Dempsey, whom I never knew, and the Kinross Prayer Group who prayed for me for so long and never gave up—for their prayers brought Christ back into my life. I will work with God and cherish Him. I pray: "Thy kingdom come. Thy will be done." AMEN - Terrence

I suppose this taught me at the time, not to question God and to be patient—for His Ways are not my ways and His timing is always perfect.

I'm Praying for You

"I have prayed for you" (Luke 22:32). When someone says, "I'm praying for you," there is no greater expression of love. The tragedy of religion without power is that it leaves you ignorant of the incredible potential of prayer. Prayer moves God and when God moves, people and situations change. There is no distance in prayer. Take as an example my story about Terrence. I live in Scotland and he lives in Hong Kong, and my late mother lived in Gibraltar. Through prayer you can project yourself into any situation, at anytime, anywhere on earth, claiming the promise, "Whatever you ask for in prayer, believe that you have received it, and it will be yours" (Mark 11:24). God comes by invitation. Your prayers open the door to Him. Any time you pray in Jesus' name, the Holy Spirit is authorised to go to work accomplishing things on your behalf that cannot be accomplished any other way. Remember that, next time someone says, "I'm praying for you".

Imagine a miracle that you would like to see; maybe the healing of a sick relative, the repairing of a broken relationship, or the redeeming of a seemingly hopeless situation. Could prayer be your answer? Could miracles become your experience?

What makes a miracle, anyway? Ultimately, you decide. Any unexplainable event that piques your curiosity and inspires your awe may be miraculous to you if you believe that a supernatural realm exists.

The top definition for "miracle" in the Merriam-Webster Dictionary is, "An extraordinary event manifesting Divine intervention in human affairs." Sceptics say that miracles may not happen, because God may not exist or if he does, He may not intervene in people's lives. But believers say that miracles happen constantly as God works in the world.

Types of Miracles

People throughout history have reported experiencing many different types of miracles, and each person's individual perspective on an event determines whether or not they consider it a miracle. Miracle stories abound among people of faith, and they seem to fall into two main categories:

- Dramatic events: Events like a terminal cancer patient's spontaneous remission or a religious figure's apparition may capture your attention as miracles. Dramatic occurrences such as an earthquake victim who's rescued after many days underneath rubble often are touted as miracles in the news.
- Quiet yet unexplainable events: You may also consider quiet yet unexplainable events to be miraculous. For example, figuring out how to solve an urgent problem after praying for guidance or meeting your future spouse and somehow knowing that you're meant to be together may be miracles in your life.

The faithful in virtually all world religions believe in miracles. The most famous miracles are those that the Bible records in both the Old and New Testaments. Many people are familiar with stories of biblical miracles, and some, such as the Old Testament's account of the Red Sea parting and the New Testament's report of Jesus' resurrection from the dead, have been depicted in popular cultural feature films. Some biblical miracles are dramatic; others are quieter but attributed to Divine intervention. But all have the same element in common, urging readers to pray and trust God.

If you believe in miracles, you're probably eager to find out what messages God may be trying to communicate through them. Each miraculous event you encounter may have something profound to teach you.

However, no single explanation may be enough to fully understand the miracles you experience. What if you have more questions than answers when you're trying to learn from miracles? You can use your questions to deepen your pursuit of truth and discover more about God and yourself in the process.

We asked the question within this chapter, 'Prayer and does it work?' I guess the answer to the question is a bit like saying, 'will doing my exercises at the gym do any good. Will they work?' Look in the mirror, what evidence do you see? The vast majority of people who exercise see the benefits, equally so, the vast majority of people who pray and practise spiritual exercises see the benefits and results. You see prayer is not about changing God, it is about changing ourselves to become more like Christ. St. Paul makes this very point that the purpose of prayer is to grant all the desires of our heart. God wants to give us everything that is good for us and prayer is one of the ways He changes our hearts to become more like His.

Dale Carnegie, a famous American writer who developed theories of self-improvement, when asked, “What is the secret of your life?” replied, “Every day I pray. I yield myself to God, the tensions and anxieties go out of me and peace and power come in. Or in the words of the poet Lord Alfred Tennyson, ‘more things are wrought by prayer than this world dreams of.’

SPIRITUAL FOOD FOR THOUGHT

Words of Encouragement

Prayer is such a wonderfully deep subject that we feel this would be a great opportunity to share with you a selection of words of encouragement and reflections on prayer that we have received at the Prayer Group in the last 31 years:

- "I want to make you whole again, each and every one of you. My healing I pour out upon you. Your prayers I answer. I meet your every need. I work in and through you by the power of my Spirit. When you have asked, I have answered."

- "My children come to me your loving Father. My heart is aflame with love for you. Why do you doubt me? Why do you go about as if you do not know me? I love you and I am always with you. As I answer your prayers, be even more bold in what you ask of me. I am not constrained by limitations or lack of resources. Bring to me the big things as well as the little things, and I will answer your prayers. Let not your minds and reason hold you back from being open to what I am capable of. Your faith and your trust in me allow me to channel my power and my strength through you for the Glory of my Kingdom."

- "You have felt my breath upon you, each one of you, as I filled you afresh with my Holy Spirit. Be uplifted. Release your burdens to me. Let them all fall away. You can depend on me - I am your certainty. I am always here for you - just a prayer away. Yet not even that far, as I know your needs before you have put them into words, my children. How I love to give to my faithful ones, even to increasing your faith when it wears thin. I build you up. I am constant in my love for you. Receive my spiritual blessings as a gift from your Father in Heaven, and share them with those I bring

into your lives, whoever they may be. It is not for you to judge them, but to love them with the love that I give you to share - to share in my strength and power and not your own."

- "No matter how difficult your situations may appear, know that I am watching over you. I will not let you stumble. Lean on me - I am your strength. Though your thoughts fly around in turmoil, though your mind goes round in circles trying to seek a way to solve your problems, and you find no peace, just stop and be still. Hand each and every situation over to me in prayer and I will give you peace. I will give you rest. I will see you through these times of trouble and turmoil. I will uphold you, and what the world throws at you will not harm you. You will be secure in my protection. Let your confidence rise within you as you allow your faith in me to increase. The ultimate victory has been secured by my Son in whom you trust - this cannot be taken away from you, my children. Be secure and confident in this knowledge. Though you are in the world, you are not of the world. My mark is upon each one of you. None of you will be lost. Rejoice in the knowledge of this certainty. The plans, insults, deceptions and wiles of the world will come to nought. They will be as dust to be blown away in the wind. They will have no substance and will be lost for ever."

- "You are welcome into my sanctuary; I have great work for you to do. Do not be afraid I am with you always. You can do anything with the power of my Holy Spirit." "Prayer is the fuel of the Holy Spirit." "Step out, follow me. There is no need to be afraid I will be with you always. You will see me all around you. You will see me in the people you meet. You will see me in the beauty of the world. You will see me in the suffering of the world."

"We pray continually that our God will make you worthy of His call, and by His power fulfil all your desires for goodness and complete all that you have been doing through faith; because in this way the name of our Lord Jesus Christ will be glorified in you and you in Him, by the Grace of our God and the Lord Jesus Christ." — 2 Thessalonians 1:11-12.

CHAPTER 7

LOVE AND FORGIVENESS

"Yes, God loved the world so much that He gave His only Son so that everyone who believes in Him may not be lost but may have eternal life." – John 3:16

Have you ever been in love? I don't mean the gushy, mushy feeling that affects your emotions, but the depth of love that cares more about the well-being of another, before your very own.

In this day and age there is a tendency to think of love as described in one word: sex. Relationships come and go and hearts are broken into pieces in the process.

What kind of love have you experienced? Is it one where you are made to feel special, or is it one where you feel used and not totally appreciated? Do you feel taken for granted and not loved and cherished?

It is quite common for these kinds of sentiments to be experienced by the vast majority of the population. The legal system and what it now allows makes it easier to end marriages. Divorce has become the 'in' word and we no longer raise our eyebrows when we hear of another unfortunate couple ending their relationship, sometimes of long standing. How painful is this?

I know of many who through no fault of their own, have ended up in situations that they would rather not have been in. They are now

carrying the wounds in their hearts of rejection, loneliness, feeling unloved and at times as if they are treated as rejects in society. Who can they turn to? Is the love and support from friends and family enough?

These individuals need to be made to feel that their purpose in life has not ended. They need to feel loved and accepted. Mistakes that have happened in their lives are not always their fault; and they have to realise that the 'blame game' is merely walking into a dead end street.

I have heard many of them saying to me, "I wonder where I went wrong?", "If only I had paid more attention to my spouse." When thinking of the other person they lost their spouse to, they have said, "What has he/she have that I haven't?' I bet they are living a happy life now."

All these thoughts are only speculative and although not wrong in themselves, they are not conducive to living a healthy, balanced, and peaceful life.

And what about forgiveness? How difficult is it to forgive someone that has seriously wronged you, or ill-treated you for the best part of your life? It takes a mammoth amount of strength and will-power to do this. Your good intentions are marred by the memory of the wrong perpetrated against you. All you can think of is: 'How can I forgive him/her when all I have experienced is pain?' Your instincts scream at you: 'get your own back!' 'I hope their life together is as much a misery as mine has become.' Does this resonate with you? If so, you need to hear words of counsel and healing that will bring you the consolation you so desperately need.

In this chapter we want to raise the idea that love and forgiveness are two sides of the same coin. Everyone has experienced situations where our willingness to forgive has been tested. It may be a divorce, an argument over money or an injustice where we feel we have not

received a fair outcome. How do you bridge that gap between perceived unfairness and a desire to get on with life leaving the past in the past? Would you like to have a new understanding of forgiveness? Then read on and near the end of the chapter there are 10 pointers to help you heal past hurts.

First, let me tell you a story of forgiveness between two brothers

Once upon a time two brothers who lived on adjoining farms fell into conflict. It was the first serious rift in 40 years of farming side by side, sharing machinery and trading labour and goods as needed without a hitch.

Then the long collaboration fell apart. It began with a small misunderstanding and it grew into a major difference and finally it exploded into an exchange of bitter words followed by weeks of silence.

One morning there was a knock on John's door. He opened it to find a man with a carpenter's toolbox. "I'm looking for a few days' work" he said. "Perhaps you would have some small jobs here and there. Could I help you?"

"Yes," said the older brother. "I do have a job for you. Look across the stream at that farm. That's my neighbour, in fact, it's my younger brother. Last week there was a meadow between us and he took his bulldozer to the river levee and now there is a stream between us. Well, he may have done this to spite me, but I'll go one better on him. See that pile of wood over there curing by the shed; I want you to build me a fence, an 8-foot fence, so I won't need to see his place anymore. Cool him down, anyhow."

The carpenter said, "I think I understand the situation. Show me the nails and the post-hole digger and I'll be able to do a job that pleases you."

The older brother had to go to town for supplies, so he helped the carpenter get the materials ready and then he was off for the day.

The carpenter worked hard all that day measuring, sawing, nailing.

About sunset when the farmer returned, the carpenter had just finished his job. The farmer's eyes opened wide, his jaw dropped.

There was no fence there at all. It was a bridge... a bridge stretching from one side of the stream to the other! A fine piece of work handrails and all and the neighbour, his younger brother, was coming across, his hand outstretched.

"You are quite a fellow to build this bridge after all I've said and done."

The two brothers stood at each end of the bridge, and then they met in the middle, taking each other's hand. They turned to see the carpenter hoist his toolbox on his shoulder. "No, wait! Stay a few days. I've a lot of other projects for you," said the older brother.

"I'd love to stay on," the carpenter said, "but, I have many more bridges to build."

(Author Unknown)

This story reminds me of a similar story in my own life. My story also is about two brothers, my husband Tony and his elder brother Roy.

Tony and Roy grew up in a very loving home, with their parents and other brother Dave. Tony thought the world of his brother Roy and certainly looked up to him. Being the youngest of the three, his outlook on life was highly influenced by his elder brother. This was evident, when later in life he followed in his brother's footsteps and went off to work abroad with an American Oil Company. Life was good for them both and their relationship strong. It was in later years that this bond between the two brothers was to be broken with the death of their mother and five years later when their dad passed away too. Tragic

circumstances were allowed to impel their lives and the brothers became estranged for twenty odd years.

Seven years ago, however, saw the turning point in both their lives as Roy was diagnosed with cancer. It is incredible how suffering and illness can sometimes be used as a catalyst to make you realise that life is too short for misgivings. It is often mere misunderstandings that create the atmosphere for warring amongst good friends, family members and spouses.

I had prayed for reconciliation for many, many years and was beginning to lose hope as nothing seemed to be happening. Suddenly, on 10th March 2008, Roy made contact with us. We found out that he was living in Oban; a place very close to our hearts, as Tony and I used to frequent it on numerous occasions, never realising that Roy was so close by. My heart leapt as I read Roy's e-mail.

Prior to this, whilst praying for both of them to be reconciled, words came to my mind that said, 'Love can build a bridge between the hearts of two people.' These words had made me think at the time that, perhaps there was every possibility our prayers would be answered.

Our first meeting with Roy was arranged for the 24th March. As we were approaching Oban I was impacted by the bridge spanning the water as I realised then that 'Love' whom I believe to be Jesus had been the bridge that brought them together once more.

I will never forget the joy and excitement in both their faces, as they hugged and embraced after being separated for so long.

The days that followed were filled with long and enthusiastic talks as there was a lot of catching up to do. Tears of joy would well up in my eyes as I heard them both voice their love for each other when they spoke on the phone, almost on a daily basis.

In October 2008 Roy joined us at a retreat at Craig Lodge in Dalmally, where he received prayer. He was touched by God in a very special

way. Two months later, on the 16th December, we received the news that his biopsy and cancer test results had come back clear. So much to be thankful for. Praise and thanks be to God. I often marvel at the power of Love and what it can achieve.

These two stories of forgiveness remind me of another story. This time it is of the famous, beautiful and dramatic story of the woman caught in adultery (John 7:53-8:11).

This is how the story goes. Jesus had gone to the Mount of Olives; then early in the morning He had come again to the temple. Many people gathered there to listen to His teachings, which they found profound and interesting. Whilst there, the Scribes and Pharisees brought a woman who had been caught in the very act of adultery and made her stand before everyone. I often wonder if this was to humiliate her in front of everyone or whether they used her as an excuse to ridicule Jesus instead and test Him so they could bring a charge against Him.

They said to Him, '"Teacher, this woman was caught in the very act of committing adultery. Now in the law Moses commanded us to stone such women. Now what do you say?" Jesus did not say a word; all He did was write with His finger on the ground.

When they kept on questioning Him, He straightened up and said to them, "Let anyone among you who is without sin be the first to throw a stone at her." And once again He bent down and wrote on the ground.

When they heard it, they went away, one by one, beginning with the elders; and Jesus was left alone with the woman standing before Him. Jesus straightened up and said to her, "Woman, where are they? Has no one condemned you?" She said, "No one, sir." And Jesus said, "Neither do I condemn you. Go your way, and from now on do not sin again."

Let's imagine the scene for a moment. The woman has been found out with a hideous sin. She was probably frightened out of her mind at the

prospect of being stoned to death. There must have been a time when she had kept her affair a secret. Hoping no-one would know of her illicit affair, she must have lived her life in total deception. Her own marriage might have been an unhappy one and she had more than likely believed she was in love with the man she had sinned with. She felt safe, cocooned in this love mirage and here she was now, totally exposed and about to meet the cruellest of deaths. Every stone that might have been hurled at her was representative of all the hurt feelings people carry when they are wronged by a partner or a friend. Feelings of; jealousy, rejection, hate, mistrust, harsh judgement, bitterness and resentment to name but a few. When you have been hurt, your first instinct is to hurt back. If you had lived in the era this woman was living in, you might have been tempted to throw the first stone at her as well.

Think of times you've been truly wronged, in small ways or big ones. Maybe someone stole something, turned others against you, broke an agreement, cheated on you, or spoke unfairly or abusively.

As the Buddha said long ago, "Getting angry with another person is like throwing hot coals with bare hands: both people get burned." You can see much the same thing internationally. Gandhi put it so well: "An eye for an eye makes the whole world blind."

But Jesus, in my opinion put it even better. 'Woman, has no-one condemned you?' 'Well, neither do I'.

For me the most remarkable aspect of this story is that Jesus was nonchalant. He appeared cool and almost offhand as He wrote with His finger on the ground. Not once, but twice. Kenneth E. Bailey, a Biblical scholar has pointed out that it was unlawful to write even two letters on the Sabbath but that writing with dust was permissible.

I believe this action on Jesus' part had a deeper meaning. He was inscribing the various sins the crowd carried in their hearts to make

them aware that their sinfulness was just as bad as the sin the woman had committed. They had no right to either judge or condemn her.

In the second scene, a brief but moving dialogue develops between Jesus and the sinner woman. They are alone, the crowds have dispersed. She has to face Him, in her shame. I wonder how she felt. She must have been quite amazed at the narrow escape she had just had.

Did she show remorse when facing Jesus? I personally think she was so overcome by His response and reaction that she had a total change of heart and was transformed by His love. What we would call in today's language, smitten by His love? This kind of forgiveness and unconditional love was something she had not experienced before. I believe, that the greater the forgiveness, the greater the love you experience. That is what happened to this woman. She must have been full of gratitude, for when someone saves your life, you are very, very grateful.

Another interesting angle on the story is that Jesus knelt down to write on the ground. Remember the woman is possibly at the lowest point in her life. By kneeling on the ground and being lower than her, Jesus in effect is saying, "If you think you have reached the lowest level, let me show you one day what will happen to me on the cross. And the Good News is it is only when we are low that we can be raised up. This is what I can do for you. I will now raise you up, I recognise you as a woman, as someone broken, yet whole. I love you as you are".

That can be a temptation, can't it? That God will only love us when we are perfect, if we have not sinned. This is not true. God loves us unconditionally and even in our brokenness. This is Good News. This is the power of forgiveness. They even say love and forgiveness are two sides of the one coin. They are free gifts which we just need to accept.

Let's come out of the story for a minute and come back to today. How many times have you felt like lashing out when you have been hurt? It is a futile exercise and all it does is tire you out with little results.

Let's turn the tables around. Put yourself in the place of the woman or man instead, for under the Jewish Law, it wasn't just the woman that had to be stoned, but also the man who had committed adultery with her. How would you feel? Perhaps you too have been wronged. But what about if you are that man or woman who went astray? Did you feel isolated and without friends? Your name has been tarnished forever. You can no longer hold your head up high, for you are walking in shame. Your sin is always before you. Who do you turn to when you need forgiveness? And by this I don't just mean the forgiveness of others, but what about yourself? Have you forgiven yourself? How difficult is it sometimes when you cannot forget the wrong you have done to another. You carry a heavy load and no amount of distraction or trying to forget will help you to erase the mistakes of your past.

This is the sad truth when we forgive or accept the forgiveness of others, but cannot forgive ourselves. Sometimes all we need is a good friend to listen to us. For me, that friend is Jesus. He is not just a good friend, but my best friend. I can talk to Him about anything and everything, knowing He will never turn me away or think any less of me. He never lets me down and He has never failed me.

This is the Good News that most people do not realise:

- There is a Saviour who forgives all your sins.
- He has overlooked all your offences.
- He has wiped the slate clean.
- You are no longer held to ransom as He has set you free from condemnation and self-hatred.

- Your debt to society has been paid by the One who loves you immensely. He does not condemn you so why do you allow others to condemn you?
- Walk high, walk tall for there is a Higher Being that will not hold your offences against you.

It is easy, the answer is simple, just don't do it again, is all He asks. Learn from your mistakes.

"Go, and do not sin again" (John 8:11). The last words of this episode show that God does not want the sinner to die, but to repent of the wrong he has committed and live.

In whatever condition we find ourselves, we can always open ourselves to a change of heart and receive forgiveness for our sins. "Neither do I condemn you; go, and do not sin again".

In order to gain a new understanding of forgiveness we can start with a realisation that God loves us as we are, there is no sin God won't forgive the repentant heart. When we know we are loved and not condemned we can in turn offer that forgiveness to other people and for us to see the dignity of the other person, not necessarily forgetting the wrong they have done, but seeing beyond the wrong and seeing the Christ that lives in them and all of us.

Now let me tell you a story of Love

"For God so loved the world that He gave His only Son so that through Him we might have life" (1 John 4:9). This kind of love is incomprehensible. Who on earth loves like that? Jesus died for everyone, He died for you and He died for me that we might be reconciled to His Father and experience God's love.

Whether you feel worthy or not to receive this love, or whether you believe in this unconditional love, the truth is Jesus died for you and

me, despite how we feel, think or believe. There is historical evidence of this fact. The just penalty for our sin, the wrong things every one of us have done, is spiritual death; separation from God. In the Old Testament times, God allowed animals to be sacrificed for the people's sin and would accept the shed blood as a substitute for the people's own life. But ever since man had first sinned, God had planned a permanent solution. The ultimate sacrifice that could pay the punishment for everyone's sin and see justice done.

The plan was this, to send His own son, Jesus who was Himself God, to be born as a human baby and live on this earth leading a perfect, sinless life, and when He had done this, to offer voluntarily His own life as a sacrifice to pay the penalty for our sin. Not just death but separation from God, the only time Jesus had ever been completely separated from His Father.

This was prophesied hundreds of years before Jesus' birth by Isaiah in chapter 53:6 "We're all like sheep who've wandered off and gotten lost. We've all done our own thing, gone our own way. And God has piled all our sins, everything we've done wrong, on Him".

And this is what He did. The fact that Jesus lived and walked on this earth is historically undeniable. There is more evidence of the existence of Jesus than there is of Julius Caesar. He was born in Bethlehem, grew up as a carpenter, and lived a perfect life never sinning once. He loved and healed people, taught them about God and was then falsely accused and crucified by the Romans outside of Jerusalem. He did all this willingly because He loved you so much that He wanted to save you from the judgement you deserve. Hebrews 12:2 says, "for the joy set before Him [Jesus] endured the cross, scorning its shame." Then Jesus came back to life again after 3 days in 'hell' since death could not hold the Son of God.

This wonderful plan is summed up in one of the most well-known Bible verses, John 3:16-18:

"This is how much God loved the world: He gave His Son, His one and only Son. And this is why: so that no one need be destroyed; by believing in Him, anyone can have a whole and lasting life. God didn't go to all the trouble of sending His Son merely to point an accusing finger, telling the world how bad it was. He came to help, to put the world right again. Anyone who trusts in Him is acquitted; anyone who refuses to trust Him has long since been under the death sentence without knowing it. And why? Because of that person's failure to believe in the one-of-a-kind Son of God when introduced to Him"

So what is our part in all this? We are called to repent; not to sin again. So you may well ask, "What is repentance?" It is turning away from that which brings death and turning to the source which brings life; just as the woman in this story did. I bet she was jolly glad she did! For when you personally know God loves you, it changes your life for the better.

If we go back to the story where Jesus says, "Let he who is without sin cast the first stone" it reminds us that Jesus' reply was made with authority in the knowledge that only God can judge. It also reveals the true meaning of Divine mercy, and leaves open the possibility for repentance. It also emphasises the great respect for the dignity of the person, which not even sin can take away.

I want to take you back to the scene where Jesus is writing on the ground. Have you ever walked along a beach and stopped at the seashore? You look for a shell, a wooden stick, or a seagull's feather and write on the sand. What do you write? For some it might be the name of someone whom you loved and is now gone, a husband or wife or child perhaps. For others it might be a memory, good or bad. You stand back, look and let the inscription take you back to moments in your life that are now in the past. Hurts arise, painful moments you'd rather forget. The swell of the sea rises in the distance with a succession of waves that have continued after a bad storm, reminding

you of the highs and lows you have experienced throughout your life. The tide then gently flows in on the seashore and washes away what you have written on the sand. Isn't this representative of how you might feel? Think about it as the word Love being inscribed on the sand instead and allow Love, meaning Jesus, to wash away all your hurts and bad memories. For me I'd rather have the inscription of LOVE on the sand. Love that represents God, for God is Love. It is that Love that washes away all my sins, hurts and bad memories of the past.

You might be thinking, "Oh this sounds easy", but the truth is that first you have to be prepared to let go of all hurtful and negative emotions to experience the fullness of love. If you do not do this as soon as you get hurt, or have experienced a brutal wrong, then these emotions will start to settle on the inside of you and start to eat you up alive in the same way cancer will eat and ravage a human body. These negative emotions will steal most, if not all of your joy, love, and peace.

Maybe someone hurt you physically or emotionally. Maybe you've survived something else more traumatic, the death through cancer of a loved one, a broken relationship, a fire, a robbery. Or maybe you've just come out of a distressing situation and though you know you'll eventually recover, you still feel pain that seems unbearable. You've been scarred and you carry it with you through most of your day.

When you're hurting some people might tell you to "get over it," or "pull yourself together". Others might say, "It's all in your head" and expect your pain to go away. But none of that brings healing and restoration to your life. So here are a few pointers to help you on your way to recovery:

1. Identify your pain

It's not always easy to identify and understand what's hurting you. Some people even stay in unhealthy relationships because they are frightened to acknowledge and recognise their many layers of pain. They are often attacked by feelings of low self-esteem and the feeling of desperation that convinces them there's no real way out.

The first step toward finding happiness after having been hurt is to understand why you were hurt, to get to the root of everything that makes the memories hard.

2. Express that pain

It is never easy to communicate how you feel to the person who hurt you; and besides they might not even understand and you end up feeling worse than if you had kept it to yourself. The best way to say what you need to say is to write all your thoughts down in a journal. Or better still, write a letter to the person who hurt you, but don't post it, just burn it after you've written it. At least you'll have got it all out, even if it is only on paper.

This will help you understand why you're hurting and what you'll do in the future to avoid similar pain so you can feel empowered instead of victimized. Research has actually proven that people who focus on lessons learned while journaling find the experience more helpful than people who don't.

3. Try to stay in the present

When you constantly relive your past, it can become like an addiction, almost like a broken record. If you keep reliving the past you are giving yourself power for your mind to stay in the past instead of moving on.

Stop torturing yourself. The challenge is to fight back instead of submitting to this desire to constantly engage the past. If this happens to you, try and silence yourself and do not keep repeating the same questions of what happened, where did I go wrong and so forth. What we are talking about here is creating new habits, healthy habits. We have to train our mind to acknowledge the past, because the past is part of us, to recognise the future is not here yet and all we have is this present moment. Make a conscious choice of rather than saying, 'Why did that happen to me?' to say, 'It took me who I was and where I've been to make me who I am now. I am now a new person and have a new life in Christ.'

In other words, it allows you to torture yourself. Regardless of what you should have done, you can't do it now. If you have post-traumatic stress disorder, you may need professional help to avoid revisiting the incident. If you don't, you need sustained effort. Fight the urge to relive the pain. You can't go back and find happiness there. You can only experience that now.

4. Stop telling the story to others

It may seem like another way to understand what happened, or maybe it feels helpful to hear someone say you didn't do anything wrong and you don't deserve to hurt. In all reality this just keeps you stuck right where you are: living your life around a memory and giving it power to control you.

No amount of reassurance will change what happened. You can't find happiness by holding onto a painful story. You can only find happiness when you let it go and make room for something better. You don't need another person's permission to let go and feel okay.

5. Forgive yourself

Maybe you didn't do anything wrong but you blame yourself. Or maybe you played a role in creating your current situation. Regardless of what happened, you need to realize that what you did is not who you are. Even if you feel immense regret, you deserve to start today without carrying that weight. You deserve a break.

You can either punish yourself and submit to misery or forgive yourself and create the possibility of happiness. It comes down to whether you decide to dwell or move on. Which do you choose: anger with yourself and prolonged pain, or forgiveness and the potential for peace?

6. Stop playing the blame/victim game

Maybe you were a victim. Maybe someone did horrible things to you, or you fell into an unfortunate set of circumstances through no fault of your own. It still doesn't serve you to sit around feeling bad for yourself, blaming other people. In fact, it only holds you back. You can't feel good if you use this moment to feel bad about another person's actions.

The only way to experience happiness is to take responsibility for creating it, whether other people made it easy for you or not. You're not responsible for what happened to you in the past but you're responsible for your attitude now. Why let someone who hurt you in the past have power over your present?

7. Don't let the pain become your identity

If everything you do and all your relationships centre on something that hurt you, it will be harder to move on. You may even come to appreciate what that identity gives you: attention, the illusion of understanding, or the warmth of compassion, for example.

You have to consider the possibility that there's a greater sense of happiness in completely releasing your story, that you'd feel better than you can even imagine if you'd stop letting your pain define you. You can have a sad story in your past without building your present around it.

8. Reconnect with who you were before the pain

It's not easy to release a pain identity, particularly if you've carried it around for a long time. It may help to remember who you were before that experience, or to consider who you might have become if it hadn't happened. You can still be that person, someone who doesn't feel bitter or angry so frequently.

If you want to feel and be peaceful and happy, start by identifying what that looks like, what you think about, what you feel, what you do, how you interact with people. Odds are this process will remind you of how you want to be and how you don't want to be.

9. Focus on things that bring you joy in the moment

You don't have to focus on completely letting go of your pain forever; you just have to make room for joy right now. Start simple. What's something you can enjoy in this moment, regardless of what pain you've experienced? Would sitting in the sun bring you joy? Would calling your sibling or a good friend bring you joy? Would going to the gym or swimming bring you joy?

Don't think about the totality of the rest of your days. That's a massive burden to carry, haven't you hurt enough? Just focus on now, and allow yourself a little peace. You'll be surprised how easily "now's" can add up when you focus on them as they come.

10. Share that joy with other people

We often isolate ourselves when we're hurting because it feels safer than showing people our vulnerability. What we fail to realise is that we don't have to feel vulnerable all the time. We can choose certain people for support and then allow ourselves time with others without involving our painful stories.

You can share a meal, a movie, a moment and give yourself a break from your anger or sadness. You don't have to carry it through every moment of your day. Don't worry if you feel you need to remember it, you'll still be able to recall it later. But as you allow yourself pockets of peace, shared with people you love, you may find you need that story a lot less.

Everyone deserves to feel happy. Everyone deserves a little peace. One more thing we all have in common: we can only provide those things for ourselves.

For some people the challenge of forgiving past hurts is too much. It just can't be done today. It needs to be done in stages. Healing is a process. If you cannot forgive one right now then why not picture that person who caused the hurt to be forgiven by God and see God as a bridge between you and that person just like the two brothers did in the story.

Before I end this chapter I'd like to recall the greatest act of love and forgiveness. Jesus went through horrendous trauma, physical pain and emotional agony, rejection, isolation, humiliation, hunger, and thirst. Even after all this he was still able to say: "Father forgive them, they know not what they do" (Luke 23:34). He never retaliated; He just loved. The supernatural power of love that forgives no matter what. He even forgave the repentant thief who was crucified with Him.

The power of love says; make love your goal. God is love and it is His power that enables us to love despite our misgivings, hurts and misunderstandings.

The spiritual life is inviting us to be nourished by the food that God is offering us every day. We need that spiritual food in order to survive. Just as we need food to nourish our bodies, spiritual food nourishes our spirits. We even say that in the Our Father; give us this day our daily bread. One of the things God is asking us to be nourished on is His Word in the Scriptures and His Love, as revealed in the real human person of Jesus Christ.

If you are finding it difficult at present in forgiving someone in your life for a misdemeanor or a hurtful situation, you might like to pray the prayer on forgiveness at the end of this chapter that we have found very helpful.

SPIRITUAL FOOD FOR THOUGHT

A Prayer for the Power to Forgive

"A man's wisdom gives him patience; it is to his glory to overlook an offence" – Proverbs 19:11

God, You told us to forgive those who hurt us.
And yet, I find this hard to do. Deliver me
from the hateful pleasure of nursing a grudge. It
brings only misery. Instead, help me want to forgive.
Then fill my heart with generosity. Make me bigger
than my little self. Help me know the incredible
pleasure of reconciliation. Amen.

What about this famous prayer ascribed to St Francis of Assisi

Lord make me an instrument of your peace;
Where there is hatred let me sow love.
Where there is injury let me sow pardon,
Where there is doubt let me sow faith,
Where there is despair let me give hope,
Where there is darkness let me give light,
Where there is sadness let me give joy.

O Divine Master, grant that I may
Not try to be comforted but to comfort,
Not try to understand but to understand.
Not try to be loved but to love.

Because it is in giving that we receive,
It is in forgiving that we are forgiven,
And it is in dying that we are born to eternal life.

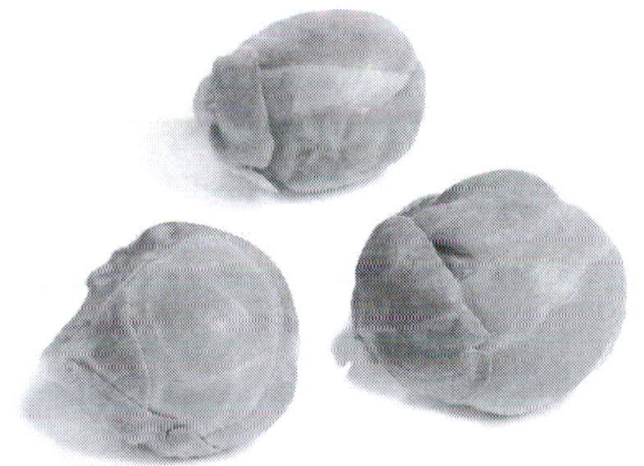

CHAPTER 8

THE CHURCH - WHY BOTHER?

"Let us hold unswervingly to the hope we profess, for He who promised is faithful. And let us consider how we may spur one another on toward love and good deeds, not giving up meeting together, as some are in the habit of doing, but encouraging one another." — Hebrews 10:23-25

I am one of 5 children. I grew up in Monifieth near Dundee; my parents were Catholic, so guess where I went every Sunday for an hour? No, it wasn't to the local park to play, then on to some yummy Italian ice cream parlour in Broughty Ferry for a knickerbocker glory; it was church.

As a day job, I write funeral eulogies.r I get to interview bereaved families and find out all about their lives growing up within that particular family unit. During these meetings, I have heard it being said on countless occasions, often from the children of the deceased, that when they were young they were 'dragged' to church. I never felt that I was dragged to church, nor did I resent the thought that I missed out on ice creams. To keep the Brussels sprout analogy going, my parents did the right thing; they taught me how to cross a road safely, they taught me to eat my vegetables and they taught me that there is more to life than just feeding the mind and the body, we have to feed our spirits.

That being said however, the truth is, many people like me in the 1970s, grew up with memories of church that were like a Brussels sprout, "Mum do I have to?" Many people when they hear the word 'church' still have negative thoughts and feelings towards the institutional church. Perhaps they come from school carol services, sitting in cold pews or from the experience of a Priest or Minister pointing the finger at the parents of noisy children in church, telling them to keep quiet in God's house.

This is no scientific statement but, from having conducted thousands of family interviews for the bereaved, there is enough anecdotal evidence to state that some people have been put off church and have a very negative image of church. They see no relevance of church whatsoever, so why bother? These people are not anti-religious, many categorise themselves as 'spiritual but not religious' but they do not see any need to go to church. Drive into any major city in Scotland and there is a good chance a former church is now a luxury block of flats or has been converted into a pub. I went into one pub in Dundee where the toilet doors had signs that said 'hymns' and 'hearse' for the males and females.

Although I was brought up to see the value of church, my personal experience of church over 48 years is a bit hokey cokey. I have been in and out and often wished the church could be shaken all about. I went to church on a weekly basis till I was aged 16. I then stopped going for a year around the age of 17. Then whilst lots of my school pals were probably going to that church that was converted into a pub in Dundee for a couple of Skol lagers, as I approached my 18th birthday, I felt a desire to go and join a Bible study class in St. Brides Church in Monifieth. A year or so later I was in a priest's training college in Glasgow aged 19.

Despite my in-out relationship with the church and Priests not being allowed to marry, I was never in-out with the God who loved me

intimately. I will always say my priesthood training years were some of the happiest of my life. I subsequently offered the next 11½ years of my life as a Priest then left the priesthood to get married. For various reasons, including the fact that my marriage was seen as an 'illegal' act in the eyes of the official Vatican church and hence could no longer receive Holy Communion on a Sunday, I stopped attending church at the age of 38. I stopped going to church for 7 years. Oh hokey cokey cokey cokey.

This chapter wants to broaden the concept of church and encourage those on the spiritual journey to find some form of church or community that will nourish them.

You would need to be living on planet Zog not to witness the steady decline of people going to church in Scotland in the late 20th century and the early 21st century. There is no need here to go into all the reasons why this is the case, a quick Google search would give you a few clues. But what I want to ask is: What is church? Do we need church? Many people in Scotland live seemingly perfect and deeply spiritual lives without going anywhere near a church, so why bother? I would even say, I felt more spiritually alive during my 7 years away from the official church than when I was a Priest. Incredible as it sounds, I became more spiritually aware and came to a deeper personal relationship with God outside the confines of the church building.

During these 7 years outside the church walls, instrumental to my spiritual awakening was a powerful ecumenical prayer group. A weekly meeting for 2 hours on a Monday night. On my very first visit I could feel that room was full of life and the Spirit. God was real and tangible. It was a bit like discovering Brussels sprouts were good for you, not because my parents were telling me to eat them, but because I had a desire to consume them. I did some research and now I made a personal choice. I wanted a real relationship with God again; I wanted to feel His presence. I now knew what was healthy for me. My

heart was aching and thirsty due to a crushing personal experience and I cried out to God for His help, for His Spirit and to know once more that He was real. I genuinely cried for the first 3 months at the Prayer Group but I knew God had called me to this holy place and powerful community of faith. It was a case of saying, "I need this, I want this". My heart had a burning desire for God's comfort. I needed to be part of a strong faith community, be amongst people who knew prayer works and re-learn from them what it means to have a spiritual life. This was my new church.

What if someone asked us to draw a picture of a church? Would we draw a building with a steeple and some stain glass windows?

Many people are familiar with the idea that the 'church' is not the building, the church is the people; it is the community. Church is the communal spiritual life of those who regularly go and sit in the pews every Sunday but also those who do not sit in the pews. These include, the sick who cannot get to church anymore, those in prison or those who have decided to stop going to church for their own personal reasons. All of these people are the 'church' even if they do not physically go to the building every Sunday at 10am. The 'church' is much more than the stone structure.

The Bible says that the 'church' is the Body of Christ, meaning that every single person in the world who believes in Jesus is part of the one church. We are all linked and connected by the fact that we share the same belief in Jesus. So collectively there is one church and Jesus Christ is the head of the church. For me, church is a place where we hang out with others who are into spiritual fitness. We can use the analogy of the gym here. Keeping fit is a great idea whether we do it alone, with friends or whether we faithfully attend the gym once a week with all the other gym users. It's all about keeping fit. Sometimes it's good to keep fit when it's just you, but many others prefer to keep fit with other people to support and encourage them.

For me, that is why we need the church. After I stopped going to the church building every Sunday at the age of 38 and started to attend a Monday weekly prayer group, I realised this was church. I needed this church. I needed to hang out with people who were spiritually fit, super fit and my goodness did these people know what the spiritual life was all about!

What I conclude from this and to answer the question, 'Why do we need the church?', is that it is so important to get the order right. Yes I was encouraged to eat my vegetables as a child but there had to come a time when I decided to eat them. At the age of 8 the order was not right. It was only later on in life, as an adult, that I saw the health benefits of eating my greens. We need to get the order right. We have to do the healthy stuff not because we are told, but because we want to and can't live without it. It took a major fall in my life to see that. As an individual, with no spiritual relationship with God my life was falling apart. Throughout that time of sorrow even the thought of my parents telling me to go to church/eat my greens was never going to work; the order was wrong. I had to decide I needed God in my life and it is by getting the order right that I have grown spiritually. I wish I had also grown physically but hey, five foot five and a half is ok for me. What comes first is the spiritual life, church comes after that; not the other way round. Perhaps when we get the spiritual foundations right then church will make more sense. Without strong spiritual roots there is a huge risk that one crisis in life can put an individual, or indeed a whole family off church for a generation. I know that to be the case. When I was a Priest, I met hundreds of people tell me why they no longer went to church; the Priest condemned them for 'living in sin', they were refused Holy Communion for being divorced and re-married or the scandals of the church that hit the headlines. But another sorrowful tale within all of this is that there were many people like me who had no depth of spirituality, no burning desire for God's presence, no other faith communities to join. So when a crisis came,

many of these people left the church and never came back. I think of the smallest verse in the Bible here, John 11:35, "Jesus wept".

I am not blaming the leaders of the church here; what good will blame do? However, to quote a comment that I saw on many a primary school report card, 'could do better', especially when it comes to spiritually nourishing the people who attend church on a Sunday. Still to this day within the Catholic Church I hear Priests talk about how missing Sunday Mass is a mortal sin or how the Priest will refuse to offer a lapsed Catholic family a Funeral Mass unless they come to see the Priest in his vestry at the forthcoming Sunday Mass. I often pick up these funerals as the families are so shocked by the church's treatment of them. The church is not about rules, yes they are important and yes we should not miss Sunday Mass. I still know my Canon Law, but as Jesus showed with the Pharisees and the woman caught in adultery, He wants our love and our faith first; obedience to church rules can come after that. How have so many got it the wrong way round. I did for many years.

Many people, including myself, were told to do it the other way; just eat your vegetables, just go to church, everything will be fine. Then one day we just go off vegetables, we discover something else, we get out of the habit and no amount of telling from my mum or from the church to do something can make us do it. What about the spiritual depth, that burning desire to live like Christ, to reach a stage in your life when you cannot live without God. It is at moments like these that I place my faith in prayer and even church. When your heart is burning for God, you can't help but pray and praise God. You now have an insatiable desire to become more like His Son Jesus Christ. As I said, I have met thousands of adults in my funeral ministry who simply say; church, why on earth would I go to church? Their arguments seem to be; it is totally irrelevant to me in my life, sorry, I now go to the park on a Sunday with my kids and we have a great time at the local ice

cream parlour eating knickerbocker glories. Yet the church has 2000 years of spiritual depth, great spiritual heroes and heroines, great examples of love and faith. That is what comes first; spirituality and a healthy and holistic relationship with Christ.

Would you want that depth of spirituality where no human failure, where no church scandal will shake your faith? Would you want to reach a depth of faith that allows you to attend church no matter the poor sermons or the bad singing? You go because the Word of God is proclaimed and it burns into your heart and you receive Communion and you are full of praise for what God has done and is still doing in the world. We are the Body of Christ. It was a body that was broken, but within that brokenness is wholeness, wholeness of faith, wholeness of love because it is His love and His faith in which we live and move and have our spiritual being.

If church is to mean anything at all, we have to appreciate its spiritual value and ancient heritage. The gym will make no sense at all if you see no value in staying physically healthy and keep on going despite the man flus and the "cannae be bothered" days. Likewise, if we want a healthy spiritual life, we have to do the spiritual exercise consistently, with conviction and belief that we are in it for the long haul. Keep going, keep faith, keep prayer and the spiritual muscle will grow. If we keep believing in prayer and keep reading the Scriptures then within time the church, as broken and sinful as it is, will be a community you need to be part of. Once we start this journey of getting ourselves spiritually fit, the church will make sense to us and we will have got the order right. Once we embark on the spiritual life, we can't take our hand off the plough (Luke 9:62) and if we do have faith, Jesus will lift the other side of the yoke and carry us through those intolerable times when nothing, including the church and our fellow human beings, makes sense. Keep ploughing, keep doing the spiritual exercises, keep developing healthy spiritual habits and through God's

power and Grace we will bear real spiritual fruit, we will understand the value and the necessity of church.

As we said earlier in this book, there are genuine health benefits to having a real and active spiritual life, just as there are health benefits to having an active physical life at the gym. The spiritual health benefits include; peace, happiness, joy, humility, patience, a sense of belonging, a lessening of the ego, a spirit of thanksgiving, a capacity to overcome hardships and a burning desire to praise God in everything. The spiritual life will help us develop healthier choices and habits and give us a peace and happiness the world cannot give (John 14:27).

When I was a Priest, I was a great functionary, an enthusiastic organiser of weekly events; organising the youth club, running adult education classes, phoning the bus company and hotel so we could have a pilgrimage to Iona on the West Coast of Scotland. I believe I was a very good and active Priest. However, my 7 years of self imposed exile outside the church because the well of my spiritual life had run dry, has sadly reminded me that I was not a prayerful Priest; my spiritual life was very immature. As a Priest, for example, we were supposed to read a prayer book called the Divine Office 3-4 times a day. We had 7 years of doing this at training college but when I was out on my own as a Priest I didn't say 'my office' as it's called. Why? Because I had no desire, no need, it was like a Brussels sprout that I did not enjoy partaking in. Now, there was no mum to tell me to eat it. Sure I could have forced myself to read this prayer book and hope that it would become a habit but ultimately I had to want to do it. There had to be a personal choice. Incredibly when I left the priesthood I gave my 3-volume Divine Office set to Maria, with whom I am now writing this book. Maria, on the other hand, during those 7 years, used it on a daily basis for a whole year and grew closer to God in the process, whilst I grew further away from Him. I have now obtained

another set of the Divine Office and now want to read these beautiful prayers and psalms and give God the praise and thanks He deserves.

When I go to Sainsbury's I decide what goes into the shopping trolley. No wonder Dr. Gillian McKeith once said; "We are what we eat". We create the healthy or unhealthy habits through our own personal choices. But I am glad after 7 years of doing the hokey cokey with the church; I have gone back to church on Sunday. I have gone back to prayer and have re-learned the importance of having a spiritual life with depth and consistency. It is a choice I wanted to make for my own wealth and health.

We don't need to go to the gym to stay physically fit and we necessarily don't need to go to the church building to stay spiritually fit. But my experience of the spiritual life has taught me that I need some form of church community in order to grow.

So find a community that helps you feel the power of prayer, singing and praise. We can find other ways of working out and I would even argue that it's not unhealthy to occasionally have time out from the church, even if it's 7 years. Find alternative places and people to nourish you spiritually. I did this through a Prayer Group but we can do it through other means:

- Reading the Bible with other people.
- Taking a more positive mindset to people.
- Listening to religious/worship music in the car.
- Developing a spirit of thanksgiving rather than complaining.
- Having a true sense of joy for the people we have in our lives.
- Going on pilgrimage to 'holy' places.
- Internet and Facebook groups that promote prayer and the spiritual life.

We do not need church per se; we can at times get by without it. But sometimes, as with Brussels sprouts it will do us no harm to add it into our diet. Over time, the more we consume, the greater the benefits. I now fully accept that church is good for me. That is why I go. It's up to you what you consume and what you believe is good for you.

It may sound strange to hear someone who was a Priest for almost 12 years tell you that in order to lead a healthy and holy spiritual life you do not need to go to church. That's not what I am saying. What I have had to discover for myself, is why I needed the church in my life. It's been a long process, a hokey cokey experience, but I am glad that I have had moments in my spiritual life when I saw no necessity for the church, because it has given me the opportunity to reassess why I need the church. I now conclude that in order to have a healthy spiritual life, I need to turn up to church on a Sunday to be spiritually fed.

Of course I fully understand anyone who makes a personal choice about not going to church. All I am encouraging you to see is the necessity to do some spiritual exercises even if you do them by yourself, outwith the church building. I applaud anyone who exercises 5 times a week and drills their body to look like a Dairylea cheese. I am equally delighted to hear that you get your exercise 'fix' by walking your dog, or you cycle to the shops instead of taking the car half a mile down the road, or you take the stairs instead of the escalator. The point is; start somewhere. One of the health benefits of going to church is fellowship, meeting up with friends, sharing stories, praying with people, for man was not called to be an island. Some of them even have nice coffee and cake in the hall afterwards. In Genesis 2:18 it says that it's not good for man to be alone.

Likewise, with prayer, it is good to realise we never pray alone, there are hundreds of thousands of people praying all over the world. Prayer is good for you just as all exercise in any shape or form is good. Eating one of your 'five a day' is a start, it's better than none a day. If we keep

developing these healthy habits it can lead to a behaviour change and that in turn, leads to real transformation taking place in our lives. If I eat Brussels sprouts once a week because I want to, that can lead to a second vegetable appearing on my plate and eating vegetables twice a week. If I keep repeating the process, over time I can change my diet, my behaviour and my health. If you can change your habits and behaviours all by yourself, through your own motivation and desire that is fantastic and you should congratulate yourself. But remember the point about this book not being a self-help book. We will struggle on the spiritual journey by ourselves, we need relationships and friendships. If you need help and you can't do it alone, seek some kind of fellowship and community. That is why we need supportive communities such as the church. The greatest support we will receive will be from Jesus Christ through His words and His Presence.

Mo Farrah is a great runner but he will tell you that much of his success was due to having a coach, an encourager, someone to run beside him on those lonely miles; someone to offer words of advice or challenge. For years and years I swam by myself. I was fairly fit, swimming 40 lengths twice a week. I felt the health benefits but something was missing and if I were honest, it was lonely and at times boring swimming by myself. Secretly I was looking for a mermaid but she never appeared. Then one day I moved house to another town, started swimming at a different pool and I met someone. We started to chat, soon we saw the sense of sharing the car journey to the pool and then over the next few years we increased the number of lengths we swam from 40, to 66, to 80 then 100 and occasionally 110. We both got fitter and more proficient; we even got the swimming coach to point out the parts of the swimming stroke that were not right, all in aid of getting fitter and fitter. It was also much more fun than swimming alone. We would encourage each other and we all need encouragers in life. The church does the same. It offers community.

It's good to have fellowship and companionship, someone to break bread with. The word panis in the word 'com-pan-y' comes from the Latin word for bread. We all know our fellow human beings sustain us and nourish us. When we 'run the race' with others there is great energy and fun for everyone and that for me is the relevance of church and why I need church. It's to do with company, fellowship and community. When we are in the gym with 100s of other committed athletes and even the beginners, we learn from them. Sometimes we just watch and learn, or we soak it all up, we absorb through osmosis, we get comfort, encouragement and information from being around other people who value their health and fitness. We grow stronger, we go deeper and we become unshakeable. Church provides an incredible support structure to sustain us in the difficult and challenging times of our lives. When we have done the exercises and we are strong, we just know that should a cold or flu come, or an attack or a crisis, the muscle is strong and we will withstand anything that comes our way in life. That for me is one of the major benefits of being part of a church community. The church community gives us perseverance when we feel like giving up and just confirms that any form of sustained spiritual exercise will get us there. That is the power of the church. We can look back over time, even those difficult times and realise we have maintained spiritual fitness. This is what I have experienced in my 38 years of doing the spiritual exercises. I now have a greater spiritual health and vitality that goes deep into the marrow and the DNA. Although my experience of church has been mixed and varied and a bit hokey cokey, I now know that church is part of my true purpose in life.

Ultimately, you will decide if you need the church, just as you will decide about what vegetables you put in your shopping basket this weekend. If we want to get to a deeper level of fitness and health it seems to be a sensible thing to listen to the advice of the spiritually strong and mature. We need good coaches and role models and the

church has 2,000 years of this. For the last 4 years, St. James' Prayer Group in Kinross has been that church community that has nourished me. I am now ready to move into the building and I have started going back to Mass every Sunday. For me, what is important is that I turn up and I do my exercises.

SPIRITUAL FOOD FOR THOUGHT

Quirky church signs

Have you ever seen those signs outside churches, especially in America? Here is a selection of some of the most popular church signs.

- Down in the mouth, have a faith lift.
- Imperfect people welcome here, you'll be in good company.
- Get off Facebook and get into my Book – God.
- Forgive your enemies, it messes their heads.
- There are some questions that just can't be answered by Google.
- Tomorrow's forecast: God reigns and the Son shines.
- Church is like a Dundee cake, sweet with a few nuts.
- iPod, iPad…try iPray.
- Can't sleep? Counting sheep? Talk to the Shepherd.
- I was addicted to the hokey cokey but then I turned myself around.
- Heaven – Deal or No Deal?
- What is missing? CH_ _ CH…UR

CHAPTER 9

WHY DO WE NEED GOD?

"They came to Jesus and woke Him up, saying, "Master, Master, we are perishing!" And He got up and rebuked the wind and the surging waves, and they stopped, and it became calm." – Luke 8:24

Black Holes in our Galaxy

A black hole is formed when a massive star dies out and collapses under the force of its own gravity, from which nothing, not even light can escape. As the star shrinks, its internal gravitational field gets greater and greater until light can no longer escape from the collapsing star.

Black Holes in our Lives

Although this talk of black holes in our galaxies is jolly interesting to cosmologists and people like me, you may be wondering why I am talking about this in a book about how to develop a healthy spiritual life. The reason is that I have experienced black holes of a different kind that have sucked the life and energy out of me and have made me question; where is God in my life?

This chapter will look at such things as, financial hardship, terminal illness/grief, and depression and try and grapple with the question of

where is God in all this? Why do we need God?

Let's start by looking at Financial Hardship.

What Is Financial Hardship?

- Financial hardship is a situation when someone suffers extreme deprivation because they don't have enough money to provide the basic comforts and necessities of life.

In this current climate of uncertainty in our world it is very hard sometimes, for a great number of people, to make ends meet.

We constantly hear about the deprivation and hunger that exists in the developing world and what our fellow human beings are suffering and enduring. Are you like me? Every time I sit down to lunch and switch the television on, there is some heart wrenching advert about those who are in dire need. The hungry of the world who do not have two pennies to rub together to feed and clothe themselves. No jobs, no future and no hope! Is it because there isn't enough food to feed the 7 billion people that there are in the world? Or is it because the food is not properly distributed in under developed countries? Could it also be the greed of the governing bodies where food and necessities only reach the privileged few?

Well, I can tell you that the world does produce enough food to feed everyone. Recent evidence suggests world agriculture produces 17 percent more calories per person today than it did 30 years ago, despite a 70 percent population increase. This is enough to provide everyone in the world with at least 2,720 kilocalories per person per day. According to World Hunger Education Service, the principal problem is that many people in the world do not have sufficient land to grow, or income to purchase, enough food.

So have the world's monetary systems failed the people they are supposed to serve? Or is it that most of the population supposedly do not live within their means and get themselves into financial hardship. Salaries too may be lower than the cost of living and no amount of budgeting or 'tightening of the belt' will resolve the ever increasing pressures of money problems.

We all have stories to tell when at times we have been in financial dire straits and sometimes no amount of tightening our belts or having empathy for those in the developing world who are in an even worst position, offers a solution to your own crisis. Where is God in all of this? Who do you turn to? The Bank, your family, or God? That would be great wouldn't it, if God could solve all our financial heartaches. Maybe He can. Let me tell you my story.

Financial Hardship

"For I know the plans that I have for you, declares the Lord, plans for welfare and not for calamity to give you a future and a hope." – Jeremiah 29:11.

I was sitting at my desk at home one late evening in the year 2002, the anxiety and distress I felt was great. For years we had struggled financially due to the loss of several of our businesses.

Prior to this, my husband had held a very responsible job with an American Oil Company, for twelve years. Our financial status in those days, I would say was pretty healthy. We lacked nothing and life was good.

I myself had worked at a well-known company both in Edinburgh and Milnathort for twenty years combined and although at times it was a struggle due to the demanding nature of my position, being a

Managing Director's Personal Assistant is never easy, financially we were very comfortable.

Life went on for both of us and our two boys and I would say it was idyllic. We used to go on regular holidays to Spain where we owned an apartment and always took the opportunity of visiting my mum and relatives who lived in Gibraltar at the time. Gibraltar was my birthplace and my home town until I married in May 1968.

In the year 1983 life started taking a new toll for us and we started spiralling downwards into what I can only describe as one of our black holes. My husband resigned from his job due to several accidents he had experienced on the oil drilling ships he was on that left him quite devastated. Fortunately he was never injured; "it's just that I've had enough", he said on his last job off the coast of Malta, as fire had raged around the ship, with little hope of escape.

Earlier on too, he had a narrow escape as he was involved in a helicopter crash in Aberdeen that left him with only his toothbrush! "Better to be left with just your toothbrush, than to lose your life", I remember saying to him.

At the time of his helicopter crash, my three year old son had accidentally taken an overdose of aspirins thinking they were sweeties! Yes and before anyone says what a careless mother I was, he had to climb on to a chair and three shelves up into a cupboard to take the dangerous medicines. Needless to say we had to rush him to hospital. One of my neighbours offered to drive me behind the ambulance in my own car and on the way there we had a car accident ourselves that brought further expense to the already diminishing funds.

With four fairly successful business ventures, recession hit us all hard. The country was struggling to keep its own economy at a reasonable level. Life became harder not just for us, but for every business that was trying to survive the economic climate. A decision had to be made

to close our alabaster and lighting business, as our debts started spiralling out of control. Our decision would also affect our overseas suppliers and indeed it did, as our lack of orders, as their sole agent for the UK and Ireland, meant that they also had to close their factory in Spain. There was nothing we could do, nowhere to turn and no-one to help us.

We were hanging on by a thread. The Bank was not willing to take us further into debt and had withdrawn their overdraft facility, which might have enabled us to get back on our feet. They refused to help in this way. I then became the sole breadwinner of our family and we struggled to make ends meet.

On the 24th December 2002 I lost my own job of 20 years and life looked bleak. As a family we tried to make the most of Christmas, which was supposed to be the season of good cheer. By this time, we still had one business left that was bringing in a trickle of money. The Bank was coming down heavy on us demanding payment of funds due. We were about to lose our home and everything that we had worked for. That was the night I sat at my desk and prayed. I prayed like I have never prayed before. I did not know what to expect as our situation became quite impossible. I knew of course, that God is the God of the impossible. I had been told that on numerous occasions, but I always felt that this applied to others and not myself.

Soon after praying, I received a call from the bank to arrange a meeting with the Bank Manager. It sounded ominous. I remember my trepidation as I walked into the foyer. I was asked to wait and whilst sitting outside the Bank Manager's office a brochure caught my eye. It read, "What's your New Year's resolution?" The answer given in the leaflet was, "I'm determined to get my finances into shape." I picked up the leaflet as it had quite an impact on me and went home. When I got home I wrote in red ink, underneath these words, "With God's help!"

The Bank Manager turned out to be a non-believer with a compassionate heart. Months of meetings were arranged where he helped me out in numerous ways, but still no overdraft, so things were tight. I chuckled at the thought of our meetings as I had not been shy in sharing with him about my New Year's Resolution. Every time we met he realised that some Superior Being was helping me to meet the challenges that came my way. He remarked at my resolution and determination and it almost felt as if he was 'egging' me on to meet the targets he set on these periodic meetings and meet them we did.

With God's help and a little help from my friend George, the Bank Manager, we were free from the massive debt we had accumulated over the years. Selling our apartment in Spain, after a two year wait, also enabled us to come out of the deep waters that we had been submerged in. With God's help and his timing, we learnt to swim and survived the stormy seas.

I can't help but think of the time when the apostles were caught in a huge storm and Jesus fell asleep in the boat, fear struck them. The storm whipped the Sea of Galilee into a fury. This kind of storm could cause shipwreck and drowning. The storm terrified the disciples. Waves covered the boat, filling it with water. But Jesus was sound asleep on a pillow, asleep in the storm. The disciples woke Jesus, crying, "Master, Master, we are perishing!" "Why are you fearful, O you of little faith?" Jesus asked His disciples. Then Jesus commanded the wind to stop blowing…and…Jesus commanded the crashing waves to lie down and be still . . . and the wind calmed . . . the sea became peaceful and still. The disciples marvelled, saying, "Who can this be, that even the winds and the sea obey Him?" (Mark 4:35-41).

That is exactly what Jesus did in our lives. He helped us. We were caught in a storm, heading for shipwreck (bankruptcy) and going under and He commanded the crashing waves to lie down and be still. He did this because He knew He had the authority to do so. The Good

News for anyone embarking on the spiritual life is that, what He does for one, He can do for another.

So if you are facing a similar financial hardship as I was in and are asking the question, “Where is God?” don’t despair for Jesus is the anchor that will stop you from drifting out to sea. All you need to do is look up to Jesus now and experience His power and might in your life today.

I did and look what He did for me. To confirm it He gave me a passage from Scripture that I have held onto since the day we became debt free. It goes like this: “ The Lord will open for you His good storehouse, the heavens, to give rain to your land in its season and to bless all the work of your hand; and you shall lend to many nations, but you shall not borrow” (Deuteronomy 28:12).

That is my experience within the spiritual life; when we come to God with any need, financial or otherwise, He will guide us out of that storm. “What about terminal illness?” I hear you say, “Where is God in all of that?”

What Is a Terminal Illness? / What is Grief?

- Terminal illness is a medical term to describe a disease that cannot be cured or adequately treated with medical intervention and that is reasonably expected to result in the death of the patient within a short period of time.
- Grief is intense sorrow, especially caused by someone's death.

In my opinion, terminal illness and grief go hand in hand.

Terminal Illness and Grief

"He heals the heartbroken and bandages their wounds."
– Psalm 147:3

Have you ever felt a wound so deep in your heart that you feel it will never heal?

As I looked out of the window into my back garden peering straight at grey skies and falling rain my heart was pained. A sense of desolation came over me. "What has become of my life?" I thought. A life I so much cherished and loved. One that was full of promise and expectation of good things to come.

My life was suddenly cut short in the year 2009. It was the year when the life of my husband and I and our children became fragmented. It seemed as if a meteorite storm had hit us and broken our hearts into smithereens. The haunting and tragic news that my beloved husband Tony was suffering from an incurable disease left us weak and timorous.

Prior to this diagnosis he had suffered a heart attack, with both my younger son and I present. Never have I felt more helpless as we watched him crying out in pain. He resisted any help, insisting he was ok and not wanting any fuss. I could not stand by and watch him suffer such excruciating pain. I ran to the phone and dialled NHS-24. The operator kept me talking for what seemed hours. All sorts of questions that my befuddled mind could not answer! "Help" I cried, "Is there anyone that can help us?" What seemed even more incredulous was when they asked to speak to him. "What, are you crazy?" I thought. "This is impossible! He is going to die and no-one cares?" I cared. I cared more than I was allowing myself to feel.

After an hour the call to NHS-24 only resulted in an out of hours doctor's home visit, who prescribed pain killers. "Should he not have been rushed to hospital?" I cried. It was the first time in this long arduous journey that I had to believe that God had it all under control. He knew my fears and that my inadequacy as a nurse was zero. I did what I knew best. I touched my husband's shoulders gently and prayed. The pain seemed to leave him and he was able to go to bed and sleep. I, however, spent the night in constant vigil, afraid he might die alone. I continued praying until my tired eyes could not stay open any longer and sleep overcame me.

Morning came and although the pain was gone, his ashen face told me that all was not well.

As the days progressed with no marked sign of improvement, apart from the fact that the pain had gone, I decided to take him to our own doctor. An ECG examination revealed an irregularity in my husband's heart that required immediate attention. The doctor admitted him to the nearest hospital and requested I drive him there as an emergency.

The tests and medical examinations revealed that he had indeed suffered a heart attack. The more sinister news came later when upon investigation; they discovered a cancerous tumour in his body.

At the time we felt hopeful that the tumour could be removed surgically and my husband would survive. Unfortunately, due to his weak heart, an operation was not possible until his heart had healed and repaired itself. Months went by and his health started improving with the heart medication he had been prescribed and our constant prayers.

Our impatience grew, however, as we realised that with every progressing month, the tumour was likely to be growing within him.

Never in my wildest dreams had I expected this. How could it have happened, when my husband had been a strong, healthy man all his life? Never one to complain, he endured everything with patience and resignation.

The weeks and months that followed were horrendous. Six months of hospital visits and check-ups left us all exhausted.

The day came for his operation and removal of the tumour. A biopsy came back after another wait of two weeks. Always hopeful that it might not be life threatening, the letter arrived. Oh God, it was malignant. It was a vicious tumour that no amount of radiotherapy or chemotherapy could annihilate.

The sad news was that the operation had not been successful as they had not been able to remove the entire tumour without damaging other organs in his body.

Months and months of living in hope, holding on to a God that seemed so far away. Two hourly daily round trips to the hospital for my husband's treatment. It was excruciating for me and I cannot even begin to imagine what it was doing to my beloved husband.

I have never been good at caring for someone with an illness, but this was something I would never have imagined. The doctor offered me her time, saying: "It is going to be tough Maria, and I am here to talk with you whenever you want. So please come and see me. I know you have been attending all the doctor's appointments with your husband, but this time it is for you". I was obviously thankful but felt I would not need her as I was strong in my Lord and He was going to help me. I was also hopeful that God would do the impossible in my husband and heal him completely.

My daily visits to the hospital were traumatic as I drove up the long distance to Dundee on my own. My husband, by this time was

spending more time in hospital than at home. One day, whilst visiting my husband in hospital, I had an encounter with God through a cancer patient who was lying in bed directly opposite my husband. I entered the ward and saw him in agony with excruciating pain. He was pacing the floor, backwards and forwards he went, and although I did not know him, my heart was breaking just witnessing the horror of his relentless pain. My husband at this juncture was still reasonably well and his pain levels were controlled. He had made friends with this young, good-looking man who reminded me of Richard Gere.

I remember his wife telling me not to tell him he looked like Richard Gere as his head would get even bigger that it already was! She was a darling and cheered everyone up every time she came into the Ward. I was grateful that she was not witnessing her husband's pain that day, for I doubt very much whether she would have been as cheerful.

As it got time to leave the hospital, I felt prompted to approach Ricky (not his real name) and asked him if he would allow me to pray with him. As he consented and I held his hand, he tightened his grip on me as the pain was too much for him to bear. I prayed gently and with tears in his eyes he thanked me. His condition was even worse than my husband's and he was terminal with a cancer I find too distressing to describe.

My long journey home, on my own, made me aware that this was a journey that I might have to make for the rest of my life. I was never alone, as my husband was my constant companion and he always drove me everywhere. Driving alone was something I felt I was going to have to get accustomed to. I have never cried out to God as much as I did that night for Ricky, for my husband Tony, for Ricky's wife and for myself; although I would not let self-pity drag me down.

The next day my regular daily visit to the hospital filled me full of hope. Ricky was in his bed, listening to music. He called me over to

thank me for praying for him as his pain had gone. It was now under control after months of intense suffering. Now wasn't God good, that at least one of my prayers was being answered. That is why this passage from Scripture means so much to me, "We know that by turning everything to their good God co-operates with all those who love Him" (Romans 8:28).

Prior to my husband's treatment and whilst waiting for his heart to heal, God gave us an abundance of Grace. By that I mean God gave me some kind of inner strength and hope to believe that perhaps both of them would be physically healed.

Tony loved his driving and his one desire was to go out every day. He was full of energy compared to my waning strength and spirit. Our daily trips became a habit. Up early, out all day, eating in his favourite places with the result that instead of losing weight with all the stress and anxiety, I started putting on weight, and so did he. He looked the picture of health; how looks can deceive when I think about it. Whilst he looked years younger, I looked like I had aged overnight. Every time I looked in the mirror, I used to think that maybe it was me that was ill, not him!

A few days prior to his chemo treatment, Tony decided to go to Tentsmuir Beach. It is a lovely picnic spot in Fife, by the sea. We used to take our boys there when they were young. As we walked in the direction of the shoreline I had another God encounter. I heard someone call my name; 'Maria'. I could not see who it was and even though I approached her, there was no recognition in my mind, as to who she might be. My husband then told me it was Tracey, a work colleague from years ago. I had lost touch with her when we both left the company we were working for. Imagine meeting her here after all these years! What was even more amazing was that she told me she now worked for Maggie's Cancer Centre in Dundee. This is a place I had seen in passing and was never very sure what it was for. She had

only just started working there and invited me to go and visit her at Maggies on my next visit to the hospital. She said it was a place for relatives and cancer patients to chill out and chill out I did!

It was a place of sanctuary for me when I needed to sort out my thoughts and get away from the environment of pain. The staff were excellent and it was where I learnt to cope with what life was presenting me with. It was a place full of hope and loving care and attention. I thank God for that encounter at the beach that gave me the respite I so desperately needed.

Sadly my husband lost the fight for his life in August 2011, as did Ricky two months later.

"And God shall wipe away all tears from their eyes; and there shall be no more death, neither sorrow, nor crying, neither shall there be any more pain: for the former things are passed away" (Revelation 21:4).

The point in sharing my story is to give encouragement to those who are going through a similar situation of suffering, pain or grief, to never lose hope either in yourself, your family and friends and in a God that is real. Where was God in all of this? Despite the deep sadness of my loss I know God is a God that cares about your life and can hold your hand whilst you are going through traumatic times. He is close to the broken-hearted and He rescues those whose spirit is crushed. God hears our prayers and rescues us from all our troubles. Do you believe this? When you are in pain, who do you turn to, where do you go? I know who I had to turn to for help and consolation. It was a God that I knew would not turn me away or be uncaring about my pain.

In every life, there is pain, loss, illness, loneliness, and death. We have no claim to a long life and still may be spared by fate. What is your pain today?

Going through heartbreak can feel like being underwater when you need to breathe. We build our lives with someone we love and care for, and then, in the blink of an eye, it's all gone. This can leave us with sorrow, anger, and some serious questions about ourselves and the future. If you're dealing with heartbreak and want to heal, try these suggestions to find the new you.

- If you are suffering from feelings of guilt after the loss of a loved one, even though the death was not your fault, forgive yourself so that you may heal. One way to forgive yourself is to believe that your loved one has forgiven you.

- Grief is a process to go through, not a destination in which to wallow. In a process, you keep putting one foot in front of the other and each little step is part of your healing.

- No person has the right to condemn you on how you repair your heart or how long you grieve because no one knows how much you are hurting. So stand firm, do not listen to others, even though they are well meaning and allow yourself to heal.

- Recovering from a broken heart takes time, so give yourself permission to heal at your own pace. Time is a great healer.

- You will begin to heal when you let go of past hurts, forgive any wrongs and learn to forgive yourself for your mistakes.

- Having a spirit of gratitude and thanksgiving is a powerful way to heal as it gives us a different perspective on life. When we have a spirit of gratitude, we become energised to live again and be glad for the life we still have.

Grieving for my beloved husband has been one of the most excruciating pains I have ever had to endure in my life. Had it not been for the love and support of my family and numerous friends, I would not have made it. For me, however, the best way to heal my broken

heart was ultimately to give God all the pieces. Broken things can become blessed things, if you let God do the mending. If God can heal a broken heart and guide us through financial storms, what about general depression? Where is God in my despondency?

What is Depression?

- Depression is typically described as severe, prolonged, feelings of despondency, desolation and dejection. I have heard it being said that depression is like drowning, except you can see everyone around you breathing.

The word depressed is a common word. People say "I'm depressed" or "I'm feeling blue, or in the doldrums" when in fact they mean "I'm fed up because I've had an argument or failed an exam, or lost my job". These ups and downs feelings of life are common and normal as feelings come and go and I am not my feelings. Most people recover quite quickly.

With true depression, you have a low mood and other symptoms each day for at least two weeks or more. Symptoms can also become severe enough to interfere with normal day-to-day activities.

The feelings usually associated with depression are when you feel melancholic, miserable, sad, unhappy, sorrowful, apathetic and these lead to 'woe is me', gloominess and ultimately you start feeling dejected. These are words you put into your own head, words that you eat and consume and ultimately believe to be true.

Events that happen in our lives can also cause us to be depressed and downhearted. Hurts and disappointments can leave us discouraged, upset and tearful.

Grief and the loss of someone close can also make us feel disconsolate, dispirited, morose and desolate. It often leads to a sense of hopelessness and despair.

Depression

> *"Why, I ask myself, are you so depressed? Why are you so upset inside? Hope in God! Because I will again give Him thanks, my saving presence and my God" – (Psalm 42:5).*

The first time I suffered from acute depression was shortly after my first baby was born. You could call it the 'baby blues' or you could call it a chemical imbalance. Whatever it was it lasted for two years.

The sudden death of my father, a year after my son was born only exacerbated my state of mind. It was a condition that seemed to be worsening. The months went by with no hope of recovery. Doctors tried their best to medicate with various pills that only brought short term relief but never got to the root of the problem.

The months went by and life became intolerable. My mind was being taken over by a depressive state that gave me no hope. The pills and drugs prescribed became my 'sweeties' that I could not do without. I was totally addicted to them and walked around like a 'zombie'. With grief gripping every fibre of my being, a one year old child to look after, and my husband working abroad in Tunisia life was becoming unbearable.

I did not know God in those days, so prayer was not an option. My husband became totally frustrated as he found himself helpless in finding a solution to my ever deepening health problem. I was stuck in a black hole and getting sucked in deeper and deeper into the darkness of my mind, with thoughts so negative that I could not see the light.

My husband gave me an ultimatum. "Throw those pills away. It's either the pills or me", he said. Now this might have seemed totally

callous and cold on his part, but he was only trying to shock me into a state of reality. I had to do something or I was going to die.

The numerous bottles of Bellergal, Valium, Librium and anti-depressant pills had to go. I knew that if I did not do something about it, not only was I going to lose my life but the person who loved me the most in this world, my beloved husband. So down the toilet they went, with me weeping at the loss of my supposedly good friends.

It was shortly after that, a good friend of mine suggested I tried Sanatogen Nerve Tonic which is a non-medication natural remedy. I took this for the next three months. Slowly but surely I recovered. To date I have never had to depend on pills again. The reason for this being that, years later God entered into my life and he has been my constant help and companion ever since. It is my belief that God came to give me life and I have always resonated with the passage that says, "The thief comes only to steal and kill and destroy; I came that they may have life, and have it abundantly" (John 10:10).

Despite the challenges of financial hardship, bereavement and depression in my life, I know that God has given me life; life in abundance. This became evident just recently, when two years after my husband's death; I suffered a bad bout of shingles.

I had been travelling abroad and locally in the U.K. every month for the best part of the first year of widowhood. I could not resist the constant invitations I had from well-meaning friends who felt they wanted to help me overcome the grief I was carrying. It was relentless and although I did enjoy the various trips and meeting loved ones and long lost friends, my heart was heavy with sadness. Everywhere I went I put on a brave face and wore a joyful mask that hid my true feelings. To all and sundry I was that brave, strong woman that could meet life challenges head on. I was stoic in my determination to get on with life and held myself together; ensuring no one saw that inside I was breaking up into tiny little pieces.

I thought I was doing well until my body crumbled under the weight of pain I had been carrying for two years. It took an intuitive doctor to discern that I was suffering once more from depression. She explained that in her opinion, I had not grieved properly for my late husband and that the shingles had occurred as a result of holding my pain inside for so long," it had to come out somehow", she said. "You have tried yourself for too long and all you have done is stuff all your emotions into a box and put the lid on it. You can no longer shut the lid as there is too much in the box". She continued by saying, "if we don't do something about it, you are going to spiral into a black hole that you will not be able to get out of." With that remark, which left me both grateful and fearful at the same time, I agreed to keep the appointment she had made for me to see her. I remember she said, "I think you should come in for a chat. I am making an appointment for you myself. If you don't come, you will need to cancel it".

She gave me two weeks and I thought long and hard about it. However, I knew then that I needed to make a decision. In earlier years, I had received a passage from Scripture that said, "Choose life, not death" (Deuteronomy 3:19). This came to mind and alerted me to the fact that I still had a life that was worth living. I owed it to my wonderful sons and I had to make the right choice, otherwise I was going to self-destruct.

The day came for my appointment with the doctor. When she saw me she verified her earlier remarks and said, "I could give you medication or send you for counselling, but somehow, with your beliefs and mindset I am not sure whether that is the right course of action".

I had shared with her that a very good friend Chris, had insisted on visiting me whilst I was at my worst with shingles. He ministered to me through prayer that helped me on the first steps to recovery.

"I believe that you would benefit more if you asked your friend to come and pray with you again and walk you through this grief you are carrying". She joked as she continued, "I don't really want to give you

any pills as I don't think they will do you any good and if I send you to a counsellor you are more than likely going to end up counselling them yourself". I laughed at this as I knew her comments to be true!

I remember phoning my friend Chris and saying to him, "I went to the doctor and the only prescription she has given me is you! Will you come and pray with me again please". I had four deep sessions of prayer with Chris, who lovingly and patiently carried me through the grieving process.

Two weeks later, I kept my promise to the doctor who wanted to check up on me and went for another appointment she had arranged for me. I will never forget her face as she saw me walking into the room. She was astounded at the difference she saw in me. Gleefully she said, "When I last saw you, you were dead. Your eyes had no life in them, but now, I see life in you. Your eyes are shining with light! I see prayer has worked for you".

Today although I still miss my husband terribly, I am no longer carrying the sheer weight of grief. I have been able to cry and the sharp pain I felt in my heart has been released.

Today I can honestly say that God's abundant love has shown me that I am never alone. He has given me the strength and grace to cope with life and rejoice in the beauty of life and all that He offers. It is indeed a beautiful world.

Within my spiritual life I now understand what Jesus meant when He said to His disciples, "If anyone wants to be a follower of Mine, let him renounce himself and take up his cross and follow Me" (Matthew 16:24). Jesus spoke these words after asking one of the disciples, Peter, "Who do you say I am?" (Matthew 16:16). One of the objectives of this book was to offer a plain and simple explanation of such things as to who God and Jesus is; and even the question, 'Where is Jesus in today's world? Where is He in my suffering and hardship?

Many people think the spiritual life and Godly things are fluffy and ephemeral thoughts, that God is a concept for the weak and feeble minded who do not have the logic, maturity or inner strength to cope with life as a human being. All I can say is, if people can cope with the challenges and stresses of life without God then I am delighted they have some sort of coping mechanism to get them through those moments when the money runs out and people we love are no longer here. I need God in my life. I need the example of another human to show me a pathway out of things like depression and suffering and for me, that exemplary human person is Jesus Christ. He is my role model, He is my comforter and consoler and I trust Him when He says 'take up your cross' because the cross is not the end of the story, the resurrection and the new life that came after the cross is the story.

Black holes may seem like black holes through a telescope. They may even seem like depressing spirals in life that we can never get out of, but this is not true. There is always another way and that way is the way Jesus showed and walked, "Anyone who loses his life for My sake will find it" (Matthew 16:25). That is the joy the spiritual life offers you and me. When we lessen our egos and our self dependency and our temptation to self-help, all by our own strength and we ask for God's strength, we will be given it. Over time, through these constant prayers and requests for God to change us, we will be changed and we will take on the mind of Christ and the path of Christ which is always the new life of Easter Sunday morning. We will rise, we will have a new enthusiasm for life, a new fire in our hearts and nothing, absolutely nothing can take that away or come between us and our love for Christ (Romans 8:31-35).

What about your Black Holes?

Have you ever heard of NASA's Nuclear Spectroscopic Telescope Array, or NuStar? It's incredible, I would encourage you to go and look at the images on the NASA website, they are mind blowing. One particular image that the telescope has captured whilst searching for

dark holes is a new dead star which appears like a heavenly high-five colourful 'Hand of God' since it looks like an open hand.

Life presents its own telescope and reveals our black holes. At different times, we need to pause and decide are these black holes in our lives precisely that, nothingness, or could these black holes be opportunities for growth and discovery.

What about you? Do you feel that life is one long hard struggle? Do you feel like sometimes you are in a vacuum or whirlpool and unable to break free? How can you get off that proverbial roundabout? How can you improve the eternal mundane sense of going round in circles, achieving nothing, and tiring yourself out? How many 'groundhog days' do you experience?

The answer is simple. Pause and reflect on the situations and circumstances in your life that are causing you harm and apply decisive measures to eliminate stress, anxiety and worry.

If you don't know how to cope with the so called black holes of life, permit me to suggest a few examples that can greatly improve your life:

- Let go of situations that are robbing you of your peace.

- Don't overemphasise or exaggerate your problems.

- Stay away from toxic people and situations that contribute to your anxiety and depression. They can make you want to live or die. They can reduce or increase your anxiety and depression. Avoid those who speak discouraging words, and spend time with those who speak good words that makes your heart glad. Proverbs 18:21 says, "Death and life are in the power of the tongue, and those who love it will eat its fruits".

- Think positive and not negative. Your thoughts are prolific. The

Psalmist said they 'multiply' within you. Random thoughts may be temporarily upsetting, but they don't produce lasting anxiety or depression. Persistent negative thought patterns will make you prisoner to your own thoughts. Break free. Take these thoughts to Christ and hand them over to Him.

- Do not allow your thoughts to multiply in your mind. Psalm 94:19 says, "When my anxious thoughts multiply within me, your consolations delight my soul".
- It's not the circumstances in your life that create the negative emotions; it's the thoughts about your circumstances. It is these thoughts that trigger the biochemistry in your brain and in turn that determines your feelings, how intense or how long they last. So you have to choose to think and see differently.
- For example; choose to forgive those that have hurt you.
- Or even better; forgive yourself for making mistakes that have dramatically changed your life for the worst.

These suggestions are not merely words, as I too have experienced moments in my life when I felt that nothing would work. However, when I made a conscious decision to apply my own advice, the results were positive and healthy for me.

It is all about choices, practising healthy habits, maintaining a positive mind-set that enables us to move towards the light and not be sucked into these dark places. I am in charge. I can decide to walk into the light. I can decide to choose life and have it to the full as Jesus told us in John's Gospel 8:12, "I am the light of the world. Whoever follows me will never walk in darkness, but will have the light of life." What strikes me here is that we have to make a choice whether we walk in the light or the dark. It's up to you.

It's been one of the constant themes of this book that, we are what we eat, be that Brussels sprouts or the words we choose to consume or believe. Why do you spend money for what is not bread, and your wages for what does not satisfy? Eat what is good, and let your soul delight itself in abundance," (Isaiah 55:2) and, "Do not labour for the food which perishes, but for the food which endures to everlasting life" (John 6:27).

We all want to live healthier. We've put ourselves on 'pause' to take a good look at our lives and where we are going wrong. If we are what we eat then the same can be said for things like prayer. We will believe in prayer as much as we pray. We will believe in God's Word as much as we read it and then take it in. The spiritual life is inviting you to get the right spiritual food, because your spiritual health and happiness depend on it. We are what we take in.

Let's have a final pause for thought. Throughout my entire life one of the things I have learnt in order to develop my spiritual fitness, is to create time to pause and be still. Pausing gives you an opportunity to reflect and listen to that inner small voice within you, whom I believe to be God. It allows me space to block out the 'noise' of the world and enter into a space of silent time and into my inner being, where I always find God. The pause also lets me hear the Good News that I constantly need to hear in order to live my life and purpose. The Good News that I hear within my daily pauses restores, refreshes, energises and brings vitality to me.

SPIRITUAL FOOD FOR THOUGHT

The Storms of Life

"O Lord God Almighty, who is like You? You are mighty, O Lord, and your faithfulness surrounds you. You rule over the surging sea; when its waves mount up, you still them"
— Psalm 89:8-9.

There are many reasons why we need God in our lives (purpose, direction, values etc.). Another reason why we need God is to help us through the so-called storms of life. Have you ever had an experience of being in a storm at sea with the waves thundering against the ship? It is a disorientating experience where we will feel knocked off balance and reaching for the sick bag! It is the same with the storms in our lives that take the equilibrium away from us.

Whatever causes our lives to be disturbed and shaken as though a storm had hit them, it is vital that we remember the words of the Bible in the reading above. It is God who rules the sea and can still the storm.

Turn to Him and He will take care of you, and give you peace if you trust Him through your storm. However fierce the waves, God will not allow you to sink, if you hold on to Him. It is our faith in Christ's calming power and our hastening to call for His help that allows Him to calm our hearts during life's storms.

Prayer:

Dear God, if it is true that I need you in order to really find "rest" for my restless soul, would you open to me the reality of the life of God in me? Would you show me this life, and how I might take hold of it? Would you give me the eyes to see and the ears to hear what no person can see or hear apart from your spirit working in me? And if Jesus is the way to this union with you, give me Jesus!

CHAPTER 10

NEW LIFE AND TRANSFORMATION

"Before I even formed you in your mother's womb, I knew all about you. Before you drew your first breath, I had already chosen you to be My prophet to speak My word to the nations." – Jeremiah 1:5

Before we can venture into this journey of New Life and Transformation we need to ask ourselves the question: 'What is life?'

Does this sound like a strange question to you? Of course we all know what is meant by the word life, but how would you define it? Do all living things move? Do they all eat and breathe? Even though we all seem to know what is meant by saying something is 'alive', it's not very easy to describe what life is. It's almost as hard as describing where life came from. Even the biologists have a tough time describing what life is. But after many years of studying living things, biologists have determined that all living organisms do share some things in common:

- Living things need to take in energy.
- Living things get rid of waste.
- Living things grow and develop.
- Living things respond to their environment.

- Living things reproduce and pass their traits onto their offspring.
- Over time, living things evolve in response to their environment.

Therefore, in order for something to be considered to have life as we know it, it must possess these characteristics.

There is one thing, in particular, that we all share in common; humans and all living creatures alike. We all have seasons or cycles in our lives. We are all born and after a period of time, whether we like it or not, we die. Look at the plants and trees of every kind and the different seasons they go through. Spring is where new growth and new life can be seen wherever you go. Every garden, every field, every pot, is teeming with life and new growth. Buds waiting to erupt into beautiful flowers, releasing their intoxicating fragrances into the air. Birds in their nests hatching their eggs and little chicks chirping for food. Newborn lambs frolicking in the fields. New life everywhere. What a wonderful time of year spring is.

Summer follows, with growth almost complete. This is where we see most plants maturing and blossoming and where colours abound. It is a time of year when we benefit from the warmer climate.

Autumn, or fall as some know it, is the season where plants start to fade away. All the leaves of the trees change into spectacular colours, apart from the evergreens. Change once again starts to take place. It is a time of preparation for the hardness and coldness of the winter months. So they regenerate, year in and year out. A constant cycle of change. It seems that one of the answers to the question, 'What is life?' is change.

So when we, as humans, think of our lives. What do we see? A human body or something else? Let's start with the beginning of life. Our beginnings are practically the same for everyone. Male seeds/ sperm and a female ovum/egg contribute to starting a new life. Once the egg

has been fertilised it immediately divides into two cells, these cells then divide again and again over the next couple of days as the cluster of cells makes its way to the womb. Here it is planted in the lining of the womb and continues dividing its cells to make billions of new cells. The female is now pregnant; full of new life within her.

The amazing thing is that each one of these cells contains the same set of chromosomes that were created at fertilisation! Over 9 months, these cells will grow into a new person, a baby. When the ovum is fertilised and becomes the first cells of the baby, these genes help to decide lots of things; whether it is a boy or girl, the colour of skin, eyes and hair.

Genes are made of DNA ('de-ox-y-ri-bo-nu-cle-ic acid', if you want the full name).

If you could see your genes they would look like beads on a necklace of DNA. These strands are called chromosomes. Usually each cell in a human body has 46 chromosomes. That first single cell has 23 chromosomes from the female and 23 from the male, which is why the baby might look like their mum or dad or grandparents and have similar traits. The chromosomes in a male are slightly different to those in a female. This is the extraordinary miracle of life.

Once you are born, you will grow up into a unique human being, there's no-one else like you in the world. Even identical twins are not exact copies of each other; they each have their own personalities.

You may look a bit like someone in your family, but there is only one of you. You are a completely unique and wonderful person.

What about God's DNA and His promise of New Life?

First, let's look at what DNA really is.

DNA, in layman's terms, is the 'blueprint' of inherited genetic molecular material for our unique identities. Our DNA comes from the combination of genes contributed by each of our biological parents. When there is a question regarding a child's parentage a paternity test, using blood samples from one or both parents, is taken. The results of this test undeniably reveal a child's biological parents through their similar DNA structure.

On April 2, 1953, James Watson and Francis Crick presented to the world for the very first time, the structure for DNA. It contains all the genetic information to create our entire bodies. DNA in our cells is very similar to an intricate computer program. DNA is made up of four chemicals, abbreviated as letters A, T, G, and C. They are by design. These letters are arranged intricately within the human cell like this: CGTGTGACTCGCTCCTGAT and so on. The order in which they are arranged instructs the cell's actions.

The amazing thing is that within the tiny space in every cell in your body, the DNA code is three billion letters long. If you were to start reading off the letters that make up your DNA information, even if you read 3 letters a second it would take you thirty-one years, even reading 24 hours a day. That is the amount of DNA information in one cell!

It has been determined that 99.9% of your DNA is similar to everyone's genetic makeup. What is uniquely you, comes in the fractional difference in how those three billion letters are sequenced in your cells. The British government identifies everyone in our country by the arrangement of a nine-digit social security number. Yet,

inside every cell in you is a three-billion-lettered DNA structure that belongs only to you. This code identifies you and continually instructs your cells' behaviour. There has never been a computer program in existence that wasn't designed, any program, and any piece of software or a message given through any language that did not have an intelligent design behind it. Dr. Antony Flew, a former atheist once questioned, "It is legitimate to ask oneself regarding this three billion letter code instructing the cell "Who wrote this script, who placed this working code, inside the cell"?

It's like walking along, and you see initials carved out in a tree that read TWB + MVB, you know the tree itself did not form that, someone wrote it. It is a precise message. It is clear communication. In the same way, the DNA structure is a complex, three-billion-lettered script, informing and directing the cell's process. On June 26, 2000, scientists completed the human genome sequencing. President Clinton, at the time, congratulating them said, "Today we are learning the language in which God created life. We are gaining ever more awe for the complexity, the beauty, the wonder of God's most Divine and sacred gift." Dr. Francis Collins, the director of the project, followed Clinton's words with his own saying, "It is humbling for me and awe-inspiring to realise that we have caught the first glimpse of our own instruction book, previously known only to God".

The purpose of this chapter is to show us that there is a greater Being who has plans to change us into who we really are; spiritual beings and Psalm 139 seems to suggest that God has a blueprint for our design.

"For You, oh God, shaped me, inside and out. You knitted me together in my mother's womb long before I took my first breath. I will offer You my grateful heart, for I am Your unique creation, filled with wonder and awe. You have approached

even the smallest details with excellence; Your works are wonderful; I carry this knowledge deep within my soul. You see all things; nothing about me was hidden from You as I took shape in secret, carefully crafted in the heart of the earth before I was born from its womb. You see all things; You saw me growing, changing in my mother's womb; every detail of my life was already written in Your book; You established the length of my life before I ever tasted the sweetness of it. Your thoughts and plans are treasures to me, O God! I cherish each and every one of them! How grand in scope! How many in number! If I could count each one of them, they would be more than all the grains of sand on earth. Their number is inconceivable!" — Psalms 139: 13-19

When looking at the DNA structure within the human body, we cannot escape the presence of intelligent (incredibly intelligent) design. This idea is even more intriguing when we look at laminin.

So what is laminin? Does anyone know what this is? A few years back, I remember listening to a fascinating talk by Louie Giglio in which he spoke about laminin. Now before you go running for your Greek lexicon or for your Bible, stop, because laminin is not in the Bible. It's a protein in your body. Every living creature has laminin inside of them. The purpose of laminin is that it basically keeps our bodies from falling apart. It holds us as one united whole. It's like the glue that holds our cells together. Could God be a critical part of our human makeup and DNA? Could it be true that we are made in His image and likeness and His spiritual DNA will sustain us, when our human DNA lets us down?

So how does laminin hold you together through tough times?

Now here is what is so amazing, laminin the very structure that holds us together looks like a cross. Go and 'Google' laminin I am sure you will be amazed with what you see.

The cellular structure that holds our body together is the shape of the cross. Does God have a sense of humour or what! Amazing isn't it? This is a glorious reminder to me that when the rough times come, and the storms of life take hold of me, what is holding my physical body together is a cellular protein in the shape of a cross. We truly are wonderfully made.

God's DNA - Is it in your spiritual man, literally?

God said, "Let us make man in our own image, in the likeness of ourselves." God created man in the image of Himself, in the image of God He created him, male and female He created them." (Genesis 1: 26-27).

Let us reflect for a second on this amazing passage in the Bible and what God is purported to have said: "Let us make man in our own image, in the likeness of ourselves". So, who is He referring to as 'our' or 'ourselves'? I believe it is the 3-in-1; God the Father, God the Son and God the Holy Spirit. Imagine being made in their image, wow! This to me is even more incredible than conception. Can you think of anything more wonderful than to have been given life by God and that in our genes, we have God's very own life? Is it not simply awesome to think that in our spirits, we also have God's own DNA?

How is this, you ask? Well, humans can reproduce only human life, but the Holy Spirit gives new life from heaven. "For God so loved the world that He gave His one and only Son, that whoever believes in Him shall not perish but have eternal life." (John 3:16)

When we receive the gift of eternal life through our acceptance of Jesus Christ as our Lord and Saviour, God breathes new life into us bringing a spiritual birth. At that moment we receive heavenly DNA into our souls in the form of the Holy Spirit. Now, we possess two sets of DNA. One physical set from our earthly parents and one spiritual from our heavenly parent. With God's DNA inside of us, the Divine life of God grows. Now, we are radically different than the rest of the world. We are part of a distinct race. We resemble our heavenly Father as evidenced by our new Christ like attitudes, motivations, perspectives, desires, goals, and new Godly value system. We have a deep desire to be a blessing to others as God has been a blessing to us. After our spiritual births we are connected eternally to God in such a way that no matter what happens in our futures, our heavenly genetic link to Him will not be broken. How can this be? Think about this. Is it scientifically possible to remove the DNA connection we have with our earthly parents? No, because new scientific breakthroughs in molecular research have proven DNA can't be completely removed or dramatically altered due to its complex structure. Is it spiritually possible to remove God's DNA from our souls once we have been given a new birth? No. We are linked eternally to Him in such a way that no matter what happens in our futures, our heavenly genetic link to God can't be broken.

In other words we won't lose or cut our eternal link with God, but we can break our relationship with Him. How? By turning our back on Him in rebellion. Similar to what a son or daughter does when they choose to disown their birth family. They may never see their family again, but whatever they do or wherever they go it will never change

the fact they have a DNA connection to their biological parents. They are still family members, if only through their shared DNA. So if we ever think we've done something to lose eternal life and our spiritual position as a member of God's family, we need to ask ourselves this question, "How can I undo my spiritual DNA or my spiritual birth or the truth that God loves me?" The answer is: We can't. "My sheep recognize My voice; I know them, and they follow me. I give them eternal life, and they will never perish. No one will snatch them away from me, for my Father has given them to me, and he is more powerful than anyone else. So no one can take them from me" (John 10: 27-29).

So the question we should ask ourselves is:

Do I want a new life, a spiritual life, this life of God living in me?

I remember a few years ago meeting a man walking along a promenade in a small village in the island of Madeira, called Jardim do Mar. He was walking his two little dogs and stopped to speak to me.

He told me he was from Bournemouth. When I asked him, "What on earth are you doing so far from home?" He said he had been coming to Madeira on holiday for many years and had decided to retire there with his wife; to get away from the pressures and stresses of life back home and to start a new life.

This man was seeking and searching for what? Peace and tranquillity? He would certainly find it in Jardim do Mar.

He couldn't speak Portuguese and said that a couple from the village who could speak English, had been helping them.

Just think: he was approaching his 70th birthday and he was having to make new friends, in a strange country, with a different culture and a different language to boot.

He told me he had been in Madeira for 6 months. I often wonder if he found what he was looking for. I sincerely hope he did as sometimes the 'grass looks greener on the other side', particularly when we are not happy with what we've got in our own life.

What do you look for when you are seeking a new life?

- Is it moving away from familiar surroundings?

I myself started a 'new life' 46 years ago when I moved to Scotland. I had tremendous expectations of what it would be like. Some were met, and some were not. I believe it was my destiny to be here in Scotland.

Do you know why you are, where you are right now?

- Because you are meant to be.

It is God's appointed time that moves us on to new phases in our lives and new places.

The man from Jardim do Mar was looking for a new life through his own circumstances. It was his choice to move abroad. I made the choice of moving from Gibraltar to Scotland.

I believe we all have choices to make to enable this new life to develop in us. But sometimes we cannot experience this new life.

So what could possibly prevent us from receiving this 'new life'?

I am going to ask you to do a little practical exercise to demonstrate what prevents us from receiving this 'new life'.

- Put your hand over your mouth; then hold your nose, now try and breathe. You can't can you? You need clear airways in order for the air to come into your lungs. Same with our spirits; if we have blockages, God cannot breathe that new life in us.

So what are these blockages?

- Fears and attitudes.

- Clinging to your past and refusing to move on.

I gave you two examples above of people moving on; the man from Bournemouth and myself. But what about the hundreds and thousands of other people who are not willing to move on? Those who are so affected by their past that they cling to their memories, whether good or bad, and are reluctant to step forward in faith.

The circumstances of their past makes them cling to their safe environments and their fears of trying something new prevents them from receiving what God has ordained for their lives.

Will you allow God to heal past memories and move you on?

When I went to Madeira I was enthralled with the place. It is a paradise island. You see beautiful life everywhere; waterfalls, rock pools, ravines as deep as the ocean, flowers of every colour, palm trees of every shape, size and colour and even the butterflies are twice as big as the ones you see in the U.K.

In fact, my late husband Tony joked with me when we were there and asked me a question: 'Where was Adam and Eve born?' And before I could answer him, he said: "In Madeira"!

Life is everywhere in Madeira and the glories of God's creation can be seen wherever you look; it is like a floating Garden of Eden.

This life as we all know is given by God and belongs to God, who remains master of life. In Genesis 2:7 it says, "Yahweh God shaped man from the soil of the ground and blew the breath of life into his nostrils, and man became a living being."

Right from the start, God has given us new life. A baby when it is first born is smacked on the bottom so that he takes his first breath. God does not spank us; he breathes into us New Life. Psalm 104:30 says, "You give breath, fresh life begins, and you keep renewing the world."

The blockages, fears and attitudes stifle our new life in Christ. John 10:10 says, "The thief comes only to steal and kill and destroy. I have come so that they may have life and have it to the full." No half measures with God. If we allow Him to work in our lives, we will experience new life every day.

Think of each new day as a new beginning. Give God the glory and praise Him for His creation. There is so much beauty around us. It is only when we have eyes to see and ears to hear that we can truly appreciate God's creation and the promise of eternal life.

The fullness of life is eternal life, which Jesus, who is Himself life, came to bring. The believer's life is hidden in Christ and implies holiness and living to God in the Spirit.

I believe this new life is breathed into us at birth and doesn't end in death but continues into eternal life. It is a life-giving union with the glorified Christ. Colossians 3:1-4 affirms this, "Since you have been raised to be with Christ, you must look for the things that are above, where Christ is, sitting at God's right hand. Let your thoughts be on things above, not on the things that are on the earth, because you have died, and now the life you have is hidden with Christ in God. But when

Christ is revealed and He is your life, you, too, will be revealed with Him in glory".

New life doesn't have to be just for when you die. New life can happen whilst we are still alive, by a change of heart, a change of attitude and a change of lifestyle.

New life is about being transformed, we cannot transform ourselves, but God can, only if we allow Him into our lives.

He can make us into new people, just as if He was breathing new life into us for the first time.

That's what it means to be dead, when there is no longer any breath in you. The breath in us is the breath of God, it is the Holy Spirit. When He breathes that new life in us, we are dead to sin, not dead in spirit. Our sins have been forgiven. That is why Jesus died on the cross to take our sins upon Himself and to give us a brand new life.

He is the restorer of all things. He is the one that can make all things new and that is His promise.

How can we experience this transformation?

"When someone becomes a Christian, he becomes a brand new person inside. He is not the same anymore. A new life has begun" (2 Corinthians 5:17).

This reminds me of the adverts you see in magazines: the new you! Have you seen them? Where they give you a makeover and you come out looking brand new? What about those before and after pictures? The sort that show how bad things were and how good they became. Do you have any of these? It is amazing what can be transformed with creative effort.

Christians celebrate Easter where they think of the transformation of Christ, before His death, hanging on the cross in weakness and after being raised from the dead with power. Easter is normally celebrated in spring. It is a sign of new life. It is a time when many plants and insects are coming to life after a period of hibernation or inactivity.

Let's think for a minute of a butterfly. Butterflies are insects that undergo a complete change or metamorphosis during their development. The life cycle of a butterfly is, first the eggs are planted. The eggs then hatch and a caterpillar appears. The caterpillar then struggles with his everyday existence, putting on weight, munching his way through the leaves, which God has provided, building up his strength.

They are very particular in their feeding habits, feeding usually only on a small number of closely related plants.

If a suitable food plant is not available, the caterpillar will starve to death rather than eat anything else. They eat and eat and grow entirely filling their skin, which does not stretch and so becomes very tight. In order that growth can continue, skin is shed more than once until they reach full size. The next stage is when the caterpillar enfolds itself into a silk cocoon and there is a period of inactivity being prepared for new life. The pupa does not move, eat or drink and since it is immobile, it is particularly vulnerable to all attacks from a variety of predators, and often for protection pupation can occur within a silk cocoon. Then the adult appears as a beautiful butterfly set free.

Caterpillars are busy munching their way through their Brussels sprouts and cabbages, though caterpillars probably enjoy them a lot more than we do, and building themselves up for the big day.

Unlike caterpillars, though, with us there's something missing which we need in order to be changed. This, of course, is a transformer. Think of it, a transformer is a device that changes an electrical voltage or

current from one level to another. Transformers are used to: Convert high voltage alternating current (AC) to desired low voltage alternating current.

I believe that God is our transformer. He is energy, as I said in an earlier chapter, and His Spirit energises our spirit and we are changed, converted, and transformed.

"And all of us, with our unveiled faces like mirrors reflecting the glory of the Lord, are being transformed into the image that we reflect in brighter and brighter glory; this is the working of the Lord who is the Spirit" (2 Corinthians 3:18).

A few guidelines on transformation

- It is God who plants the seed in us to change our attitudes and misgivings in life.
- He feeds us with His Word (the Bible).
- We have to be very particular who and where we feed from. If we do not feed from the Word of God, we can spiritually starve and die.
- We need to stay close to God; He gives us the means to overcome our trials and sufferings.
- Pray and ask God to give you this New Life.

There are many instances in the Bible where people were transformed by God.

- The adulteress (already mentioned in the chapter on Love and Forgiveness).

- The apostle Paul on his way to Damascus. A light hit him from heaven. His attitude was completed changed.

God totally transformed the lives of these people. They surrendered to Him and decided to follow Him and because of that, they experienced New Life, they were set free.

When we experience transformation in Christ we know it, it shows. We manifest the fruits of the Holy Spirit, amongst other things.

Christians have already received the Holy Spirit, but sometimes we need to do more than just that. The secret to new life is to open your heart to God and let the Holy Spirit work in you. In order to be transformed you need to have a change of heart and a change of attitude to your present circumstances. Remember, everyone has a God-shaped hole in their heart that only God can fill.

"Do not model your behaviour on the contemporary world, but let the renewing of your minds transform you, so that you may discern for yourselves what is the will of God, what is good and acceptable and mature" (Romans 12:1, 2).

That is God's plan for every one of us; that we be transformed into the image and likeness of His Son Jesus. There is a song that is sung by Christians: "Open the eyes of my heart Lord". Transformation comes when we open our hearts to God. Yes, we need to think differently, but this transformation only happens when our hearts have been touched by God's grace and we have experienced repentance, conversion and a turning back to God. When we have fallen in love with God because of what He has done for us. Just like the woman that anointed His feet and cried tears of repentance and thanksgiving (Luke 7:36-50).

Through the Holy Spirit we are being transformed more and more into the Divine nature, we are being re-created, we are being 'made new'. Our lives are being drawn into intimacy with God.

There's a passage in Ephesians 2 which encourages us to see the before and after of the Christian, and links it to the experience of Jesus at Easter. "For we are God's workmanship, created in Christ Jesus to do good works, which God prepared in advance for us to do" (Ephesians 2:10).

Can you imagine a God who knows your inner most being, who has knit together your DNA and His desire is to mould and shape you into the person you are meant to be and will be one day?

Christ the Sculptor

There is a story of a man who was really interested in sculpturing, and wanted to learn how to sculpture, so he sought out the best expert in the country, and visited him to see him in action, sculpting something.

He came into the hall where this famous sculptor worked, and watched as a large block of stone was brought in. This guy looked at the stone. It was big and ugly, and he didn't have much hope for it.

The sculptor chose some tools and began chipping away, bit by bit, sometimes taking big bits out, and other times very small bits with his hammer and chisel.

Gradually, over a long period of time, the observer could see what the sculptor was transforming this block of stone into. It was the most lifelike sculpture of a horse he had ever seen. A horse in mid-gallop, mane blowing behind it in the wind, every muscle and tendon clear and visible.

The observer was stunned. It was so beautiful. Finally, when the sculptor had finished, the observer plucked up enough courage to go up to him and congratulate him. He asked in amazement, "How do you do it, this horse is so lifelike!"

How do you transform such an ugly looking block of stone into something so beautiful?" The sculptor replied, "It's easy. I just chop off anything that doesn't look like a horse."

Imagine that you are that block of stone, undergoing that process of gradual transformation and change.

Imagine that this master sculptor is Jesus, who through his abilities and talents has the ability to make you into a beautiful sculpture.

When Jesus looks at you, He can't see the bad bits as being part of you, but only as things to chip away at, as part of the process of perfecting His carving.

One of the keys to being made into the person that God wants us to be is submission; submission to the master sculptor who is at work in our lives changing us.

We are so preoccupied with our bad parts and yet to God, these are not parts of us at all, but a result of the fall and sin entering the world.

So when Jesus looks at us, He doesn't see the ugly big blocks of stone that we are, He sees what God made us to be; God's workmanship, beautiful masterpieces in His collection.

St. Ignatius, one of the early church fathers, said, "A thick and shapeless tree trunk would never believe that it could become a statue, admired as a miracle of sculpture, and would never submit itself to the chisel of the sculptor, who sees by her genius what she can make of it."

We must not be too preoccupied with the parts of us that aren't really part of us. Submitting to the work of Christ in our lives involves trusting Him completely. He is the master craftsman, and He sees what is necessary to get rid of first. He sees the priorities, and what our priorities are will not necessarily be His.

We have to submit ourselves to what God wants us to do as part of this transformation process. In Ephesians, chapter 2, verse 10 St. Paul says that we are created in Christ Jesus to do good works, which God prepared in advance for us to do.

These good works are going to be completely different for each one of us. For some of you it will involve being the best teacher you can, or the best mum, best dad, and so on and for others something completely different.

But the extent to which we embrace these good works is going to help our transformation. God, through what He has planned for us, has got a lot He wants to teach us and show us, and we need to be open to these things.

Submit to Christ's sculpting, and submit to God's plan for you.

Remember the story I shared and remember the way in which the sculptor saw so clearly what the horse was going to look like. Well, in heaven, we are all going to see ourselves and each other as God really intended us to be, without all of our problems and issues, and each and every one of us are going to be masterpieces.

I would encourage you now to spend some time in silence. Imagine yourself as the statue that Christ is working on –

- Are you submitting to His craftsmanship?
- Do you see that when Christ looks at you all He sees is your beauty?
- Do you trust enough in God's plan for you and your transformation, to be open to His plans for you?

Finally, I find it strange that so many Christians, focus so much on their failings and their sins that they have such a negative self-image of themselves. They find it hard to believe sometimes that they can be

made into something beautiful – the things that they struggle with seem so deep and so much a part of them, and whatever they do they can't get rid of them. There are just some sins in all of our lives, that we repeat over and over and over again. We really hate ourselves for it, and yet we can't stop ourselves. They seem so much a part of who we are.

Does this sound familiar? Of course, everyone has his or her own problems that we struggle with; we all know that no one is perfect. Yet for some people, focusing on their failings becomes such an obsession. We seem to ignore Bible passages that say, "We are God's workmanship" (Ephesians 2:10). Or we think that we are the exception that everyone else is God's workmanship, but I am the exception that proves the norm, the one that God screwed up on.

So for those of you that have ever felt this way, here are the keys to achieving high self-esteem:

- Talk with God about everything.
- Detox and avoid all toxins.
- Surround yourself with positive and supportive friends.
- Have fun, laugh and play often.
- Treat yourself with respect.
- Forgive everyone and everything, especially yourself.
- Only engage in actions that you feel good about.
- Keep your promises to yourself and others.
- Take good care of your physical body (eat your Brussels sprouts)!
- Release the past and anything that has served its purpose.

- Let go of all guilt, shame or regrets.
- Don't gossip.
- Spend time daily on your priorities.
- Be lovingly honest with yourself and others.
- Trust and follow God's guidance.

Worry never helps anything, but prayer helps everything. My dad used to always say: 'if you worry you die; and if you don't worry you die also. So why worry?

Remember that God is with us at every stage of our lives and all that happens to us are just seasons in our lives. Things come and go and change. But as long as you hold on to the anchor of your lives, you will not drift aimlessly, with any sense of direction. Let God be the rudder of your life. Give Him a try, you will not regret it.

SPIRITUAL FOOD FOR THOUGHT

Masterpiece Restored

Everybody is different
No two people are the same
Each one an original masterpiece
In an individual frame
The pictures have been damaged
They are dirty, discoloured, scarred
Some have been so near the flames
They are badly blistered and charred

There are a number of paintings,
Authentic they seem at first sight
But if the surface is gently scraped
You'll find that all is not right
They've been restored by friends of the artist
Who thought they knew what he'd planned
They've completely destroyed the original
Spoiled the work of the Masters hand

When an artist begins restoration
He first clears the dirt and the grime
Slowly revealing the picture that was
Before the ravage of time
Next he restores damaged paint-work
Carefully matches each colour and shade
He does not repaint as an all action scene
What began as a quiet leafy glade

Here's some advice to you friends of the artist
Who restore men damaged by sin
Simply introduce them to Jesus
Let Him change their lives from within

Pictures which have been altered or changed
Are the hardest of all to restore
So leave it to God let Him start from scratch
Don't get in His way any more

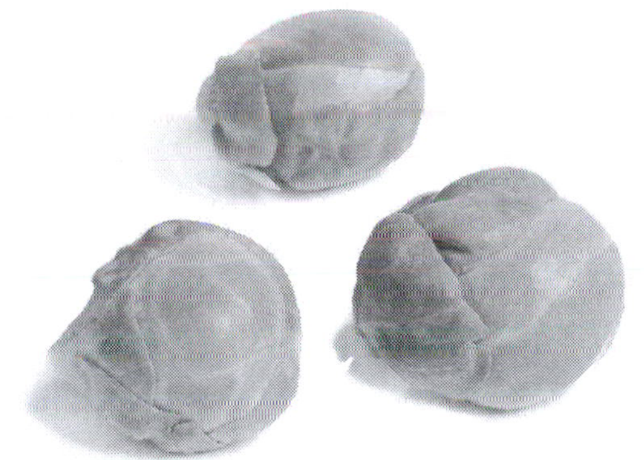

CHAPTER 11

THE MASTER GARDENER

"Then God said, 'let the land produce vegetation: seed-bearing plants and trees on the land that bear fruit with seed in it, according to their various kinds.'" — Genesis 1:11-12

As I write this chapter in May 2014, the Royal Horticultural Society (RHS) Chelsea Flower Show is taking place in the grounds of the Royal Hospital Chelsea in London. It was formally known as the Great Spring Show. It is a garden show held for five days by the RHS. It is the most famous flower show in the United Kingdom, and perhaps the biggest in the world, attracting around 157,000 visitors from all continents.

Every year the grounds of the Royal Hospital Chelsea are transformed into show gardens, inspirational small gardens and vibrant horticultural displays. Rare plants never before seen in cultivation have been used, for example at the Cave Pavilion designed by Sophie Walker. The one garden that has captivated me is the M&G Garden, designed by Cleve West, which has won the gold medal. This garden is based on the paradise garden that was invented by the Persians more than 2,000 years ago and uses water, shade and planting for sanctuary and contemplation.

I would like you to imagine being in the peace and serenity of this garden. The concept of this garden of paradise is centred on water flowing from a tall, octagonal fountain made from limestone and flint

in a sunken terrace. Roots of the Tree of Life have been engraved into stone wall panels, with four trees planted around the fountain representing the elements of earth, water, air and fire. The plants for the garden were carefully chosen for their sensory qualities. These, together with stone elements and running water, infused this 21st century refuge with a sense of timelessness, an essence of paradise.

What a wonderful reminder that gardening today has its roots in ancient history.

In July of this same year, London will again be the focus for the next major garden show, the RHS Hampton Court Flower Show. The organisers of this show are looking forward to see what the designers have in store for them in the Conceptual Gardens, which have the theme of the Seven Sins.

There are RHS Flower Shows throughout the year in other cities in Great Britain, attracting more than 700,000 visitors and reaching millions more via the media. But it is not only Britain that displays such floral splendour. Flower Shows are held throughout the world. So it is safe to say that thousands upon thousands of people throughout the world are attracted to flowers, plants and gardens. Each one imbued with their own personal recollection of a special moment in their life. Florists all over the world, tenderly create loving floral arrangements for special occasions such as, a wedding, a new birth, an anniversary, a special birthday, a funeral. Catering to many people with varying preferences as they arrange their floral tributes for those they love and appreciate. Flowers of every colour and shade are used; various hybrids and varieties, but all serving the same purpose – to show love and brighten up someone's day.

It is customary when boy meets girl for the first time for flowers to be given. Sometimes a single rose, to declare their love for each other. But what happens as time goes by and you take each other for granted,

and the proverbial song 'You don't bring me flowers anymore', made famous by Barbara Streisand and Neil Diamond, resonates within your being?

Every now and then we should stop and smell the roses, the orchids and the irises. You get the point?

As you journey with us through this chapter, I would encourage you to harness your inner gardener, for there is within each and every human being an in-built love of gardens, flowers and plants. The intoxicating aroma and fragrance of the beautiful flowers of paradise are there for all to smell and enjoy.

The purpose of this chapter is to build on the question of what is it that makes us human, why are we different from the plants and all the other things that God made? The Adam and Eve story reminds us we are different because we have an ability to know the difference between what is healthy and what is not so healthy for us. What is more, when we begin the spiritual life and start hearing God's words and His view on living a full life, we will understand that although there will be times when we endure the cross and suffering, be that financial, emotional or spiritual, we will never be alone. If these experiences seem like a pruning or a cutting back and we are changing our attitudes and behaviours then it is because God, as the Master Gardener, wants us to bloom and flourish and make His Presence known through us to the world. If, for example we experience a pruning of fear to hope, disunity to unity, apathy to enthusiasm or from hate to love, then know your spiritual life is real and that proverbial six-pack is building.

I would urge you now, to become like a little child, whether you believe it to be true or not, and go beyond the realm of reasoning and understanding. Enter in, if only briefly, to the story of creation with us.

The story of Adam and Eve (Genesis 2:4-24)

"This is the account of heaven and earth when they were created, at the time when the Lord God made earth and heaven.

Wild bushes and plants were not on the earth yet because the Lord God hadn't sent rain on the earth. Also, there was no one to farm the land. Instead, underground water would come up from the earth and water the entire surface of the ground.

Then the Lord God formed the man from the dust of the earth and blew the breath of life into his nostrils. The man became a living being.

The Lord God planted a garden in Eden, in the east. That's where he put the man whom he had formed. The Lord God made all the trees grow out of the ground. These trees were nice to look at, and their fruit was good to eat. The tree of life and the tree of the knowledge of good and evil grew in the middle of the garden.

A river flowed from Eden to water the garden. Outside the garden it divided into four rivers. The name of the first river is Pishon. This is the one that winds throughout Havilah, where there is gold. (The gold of that land is pure. Bdellium and onyx are also found there.) The name of the second river is Gihon. This is the one that winds throughout Sudan. The name of the third river is Tigris. This is the one that flows east of Assyria. The fourth river is the Euphrates.

Then the Lord God took the man and put him in the Garden of Eden to farm the land and to take care of it. The Lord God commanded the man. He said, "You are free to eat from any tree in the garden. But you must never eat from the tree of the knowledge of good and evil because when you eat from it, you will certainly die."

Then the Lord God said, "It is not good for the man to be alone. I will make a helper who is right for him."

The Lord God had formed all the wild animals and all the birds out of the ground. Then he brought them to the man to see what he would call them. Whatever the man called each creature became its name. So the man named all the domestic animals, all the birds, and all the wild animals.

But the man found no helper who was right for him. So the Lord God caused him to fall into a deep sleep. While the man was sleeping, the Lord God took out one of the man's ribs and closed up the flesh at that place. Then the Lord God formed a woman from the rib that He had taken from the man. He brought her to the man.

The man said, "This is now bone of my bones and flesh of my flesh. She will be named woman because she was taken from man."

That is why a man will leave his father and mother and will be united with his wife, and they will become one flesh. The man and his wife were both naked, but they weren't ashamed of it.

One day, Adam and Eve were gathering berries for dinner when Eve heard a silky voice behind her.

"Has God told you that you can eat the fruit from all the trees?" the voice asked softly. Eve turned around to see a snake talking to her. "God has told us we can eat all the fruit except for what grows on The Tree of the Knowledge of Good and Evil," Eve told the serpent.

"Oh come now, that's silly! I hardly think such a lovely fruit would do you any harm," the serpent lied. "God knows that if you eat from The Tree of the Knowledge of Good and Evil you'll become just like God, and will be able to decide for yourself what is right and what is wrong."

The woman looked at the fruit and thought how tasty it looked. She thought how wonderful it would be to be as wise and powerful as God. She believed the serpent's lie and ate the fruit and also gave some to Adam, who was with her, and he took a bite as well.

She felt a strange feeling in the pit of her stomach. She fidgeted and wondered what was wrong with her. Suddenly she realized that she was feeling guilty, she had disobeyed God and knew she'd done something wrong.

When God asked them if they had eaten from The Tree of the Knowledge of Good and Evil that He had told them not to touch, they blamed each other for their sins.

The Master Gardener tenderly prunes us to bear good fruit

The story of humanity's sin begins with a tree and ends on a tree: first, the tree of the knowledge of good and evil; and finally, the cross on which Jesus dies. The first tree offers fruit that leads to death, but the second offers a death that leads to eternal life.

After reading this story, we could quite easily say that God had intended for Adam and Eve to be the first gardeners in His Garden of Eden. They were given something precious to tend and care for and they wasted it by turning their backs on God. Notice how they blamed one another for their sins. They would not take accountability for their own actions or mistakes. All they did was point the finger at each other. Since Adam and Eve, people have been blaming others for their own mistakes.

What about you? How often have you pointed the finger at another, perhaps a friend you have fallen out with, or your spouse? Just remember this, that for every time you point the finger at another, in

judgement or condemnation, there are three fingers pointing back at you!

God's Garden of Eden must have been out of this world; sheer stunning beauty, with plants of paradise abounding. Isn't it funny how nowadays every single gardener and flower show is trying to captivate that same beauty that Adam and Eve once enjoyed in God's garden? I remember when I went to Madeira the plants of paradise were prolific on the island. Never had I seen flowers so strikingly beautiful. As Tony and I walked through the gardens all lush and inviting, it truly felt as if we were walking in the Garden of Eden. Thank goodness we did not meet up with any serpents enticing us to turn our backs on God!

A gardener tends his garden with a lot of tender loving care. He treats his plants, vegetables and fruit with the utmost attention. He tends to his vines, shrubs and roses and prunes them to encourage growth. The pruning has to be done at the right time of the year. You have to know what you are doing. I remember pruning some rose bushes and ended up killing them as I either over-pruned them, or pruned them at the wrong time of the year.

I wasn't really born with the proverbial green thumb. You either have green fingers or not, that is why botanical gardens and other stately estates with beautiful gardens employ the right people to do the job. The gardeners know what they are doing. They prune in season to encourage growth and feed their crops at the appropriate time in order that all their vegetables and plants flourish with the right nourishment.

If you are a gardener you will understand how important it is to ensure that you know your garden inside out. If you work as a gardener for someone else it is equally important that you tend your employer's garden with the same care and attention as you would your own. The people whose gardens you tend merit your trust and through time strong relationships are developed as they see their gardens maturing

and looking beautiful. Quite often you gain their respect and admiration as they see their gardens being transformed by the work of your hands.

Our lives are like a garden, well-tended, or full of weeds. In order to proudly display a well-kept garden it needs to be looked after; good seeds need to be planted in order to produce beautiful plants and vegetation. Just think, your mind is a garden; your thoughts are the seeds. You can grow flowers, or you can grow weeds.

Ever seen a lawn full of weeds? Mine is a bit like that and it is looking rather tired after being down for 40 years! So what do you do when your garden is full of weeds? Do you call in the experts or do you allow the weeds to take over?

Some weeds are very deep rooted and difficult to pull up or get rid of, unless you are a gardener with years of experience who knows what to do.

According to Genesis, God was the world's first gardener and the Master Gardener of the universe. Once we begin to take the spiritual life seriously, it will become apparent that the Master Gardener may want to change or prune us.

The vine and the branches

"I am the true vine, and my Father is the gardener. He cuts off every branch in me that bears no fruit, while every branch that does bear fruit He prunes so that it will be even more fruitful. You are already clean because of the word I have spoken to you. Remain in me, as I also remain in you. No branch can bear fruit by itself; it must remain in the vine. Neither can you bear fruit unless you remain in me.

I am the vine; you are the branches. If you remain in me and I in you, you will bear much fruit; apart from me you can do nothing. If you do

not remain in me, you are like a branch that is thrown away and withers; such branches are picked up, thrown into the fire and burned. If you remain in me and my words remain in you, ask whatever you wish, and it will be done for you. This is to my Father's glory, that you bear much fruit, showing yourselves to be my disciples" (John 15:1-8).

What about your spiritual life? Is that as healthy as it could be? Or do you need the Master Gardener to come and tend to your soul?

Are you suffering from deep-seated roots that are going deeper and deeper and affecting your health and way of thinking? I would say this to you then, be careful with what seeds you allow to take root in the garden of your heart as not all seeds bear good fruit.

Who's going to argue with that? Many prizes were handed out at the Chelsea Flower Show this year but we could even go further and crown God with the title of "Master Gardener" of the universe. Which is to say, the entire universe is God's garden where consciousness is grown and life is realized. Within this garden, God has created the perfect medium for spirit and consciousness to pass through and complete the cycle of life. It is here in the fabric of space and time where His Seeds of life are sown in faith and grown with love. It is here in this garden of the Divine where we find our self and our life. It is here in the garden of the soul where we know we are growing toward a holy and glorious purpose. Like the plants of the earth, our purpose is to grow, mature and produce fruit at the hands of the Master Gardener who nurtures us with the light of knowledge and the water of love. Yes indeed, God is a gardener on the highest level. Yet, not only is God the Gardener, but God is also the Sun, the power that gives us the energy to grow and mature. "I am the true vine, and my Father is the gardener" (John 15:1).

So what are some of these seeds that have taken root and buried themselves deep in your subconscious?

- Bitterness
- Resentment
- Jealousy
- Envy
- Unforgiveness
- Hurts
- Painful past experiences
- Broken relationships
- Repressed grief
- Bad memories

The seeds we sow create the atmosphere we walk in or in layman's terms: 'you reap, what you sow.'

What would be the cost to me if I allowed the Master Gardener to work in me and allow, healing, wholeness and reconciliation to take place?

God is not only the Master Gardener, but He also uses us as gardeners in His world. He gives us seeds to plant. If we don't plant them, they will not grow.

So, what kinds of seeds are you sowing? Not just in others but in yourself? Are you sowing seeds that encourage others and help them to grow into the people they are meant to be, such as, love, joy, peace, patience, kindness, goodness, trustfulness, gentleness and self-control. Or are your seeds bringing others down?

I'll give you a classic example. Take the seed of Discouragement -v- Encouragement. Three ladies stopped to speak after a service at my local church. One of them said to the other, "Oh my, you are looking

so tired". The other said, "Oh I love your hair; it is looking ever so nice". Which of the two do you think uplifted the person most?

We all do it, don't we? Without realising it, what comes out of our mouths shows what kind of person we are. Like a tree, if it is rotten inside it will only produce bad fruit, but if it is sound, it will produce good fruit.

I always have to consider this and am fully aware that sometimes what comes out of my mouth is not necessarily the good fruit I am supposed to be producing. So let us consider the kind of fruit we have the potential to grow in us and the seeds we may be planting. Such as:

Fear -v- Hope

- Fear – is an unpleasant feeling of anxiety or apprehension caused by the presence or anticipation of danger.
- Hope – Jesus is the Anchor of Hope.

Disbelief -v- Belief

- Disbelief – an inability or refusal to accept that something is true or real.
- Belief – an acceptance that something exists or is true, especially one without proof.

Doubt -v- Faith

- Doubt – a status between belief and disbelief, involves uncertainty or distrust or lack of sureness of an alleged fact, an action, a motive, or a decision.

- Faith – is the assurance of things you have hoped for, the absolute conviction that there are realities you've never seen.

Disunity -V- Unity

- Disunity – a lack of agreement or harmony.
- Unity – the state of being united or joined as a whole. 'I appeal to you, brothers and sisters, in the name of our Lord Jesus Christ, that all of you agree with one another so that there may be no divisions among you and that you may be perfectly united in mind and thought.' (1Corinthians 1:10).

Hate -V- Love

- Hate – intense dislike; feelings of hate and revenge.
- Love – love is but acceptance of the other, whatever he or she is. God is love.

Unfriendliness -V- Friendliness

- Unfriendliness – not amicable; not friendly or kindly in disposition; unsympathetic, aloof, hostile, antagonistic, cold.
- Friendliness – the quality of being friendly; affability; amiability, geniality, congeniality, cordiality, good nature, good humour, warmth, affection, affectionateness. "Be friends with one another and forgive each other as soon as a quarrel begins." (Colossians 3:13).

Apathy -v- Enthusiasm

- Apathy – total disinterest or indifference.
- Enthusiasm – intense and eager enjoyment, interest, or approval.

Selfishness -v- Selflessness

- Selfishness – is placing concern with oneself or one's own interests above the well-being of others.
- Selflessness – renunciation of your own interests in favour of the interests of others. Dying to self – 'Unless a grain of wheat falls into the earth and dies, it remains just a grain of wheat; but if it dies, it bears much fruit" (John 12:24).

Impatience -v- Patience

- Impatience – intolerance of anything that thwarts, delays or hinders.
- Patience – the capacity to accept or tolerate delay, problems or suffering without becoming annoyed or anxious.

Unkindness -v- Kindness

- Unkindness – lack of sympathy, insensitiveness, unhelpfulness, inconsideration, thoughtlessness.
- Kindness – the quality of being warm-hearted, understanding, helpful.

All of your actions are like a seed, for sooner or later, it will bear fruit. Just make sure it is good fruit and not rotten. Plant in season or your seed will not grow.

Love, light, and life flow from the vine through us and into the fruit. In the fruit are seeds. The seeds continue to grow and multiply in the lives of others. When a Christian stays connected to Jesus and walks in goodness, the fruit produced can change the world. God wants us to grow in maturity and bear fruit, which will produce seed so that seed can then be replanted and bear even more fruit.

The other thing to consider is that you will never grow an abundant crop in life's garden until you learn to plant "seeds of faith and encouragement". And when it comes to God, you just can't out plant Him! So plant the seeds, don't just keep them in the packet.

The analogy of God being the Master Gardener sits well with me. Does it with you? I have found that God is extremely patient with me and He is the same with others. He does not push us into submission, for He is the perfect gentleman and He has given us free will to make our own choices. God is also good. In fact, He is very good. "O taste and see that the Lord is good" (Psalm 34:8).

For me, the proof is in the pudding. You have to taste what you eat before you can tell whether it is good. Take for example the classic Brussels sprout. People have varying tastes. For some this tiny little vegetable looks appetising, but for others it is repugnant. Just looking at it makes them feel sick. Brussels sprouts have many good and healthy elements, as Neil has already explained. Those that will benefit most from eating the Brussels sprout are those who taste, see it is good and partake of its health benefits.

I always remember my dad, when sitting at table to eat. My mum was a great cook and her meals were always delicious. On the odd occasion, however, the Brussels sprout would inevitably make its way onto my plate. My face would change colour at the thought of putting such a tasteless, in my opinion, food in my mouth. My mum would probably have said: 'if you don't like it, leave it!' My dad, however,

knew that this offenceless little vegetable was good for me and would insist at first that at least I tasted it. His words: 'taste it and if you don't like it, then you can leave it.' A more gentle approach that sometimes paid its dividends.

My mum, probably after cooking all day, could not be bothered with this cantankerous child and preferred to close the subject for the sake of peace. My dad, in his wisdom, knew that I had a choice and allowed me to make that choice but did not want me to lose out on the benefits it would bring me by eating this vegetable. He knew that if I tasted it, there was every chance I might have liked it and that was half the battle won.

It was years later when I married my husband Tony, who was Scottish, and his own mum who gave me the well-known dish, 'stovies' that I developed a taste and liking for this innocuous little green vegetable. To this day I have never looked back.

To finish this chapter, I would just like to give you all some additional seeds that you can sow:

- Prayer fertilizes the soil – so use it and spread it.
- God protects us in all the seasons of our lives, so whatever you are going through just now, know that God is with you and He is protecting you.
- God makes room for everyone. He has no favourites. So do not be afraid to approach Him and ask for His help.
- If you are a Broken Vessel, allow God to heal you; ask for prayer.
- Don't be pot bound full of deep roots. Allow God to use the potential He sees in you.
- A seed is no more than a flower in disguise. So see things as they could be, not as they are.

And finally, a little reminder: God has planted seeds of greatness in every person, and His plan for your life is for those seeds to sprout and grow and produce in you a life of health, wealth and happiness. From the very start of creation it was God's plan for people to enjoy life. Men and women were the ultimate, the highest pinnacle of creation. Men and women were created in the image of God; he was the reason for the creation. God did not plan for His people to be sick, to be poor, and to be in bondage; He planned for us to be on top of the world. When God created Adam, He did it in such a way that in order for Adam to achieve greatness there had to be a co-operative effort between God and Adam. This is a vital point. We often think of Adam as being a perfect creature, yet God created him with the potential to grow and develop. God said to Adam, "Be fruitful and multiply, fill the earth, and conquer it, and have dominion over all the wild animals" (Genesis 1:28). God placed Adam and Eve in the Garden of Eden. As I've already said, they were the first gardeners. God wanted them to tend His Garden. They had a job to do and a part to play in developing God's seeds in their lives. God's desire for us is the same as His desire for Adam and Eve. God wanted them to take what had been given them in creation, and make it productive, make it grow, make it develop. God uses us as gardeners too - so, be a gardener for God. I promise you, it's fun all the way!

SPIRITUAL FOOD FOR THOUGHT

Seeds and the Sons of the Kingdom

The Word of God was just a seed
alive in Mary's womb,
that very seed burst into life
as He escaped the tomb.
Though the seed was buried
it sprouted down deep roots,
preparing ground for everyone
to recognize the truth.

The grains of faith like mustard seeds
lie dormant in our hearts
as we feed and water them
something new will start.
The faith that He has granted us
can grow and grow and grow
and before we even know it
the branches start to show.

The seeds produced from our lives
may travel far and wide,
we may not see the fruit of them
but we sense the Father's pride.
That they won't fall on rocky ground
is something that we pray,
He'll break up the fallow ground
and roots will make a way
into ground that is prepared

to hear the Father's words,
a joy and fruitfulness to come
an attracting of the birds.

Seeds are scattered everywhere
and they push their way to life,
buried deep within the ground
where it's as black as night.
As the grain surrenders
there, new life is born
and out from underneath the earth
it takes on a new form.
Life breaks forth and opens up
through the seeds within our lives
fresh faith will move the mountains
these beginnings don't despise.

Learning ways of wisdom;
how to direct His power,
awareness of the seasons,
the times the days the hour.
Preparing ground for future days
where nutrients combine,
to grow us into fruitfulness
in the glorious sunshine.

Prayer for growth

Lord may I bear much fruit with the seeds you have planted in me. May I become a mature fruitful branch filled with seed-laden fruit that will result in much more seed-producing fruit; so that you, our Heavenly Father will be pleased to call this fruit your own. Then I will be profitable to your kingdom and hear you say… "well done good and faithful servant….enter into the joy of the Lord."

— Matthew 25: 21

CHAPTER 12

WE ARE WHAT WE EAT – TASTE AND SEE THAT THE LORD IS GOOD

"Taste and see that the Lord is good! How blessed is the person who trusts in Him!" – Psalm 34:8

Many years ago I remember completing one of those psychological personality profiles and one of the questions asked, "Do you live to eat or eat to live?" I can't quite remember what my response to all the questions asked in the profile said about my personality. However, with this particular question, I said, 'I eat to live rather than live to eat'. Sure like everyone I enjoy a nice meal but fundamentally, for me, food is energy. I take it on board to keep strong and healthy. To some people food is a religion, it's their job, and it's their hobby or passion. But if I had to choose a passion between being hungry for God and hungry for the flavours and tastes of food, I will choose God.

They say it takes seven years for the cells in our body to be replaced and these cells are made from the food we eat. So I need to keep a careful watch to what's going into my mouth. But I know too God the

Father has a deep concern as to who I am becoming; what my mind, body and spirit are consuming. From the beginning of time, God has had an interest in what we put into our bodies after he told Adam and Eve to eat from the Tree of Knowledge. God gave us freedom to choose. We see that right throughout the Old Testament where the people of Israel sometimes chose to follow God's way and at other times they turned their backs on Him. This was the situation Jesus saw for Himself when he was on this earth. He knew that men and women had an inherent weakness and flaw to choose things that were not particularly good for them. The day before he died, His best and most trusted friend on earth, Peter, denied 3 times that he even knew of this man Jesus. The Good News is; despite Jesus' death, there was a Master Plan. St. John in his Gospel tells us that at the beginning of time God has a plan (John 1:1-18). The plan being, that one day God the Father would reveal the fullness of His love to us through His Son and after Jesus had completed His purpose on earth the Holy Spirit would be sent to live in us and be part of our DNA. God's plan was to give us a new spiritual diet so that we could grow into the image and likeness of His Son Jesus Christ. God wants us to be holy, healthy and happy.

Now some people may laugh at the thought of being holy, surely that is what those statues of saints in churches all over the world are alluding to. Holy people who have halos over their heads. The sculptor has chiselled them to have perfect porcelain skin and no defects. They have serene smiles that say, "Yip I am so different to you guys, I am holy and perfect".

Yes to be holy is to be different; it is to be set-apart, separated. It's not to be perfect however. Holy people are imperfect, they are broken, and they are scarred and chipped at the edges. But like a supreme athlete, despite their flaws and the difficulties of life, holy people have almost perfect faith and almost perfect love for God. Holy people are so like Christ on this earth and that is what makes them holy and separate.

But it's a different kind of separation. It's a separation from sin and death, from apathy and fear, from bitterness and a "cannae be bothered" take on life.

The cross as the Game Changer

One of the central messages that God wants to teach us and one of the central messages of this book; is this idea of separation. Once upon a time, even in Adam and Eve days, we had an ability to choose good and bad in life. We have a choice to either want to be close to God or to be separated from Him. There was the immense temptation within the human spirit to choose the unhealthy things that were not good for us like greed, selfishness, revenge, pride and sloth. These weaknesses were even given a name, "The 7 Deadly Sins". That is where the separation took place. There was throughout the course of history, no solution or fix to this temptation. At this stage in history we were still bound by our 'fallen nature' to do what we wanted to do and reject what God wanted us to do. It was like human beings had a debilitating virus that took the joy from their lives; we were in some kind of limbo state.

St. John confirms (John 1:1-18) something new happened when God sent His only Son Jesus Christ. The Word became flesh; God became man, almost saying, "Hey I understand your fallen human condition". Jesus knew this and the propensity for men and women to choose to be separated from God rather than be close to God. Jesus said He was going to bring a radical solution to this separation and it was called the cross. Jesus only spent 3 years of His life preaching, teaching and healing and even from the earliest days of His 3-year ministry He told His closest friends that He was going to suffer and die on the cross. They did not understand until after the event what the cross meant and when the 4 writers of the Gospel wrote down Jesus' life story and St. Paul started to write his letters, it is abundantly clear that the cross is

the game changer. This is the one event in history that changes the world and everything within the human condition. After the cross humanity would be turned upside down and there would be a new separation.

You see, before the cross the separation was; we had a propensity to be drawn away from Godly things. Our natural state was to choose the unhealthy options; we did not at this point in time have the fullness of capacity to be holy, to have the mindset of Christ.

That all changed with the cross and with a baptism or rebirth in God's Spirit.

Nicodemus, an elderly Jew asked that very question. Nicodemus thinks it crazy to have talk that says we have to be born again in the Spirit. But Jesus insists. "I tell you most solemnly, "Unless a man is born from above, he cannot see the Kingdom of God" (John 3:5).

But here's the Good News; here's the game changer. Because of what God has done by sending His Son to die on the cross, and risen from the dead, the gift of the Holy Spirit was offered to everyone. Now for the first time ever the natural propensity of men and women is to be united to God in faith not separated from Him anymore.

Once we were naturally separated or fallen but now, through the cross we are naturally united and this is something no one can take away from us. St. Paul had this amazing certainty that nothing could ever separate us from God because of the game changer; the cross. This is what he said to people who were living in Rome sometime in early to mid 50 AD, "For I am sure that neither death nor life, nor angels nor rulers, nor things present nor things to come, nor powers, nor height nor depth, nor anything else in all creation, will be able to separate us from the love of God in Christ Jesus our Lord" (Romans 8:38-39).

This is what was spoken about on p218 of this book:

"When we receive the gift of eternal life through our acceptance of Jesus Christ as our Lord and Saviour, God breathes new life into us bringing a spiritual birth. At that moment we receive heavenly DNA into our souls in the form of the Holy Spirit. Now, we possess two sets of DNA. One physical set from our earthly parents and one spiritual from our heavenly parent. With God's DNA inside of us, the Divine life of God grows. Now, we are radically different than the rest of the world. We are part of a distinct race. We resemble our heavenly Father as evidenced by our new Christ like attitudes, motivations, perspectives, desires, goals, and new godly value system. We have a deep desire to be a blessing to others as God has been a blessing to us. After our spiritual births we are connected eternally to God in such a way that no matter what happens in our futures, our heavenly genetic link to Him will not be broken."

So if there is any kind of separation now it is a separation from selfishness, a separation from sin and even a separation from death.

In the beginning our natural state had no solution to sin, death, selfishness, apathy and greed; now there is a solution. The solution being; that we are united and eternally part of God's life and love which is the antithesis of sin, death, selfishness, apathy and greed. Hence we have a new kind of separation but thankfully it is a good kind of separation. It's a separation from the things of life that drags us down.

"Ah", I hear you cry, "If that is the case then why is there still death, sin, selfishness, apathy and greed in the world. If God were real He would have totally got rid of these things and made us perfect and holy."

That is the point; we already have access to perfection and holiness because of Christ. If we stay close to Jesus in everything we say and do, if we truly believe that there is no separation now, like there once

was, then there is nothing to fear spiritually. We have everything we need spiritually. We have all the love, the life, the joy, the hope, the passion for life we need to lead whole/holy lives. That is what we are now, in Christ. Because of the cross and resurrection, we are spiritual beings first and physical beings second. Yes we have physical bodies and yes we will still be tempted to choose to be selfish, greedy, fearful or hopeless but that is not the choice God wants us to make. God has planted His DNA, His Spirit in us; nothing can take that away or separate us from God. But still we have to make daily choices in our physical lives just as we make daily choices between the Brussels sprout and the banoffee pie. The struggle, the tension is where we live out our faith, where we become holy and more like Christ. Remember too, we are not alone in this struggle. That is why this is not purely a self-help book. Self-help is great up to a point but it can only take us so far. At times we need a coach whispering the right words of guidance and encouragement. We need to do some daily exercises like prayer, reading the Bible, having a spirit of thanksgiving and praise. With God's help and Grace we will become holy, we will become more like Christ. That has been God's eternal plan since the days of Adam and Eve.

From the days of Adam and Eve to the moment Jesus died on the cross there was a pull of the ego that says, "I can live life all by myself, through my own reasoning, logic and strength". Then the game changed with the blood of the cross. Now the pull is, "With Christ I can do all things" (Philippians 4:13). The holy person is someone who knows they are not under the bondage of sin or the ego anymore, they are not an island and they are in a relationship with a living God who has an eternal plan for every one of us. The plan being, separation from sin and death and unity with Grace and life. It is God's will that we should be holy, that we should be like His Son Jesus Christ but, like Adam and Eve in the Garden of Eden, God still gives us a choice just as we have a choice this very night what we put on our dinner plates and what we put into our bodies because we are what we eat.

This begs the question, "What are we consuming?" If we are what we eat then what dieticians and nutritionists are we listening to? What words and voices are we taking on board? Have we placed ourselves in the right locations to even hear these words? If God's word is Spirit and life, where are we hearing His word? How often are we hearing this word? Who is reminding us to stay spiritually healthy and who is encouraging us to keep going on the journey when we have severe hunger pains? Who is feeding you? What is feeding you? If you are open to the spiritual life, the Good News is, the message will get through. God will make sure of that. Listen anyone who has ears (Mark 4:9).

During the last 12 months in the U.K. there has been a national effort to get people from phoning 999 for non-emergency calls. Newspapers have reported incredible stories of how in the past, people have used 999 to ask how long it will take a turkey to cook in an oven, or because someone had broken their laptop computer and wanted a lift to the shops to get a new one. As a result U.K. Police have now issued a new emergency number, it's 101. How many years will it take for everyone in the U.K. to get this message that you dial 101 instead of 999 for non-emergency calls? Perhaps 10 years. It's the same with the healthy eating message about our 5-a-day; how long will it take for that message to seep into the consciousness and behaviours of your average Joe? It's the same with the spirituality message. We need to be in places where we hear the right messages. We need people who are encouraging us with the right messages. This is when we choose, what kind of pathway we want, as Deuteronomy 30:19 says 'I set before you life, or death...choose life'.

Since we must make a choice one way or another; we must choose what we put into our bodies, it follows that there are certain standards that appeal to us. Who's standards are we following? Who is your hero? Who are you looking up to or into in life? When you reach the

end of your days what legacy do you want to leave behind? I see this in my funeral ministry time after time. There are some people who live life to the full and live like they are never going to die and on the other hand there are others who have died but never fully lived, never fully experienced the depth of life they are meant to have this side of heaven.

My 9-year-old daughter has been hearing this message of healthy eating choices during all her years at school along with other messages about care for the environment. Undoubtedly, these messages, over time, will get through. Sure she will still eat donuts now and again and may occasionally throw her sweet wrappers on the living room floor. But the message has been delivered. I guess that brings me back to where I started this book, sat at home around the Christmas table aged 9 and thinking, "I do not want to eat these Brussels sprouts, they are yuk, maybe my mum won't notice if I hide them under some roast potatoes and smother them in gravy." Fast-forward forty years and now I choose the message for myself; as this is what I desire in my body. I am certainly not perfect and don't eat my 5-a-day everyday but I now have a deeper desire to do this as I now know what is good for me. Which is a message I am sure my mum said all those year ago, "Eat your vegetables Neil, they are good for you".

So I now go to my local supermarket with that message still there. I have even taken that message one stage further, to a deeper level that my mum had not asked for. I now read the food labels or have a quick scan at the red and green warning labels we find on many food packages. Woo cowboy! That Rocky Road Cheesecake Wedge has 34% fat of which 67% are saturated fat. Danger, danger, danger! So I ate half a slice instead. What an exciting life aged 48; I read food labels. But that has also moved into my spiritual life too. I now look at other things in greater depth now. In days gone by a quick prayer and a weekly visit to church was all I desired. That then stopped for 7 years and so I asked God for the Grace to come back to Him with a

greater depth, a greater faith, a greater love and a greater desire for the spiritual exercises my spirit needed. That is where I am now. I still 'eat to live' as that personality profile showed. But I also have a desire to 'live' for eating and consuming those things that are good for my spirit. It's not always an easy road; even that cheesecake I ate the other day was called 'Rocky Road'. Honest I only ate half of one slice!

Who is feeding us? We are what we eat. I need to hear Bible stories on a more regular basis. I now want to have more time to pray and I like to listen to praise music. For many years I thought church was irrelevant but I have gone back even though it is not perfect. I know God's Presence is there in His Word every time it is spoken and I need that voice so that I can compare it to the many other competing voices in my life. If only we had a red and green danger sign for voices like we have for saturated fats.

If you want to know what you are eating right now look in your fridge. Our fridges and cupboards will tell us a lot about who we are. What if someone asked you to lay out a spiritual plate for them, what things would you expect to see on that plate? Will these be in your store cupboard? Why not allow God that freedom to guide you towards what you should be consuming? Our choices reflect our identity and values and reveal our spiritual health. It is the choosing that makes the difference and it's always our choice and I hope this book, in some small way, has helped you with that choice.

The spiritual life is calling us to make a distinction between the healthy and the not so healthy. The choice is always ours. Do you want to think and act differently? Would you like a Christ like mindset that aims to produce good fruit? God wants us to stand out and shine in the world because He made us, we belong to Him, His DNA is in our cell structure or spirit.

We can easily forget the words parents, teachers and educators have spoken from days gone by; be these words about Brussels sprouts or whatever. We can forget promises that have been made to us with the

passing of time. We can forget core messages whether it's healthy eating, Police phone numbers or just how much someone loves us. That is why we constantly need to hear all these messages. We need to be reminded of the Good News so that the fire will rage again. By that I mean God's Spirit burning within us.

This book has set out to offer gentle reminders of these messages we need to hear. We need to hear that the Bible is not an irrelevant dusty old book but it is a collection of books designed to help and guide us through life. We need to hear that God is not some nebulous individual sitting on a cloud totally uninterested in what is going on in our lives. We need to hear that He was a true historical person, He is the only Son of God who fully understands our human nature and that Jesus was a game changer, we now have everything we ever need for a full and happy life if we chose to have it.

Within this book we have shown you 'appetisers' to starting and growing within the spiritual life. We have written this book for people who, for various reasons, have not found the spiritual guidance and nourishment they have been looking for or they have, through time and the 'trauchles' of life, (old Scots word for 'troubles') forgotten what the spiritual life can do for them and the genuine happiness it can offer. We have attempted to unpack, through story and commentary, the basics of; the Bible, God, Jesus, The Spirit, why we need God, Church, prayer, sin, love and forgiveness and how because of the game changer that was Jesus' death on the cross, there is a Master plan, from a Master Gardener who has a burning desire to transform us and give us a new life and new spirit within us, as the Prophet Ezekiel foretold. Throughout the book we have used analogies of healthy eating, going to the gym and the humble Brussels sprout to give this book a different take on the spiritual life and why the spiritual life is good for us.

We hope this has been an enriching and encouraging book and you have seen what the spiritual journey has been like for two ordinary

people who believe that with Christ in their lives extra-ordinary things happen. It won't take away the sorrows and challenges of losing a loved one, depression or financial hardship. But we have shown you a way out of these black holes and sought to raise your spirit with the truth that we are never alone.

God is faithful in His promises to give us all the good things we need in life and all we have to do is believe, have faith and do the exercises. The spiritual muscle will grow; our lives will be transformed because people who love us, as God the Father and His Son do, will give us the strength (His Spirit) to cope with anything. More than that the Spirit will give us a burning desire to want more of Him until it is no longer I that live but Christ that lives in me. With God on our side, we are never separated from Him; there has been a breakthrough and a game changer. With God's spirit, His faith, His power and His love living in us, we will develop a spiritual 'six- pack' maybe even a 'nine-pack'. Choose to listen and be fed by this Good News and you will see the results: love, joy, peace, patience, kindness, goodness, faithfulness, gentleness and self-control.

That has been the aim of this book to offer simple yet powerful Good News and we hope that the spiritual journey you are now on and the New Life you have in Christ and His Spirit will allow you to, "Taste and see that the Lord is Good" (Psalm 34:8).

SPIRITUAL FOOD FOR THOUGHT

Fruits of the Spirit

May you know the Joy, which remains
Even through times of sorrow.
Have the Peace, which dispels anxiety
As you face an unknown tomorrow.

Have Patience when your plans are destroyed
To start again and not be annoyed.
Show Kindness to all – yes be kind
To the 'junkie' stoned out of his mind.

Overcome evil with Goodness,
You'll find it's the only way,
To oppose the powers of darkness
Which surround us every day.

Show Faithfulness and commitment,
Be there! – when you say.
Be willing to be taken for granted
In the 'Me first' world of today.

To be strong is to be assertive
You will be told at length.
This is a delusion
In Gentleness is strength.

To give expression to your feelings
Can be a good thing on the whole.
Where others may be affected
Exercise Self-control.

These are the Fruits of the Spirit,
Who proceeds from the Father above.
And yet they all count for nothing
If they are not motivated by Love.

Ian Young © (used with permission from author)

ABOUT THE AUTHORS

Maria Bartlett has been the Spiritual Leader of St. James Prayer Group in Kinross for 31 years and has run countless retreats and workshops to lead people into a deeper relationship with God. She was one of the founding members of Healings Rooms in Kinross, Scotland. When asked to sum up life she said, 'Life is like a book, every day is a new page'.

Neil Dorward works as a Funeral Celebrant in Central Scotland and was a Catholic Priest for 11 years. He wrote a book on the subject of Civil Funerals called *The Guide to a Dead Brilliant Funeral Speech* and is the President of the Professional Speaking Association in Scotland. When asked to sum up life he said, 'Life is like me, short and sweet'.

NOTES

Notes

Made in the USA
Charleston, SC
09 December 2014

Contents

All things are possible until they are proved impossible –
and even the impossible may only be so, as of now.
Pearl Buck, A Bridge for Passing (1962)

About the authors

Vivian A Elwell MB BS, MRCS, BA (Hons), MA (Cantab)
Currently working as a Specialist Registrar in Neurosurgery, Vivian held posts in Accident and Emergency, Orthopaedics, Neurosurgery, and General Surgery with the Surgical Rotation at St Mary's Hospital, Imperial College NHS Trust, London.

Vivian is an author of undergraduate and post-graduate medical textbooks: *Essential OSCE Topics for Medical and Surgical Finals* (Radcliffe 2008), *The Insider's Guide to the MRCS Clinical Examination* (Radcliffe 2009), and *OSCEs for the MRCS Part B: A Bailey and Love Revision Guide* (Hodder Arnold 2009).

She taught clinical skills to medical students and doctors, and was an anatomy demonstrator at the Imperial College School of Medicine, London. She served on the Imperial College School of Medicine Curriculum Development Committee.

Vivian's awards include: the Swinford Edward Silver Medal Prize for her OSCE Examination, the Columbia University Research Fellowship at Columbia College of Physicians and Surgeons in New York City, the Columbia University King's Crown Gold and Silver Medal Awards, the Kathrine Dulin Folger Cancer Research Fellowship and the "Who's Who of Young Scientists Prize." In 2010, Vivian was a finalist for the BMA's Junior Doctor of the Year Award.

Vivian earned a Bachelor's Degree in Biological Sciences at Columbia College, Columbia University, and a MA from the University of Cambridge. She earned a Bachelor of Medicine and Bachelor of Surgery from the Imperial College School of Medicine. She is a member of the Royal College of Surgeons and is a College Instructor on the "Care of the Critically Ill Surgical Patient (CCrISP)" course.

Jonathan M Fishman BM BCh (Oxon), MRCS (Eng), DOHNS (RCS Eng), BA (Hons), MA (Cantab)
Jonathan is an Oxford Specialist Registrar in ENT and a member of the Royal College of Surgeons. He graduated with a First Class Honours Degree in Natural Sciences from Sidney Sussex College, University of Cambridge, and completed his clinical training at St John's College, University of Oxford. He has held posts in Accident and Emergency, ENT, General Surgery and Neurosurgery, as part of the surgical rotation at St Mary's Hospital, Imperial College, London.

Jonathan has extensive teaching experience and is the primary author of three undergraduate and three postgraduate medical textbooks, including the highly successful *History Taking in Medicine and Surgery* (Pastest Publishing, 2005; 2nd Edition, 2010). He spent part of his medical training at both Harvard University and the NASA Space Center.

Jonathan was awarded Taylor and Howard-Agg Scholarships at Sidney Sussex College, Cambridge, and has been awarded the highly prestigious title of 'Lifelong Honorary Scholar' by the University of Cambridge, for academic excellence. He has been awarded a fellowship from the British Association of Plastic Surgeons for research at NASA, and from Cambridge University for research at Harvard University.

Jonathan is committed to a career in academic ENT, with a strong emphasis on research and teaching. In 2009, he was awarded a Royal Society of Medicine GlaxoSmithKline Fellowship Award for his academic achievements to date. In 2010, he was awarded a Foreign and Commonwealth Office UK-USA Stem Cell Collaboration Fellowship, in addition to a Royal College of Surgeons of England Surgical Research Fellowship.

In 2011, he was awarded a prestigious Medical Research Council Clinical Research Training Fellowship.

Rajat Chowdhury BM BCh (Oxon), MRCS, BSc (Hons), MSc (Lond), MA (Oxon)

Rajat is a Specialist Registrar in Radiology and has held posts in Accident and Emergency, Orthopaedics & Trauma, Cardiothoracic Surgery, General Surgery, and Plastic Surgery with the Surgical Rotation at St Mary's Hospital, Imperial College NHS Trust, London. He completed his medical studies at Oxford University, May Clinic and Harvard University. He is a member of the Royal College of Surgeons.

He taught clinical skills to medical students and doctors in Oxford and London, and tutored Biochemistry and Genetics students at Oxford University. He was an anatomy demonstrator at the Imperial College School of Medicine, London, and was President of Oxford's Hugh Cairns Surgical Society. He is currently pursuing a Postgraduate Certificate in Medical Education.

Rajat's academic awards include: Oxford University's Bristol Myers Squibb Prize in Cardiology; The Radcliffe Infirmary Prize in Surgery; GlaxoSmithKline Medical Fellowship; the Warren Scholarship for Paediatric Studies at the University of Toronto; Exhibition and Kennedy scholarships to Harvard University. Rajat was also awarded Bachelors and Masters Degrees from University College London. In 2009, Rajat won the prestigious British Society of Interventional Radiology Specialist Registrar Prize. In 2010, he was elected to the chair of the National Trainee Committee of the British Institute of Radiology. Rajat has been awarded a NICE Scholarship and plans to become a future NHS leader. He is also the lead author of *Radiology at a Glance* (Wiley-Blackwell 2010) and *Consent in Surgery* (Radcliffe 2010).

Preface

This book has been written as an accompaniment to *Bailey and Love's Short Practice of Surgery* with the MRCS examination in mind. It is dedicated to the Intercollegiate MRCS Part A Examination, which is the first part of the Intercollegiate MRCS Examination. This new examination was introduced in the Autumn of 2008 and replaced the MRCS Parts 1 and 2 examinations, in line with the new pattern of surgical training in the UK. The examination syllabus, format and content are common to The Royal College of Surgeons of Edinburgh, The Royal College of Surgeons of England and The Royal College of Physicians and Surgeons of Glasgow. This examination is designed and set by the Royal Colleges of Surgeons to test the knowledge, skills and attributes acquired during core surgical training.

The Intercollegiate MRCS Part A examination comprises of two MCQ papers taken on the same day. Each paper is 2 hours in duration. The first paper covers 'Applied Basic Sciences' (single best answer (SBA) format) and the second paper covers 'Principles of Surgery-in-General' (extended matching questions (EMQ) format). A minimum mark must be obtained in both papers, in addition to attaining the total pass mark to obtain an overall pass in the Intercollegiate Part A Examination. Successful completion of the Intercollegiate Part A Examination qualifies the trainee surgeon to enter the Intercollegiate Part B Objective Structured Clinical Examination.

This book is based on our highly successful *Insider Medical MRCS Courses,* and the feedback obtained from candidates who sat the examination. We have, therefore, written this book with the aim of targeting high-yield topics that are likely to be faced and offer methods to tackle the challenges that may be posed in the examination. We have drawn from our breadth of experience of teaching at both the undergraduate and postgraduate levels and have identified common pitfalls.

A thorough understanding of applied basic science and the ability to problem-solve underpins surgical science and sets the foundation for future surgical practice. Whilst it is not feasible to cover the complete syllabus within the remit of this book, we have selected the most important and high-yield topics to facilitate examination study and revision. The style of questions mimics those found in the real examination and these will therefore serve well as mock papers. We are confident that this book will assist any trainee surgeon in their revision for the MRCS Part A Examination and, in doing so, refine their analytical approach to all areas of their surgical practice.

Vivian A Elwell
Jonathan M Fishman
Rajat Chowdhury

Acknowledgements

This book would not have been possible without the help, encouragement and ongoing support of the following individuals:

Mrs Carole D Elwell, Mr Nigel D Mendoza, Mr John A Cervieri Jr., Mrs Eva-Inge Cervieri, Dr George Leib, Mrs Ingrid Leib, Dr Sandra J Ginsberg, Dr Colette M Magnant, Dr Irene Gage, Dr David S Fishman, Mrs Wendy F Fishman, Miss Caroline Graham, Mrs Julia Sender, Dr Laura Fishman, Dr Madhuchanda Bhattacharyya, Miss Monika Chowdhury, Mrs Archana Chowdhury, Mr Ashit Chowdhury, Dr Stephen Harden and Dr Joanna Fairhurst.

Introduction: The Insider's Guide to the MRCS Part A

So you want to be a surgeon? Fantastic choice! The road to enlightenment begins with the first test – the *Intercollegiate MRCS Part A Examination*.

Studying for examinations is often not the most pleasant experience. However, this examination is not peppered with esoteric topics but ones that you will find genuinely useful in your daily practice, even at your junior stage.

The Part A examination consists of two MCQ papers of multiple-choice questions, each of two hours' duration taken on the same day. The papers cover generic surgical sciences and applied knowledge.

- Paper 1 covers **applied basic science** and consists of 135 single best answer questions (SBAs). Each question contains five possible answers, of which there is only one single best answer.
- Paper 2 covers **principles of surgery-in-general** and consists of 135 extended matching answer questions (EMQs). Each theme contains a variable number of options and clinical situations. Only one option, however, will be the most appropriate response to each clinical situation. It is possible for one option to be the answer to more than one of the clinical situations.

To achieve a 'pass', a minimum level of competence in each of the two papers will be required in addition to achieving or exceeding the pass mark set for the combined total mark for the whole of Part A. There are equal marks for each question and there is no negative marking. In other words, marks will not be deducted for a wrong answer.

Preparing for an examination is never straightforward and you are often faced with a vast range of revision sources, from traditional textbooks to scientific journals. The secret to passing any kind of MCQ exam is to practice as many questions as possible. Sitting in front of large textbooks will help to a degree, but it is important to get a feel for the type of questions that may appear in the exam and then to focus revision on reading around the questions. Inevitably, at some stage during the revision process you will want to test yourself on exam-style questions, so this book aims to fulfil that need. The questions are grouped into single best answers and extended matching questions as in the real examination, and the explanations have been divided into separate chapters so that you can attempt the questions under mock examination conditions, or use each question as a syllabus guide.

Most questions will require you to read a **clinical vignette** and will therefore test both your knowledge and correct application. There may be more than one answer that could fit each question, but there will always be one answer that is considered *the best answer*. Beware of absolute terms such as 'always' and 'never': these are rarely ever the best answer!

One of the first techniques in approaching these types of questions is to cover up the answers initially, read the question and suggest an answer. Then look for the answer in the options available. If the answer appears, you have a very high chance of being correct. You should check that the other answers are in fact incorrect, before selecting your final answer. If you are unable to answer the question initially, work your way down the list and start by eliminating those answers that you definitely feel are incorrect.

These new questions take time to read as they can be several lines long, so you must keep a careful eye on the time you spend on each. There is no obligation to answer the questions in the order they appear, but you must keep a close check on those that you wish to revisit later. If there are any questions you are unsure of, we recommend that you asterisk that particular question so that if you have time, you can come back to it at the end. If you run out of time, it is well worth guessing any answer for the outstanding questions – you have nothing to lose and may well get lucky.

Research has shown that changing your answer in the exam is neither good nor bad: if you have a good reason for changing your answer, then change it. It is a myth that people always change from 'right' to 'wrong', in that it is those questions that you will remember and review after the exam. You will not remember the questions you changed from wrong to right!

Although everyone may tell you before the exam **'read the question'**, it is imperative to do so in the MCQ exam. Underline the key words, and do not be caught out, as so often people are, when the question says which of the following is false as opposed to being true! When you have finished the exam, make a final check that you have answered **all** the questions.

Finally, remember that common things are common. The examination is testing your ability to diagnose and manage common and important conditions to be a safe and competent surgeon.

Turn your passion into perfection. Happy studying, and good luck!

Section 1
Applied Basic Sciences

Single best answer questions

1. **A 21-year-old footballer presents to A&E with a stabbing pain above his right knee joint. He states the pain came on suddenly while he was sprinting. On examination he is unable to extend the leg and he walks with a limp. There is suprapatellar swelling and an absent knee jerk. What is the likely diagnosis?**
   A Fracture of patella
   B Injury to posterior cruciate ligament
   C Tear of adductor magnus muscle
   D Tear of biceps femoris muscle
   E Tear of quadriceps tendon

2. **During strenuous exercise, what else occurs besides tachycardia?**
   A Rise in $Paco_2$
   B Increased stroke volume
   C Rise in mixed venous blood O_2 saturation
   D No change to blood pressure
   E Increased renal blood flow

3. **A patient is found to have thrombophlebitis migrans. What other condition must be considered?**
   A Venous insufficiency
   B Diabetes mellitus
   C Bronchial carcinoma
   D Lyme disease
   E Beckwith–Wiedemann syndrome

4. **A 42-year-old lady is involved in a road traffic accident. She presents with a dislocated shoulder. The shoulder is relocated by you in A&E but afterwards you notice there is winging of the scapula. Which nerve or muscle is likely to be damaged?**
   A Axillary nerve
   B Teres major
   C Radial nerve
   D Long thoracic nerve of Bell
   E Deltoid

5. **Which cells cannot regenerate?**
   A Peripheral nerve cells
   B Schwann cells
   C Renal tubular cells
   D Mucosal cells
   E Liver cells

6. **Which of the following is a feature of metastatic spread?**
   A Commonly occurs transluminally
   B Basal cell carcinomas commonly spread via lymphatics
   C Osteosarcomas commonly spread via lymphatics
   D Prostatic carcinoma commonly spreads via the blood
   E Spread follows the pattern of venous drainage

7. **A 35-year-old man is knocked off his cycle and hits his head on a kerb. He is brought into hospital with a fluctuating score on the Glasgow Coma Scale. He underwent a CT head scan which shows a biconvex-shaped haematoma. What other finding is he most likely to have?**
   A Midline shift
   B Subdural haemorrhage
   C Skull fracture
   D Subarachnoid haemorrhage
   E Papilloedema

8. **In wound healing, which cells are responsible for wound contraction?**
   A Fibroblasts
   B Macrophages
   C Reticulocytes
   D Giant cells
   E Lymphocytes

9. **Which is a feature of an adenoma?**
   - A Typically encapsulated
   - B Can arise in transitional epithelial cells
   - C Typically invades the basement membrane
   - D Typically annular lesions
   - E Does not contain dysplastic cells

10. **A singer complains of not being able to sing high notes following her thyroidectomy. What is the likely cause?**
   - A Damage to the recurrent laryngeal nerve
   - B Damage to the external laryngeal nerve
   - C Damage to the vagus nerve
   - D Tracheal stenosis
   - E Vocal cord hemiparalysis

11. **During fracture healing, what type of bone makes up the provisional callus?**
   - A Cortical bone
   - B Cancellous bone
   - C Cartilage
   - D Woven bone
   - E Lamellar bone

12. **Radiotherapy can be the sole treatment for which of the following cancers?**
   - A Adenocarcinoma of the oesophagus
   - B Rectal carcinoma
   - C Anal cancer
   - D Gastric carcinoma
   - E Phylloides breast tumour

13. **A woman has a pleomorphic adenoma. She is undergoing a total parotidectomy. Which important vascular structure should the surgeon be most aware of?**
   - A Facial artery
   - B Facial vein
   - C External carotid artery
   - D Retromandibular vein
   - E Internal jugular vein

14. **What is the cardiac index?**
   - A Stroke volume × heart rate
   - B Mean arterial pressure × systemic vascular resistance
   - C Cardiac output divided by body weight
   - D Cardiac output divided by heart rate
   - E Cardiac output divided by body surface area

15. **A patient is known to have exposure to beta-naphthylamine. What is he/she at increased risk of developing?**
   - A Small-cell lung carcinoma
   - B Bladder cancer
   - C Breast cancer
   - D Chemical pneumonitis
   - E Lymphoma

16. **A 70-year-old man suffers an ischaemic stroke and develops a left homonymous hemianopia. Where is the likely infarct?**
   - A Left frontal lobe
   - B Right frontal lobe
   - C Left occipital lobe
   - D Right occipital lobe
   - E Left temporal lobe

17. **When does the heart rate decrease?**
   - A After a meal
   - B On inspiration
   - C Pressure on the eyeball
   - D Pressure on the sinoatrial node
   - E Exercise

18. **Which of the following suggests that respiratory failure is chronic rather than acute?**
   - A Plasma bicarbonate of 39 mmol/L
   - B Pao_2 of 9 kPa
   - C Pao_2 of 7 kPa
   - D Arterial pH of 7.2
   - E Hypoventilation

19. **A 12-year-old boy develops acute tonsillitis. He starts to complain of pain in the ear. What nerve is likely to be involved?**
   - A Superior laryngeal
   - B Glossopharyngeal
   - C Facial
   - D Hypoglossal
   - E Lesser palatine

20. **A man undergoes an open inguinal hernia repair. During the procedure the spermatic cord is visualized. What structures does this contain?**
   - A Dartos muscle
   - B Femoral branch of the genitofemoral nerve
   - C Ilioinguinal nerve
   - D Inferior epigastric artery
   - E Pampiniform plexus

21. **When performing a left nephrectomy from a posterior approach, which of the following structures are encountered before reaching the kidney?**
A Peritoneum
B Suprarenal gland
C Subcostal nerve
D Tail of pancreas
E Right hemidiaphragm

22. **When performing a right hemicolectomy, which of the following structures is encountered during dissection?**
A Caudate lobe of liver
B Inferior vena cava
C Third part of duodenum
D Right ureter
E First part of duodenum

23. **What structure does the pancreas overly?**
A Right kidney
B Left kidney
C Right adrenal gland
D Left adrenal gland
E Gall bladder

24. **What causes a reduction in pulmonary functional residual capacity?**
A Asthma
B Pulmonary fibrosis
C Emphysema
D Pneumonia
E Pulmonary oedema

25. **Which is a feature of the physiology of angiotensin II?**
A Stimulates renin release
B Inhibits aldosterone release
C Weak arteriolar vasoconstriction
D Converted from angiotensin I in the liver
E Released in hypovolaemia

26. **Which displaces the oxygen–haemoglobin curve to the left?**
A A decrease in pH
B Anaemia
C A rise in Pco_2
D A fall in Pco_2
E Pyrexia

27. **What factor decreases coronary perfusion?**
A Hypoxia
B Antidiuretic hormone (ADH)
C Alpha stimulation
D Beta stimulation
E Glyceryl trinitrate (GTN) spray

28. **Resection of the terminal ileum is associated with malabsorption of which of the following substances?**
A Calcium
B Folic acid
C Cholesterol
D Bile salts
E Potassium

29. **Which is a feature of the action of insulin?**
A Promotes protein synthesis
B Promotes gluconeogenesis
C Inhibits potassium entry into cells
D Promotes calcium release from bone
E Promotes phosphate release from bone

30. **Which causes prolonged vomiting due to pyloric stenosis?**
A A drop in serum urea
B A drop in bicarbonate
C A rise in serum potassium
D A rise in serum chloride
E A rise in arterial Pco_2

31. **Extracellular fluid differs from intracellular fluid by which of the following?**
A Lower chloride concentration
B Higher potassium concentration
C Greater volume
D Lower protein concentration
E Lower pH

32. **Which is a feature of raised intracranial pressure?**
A Caused by shearing injury to the scalp
B Occurs immediately after an acute subdural haematoma
C Leads to a rise in cerebral perfusion pressure
D Causes constriction of the ipsilateral pupil
E Can lead to a rise in blood pressure and bradycardia

33. **Which is a feature of metabolic acidosis?**
A There is negative base excess
B Bicarbonate is the main intracellular buffer
C Proteins and phosphates are the main extracellular buffer
D Compensation occurs by a decrease in alveolar ventilation
E Bicarbonate infusion is the mainstay of treatment

34. Which is a feature of the posterior third of the tongue?
- A Filiform papillae
- B Fungiform papillae
- C Sensory innervations from the internal laryngeal nerve
- D Sensory innervations from the chordae tympani
- E Villiform papillae

35. Which is a feature of the knee joint?
- A The popliteus tendon is extracapsular
- B The suprapatellar bursa does not communicate with the joint
- C The anterior cruciate ligament is supplied by the middle geniculate artery
- D The iliotibial tract inserts into the fibula
- E Rotation occurs above the meniscus

36. Which is a feature of the hepatic artery?
- A Supplies the same amount of blood to the liver as the portal vein
- B Provides the same amount of oxygen to the liver as the portal vein
- C Contains blood with the same oxygenation as the portal vein
- D Does not supply blood to hepatic metastases
- E Divides the liver into anatomical segments

37. Metabolic alkalosis is commonly seen in patients with which of the following?
- A Pancreatic fistula
- B Aspirin poisoning
- C Protracted vomiting
- D Hypoglycaemia
- E Hyperventilation

38. Osteomyelitis is most commonly caused by which microbe in adults?
- A *Staphylococcus aureus*
- B *Escherichia coli*
- C *Staphylococcus epidermidis*
- D *Pseudomonas* sp.
- E *Streptococcus viridans*

39. Which is a feature of a keloid scar?
- A May respond to pressure dressing
- B Occurs within the limits of the surgical wound
- C Is most common on flexure surfaces of the limbs
- D Can be prevented by subcuticular sutures
- E May be re-excised with good results

40. Splenectomy patients are at particular risk of overwhelming sepsis from which organisms?
- A Anaerobic bacteria
- B *Bacteroides fragilis*
- C *Haemophilus influenzae*
- D Fungi
- E *Staphylococcus aureus*

41. A boy is found to have haemophilia B. What pathological problem does he have?
- A Deficiency of platelets
- B Deficiency of factor VIII
- C Deficiency of factor IX
- D Deficiency of factor X
- E Deficiency of factor XI

42. A patient is found to have chronic iron deficiency anaemia. What symptom might he also describe?
- A Dysphagia
- B Vomiting
- C Diarrhoea
- D Dysuria
- E Nausea

43. What features would you expect to find in a patient with haemorrhagic shock?
- A Decrease in catecholamine secretion
- B Oxygen–haemoglobin dissociation curve shifted to the right
- C Stimulation of aortic chemoreceptors
- D Increase in tidal ventilation
- E Decrease in antidiuretic hormone (ADH) secretion

44. Gastrointestinal consequences of major burns include which of the following?
- A Splanchnic vasodilation
- B Acute gastric dilatation
- C Cushing's ulcers
- D Terminal ileal hyperplasia
- E Mechanical bowel obstruction

45. When is nitrogen balance positive?
- A In sepsis
- B During the first 3 days following surgery
- C During growth
- D While adrenocorticotropic hormone (ACTH) levels are high
- E Following bone fractures

46. **Hormones of the anterior pituitary include which of the following?**
A Prolactin
B Oxytocin
C Thyroxin
D Antidiuretic hormone (ADH)
E Vasopressin

47. **Which is a feature of the scalenus anterior muscle?**
A Attaches into the anterior tubercles of the transverse processes of C1–C7 vertebrae
B Attaches to the scalene tubercle of the 2nd rib
C Has the subclavian vein passing posterior to it
D Has the subclavian artery passing anterior to it
E Lies deep to the prevertebral layer of the deep cervical fascia

48. **What is the normal glomerular filtration rate?**
A 50 mL/min
B 75 mL/min
C 100 mL/min
D 125 mL/min
E 150 mL/min

49. **What is the commonest cancer in the UK?**
A Colorectal cancer
B Lung cancer
C Breast cancer
D Melanoma
E Leukaemia

50. **What is the 5-year survival rate of carcinoma of the pancreas?**
A 5 per cent
B 15 per cent
C 30 per cent
D 50 per cent
E 60 per cent

51. **Regarding enteral tube feeding, which statement is true?**
A Requires just as much monitoring as parental feeding
B Continuous feeding with iso-osmolar fluids may cause diarrhoea
C Elemental fluids require minimal digestion by the patient
D Maintains the structural, but not the functional, integrity of the small bowel
E Fluids should contain glucose rather than sucrose to lower the osmolality

52. **Which statement applies to the original Dukes' classification for colorectal carcinoma?**
A Is a tumour grading scale
B Accurately defines the number of lymph nodes involved
C Distinguishes tumours that penetrate the muscularis mucosa from those that are confined by the mucosa
D Does not take into account the presence of metastases
E Highlights the improved prognosis in those patients with villous rather than tubular carcinoma

53. **In acute osteomyelitis of a long bone, which statement applies?**
A If blood-borne, is usually caused by streptococci
B Acute inflammation causes a rise in intraosseous pressure
C The involucrum is a focus of dead bone
D Early radiographs will demonstrate rarefaction and periosteal new bone formation
E *Pseudomonas* tends to occur in patients with sickle cell disease

54. **In intestinal anastomatic leaks, which statement applies?**
A Are apparent 10–14 days after surgery
B Abdominal pain, pyrexia and tachycardia are suggestive of a leak
C The appearance of bowel contents through the abdominal wound is proof of an anastomatic leak
D Early leaks are best tested by local surgical repair
E Late leaks are treated by urgent laparotomy, abdominal washout and repair

55. **Which of the following chemotherapeutic drugs is an alkylating agent?**
A Cyclophosphamide
B Doxorubicin (Adriamycin)
C 5-Fluorouracil (5-FU)
D Vincristine
E 6-Mercaptopurine

56. **Which statement applies to metastatic calcification?**
    A Occurs in normal tissue
    B Is characterized by psammoma bodies
    C Has normal blood levels of calcium
    D Characteristically occurs in osteoarthritis
    E Is associated with degenerated foci in leiomyomas and has caseous nodules

57. **Complications of an above-knee amputation include which of the following?**
    A Joint contractures affecting the hip joint
    B Sudek's atrophy
    C Myoglobinuria
    D Neuroma formation
    E Amyloid deposition

58. **Which statement applies to the cephalic vein?**
    A Begins in the region of the anatomical snuffbox
    B At the elbow is deep to the lateral cutaneous nerve of the forearm
    C Ends by joining the brachial vein
    D Is medial to the biceps muscle in the arm
    E Has no valves

59. **Thyrotoxicosis is characterized by which of the following?**
    A Weight gain
    B Proximal myopathy
    C Enopthalmos
    D Hypertrophy of the vascular elastic lamina
    E Nose bleeds

60. **Which is a product of occlusion of the right posterior cerebral artery?**
    A Blindness in the right eye
    B Left homonymous hemianopia
    C Bilateral hemianopia
    D An absent light reflex
    E Extraocular muscle paralysis

61. **The adductor (subsartorial) canal contains which of the following?**
    A Vastus lateralis muscle in its lateral aspect
    B Profunda femoris vessels
    C Femoral arterial branch, which takes part in the anastomosis around the knee joint
    D Vastus medialis muscle
    E Adductor longus muscle

62. **Which is a feature of a cervical rib?**
    A A cause of brachial artery aneurysm
    B Best diagnosed by posteroanterior (PA) chest radiograph
    C Compresses the upper trunk of the brachial plexus
    D A cause of thoracic outlet syndrome
    E Most commonly symptomatic in the 50–60 years age group

63. **Which statement applies to a 5 cm abdominal aortic aneurysm?**
    A Has an annual risk of rupture of 80 per cent
    B Involves the renal artery origin in 15 per cent of cases
    C If the aortic aneursym grows at a rate of more than 5 mm/year, elective surgery should be considered
    D Is more common in builders
    E Is a cause of toe gangrene

64. **Which statement applies to the hepatic portal vein?**
    A Is formed by the union of the splenic and superior mesenteric veins
    B Runs behind the epiploic foramen
    C Lies anterior to the common hepatic artery
    D Originates behind the body of the pancreas
    E Approximately 25 per cent of hepatic blood flow is derived from the hepatic portal vein

65. **Which statement applies to chronic lower limb ulceration?**
    A Affects 10 per cent of the elderly population
    B Is most commonly caused by arterial disease
    C Is linked to varices
    D Predisposes to malignant change
    E Should be treated by compression bandaging if the ankle–brachial pressure index (ABPI) is less than 0.5

66. **Which statement applies to lymphoedema?**
    A Affects the lower limbs in 80 per cent of cases
    B Presents with bilateral limb swelling
    C Is diagnosed by ultrasound

D Is most commonly iatrogenic in aetiology
E Is best treated by graded compression stockings

67. **Which statement regarding Hodgkin's disease is true?**
A Typically seen in the gastrointestinal tract
B May be classified using the Rappaport classification
C Is characterized by Reed–Sternberg cells
D The lymphocyte-depleted type is associated with a more favourable prognosis
E Usually presents with painful lymphadenopathy

68. **What is supplied by the facial nerve?**
A Palatoglossus muscle
B Medial pterygoid muscle
C Masseter muscle
D Temporalis
E Parasympathetic fibres to the submandibular gland

69. **Which is a feature of the submandibular duct?**
A Lies between mylohyoid and hyoglossus muscle
B Is 10 cm long
C Develops from the endoderm
D Is closely related to the facial nerve
E Opens into the mouth at the side of the cheek

70. **Which is a feature of the Eustachian tube in a child?**
A Extends from the middle ear to the oropharynx
B Is at more of a horizontal angle than in an adult
C Is longer in length than in an adult
D Is cartilagenous
E Is derived from the second pharyngeal pouch

71. **In intussusception in children, which statement applies?**
A Occurs more commonly in girls
B The commonest form is ileo-ileal
C Is characterized by severe colicky abdominal pain with pain-free intervals
D There is an association with Henoch–Schönlein purpura
E Usually occurs in the 2–3 years age group

72. **Which statement is true of Sjögren's syndrome?**
A Is a condition in which the patient has wet eyes and mouth
B Is most commonly seen in young men
C Is characterized by beta-pleated sheets
D Is associated with autoimmune diseases
E Predisposes to adenocarcinoma

73. **Which applies to rigid sigmoidoscopy?**
A Is useful in the examination of haemorrhoids
B Will usually demonstrate the first 25 cm of sigmoid colon
C Allows the biopsy of rectal tumours without anaesthetic
D Is the best way of obtaining tissue to diagnose Hirschsprung's disease
E Causes perforation in about 5 per cent of patients

74. **Which of the following is associated with hyperparathyroidism?**
A Paravertebral ossification
B Peptic ulcer
C Retinal haemorrhages
D Aortic stenosis
E Hoarse voice

75. **Which statement applies to the posterior triangle of the neck?**
A Is bounded by the lateral third of the clavicle inferiorly
B Has a roof formed by the prevertebral fascia
C Has a roof pierced by the external jugular vein
D Is bounded by the anterior border of sternocleidomastoid
E Contains the carotid sheath

76. **Which statement applies to the tongue?**
A Develops from the first and third branchial arches
B Has taste buds supplied by the hypoglossal nerve
C Is supplied by the facial artery
D Has a profuse anastomosis of blood vessels across the midline
E Deviates to the left in lesions of the left glossopharyngeal nerve

77. Which statement is true of postcricoid carcinoma?

A Is more common in patients with Plummer–Vinson syndrome
B Is highly radiosensitive
C Is associated with workers exposed to iron
D Has a 5-year survival rate of more than 60 per cent
E Is more common in males

78. In a 65-year-old women with a retrosternal goitre discovered on a routine chest X-ray, which of the following statements is appropriate?

A Thyroid dysfunction is unlikely
B Stridor is likely if the trachea is deviated to one side
C Thyroid antibodies will be present
D Thyroid malignancy is common
E Recurrent laryngeal nerve palsy is common

79. Which of the following statements is true of salivary gland carcinoma?

A Typically occurs in the minor salivary glands
B Is related to smoking
C Occurring in the parotid gland results in Frey's syndrome
D In the parotid gland can be reliably diagnosed by fine-needle aspiration
E Is characteristically sensitive to radiotherapy

80. Which of the following statements is true of Colles' fracture?

A Is a cause of carpal tunnel syndrome
B Results in palmar displacement of the distal fractured fragment
C Extends into the wrist (radiocarpal) joint
D Is typically associated with compression of the ulnar nerve
E Involves the ulnar styloid process

81. When a person lifts his right leg and stands unaided with only his left foot on the ground, the iliac crest on the right side does not descend (negative Trendelenburg sign) provided that one of the following applies. Which?

A The right gluteus medius muscle is actively contracted
B The left hip joint is not congenitally dislocated
C The right superior gluteal nerve is intact
D The left psoas muscle is actively contracted
E The neck of the right femur is not been shortened by a healed fracture

82. Which of the following describes laminar flow in a blood vessel?

A Has maximum velocity in the centre
B Is a flow regime characterized by low momentum diffusion and high momentum convection
C Produces the highest concentration of cells at the periphery of the vessel
D Reynolds numbers of greater than 2300 are generally considered to be of a laminar type
E Is considered to be 'rough' whereas turbulent flow is considered to be 'smooth'

83. The clinical features of a lumbar disc prolapse affecting root S1 may include which of the following?

A Paraesthesia on the medial aspect of the foot
B A positive femoral stretch
C Weakness and wasting of the muscles that dorsiflex the foot
D Limitation of straight-leg raising
E An impaired knee jerk

84. Which is true of umbilical hernias in children?

A Are a rare problem (1 in 10 000)
B Are commonly associated with incarceration of the bowel
C Are most commonly found in Caucasian children
D Are typically associated with a patent vitello-intestinal duct
E Have small orifices and characteristically close spontaneously before the age of 5 years

85. A patient is suspected of having a haemolytic transfusion reaction. How should the patient best be managed?

A Removal of inessential foreign body irritants (nasogastric tube, Foley's catheter)
B Fluid restriction

C 0.1 M HCl infusion
D Steroids
E Fluids and mannitol

86. **Which of the following statements concerning access to the abdomen is true?**
A Muscle-splitting incisions are more painful than cutting incisions
B Failure to close the peritoneum increases the incidence of adhesions
C Collagenase dissolves sutures near wound edges
D The Veress needle in laparoscopic surgery is inserted under direct vision
E Burst abdomen is preceded by serosanguinous discharge

87. **Which of the following is true of pseudomembranous colitis?**
A Does not cause colonic bleeding
B Is caused by *Clostridium perfringes*
C Is the result of metronidazole administration
D Is a cause of toxic dilation of the stomach
E Responds to treatment with vancomycin

88. **The diagnosis of acute cholecystitis can be reliably confirmed by which of the following?**
A Ultrasound
B Plain radiograph
C Abdominal radiograph
D Oral cholecystography
E Liver function tests

89. **According to the modified Glasgow scoring system, indices of poor prognosis in severe pancreatitis at 48 hours include which of the following?**
A Albumin of 30 g/L
B Urea of 10 mmol/L
C Corrected serum calcium of 2.98 mmol/L
D Arterial Po_2 of 10 kPa
E Blood glucose of 6 mmol/L

90. **Which statement is true of the rectum?**
A Has a venous drainage into the superior mesenteric vein
B Has a lymphatic drainage to the superficial inguinal nodes
C Is supplied by the superior mesenteric ganglia
D Is anteriorly bounded by the seminal vesicles and prostate
E Receives its main arterial blood supply from the middle rectal artery

91. **What is a characteristic feature of the liver?**
A It weighs 750 g
B It receives 60 per cent of the body's total cardiac output
C It drains through hepatic veins into the superior vena cava
D It receives its nerve supply from the right vagus via the superior mesenteric ganglia
E It is attached to the diaphragm by the falciform ligament

92. **Which statement regarding choledochal cysts is true?**
A Rarely present beyond childhood
B Iron deficiency may develop
C Dumping syndrome may develop
D Incapacitating diarrhoea is not infrequent
E Recurrent duodenal ulcers usually follow an aggressive course

93. **Which of the following is true of talipes equinovarus?**
A Is a structural deformity of the midfoot and forefoot
B Is bilateral in fewer than 10 per cent of cases
C Is more common in females
D Is initially treated by correction of the equines deformity first
E Is treated by operative correction and may result in articular damage and foot stiffness

94. **Concerning bone tumours, which is true?**
A There is an association between osteosarcoma and Paget's disease of the bone
B Chondosarcomas most commonly occur in young children
C Chemotherapy has a limited role in overall management
D Metastasis usually occurs via lymphatics
E Pain is rarely a presenting feature

95. **The posterior relations of the kidney include which structure?**
A Rectus abdominis muscle

B Femoral nerve
C Long thoracic nerve of Bell
D Costodiaphragmatic recess of the pleura
E Lumbar sympathetic trunk

96. Which statement is true of Meckel's diverticulum?
A Is present in 20 per cent of the population
B Arises from the mesenteric border of the jejunum
C May contain heterotropic pancreas
D Is present only in males
E Is a diverticulum of the bladder

97. Which of the following is a recognized curative treatment option for localized carcinoma of the prostate?
A Radiotherapy
B Lithotripsy
C Hormonal treatment
D Cytotoxic therapy
E Tamsulosin

98. Which of the following statements is true for a patient who has been maintained on haemodialysis for 10 years?
A Will need a parathyroidectomy shortly after renal transplant
B Will have vascular calcification, which will resolve after parathyroidectomy
C Is no more likely to have secondary hyperparathyroidism than someone on continuous ambulatory peritoneal dialysis (CAPD) for the same period
D Could have osteoporosis if has taken aluminium hydroxide over this time
E Will need bisphosphonates after parathyroidectomy

99. In relation to breast carcinoma, which statement is true?
A Will affect 1 in 15 women
B Is more common in multiparous women
C Is more common in women with late menarche
D Is more common in women who breast-feed
E Has a 60 per cent chance of occurring in patients with a first-degree relative who had a premenopausal breast cancer

100. Concerning statistical analysis of a population with a normal (Gaussian) distribution, which is true?
A The population may be uniquely defined by its mean and its median values
B About 95 per cent of the population lies within one standard deviation of the mean
C It would be inappropriate to apply a chi-squared test because the distribution is not linear
D Non-parametric tests could be used
E Fewer than 5 out of 1000 of the population would be expected to be more than two standard deviations from the mode

101. Which of the following cells secrete intrinsic factor?
A Goblet cells
B Kupffer cells
C Peptic cells
D Chief (zymogenic) cells
E Parietal cells

102. Splenectomy increases susceptibility to which of the following organisms?
A *Streptococcus pyogenes*
B *Schistosoma haematobium*
C *Bacteroides fragilis*
D *Neisseria meningitidis*
E *Staphylococcus aureus*

103. Cardiac output is decreased under what circumstances?
A During stimulation of sympathetic nerves to the heart
B On cutting the vagus nerves to the heart
C By increasing the end-diastolic volume of the heart
D As a result of decreased pressure within the carotid sinus
E Upon assuming the upright position

104. Which statement is true for flow through a vessel or lumen?
A It is inversely proportional to the pressure head of flow
B It is inversely proportional to the radius
C It is directly proportional to the length of the tube
D It is directly proportional to the viscosity of blood passing through the tube
E It is directly proportional to the fourth power of the radius

105. **You request preoperative lung function tests on a patient with longstanding emphysema. What is true of the functional residual capacity?**
   A It is the sum of the tidal volume and residual volume
   B It is the sum of the inspiratory reserve volume, the expiratory reserve volume and the tidal volume
   C It can be measured directly by spirometry
   D It is the sum of the residual volume and the expiratory reserve volume
   E It is the volume of air that remains in the lung after forced expiration

106. **Which statement is true of lung compliance?**
   A Is defined as the change in pressure per unit volume
   B Is synonymous with elastance
   C Is increased in emphysema
   D Is equal in inflation and deflation
   E Is reduced by the presence of surfactant

107. **Which of the following hormones is secreted by the anterior pituitary gland?**
   A Testosterone
   B Oxytocin
   C Thyroid-stimulating hormone (TSH)
   D Corticotropin-releasing hormone (CRH)
   E Antidiuretic hormone (ADH)

108. **The oxygen–haemoglobin dissociation curve is shifted to the left by what?**
   A An increase in Pco_2
   B A fall in pH
   C A rise in temperature
   D An increase in 2,3-DPG
   E Fetal haemoglobin

109. **Which of the following cells are cytotoxic?**
   A CD4 T-cells
   B CD8 T-cells
   C B-cells
   D TH1 cells
   E TH2 cells

110. **A 3-week-old baby exhibits projectile vomiting shortly after feeding, and failure to thrive. On examination, an olive-shaped mass is palpable in the right upper quadrant of the abdomen. A clinical diagnosis of pyloric stenosis is made. What biochemical laboratory features would support the diagnosis?**
   A Hypokalaemia, metabolic alkalosis, low urinary pH
   B Hyperkalaemia, metabolic acidosis, high urinary pH
   C Hypokalaemia, metabolic acidosis, high urinary pH
   D Hyperkalaemia, metabolic alkalosis, low urinary pH
   E Hypokalaemia, metabolic alkalosis, high urinary pH

111. **A sample of cerebrospinal fluid (CSF) is obtained following a lumbar puncture. What is a feature of normal CSF?**
   A Is produced within arachnoid granulations
   B Has a composition identical to that of plasma
   C Has a protein content that is 0.5 per cent that of plasma
   D Has a higher potassium content than that of plasma
   E Its pH is heavily buffered

112. **A patient on the surgical ward has chronic renal impairment. The plasma creatinine is 225 μmol/L and the glomerular filtration rate (GFR) is 25 mL/min. Which statement is correct regarding the patient's renal function?**
   A The GFR is the main factor determining the rate of urine production
   B GFR can be measured by para-aminohippuric acid (PAH)
   C The normal GFR is 50 mL/min
   D Inulin clearance can be used to estimate GFR
   E A normal plasma creatinine implies normal renal function

113. **Gastric acid secretion is stimulated by which of the following?**
   A Somatostatin
   B Gastrin
   C Secretin
   D The glossopharyngeal nerve
   E Cholecystokinin

114. **Carbon dioxide is principally transported in the blood in which form?**
   A CO_2 physically dissolved in solution
   B Carboxyhaemoglobin

C Bicarbonate
D Carbaminohaemoglobin
E Carbonic anhydrase

115. The plateau phase of the cardiac action potential is due to what?
A Magnesium influx
B Potassium influx
C Calcium influx
D Chloride efflux
E Sodium influx

116. A patient with a 6 cm abdominal aortic aneurysm is scheduled for elective repair. As part of the preoperative work-up, an echocardiogram is requested. The ejection fraction is defined as what?
A The ratio of end-diastolic volume to stroke volume
B The ratio of stroke volume to end-diastolic volume
C End-diastolic volume minus end-systolic volume
D End-systolic volume divided by stroke volume
E The ratio of stroke volume to end-systolic volume

117. Bile salt reuptake principally occurs where?
A In the duodenum
B In the jejenum
C In the ileum
D In the colon
E In the caecum

118. A 40-year-old patient is brought into the A&E unit with head injury. The cardiovascular effects of raised intracranial pressure include (BP = blood pressure; HR = heart rate; CPP = cerebral perfusion pressure):
A ↓ BP, ↓ HR, ↓ CPP
B ↓ BP, ↑ HR, ↓ CPP
C ↑ BP, ↑ HR, ↓ CPP
D ↑ BP, ↓ HR, ↓ CPP
E ↓ BP, ↑ HR, ↑ CPP

119. A patient is diagnosed with Conn's syndrome. Aldosterone is secreted from where?
A Liver
B Zona glomerulosa of the adrenal cortex
C Juxtaglomerular apparatus
D Adrenal medulla
E Zona fasciculata of the adrenal cortex

120. Which of the following gastrointestinal fluids is richest in potassium?
A Salivary
B Pancreatic
C Gastric
D Bile
E Small bowel

121. Which one of the following is the most potent inhibitor of gastric acid secretion?
A Chlorphenamine
B Misoprostol
C Ranitidine
D Omeprazole
E Gaviscon®

122. The following changes occur at birth:
A The left umbilical vein becomes the ligamentum venosum
B The urachus becomes the medial umbilical ligament
C The ligamentum arteriosum is a remnant of the umbilical arteries
D The foramen ovale closes in all cases at birth
E The vitellointestinal duct may persist as a Meckel's diverticulum

123. With regard to phototransduction:
A Photoreceptors depolarize in response to light exposure
B It is a vitamin D-dependent process
C Upon exposure to light, cGMP levels within the photoreceptor fall
D Opening of cGMP-gated cation channels occurs in response to light
E Light photons are absorbed by transducin

124. Which of the following is a feature of the adaptive (acquired) immune response?
A Acute inflammation
B Secretion of tears
C Natural killer cells
D Surface epithelia
E Self/non-self discrimination

125. **With regard to the thyroid gland, which of the following is true?**
A Tri-iodothyronine is the principal hormone of the gland
B Calcitonin is produced by follicular cells
C Organification involves the binding of tetra-iodothyronine to amino acids
D It is stimulated to produce thyroxine (T4) by TRH
E Thyroglobulin is stored in the colloid of follicles

126. **Which one of the following is a depolarizing neuromuscular blocker?**
A Atracurium
B Atropine
C Guanethidine
D Suxamethonium
E Neostigmine

127. **With regard to genital development:**
A The mesonephric (Wolffian) ducts differentiate into the female genitalia
B Female development is hormonally regulated through the actions of anti-Mullerian hormone and testosterone
C Gender is principally determined by the presence or absence of two X chromosomes
D Anti-Mullerian hormone is secreted by Leydig cells
E The testes and ovaries descend from their original position at the 10th thoracic level

128. **With regard to visual field pathways:**
A The axons contained within the optic nerve are derived from photoreceptors
B The optic tracts synapse in the medial geniculate nucleus of the thalamus
C Decussation is complete at the optic chiasm
D The macula region is grossly over-represented in the visual cortex
E Compression at the optic chiasm results in a homonymous hemianopia

129. **With regard to neutrophils (polymorphonuclear leucocytes):**
A They are the predominant cell type in chronic inflammation
B They have bilobed nuclei
C They have a life-span of only a few hours in inflamed tissue
D They may fuse to form multinucleate giant cells
E They carry out oxygen-dependent microbial killing by lysosomal enzymes

130. **Which one of the following regarding myoglobin in skeletal muscle is correct?**
A It binds and stores oxygen for rapid release during falling Po_2
B It contains a magnesium cofactor
C It releases oxygen at high Po_2
D It exhibits cooperative binding with O_2 (sigmoid dissociation curve)
E It is devoid of iron

131. **The following are classes of antihypertensive agents, *except*:**
A ACE inhibitors
B Beta-blockers
C Alpha-blockers
D Angiotensin II receptor antagonists
E Calcium-channel agonists

132. **With regard to development of the limbs:**
A Occurs in the second trimester of pregnancy
B Shaping of the hands and feet is brought about through apoptosis
C Is independent of the apical ectodermal ridge
D Thalidomide most commonly causes clinodactyly
E Under some circumstances limb regeneration occurs to a small degree in adult humans following amputation

133. **With regard to the organization of the cerebral cortex:**
A The right cerebral hemisphere is normally dominant
B The primary visual cortex is located within Brodmann area 17
C The primary auditory cortex is located within Broca's area
D The primary motor cortex is located within the post-central gyrus
E The primary somatosensory cortex is located within the pre-central gyrus

134. **The germinal centre of a lymph node:**
A Contains mainly T-lymphocytes

B Contains Langerhans dendritic cells
C Generates immunoglobulin-producing plasma cells
D Is characteristically enlarged in established infectious mononucleosis
E Contains the cords and sinuses

135. All eukaryotic cells have membrane-bound organelles. Which one of the following organelles is self-replicating?
A Golgi body
B Ribosome
C Rough endoplasmic reticulum
D Mitochondria
E Lysosome

136. With regard to antidiabetic agents, which drug stimulates release of insulin from the pancreas?
A Actrapid
B Gliclazide
C Metformin
D Rosiglitazone
E Acarbose

137. With regard to development of the kidney:
A It is derived from endoderm
B The transcription factor WT-1 is necessary for the competence of the mesenchyme to be induced
C There are two phases of kidney development
D The kidneys descend during development to their final site
E The metanephric blastema gives rise to the collecting ducts

138. With regard to cerebrospinal fluid (CSF):
A It is produced by arachnoid granulations
B It is produced at a rate of 30 mL/min
C It is situated within the subdural space
D It flows between the lateral ventricles and third ventricle via the Foramen of Magendie
E It turns over approximately 4–5 times daily

139. With regard to antibodies (immunoglobulins):
A They are produced by mast cells
B The antigen binding region is located in the constant region
C Antibody class is defined by the structure of the light chain
D Diversity is partly achieved through somatic hypermutation
E They are composed of one heavy chain and two light chains

140. A patient is diagnosed as having iron deficiency anaemia. Which of the following is the peripheral blood film likely to show?
A Macrocytic anaemia
B Microcytic anaemia
C Ring sideroblasts
D Sickle-shaped cells
E Howell–Jolly bodies

141. Which one of the following diuretics acts mainly on the distal convoluted tubule to decrease water reabsorption?
A Furosemide
B Acetazolamide
C Bendroflumethiazide
D Metolazone
E Vasopressin

142. With regard to diaphragmatic development:
A Is formed by the fusion of two separate elements
B Develops in the thoracic region
C The left pleuroperitoneal canal is larger and closes later than the right
D The central tendon arises from the pleuroperitoneal membranes
E The septum transversum migrates cranially (rostrally) in development

143. With regard to cerebrospinal fluid (CSF) composition:
A CSF is produced through a passive process
B The composition of CSF is identical to that of plasma
C The protein content of CSF is 0.5 per cent that of plasma
D The potassium content of CSF is higher than that of plasma
E The pH of CSF is heavily buffered

144. With regard to IgM antibodies:
A They cross the placenta

B They are characteristically produced in a secondary immune response
C They can activate complement
D They are usually found lining mucosal surfaces
E They are usually monomeric

145. Epinephrine is an endogenous catecholamine. Its effects include which one of the following?

A Decreased glucagon secretion by pancreatic alpha cells
B An effect mainly on alpha-adrenoceptors
C Increased glycogen synthesis in liver
D Increased glycogen synthesis in muscles
E Increased lipolysis

146. Which antibiotic acts by inhibiting protein synthesis?

A Penicillin
B Erythromycin
C Cefuroxime
D Trimethoprim
E Co-trimoxazole

147. With regard to craniofacial development:

A The human face forms from the fusion of four swellings
B Alcohol is the most common cause of holoprosencephaly
C The palate forms from the medial extensions of the mandibular swellings
D Craniofacial abnormalities account for 5 per cent of all human congenital defects
E The nasolacrimal groove forms between the medial and lateral nasal processes

148. The speed of nerve conduction decreases with:

A Increasing axonal diameter
B Increasing membrane capacitance
C Decreasing axonal resistance
D Myelination by Schwann cells
E Increasing temperature

149. The human major histocompatibility complex (MHC):

A Resides on chromosome 11
B Is composed of six human leukocyte antigen (HLA) genes
C Codes for three classes of antigens
D Will be identical in dizygotic twins
E Codes for blood group antigens

150. Which one of the following statements regarding von Willebrand's disease is true?

A It commonly exhibits an autosomal dominant pattern of inheritance
B It presents with reduced bleeding times
C It always has associated reduced factor VIII levels
D It is associated with reduced or abnormal platelets
E It is X-linked recessive

151. Which one of the following lipid-lowering agents acts by inhibiting HMG CoA reductase?

A Nicotinic acid
B Bezafibrate
C Colestyramine
D Simvastatin
E Omega-3 fatty acids

152. With regard to intestinal development:

A The gut is a mesodermal derivative
B The whole of the foregut apart from the stomach undergoes rotation
C The stomach is a midgut derivative
D Rupture of the cloacal membrane creates the mouth
E Midgut development involves herniation of bowel into the umbilicus

153. With regard to skeletal muscle fibres:

A They are each normally innervated by more than one motor neurone
B They become less excitable as the extracellular ionized calcium levels fall
C Calcium is taken up by the sarcotubular system when they contract
D Actin and myosin filaments shorten when they contract
E They contain intracellular stores of calcium ions

154. With regard to the major histocompatibility complex (MHC):

A CD4 (helper) T-cells recognize antigen only in the context of MHC Class I
B Class II MHC is expressed on all nucleated cells of the body
C Class II MHC contains β_2-microglobulin
D Class II MHC presents exogenous antigens
E Class II MHC is expressed in low levels on the surface of dendritic cells

155. **In acute inflammation, which is the predominant cell type involved?**
   A Basophil
   B Eosinophil
   C Lymphocyte
   D Monocyte
   E Neutrophil

156. **Which antiarrhythmic drug acts by inhibiting potassium channels?**
   A Lignocaine
   B Atenolol
   C Amiodarone
   D Verapamil
   E Diltiazem

157. **With regard to the branchial arches:**
   A Apart from the first cleft, the other branchial clefts are normally obliterated by overgrowth of the second branchial arch
   B Six pairs of branchial arches develop in humans
   C The muscles of facial expression are first-arch derivatives
   D All parathyroid glands originate from the same branchial arch
   E The tongue principally develops from the second branchial arch

158. **With regard to nerve fibres:**
   A Impulses can travel in one direction only
   B They continue to conduct impulses when extracellular sodium is replaced by potassium
   C An action potential has an amplitude varying directly with the strength of the stimulus
   D The equilibrium potential for an ion species depends on the ratio of the concentrations of the ion outside to inside of the cell
   E Resting nerve cell membranes are more permeable to Na^+ ions than to K^+ ions

159. **The classic pathway of complement activation:**
   A Starts with the activation of the C3 component
   B Is activated by lipopolysaccharide cell-wall constituents
   C Is activated by IgA immune complexes
   D Is activated by IgM immune complexes
   E Is evoluntionarily older than the alternative pathway

160. **The plateau stage of the cardiac action potential is caused by which one of the following mechanisms?**
   A Ingress of calcium ions
   B Ingress of potassium ions
   C Efflux of potassium ions
   D Ingress of sodium ions
   E Efflux of sodium ions

161. **Which of the following anti-Parkinsonian drugs is a COMT (catechol-O-methyltransferase) inhibitor?**
   A Selegiline
   B L-Dopa
   C Entacapone
   D Benzatropine
   E Bromocriptine

162. **With regard to development of the nervous system:**
   A Neural tube development requires signals from the underlying mesoderm
   B The nervous system is derived from endoderm
   C Neural tube defects originate during the final trimester of pregnancy
   D The notochord forms the spinal cord in adults
   E Neural tube defects result from the incomplete migration of neural crest cells

163. **With regard to smooth (visceral) muscle:**
   A Excitation depends more on the influx of extracellular calcium than release from internal stores
   B It contains no actin or myosin filaments
   C It classically relaxes when it is stretched
   D It contains an extensive T-tubular system
   E It is innervated through somatic motor nerve endings

164. **A young man has a skull fracture involving the posterior cranial fossa. The fracture is most likely to have injured:**
   A The temporomandibular joint (TMJ)
   B The temporal lobe
   C Mandibular division of trigeminal nerve (Vc)
   D Abducens nerve in the cavernous sinus

E Cranial nerve VIII as it enters the internal acoustic meatus

165. **The incubation period for hepatitis A is:**
A 2–10 days
B 15–40 days
C 40–60 days
D 60–160 days
E More than 160 days

166. **In the treatment of asthma, the drug salbutamol principally acts by which of the following mechanisms?**
A α_1-adrenoceptor antagonism
B β_1-adrenoceptor agonism
C β_2-adrenoceptor agonism
D β_2-adrenoceptor antagonism
E Muscarinic antagonism

167. **A Meckel's diverticulum:**
A Is a remnant of the urachus
B Is found in 10 per cent of the population
C Is most commonly situated immediately adjacent to the vermiform appendix
D Is completely asymptomatic and an incidental finding
E May contain ectopic tissue

168. **With regard to the structure of cardiac muscle:**
A The T-tubules are located at the junction of the A and I bands
B It has no visible striations in the cytoplasm
C It has an underdeveloped sarcoplasmic reticulum
D Specialized intercellular junctions exist between myocytes
E Muscle fibres are typically multinucleate with peripherally located nuclei

169. **With regard to the acute-phase response:**
A Bacterial endotoxin induces the acute-phase response
B Exogenous pyrogens act on the liver to release tumour necrosis factor (TNF)α
C The acute-phase response is mediated through interleukin-10
D Serum albumin levels increase during the acute-phase response
E TNFα decreases catabolic activity

170. **Which one of the following areas of the central nervous system contains structures that are considered to be the phylogenically the oldest parts of the brain:**
A Frontal lobe
B Limbic system
C Cerebellum
D Visual cortex
E Parietal lobe

171. **With regard to organelles:**
A Smooth endoplasmic reticulum makes polypeptides
B Mitochondria perform anaerobic respiration
C Mitochondria can multiply independently
D Prokaryotic cells have membrane-bound organelles
E The Golgi apparatus is involved in the degradation of proteins

172. **Which one of the following cranial nerves carries parasympathetic fibres?**
A V
B IV
C VI
D III
E II

173. **With regard to properties of cardiac muscle:**
A A fused tetanic response can be produced by repetitive stimulation
B The cardiac muscle action potential lasts approximately 2–3 ms
C Excitation–contraction coupling requires calcium-induced calcium release
D The force of contraction is independent of the length of the muscle fibre
E The plateau phase of the cardiac action potential is principally due to sodium influx

174. **With regard to fever:**
A It results from the direct action of microorganisms on the brain
B It depends on the action of prostaglandins within the hypothalamus
C It is always maladaptive and serves no purpose
D It only results from infectious causes

E The antipyretic action of aspirin results from boosting of the immune response

175. A patient presents with a torn medial collateral ligament of his left knee. Which of the following signs may be elicited on physical examination?

A Posterior displacement of the tibia
B Anterior displacement of the tibia
C Abnormal lateral rotation during extension
D Abnormal passive abduction of the extended knee
E Inability to lock knee on full extension

176. Which of the following is a technique used to identify specific sequences of DNA?

A Northern blotting
B Southern blotting
C Polymerase chain reaction (PCR)
D Western blotting
E Reverse-transcription PCR

177. Which one of the following is true concerning the larynx?

A The posterior crico-arytenoids are the only muscles that separate the vocal cords
B All the intrinsic muscles are supplied by the recurrent laryngeal nerve
C The vocal cords are lined by pseudostratified columnar ciliated epithelium ('respiratory' epithelium)
D The epiglottis is composed largely of hyaline cartilage
E The cricoid cartilage and tracheal rings are all complete rings of cartilage

178. With regard to chemical neurotransmitters:

A Noradrenaline is the predominant neurotransmitter found between first- and second-order sympathetic neurones
B The nerve endings of second-order parasympathetic neurones release acetylcholine that acts on nicotinic cholinergic receptors
C The neuromuscular junction releases acetylcholine that acts on muscarinic cholinergic receptors
D The nucleus accumbens and substantia nigra are rich in dopamine
E The locus coeruleus and periaqueductal grey are rich in acetylcholine

179. Which of the following is *not* an immunologically privileged site?

A Central nervous system
B Skin
C Eye
D Uterus
E Testis

180. Pathogenic bacteria enter the body by various routes, and entry mechanisms are critical for understanding the pathogenesis and transmission of the each agent. Which pathogen is correctly linked with its mode of entry?

A *Neisseria meningitidis* – sexually transmitted entry
B *Corynebacterium diphtheriae* – food-borne entry
C *Clostridium tetani* – inhalation entry
D *Borrelia burgdorferi* – arthropod vector-borne entry
E *Rickettsia rickettsii* – contaminated wound with soil entry

181. With regard to gene expression:

A Translation occurs in the nucleus of eukaryotes
B Introns code for proteins
C DNA polymerases manufacture DNA in a 3′–5′ direction
D RNA polymerase II gives rise to protein encoding mRNA
E Codons are formed from groups of three amino acids

182. Concerning the thyroid gland, which one of the following is correct?

A Blood supply is through the internal carotid and subclavian arteries
B Embryologically starts out at the foramen caecum of the tongue
C Venous drainage is by way of the external jugular vein
D Produces thyroid stimulating hormone (TSH)
E Is attached to the thyroid cartilage by Berry's ligament

183. **Opioids:**
   A Commonly cause diarrhoea
   B Act only centrally
   C Mediate most of their beneficial effects and side-effects through ς-receptors
   D Lead to tolerance
   E Can be reversed by flumazenil

184. **Type I hypersensitivity:**
   A Is caused by antigen reacting with IgM antibodies
   B Results in mast-cell degranulation
   C Is characterized by the Arthus reaction
   D Takes 48–72 hours to develop
   E Is caused by the formation of antibody–antigen complexes

185. **Which one of the following statements concerning referred pain is true?**
   A Pain from the transverse colon is usually referred to the midline area below the umbilicus
   B Somatic pain is usually referred in a diffuse, poorly localized pattern
   C The mechanism of referred pain is well understood
   D Diaphragmatic pain is usually referred to the inguinal area
   E Pain from an inflamed appendix is referred to the medial thigh

186. **With regard to cell division:**
   A Transfer of genetic information between homologous chromosomes occurs in metaphase I of meiosis
   B Mitosis always produces genetically identical daughter cells
   C It is controlled externally by cyclins
   D Cyclins are activated by dephosphorylation
   E p53 is an oncogene

187. **With regard to the tongue:**
   A All muscles of the tongue are innervated via the hypoglossal nerve
   B Special taste sensation on the anterior two-thirds of the tongue is through the mandibular division of the trigeminal nerve
   C It is composed of smooth musculature
   D Genioglossus muscle protrudes the tongue
   E Its epithelium is of the glandular columnar variety

188. **With regard to the relationship of the electrocardiogram to the cardiac cycle:**
   A The P-wave results from atrial repolarization
   B The QRS complex is due to ventricular repolarization
   C The Q-T interval gives a rough indication of the duration of ventricular systole
   D The first heart sound occurs at the same time as the P-wave
   E The second heart sound occurs at the same time as the QRS complex

189. **Type III hypersensitivity:**
   A Is mediated by specifically sensitized T-lymphocytes
   B May cause allergic rhinitis
   C Is a feature of nickel sensitivity
   D May occur in systemic lupus erythematosus
   E Is cell-mediated

190. **Which one of the following proteins binds to penicillin?**
   A Alanine racemase
   B 30S ribosomes
   C Porin
   D Transpeptidase
   E Peptidoglycan

191. **With regard to DNA:**
   A Adenine pairs only with thymine
   B Cytosine always pairs with guanine
   C The DNA double helix has 12 base-pairs per turn
   D Uracil is an example of a purine base
   E All bases are paired by two non-covalent hydrogen bonds

192. **With regard to the parathyroid glands:**
   A They secrete calcitonin
   B They are always four in number
   C They are third branchial pouch derivatives
   D They are all supplied by the inferior thyroid artery
   E They have an invariable position in the neck

193. **A woman has warts caused by human papilloma virus (HPV). The infectious HPV is most likely to be found:**
   A In terminally differentiated squamous cells

B In the basal layer of the warts
C In the surface cell layer of the warts
D In transformed cancer cells
E Throughout the warts

194. **Hyperacute rejection:**
A Is a cell-mediated response
B Occurs 48 hours after transplantation
C Can occur in autografts
D May be reversed by high-dose steroids
E May be minimized by blood-group matching

195. **A total of 100 hypertensive patients are followed over a 4-week period for the effects of a diuretic drug on potassium concentrations. The statistical test used to compare the potassium serum levels before and after medication is most likely to be:**
A Discriminant analysis
B Paired *t*-test
C Regression analysis
D Pearson correlation
E Chi-squared test

196. **Gene transcription is initiated by:**
A Exons
B Promoters
C Silencers
D Introns
E Enhancers

197. **With regard to extra-ocular muscles:**
A Superior rectus is supplied by the trochlear nerve
B Levator palpebrae superioris is supplied solely by the occulomotor nerve
C The superior oblique muscle is innervated by the occulomotor nerve
D Lateral rectus is supplied by the abducens nerve
E The inferior oblique muscle moves the eye inferiorly

198. **Which of following substances is a vasodilator?**
A Angiotensin II
B Nitric oxide
C Noradrenaline
D Vasopressin
E Thromboxane A2

199. **Autoimmune diseases:**
A Are usually congenital
B Are overall more common in men than in women
C Arise when an immune response is mounted against a foreign antigen
D Result from a breakdown in immunological tolerance
E Are always humoral-mediated

200. **Hodgkin's lymphoma can be distinguished from other forms of lymphoma by the presence of:**
A Reed–Sternberg cells
B Philadelphia chromosome
C Auer rods
D Decreased quantities of leukocyte alkaline phosphatase
E Pappenheimer bodies

201. **A disease inherited as an autosomal dominant disorder:**
A Requires that both parents carry the abnormality
B Usually prevents reproduction
C Affects males and females equally
D Affects all the children of the affected adult
E May be transmitted by a carrier who does not manifest the disease

202. **With regard to the Palatine tonsil:**
A It lies on the middle pharyngeal constrictor muscle
B It is supplied by the superior pharyngeal artery
C It is lined by columnar epithelium
D Inflammation may cause referred pain to the ear
E Bleeding after tonsillectomy is usually due to arterial bleeding

203. **With regard to coronary blood flow:**
A Blood flow to the left ventricle increases in early systole
B Local metabolic activity is the chief factor determining rate of blood flow to the heart
C Coronary blood flow to the left ventricle increases in hypothermia
D Coronary blood flow is increased in aortic stenosis

E The myocardium extracts 25 per cent of the oxygen from the coronary blood

204. **With regard to bacterial structure and classification:**
A Gram-positive bacteria contain lipopolysaccharide
B Gram-positive bacteria retain an iodine purple dye complex
C Gram-negative bacteria possess thicker layers of peptigoglycan than Gram-negative bacteria
D The endotoxin part of lipopolysaccaride is the O-antigen portion
E All cocci are Gram-positive

205. **Derivatives of the hindgut are typically supplied by the:**
A Coeliac artery
B Ductus arteriosus
C Inferior mesenteric artery
D Superior mesenteric artery
E Umbilical artery

206. **Which one of the following is an autosomal dominant disorder?**
A Christmas disease
B Phenylketonuria
C Haemophilia A
D Cystic fibrosis
E Marfan's syndrome

207. **The spinal accessory nerve supplies which of the following muscles?**
A Buccinator
B Latissimus dorsi
C Trapezius
D Stylopharyngeus
E Palatoglossus

208. **With regard to cardiac conducting tissue:**
A Purkinje fibres lead to contraction of the apex before the base of the heart
B Sinoatrial node cells are found in both atria
C Sinoatrial node cells are unable to generate impulses when completely denervated
D Sinoatrial node cells are connected to the AV node by fine bundles of Purkinje tissue
E The pacemaker of the heart is the region of the heart that has the slowest intrinsic firing rate

209. **Splenectomy increases susceptibility to which of the following organisms?**
A *Streptococcus pyogenes*
B *Schistosomiasis haematobium*
C *Bacteroides fragilis*
D *Neisseria meningitidis*
E *Staphylococcus aureus*

210. **During a cholecstectomy, the cystic artery must be located and ligated. This arterial supply most commonly arises from the:**
A Gastroduodenal artery
B Hepatic artery proper
C Right hepatic artery
D Left hepatic artery
E Superior pancreatico-duodenal artery

211. **A teenager would like genetic counselling. His mother has phenylketonuria, or PKU (which is inherited as autosomal recessive). He has a brother with PKU. What is the chance that he is a carrier of the disease?**
A 0 per cent
B 25 per cent
C 50 per cent
D 75 per cent
E 100 per cent

212. **With regard to the parotid gland:**
A It contains within it branches of the facial nerve deep to the retromandibular vein
B It consists of superficial, middle and deep lobes
C Secreto-motor innervation is via the glossopharyngeal and auriculotemporal nerves
D Its duct pierces the masseter muscle to enter the mouth opposite the upper second molar tooth
E It produces mainly a mucous secretion

213. **With regard to circulating red blood cells (erythrocytes):**
A They have a normal lifespan of 6–8 weeks
B They are broken down in the bone marrow
C They contain the enzyme glutaldehyde anhydrase

D They lack nuclei and mitochondria
E They swell to bursting point when suspended in 0.9% saline

214. With regard to *Helicobacter pylori* (*H. pylori*):
A It is a Gram-positive organism
B It is a known carcinogen
C Approximately 5 per cent of the population are infected with *H. pylori*
D It is destroyed by the acidic environment present within the stomach
E Infection can be prevented through vaccination

215. Cells in the pancreas that secrete glucagon and insulin are:
A A- and B-cells
B Acinar cells
C D cells
D Pancreatic D1 cells
E Pancreatic polypeptide cells

216. Which one of the following karyotypes is associated with short stature?
A 45XO
B 46YO
C 46XO
D 47XYY
E 47XXY

217. With regard to the cavernous sinus:
A It contains the external carotid artery
B It lies within the anterior cranial fossa
C The pituitary and sphenoidal air sinus lie in its medial wall
D Blood flows from anterior to posterior by way of valves
E It contains the optic nerve

218. Which of the following is true of erythrocytes?
A They travel at slower velocity in venules than in capillaries
B They are normally spherical
C They make little contribution to the buffering capacity of the blood
D Following haemolysis, erythrocytes release erythropoietin which stimulates the production of more erythrocytes
E They deform as they pass through the capillaries

219. Cholera:
A Is transmitted by the blood-borne route
B Is caused by infection with *Shigella sonnei*
C Is usually accompanied by marked mucosal inflammation and ulceration
D Is caused by a toxin which increases adenylate cyclase activity
E Is caused by endotoxin

220. The glossopharyngeal nerve provides the parasympathetic innervation of the:
A Submandibular salivary gland
B Sublingual salivary gland
C Parotid salivary gland
D Lacrimal gland
E Nasal mucous glands

221. With regard to Down's syndrome:
A Alzheimer's in seen in all individuals by the age of 45 years
B It is caused by trisomy 23
C It most commonly results from a chromosomal translocation
D The risk of having a child with Down's syndrome is approximately 1 in 1000 if the mother is 30 years old
E Individuals most commonly die prematurely from lung cancer

222. Which of the following muscles is *not* a muscle of mastication?
A Medial pterygoid
B Buccinator
C Masseter
D Lateral pterygoid
E Temporalis

223. With regard to blood clotting:
A The haemostatic response comprises two key events
B Blood platelets have a small single-lobed nucleus
C The conversion of fibrinogen to fibrin is catalysed by prothrombin
D It is reversed by plasmin (fibrinolysin)
E Liver failure results in a prothrombotic state

224. With regard to hepatitis B:
A It is an RNA virus
B Infection is more commonly cleared if acquired in childhood than later in life

C It is the second commonest human carcinogen worldwide
D It is commonly acquired by the faeco-oral route
E It is effectively treated by hepatitis B vaccination

225. A skydiver lands forcefully on his right lower limb and suffers a fracture of the acetabulum, with a dislocation of the femoral head into the pelvis. The acetabulum is formed by the ilium, ischium and pubis. These three bones are completely fused by:
A Birth
B 6 years of age
C Puberty
D 16 years of age
E 23 years of age

226. Huntington's disease (Huntington's chorea):
A Is an autosomal recessive condition
B Is a CTG trinucleotide repeat disorder
C Causes polyglutamine repeats within the fibrillin protein
D Is characterized clinically by a triad of bradykinesia, rigidity and tremor
E Exhibits a genetic phenomenon known as 'anticipation'

227. With regard to the Circle of Willis (circulus arteriosus):
A It is formed from the anastomosis of the internal and external carotid arteries
B The anterior communicating artery joins the two anterior cerebral arteries
C The posterior cerebral artery is the terminal branch of the internal carotid artery
D The posterior communicating artery joins the two posterior cerebral arteries
E It is fascinating, but clinically unimportant

228. With regard to the microcirculation and formation of lymph:
A At the arterial end of the capillary, the plasma colloid osmotic pressure exceeds the capillary hydrostatic pressure
B At the venous end of the capillary, the capillary hydrostatic pressure exceeds the plasma colloid osmotic pressure
C Oedema results from a rise in colloid osmotic pressure
D Interstitial fluid hydrostatic pressure is normally negative
E All the fluid that is filtered from the capillary flows into lymph vessels

229. Human immunodeficiency virus (HIV):
A Is a DNA virus
B Contains RNA polymerase
C Is transmitted by the faeco-oral route
D Establishes persistence through antigenic variation
E Principally targets CD8 T-cells

230. Typical physical and laboratory findings in hyperthyroidism include which of the following:
A Bradycardia
B Delayed reflexes
C High serum cholesterol
D Thick, rough skin
E Tremor

231. With regard to cystic fibrosis:
A Inheritance is sex-linked
B It is caused by a genetic defect on chromosome 6
C It is the most common inherited disease in Caucasians
D Patients can expect a normal life expectancy
E Gene therapy is a well established treatment option

232. With regard to the cranial meninges:
A The dura mater is a single layer thick
B The pia mater is the outermost layer (closest to the skull)
C A subdural haematoma lies in the plane between the dura and arachnoid mater
D A subarachnoid haematoma forms on the outside of the dura mater
E The dura mater is poorly innervated

233. With regard to the cerebral circulation:
A Cerebral blood flow is mainly governed by cardiovascular reflexes
B Cerebral blood flow is very sensitive to changes in the pCO_2 of the perfusing blood
C Cerebral blood flow increases steeply with increasing blood pressure

D It comprises functional end-arteries
E Raised intracranial pressure results in hypotension and tachycardia

234. With regard to influenza:
A It is a DNA virus
B It belongs to the Picornaviridae family of viruses
C Antigenic drift is responsible for pandemics
D Mutations in the haemagglutinin molecule are responsible for antigenic drift
E It can be prevented by administration of a live vaccine

235. Risk factors for developing osteoporosis include:
A Obesity
B Low calcium intake
C Late menopause
D Excessive rigorous physical exercise
E Abstinence from alcohol

236. Haemophilia A:
A Is more common in females than males
B Is due to an abnormal gene on the Y chromosome
C Is synonymous with Christmas disease
D Is due to a deficiency in factor IX
E Affects the intrinsic, rather than the extrinsic, pathway for blood coagulation

237. With regard to the facial nerve:
A It carries taste sensation from the posterior third of the tongue
B It innervates the levator palpebrae superioris muscle
C It is secreto-motor to the lacrimal gland
D It is associated with the third branchial arch
E It supplies the principal muscles of mastication

238. Which one of the following statements concerning lung volumes is true?
A The functional residual capacity is the sum of the tidal volume and residual volume
B The vital capacity is the sum of the inspiratory reserve volume, the expiratory reserve volume and the tidal volume
C The functional residual capacity can be measured directly by spirometry
D The residual volume is the volume of air left in the lungs after normal quiet expiration
E The normal tidal volume is approximately 2 litres

239. The pathogenicity of the tubercle bacillus is primarily due to which one of the following?
A Ability to multiply within macrophages
B Delayed hypersensitivity reaction against the bacteria
C Direct toxic effect on host cells
D Effective antibody response
E Necrosis caused by expanding granulomas

240. A 36-year-old man has a neck tumour. It has damaged his left cervical sympathetic chain ganglion. Which of the following physical signs would you expect:
A Increased sweat secretion on the left side of the face
B Lateral deviation of the left eye
C Pale skin on the left side of his face
D Ptosis on the left
E Pupil dilatation of the left eye

241. With regard to sickle cell anaemia:
A The inheritance pattern is autosomal dominant
B It is caused by a mutation within the haemoglobin alpha chain
C Mutation is a valine–alanine substitution
D It is more common in regions of the world in which malaria is endemic
E It causes splenomegaly in adulthood

242. With regard to the spinal cord and vertebral column:
A The spinal cord terminates at the level of L4
B The intervertebral joints are secondary cartilaginous joints
C It is supplied by two anterior spinal arteries and one posterior spinal artery
D Batson's vertebral venous plexus contains valves
E Intervertebral disc prolapse at L4/5 causes L4 root compression

243. With regard to surfactant:

A It increases the surface tension of the film of liquid lining the alveoli
B It reduces lung compliance
C It is secreted by type I pneumocytes
D The surface tension of fluid containing surfactant increases as the surface area of the fluid decreases
E It helps to prevent the formation of pulmonary oedema

244. *Mycobacterium* tuberculosis:

A Is a Gram-negative organism
B Is an anaerobic microorganism
C Typically affects the apical lung in post-primary TB
D Is treated with penicillin
E Is impossible to acquire following BCG vaccination

245. What are the insensible losses of water (i.e. skin and lung) over 24 hours in a typical adult male at room temperature?

A 0 mL
B 100–300 mL
C 500–1000 mL
D 2500–3500 mL
E 4000–5000 mL

246. With regard to disorders of haemoglobin:

A Sickle cell disease is due to the decreased production of normal globin
B Haemoglobin binds more avidly to oxygen than carbon monoxide
C Defective haem synthesis results in porphyria
D Thalassaemia is due to the production of abnormal globin
E Cyanide kills by blocking the interaction between oxygen and haemoglobin

247. With regard to the breast:

A It drains to the tracheobronchial group of lymph nodes
B It is supplied mainly by the anterior intercostal arteries
C It sits on the pectoralis minor muscle
D Lymphatics of the breast have connections with those of the opposite breast
E It involutes during pregnancy

248. With regard to pulmonary blood flow:

A Dilatation of pulmonary blood vessels occurs in response to hypoxia
B The pulse pressure in the pulmonary artery is about the same as that in the aorta
C During exercise, blood flow to the upper portion of the lung increases
D The ventilation/perfusion ratio is the same in all parts of the lung in a standing man
E Pulmonary vascular resistance is six times greater than that of the systemic circulation

249. With regard to tetanus:

A It is caused by a Gram-negative bacillus
B It is caused by an aerobic organism
C It results from the secretion of exotoxin
D It is caused by *Clostridium perfringens*
E It is caused by bacterial invasion of the nervous system

250. Nitric oxide (NO) results in induction of vascular smooth muscle relaxation in response to acetylcholine. The production of NO requires which amino acid?

A Lysine
B Glutamine
C Cysteine
D Aspargine
E Arginine

251. With regard to ABO blood grouping:

A Blood group O is the universal recipient
B The mode of inheritance is autosomal recessive
C Blood group AB is the universal donor
D Blood group O is recessive to A and B
E Individuals of blood group O are resistant to *Plasmodium vivax*

252. With regard to the intercostal spaces:

A The neurovascular bundle lies between the external intercostal and inner intercostal muscle layers
B The direction of fibres of the external intercostal muscle is downwards and medial
C The intercostal vein lies below the intercostal nerve
D The neurovascular bundle lies in a groove just above each rib

E The intercostals are the main muscles of respiration

253. With regard to chemoreceptors:

A The carotid bodies have a blood flow per unit volume similar to that of the brain
B The carotid bodies are stretch receptors in the walls of the carotid arteries
C Central chemoreceptors are located in the aortic arch
D Carotid bodies primarily respond to hypoxia
E The response of the peripheral chemoreceptors to arterial pCO_2 is more important than that of the central chemoreceptors

254. With regard to malaria:

A It is caused by a virus
B It is transmitted by the Aedes mosquito vector
C The most virulent strain is *Plasmodium malariae*
D It may cause blackwater fever
E It is effectively prevented by vaccination

255. The neurotransmitters adrenaline, noradrenaline and dopamine are derived from which amino acid?

A Tyrosine
B Arginine
C Aspargine
D Phenylalanine
E Tryptophan

256. Adult polycystic kidney disease:

A Is inherited as an autosomal recessive condition
B Affects only one kidney
C Is associated with berry aneurysms of the Circle of Willis
D Commonly presents at birth
E Is due to a mutation in polycystin-1 in all cases

257. With regard to the oesophagus:

A It is a segmental muscular tube composed entirely of smooth muscle
B Epithelium is always stratified squamous throughout its whole length
C Blood supply is from the descending thoracic aorta along its entire length
D It lacks a true serosal surface
E It measures approximately 40 cm in length

258. With regard to carbon dioxide transport:

A Carbon dioxide is mainly carried in the blood in its dissolved form
B It is carried as carboxyhaemoglobin on the haemoglobin molecule
C The Haldane effect describes changes in the affinity of the blood for CO_2 with variations in the PaO_2
D Venous blood has a higher pH than arterial blood
E Carbon dioxide is less soluble in plasma than is oxygen

259. With regard to the malaria life cycle:

A Sporozoites invade erythrocytes
B Parasites may remain dormant in the liver as hypnozoites
C Trophozoites invade hepatocytes
D Schizonts are contained within the mosquito's salivary glands
E Fertilization and formation of a zygote occurs in humans

260. A 42-year old woman has a genetic defect and cannot produce J-chains that are important in the structure of immunoglobulins. Most likely she will have:

A Increased serum IgM and decreased IgE
B Increased IgA in the intestine
C Decreased serum IgM
D Decreased mature T-lymphocytes
E Decreased mature B-cells

261. The decline in incidence of serious infections during the nineteenth and twentieth centuries is mainly due to:

A Better sanitation
B Antibiotics
C Immunization programmes
D A decline in the virulence of organisms
E Advances in medical science

262. With regard to oesophageal constrictions:

A The lower oesophageal sphincter is a true anatomical sphincter
B They may be caused by the right principal bronchus
C The narrowest part of the oesophagus is at the level of cricopharyngeus

D They may be caused normally by the left atrium
E They may be caused by the descending thoracic aorta

263. Which one of the following is true of the haemoglobin oxygen/dissociation curve?
A It is a rectangular hyperbola
B It is shifted to the left by an increase in $P\text{CO}_2$
C Fetal haemoglobin shifts the curve to the right
D The Haldane effect describes the changes in affinity of the haemoglobin chain for oxygen following variations in $P\text{CO}_2$
E The shape of the curve is explained by the physico-chemical properties of haemoglobin

264. With regard to schistosomiasis:
A It is caused by a protozoan
B The intermediate host is the sandfly
C *Schistosoma mansoni* causes urinary schistosomiasis
D Disease results from the immune response to schistosome eggs
E It is treated with quinine

265. An 83-year-old man has chest pain, breathlessness and ankle oedema. On clinical examination, cardiomegaly is identified and a subsequent diagnosis of viral myocarditis is made. Which of the following microorganisms is most likely responsible for this illness:
A Rhinovirus
B Mumps
C Coronavirus
D Adenovirus
E Coxsackie B

266. Which one of the following changes in disease patterns have occurred in Europe and North America over the past 50 years?
A The death rate from lung cancer in females has fallen
B The death rate from lung cancer in males has risen in recent years
C The numbers infected with the HIV virus has fallen
D The death rate from suicide has fallen
E The death rate from gastric carcinoma has fallen

267. With regard to the diaphragm:
A It is composed of smooth muscle
B It contracts with expiration
C It forms the main muscle of respiration at rest
D Motor innervation is through right and left phrenic nerves and lower intercostal nerves
E Sensation is via lower intercostals nerves only

268. At high altitude when the atmospheric pressure is halved, which one of the following changes occurs?
A Decreased pulmonary arterial pressure
B Decreased arterial pH
C Increased arterial $P\text{O}_2$
D Decreased pulmonary ventilation
E Increased blood viscosity

269. Prions:
A Are infectious microorganisms
B Are destroyed by sterilization
C Contain nucleic acid
D Cause disease by inducing mutations in the DNA of the host
E Are responsible for causing Kuru in humans

270. Which of the following is the best neutrophil and macrophage chemotactant?
A C5a
B HLA-A
C HLA-B
D J-chain
E Variable region of heavy-chain IgG

271. The most common cause of death from cancer in women is currently:
A Ovarian cancer
B Breast cancer
C Lung cancer
D Endometrial cancer
E Colon cancer

272. With regard to diaphragmatic openings:
A The inferior vena cava passes through the muscular part of the diaphragm at T8

B The aortic opening lies at the T10 level
C The oesophageal opening transmits the right phrenic nerve
D The left phrenic nerve passes with the oesophagus through the oesophageal opening
E The sympathetic trunks pass posterior to the medial arcuate ligament

273. With regard to gas exchange:
A The rate of diffusion across the alveolar wall is directly proportional to its thickness
B Under resting conditions, equilibration between alveoli PO_2 and red blood cell PO_2 occurs one-third of the way along the pulmonary capillary
C At rest, the red blood cell spends approximately 5 seconds within the pulmonary capillary
D The rate of diffusion across the alveolar wall is inversely proportional to the surface area available for diffusion
E Chlorine is the gas of choice for measuring the diffusion properties of the lung

274. Which of the following definitions is correct?
A Hyperplasia is an increase in tissue growth through an increase in cell size
B Dysplasia is a change from one type of differentiated tissue to another
C Carcinoma-in-situ is a carcinoma with stromal invasion
D Anaplasia is almost a complete lack of differentiation
E Metaplasia is the disordered development of cells with loss of organization

275. A 92-year-old man has died secondary to lobar pneumonia. At post-mortem he is diagnosed with red hepatization. What pathological process within the lung was responsible?
A Desquamation of tracheal and bronchial epithelial cells
B Fibroblast proliferation
C Alcoholic toxic necrosis
D Leucocytes, erythrocytes and fibrin filling of the alveolar spaces
E Pleural deposits of fibrin and low molecular proteins

276. Which one of the following diseases is water-borne?
A Tuberculosis
B Cholera
C Hepatitis C
D Bubonic plague
E Malaria

277. With regard to the thoracic duct:
A It drains into the confluence of the right internal jugular and subclavian veins
B It lies anterior to the oesophagus as it passes through the diaphragm
C It crosses the midline at the level of T5
D It has no valves
E If it is injured, a haemothorax may result

278. With regard to the mechanics of respiration:
A Compliance is defined as the change in pressure per unit volume
B Compliance is synonymous with elastance
C Sighing serves no physiological purpose
D The lung follows the same behaviour in inflation and deflation
E Emphysema results in increased lung compliance

279. Which one of the following statements is true?
A Adenoma is a malignant tumour of glandular epithelium
B Sarcoma is a benign tumour of connective tissue
C Leiomyosarcoma is a malignant tumour of skeletal muscle
D Lymphoma is a benign tumour of lymphoid cells
E Liposarcoma is a malignant tumour of adipose tissue

280. Budd–Chiari syndrome is:
A A congenital inability to metabolize bilirubin
B A dietary deficiency of an essential amino acid
C Agenesis of the hepatic lobe
D Occlusion of the hepatic venous drainage

E Malignant transformation of the biliary epithelium

281. **Which one of the following is true concerning retrospective and prospective studies?**
A Prospective studies are also known as case–control studies
B Prospective studies allow direct determination of incidence rates
C The retrospective approach has the advantage that there is little or no bias
D In a prospective study, the cohort consists of people who are found to have the disease in question
E The prospective approach is usually used to determine the aetiology of a rare disease

282. **With regard to the lungs:**
A The left lung has three lobes
B The horizontal fissure is present in the left lung
C Each lung has eight bronchopulmonary segments
D A foreign body is more likely to enter the left bronchus than the right
E The lungs receive a dual blood supply

283. **Which one of the following is true of haemoglobin?**
A Most haemoglobin circulates as free protein in plasma
B Oxygen attaches to the globin chains
C Each haemoglobin molecule combines with eight oxygen atoms
D In normal adult haemoglobin, iron exists in the ferric state
E Normal adult haemoglobin contains two alpha and two gamma chains

284. **With regard to metaplasia:**
A It is irreversible
B It is most important in the upper oesophagus
C Metaplasia in the bronchus involves a change from columnar to stratified squamous epithelium
D It is harmless
E Barrett's oesophagus involves a change from glandular to stratified squamous epithelium

285. **A 52-year-old man presents with episodic hypertension, an adrenal mass and elevated catacholamines. The most likely diagnosis is:**
A Adrenal cortical carcinoma
B Adrenal cortical hyperplasia
C Phaeochromocytoma
D Ganglioneuroma
E Neuroblastoma

286. **Which one of the following studies is regarded as the gold standard in epidemiological research?**
A Cross-sectional study
B Case–control study
C Case report
D Randomized controlled trial
E Non-randomized controlled trial

287. **With regard to the pleura:**
A The pleura ends level with the 12th rib posteriorly
B It extends above the clavicle superiorly
C The visceral layer is richly innervated
D It extends above the neck of the 1st rib superiorly
E The pleural reflection on the right side matches that on the left side identically

288. **Which one of the following is true of erythropoietin?**
A It is a polypeptide
B Secretion is decreased at high altitude
C In adults, it is mainly made in the liver
D It acts via a secondary messenger
E Production is decreased by local hypoxia

289. **Which of the following is a defining characteristic of a malignant tumour?**
A Increase in size with time
B Chromosomal abnormalities
C Presence of a pseudo-capsule
D Invasion beyond the basement membrane
E Well-ordered maturation

290. **Following a lethal overdose of paracetamol, the post-mortem will demonstrate:**
A Pulmonary necrosis
B Hepatic necrosis
C Acute renal tubular necrosis

D Splenic infarction
E Meningeal inflammation

291. You are involved in running a diabetes screening service. Two thousand people, aged between 60 and 75, are screened. Both the mean and median random glucose measurement is 9.5 and the standard deviation is 1.4. Which statement is correct?

A Five per cent of subjects will have a glucose greater than 10.9
B The distribution is not a normal distribution
C Ninety-five per cent of subjects will have a blood glucose between 6.7 and 12.3
D Sixty-eight per cent of subjects have a blood glucose between 6.7 and 12.3
E Ninety-five per cent of the observations lie between two standard errors of the mean

292. With regard to the pericardium:

A It is two layers thick
B It is poorly innervated
C It is responsible for the formation of the transverse and oblique sinuses
D Pericardiocentesis may be detrimental in the management of cardiac tamponade
E It is essential in order to maintain a normal cardiac output

293. Which one of the following is true of aldosterone?

A It is a steroid hormone secreted by the adrenal medulla
B Production is decreased by angiotensin-converting enzyme inhibitors
C Secretion results in increased potassium reabsorption from the nephron
D Secretion results in a rise in urinary pH
E Production ceases following the removal of the kidneys and their juxtaglomerular cells

294. Which of the following are cytological features of malignancy?

A Hyperchromatism
B Pyknosis
C Karyorrhexis
D Decreased nuclear to cytoplasmic ratio
E Low mitotic index

295. A 63-year-old male has a progressive history of congestive cardiac failure. At post-mortem, the heart demonstrates extensive replacement of the myocardium by an acellular, eosinophilic material. This material is most likely to be:

A Cholesterol
B Calcium salt deposits
C Myocyte fibrinoid necrosis
D Post-infarctive cicatrix (scar)
E Amyloid

296. Which one of the following statements is true?

A The standard error provides a measure of the spread of observations around the mean
B The standard deviation is equal to the standard error divided by the square-root of the sample size
C The standard error is generally larger than the standard deviation
D In a positively skewed distribution, the median is greater than the mode, but greater than the mean
E The mean and standard deviation of a random sample will generally be different from the mean and standard deviation of the true population

297. Which of the following regarding the coronary arteries is correct:

A The sinoatrial node is supplied by the left coronary artery in most cases
B The atrioventricular node is supplied by the left coronary artery in most cases
C The circumflex artery is a branch of the right coronary artery
D Occlusion of the anterior interventricular artery (left anterior descending artery) results in an anterior myocardial infarction
E Angina is always due to atherosclerosis of the coronary vessels

298. With regard to the renin–angiotensin system:

A Angiotensinogen is secreted by the juxtaglomerular apparatus
B The lung catalyses the conversion of angiotensinogen to angiotensin I
C Activation results in the stimulation of aldosterone release

D Angiotensin II is a potent vasodilator
E Angiotensin-converting enzyme is found principally in the liver

299. Carcinomas most often metastasize by which of the following routes?
A Bloodstream
B Lymphatics
C Trans-coelomic
D Peri-neural
E Implantation

300. A 73-year-old man works in a plastics factory and is exposed to vinyl chloride. This industrial exposure has increased his likelihood of developing:
A Focal nodular hyperplasia
B Hepatic adenoma
C Hepatic angiosarcoma
D Hepatic fibroma
E Hepatocellular carcinoma

301. In a certain trial, the mean ± standard error is 0.5 ± 0.2, with a *p*-value under 0.005. This implies that:
A Ninety-five per cent of the values lie between 0.1 and 0.9
B This difference would have arisen by chance alone less than one time in 200
C This difference would have arisen by chance alone less than one time in 20 000
D One can be 95 per cent confident that the true population mean lies somewhere within the interval 0.3–0.7
E There is a 2.5 per cent chance that the true population mean lies outside the range 0.1–0.9

302. With regard to the inguinal canal:
A The superficial inguinal ring is a hole in transversalis fascia
B The canal runs from the anterior superior iliac spine to the pubic tubercle
C The conjoint tendon is formed by fusion of external and internal oblique muscles
D The posterior wall of the canal is bounded by transversalis fascia and the conjoint tendon medially
E A direct inguinal hernia passes through both the deep and superficial inguinal rings

303. With regard to the juxtaglomerular apparatus:
A The macula densa is a specialized region of the afferent arteriole
B Renin is secreted at the macula densa
C Renin is secreted in response to a raised sodium at the macula densa
D A fall in pressure in the afferent arteriole promotes renin secretion
E The juxtaglomerular (granular) cells are located in the wall of the distal convoluted tubule

304. Which of the following malignant neoplasms rarely metastasizes to distant sites:
A Bronchial carcinoma
B Breast carcinoma
C Astrocytomas
D Renal-cell carcinoma
E Melanoma

305. A 56-year-old man presents with a productive cough and weight loss. Chest X-ray demonstrates a large hilar mass. Sputum cytology shows oval cells with hyperchromatism, paucity of cytoplasm and inconspicuous nuclei. These malignant cells are most likely associated with:
A Clara cells
B Metaplastic bronchial epithelial cells
C Neuroendocrine cells
D Type I alveolar pneumocytes
E Type 2 alveolar pneumocytes

306. The following table shows the results for a screening test for pancreatic cancer in 100 people:

	Disease positive	*Disease negative*
Test positive	4	5
Test negative	1	90

Which of the following is true?
A The positive predictive value is 0.95
B The sensitivity is 0.95
C The specificity is 0.8
D The negative predictive value is 0.99
E The sensitivity and specificity depends on the disease prevalence

307. **With regard to the epiploic foramen (of Winslow), which of the following is true?**
A The posterior wall is formed from the lesser omentum
B The portal vein lies in its posterior wall
C Superiorly lies the quadrate lobe of the liver
D The common bile duct sits in the free edge of the greater omentum anteriorly
E It forms the entrance to the lesser sac

308. **With regard to antidiuretic hormone (arginine vasopressin):**
A It increases in response to a loss of circulating volume of at least 10 per cent
B It is secreted by the pars distalis (adenohypophysis)
C Increased secretion occurs in response to hypo-osmolar blood
D It causes water reabsorption from the Loop of Henle
E Insufficiency results in diabetes mellitus

309. **Sarcomas:**
A Are derived from epithelium
B Are more common than carcinomas
C Have a peak incidence in those less than 50 years of age
D Metastasize more commonly by lymphatic than haematogenous routes
E Have a long in-situ phase

310. **One sensitive indicator of heavy alcohol dependence is:**
A Decreased mean cell volume (MCV)
B Decreased serum alkaline phosphatase
C Elevated serum creatinine
D Elevated serum gamma-glutamyl transpeptidase
E Elevated serum indirect bilirubin

311. **Which of the following are features of small bowel?**
A Valvulae conniventes
B Haustra
C Sacculations
D Appendices epiploicae
E Taeniae coli

312. **With regard to acid–base balance:**
A The normal pH of arterial blood is 7.85–7.95
B The pH of the blood fluctuates widely
C The kidneys respond most rapidly to a change in pH
D The kidney is able to generate new bicarbonate from glutamine
E The renal tubule reabsorbs hydrogen ions and actively excretes bicarbonate

313. **Which is true of tumour kinetics?**
A The smallest clinically detectable tumour is 1000 cells
B Tumour growth obeys Gompertzian kinetics
C In most tumours, the growth fraction is greater than 90 per cent
D Tumour growth is characterized by contact inhibition
E The clinical phase of tumour growth is long in comparison to the preclinical phase

314. **The activity of what structure in the pons is suppressed by opiates, clonidine and GABA, and produces the most noradrenergic input to the brain?**
A Substantia nigra
B Nucleus solitarius
C Nucleus pulposus
D Mammillary bodies
E Locus coeruleus

315. **With regard to the gall bladder:**
A Epithelium is stratified squamous
B It has a normal capacity of around 10 mL
C It is supplied by the cystic artery, a branch of the left hepatic artery
D It is stimulated to contract by cholecystokinin
E It is essential for life

316. **With regard to renal blood flow:**
A The kidneys receive 5 per cent of the cardiac output
B Angiotensin II vasoconstricts the afferent more than the efferent arteriole
C It can be accurately measured by the use of inulin
D The low blood flow in the vasa recta assists in the formation of concentrated urine
E A fall in arterial blood pressure decreases glomerular filtration rate (GFR)

317. With regard to angiogenesis:

A It is the process of programmed cell death
B It is highly dependent on vascular endothelial growth factor (VEGF)
C It is impaired when tumours grow larger than 1 mm^3
D It is always pathological
E Granulation tissue is rich in cytokines that inhibit angiogenesis

318. Serum electrolytes reveal sodium 150 mEq/L and potassium 5.2 mEq/L. The most likely diagnosis is:

A Alzheimer's disease
B Delirium
C Pick's disease
D Secondary dementia
E Seizure disorder

319. With regard to gall bladder disease:

A Courvoisier's law states that in the presence of obstructive jaundice an impalpable gall bladder is always due to gallstones
B It may refer pain to the right shoulder tip
C The surface marking of the gall bladder is the right sixth intercostal space, mid-clavicular line
D Gallstones are usually composed of calcium carbonate
E Gallstones always cause symptoms

320. With regard to glomerular filtration:

A The GFR is the main factor determining the rate of urine production
B GFR can be measured by para-aminohippuric acid (PAH)
C The normal GFR is 50 mL/min
D The glomerular filtration barrier comprises three layers
E A normal plasma creatinine implies normal renal function

321. An increased frequency of tumours caused by occupational carcinogen exposure has been proven in the following groups, *except*:

A Transitional cell carcinoma bladder in dye workers
B Scrotal carcinoma in chimney sweeps
C Mesothelioma with asbestos exposure
D Hepatocellular carcinoma with polyvinyl chloride exposure
E Malignant melanoma with sunlight exposure

322. Which of the following decreases insulin resistance:

A Cortisol
B Exercise
C Obesity
D Pregnancy
E Growth hormone

323. With regard to the liver:

A It is completely surrounded by peritoneum
B The ligamentum venosum is a remnant of the umbilical vein
C It receives oxygen from the hepatic artery only
D It is surrounded by Gerota's fascia
E The right subhepatic space or hepatorenal pouch (of Rutherford–Morison) is the most dependent part of the peritoneal cavity

324. With regard to tubular function:

A Fifty per cent of the filtered sodium is reabsorbed in the distal convoluted tubule
B Most glucose is reabsorbed in the Loop of Henle
C The ascending limb of the Loop of Henle is permeable to water
D Drinking seawater is better than drinking nothing at all if lost at sea
E The maximum concentrating ability of the human kidney is 1200 mOsm/L

325. For which one of the following tumours is there an association with Epstein–Barr virus (EBV) infection?

A Bronchial carcinoma
B Cervical carcinoma
C Burkitt's lymphoma
D Hepatocellular carcinoma
E Kaposi's sarcoma

326. Which of the following is the most common thyroid neoplasm in the UK?

A Medullary thyroid cancer
B Lymphoma
C Papillary thyroid cancer

D Follicular cancer
E Metastases

327. With regard to portosystemic anastomoses:
A They occur at sites at which arterial blood meets venous blood
B They feature at the lower end of the oesophagus
C They become highly significant in renal failure
D They are most clinically significant at the lower end of the anal canal
E They feature at the splenic hilum

328. With regard to saliva:
A Secretion is equivalent to 200 mL/day
B Secretion from the parotid gland is mainly mucinous
C It contains the trypsin enzyme
D It is richer in potassium than any other gastrointestinal secretion
E Secretion is a passive process

329. With regard to oncogenes:
A They behave in a dominant fashion
B They encode proteins that negatively regulate growth
C BRCA1 is an oncogene implicated in breast carcinoma
D Transcription of oncogenes is dysregulated in normal cells
E Oncogenes are present only in tumour cells

330. The neurotransmitter released from the cerebellar Pukinke cells is:
A Glutamate
B GABA
C Acetylcholine
D Glycine
E Serotonin

331. With regard to the spleen:
A It lies under cover of ribs 9–11 on the right
B It is the major site of erythropoietin secretion
C It is normally the site of haematopoiesis in adults
D Accessory spleens are rare
E Splenectomized patients are at high risk of post-splenectomy sepsis

332. Which of the following cells secretes intrinsic factor?
A Goblet cells
B Kupffer cells
C Peptic cells
D Chief cells
E Parietal cells

333. With regard to tumour suppressor genes:
A They encode proteins that positively regulate growth
B They behave in a dominant fashion
C Gain-of-function of tumour suppressor genes results in neoplastic growth
D p53 and Rb-1 are tumour suppressor genes
E p53 normally functions as an anti-apoptotic factor

334. Which one of the following muscles is innervated by the facial nerve?
A Temporalis
B Anterior belly of digastric
C Buccinator
D Masseter
E Lateral pterygoid

335. With regard to the transpyloric plane (of Addison):
A It is half way between the suprasternal notch and umbilicus
B It lies at the level of T12
C It lies at the origin of the inferior mesenteric artery
D It lies level with the hilum of the kidneys
E It is the point at which the aorta bifurcates

336. With regard to gastric acid secretion:
A It is inhibited by gastrin
B It is potentiated by histamine
C It commences only when food enters the stomach
D It is stimulated by the glossopharyngeal nerve
E It is stimulated by somatostatin

337. Retinoblastoma:
A Is inherited as an autosomal recessive condition
B Is due to a defective gene located on chromosome 5

C Is familial in 90 per cent of cases
D In its inherited form, carries minimal risk of extraretinal malignancies
E Results from loss of heterozygosity of the normal Rb gene

338. From which branchial (pharyngeal) pouch does the inferior parathyroid gland arise?
A First
B Second
C Third
D Fourth
E Fifth

339. With regard to the adrenal gland (suprarenal gland):
A The suprarenal vein on each side drains into the corresponding renal vein
B The adrenal gland is situated within the same fascial compartment as the kidney
C The zona glomerulosa forms the innermost layer of the adrenal cortex
D The anterior surface of the right adrenal gland is overlapped by the inferior vena cava
E The adrenal medulla is derived from embryonic mesoderm

340. Which one of the following is true of gastrin?
A It is secreted in the body of the stomach
B It is stimulated by low pH
C It stimulates gastric acid production
D It inhibits gastric motility
E Decreased secretion results in the Zollinger–Ellison syndrome

341. Lung carcinoma:
A Is the third most common cause of death from neoplasia in the UK
B Has rarely metastasized at the time of presentation
C May produce paraneoplastic syndromes
D Is most commonly due to small-cell (oat-cell) carcinoma
E Is most commonly caused by asbestos exposure

342. Prokaryotes differ from eukaryotes in that prokaryotes have:
A Peptidoglycan
B Sterols in their membranes
C 2 to 6 chromosomes
D An endoplasmic reticulum
E Larger 80S ribosomes

343. With regard to the vermiform appendix:
A It is most often situated in a pelvic position
B It receives blood via the right colic branch of the superior mesenteric artery
C It lies at McBurney's point (half way between the anterior superior iliac spine and umbilicus)
D It is unimportant in humans
E It is a retroperitoneal structure

344. With regard to the exocrine pancreas:
A It secretes digestive juices with a pH of 4–5
B It develops from a single ventral pancreatic bud
C Secretion is inhibited by cholecystokinin
D The main stimulation for secretion occurs during the intestinal phase
E It produces secretin

345. Which one of the following is the commonest intracerebral neoplasm:
A Astrocytoma
B Oligodendroglioma
C Meningioma
D Neuronal tumour
E Secondary carcinoma

346. A 67-year-old male undergoes an elective right colectomy for adenocarcinoma of the caecum. If distant non-nodal metastases are discovered, which organ would be affected first?
A Brain
B Lung
C Adrenal
D Liver
E Bone

347. With regard to acute appendicitis:
A It is most common at the extremes of age
B It may result in thrombosis of the appendicular artery (endarteritis obliterans)
C It often resolves with conservative management such as antibiotics
D If untreated it is rarely life-threatening
E Classically it refers pain to the epigastric region

348. Which one of the following is true of pancreatic enzymes:
- A Trypsin is a powerful activator of other pancreatic proteolytic enzymes
- B The pancreas secretes enterokinase (enteropeptidase)
- C Chymotrypsinogen activates trypsinogen to form trypsin
- D The pancreas secretes proteases in their activated form
- E The pancreas normally contains a trypsin activator

349. Which one of the following is the commonest malignant tumour of bone?
- A Chondroblastoma
- B Giant-cell tumour
- C Osteosarcoma
- D Chondrosarcoma
- E Secondary carcinoma

350. A research assistant is studying the production of an anthrax vaccine. He must destroy all vegetative cells and spores of *Bacillus anthracis* that have contaminated the pipette. What agent should he use?
- A Boiling
- B Ethanol alcohol
- C Oxidizing agents
- D Autoclaving
- E Anionic detergents

351. With regard to the greater omentum:
- A It has no surgical importance
- B It is supplied by the right and left gastric arteries
- C It is two layers thick
- D It provides a route of access to the lesser sac
- E The anterior layers descend from the lesser curvature of the stomach

352. With regard to the endocrine pancreas:
- A It secretes hormones into a highly branched ductal system
- B Glucagon is secreted from β-islet cells
- C Islets of Langerhans make up only 2 per cent of the volume of the gland
- D Somatostatin is secreted from α-islet cells
- E Glucagon stimulates glycogenesis

353. Apoptosis:
- A Is always a pathological event
- B Involves the death of large contiguous areas of cells
- C Is usually accompanied by inflammation
- D May be seen in histological section
- E Leaves a permanent clump of cellular debris

354. The virus responsible for causing acquired immunodeficiency sydrome (AIDS) has which one of the following features?
- A A double-stranded genome
- B Lacks a viral evelope
- C Lacks reverse transcriptase
- D Is a member of the adenovirus group
- E Destroys CD4 T-lymphocytes

355. With regard to the ureters:
- A They are lined by stratified squamous epithelium
- B They enter the bladder obliquely forming a flap valve
- C The point of narrowest calibre is at the pelviureteric junction
- D The arterial supply of the lower third of the ureter is by way of the descending abdominal aorta
- E In the female, the ureters are crossed below by the uterine arteries in the broad ligament

356. Which one of the following is true of bile?
- A Bile salts are derived from the waste products of haemoglobin
- B It is actively concentrated in the gall bladder
- C Thirty per cent is reabsorbed by the enterohepatic circulation
- D Bile contains enzymes required for the digestion of fat
- E Accumulation of bile salts is responsible for causing jaundice

357. With regard to acute inflammation:
- A The predominant cell type involved is the macrophage
- B Inflammation is usually initiated by cell-mediated immunity
- C Inflammation may last for many months
- D Inflammation is intimately connected with the clotting system
- E Inflammation is always due to infection

358. A man is bleeding from the carotid artery. In order to temporary control the bleeding, the surgeon should compress the artery against the anterior tubercle of which of the following?

A Second cervical vertebra
B Third cervical vertebra
C Fouth cervical vertebra
D Fifth cervical vertebra
E Sixth cervical vertebra

359. With regard to the spermatic cord:

A It contains within it the ilioinguinal nerve
B It contains the femoral branch of the genitofemoral nerve
C It is surrounded by two fascial coverings
D It contains the pampiniform plexus
E It has dartos muscle contained in its wall

360. With regard to intestinal absorption:

A A greater volume of water is absorbed from the colon than from the small intestine
B Gastric acid assists in the absorption of iron
C Glucose is absorbed by a potassium-cotransport mechanism
D Vitamin B_{12} is absorbed from the duodenum
E Sodium is absorbed at a rate proportional to body needs

361. The following are possible outcomes of acute inflammation, *except*:

A Resolution
B Chronic inflammation
C Abscess formation
D Amyloidosis
E Death

362. A man falls on an outstretched hand. X-rays indicate an anterior dislocation of one of the carpal bones. Which carpal bone is most commonly dislocated?

A Capitate
B Lunate
C Scaphoid
D Trapezoid
E Triquetrum

363. With regard to the testis:

A It is supplied by the testicular artery which arises from the internal iliac artery
B It drains via the pampiniform plexus to the inferior vena cava
C Lymph drainage is to the inguinal group of lymph nodes
D It is supplied by T10 sympathetic nerves
E A fluid collection around the testis is known as a varicocele

364. In the setting of starvation:

A Glycogen stores last for two weeks
B Glucose is the only metabolic fuel that can be used by neurones
C The brain uses free amino acids when glucose levels begin to fall
D Protein is spared until relatively late
E Death occurs at around 21 days

365. With regard to chronic inflammation:

A It is always preceded by an acute inflammatory phase
B It usually heals by organization and repair
C It is characterized by less tissue destruction than acute inflammation
D It usually results in resolution
E Neutrophils are the predominant cell type

366. Under normal conditions, virtually 100 per cent of the filtered load of glucose is reabsorbed by the kidney tubules. Which part of the nephron shown in Figure 1 is expected to have the highest reabsorption of glucose?

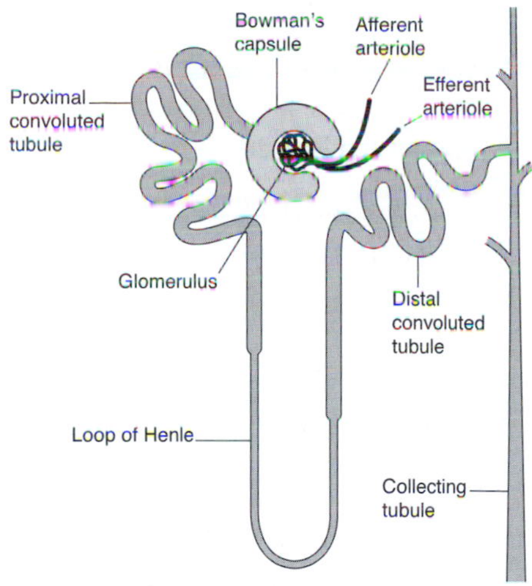

Figure 1 The nephron.

A Proximal convoluted tubule
B Thin descending Loop of Henle

C Thick ascending limb of Loop of Henle
D Distal convoluted tubule
E Collecting duct

367. With regard to the ovary:
A It is retroperitoneal
B It lies medial to the obturator nerve and anterior to the ureter
C It drains lymph to the internal iliac nodes
D It receives a parasympathetic supply from the pudendal nerve
E It gives rise to referred pain in the suprapubic region

368. Which one of the following hormones is secreted by the anterior pituitary?
A Testosterone
B Oxytocin
C Thyroid-stimulating hormone (TSH)
D Corticotropin-releasing hormone (CRH)
E Antidiuretic hormone (ADH)

369. Which of the following inflammatory processes often involves granulomas?
A Lobar pneumonia
B Bronchopneumonia
C Tuberculosis
D Granulation tissue
E Ulcerative colitis

370. An intravenous drug user presents with pyrexia and haematuria. Clinical examination demonstrates splenomegaly and splinter haemorrhages. Of which of the following heart valves would vegetations be expected?
A Aortic
B Pulmonary
C Mitral
D Tricuspid
E Bicuspid

371. With regard to the rectum:
A It is drained by tributaries of both the inferior mesenteric and internal iliac veins
B It is suspended by a mesentery
C It receives its blood supply from the external iliac artery
D It is lined by transitional epithelium
E It is supplied by parasympathetic nerve fibres from the vagus

372. Which one of these statements regarding type 2 diabetes mellitus is true?
A It usually presents with weight loss
B Ketones are found
C It is associated with HLA DR3/4
D Identical twins show 90 per cent concordance
E It usually presents in the teen years

373. With regard to wound healing:
A Granulation tissue actively contracts
B Granulation tissue is defined by the presence or absence of granulomas
C Repair implies the complete restitution of normal tissue architecture and function
D In first-intention healing, the wound is unapposed
E Scar formation is absent in second-intention healing

374. A 62-year-old industrial chemist presents with painless haematuria, urinary frequency and urgency. He is diagnosed with bladder cancer. Which is the most likely type?
A Adenocarcinoma
B Sarcoma
C Papilloma
D Squamous cell carcinoma
E Transitional cell carcinoma

375. With regard to the uterus:
A It usually lies in a retroverted, anteflexed position
B The broad ligament is a remnant of the gubernaculum
C The Pouch of Douglas lies between the bladder anteriorly and uterus posteriorly
D The ovarian artery is intimately related to the ureter
E The ureter is closely related to the lateral fornix of the cervix

376. In diabetes mellitus:
A A fasting glucose of 6.5 mM is compatible with a diagnosis
B A random glucose of 9 mM on two occasions is compatible with a diagnosis
C A fasting glucose of 7.5 mM on two occasions is consistent with a diagnosis
D A glucose of 10 mM after a 2-hour glucose tolerance test is compatible with a diagnosis

E A 50 g glucose challenge is used in the glucose tolerance test

377. Which one of the following tissues is likely to regenerate following damage?

A Cerebral cortex
B Peripheral neurones
C Skeletal muscle
D Cardiac muscle
E Spinal cord

378. Deficiencies of which of the following factors usually predispose to thrombosis rather than bleeding?

A Factor V
B Factor VIII
C Factor IX
D Factor X
E Factor XII

379. With regard to the blood supply of the stomach:

A The right half of the lesser curvature is supplied by the right gastoepiploic artery
B The left half of the greater curvature is supplied by the left gastric artery
C The fundus of the stomach is supplied by the left gastric artery
D The gastroduodenal artery is a branch of the common hepatic artery
E The right gastric artery is most commonly implicated in a bleeding duodenal ulcer

380. Which one of these statements regarding insulin is true?

A Insulin receptors use cAMP as their signal transducer
B It is secreted by alpha-cells of the pancreas
C Secretion is stimulated by somatostatin
D It is an anabolic hormone
E Release is inhibited by the ingestion of amino acids

381. With regard to necrosis:

A It is a physiological or pathological process
B Single cells are involved
C Liquefactive necrosis classically occurs in the brain
D Necrotic cells are phagocytosed by adjacent cells
E Caseous necrosis is the commonest type

382. A Swan–Ganz catheter is inserted into a patient with acute respiratory distress syndrome (ARDS). His pulmonary artery pressure is 6 mmHg. The same pressure would be expected in which of the following structures?

A Aorta
B Left atrium
C Left ventricle
D Right atrium
E Systemic veins

383. With regard to the femoral triangle, which of the following is correct?

A The femoral vein lies lateral to the femoral artery
B The femoral nerve lies within the femoral sheath
C The femoral artery lies at the mid-point of the inguinal ligament
D The femoral nerve is the most medially placed structure
E Cloquet's node lies most medially within the femoral canal

384. With regard to the hypothalamo-pituitary axis:

A Oxytocin is synthesized in the posterior pituitary gland
B Prolactin is under dominant inhibitory regulation
C Thyroxine is a steroid hormone
D Thyroid-stimulating hormone (TSH) acts via tyrosine kinase receptors
E GH binds to intracellular receptors

385. Which one of the following is the best definition of gangrene?

A Digestion of living tissue by saprophytic bacteria
B Digestion of dead tissue by saprophytic bacteria
C Gas production in dead tissue
D Necrosis of tissue caused by bacterial toxins
E Necrosis of tissue caused by ischaemia

386. A woman has episodic abdominal pain which is worse after fatty meals. Which hormone is responsible for her post-prandial worsening of symptoms?

A Somatostatin
B Secretin

C Pepsin
D Cholecystokinin
E Gastrin

387. With regard to the shoulder (glenohumeral) joint:
A It is a ball-and-socket fibrocartilagenous joint
B It has high mobility at the expense of stability
C It is supported mainly by way of ligaments
D It lies in close relation to the musculocutaneous nerve
E It most commonly dislocates posteriorly

388. Which one of the following is true of cortisol?
A It is a protein
B It lowers blood glucose
C It is an anabolic hormone
D It is stimulated by renin
E It has a peak hormonal concentration in the morning

389. Which one of the following increases the risk of thrombosis?
A Immobility
B Thrombocytopenia
C Reduced blood viscosity
D An intact endothelium
E Heparin

390. When inserting a subclavian central line, the first bony landmark that can be palpated below the inferior margin of the medial portion of the clavicle is:
A Acromion
B Atlas
C First rib
D Second rib
E Third rib

391. With regard to the hip joint, which of the following is true?
A The blood supply to the femoral head arises from a single source
B It may refer pain to the knee
C It is the most commonly dislocated joint in the body
D It lies deep to the sciatic nerve
E The fibrous capsule is strengthened by two ligaments

392. With regard to calcium homeostasis:
A The active form of vitamin D is 25-hydroxycholecalciferol
B PTH secretion is stimulated by the pituitary gland
C Activated vitamin D decreases calcium absorption from the intestine
D PTH acts directly on osteoblasts in bone
E In the kidney, PTH increases calcium excretion and increases phosphate reabsorption from the urine

393. With regard to an embolus:
A It most often arises from a thrombus formed within arteries
B It is the same as a thrombus
C Embolus due to thrombus is impossible to distinguish from post-mortem clot
D Embolus is always due to thrombus
E It generally has a worse outcome than thrombus

394. Which of the following veins empties into the left renal vein?
A Hepatic
B Left suprarenal
C Right gonadal
D Left phrenic
E Right renal

395. With regard to the anatomical snuffbox:
A Tenderness at its base is indicative of a fractured hamate
B It is bounded medially by the abductor pollicis longus
C The basilic vein begins in its roof
D The skin overlying it is supplied by cutaneous branches of the median nerve
E The pulsation of the radial artery may be felt at its base

396. With regard to thyroxine:
A The thyroid gland produces more T3 than T4
B TRH directly results in thyroxine release from the thyroid gland
C Thyroxine promotes the growth and development of the brain
D Thyroxine decreases basal metabolic rate
E Thyroxine acts on cell surface receptors

397. **Ischaemia:**
A Refers to generalized tissue death due to toxins, trauma or vascular occlusion
B Is synonymous with the term 'infarction'
C Is an abnormal reduction of the blood supply to, or drainage from, an organ or tissue
D Is always due to vascular occlusion
E Leads to a worse outcome in tissues with a collateral circulation

398. **The Brunner glands secrete an alkaline product that helps maintain an optimal pH for pancreatic enzyme activity. Where are these glands located?**
A At the base of the villi throughout the small intestine
B Epithelium of the Ampulla of Vater
C Submucosa of the ileum
D Submucosa of the jejunum
E Submucosa of the duodeneum

399. **With regard to the knee joint:**
A It is a synovial, pivot joint
B The cruciate ligaments are intracapsular and intrasynovial
C The suprapatellar bursa (pouch) communicates with the knee joint
D Inflammation of the prepatellar bursa is known as 'clergyman's knee'
E The menisci play an important role in the locking and unlocking mechanism of the knee joint

400. **During diabetic ketoacidosis:**
A The pH of the blood is high
B Cheyne–Stokes breathing is characteristic
C Hyperkalaemia occurs
D Blood glucose levels are typically low
E Volume status is euvolaemic

401. **With regard to acute myocardial infarction:**
A It usually results from an embolus
B It always causes chest pain
C It induces acute inflammatory changes, maximal at 1–3 days post-infarct
D Infarcts less then 12 hours old are clearly visible on macroscopic examination
E The infarcted tissue is replaced by new cardiac muscle

402. **A woman sprains her ankle while running down a flight of stairs. Which ligament did she most likely injure?**
A Deltoid
B Anterior talo-tibial
C Medial collateral
D Calcaneo-fibular
E Calcaneo-tibial

403. **With regard to the brachial plexus:**
A It has principal root values C6–T2
B The serratus anterior muscle is innervated by the subscapular nerve
C A lesion involving the lower roots of the brachial plexus results in a classic Erb–Duchenne palsy
D Cords lie in relation to the third part of the axillary artery
E Roots lie in the neck between the scalenus anterior and medius muscles

404. **With regard to adrenal gland disorders:**
A Adrenal insufficiency results in hypokalaemia and hypernatraemia
B Conn's syndrome results in hyperkalaemia
C Cushing's disease is due to a cortisol-producing tumour of the adrenal cortex
D Phaeochromocytoma is due to oversecretion of cortisol by a tumour of the adrenal medulla
E Congenital adrenal hyperplasia (adrenogenital syndrome) results in virilization and salt wasting

405. **Atherosclerosis:**
A Is irreversible
B Most commonly occurs at branching points within the circulation
C Is a disease that primarily affects the tunica media of arteries
D Is accompanied by acute inflammation
E Is accelerated by hypocholesterolaemia

406. **What structure is involved in tarsal tunnel syndrome with heel pain?**
A Anterior tibial artery
B Deep peroneal nerve
C Peroneal artery
D Superficial peroneal nerve
E Tibial nerve

407. With regard to the brachial plexus:

A The ulnar nerve arises from the posterior cord
B The radial nerve arises from the lateral cord
C The musculocutaneous nerve arises from the lateral cord
D The median nerve arises from the anterior cord
E The axillary nerve arises form the lateral cord

408. Which one of the following is true of testosterone?

A Secretion occurs only in males
B It is secreted from the Sertoli cells of the testis
C It is a peptide hormone
D It is essential for spermatogenesis
E It depends on FSH for secretion

409. Which of the following regarding local anaesthetics is true?

A Cocaine is an amide
B Addition of adrenaline increases systemic absorption of the local anaesthetic
C One of the first signs of toxicity is perioral paraesthesia
D They work by blocking potassium channels in the nerve endings
E They inhibit the propagation of impulses in Aβ fibres first

410. A surgeon's finger is placed in the epiploic Foramen of Winslow. The superior margin is:

A Common bile duct
B First part of the duodenum
C Head of pancreas
D Hepatic veins
E Caudate lobe of the liver

411. With regard to the carpal tunnel:

A It is a fibro-osseous tunnel containing the extensor tendons
B It contains within it the ulnar nerve and artery
C Entrapment of the median nerve within it is known as cubital tunnel syndrome
D It contains ten tendons within it
E It contains within it the palmar cutaneous branch of the median nerve

412. With regard to the female reproductive system:

A The menopause is associated with an increase in follicle stimulating hormone
B Oestrogen concentration peaks just prior to menstruation
C Both oestrogen and progesterone are necessary for ovulation to take place
D Oestrogen production is confined to ovarian tissue
E Fertilization of the human ovum normally takes place in the uterus

413. Aspirin (acetylsalicylic acid):

A Is a lipo-oxygenase inhibitor
B Inhibits the coagulation cascade
C Inhibits platelet aggregation
D Is a reversible cyclo-oxygenase inhibitor
E Works by acetylating an aspartate residue at the active site

414. Cancer of the testis most likely metastases to which set of lymph nodes?

A Aortic
B Deep inguinal
C Superficial inguinal
D Common iliac
E Internal iliac

415. With regard to the arterial supply of the lower limb:

A The femoral artery is a direct continuation of the common iliac artery
B The posterior tibial pulse is posterior to the lateral malleolus at the ankle
C The popliteal pulse is the most superficial structure within the popliteal fossa
D The femoral pulse lies at the mid-point of the inguinal ligament
E The dorsalis pedis pulse is lateral to the extensor hallucis longus tendon

416. With regard to thermoregulation:

A Brown fat (non-shivering thermogenesis) plays a significant role in adults
B Acclimatization of the sweating mechanism occurs in response to heat
C Apocrine sweat glands play an important role in heat loss by evaporation
D Thermoregulation is one of the principal functions of the thalamus

E Heat adaptation takes approximately 3–5 days to develop

417. Aspirin damages the gastric mucosa through which of the following mechanisms?

A Reduced surface mucus secretion
B Increased mucosal blood flow
C Increased surface bicarbonate secretion
D Reduced acid secretion by gastric parietal cells
E Delayed gastric emptying

418. Internal haemorrhoids are painless and only sensitive to stretch. They are formed from folds of the mucous membrane and the submucosa of the anal canal which contain varicose branches of the:

A Superior rectal vein
B Inferior rectal vein
C Superior rectal artery
D Middle rectal artery
E Inferior rectal artery

419. With regard to the superficial veins of the extremities:

A The cephalic vein lies within the deltopectoral groove
B The long (great) saphenous vein lies behind the medial malleolus at the a nkle
C The short (small) saphenous vein enters the femoral vein
D The basilic vein pierces clavipectoral fascia
E The long saphenous vein has no tributaries draining into it

420. With regard to antiemetics:

A Cyclizine acts on the histaminergic system
B Ondansetron primarily acts on the dopaminergic system
C Prochlorperazine acts on the cholinergic system
D Metoclopramide is the drug of choice for motion sickness
E Metoclopramide is the antiemetic of choice in Parkinson's disease

421. A 'claw hand' is usually associated with injury to which of the following nerves?

A Axillary nerve
B Musculocutaneous nerve
C Radial nerve
D Median nerve
E Ulnar nerve

422. With regard to the hand:

A All the lumbricals are supplied by the median nerve
B All the interossei are supplied by the ulnar nerve
C The palmar interossei abduct the fingers
D It is supplied by a single palmar arterial arch
E Dupuytren's contracture is caused by ischaemic contracture of the intrinsic muscles of the hand

423. Which one of the following agents is a thrombolytic?

A Warfarin
B Aspirin
C Fibrinogen
D Streptokinase
E Heparin

SBA answers and explanations

1E: Tear of quadriceps tendon

A 21-year-old male has sustained an injury of sudden onset, associated with swelling and an inability to extend at the knee joint and an absent knee reflex. This is consistent with an injury to the quadriceps group of muscles that lie in the anterior compartment of the thigh and act as the principal extensors of the knee joint. The mechanism of injury is inconsistent with a fractured patella.

2B: Increased stroke volume

During strenuous exercise there is an increase in heart rate, stroke volume and cardiac output. Remember cardiac output is a function of heart rate and stroke volume. During exercise, there is an increase in respiratory rate (hyperventilation) which will lead to a reduction in P_aCO_2. During exercise the oxygen demand of skeletal muscle rises, therefore leading to a reduction in mixed venous blood oxygen concentration. Renal blood flow is autoregulated, so renal blood flow is preserved and will tend to remain the same. Mean arterial blood pressure is a function of cardiac output and total peripheral resistance and will increase with exercise, mainly as a result of the increase in cardiac output that occurs.

3C: Bronchial carcinoma

Thrombophlebitis migrans (or migratory thrombophlebitis) is a condition that results in recurrent episodes of venous inflammation (phlebitis) associated with thrombosis, that occurs in different locations (migratory). It is generally caused by inflammatory, or malignant, conditions where the patient is tipped into a hypercoagulable state. When associated with malignant conditions it is known as Trousseau's syndrome and is generally associated with visceral malignancies (adenocarcinomas), such as gastric, pancreatic, bronchial carcinomas. It is a non-metastatic (or paraneoplastic) effect of malignancy and is related to factors secreted by tumours.

4D: Long thoracic nerve of Bell

The serratus anterior muscle acts to protract the upper limb at the shoulder joint (the 'boxing' muscle). It is innervated by the long thoracic nerve of Bell which is a branch of the brachial plexus and has root values C5, 6 and 7. This may be remembered by the old aphorism 'C5, 6, 7 – Bells of Heaven'. A problem with either the nerve or muscle (e.g. nerve injury following axillary lymph node clearance for breast cancer, some forms of muscular dystrophy) leads to loss of the normal function of the muscle and winging of the scapula when the patient is asked to push against a wall. This is an important clinical sign.

5C: Renal tubular cells

Peripheral nerve cells, unlike nerve cells of the central nervous system, do regenerate following injury. It is a slow process that occurs at about 1 mm/day and may be followed with nerve conduction studies. Schwann cells are responsible for myelination of nerve fibres which increases the axonal speed of conduction. Following injury (Wallerian degeneration), they are able to regenerate. Mucosal cells are epithelial cells which behave like stem cells and can therefore continuously renew themselves. Liver cells (hepatocytes) under certain circumstances can be stimulated to divide. Renal tubular cells lack the ability to regenerate following injury. This is why renal blood flow is so carefully autoregulated. It is also why acute tubular necrosis is taken so seriously, because damage to renal tubular cells is irreversible and will lead to end-stage renal failure, requiring renal replacement therapy in the form of dialysis or transplantation.

6D: Prostatic carcinoma commonly spreads via the blood

Metastasis may be defined as the survival and growth of cells that have migrated or have otherwise been transferred from a malignant tumour to a site or sites distant from the primary.

Tumours commonly spread via the lymphatic and haematogenous routes, so spread generally follows the pattern of these two routes. Other routes are less common (transcoelomic, perineural spread, through cerebrospinal fluid, iatrogenic). Although there are some exceptions, as a general rule, adenocarcinomas spread via the lymphatic route and sarcomas typically spread haematogenously (through the bloodstream). Therefore osteosarcomas typically spread via the bloodstream. Basal cell carcinomas rarely metastasize (thereby excluding answer B) and tend to cause destruction through local invasion. Adenocarcinoma of the prostate tends to metastasize haematogenously through the basivertebral vertebral venous plexus to bone.

7C: Skull fracture

A biconvex-shaped haematoma on a head CT scan is consistent with an extradural haematoma (unlike a crescenteric-shaped haematoma which is caused by a subdural haematoma) and this would explain the patient's fluctuating GCS score. Extradural haematomas are caused by arterial bleeds (typically the important middle meningeal artery which is a branch of the maxillary artery and passes through the foramen spinosum). Usually the artery is torn during a traumatic episode around the region of the pterion which is the weakest part of the skull. The middle meningeal artery forms a close relation to the pterion of the skull. A fracture in this region leads to a torn middle meningeal artery and an extradural haematoma. Management is resuscitation with immediate evacuation through burr holes to prevent a deterioration in neurological function.

8A: Fibroblasts

The stages of wound healing include:

- haemostasis/coagulation
- acute inflammation
- formation of granulation tissue (endothelial cells, fibroblasts, macrophages)
- angiogenesis
- epithelialization, fibroplasia, wound contraction (myofibroblasts)
- remodelling.

During the wound contraction phase (which is responsible for forming a mature scar), fibroblasts change phenotypes and take on contractile properties (forming myofibroblasts). They are primarily responsible for drawing the two wound edges together. Macrophages are responsible for engulfing foreign and particulate matter through phagocytosis and also release cytokines that assist in the inflammatory and healing phases of the injury response. Reticulocytes are immature red blood cells (erythrocytes) and play no significant role in wound contraction. Giant cells are formed from a coalescence of macrophages and are seen in granulomatous conditions but again play no significant role in wound contraction.

9A: Typically encapsulated

An adenoma is defined as a benign tumour of epithelial cells. Table 1 distinguishes the main features of benign and malignant tumours.

Table 1 Features of benign and malignant tumours

Benign	Malignant
Non-invasive	Invasive
No metastasis	Capable of metastasis
Resembles tissue of origin (well-differentiated)	Variable resemblance to tissue of origin
Slowly growing	Rapidly growing
Normal nuclear morphology	Abnormal nuclear morphology
Well circumscribed	Irregular border
Rare necrosis/ulceration	Common necrosis/ulceration

Benign tumours do *not* spread beyond the basement membrane, nor metastasize to distant sites. They are typically encapsulated and have a pseudocapsule caused by compression of the normal surrounding tissues as a result of their slow growth.

Some cells may be dysplastic within a benign tumour (dysplasia means 'precancerous', or disordered, cells but importantly without the ability to invade through the basement membrane and metastasize to distant sites, so technically by definition are still benign). Dysplasia represents an important step in the progression to a malignant tumour and severe dysplasia is synonymous with carcinoma-in-situ. Examples of adenomas that may contain dysplastic cells include some types of bowel polyps (e.g. tubular, villous and tubulovillous polyps/adenomas).

Most adenomas are solid nodules, rather than being annular or circumferential lesions. Rectal carcinomas (that are malignant) can form annular or circumferential lesions.

10B: Damage to the external laryngeal nerve

Two important nerves are at risk in a thyroidectomy.

- The recurrent laryngeal nerve supplies all the intrinsic muscles of the larynx with the exception of the cricothyroid muscle. Damage on either side leads to vocal fold paralysis and resulting hoarseness. Bilateral injury leads to stridor which may necessitate a tracheostomy to maintain a reasonable airway (Semon's law).
- The external branch of the superior laryngeal nerve supplies the cricothyroid which is responsible for lengthening and shortening of the vocal cords, thereby controlling voice pitch.

11D: Woven bone

During fracture healing, provisional callus is composed of woven bone. This is gradually replaced with lamellar bone. Woven bone is characterized by a haphazard organization of collagen fibres and is mechanically weak. Lamellar bone has a regular parallel alignment of collagen into sheets (lamellae) and is mechanically strong.

12C: Anal cancer

The key word in this question is 'sole'. Anal carcinoma is the only cancer featured in the list that may be treated solely with radiotherapy. Current best available treatments for the other cancers require combination treatments (surgery, chemotherapy, radiotherapy).

13D: Retromandibular vein

There are several important structures to be aware of during parotid surgery. From superficial to deep are the following structures:

- facial nerve (VII cranial nerve)
- retromandibular vein – often large and responsible for causing troublesome bleeding
- external carotid artery – deep and rarely encountered.

Also at risk is the great auricular nerve (sensory to the ear-lobe and angle of mandible) and the risk of Frey's syndrome (gustatory sweating caused by misdirected reinnervation to the sweat glands through injury to the parasympathetic secretomotor fibres of the auriculotemporal nerve).

14E: Cardiac output divided by body surface area

The cardiac index is defined as the cardiac output relative to body surface area, thus relating heart performance to the size of the individual. The unit of measurement is litres per minute per square metre (L/min/m^2). Cardiac output (CO) is a function of heart rate (HR) and stroke volume (SV): $CO = HR \times SV$. Mean arterial blood pressure (MABP) is a function of cardiac output (CO) and total peripheral resistance (TPR): $MABP = CO \times TPR$.

15B: Bladder cancer

Beta-naphthylamine is a carcinogen that increases the risk of transitional cell carcinoma of the bladder. It was commonly used by workers in the aniline dye industry.

16D: Right occipital lobe

The man has a left homonymous hemianopia which means he is unable to view objects in the left visual field. This information is processed by the right primary visual cortex which lies in the right occipital lobe.

17C: Pressure on the eyeball

Heart rate increases when physiological demand increases (e.g. increased blood flow to skeletal muscles during exercise, to the gut after a heavy meal). Pressure on the sinoatrial node results in activation of the Bainbridge reflex (or atrial reflex) whereby an increase in heart rate occurs as a result of an increase in atrial pressure. During inspiration, intrathoracic pressure decreases. This triggers increased venous return which causes an increased heart rate through the Bainbridge reflex and Frank–Starling's law. Various vagotonic manoeuvres (e.g. Valsalva manoeuvre, carotid sinus massage, pressure on eyeballs, ice-water facial immersion, swallowing of ice-cold water) result in increased parasympathetic tone through the vagus nerve which results in a decrease in heart rate. Such manoeuvres may be clinically useful in terminating supraventricular arrhythmias.

18A: Plasma bicarbonate of 39 mmol/L

Respiratory failure is associated with hypoxia and either a normal/low CO_2 (type 1 respiratory failure) or a raised CO_2 (type 2 respiratory failure). Type 2 respiratory failure in the setting of a raised carbon dioxide leads to a respiratory acidosis. When respiratory failure is chronic, rather than acute, pH compensation occurs through the kidneys.

Renal compensation occurs whereby the renal tubules act to increase the resorption of bicarbonate thereby normalizing the plasma pH (a normal bicarbonate range is 22–30 mmol/L, so 39 mmol/L is raised). This is why patients with long-term, stable chronic obstructive pulmonary disease often have a normal pH but a raised plasma CO_2 and bicarbonate on their arterial blood gases. Renal compensation takes several days before it is fully functional (hence it is a sign of chronic respiratory failure, rather than acute).

19B: Glossopharyngeal nerve

The palatine tonsils are closely related to the glossopharyngeal nerve (cranial nerve IX) which is also the same nerve that supplies the middle ear (Jacobson's nerve). Pain from the tonsils is therefore commonly misinterpreted by the body as coming from the ear when it is in fact not. Referred otalgia is common after tonsillectomy and is also commonly seen in patients presenting with tonsillar and/or base of tongue tumours.

20E: Pampiniform plexus

The contents of the spermatic cord may be remembered by the "Rule of 3's" as follows:

- 3 *constituents*: vas deferens (round ligament uterus in females), lymphatics, obliterated processus vaginalis
- 3 *arteries*: testicular artery, artery to vas (a branch of the superior/inferior vesical), cremasteric artery (a branch of the inferior epigastric)
- 3 *nerves*: genital branch of the genitofemoral (motor to cremaster muscle, sensory to cord), ilioinguinal nerve (inside the inguinal canal but outside the cord), autonomics
- 3 *veins*: pampiniform venous plexus, vein from vas, cremasteric vein
- 3 *fascial coverings*: internal spermatic fascia, external spermatic fascia, cremasteric muscle and fascia.

The ilioinguinal nerve is inside the inguinal canal, but importantly lies outside the spermatic cord. The dartos muscle lies within the scrotal layers and is not to be confused with the cremaster muscle.

21C: Subcostal nerve

When the kidney is approached surgically through a posterior approach, the subcostal nerve is usually superficial and encountered before reaching the kidney. The kidney lies extraperitoneally (retroperitoneal) and therefore A is incorrect. B and D are incorrect because the question is asking which structure is encountered before reaching the kidney. E is incorrect because the left kidney is being operated on and therefore the right hemidiaphragm should not be encountered. Always remember to read the question carefully!

22D: Right ureter

There are three important structures at risk in a right hemicolectomy that also form important relations to the right hemicolon:

- right ureter
- right gonadal vessels
- second part of the duodenum.

Vigilance and careful identification of these structures are needed to prevent inadvertent injury to them at the time of surgery.

23B: Left kidney

The head of the pancreas is related to the hilum of the right kidney but does not overlie it. It is, however, anterior to the left kidney.

24B: Pulmonary fibrosis

Pulmonary functional residual capacity (FRC) is the volume of air present in the lungs at the end of passive expiration. Obstructive diseases (e.g. emphysema, chronic bronchitis, asthma) lead to an increase in FRC due to an increase in lung compliance and air trapping. Restrictive diseases (e.g. pulmonary fibrosis) result in stiffer, less compliant lungs and a reduction in FRC.

25E: Released in hypovolaemia

Angiotensin II is one of the most potent vasoconstrictors in the human body. It is released as part of the renin–angiotensin system and is derived from angiotensin I (Figure 2). Angiotensinogen is converted to angiotensin I by renin. Angiotension I is converted to angiotensin II by angiotensin-converting enzyme (ACE) in the lungs. Angiotensin II stimulates secretion of aldosterone from the adrenal cortex (zona glomerulosa layer).

Hypovolaemia results in a decrease in intrarenal blood pressure which is sensed by the juxtaglomerular apparatus of the kidney, resulting in renin secretion and a rise in the levels of angiotension II.

26D: A fall in $P\text{CO}_2$

The oxygen–haemoglobin dissociation curve is shifted to the right by a fall in pH (increased hydrogen ion concentration, or acidosis), a rise in temperature, an increase in 2,3-DPG (2,3-diphosphoglycerate), a rise in $P\text{CO}_2$, exercise and HbS (sickle-cell haemoglobin). The dissociation curve is shifted to the left by a rise in pH, a fall in temperature, a decrease in 2,3-DPG, a fall in $P\text{CO}_2$, fetal haemoglobin, high carbon monoxide levels (carboxyhaemoglobin) and methaemoglobinaemia (Figure 3).

Anaemia has no effect on the dissociation curve as the graph represents the degree of oxygen saturation of the existing haemoglobin, rather than the amount, or concentration, of haemoglobin in the blood.

27A: Hypoxia

The dominant control process of coronary perfusion is metabolic hyperaemia. GTN spray is used in angina and increases coronary blood flow through the vasodilatatory action of nitric oxide. Alpha-adrenoceptor stimulation increases systemic blood pressure and thereby increases coronary artery perfusion. All beta-adrenoceptor agonists dilate the coronary vessels thereby increasing coronary perfusion. ADH, or vasopressin, causes a strong vasoconstriction in most tissues, but the cerebral and coronary vessels, by contrast, respond to vasopressin with an EDRF-mediated

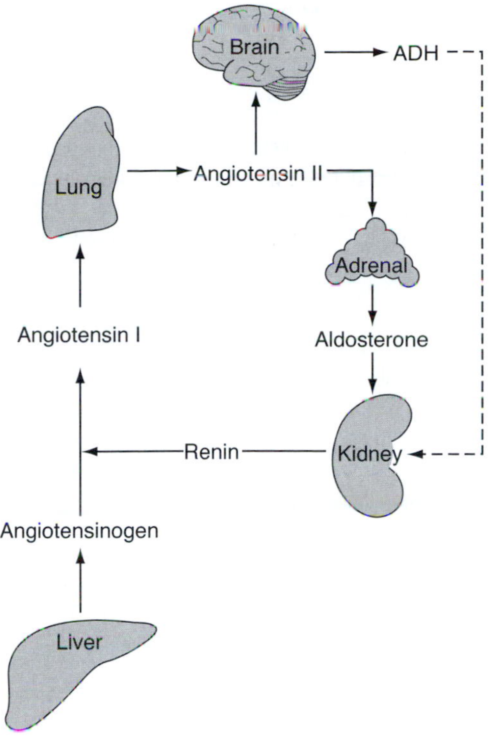

Figure 2 The renin–angiotensin–aldosterone system. Angiotensin I is a decapeptide and angiotensin II is an octapeptide. Renin is a proteolytic enzyme; angiotensin II is a converting enzyme. ADH, antidiuretic hormone.

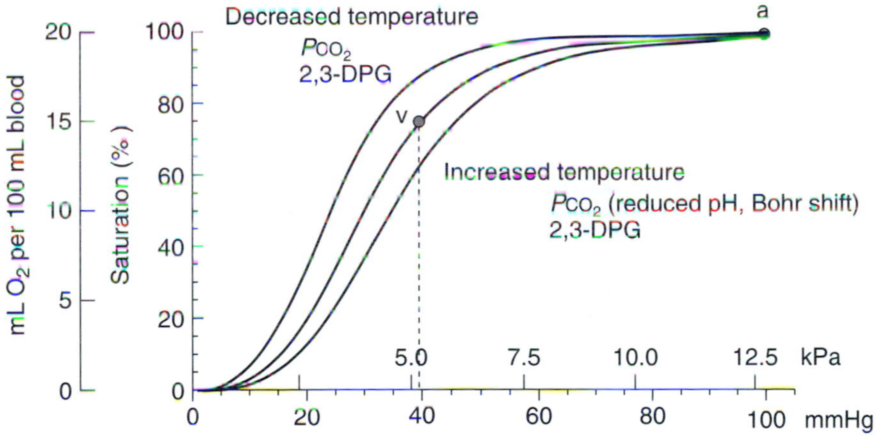

Figure 3 The carriage of oxygen by blood. v, venous; a, arterial.

dilatation (thereby increasing coronary flow). Vasopressin thus produces a redistribution of cardiac output in favour of brain and heart, which seems appropriate in hypovolaemia. Hypoxia reduces myocardial contractility and thereby decreases coronary perfusion.

28D: Bile salts

Resection of the terminal ileum interferes with the enterohepatic circulation, which is the route by which bile salts are recirculated in the body. Resection of the terminal ileum (e.g. in Crohn's disease) may therefore lead to a deficiency in bile salts. The clinical consequences of this are an increased risk of cholesterol gallstones. Vitamin B_{12} is also reabsorbed in the terminal ileum, so resection may also lead to deficiencies in vitamin B_{12} levels through malabsorption.

29A: Promotes protein synthesis

Insulin is produced by the beta-cells of the islets of Langerhans in the pancreas and has various actions, including: promoting uptake of glucose into cells; glycogen synthesis (glycogenesis); protein synthesis; stimulation of lipogenesis (formation of fat). Insulin functions to drive potassium into cells and is used to treat hyperkaelamia. Parathyroid hormone and activated vitamin D are the principal hormones involved in calcium/phosphate metabolism, rather than insulin.

30E: A rise in arterial $P\text{CO}_2$

Prolonged vomiting will lead to a hypochloraemic metabolic alkalosis (a rise in pH; raised bicarbonate), in addition to causing a hypokalaemia as gastric juices are rich in potassium. A hypovolaemic state will ensue with a raised urea concentration. pH compensation occurs through the respiratory system, resulting in hypoventilation which will tend to increase arterial $P\text{CO}_2$ levels.

31D: Lower protein concentration

Intracellular fluid contains a higher concentration of potassium, phosphate, protein and magnesium, but extracellular fluid contains a higher concentration of sodium, calcium and chloride and bicarbonate (Figure 4). Roughly two-thirds of the total body water content is intracellular and one-third is extracellular. The intracellular compartment is more acidic (lower pH; higher hydrogen ion concentration) due to nucleic acids (DNA and RNA) present within cells. The protein content inside cells is higher than the extracellular compartment; osmotic shock (cell lysis) is prevented by the $3Na^+/2K^+$-ATPase pump.

EXTRACELLULAR			INTRACELLULAR	
Na^+	143 mM	>	10 mM	Na^+
K^+	4 mM	<	140 mM	K^+
Ca^{2+}	1.5 mM	>	0.1 μM	Ca^{2+}
Mg^{2+}	1.0 mM	<	58 mM	Mg^{2+}
Cl^-	118 mM	>	10 mM	Cl^-
HCO_3^-	24 mM	>	10 mM	HCO_3^-
pH	7.4	>	7.0	pH

Figure 4 The ionic composition of intracellular and extracellular spaces.

32E: Can lead to a rise in blood pressure and bradycardia

The pressure–volume relationship between intracranial pressure (ICP), volume of cerebrospinal fluid (CSF), blood, and brain tissue, is known as the Monro–Kellie doctrine, or the Monro–Kellie hypothesis. This states that the cranial compartment is incompressible, and the volume inside the cranium is a fixed volume. The cranium, along with the relatively inelastic dura, forms a rigid container, such that the increase in any of its contents – brain, blood, or CSF – will tend to increase the ICP. This in turn will result in a fall in CPP, because CPP = MABP – ICP, where MABP is the mean arterial blood pressure. To compensate for a fall in CPP, the Cushing's reflex/response occurs, resulting in a rise in mean arterial blood pressure and, through the baroreceptor reflex, this causes a reflex bradycardia.

Raised intracranial pressure would not be caused by a shearing injury to the scalp as the injury sustained is outside the cranial vault. Following an acute subdural haematoma there is often a delay before a rise in ICP, because these are often caused by slow venous bleeds, and compensatory mechanisms occur to maintain the ICP within the normal range (displacement of CSF into the spinal canal; ability of the falx or tentorium to stretch). Chronic subdural haematomas, on the other hand, can result in a rise in ICP when compensation can no longer occur.

When the rise in ICP is significant, 'coning' may occur with compression of the 3rd cranial nerve on one side, causing a fixed, dilated pupil on the ipsilateral side.

33A: There is negative base excess

In metabolic acidosis there is a negative base excess. Bicarbonate is the main extracellular buffer, not intracellular. The main intracellular buffers are phosphate and proteins. Compensation in metabolic acidosis occurs through hyperventilation (an increase in alveolar ventilation) and blowing off of CO_2. The mainstay of treatment is to treat the underlying cause (e.g. treatment of hypoxia, shock, hypovolaemia, sepsis). Bicarbonate infusions are used as a last resort since they shift the oxygen–haemoglobin dissociation curve to the left.

34C: Sensory innervations from the internal laryngeal nerve

The posterior one-third of the tongue is innervated (light touch and special taste sensation) by branches of the glossopharyngeal (IX) and vagus (X) nerves. The chorda tympani supplies special taste sensation to the anterior two-thirds of the tongue, and light touch to the anterior two-thirds of the tongue is supplied by the lingual nerve.

Filiform (for gripping food) and fungiform (for sweet/salty taste) papillae are found on the anterior aspect of the tongue. Valate papillae are found further back but still on the anterior two-thirds of the tongue and are concerned with bitter taste. Foliate papillae are found on the sides of the tongue and are concerned with sour taste. The mucous membrane covering the posterior one-third of the tongue is devoid of papillae but has a nodular irregular surface caused by the presence of underlying lymphoid tissue, the lingual tonsil.

35C: The ACL is supplied by the middle geniculate artery

The popliteus tendon penetrates the capsule and is covered by synovial membrane. The suprapatellar bursa communicates with the joint space. The middle geniculate artery pierces the joint capsule to supply it and the cruciate ligaments. The iliotibial tract is attached to a smooth round facet on the anterolateral aspect of the lateral condyle of the tibia. Flexion occurs in the upper compartment and rotation in the lower compartment of the knee.

36B: Provides the same amount of oxygen to the liver as the portal vein

The liver has a rich blood supply derived from two sources: two-thirds from the portal vein, the remaining one-third from the hepatic artery. Portal vein blood is rich in nutrients absorbed from the intestine, but has a relatively low oxygen tension. Hepatic arterial blood contains few nutrients but is rich in oxygen. The hepatic artery supplies roughly 50 per cent of the oxygen delivered to the liver and the portal vein the other 50 per cent of hepatic oxygen supply. The liver is divided into segments by planes defined by the main hepatic veins (Couinaud classification). Purposeful embolization of hepatic arterial branches may be used to treat hepatic metastases.

37C: Protracted vomiting

Metabolic alkalosis is commonly seen in protracted vomiting where there is a loss of hydrochloric acid. Aspirin (salicylic acid) poisoning will lead to a metabolic acidosis with a raised anion gap. A pancreatic fistula will lead to loss of bicarbonate-rich (alkaline-rich) digestive juices, resulting in a metabolic acidosis (normal anion gap). Hyperventilation will cause a respiratory, rather than a metabolic, alkalosis. Hypoglycaemia will lead to a metabolic acidosis secondary to lactic acidosis and the production of ketone bodies.

38A: Staphylococcus aureus

Osteomyelitis is most commonly caused by *S. aureus* in all age groups.

39A: May respond to pressure dressing

Keloid scars extend beyond the margins of the wound (unlike hypertrophic scars which are confined to the wound margins). Keloid scars are most common on the sternum and deltoid area. Re-excision will usually lead to recurrence. Steroid injections (e.g. triamcinolone) may reduce keloid scar formation around the time of surgery. Pressure dressings also help. The use of subcuticular sutures will not reduce keloid formation.

40C: Haemophilus influenzae

Splenectomized patients are at high risk of postsplenectomy sepsis, especially from encapsulated organisms such as:

- *Haemophilus influenzae*
- *Neisseria meningitidis* (meningococcus)
- *Streptococcus pneumoniae* (pneumococcus).

They are prevented by administering the relevant vaccinations and giving prophylactic penicillin. Patients are also at risk of malaria (especially *Plasmodium falciparum*).

41C: Deficiency of factor IX

Haemophilia B (also known as Christmas disease) is less common than haemophilia A and is due to a deficiency in factor IX. Haemophilia A is due to a deficiency in factor VIII.

42A: Dysphagia

Iron deficiency may be associated with a postcricoid web resulting in dysphagia, koilonychia (spoon-shaped nails), glossitis and angular cheilitis. The association is known as Plummer–Vinson syndrome (also known as George–Paterson–Brown-Kelly syndrome, or sideropenic dysphagia). Such patients are usually female and are at an increased risk of postcricoid tumours.

43D: Increase in tidal ventilation

During haemorrhagic shock, catecholamine levels increase as a result of secretion by the adrenal medulla during the 'fright, fight or flight' (stress) response. A hypovolaemic state stimulates antidiuretic hormone (ADH) secretion. Hypoxia as a result of haemorrhage stimulates chemoreceptors, resulting in increased ventilation (tidal ventilation). The carotid body peripheral chemoreceptors are most sensitive. There is also stimulation of baroreceptors located in the carotid sinus and aortic arch, that act to maintain blood pressure. Haemorrhagic shock leads to hypothermia and a reduction in $P\text{CO}_2$ (secondary to hyperventilation) and consequently a shift in the oxygen–haemoglobin dissociation curve to the left, thereby increasing the affinity of haemoglobin for oxygen.

44B: Acute gastric dilatation

Major burns are associated with splanchnic vasoconstriction on both the arteriolar and venous sides of the circulation. Curling's ulcers are stress ulcers related to major burns, not to be confused with Cushing's ulcers which occur in the setting of head injury. They were once a common complication of major burns and commonly resulted in perforation and haemorrhage, more often than other forms of intestinal ulceration, with correspondingly high mortality rates. Major burns are associated with paralytic ileus, rather than mechanical bowel obstruction.

45C: During growth

Following trauma, sepsis, surgery or any other catabolic state, nitrogen balance is negative. Metabolic rate increases and protein from muscle stores is mobilized for repair and energy, which results in increased urea production and a net nitrogen loss. This may be prolonged for many weeks if sepsis or multiorgan failure occurs. Adrenocorticotropic hormone (ACTH) stimulates cortisol secretion, leading to a catabolic state and a negative nitrogen balance. During growth there is a positive nitrogen balance as protein synthesis occurs.

46A: Prolactin

The anterior pituitary gland (adenohypophysis or pars distalis) synthesizes and secretes the following six hormones: FSH (follicle-stimulating hormone), LH (luteinizing hormone), growth hormone, prolactin, ACTH (adrenocorticotropic hormone) and TSH (thyroid-stimulating hormone). The posterior pituitary gland (neurohypophysis) produces only two hormones: ADH (antidiuretic hormone, also known as vasopressin) and oxytocin. These hormones are synthesized by the hypothalamus and then stored and secreted by the posterior pituitary gland into the bloodstream.

47E: Lies deep to the prevertebral layer of the deep cervical fascia

Scalenus anterior arises from the anterior tubercles of the transverse processes of the 3rd, 4th, 5th and 6th cervical vertebrae and descends almost vertically to insert into the scalene tubercle on the inner border of the 1st rib and into the ridge on the upper surface of the rib in front of the subclavian grove. It lies deep to the prevertebral layer of the deep cervical fascia in the posterior triangle of the neck. The important anterior relations include the phrenic nerve and subclavian vein. Important posterior relations include the second part of the subclavian artery and the roots of the brachial plexus (anterior rami of lower cervical and first thoracic nerves).

48D: 125 mL/min

The normal glomerular filtration rate (GFR) in humans is 125 mL/min. After the age of 40, GFR decreases progressively by about 0.4–1.2 mL/min per year.

49B: Lung cancer

The three most common cancers in the female population in the UK in descending order of frequency are lung, breast and colorectal. In the male population the three most common in descending order of frequency are lung, prostate and colorectal.

50C: 30 per cent

Patients diagnosed with pancreatic cancer typically have a poor prognosis, partly because the cancer usually causes no symptoms early on, leading to locally advanced or metastatic disease at the time of diagnosis. Median survival from diagnosis is around 3–6 months. Even in those suitable for resectional surgery, 5-year survival rates are still only 30 per cent.

51C: Elemental fluids require minimal digestion by the patient

Enteral tube feeding may be administered in the presence of a functional gastrointestinal tract and may be achieved by a nasogastric tube, gastrostomy or enterostomy. Most patients will tolerate a non-lactose, iso-osmolar non-elemental feed, but those suffering from intestinal fistulae, short bowel syndrome or inflammatory bowel disease benefit from an elemental diet which requires minimal digestion. Diarrhoea is a possible complication, but less likely if feeds are given continuously rather than in bolus and if iso-osmolar rather than hyperosmolar fluid administration. Osmolality is increased when the feed contains glucose, and is lowered when the feed contains sucrose or glucose polymers as the carbohydrate source. Enteral feeding is more cost-effective, safer and requires less monitoring than parental feeding. Moreover, the enteral route allows maintenance of the structural and functional integrity of the intestine.

52D: Does not take into account the presence of metastases
Duke's classification is a histological staging system (defines how far the tumour has spread). The individual stage gives valuable information for the prognosis and management of the patient. A grading system describes the degree of cellular differentiation. Stage A represents a tumour confined to the wall of the bowel, stage B when the tumour has penetrated the serosal surface and stage C when there is local lymph node involvement. Stage D was added later and represents widespread distant metastases, as this is a histological not a clinical staging system. A more detailed method is the TNM system which addresses many more details about tumour spread.

53B: Acute inflammation causes a rise in intraosseous pressure
Osteomyelitis is an infection of bone caused by pyogenic bacteria. *Staphylococcus aureus* is the commonest causative organism. Acute inflammation causes a rise in intramedullary pressure resulting in pain and vessel thrombosis. The classical pathological sequelae are as follows. Bone death results in the formation of a sequestrum, but healing is by new bone formation (the involucrum). A cloacae forms (holes in the involucrum through which pus formed in the medulla discharges). Finally, a tract from drainage from cloaca to the skin is apparent (sinus). Early plain radiographs are often normal, but after 7–10 days bone rarefaction, periosteal new bone and sequestra may be seen. Patients with sickle cell disease are prone to osteomyelitis caused by *Salmonella*.

54B: Abdominal pain, pyrexia and tachycardia are suggestive of a leak
Anastomoses involving the large bowel are more likely to leak than the small bowel. The small bowel has a better blood supply (perfusion), more fluid contents and lower intraluminal pressure compared to the large bowel. Surgical technique plays an important role in preventing leakage. Anastomatic leaks may be apparent in the immediate postoperative period, but it is more usual for signs and symptoms to develop at day 5/6 when bowel peristalsis commences. Abdominal pain, pyrexia and tachycardia are all suggestive of a leak. The appearance of bowel contents through the abdominal wound is not proof of a leak. Extensive dissection may be caused by injury to an unrelated portion of bowel, which had necrosed and leaked. In general, early leaks are best treated by exterioration of the anastomatic ends, or by creating a proximal defunctioning stoma. Late leaks often result in adhesions, abscesses or fistulae. Urgent laparotomy is rarely indicated and conservative management should be adopted.

55A: Cyclophosphamide
The main alkylating agents in regular use are cyclophosphamide, chlorambucil, melphelan and nitrogen mustard. Their mechanism of action is that they bind to proteins and DNA, thereby inhibiting their normal function. Both 5-FU and 6-mercaptopurine are classified as antimetabolites because they inhibit specific synthetic pathways and prevent cell division. Vincristine is a vinca alkaloid, which disrupts the integrity the spindle apparatus and arrest cells during mitosis.

56A: Occurs in normal tissue
Metastatic calcification is a process that involves calcium deposition in normal tissue due to elevated serum calcium levels in the blood. Altered calcium metabolism results in increased absorption, or decreased excretion of calcium and related minerals. Metastatic calcification is a different process to dystrophic calcification (normal serum calcium levels in the blood) and associated with tissue abnormalities or degeneration resulting in mineral deposition. Dystrophic calcification is the calcification occurring in degenerated or necrotic tissue, as in hyalinized scars,

degenerated foci in leiomyomas, and caseous nodules. This occurs as a reaction to tissue damage. The former process is general in nature and the latter is a localized phenomenon. Psammoma bodies are associated with the following tumours: papillary carcinomas (thyroid, renal cell, ovarian), meningiomas, mesotheliomas and prolactinomas.

57D: Neuroma formation

Joint contractures affecting the hip joint are a contraindication to offering a patient an above-knee amputation. Sudek's atrophy is the type I form of complex regional pain syndrome and does not demonstrate nerve lesions. This is not commonly associated with amputation. Myoglobinuria is the presence of myoglobin in the urine and is associated with rhabdomyolyis or muscle destruction. Amputation neuroma is a tumour that may occur near the stump following an amputation. Amyloid is a family of unusual proteins, all characterized by beta-pleated sheets, and associated with chronic infections, chronic inflammatory diseases and certain neoplasms.

58A: Begins in the region of the anatomical snuffbox

The cephalic vein is a superficial vein of the upper limb that arises within the anatomical snuffbox. It communicates with the basilic vein by the median cubital vein at the elbow and is located in the superficial fascia along the anterolateral surface of the biceps muscle. At the elbow, it is superficial to the lateral cutaneous nerve of the forearm. Superiorly, the cephalic vein passes between the deltoid and pectoralis major muscles (deltopectoral groove) and through the deltopectoral triangle, where it empties into the axillary vein. As it is a vein, it contains valves.

59B: Proximal myopathy

The patient is generally a young female and the condition may be familial. The thyroid is usually moderately diffusely enlarged and soft and a bruit may be heard. The patient may be hot, with moist and warm skin due to peripheral vasodilatation. Weight loss may be a feature despite increased food intake. Fine hand tremor with hyperkinesias and increased bowel mobility is also common. Cardiac enlargement and abnormal heart sounds are suggestive of Cushing's syndrome. Eye signs are usual. Menstrual irregularity and infertility are common.

60B: Left homonymous hemianopia

Occlusion of the posterior cerebral artery results in the following signs and symptoms:

- contralateral loss of pain and temperature sensations
- prosopagnosia with bilateral lesions of the lingual and fusiform gyri
- medial midbrain syndrome (Weber's syndrome)
- contralateral deficits of cranial nerves: facial (UMN), vagus and hypoglossal nerves
- ipsilateral deficit of occulomotor nerve (ophthalmoplegia)
- visual field defects (contralateral homoymous hemianopia with macular sparing)
- Horner's syndrome
- visual agnosia
- palinopsia, micropsia and macropsia (illusory phenomena)
- achromatopsia and dyschromatopsia (disorders of colour vision)
- memory impairment (amnesia).

61C: Femoral arterial branch, which takes part in the anastomosis around the knee

The adductor canal contains the femoral artery, femoral vein, and branches of the femoral nerve (the saphenous nerve and nerve to vastus medalis). The boundaries of the adductor canal are as follows:

- lateral: vastus medialis muscle
- posteromedially: adductor longus and adductor magnus muscles
- anteriorly: sartorius muscle
- roof: the sartorius and the subsartorial fascia.

62D: A cause of thoracic outlet syndrome

A cervical rib is an extra rib, which arises from the 7th cervical vertebra. It is a congenital abnormality that is located above the 1st rib. Thoracic outlet syndrome is caused by compression of the lower trunk of the brachial plexus or subclavian artery. It is associated with the formation of subclavian aneurysms. Chest radiographs with apical lordotic views and cervical spine radiographs are recommended. Onset is from the second to eighth decade with a peak in the fourth decade. It is more common in females.

63E: Is a cause of toe gangrene

An aneurysm is an abnormal dilation of a blood vessel. Abdominal aortic aneurysms between 5 and 5.9 cm have a growth rate 0.43 cm/year and an annual risk of rupture of 3–15 per cent. Ninety per cent of abdominal aortic aneurysm are infrarenal (below the level of the kidneys). If the aortic aneurysm grows at a rate of more than 1 cm/year, surgical treatment should be performed electively. It is associated with positive family history, smoking, atherosclerosis and other causes (infection, inflammation, trauma, etc.). There is no causative link with builders. Complications of aneurysms include: thrombosis, embolism, pressure effects, haemorrhage or ischaemia.

64A: Is formed by the union of the splenic and superior mesenteric veins

The hepatic portal vein is the venous drainage from the gastrointestinal tact and spleen into the liver. It is formed by the confluence of the superior mesenteric and splenic veins. The anterior boundaries of the epiploic foramen of Winslow is the hepatic portal vein. The portal vein is posterior to the common hepatic artery. The hepatic portal vein orginates behind the neck of the pancreas. Approximately 75 per cent of hepatic blood flow is derived from the hepatic portal vein, while the remainder is from the hepatic arteries.

65D: Predisposes to malignant change

Ulceration of the lower limb affects 1 per cent of the adult population and approximately 3.6 per cent of people over the age of 65. The majority of chronic lower limb ulceration is attributed to venous disease. Venous ulcers occur when there is venous insufficiency or following deep venous thrombosis in which the valves have been destroyed following recanalization. In both, the common denominator is venous stasis. Chronic limb ulceration is linked to Marjolin's ulcers (an aggressive ulcerating squamous cell carcinoma in areas of previously damaged skin). The use of compression bandages or graduated compression stockings exerts a pressure of 40 mmHg at the ankle. An ABPI of less than 0.5 is contraindicated for compression bandaging.

66A: Affects the lower limbs in 80 per cent of cases

Lymphoedema is the accumulation of tissue fluid as a result of a fault in the lymphatic system. It commonly affects the legs, arms, genitalia and face. Lymphoedema affects the legs in 80 per cent of cases. Lymphoedema presents with unilateral limb swelling. It may be classified as primary (unknown aetiology) or secondary due to infection/inflammation. Lymphoedema should be distinguished from systematic diseases (cardiac or renal failure), venous disease (post-thrombotic syndrome) or rarer causes (arteriovenous malformations). Delayed ilio-inguinal uptake of radionucleotide rhenium–antimony labelled technetium is diagnostic. Treatment of lymphoedema is conservative (compression stocks), medical (diuretics), or surgical (debulking operations: Homan's procedure, lymphovenous shunts and lymphatic bypass).

67C: Is characterized by Reed–Sternberg cells

Hodgkin's disease often presents with painless enlargement of one or more lymph nodes (usually in the cervical region) and is characterized histologically by the presence of Reed–Sternberg cells. Non-Hodgkin's disease is commonly seen in the gastrointestinal tract. The Ann Arbour system divided Hodgkin's disease into four stages, according to its extent, with A or B subtypes according to absence or presence of constitutional systems. The lymphocyte-depleted type of Hodgkin's disease is associated with the worse prognosis.

68E: Parasympathetic fibres to the submandibular gland

The facial nerve is the seventh (VII) of twelve paired cranial nerves. It emerges from the brainstem between the pons and the medulla, controls the muscles of facial expression, and provides taste sensations for the anterior two-thirds of the tongue and oral cavity. It also supplies preganglionic parasympathetic fibres to many head and neck ganglia (including the submandibular and sublingual glands via the chorda tympani). The vagus nerve (CN X) supplies the palatoglossus muscle and the trigeminal nerve (CN V) supplies the medial pterygoid, masseter and temporalis muscles.

69A: Lies between mylohyoid and hypoglossus muscle

The submandibular (Wharton's) duct is 5 cm long. First it lies between mylohyoid and hyoglossus muscles and then between the sublinguinal gland and geniohyoid muscle. The duct develops in the ectoderm from a groove in the floor of the mouth. It opens into the floor of the mouth adjacent to the frenulum. The facial nerve (CN VII) runs through the parotid gland.

70B: Is at more of a horizontal angle than in an adult

The Eustachian tube links the nasopharynx to the middle ear. It is noted to be more horizontal in shape in children compared to adults. A portion of the tube (1/3) proximal to the middle ear is comprised of bone and the remainder is composed of cartilage. It is derived from the first pharyngeal pouch. Otitis media commonly affects the Eustachian tube. Children under 7 years of age are more susceptible to this condition because the Eustachian tube is shorter and at more of a horizontal angle than in the adult ear.

71D: There is an association with Henoch–Schönlein purpura

Intussusception is an invagination of a portion of bowel into its own lumen. It occurs most commonly in boys aged 3–12 months. The majority of intussusceptions are ileo-colic, but ileo-ileal, ileo-ileocolic and colo-colic have also been described. Henoch–Schönlein purpura is a systemic vasculitis characterized by deposition of immune complexes containing the antibody IgA into the skin and kidney. There is an association with intussusception.

72D: Is associated with autoimmune diseases

Sjögren's syndrome is an autoimmune disease characterized by dryness of the mouth and eyes. There is a female predominance with an average age of onset in the late forties. Amyloid comprises a family of unusual proteins, all of which have characteristic beta-pleated sheet structure, and is not directly related to Sjögren's disease. Five per cent of patients with Sjögren's disease will develop lymphoma.

73C: Allows the biopsy of rectal tumours without anaesthetic

Rigid sigmoidoscopy examines the rectum. It rarely causes serious complications (<1 per cent). At about 15 cm the rectosigmoid junction will be encountered and usually this can be negotiated to show about 10 cm of the sigmoid. A proctoscope is used to examine haemorrhoids. Partial-thickness rectal biopsies are easy to carry out in clinic without anaesthesia. In the diagnosis of Hirschsprung's disease, a full-thickness biopsy at the anorectal junction is taken, usually under general anaesthetic or using a small anal retractor in neonates.

74B: Peptic ulcer

Parathyroid hormone increases serum calcium levels at the expense of phosphate. In 70 per cent of cases the condition is asymptomatic. Symptomatic forms are described as 'stones' (nephrolithiasis and nephrocalcinosis), 'bones' (bone pain and arthralgia), 'groans' (peptic ulcer disease and pancreatitis) and 'psychic overtones'. Calcium may increase gastrin secretion, which in turn may lead to peptic ulcer disease. The calcium may deposit in the eye leading to cataract formation. Hoarseness due to laryngeal spasm is associated with hypoparathyroidism.

75C: Has a roof pierced by the external jugular vein

The boundaries of the posterior triangle of the neck are: posterior border of sternocleidomastoid, anterior border of trapezium and the medial third of the clavicle. The roof is formed by investing fascia, platysma and the external jugular vein. The floor is comprised of prevertebral fascia covering muscles, subclavian artery, trunks of the brachial plexus and cervical plexus. The carotid sheath is contained in the anterior triangle of the neck.

76A: Develops from the first and third branchial arches

The tongue is a branchial arch derivative and is derived from the first and third branchial arches. Special taste to the anterior two-thirds of the tongue is from the chorda tympani nerve (a branch of the facial nerve, VII) and special taste sensation to the posterior one-third of the tongue derives from the glossopharyngeal nerve (IX). Somatic touch to the anterior two-thirds of the tongue is by way of the lingual nerve (Va) and to the posterior one-third is by way of the glossopharyngeal nerve (IX), as is the case with special taste.

The hypoglossal nerve (XII) supplies all the intrinsic muscles of the tongue, with the exception of palatoglossus which is supplied by the pharyngeal plexus of nerves (IX, X, sympathetics). A left hypoglossal nerve palsy will result in a deviated tongue to the left on tongue protrusion (but note the question says glossopharyngeal nerve!).

The tongue receives its blood supply primarily from the lingual artery, a branch of the external carotid artery. The fibrous septum dividing the two halves of the tongue prevents any significant anastomosis of blood vessels across the midline. In contrast, a significant feature of the tongue's lymphatic drainage is that lymph from one side, especially of the posterior part, may reach nodes on both sides of the neck (in contrast to the blood supply which remains unilateral). Because the lymphatic plexus freely communicates across the midline, cancer of the tongue frequently metastasizes bilaterally.

77A: Is more common in patients with Plummer–Vinson syndrome

Postcricoid tumours are more common in females. They are associated with iron deficiency anaemia and patients with Plummer–Vinson syndrome (also known as George–Paterson–Brown–Kelly syndrome) are at higher risk of developing such tumours. Such tumours require multimodal (combination) therapy (radiotherapy, chemotherapy and surgery). If surgically operable, they can be safely resected and reconstructed with a good chance of cure with minimal morbidity.

Postcricoid tumours are highly lethal with a poor prognosis and a 5-year survival generally ranging from 15 to 20 per cent.

78A: Thyroid dysfunction is unlikely

Retrosternal goitres are usually benign and multinodular. Although any thyroid malignancy can extend retrosternally (but especially anaplastic thyroid carcinomas and lymphomas), most cases are benign. In most cases the patient remains euthyroid with normal thyroid function tests and normal thyroid autoantibody tests. Tracheal deviation is not necessarily associated with stridor and many patients solely complain of shortness of breath on exertion. Recurrent laryngeal nerve palsy is a sign of thyroid malignancy and, as mentioned, most retrosternal goitres are benign.

79D: In the parotid gland can be reliably diagnosed by fine-needle aspiration

Although tumours seen within the minor salivary glands are more commonly malignant, malignant salivary gland carcinomas are still far more common in the major salivary glands (parotid, submandibular, sublingual). Frey's syndrome (gustatory sweating) is a postoperative complication of parotid surgery and is due to misdirected reinnervation of the secretomotor fibres of the auriculotemporal nerve into the sweat glands.

Salivary gland carcinomas are best diagnosed by ultrasound-guided fine-needle aspiration cytology (if the result is positive), although a negative test (benign result) does not exclude the presence of malignancy as the needle may have been directed into the wrong place. Risk factors for salivary gland malignancies include prior radiation treatment. Tobacco and alcohol, which are highly associated with head and neck squamous cell carcinoma, have not been shown to play a role in the development of malignancies of the salivary glands. Salivary gland carcinomas are relatively resistant to radiotherapy. Carefully planned and executed surgical excision is the primary treatment for all primary salivary gland tumours.

80A: Is a cause of carpal tunnel syndrome

Colles' fracture is a distal fracture of the radius that is a known cause of carpal tunnel syndrome (compression of the median nerve in the carpal tunnel). It rarely results in ulnar nerve compression. A Colles' fracture is extra-articular by definition and does not extend into the wrist joint, otherwise this would make it an intra-articular fracture (Barton's fracture). The distal fragment in a Colles' fracture is displaced dorsally, unlike in a Smith's fracture where the distal fragment is displaced volarly (ventrally). Associated fracture of the ulnar styloid process may occur in more than 60 per cent of cases, although this does not form part of the true Colles' fracture (especially as it may not occur in all cases) and is a common associated injury.

81B: The left hip joint is not congenitally dislocated

The Trendelenburg test is a favourite of examiners, so it is worth spending a moment discussing it. Put simply, the test is an assessment of insufficiency of the hip abductor system.

Ask the patient to stand on his or her good leg and flex the other leg at the knee. The opposite side of the pelvis should rise to help to balance the trunk on the leg by bringing the centre of gravity over the weight-bearing foot. This involves the use of the hip abductors – the gluteus medius and minimus. This manoeuvre is then repeated by asking the patient to stand on the bad leg. The test is positive if the opposite side of the pelvis falls and the patient has difficulty standing. You may notice that the patient throws the upper part of the body over the affected hip in order to compensate for the loss of balance due to the pelvic dip on the contralateral side (Trendelenburg lurch).

In this scenario the left gluteal abductors (and left superior gluteal nerve), but not the psoas muscle, are working.

A Trendelenburg test can be positive for two main reasons – neurological or mechanical. Neurological causes can be due to generalized motor weakness as seen with myelomeningocele and spinal cord lesions, or more specific problems, such as superior gluteal nerve dysfunction/injury (e.g. following hip surgery). The mechanical causes include conditions that affect the abductor muscle lever arm, such as:

- congenital dislocation of the hip
- coxa vara
- fractures of the femoral neck
- dislocation or subluxation of the hip joint
- neuromuscular diseases (e.g. poliomyelitis)
- pain arising in the hip joint, inhibiting the gluteal muscles.

These conditions shorten the length of the muscle from its origin to its insertion, and significantly reduce its strength.

It should be noted that the test is not valid in children below the age of 4 years, and that it has a 10 per cent false-positive rate due to pain, generalized weakness, poor cooperation or bad balance.

82A: Has maximum velocity in the centre

In a vessel, laminar flow is governed by Poiseuille's law. Flow is maximal in the centre of a tube, with the highest concentration of cells in the centre. For flow in a pipe, laminar (smooth) flow occurs when the Reynold's number is less than 2300 and turbulent (rough) flow occurs when it is greater than 4000. Turbulent flow is a fluid regime characterized by chaotic, stochastic property changes. This includes low-momentum diffusion, high-momentum convection, and rapid variation of pressure and velocity in space and time.

83D: Limitation of straight-leg raising

A right S1 radiculopathy secondary to a lumbar disc protrusion would result in right-sided pain in the posterior aspect of the leg and ankle, reduced power in plantar flexion and reduced sensation in the lateral foot, and reduced/absent ankle jerk. A femoral stretch test assesses for irritation of higher nerve roots (L4 and above). The straight-leg raise test (Lasègue's sign or Lasègue test) determines whether a patient with low back pain has an underlying herniated disk, mostly located at L5, S1 or S2 spinal nerves.

84E: Have small orifices and characteristically close spontaneously before the age of 5 years

Congenital umbilical hernia is a congenital malformation, common in infants of African descent. Among adults, it is three times more common in women than in men; among children, the gender ratio is roughly equal. Umbilical hernias in children are common with an incidence of 1 in 10. Obstruction and strangulation of the underlying hernia is rare because the underlying defect in the abdominal wall is larger compared to inguinal hernia of the newborn. The size of the base of the herniated tissue is inversely correlated with risk of strangulation (i.e. narrow base is more likely to strangulate). A persistence of a patent vitelline duct permits an intermittent discharge of enteric contents from the umbilicus. It is a very rare abnormality and may be associated with umbilical polyps. When the hernia's orifice is small (<2 cm), 90 per cent close by 5 years.

85E: Fluids and mannitol

Haemolytic transfusion reactions lead to hypotension and oliguria. The increased haemoglobin in the plasma will be cleared via the kidney, which leads to haemoglobinuria. Inserting a urinary catheter with subsequent demonstration of oliguria and haemoglobinuria not only confirms the diagnosis, but is also useful in monitoring therapy. Treatment commences with discontinuation of the transfusion, followed by aggressive fluid resuscitation to support the hypotensive episode and increased urine output. Inducing diuresis through fluid resuscitation and osmotic diuretics is an important step to eliminate the haemolysed red cell membranes and help prevent renal failure. Alkalinization of the urine (pH >7) helps prevent haemoglobin aggregation and renal failure. Steroids have a limited role in this context.

86E: Burst abdomen is preceded by serosanguinous discharge

Cutting through muscle produces more postoperative pain than muscle splitting incisions where the anatomical planes between muscle fibres are used. There is no evidence that closing the peritoneum reduces the development of adhesions. The release of collagenase near wound edges weakens the skin and therefore sutures should be placed 1 cm away. The tip of the first trocar cannot be visualized before the camera is inserted unless a small laparotomy incision is made. The 'pink sign' indicates impending wound disruption.

87E: Responds to treatment with vancomycin

Pseudomembranous colitis, also known as antibiotic-associated diarrhoea (AAD), is an infection of the colon. The main causative agent is *Clostridium difficile*. Patients present with diarrhoea, fever, abdominal pain and rectal bleeding. In severe cases, life-threatening complications can develop, including toxic megacolon. A major risk factor for this condition includes recent antibiotic usage. Clindamycin is the antibiotic classically implicated as the causative agent, but any antibiotic can cause the condition. Due to frequent administration, cephalosporin antibiotics (cefazolin and cephalexin) account for a large percentage of cases. Medical treatment of this condition includes metronidazole or vancomycin.

88A: Ultrasound

There are no blood tests that are specific and sensitive to establish the diagnosis of acute cholecystitis. (Raised alkaline phosphatase, bilirubin, WBC and CRP are only suggestive of the underlying diagnosis.) However, ultrasound, CT scan and hepatobiliary scintigraphy with technetium-99m DISIDA (bilirubin) analogue are all sensitive and specific modalities for the diagnosis of acute cholecystitis. Plain radiographs are not beneficial.

89A: Albumin of 30 g/L

The modified Glasgow scoring system is an indicator of prognostic severity (Table 2). One point is scored for each criterion met on admission and again at 48 hours after admission (1–2 points is associated with a mortality of <1 per cent, 3–4 points with 15 per cent, and 6 points with a mortality approaching 100 per cent).

Table 2 Modified Glasgow scoring

Po_2	<8 kPA (60 mmHg)
Age	>55 years
Neutrophils/WCC	>15 × 10^9/L
Ca (corrected)	<2 mmol/L
Raised urea	>16 mmol/L
Enzymes (LDH)	>600 IU/L
Albumin	<32 g/L
Sugar (glucose)	>10 mmol/L

90D: Is anteriorly bounded by to the seminal vesicles and prostate

The blood supply of the rectum is supplied by the superior rectal artery (first two-thirds of rectum) and the middle rectal artery (last third of rectum). The venous drainage is the superior and middle rectal veins. The nerve supply comprises the inferior anal nerves and inferior mesenteric ganglia. The lymphatic drainage comprises the inferior mesenteric, pararectal and internal iliac lymph nodes. In males, the anterior border of the rectum comprises the rectovesical pouch, small bowel, Denonvillier's fascia, bladder, vas, seminal vesicles and prostate.

91E: Is attached to the diaphragm by the falciform ligament

The liver weighs 1500 g and is the largest organ in the body. It receives 30 per cent of the body's total cardiac output (1500 mL blood flow/min). The liver is drained by the hepatic veins into the inferior vena cava. The nerve supply of the liver is by the right vagus nerve via the celiac ganglia and left vagus, which is supplied directly into the porta hepatis. Sympathetic innervation is carried on vessels. The liver is attached to the diaphragm by the falciform ligament.

92B: Iron deficiency may develop

Choledochal cysts are dilations of the bile duct that may present with cholangitis, biliary obstruction or as an abdominal mass. They are major risk factors for cholangiocarinoma and are rare except in the Far East. One-third of cases present in adulthood. Treatment consists of excising the cyst and fashioning a Roux-en-Y choledochojejunal anatomosis. Multiple intrahepatic dilations occur in Caroli's disease, which is associated with cirrhosis and with medullary sponge kidney. Of note, Casoni's complement fixation test is for hydatid disease.

93E: Is treated by operative correction and may result in articular damage and foot stiffness

Talipes equinovarus is a structural deformity of the hindfoot and forefoot. Conservative treatment should address the problem by stretching and splinting in the following order: first the forefoot adduction, then the supination, and finally the equines deformity. It is more common in males and is bilateral in 30–50 per cent of cases.

94A: There is an association between osteosarcoma and Paget's disease of the bone

Bone tumors are rare. The three predominant malignant tumours are the osteosarcomas, chondrosarcomas and Ewing's sarcoma. Chondrosarcomas commonly occur in the middle-aged and elderly. Chemotherapy is now given routinely for osteosarcomas and Ewing's sarcoma, but has a limited role for chondrosarcomas. Metastasis usually occurs via the bloodstream. Pain and swelling are the two most common features.

95D: Costodiaphragmatic recess of the pleura

The posterior relations of the kidney include:

- diaphragm and costo-diaphragmatic recess of the pleura
- psoas muscle
- quadratus lumborum muscle
- 12th rib
- subcostal neurovascular bundle (vein, artery and nerve)
- iliohypogastric and ilio-inguinal nerves.

96C: May contain heterotropic pancreas

Meckel's diverticulum is the anatomical remnant of the vitello-intestinal duct. In the developing fetus the vitello-intestinal duct connects the primitive midgut to the yolk sac and plays a part in intestinal rotation. It is present in 2 per cent of the population. It is often observed as a 5 cm intestinal diverticulum projecting from the antimesenteric wall of the ileum and about 60 cm from the ileocaecal valve. Its blind end may contain ectopic tissue, namely gastric mucosa (10 per cent of cases), liver, pancreatic tissue, carcinoid or lymphoid tissue. It is about twice as common in males.

97A: Radiotherapy

Recognized curative treatment for localized carcinoma of the prostate includes primarily surgery, radiation therapy, and proton therapy. Alternative treatments (hormonal therapy, chemotherapy, cryosurgery, and high-intensity focused ultrasound (HIFU)) can halt the progression of disease, but not provide a cure. Tamsulosin is an α_{1a}-selective alpha-blocker used in the symptomatic treatment of benign prostatic hyperplasia (BPH).

98C: Is no more likely to have secondary hyperparathyroidism than someone on CAPD for the same period

Patients with end-stage renal failure, whether they are on haemodialysis or continuous ambulatory peritoneal dialysis (CAPD), are at an increased risk of secondary hyperparathyroidism – an increase in parathyroid hormone as a physiological response to hypocalcaemia as a result of low levels of activated vitamin D in chronic renal failure. Many years following renal transplantation, a condition known as tertiary hyperparathyroidism may develop where the parathyroid glands begin to function autonomously and complications may ensue. In such situations a parathyroidectomy may be indicated. Bisphosphonates following surgery would be counterproductive as they would lower calcium even further (bisphosphonates inhibit osteoclasts and thereby decrease calcium). Vascular calcification causes hardening and sclerosis of the blood vessels and is irreversible. Patients on haemodialysis who have taken aluminium hydroxide (to control high levels of phosphate) over long periods are at increased risk of osteomalacia (not osteoporosis).

99A: Will affect 1 in 15 women

Breast carcinoma is the most common female cancer in the UK. There is a genetic element (i.e. BRAC 1 and 2 genes) to the disease, but the risk is only about three times the normal in those with a first-degree relative with pre-menopausal disease. Oestrogen exposure has been linked. For example, early menarche, late menopause and nulliparous women are at a higher risk. Breast feeding is protective.

100D: Non-parametric tests could be used

A normal distribution is shown be a symmetrical bell-shaped curve on a graph. A population is defined in terms of its mean and its standard deviation. The mean, median and mode have the same value. A chi-squared test can be applied to a normally distributed population, whereas non-parametric tests can be applied whether a population is distributed normally or otherwise. One standard deviation from the mean contains 68 per cent of the population, two standard deviations include 95 per cent, and three standard deviations include 99.7 per cent. Twenty-five out of 1000 individuals (2.5 per cent) would be expected to be more than two standard deviations from the mode.

101E: Parietal cells

Goblet cells are mucus-secreting cells, widely distributed throughout epithelial surfaces, but especially dense in the gastrointestinal and respiratory tracts. Kupffer cells have phagocytic properties and are found in the liver; they participate in the removal of ageing erythrocytes and other particulate debris. The gastric mucosa contains many cell subtypes, including acid-secreting cells (also known as parietal or oxyntic cells), pepsin-secreting cells (also known as peptic, chief or zymogenic cells) and G-cells (gastrin-secreting cells). Peptic cells synthesize and secrete the proteolytic enzyme, pepsin. Parietal cells actively secrete hydrochloric acid into the gastric lumen, accounting for the acidic environment encountered in the stomach. However, parietal cells are also involved in the secretion of the glycoprotein, intrinsic factor.

Intrinsic factor plays a pivotal role in the absorption of vitamin B_{12} from the terminal ileum. Autoimmune damage to parietal cells leads to a lack of intrinsic factor and hydrochloric acid, leading to vitamin B_{12} deficiency and achlorhydria. This is known as pernicious anaemia. Pernicious anaemia is associated with a 3-fold increase in gastric cancer risk.

102D: Neisseria meningitidis

The spleen plays an important role in the removal of dead and dying erythrocytes and in the defence against microbes. Removal of the spleen (splenectomy) leaves the host susceptible to a wide array of pathogens, but especially to encapsulated organisms.

Certain bacteria have evolved ways of evading the human immune system. One way is through the production of a 'slimy' capsule on the outside of the bacterial cell wall. Such a capsule resists phagocytosis and ingestion by macrophages and neutrophils. This allows them not only to escape direct destruction by phagocytes, but also to avoid stimulating T-cell responses through the presentation of bacterial peptides by macrophages. The only way that such organisms can be defeated is by making them more 'palatable' by coating their capsular polysaccharide surfaces in opsonizing antibody.

The production of antibody against capsular polysaccharide primarily occurs through mechanisms that are independent of T-cells. The spleen plays a central role in both the initiation of the antibody response and the phagocytosis of opsonized encapsulated bacteria from the bloodstream. This helps to explain why the asplenic individuals are most susceptible to infection from encapsulated organisms, notably *Streptococcus pneumoniae* (pneumococcus), *Neisseria meningitidis* (meningococcus) and *Haemophilus influenzae*.

The risk of acquiring these infections is reduced by immunizing individuals against such organisms and by placing patients on prophylactic penicillin, in most cases for the rest of their life. In addition, asplenic individuals should be advised to wear a MedicAlert bracelet to warn other healthcare professionals of their condition.

103E: Upon assuming the upright position

Stimulation of the sympathetic nervous system results in a rise in heart rate and stroke volume and therefore cardiac output increases. Cutting the vagus nerves to the heart results in an increase in heart rate because of the abolition of vagal tone and therefore cardiac output increases.

If the end-diastolic volume of the heart (preload) is increased, under normal physiological circumstances, cardiac output is increased by the Frank–Starling mechanism. The exception is in the failing heart where the law of LaPlace becomes more important and cardiac output actually falls.

Arterial blood pressure is homeostatically regulated through the action of baroreceptors, principally located in the carotid sinus and the wall of the aortic arch. If the carotid sinus pressure is reduced, the baroreceptors become inactive and lose their inhibitory effect on the vasomotor centre in the brainstem. The result is activation of the sympathetic nervous system. This produces a rise in heart rate, stroke volume, mean systemic filling pressure and venous return, leading to an increase in cardiac output and return of the mean arterial blood pressure to its original value.

Cardiac output falls when one stands up owing to the pooling of blood on the venous side of the circulation, which has a large capacitance. Stepping out of a hot bath exacerbates this pooling effect because superficial cutaneous veins dilate in response to heat, increasing their capacitance even further. Under normal circumstances, activation of the baroreceptor reflex compensates to some degree, preventing syncope. However, in the elderly, or in patients on antihypertensives, inadequate compensation from the baroreceptor reflex may result in a vasovogal syncope, or othostatic hypotension.

104E: It is directly proportional to the fourth power of the radius

The Hagen–Poiseuille law states that the flow through a vessel is:

- *directly* proportional to the *pressure* head of flow
- *directly* proportional to the *fourth power* of the radius
- *inversely* proportional to the *viscosity*
- *inversely* proportional to the *length* of the tube.

The radius of the tube is therefore the most important determinant of flow through a blood vessel. Thus, doubling the radius of the tube will lead to a 16-fold increase in flow at a constant pressure gradient. The implications of this are several fold.

First, owing to the fourth-power effect on resistance and flow, active changes in radius constitute an extremely powerful mechanism for regulating both the local blood flow to a tissue and central arterial pressure. The arterioles are the main resistance vessels of the circulation and their radius can be actively controlled by the tension of smooth muscle within its wall.

Second, in terms of intravenous fluid replacement in hospital, flow is greater through a peripheral cannula than through central lines. The reason is that peripheral lines are short and wide (and therefore of lower resistance and higher flow) compared to central lines, which are long and possess a narrow lumen. A peripheral line is therefore preferential to a central line when urgent fluid resuscitation, or blood, is required.

105D: The sum of the residual volume and the expiratory reserve volume

Spirometry traces are easy to understand if you remember the following two rules:

1. There are four lung volumes and five capacities that you need to remember.
2. A capacity is made up of two or more lung volumes.

The *four lung volumes* are:

- *Tidal volume* = volume of air inspired or expired with each normal breath in quiet breathing; approximately 500 mL
- *Residual volume* = volume of air that remains in the lung after forced expiration
- *Inspiratory reserve volume* = extra volume of air that can be inspired over and above the normal tidal volume
- *Expiratory reserve volume* = extra volume of air that can be expired by forceful expiration after the end of a normal tidal expiration.

The *five lung capacities* are:

- *Functional residual capacity* = volume of air that remains in the lung at the end of quiet expiration, equal to the sum of the residual volume and the expiratory reserve volume
- *Inspiratory capacity* = inspiratory reserve volume + tidal volume

- *Expiratory capacity* = expiratory reserve volume + tidal volume
- *Vital capacity* = inspiratory reserve volume + tidal volume + expiratory reserve volume (or total lung capacity – residual volume)
- *Total lung capacity* = vital capacity + residual volume.

The residual volume (and therefore functional residual capacity and total lung capacity) cannot be measured directly by spirometry. They are measured by either whole-body plethysmography, or by using the helium dilution or nitrogen washout techniques.

106C: Is increased in emphysema

Compliance is expressed as volume change per unit change in pressure. Elastance is the reciprocal of compliance. The pressure–volume curve of the lung is nonlinear with the lungs becoming stiffer at high volumes. The curves which the lung follows in inflation and deflation are different; this behaviour is known as 'hysteresis'. The lung volume at any given pressure during deflation is larger than during inflation. This behaviour depends on structural proteins (collagen, elastin), surface tension and the properties of surfactant.

Surfactant is formed in, and secreted by, type II pneumocytes. The active ingredient is dipalmitoyl phosphatidylcholine. It helps prevent alveolar collapse by lowering the surface tension between water molecules in the surface layer. In this way it helps to reduce the work of breathing (makes the lungs more compliant) and permits the lung to be more easily inflated.

Various disease states are associated with either a decrease or an increase in the lung compliance. Fibrosis, atelectasis and pulmonary oedema all result in a decrease in lung compliance (stiffer lungs). An increased lung compliance occurs in emphysema where an alteration is elastic tissue is probably responsible (secondary to the long-term effects of smoking). The lung effectively behaves like a 'soggy bag' so that a given pressure change results in a large change in volume (i.e. the lungs are more compliant). However, during expiration the airways are less readily supported and collapse at higher lung volumes, resulting in gas trapping and hyperinflation.

107C: Thyroid-stimulating hormone

The pituitary gland (hypophysis) is the conductor of the endocrine orchestra. It is divided into an anterior part and a posterior part. The *anterior pituitary* (adenohypophysis or pars distalis) secretes six hormones, namely:

- FSH/LH: reproduction
- ACTH: stress response
- TSH: basal metabolic rate
- GH: growth
- prolactin: lactation.

The *posterior pituitary* (neurohypophysis or pars nervosa) secretes only two hormones:

- ADH (vasopressin): osmotic regulation
- oxytocin: milk ejection and labour

Testosterone is produced from Leydig cells in the testis and from the adrenal glands. CRH is produced by the median eminence of the hypothalamus.

108E: Fetal haemoglobin

The haemoglobin oxygen dissociation curve is sigmoidal in shape, which reflects the underlying biochemical properties of haemoglobin. The significance of the sigmoidal curve is that haemoglobin becomes highly saturated at high oxygen partial pressures (and is therefore highly efficient at collecting oxygen), and releases a significant amount of oxygen at pressures that are fairly low, but not extremely so (with the result that haemoglobin is highly effective at supplying oxygen where it is needed).

The effect of things that shift the curve to the right (raised CO_2, lowered pH, increased temperature, increase in 2,3-DPG) is to increase oxygen availability in the tissues. The effect of CO_2/H^+ on O_2 carriage is known as the Bohr shift or effect. This is exactly what is needed in metabolizing tissues; release of acids or CO_2 thus liberates O_2 to fulfil the metabolic needs of the tissue. Do not confuse this with the effect of changes in O_2 on CO_2 carriage, which is called the Haldane effect.

A shift of the oxygen dissociation curve to the left is characteristic of fetal haemoglobin. When compared with adult haemoglobin, it is composed of two alpha and two gamma chains, instead of the usual two alpha and two beta chains of adult haemoglobin. This arrangement assists in the transfer of oxygen across the placenta from the maternal to the fetal circulation. The corollary of this is that fetal tissue oxygen levels have to be low to permit the release of oxygen from the haemoglobin.

109B: CD8 T-cells

Lymphocytes can be divided into two main subtypes – T-cells and B-cells. B-cells (or plasma cells) secrete antibodies. T-cells can be divided into two further subtypes – CD4 T-cells and CD8 T-cells. CD4 (helper) T-cells can recognize antigen only in the context of MHC Class II, whereas CD8 (cytotoxic) T-cells recognize cell-bound antigens only in association with Class I MHC. This is known as MHC restriction.

CD4 and CD8 T-cells perform distinct but somewhat overlapping functions. The CD4 helper T-cell can be viewed as a master regulator. By secreting cytokines (soluble factors that mediate communication between cells), CD4 helper T-cells influence the function of virtually all other cells of the immune system including other T-cells, B-cells, macrophages and natural killer cells. The central role of CD4 cells is tragically illustrated by the HIV virus which cripples the immune system by selective destruction of this T-cell subset. In recent years two functionally different populations of CD4 helper T-cells have been recognized – TH1 cells and TH2 cells, each characterized by the cytokines that they produce. In general, TH1 cells facilitate cell-mediated immunity, whereas TH2 cells promote humoral-mediated immunity.

CD8 cytotoxic T-cells mediate their functions primarily by acting as cytotoxic cells (i.e. they are T-cells that kill other cells). They are important in the host defence against cytosolic pathogens. Two principal mechanisms of cytotoxicity have been discovered – perforin–granzyme-dependent killing and Fas–Fas ligand dependent killing.

110A: Hypokalaemia, metabolic alkalosis, low urinary pH

Following a diagnosis of pyloric stenosis, the first concern is to correct the metabolic abnormalities that invariably coexist with the condition. The serum electrolytes and capillary gases should be measured and corrected prior to surgery.

With prolonged vomiting, the infant becomes dehydrated, with a hypochloraemic metabolic alkalosis. The alkalosis is a result of loss of unbuffered hydrogen ions in gastric juice with concomitant retention of bicarbonate.

Fluid loss stimulates renal sodium reabsorption, but sodium can be reabsorbed only either with chloride, or in exchange for hydrogen and potassium ions (to maintain electroneutrality). Gastric juice has a high concentration of chloride and patients losing gastric secretions become hypochloraemic. This means that less sodium than normal can be reabsorbed with chloride.

However, it appears that the defence of extracellular fluid volume takes precedence over acid–base homeostasis and further sodium reabsorption occurs in exchange for hydrogen ions (perpetuating the alkalosis) and potassium ions (leading to potassium depletion). This explains the apparently paradoxical finding of acidic urine in patients with pyloric stenosis. Potassium is also lost in the gastric juice and thus patients frequently become potassium-depleted and yet are losing potassium in their urine.

111C: Has a protein content that is 0.5 per cent that of plasma

Most of the CSF is produced by the choroid plexus, which is situated in the lateral, third and fourth ventricles. CSF is absorbed directly into the cerebral venous sinuses through the arachnoid villi, or granulations, by a process known as mass or bulk flow.

The composition of CSF is different from plasma. The concentrations of K^+, Ca^{2+}, bicarbonate and protein are lower in CSF than in plasma. This is to prevent high concentrations of these electrolytes inadvertently exciting neurones present within the brain substance. The potassium content of the CSF in this respect is particularly important. Further buffering of the K^+ content of CSF takes place through astrocytes.

Likewise, the low protein content of the CSF (the CSF protein content is 0.5 per cent that of plasma) is deliberate to prevent some proteins and amino acids acting as 'false neurotransmitters'. The CSF is more acidic than plasma because pH of the CSF plays a critical role in the regulation of pulmonary ventilation and cerebral blood flow. Another reason why the CSF protein is kept deliberately low is to prevent proteins buffering pH. The result is that the pH of the CSF accurately reflects carbon dioxide levels of the blood. In this way changes in pH act as a powerful regulator of the respiratory system (through the action of pH on central chemoreceptors) and on cerebral blood flow.

112D: Inulin clearance can be used to estimate GFR

In the normal adult human the GFR (or normal renal clearance) averages 125 mL/min, or 180 L/day. The entire plasma volume (about 3 L) can therefore be filtered and processed by the kidney approximately 60 times each day. The rate of urine production in humans is dominated by tubular function and not by GFR. The GFR remains relatively constant through autoregulation.

After 35 years of age, GFR falls at about 1 mL/min/year. By the age of 80, GFR has fallen to about 50 per cent of its youthful level. GFR can decrease by as much as 50 per cent before plasma creatinine rises beyond the normal range. Consequently, a normal creatinine does not necessarily imply normal renal function, although a raised creatinine does usually indicate impaired renal function.

A substance used to measure the GFR must be freely filtered at the glomerulus, not be secreted by the tubules, not be reabsorbed, not be metabolized or synthesized in the body, not alter the renal function/GFR, be non-toxic and soluble in plasma. Such a substance is the polyfructose molecule, inulin. However, it is too cumbersome to use in routine clinical practice. Instead, GFR is more commonly quantified by measuring the 24-hour urinary creatinine excretion. Para-aminohippuric acid is used to measure renal blood flow and not GFR.

113B: Gastrin

Gastric acid is *stimulated* by three factors:

- acetylcholine, from parasympathetic neurones of the vagus nerve that innervate parietal cells directly
- gastrin, produced by pyloric G-cells
- histamine, produced by mast cells. This stimulates the parietal cells directly and also potentiates parietal cell stimulation by gastrin and neuronal stimulation. H_2 blockers such as ranitidine are therefore an effective way of reducing acid secretion.

Gastric acid is *inhibited* by three factors:

- somatostatin
- secretin
- cholecystokinin.

There are *three classic phases of gastric acid secretion*:

- *Cephalic* (preparatory) phase [significant]: results in the production of gastric acid before food actually enters the stomach – triggered by the sight, smell, thought and taste of food acting via the vagus nerve
- *Gastric* phase [most significant]: initiated by the presence of food in the stomach, particularly protein-rich food
- *Intestinal* phase [least significant]: the presence of amino acids and food in the duodenum stimulate acid production.

114C: Bicarbonate

Carbon dioxide is transported in the blood in various forms:

- Bicarbonate accounts for about 80–90 per cent of the total CO_2 in the blood
- Carbamino compounds account for 5–10 per cent
- Only 5 per cent is physically dissolved in solution.

Carbon dioxide is carried on the haemoglobin molecule as carbamino-haemoglobin; carboxyhaemoglobin is the combination of haemoglobin with carbon monoxide.

Erythrocytes contain the enzyme carbonic anhydrase that catalyses the reaction $CO_2 + H_2O = H^+ + HCO_3^-$ and requires zinc as a cofactor. This plays an important role in carbon dioxide transport and in the buffering of pH.

115C: Calcium influx

The most important source of activator calcium in cardiac muscle remains its release from the sarcoplasmic reticulum. Calcium, however, also enters from the extracellular space during the plateau phase of the action potential. This calcium entry provides the stimulus that induces calcium release from the sarcoplasmic reticulum (calcium-induced calcium release).

The result is that tension generated in cardiac, but not in skeletal, muscle is profoundly influenced both by extracellular calcium levels and by factors that affect the magnitude of the inward calcium current. This is of practical value in two key clinical situations; in heart failure where digoxin is utilized to increase cardiac contractility (by increasing the intracellular calcium concentration) and in hyperkalaemia where calcium gluconate is used to stabilize the myocardium.

The plateau phase of the action potential in cardiac muscle (principally due to calcium influx) maintains the membrane at a depolarized potential for as long as 500 ms. The result is that the cell membrane is refractory throughout most of the mechanical response, largely due to the inactivation of fast sodium channels. This prevents tetany upon repetitive stimulation which would be detrimental to cardiac output. Furthermore, the prolonged refractory period in cardiac muscle allows the impulse that originates in the sinoatrial node to propagate throughout the entire myocardium just once, thereby preventing re-entry arrhythmias.

116B: The ratio of stroke volume to end-diastolic volume

During diastole, filling of the ventricles normally increases the volume of each ventricle to about 120 mL. This volume is known as the end-diastolic volume. Then, as the ventricles empty in systole, the volume decreases about 70 mL, which is known as the stroke volume. The remaining volume in each ventricle, about 50 mL, is known as the end-systolic volume and acts as a reserve which can be utilized to increase stroke volume in exercise.

The fraction of end-diastolic volume that is ejected is called the 'ejection fraction' – usually equal to about 60 per cent. The ejection fraction is often used clinically as an indirect index of contractility. It is a particularly useful in assessing the state of the myocardium prior to aortic aneurysm repair where cross-clamping of the aorta places particular stress on the myocardium.

117C: In the ileum

Between 90 and 95 per cent of the bile salts are absorbed from the small intestine and then excreted again from the liver; most are absorbed from the terminal ileum. This is known as the enterohepatic circulation. The entire pool recycles twice per meal and approximately 6 to 8 times per day.

Disruption of the enterohepatic circulation, either by terminal ileal resection or through a diseased terminal ileum (e.g. Crohn's disease), results in decreased fat absorption and cholesterol gallstone formation. The latter is believed to result because bile salts normally make cholesterol more water-soluble through the formation of cholesterol micelles. Loss of reuptake also results in the presence of bile salts in colonic contents, which alters colonic bacterial growth and stool consistency.

118D: ↑BP, ↓HR, ↓CPP

The important relationship between cerebral perfusion pressure (CPP), mean arterial blood pressure (MABP) and intracranial pressure (ICP) is as follows: CPP = MABP – ICP. It stems from the fact that the adult brain is enclosed in a rigid, incompressible box, with the result that the volume inside it must remain constant (Monro–Kelly doctrine). A rise in intracranial pressure therefore decreases cerebral perfusion pressure (and hence cerebral blood flow).

In raised intracranial pressure, as the brainstem becomes compressed, local neuronal activity causes a rise in sympathetic vasomotor drive and thus a rise in blood pressure. This is known as the Cushing's reflex. This elevated blood pressure evokes a bradycardia via the baroreceptor reflex. The Cushing's reflex helps to maintain cerebral blood flow and protect the vital centres of the brain from loss of nutrition if the intracranial pressure rises high enough to compress the cerebral arteries.

119B: Zona glomerulosa of the adrenal cortex

The adrenal gland comprises an outer cortex and an inner medulla, which represent two developmentally and functionally independent endocrine glands within the same anatomical structure. The adrenal medulla secretes adrenaline (70 per cent) and noradrenaline (30 per cent). The adrenal cortex consists of three layers, or zones. The layers from the surface inwards may be remembered by the mnemonic GFR:

G = zona glomerulosa (secretes aldosterone)
F = zona fasciculata (secretes cortisol and sex steroids)
R = zona reticularis (secretes cortisol and sex steroids).

Aldosterone is a steroid hormone that facilitates the reabsorption of sodium and water and the excretion of potassium and hydrogen ions from the distal convoluted tubule and collecting ducts. Conn's syndrome is characterized by increased aldosterone secretion from the adrenal glands.

120A: Salivary

In humans, about 1–1.5 litres of saliva are secreted each day. Secretion is an active process. The two-stage hypothesis of salivation states that a primary secretion is first formed by secretory end-pieces (that resembles an ultrafiltrate of plasma), which is then modified as it flows along the duct system. Na^+ and Cl^- are absorbed and K^+ and HCO^{3-} are secreted as saliva flows along the ductal system. In addition, the ducts have a low water permeability.

The final saliva is hypotonic with respect to plasma and contains a higher potassium concentration than any other gastrointestinal secretion of the body. Any abnormal state in which saliva is lost to the exterior of the body for long periods can lead to a serious depletion of potassium, leading in occasional circumstances to serious hypokalaemia and paralysis.

121D: Omeprazole

Three main classes of drugs are used to combat gastric hyperacidity. From least to most potent they are:

- antacids
- H_2-receptor antagonists
- proton pump inhibitors (PPIs).

Only the H_2-receptor antagonists and PPIs reduce the secretion of acid from parietal cells. Of these, the PPIs (e.g. omeprazole, lansoprazole) are the most potent and have the longest duration of action. The reasons for this are two-fold. First, PPIs target the terminal stage in gastric acid secretion, namely the proton pump which is directly responsible for secreting H^+ ions into the gastric lumen. Second, the irreversible nature of the proton pump inhibition means that acid secretion only resumes after the synthesis of new enzyme. PPIs are extremely effective in promoting ulcer healing, even in patients who are resistant to H_2 antagonists.

H_2-receptor antagonists, however, should not be regarded as obsolete since they have a faster onset of action compared with PPIs. They are, however, less potent in inhibiting gastric acid secretion and have a relatively short duration of action compared with PPIs. H_2 antagonists (e.g. cimetidine, ranitidine) competitively inhibit histamine actions at all H_2 receptors. Acid secretion is not mediated via H_1 receptors, so chlorphenamine has no effect on acid secretion.

Antacids have no effect on the secretion of gastric acid from parietal cells but exert their effect by neutralizing the acid that is produced. Their efficacy is limited because the rise in pH stimulates gastrin secretion, which in turn stimulates more acid release (the 'acid rebound effect'). This effect does not occur with H_2-receptor antagonists and PPIs which act directly on parietal cells. Alginates (e.g. Gaviscon) are sometimes used and are believed to increase adherence of mucus to the mucosa, thereby increasing mucosal resistance to acid-pepsin attack.

Misoprostol is a synthetic prostaglandin analogue that promotes ulcer healing by stimulating protective mechanisms in the gastric mucosa (increased mucus, bicarbonate and blood flow) and by reducing acid secretion. It is sometimes co-administered with NSAIDs in the elderly to prevent peptic ulcer disease. However, misoprostol is not as efficacious as a PPI and use is limited by its tendency to cause troublesome diarrhoea.

122E: The vitellointestinal duct may persist as a Meckel's diverticulum

There are many important changes that take place at birth:

- The urachus (allantois) becomes the single, median umbilical ligament
- The umbilical arteries become the right and left, medial umbilical ligaments, respectively
- The ductus venosus becomes the ligamentum venosum
- The left umbilical vein becomes the ligamentum teres (round ligament) in the free edge of the falciform ligament
- The ductus arteriosus becomes the ligamentum arteriosum
- In 2 per cent of cases the vitellointestinal duct may persist as a Meckel's diverticulum
- The foramen ovale in most cases obliterates at birth to become the fossa ovalis, but remains patent into adulthood in some 20 per cent of cases.

Aberrations of this normal developmental process may lead to problems in adulthood. Failure of the urachus (which normally runs from the bladder to the umbilicus) to obliterate correctly may lead to a urachal fistula, sinus, diverticulum or cyst, often with leakage of urine from the umbilicus. Failure of the ductus arteriosus to obliterate at birth leads to a patent ductus arteriosus, resulting in non-cyanotic congenital heart disease. In 2 per cent of cases, the vitello-intestinal duct persists as a Meckel's diverticulum with its associated complications. In 20 per cent of cases the foramen ovale fails to obliterate completely at birth resulting in a patent foramen ovale. This may become the site for paradoxical embolism (where venous thrombus migrates and enters the systemic circulation through a patent foramen ovale), resulting in stroke.

123C: Upon exposure to light, cGMP levels within the photoreceptor fall

Phototransduction is the process by which light energy in the form of photons is converted to a change in membrane potential of the photoreceptor cell (rod or cone):

Incident light photons
→ Conformational change of rhodopsin

→ Activation of G-protein, transducin
→ Activation of cGMP phosphodiesterase
→ Decreased intracellular cGMP
→ Closure of Na^+ channels
→ Hyperpolarization
→ Decreased release of neurotransmitter
→ Response in bipolar cells and other retinal neurones.

The outer segment of the rod contains internal membranous discs which contain the light-sensitive protein, rhodopsin. Rhodopsin consists of opsin (seven transmembrane protein, or serpentine receptor) bound to retinal (the light-absorbing portion), a derivative of vitamin A. Deficiencies of vitamin A can therefore lead to night blindness and if untreated to deterioration of receptor outer segments and eventually total blindness. Slight differences among the opsins of each of the three types of cone results in differences in the wavelengths absorbed preferentially by each photopigment.

In the dark, non-selective cation channels in the outer segment are bound to cGMP and open, causing a predominant Na^+ influx. This is known as the 'dark current'. The level of cGMP in the outer segment depends on its rate of synthesis (by guanylate cyclase) and degradation (by phosphodiesterase). Absorption of a photon of light leads to isomerization of retinal (from the 11-*cis* to the all-*trans* configuration), structural activation of rhodopsin and activation of the G-protein, transducin. Activated transducin produces a fall in cGMP, closure of cGMP-gated cation channels and hyperpolarization. The hyperpolarization reduces the release of synaptic transmitter (glutamate) and this generates a signal that ultimately leads to action potentials in ganglion cells (the output cells of the retina). The action potentials are transmitted to the brain. In a sense, therefore, our photoreceptors are really 'dark receptors', depolarizing and releasing more transmitter as the level of illumination decreases. Presumably because we spend less than half our time in darkness, this arrangement is not as metabolically inefficient as it sounds at first.

This seemingly cumbersome process occurs very rapidly and results in great amplification. Photoactivation of a single rhodopsin molecule can lead to the hydrolysis of more than 10^5 molecules of cGMP per second. The amplification helps to explain the remarkable sensitivity of photoreceptors; rods are capable of producing a detectable response to as little as one photon of light. Several forms of retinitis pigmentosa, an inherited disorder of photoreceptors leading to blindness, are due to mutations within genes encoding members of the photoreceptor visual transduction cascade.

124E: Self/non-self discrimination

Innate (natural) immunity comprises:

- physical barriers (skin, mucosal membranes)
- physiological factors (pH, temperature, oxygen tension; e.g. low pH of stomach inhibits microbial growth, commensal flora)
- protein secretions (e.g. lysozyme in saliva and tears, complement, cytokines, acute phase proteins)
- phagocytic cells (neutrophils, macrophages, natural killer cells)
- acute inflammation (including mast cells, histamine etc.).

The two key features of adaptive (acquired) immunity are its specificity and memory.

The adaptive (acquired) arm of the immune response operates through both humoral and cell-mediated mechanisms and has a number of key features. Immunological tolerance is the exposure to self components in fetal life that leads to a state of specific immunological unresponsiveness (anergy). In adulthood the adaptive immune system is therefore able to discriminate self from non-self which is essential in preventing one's own immune system mounting a response against tissues. It may become defective resulting in autoimmune disease.

Immunological memory is a feature of the adaptive immune response and is essential for the rapid response to subsequent exposure of antigens. This concept is central to understanding how vaccines work.

125E: Thyroglobulin is stored in the colloid of follicles

The thyroid gland produces three hormones: tetra-iodothyronine (T4), which is the principal hormone; tri-iodothyronine (T3), which has shorter duration but is more potent than T4; and calcitonin, which is produced by parafollicular C-cells and is involved in calcium balance. The steps in the production of T4 and T3 can be summarized as follows:

- An active pump concentrates iodine into the thyroid follicular cells
- Iodine is oxidized into its active form (by peroxidase)
- Iodine binds with tyrosine, to form tyrosyl units (organification)
- Tyrosyl units bind to a protein core, to form thyroglobulin
- Tyrosyl units combine while bound to the protein core, to form either T3 or T4
- Thyroglobulin molecules are stored as colloid in follicles
- TRH (from the hypothalamus) stimulates the anterior pituitary gland to produce TSH
- TSH (thyroid stimulating hormone) stimulates the release of T3 and T4 into the blood.

126D: Suxamethonium

Neuromuscular blockers are commonly used drugs in anaesthetics. By specific blockade of the neuromuscular junction (NMJ) they relax skeletal muscles and induce paralysis. This enables light levels of anaesthesia to be employed with adequate relaxation of the muscles of the abdomen and diaphragm, thereby facilitating surgery. They also relax the vocal cords and allow the easy passage of a tracheal tube at anaesthetic induction, a procedure known as endotracheal intubation. They can be used *only* when mechanical ventilation is available because such drugs also paralyse the main muscles of respiration. Neuromuscular blockers can be divided into two main types: depolarizing and non-depolarizing.

Non-depolarising blockers (e.g. atracurium), also known as competitive muscle relaxants, compete with acetylcholine for receptor sites at the NMJ and their action can be reversed with anticholinesterases, such as neostigmine. Atropine is a muscarinic antagonist and is often given with neostigmine in order to prevent the muscarinic (parasympathomimetic) side effects of anticholinesterases (such as bradycardia, excessive salivation etc.).

Depolarizing blockers (e.g. suxamethonium, also known as succinylcholine) act by mimicking the action of acetylcholine at the NMJ but hydrolysis is much slower than for acetylcholine because it is resistant to degradation by cholinesterase. Depolarization is therefore prolonged, resulting in sodium-channel inactivation and neuromuscular blockade. Unlike non-depolarizing agents, its action cannot be reversed and recovery is spontaneous. Indeed, anticholinesterases such as neostigmine potentiate the neuromuscular block. Anticholinesterases are also used in myasthenia gravis to enhance neuromuscular transmission by prolonging the action of acetylcholine.

Suxamethonium has a half-life of only a few minutes and is rapidly hydrolysed by pseudocholinesterase. In patients with deficient or atypical pseudocholinesterase enzyme (an autosomal recessive condition), the metabolism is reduced and the half-life and duration of action of suxamethonium are prolonged, resulting in 'scoline apnoea', or prolonged paralysis. Assisted ventilation should be continued until muscle function is restored. In addition, suxamethonium may be responsible for triggering malignant hyperthermia in susceptible individuals – an autosomal dominant disorder that results in intense muscular spasm and hyperpyrexia and is associated with a high mortality.

Guanethidine inhibits the release of noradrenaline from postganglionic sympathetic nerve terminals. It has largely fallen out of use but is extremely effective in lowering blood pressure and may be useful in cases of resistant hypertension.

127E: The testes and ovaries descend from their original position at the 10th thoracic level

Genital development is principally determined by the presence or absence of a Y chromosome. Thus XO individuals (Turner's syndrome) are female and XXY individuals (Klinefelter's syndrome) are male. Presence of the sex-determining region of the Y chromosome (SRY) results in male development, absence of SRY leads to female development.

If the embryo is male, the SRY gene is transcribed and this initiates a cascade of events. The sex cord form the seminiferous tubules, some of the support cells become Sertoli cells and produce a hormone known as anti-Mullerian hormone (AMH), while other support cells become Leydig cells and secrete testosterone. This has the consequence that the paramesonephric (Mullerian) ducts regress due to AMH and the external genitalia become male (conversion of testosterone to dihydrotestosterone in the genital fold results in the formation of the penis and scrotum). The mesonephric (Wolffian) ducts grow to form the vas deferens and associated ducts. In females, where there is no SRY gene, the support cells do not form Sertoli cells. This has the consequence that no AMH is produced and no testosterone-secreting cells develop. The paramesonephric (Mullerian) ducts remain and form the uterus and fallopian tubes, the mesonephric (Wolffian) ducts regress and female external genitalia develop (labia majora and minora, clitoris). Aberrations of this process may lead to ambiguous genitalia and problems with gender assignment.

During embryonic and fetal life, the testes and the ovaries both descend from their original position at the 10th thoracic level. This explains the long course taken by the gonadal arteries and the site of referred pain from the gonads to the umbilicus (T10 dermatome). Descent is genetically, hormonally and anatomically regulated and depends on a ligamentous cord known as the gubernaculum. Furthermore, descent of the testis through the inguinal canal into the scrotum depends on an evagination of peritoneum known as the processus vaginalis. This normally obliterates at birth. Gonadal descent is a complicated process and therefore there are many ways in which it can go wrong. Most commonly, an undescended or maldescended testis may occur (cryptorchidism). A patent processus vaginalis may lead to the formation of a congenital hydrocele, or inguinal hernia.

128D: The macula region is grossly over-represented in the visual cortex

The visual pathway may be summarized as follows:

- Photoreceptors (rods, cones) within the retina convert light energy into electrical impulses (phototransduction)
- This is transmitted to ganglion cells, directly via bipolar cells, or indirectly via horizontal and amacrine cells
- Ganglion cells are the output cells of the retina. Axons from ganglion cells converge at the optic disc (blind spot) and travel in the optic nerve
- Incomplete decussation occurs at the optic chiasm; those from the nasal half of each retina (corresponding to the temporal halves of the visual field) cross over (decussate), while those from the temporal halves of each retina stay on the same side
- The optic tracts synapse in the various layers of the lateral geniculate nucleus of the thalamus before being relayed to the primary visual cortex in the occipital lobe via the optic radiation.

The macula is a region of the retina that subserves highest visual acuity. It is grossly over-represented in the visual cortex in a phenomenon known as 'cortical magnification'. This may partly explain why lesions located within the visual cortex may result in macula sparing.

The effects of lesions to the visual pathway may be easily predicted utilizing the above information:

- Lesions anterior to the optic chiasm (i.e. a transected optic nerve) result in a unilaterally blind eye

- Lesions of the optic chiasm (commonly from a pituitary tumour) result in a bitemporal hemianopia
- Lesions posterior to the optic chiasm (commonly due to ischaemic events) result in a homonymous hemianopia, with or without macula sparing.

129C: They have a life-span of only a few hours in inflamed tissue

Neutrophils are the most common type of leukocyte in the blood. They are present in large numbers in acute inflammation, but in chronic inflammation macrophages predominate. They have multilobed rather than bilobed nuclei, with 4–5 lobes but rising to 6–7 lobes in patients with vitamin B_{12} or folate deficiency. The ability to form multinucleate giant cells is a characteristic of macrophages rather than neutrophils and is classically seen in granulomatous conditions such as tuberculosis.

The phagocytic ability of neutrophils plays a vital role in the host defence against infection. Microbial killing results from both oxygen-dependent and oxygen-independent mechanisms. The former is more important and depends on the 'respiratory burst'. The respiratory burst follows activation of cell membrane NADPH oxidase by phagocytosis and results in the formation of powerful bacteriocidal agents (H_2O_2, superoxide anion and singlet oxygen). Oxygen-independent microbial killing is carried out by lysosomal enzymes, such as lysozyme. The importance of oxygen-dependent bacterial mechanisms is illustrated by the congenital disorder, chronic granulomatous disease. It results from inherited defects in the genes encoding several components of NADPH oxidase, rendering the patient susceptible to recurrent bacterial infections.

Neutrophils have a life-span of only a few hours in an inflammatory lesion, sometimes less. A severe local infection quickly becomes a graveyard of thousands of neutrophils. Their content, especially enzymes, spill out and may cause additional damage to host tissues. This is known as immune pathology and is the price to be paid for having a sophisticated immune system.

130A: It binds and stores oxygen for rapid release during falling $P\text{O}_2$

Myoglobin is a single-chain globular protein containing a haem group (iron-containing porphyrin) with eight alpha helices and a hydrophobic core. Being monomeric, it has instant binding with oxygen rather than the cooperative binding seen in haemoglobin. It has a hyperbolic dissociation curve. Its function is to store oxygen in muscle tissues for rapid release during times of need, as in exercise.

131E: Calcium-channel agonists

The following classes of antihypertensive drugs are currently in use (remembered by AAABCD):

- ACE inhibitors
- angiotensin II receptor antagonists
- alpha-blockers
- beta-blockers
- calcium-channel blockers (antagonists)
- diuretics.

Lowering raised blood pressure has successfully been shown (in both primary and secondary preventative settings) to reduce the risk of stroke, coronary events, heart failure and renal failure.

The choice of antihypertensive drug will depend on the relevant indications or contraindications for the individual patient. A single agent may not be enough, so additional blood-pressure–lowering drugs may have to be added until the blood pressure is well-controlled.

Alpha-blockers have largely been superseded by the other classes of antihypertensive agents. However, they still play an important role in the management of phaeochromocytoma (an adrenaline-secreting tumour of the adrenal medulla). In such instances α-receptors must be blocked prior to β-receptor blockade in order to prevent a dangerous hypertensive crisis developing.

Angiotensin II receptor antagonists are generally used as second-line agents when patients are unable to tolerate an ACE inhibitor. From 15 to 30 per cent of patients taking ACE inhibitors develop an intractable cough which is believed to result from the accumulation of bradykinin (angiotensin converting enzyme normally assists in the degradation of bradykinin and its derivatives). In such cases the patient may benefit from conversion to an angiotensin II receptor antagonist.

132B: Shaping of the hands and feet is brought about through apoptosis

The limb is the organ whose development is probably best understood and to understand abnormalities it is necessary to understand how the limb develops. Limb development takes places over a 4-week period, and by the end of the eighth week all the components of the upper and lower limbs are distinct. During this critical period, limb development is susceptible to the harmful effects of environmental teratogens, resulting in limb anomalies.

The limbs develop from small protrusions (the limb buds) that arise from the body wall of the embryo. Positioning and patterning the limb involves cellular interactions between the ectoderm surrounding the limb bud (apical ectodermal ridge) and the mesenchymal cells that form the core of the limb bud.

As the limb grows out the cells acquire a positional value that relates to their position in the bud with respect to all three axes, proximodistal, anteroposterior and dorsoventral. These positional values largely determine how the cells will develop. The positional value of the cells is acquired in the progress zone at the tip of the growing bud. Thalidomide, a drug commonly used in the late 1950s and early 1960s for morning sickness, was later found to interfere with the normal processes of limb development resulting in major limb defects such as phocomelia (short, ill-formed limbs resembling the flippers of a seal) and amelia (absent limbs).

Separation of the digits occurs by apoptosis (or programmed cell death). This is a good example of a situation in which apoptosis is physiological, rather than pathological.

Adult human limbs never regenerate following amputation, under any circumstances. Adult human limb loss is permanent and irreversible. Some amphibians, however, are unique among vertebrates in being able to regenerate entire limbs. This relates to their ability to revert to an embryonic state (dedifferentiate) in order to recapitulate embryogenesis. Elucidation of the mechanisms involved in amphibians and their possible relationship to limb development in higher organisms may one day enable us to regenerate a lost limb following an amputation.

133B: The primary visual cortex is located within Brodmann area 17

The human cerebral cortex is divided into about 50 distinct areas known as Brodmann areas, based on histological structural differences. The numbered areas have come to refer to the different functional areas of the human cortex.

In general, sensory signals from all modalities of sensation terminate in the cerebral cortex posterior to the central sulcus (with the primary somatosensory cortex area lying in the postcentral gyrus). On the other hand, the portion of the cortex anterior to the central sulcus is devoted almost entirely to motor control (with the primary motor cortical area lying in the precentral gyrus). A good way to remember this is 'Marks & Spencer' or 'M&S', with motor in front and sensory behind the central sulcus.

Visual signals terminate in the occipital lobe (Brodmann area 17 corresponds to the primary visual cortex) and auditory signals terminate in the temporal lobe (Heschl's gyrus).

There are two primary language centres within the brain: Broca's and Wernicke's areas. Broca's area is situated in the frontoparietal area and is concerned with the expression of speech. Wernicke's area lies in the temporoparietal area and deals primarily with the comprehension of speech. In the majority of people, the left cerebral hemisphere is dominant so that a stroke affecting the left cerebral cortex (resulting in a right-sided hemiparesis) interferes with the language centres, producing a corresponding dysphasia.

134C: Generates immunoglobulin-producing plasma cells

The germinal centres of lymph nodes contain mainly B-lymphocytes and follicular dendritic cells. Follicular dendritic cells are able to trap antigen on their cell surface for long periods. They help to initiate a B-cell response to antigens entering the lymph node and play an important role in affinity maturation (a process which results in an increase in the affinity of the antibodies produced during the course of a humoral immune response). Follicular dendritic cells should not be confused with Langerhans' dendritic cells which are professional antigen presenting cells found in the skin.

The cords and sinuses of a lymph node are situated in the medulla. The medullary cords are rich in plasma cells, whereas the sinuses are rich in macrophages. The paracortical zone (or interfollicular area) is rich in T-lymphocytes.

There is characteristically an expansion of the paracortex, rather then the germinal centres, in infectious mononucleosis (and many other viral infections), so-called reactive hyperplasia. This manifests clinically as lymphadenopathy.

135D: Mitochondria

Mitochondria are found in all eukaryotic cells. They contain their own DNA and are thought to be symbiotic prokaryotes that have been assimilated into eukaryotic cells in our biological past (endosymbiotic theory). They replicate by mitosis to form a clonal population. All the mitochondrial DNA in humans is derived from the clonal population of the ovum and therefore are maternally inherited.

136B: Gliclazide

Sulphonylureas (gliclazide and glibenclamide) are indicated when diet fails to control hyperglycaemia. Sulphonylureas stimulate insulin release from the pancreas, and are therefore of use only in patients who still have residual pancreatic islet cell function. Side effects include weight gain and hypoglycaemia.

Metformin increases the sensitivity to insulin at the receptor level, but should be avoided in patients with impaired renal function. Side effects include lactic acidosis, nausea, vomiting and diarrhoea.

Rosiglitazone is an example of a thiazolidinedione. This class of drugs act by increasing the sensitivity of insulin by binding to a nuclear receptor called PPAR-γ. It is not a first-line treatment and should be used in combination with metformin or a sulphonylurea. Rosiglitazone is currently contraindicated in heart failure as it is thought to worsen this condition.

Acarbose acts by delaying the digestion and absorption of starch and sucrose, through the inhibition of intestinal alpha-glucosidases. Its main side-effect is flatulence.

137B: The transcription factor WT-1 is necessary for the competence of the mesenchyme to be induced

The kidney develops from the intermediate column of mesoderm. There are three phases of kidney development, the definitive kidney developing in the last phase:

- stage 1: pronephros – primitive tubules
- stage 2: mesonephros – functional in the embryo, producing a dilute urine important in maintaining the composition of the amniotic fluid. They also contribute to the male genital system.
- stage 3: metanephros – true, hind kidneys.

The definitive metanephroi are induced early in the fifth week by the ureteric buds that sprout from the mesonephric ducts. The ureteric bud induces the mesenchymal cells to condense around it, forming the metanephric blastema. The development of the ureteric bud and the metanephric blastema depends on reciprocal induction, neither being able to develop in the absence of the other. The metanephric blastema causes the ureteric bud to grow and bifurcate and the ureteric bud induces the mesenchyme to differentiate into nephrons. If the ureteric bud does not reach/

signal properly to the surrounding mesenchyme, or vice versa, a kidney will not form (renal agenesis). If the ureteric bud bifurcates prematurely, a bifid ureter may result. Alternatively, if two ureteric buds develop an ectopic ureter may result.

The ureteric bud branches and gives rise to the collecting ducts and ureters; the metanephric blastema gives rise to the tubules, or nephrons.

The transcription factor and tumour suppressor gene, WT-1, is expressed in metanephric blastema, making it competent to receive signals from the ureteric bud that are essential for its induction. Mutations in the gene are associated with a cancer of the kidney in children known as Wilm's tumour.

The kidneys ascend from their original sacral location to a lumbar site. The mechanism responsible is not understood, but the differential growth of the lumbar and sacral regions of the embryo may play a role. Several anomalies can arise from variations in this process of ascent. A kidney may fail to ascend, remaining as a pelvic kidney. The inferior poles of the two metanephroi may fuse during ascent, forming a U-shaped horseshoe kidney. During ascent this kidney comes caught under the inferior mesenteric artery and therefore does not reach its normal site.

138E: It turns over approximately 4–5 times daily

Cerebrospinal fluid (CSF), situated within the ventricles and the subarachnoid space, bathes the surface of the brain and spinal cord, supplies nutrients to it, protects it and reduces its effective buoyancy. It also plays an important homeostatic role and is crucial for maintaining a constant external environment for neurones and glia. In humans the volume is about 150 mL and its rate of production is 0.5 mL/min (or approximately 30 mL/hour or 600 mL/day). Thus, the CSF turns over about four times daily.

Most of the CSF is produced by the choroid plexus, which is situated in the lateral, third and fourth ventricles. It flows between the lateral ventricles and third ventricle via the interventricular foramen (of Monro). The third and fourth ventricles communicate via the cerebral aqueduct (or Aqueduct of Sylvius). The fourth ventricle communicates with the spinal cord by way of the single median Foramen of Magendie and the two laterally placed Foramina of Luschka. CSF is absorbed directly into the cerebral venous sinuses through the arachnoid villi, or granulations, by a process known as 'mass or bulk flow'.

Occasionally the above physiology is disrupted and it becomes the centre of a pathological process. Hydrocephalus is an increase in the volume of CSF within the cerebral ventricles. It may arise from the oversecretion of CSF, impaired absorption of CSF, or obstruction of CSF pathways.

139D: Diversity is partly achieved through somatic hypermutation

Antibodies (immunoglobulins) are a heterogeneous group of proteins produced by plasma cells and B-lymphocytes that react with antigens. All have a similar structure with two heavy chains and two light chains. In addition, antibodies are made up of variable and constant regions. The antigen binding region is located in the variable region, whereas the complement fixing and antibody receptor binding activity is found in the constant region. The structure of the heavy-chain constant region determines the class of the antibody (i.e. IgG, IgM, IgA, IgE etc.). Although mast cells do not produce antibodies, they contain immunoglobulin receptors on their cell surfaces. As a result mast cells are able to bind pre-formed IgE on their cell surface which plays an important role in allergy and anaphylaxis (type I hypersensitivity reaction).

Any individual has about 10^{10} different antibodies. This astonishing degree of diversity arises through four main processes:

- pairing of different combinations of heavy and light chains
- recombination of V, D and J segments (VJ for light chains)
- variability in the joins of the recombined segments through imprecise joining by recombinatorial machinery and by the addition of extra random nucleotides by terminal deoxynucleotide transferase

- somatic hypermutation – a poorly understood mechanism for introducing mutations into V regions of activated B-cells (antigen driven).

A malignant tumour of plasma cells may result in the overproduction of a monoclonal population of immunoglobulins. This is known as multiple myeloma.

140B: Microcytic anaemia

Iron-deficiency anaemia is the most common cause of hypochromic, microcytic anaemia. Iron-deficiency anaemia occurs when the dietary intake or absorption of iron is insufficient and haemoglobin, which contains iron, cannot be formed. The principal cause of iron-deficiency anaemia in pre-menopausal women is blood lost during menses. Iron-deficiency anaemia is characterized by pallor, fatigue and weakness. Because it tends to develop slowly, adaptation occurs and the disease often goes unrecognized for some time. Hair loss and light-headedness can also be associated with iron-deficiency anaemia.

The blood smear of a patient with iron-deficiency shows many hypochromatic and rather small red blood cells (RBCs), and may also show poikilocytosis (variation in shape) and anisocytosis (variation in size). With more severe iron-deficiency anaemia the peripheral blood smear may show target cells, hypochromic pencil-shaped cells, and occasionally small numbers of nucleated RBCs (reticulocytes). The diagnosis of iron-deficiency anaemia will be suggested by appropriate history (e.g. anaemia in a menstruating woman) and by diagnostic tests such as a low serum ferritin, a low serum iron level, an elevated serum transferrin and a high total iron-binding capacity (TIBC). Serum ferritin is the most sensitive laboratory test for iron-deficiency anaemia.

If the cause is dietary iron deficiency, iron supplements, usually with ferrous sulphate or ferrous gluconate, will usually correct the anaemia.

141C: Bendroflumethiazide

Thiazide diuretics, which include bendroflumethiazide and metolazone, act mainly on the distal convoluted tubule where sodium reabsorption is inhibited. Water accompanies the sodium. Common side effects include hypokalaemia, hyperuricaemia and impaired glucose tolerance. Potassium loss arises from two distinct mechanisms that are not mutually exclusive. First, an increased sodium load in the collecting ducts stimulates sodium absorption in exchange for potassium secretion. Second, the high flow rate of filtrate produced by these diuretics will also favour potassium excretion by continually flushing it away, increasing the gradient from cell to lumen.

Acetazolamide is a carbonic anhydrase inhibitor, which acts by reducing bicarbonate reabsorption from the proximal tubule. Excretion of bicarbonate, sodium and water is therefore increased.

Furosemide is a loop diuretic which inhibits sodium and chloride reabsorption from the thick ascending Loop of Henle (acting on the $Na^+/K^+/2Cl^-$ transporter). As with thiazide diuretics, side-effects include hypokalaemia, hyperglycaemia and hyperuricaemia.

Vasopressin (ADH) acts by increasing the number of aquaporins, or water channels, in the collecting ducts, which increases the reabsorption of water.

Potassium-sparing diuretics (e.g. spironolactone, amiloride) also act on the distal convoluted tubule and collecting ducts to reduce sodium reabsorption and subsequently water reabsorption. Aldosterone stimulates sodium and subsequent water reabsorption from the distal convoluted tubule.

142C: The left pleuroperitoneal canal is larger and closes later compared with the right

The diaphragm is a composite musculotendinous structure formed in the embryo by the fusion of four separate elements:

- septum transversum (giving rise to the non-muscular central tendon)
- pleuroperitoneal membranes – closes the primitive communication between the pleural and peritoneal cavities (forms the bulk of the diaphragmatic muscle)

- a peripheral rim derived from the body wall (paraxial mesoderm)
- dorsal oesophageal mesenchyme (forms the left and right crura).

The septum transversum develops within the cervical region. This explains how the diaphragm derives its innervation from the phrenic nerve ('C3, C4, C5, keeps the diaphragm alive!'). Caudal translocation of the septum transversum is accompanied by elongation of the phrenic nerves and explains the long course of the phrenic nerves (from the cervical roots) through the thoracic cavity.

In a congenital diaphragmatic hernia, one of the pleuroperitoneal canals (which forms a communication between the pleural and peritoneal cavities, respectively) fails to close off through failure of pleuroperitoneal membrane development. This allows the developing abdominal viscera to bulge into the pleural cavity. If the mass of displaced viscera is large enough, it will stunt the growth of lung on that side, resulting in pulmonary hypoplasia and respiratory insufficiency, which may be fatal. The left side is involved four to eight times more often than the right, primarily because the left pleuroperitoneal canal is larger and closes later than the right, but also because of the liver on the right side.

143C: The protein content of cerebrospinal fluid is 0.5 per cent that of plasma

The constituents of the CSF are regulated by an active process that takes place within the choroid plexus. Thus the composition of CSF is different from that of plasma. Of importance to mention are the concentrations of K^+, Ca^{2+}, bicarbonate and protein that are lower in CSF than in plasma. This is to prevent high concentrations of these electrolytes inadvertently exciting neurones present within the brain substance. The potassium content of the CSF in this respect is particularly important. Further buffering of the K^+ content of CSF take place through astrocytes.

Likewise, the low protein content of the CSF (the CSF protein content is 0.5 per cent that of plasma) is deliberate to prevent some proteins and amino acids acting as 'false neurotransmitters'. The CSF is more acidic than plasma because pH of the CSF plays a critical role in the regulation of pulmonary ventilation and cerebral blood flow. Another reason why the CSF protein is kept deliberately low is to prevent proteins buffering pH. The result is that the pH of the CSF accurately reflects carbon dioxide levels of the blood. In this way changes in pH act as a powerful regulator of the respiratory system (through the action of pH on central chemoreceptors) and on cerebral blood flow.

144C: They can activate complement

IgM antibodies are usually pentameric, whereas IgG is monomeric and IgA is usually found as a dimer linked by a J-chain. IgM antibodies are characteristic of a primary immune response; IgG antibodies predominate in a secondary immune response. IgM is an effective activator of complement when it has bound specific antigen. IgA, rather than IgM, is found lining mucosal surfaces and is secreted into breast milk; IgA is therefore known as secretory immunoglobulin.

IgM cannot cross the placenta, whereas IgG can. The consequences of this are three-fold. First, if IgM antibodies directed against infectious organisms are found in the fetal blood, they are an indicator of intra-uterine infection. Second, antibodies to ordinary ABO blood groups (anti-A and anti-B) are usually of the IgM type and hence do not cross the placenta. Third, because IgG can cross the placenta, whereas IgM cannot, it explains why rhesus haemolytic disease of the newborn is uncommon with the first pregnancy (the initial exposure to rhesus antigen evokes the formation of IgM antibodies). Subsequent exposure during a second or third pregnancy generally leads to a brisk IgG antibody response.

145E: Increased lipolysis

Adrenaline acts mainly on beta-adrenoceptors (unlike noradrenaline which acts mainly on alpha-adrenoceptors) and has numerous metabolic effects. It has direct effects on adipose tissue inducing hormone sensitive lipases, thereby promoting lipolysis and releasing fatty acids into the bloodstream. Increased glycogenolysis in the liver releases large amounts of glucose into the bloodstream. Glycogen synthesis in the liver and in muscles is inhibited. Glycogenolysis in muscles does not increase blood glucose as the glucose generated remains within the muscles for rapid metabolism.

146B: Erythromycin

Penicillins and cephalosporins (which includes cefuroxime, cefotaxime, ceftriaxone) inhibit bacterial cell wall synthesis through the inhibition of peptidoglycan cross-linking. This weakens the cell wall of bacteria and renders them susceptible to osmotic shock. Macrolides (such as erythromycin), tetracyclines, aminoglycosides and chloramphenicol act by interfering with bacterial protein synthesis. Sulphonamides (e.g. trimethoprim, co-trimoxazole) work by inhibiting the synthesis of nucleic acid (Table 3).

Table 3

Mechanism of action	Examples
Inhibition of cell wall synthesis	Penicillins, cephalosporins, vancomycin
Inhibition of protein synthesis	Macrolides, tetracyclines, aminoglycosides, chloramphenicol, clindamycin
Inhibition of nucleic acid synthesis	Sulphonamides, trimethoprim, quinolones, metronidazole, rifampicin
Inhibition of cell membrane synthesis	Lincomycins, polymyxins

147B: Alcohol is the most common cause of holoprosencephaly

The human face forms from the fusion of five facial swellings:

- median frontonasal prominence (in front of forebrain)
- bilateral maxillary swellings (first arch derivative)
- bilateral mandibular swellings (first arch derivative).

All appear by the end of the fourth week of development.

In the fifth week of development, a pair of ectodermal thickenings appear on the frontonasal process called the nasal placodes. In the sixth week, the nasal placode divides into medial and lateral nasal processes. The groove between the lateral nasal process and the adjacent maxillary swelling is called the nasolacrimal groove. This later forms the nasolacrimal duct that drains excess tears from the conjunctiva of the eye into the inferior meatus of the nasal cavity. The palate forms from medial extensions of the maxillary swellings, the palatine shelves, which fuse with one another in the midline. An appreciation of the five facial swellings helps to explain how the different parts of the face are separately innervated by the different branches of the trigeminal nerve.

In this remodelling process all the different parts must be in register to ensure perfect fusion. This is complex both temporally and spatially, so craniofacial development is highly sensitive to perturbations. Indeed craniofacial abnormalities account for a third of all human congenital defects. Anomalies in the fusion of the five facial swellings result in facial clefts: for example, cleft lip results when the maxillary swelling fails to fuse correctly with the medial nasal process, and cleft palate from incomplete fusion of the palatine shelves. These can be of variable severity, are sometimes bilateral and have a number of causes.

The term holoprosencephaly refers to a spectrum of malformations of the head midline, including abnormal development of the forebrain, medial nasal processes and associated midfacial structures (e.g. nasal bones and septum). In severe cases this may result in a single nostril (cebocephaly) with close-set eyes (hypotelorism), or even a single eye (cyclopia). It is most commonly caused by alcohol consumption during the first month of pregnancy, being the most disabling manifestation of fetal alcohol syndrome, and alcohol is now regarded as the commonest cause of congenital mental retardation in the western world.

148B: Increasing membrane capacitance

The speed of nerve conduction increases with:

- increasing axonal diameter which decreases axonal resistance
- myelination (insulation of axons) by Schwann cells in the peripheral nervous system, or oligodendrocytes in the central nervous system
- increasing temperature
- decreasing membrane capacitance.

Capacitance slows down passive conduction because some of the current has to be used to charge or discharge the capacitance before it can spread further.

The effect of temperature on axonal velocity is easily understood by remembering what happens to one's hands when playing in the snow on a cold day. Most will be able to recall that hands go numb, but retain the ability to feel pain. The reason is straightforward and is based on axonal velocity. Light touch is carried by myelinated, Aβ nerve fibres. As the temperature decreases, the velocity of impulse propagation decreases until a point comes at which the amplitude of impulse is insufficient to regenerate the action potential at the next Node of Ranvier. Cooling has the further effect of slowing sodium conductance at the Nodes of Ranvier. Saltatory conduction is therefore disrupted; the result being that the hands are numb. Pain, on the other hand, is carried by unmyelinated C fibres. The generation of action potentials is not therefore restricted to the Nodes of Ranvier and pain sensation is preserved until far lower temperatures are reached.

The myelin sheath increases velocity by three mechanisms: first, by insulating the axon; second, by decreasing membrane capacitance; and third, by restricting the generation of axon potentials to the Nodes of Ranvier. The importance of myelination in increasing the speed of nerve conduction is illustrated by certain disease states where the myelin sheath is absent or lacking. One example is the condition multiple sclerosis which is a chronic, inflammatory, demyelinating condition resulting in multifocal lesions within the white matter of the central nervous system. The equivalent disease process within the peripheral nervous system is known as Guillain–Barré syndrome. Both result in neurological deficits, such as motor weakness and sensory loss as a result of the decreased velocity of impulse propagation down nerve fibres.

149B: Is composed of six human leukocyte antigen (HLA) genes

The human MHC is situated on chromosome 6. There are six pairs of allelic genes (A, B, C, DP, DQ, DR). The human MHC will be identical only in monozygotic (identical) twins. There are two classes of MHC antigens: class I antigens are expressed on the surface of all nucleated cells; class II are expressed only on the surfaces of cells such as antigen-presenting cells.

150A: It commonly exhibits an autosomal dominant pattern of inheritance

Von Willebrand disease is the most common hereditary bleeding disorder. It is caused by an abnormality, either quantitative or qualitative, of the von Willebrand factor, which is a large multimeric glycoprotein that functions as the carrier protein for factor VIII. Von Willebrand factor is also required for normal platelet adhesion. Von Willebrand disease can be classified into three main types:

- Type 1 accounts for 70–80 per cent of cases. It is characterized by a partial quantitative decrease of qualitatively normal von Willebrand factor and factor VIII. An individual with type 1 disease generally has mild clinical symptoms, and this type is usually inherited as an autosomal dominant trait; however, penetrance may widely vary in a single family.
- Type 2 accounts for 15–20 per cent of cases. It is a variant with primarily qualitative defects of von Willebrand factor. It can be either autosomal dominant or autosomal recessive.
- Type 3 is the most severe form. In the homozygous patient, it is characterized by marked deficiencies of both von Willebrand factor and factor VIII in the plasma, and the absence of von

Willebrand factor from both platelets and endothelial cells. It is characterized by severe clinical bleeding and is inherited as an autosomal recessive trait.

Investigations commonly reveal a normal platelet count and prothrombin time, with a prolonged activated partial thromboplastin time (APTT) and bleeding time.

151D: Simvastatin

Statins reduce cholesterol by competitively inhibiting HMG CoA reductase, an enzyme involved in cholesterol biosynthesis. They are more effective at lowering both total and LDL cholesterol than other classes of drugs, but are less effective than fibrates in reducing triglycerides. Side effects include myopathy and deranged liver function.

Nicotinic acid acts by inhibiting the release of VLDL, lowering plasma triglycerides and cholesterol, and increasing HDL. Its side effects include dizziness and flushing, which limit its use.

Fibrates stimulate lipoprotein lipase activity and work mainly to decrease triglycerides as well as moderately decreasing LDL and increasing HDL cholesterol.

Colestyramine (and other anion exchange resins) act by increasing the excretion of bile acids, and thus more cholesterol is converted into bile acid.

152E: Midgut development involves herniation of bowel into the umbilicus

The gut is an endodermal derivative created from a midline gut tube through a complex series of rotations. The gut is divided into three distinct territories:

- foregut = mouth up to second part of duodenum
- midgut = second part of duodenum up to two-thirds along the transverse colon
- hindgut = two-thirds along the transverse colon up to the anus.

This distinction is important developmentally, anatomically and clinically.

One consequence of the midline development of the gut is that visceral pain arising from the intestine often refers to the midline in the adult. Thus, foregut pain typically refers to the epigastric region, midgut pain to the peri-umbilical region and hindgut pain to the suprapubic region.

The cranial end of the embryological gut tube is capped by the buccopharyngeal membrane and the caudal end by the cloacal membrane. Both later rupture, forming the orifices of the body (i.e. the mouth and anus, respectively).

The stomach forms the thoracic part of the foregut. The dorsal wall of the stomach grows faster than the ventral wall, resulting in a dorsal 'greater curvature' and a ventral 'lesser curvature'. Subsequently the stomach rotates 90 degrees about the craniocaudal axis. As a result the greater curvature lies to the left. This has the consequence that the two vagus nerves that initially flanked the stomach on the left and right now lie posterior and anterior in the region of the stomach (remembered by the mnemonic RIP, or right is posterior). An additional tilting caudally orients the greater curvature so that it lies inferiorly.

Excessive growth of the midgut results in its herniation into the umbilicus, forming the primary intestinal loop. This loop undergoes a 90-degree rotation counterclockwise. Subsequently the midgut is rapidly retracted into the abdomen. As it does so, it rotates counterclockwise a further 180 degrees. Finally the caecum moves inferiorly to give the definitive organization of the intestine. If the anterior abdominal wall does not close completely, loops of midgut may remain outside the abdominal cavity at birth, forming a condition known as omphalocele, or gastroschisis. Abnormal rotation of gut can cause a spectrum of anomalies; for example, there may be freely (malrotated) suspended coils of intestine that are prone to volvulus, causing constriction of its blood supply.

153E: They contain intracellular stores of calcium ions

A single motor neurone supplies a group of muscle fibres in what is known as a motor unit. The more precise the movement, the fewer the muscle fibres supplied by one motor neurone. However, each muscle fibre is innervated by only one motor neurone.

Mammalian skeletal muscle is optimally organized for rapid excitation of muscle contraction in a process known as 'excitation–contraction coupling'. Calcium is released from the intracellular stores (sarcotubular system) when skeletal muscle contracts. Calcium reuptake occurs through an active mechanism requiring a calcium pump. During contraction the actin and myosin filaments do not shorten but slide together over one another (sliding filament theory).

Decreasing extracellular calcium increases excitability and may lead to spontaneous contractions (tetany), possibly by increasing sodium permeability. In hypocalcaemia this may manifest clinically as Chvostek's sign (activation of the facial nerve and muscles by merely tapping the skin) or Trousseau's sign (carpopedal spasm producing the '*main d'accoucheur*'). Fatal spasm of the larynx and seizures may later ensue if calcium levels are not corrected. Hyperventilation (overbreathing) may cause a similar effect through the respiratory alkalosis that it generates. Amino acids buffer the change in pH by loosing protons to the plasma and in doing so become negatively charged. This negative charge binds free calcium in the plasma, resulting in hypocalcaemia.

154D: Class II MHC presents exogenous antigens

Two principal classes of MHC exist; both play as important role in antigen presentation and recognition by T-cells. Class I MHC molecules are made up of one heavy chain and a light chain called β_2-microglobulin. Class II molecules do not contain β_2-microglobulin and consist of two chains of similar size.

Almost all nucleated cells of the body express MHC class I molecules on their cell surfaces. Hepatocytes express relatively low levels of class I MHC. This may explain why infection by certain hepatitis viruses (namely hepatitis B and C) or Plasmodium protozoa (the cause of malaria) commonly leads to a chronic carrier state in the host. Non-nucleated cells such as erythrocytes express little or no class I MHC; infection in the interior of red cells (such as malaria) can therefore go undetected. Class II MHC molecules are constitutively expressed only by certain cells involved in immune responses, though they can be induced in a variety of cells. Class II MHC molecules are richly expressed on the surface of dendritic cells.

The two classes of MHC are specialized to present different sources of antigen. MHC class I molecules present endogenously synthesized antigens (e.g. viral proteins). MHC class II molecules present exogenously derived proteins (e.g. extracellular microbes) that are first internalized and processed in the endosomes or lysosomes. Class I MHC molecules present peptides generated in the cytosol to CD8 T-cells, whereas MHC class II molecules present peptides degraded in intracellular vesicles to CD4 T-cells.

155E: Neutrophil

The predominant cell type seen in acute inflammation is neutrophils. These generally infiltrate the area over 24 hours, and after 24–48 hours they are replaced by macrophages.

156C: Amiodarone

This question requires knowledge of the Vaughan Williams classification of antiarrhythmic drugs. Lignocaine is a class 1B drug and blocks sodium channels. Procainamide, a class 1A drug, and flecainide, a class 1C drug, also block sodium channels. All class I drugs have membrane stabilizing properties.

Class II drugs comprise the beta-blockers. They are believed to work by blocking the pro-arrhythmic effects of catecholamines and the sympathetic nervous system.

Class III drugs (e.g. amiodarone, sotalol) act through the blockade of potassium channels. They work by prolonging the action potential, thereby increasing the refractory period and hence suppressing ectopic and re-entrant activity. Note sotalol has both class II and class III actions.

Class IV includes drugs such as verapamil and diltiazem which act by blocking calcium channels.

157A: Apart from the first cleft, the other branchial clefts are normally obliterated by overgrowth of the second branchial arch

The pharyngeal, or branchial arches, are the mammalian equivalent of the gill arches in fish. In humans, there are five pairs of branchial arches that develop in a craniocaudal sequence (equivalent to gill arches 1, 2, 3, 4, 6). Note that the fifth branchial arch never forms in humans, or forms as a short-lived rudiment and promptly regresses. Each arch contains a central cartilaginous element, striated muscle, cranial nerve and aortic arch artery, surrounded by ectoderm on the outside and lined by endoderm. The arches are separated externally by ectodermally lined branchial clefts and internally by endodermally lined branchial pouches.

- The first arch gives muscles of mastication
- The second arch gives muscles of facial expression
- The third and fourth arches give muscles of vocalization and deglutition
- The sixth arch gives the intrinsic muscles of the larynx.

Certain key features concerning the branchial arches are worth remembering. First, the superior parathyroid glands develop from the fourth branchial pouch; the inferior parathyroids, along with the thymus, are third-pouch derivatives. Consequently, the inferior parathyroids may migrate with the thymus down into the mediastinum, hence its liability to end up in unusual positions.

The tongue is derived from several sources. The anterior two-thirds of the tongue mucosa is a first-arch derivative, whereas the posterior one-third is contributed to by the third and fourth arches. The tongue muscles, in contrast, are formed from occipital somite mesoderm. For this reason, the motor and sensory nerve fibres of the tongue are carried by separate sets of cranial nerves.

The thyroid gland arises from between the first and second arches as a diverticulum (thyroglossal duct) which grows downwards leaving the foramen caecum at its origin. Incomplete thyroid descent may give rise to a lingual thyroid, or a thyroglossal cyst.

Apart from the first branchial cleft (which forms the external ear), the other clefts are normally obliterated by overgrowth of the second pharyngeal arch, enclosing the remaining clefts in a transient, ectoderm-lined, lateral cervical sinus. This space normally disappears rapidly and completely. It may persist in adulthood as a branchial cyst or fistula.

158D: The equilibrium potential for an ion species depends on the ratio of the concentrations of the ion outside to inside of the cell

In axons, impulses can travel in both directions (orthodromic and antidromic) from a point of electrical stimulation. Antidromic activity explains certain clinical phenomena such as how infection of a dorsal root by herpes zoster virus causes the segmental cutaneous hyperaemia characteristic of shingles. The amplitude of the action potential generated by an excitatory stimulus is independent of the stimulus strength; this is known as the 'all or nothing' law. This means stimulus intensity is coded for by frequency rather than through the amplitude of action potential.

The resting membrane potential is dependent on the electrogenic sodium–potassium ATPase pump and the relative intracellular and extracellular concentrations of ions on each side of the nerve cell membrane, as well as their relative permeabilities across the membrane. This establishes both a concentration (chemical) gradient and an electrical gradient across the nerve cell membrane – an electrochemical gradient. The equilibrium potential for a given ion species depends on the ratio of the concentrations of the ion outside to that inside the cell (the Nernst potential or equation). The Goldman constant-field (or Goldman–Hodgkin–Katz) equation is a more general form of the Nernst equation which allows for different permeabilities. Resting nerve cell membranes are about 100 times more permeable to K^+ ions than to Na^+ ions.

If extracellular sodium is replaced by potassium it would follow from the Nernst equation that this would depolarize the fibres completely. The resulting depolarization inactivates sodium channels and blocks the propagation of impulses down nerves. This is why hyperkalaemia is so dangerous. Cardiac muscle is especially sensitive to small changes in extracellular potassium concentrations and death often ensues from cardiac standstill.

159D: Is activated by IgM immune complexes

The complement system consists of a large number of distinct plasma proteins, triggering a cascade of reactions where the activation of one complement component results in the activation of another. This amplifies the effector molecules of the complement system. The main consequences of complement activation are opsonization of pathogens, the recruitment of inflammatory cells and direct killing of pathogens. There are two principal pathways of complement activation, the alternative and classical. The alternative pathway is the evolutionary older of the two pathways but the classical pathway was discovered first, hence the term classical pathway.

The alternative pathway is activated by the lipopolysaccharide of cell wall constituents, whereas the classical pathway is activated by IgM or IgG (but not IgA) which has bound to its specific antigen. Thus, in a transfusion reaction IgM from the recipient's blood binds to the incompatible donor red cells leading to complement activation, haemolysis and acute renal failure. The alternative pathway begins with the activation of the C3 component, but the classical pathway starts with the activation of the C1 component.

160A: Ingress of calcium ions

The cardiac action potential is divided into a number of phases (Figure 5):

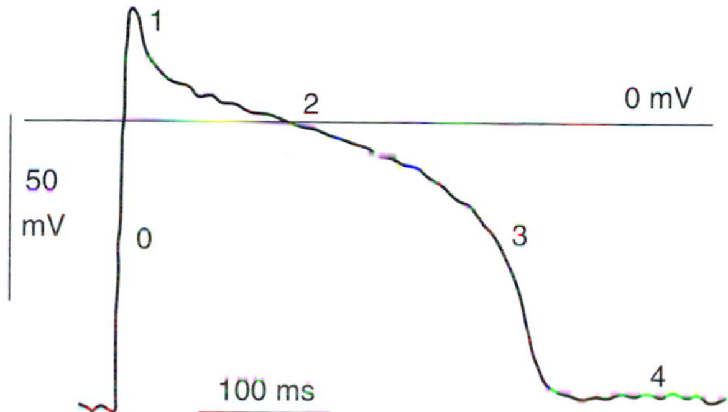

Figure 5 The cardiac plateau

- 0 – rapid depolarization (caused by the rapid influx of sodium ions)
- 1 – early repolarization (caused by the inactivation of sodium channels and the outward passage of potassium ions)
- 2 – plateau phase (caused predominantly by the ingress of calcium ions and the efflux of potassium ions)
- 3 – late repolarization (caused predominantly by the efflux of potassium ions)
- 4 – diastolic phase.

161C: Entacapone

Parkinson's disease is a progressive neurodegenerative disorder characterized clinically by a triad of bradykinesia, rigidity and resting tremor. It results from the decreased production of dopamine from the substantia nigra of the basal ganglia. Direct replacement with dopamine is not possible since dopamine does not cross the blood–brain barrier.

L-Dopa (levodopa) is the amino-acid precursor of dopamine, and is able to cross the blood–brain barrier, where it is converted (decarboxylated) to dopamine. L-Dopa acts by directly replenishing depleted striatal dopamine. It is given with a dopa-decarboxylase inhibitor (e.g. carbidopa), that does not cross the blood–brain barrier. This reduces the peripheral conversion of L-dopa to dopamine, thereby limiting side effects such as nausea, vomiting and cardiovascular effects (particularly hypotension).

Bromocriptine, cabergoline, ropinirole and pergolide are all dopamine agonists. They may be used alone, or in combination with L-dopa.

Selegiline inhibits the enzyme, MAO–B (monoamine oxidase B) for which dopamine is a substrate. It reduces the metabolism of dopamine in the brain and potentiates the action of L-dopa.

Entacapone inhibits the enzyme COMT (catechol-O-methyltransferase). By inhibiting this enzyme it slows the elimination of L-dopa. It prolongs the duration of a single dose, in addition to smoothing out any fluctuations in the plasma concentration of L-dopa.

Muscarinic antagonists, such as benzatropine, may play a role in the management of Parkinson's disease and are particularly useful when the resting tremor is the predominant symptom.

162A: Neural tube development requires signals from the underlying mesoderm

The nervous system arises from a special type of ectoderm that has been neurally induced to form neuroectoderm. The first stage in neurulation (i.e. development of the nervous system) is the establishment in the ectoderm of a region of cells that acquire neural competence (neural induction). The second stage is the morphogenetic process of neurulation that transforms the neuroepithelial sheet into the neural tube.

Neurulation involves communication between the mesoderm and the overlying ectoderm. The mesoderm primarily involved is the notochord, a dense rod of axial mesoderm that is very important in patterning the embryo early in development, but forms only the nucleus pulposus in the adult (in the centre of the intervertebral disc) and the apical ligament of the dens. Signals (specialized secreted proteins) are secreted by the notochord and induce the specialization of the overlying ectoderm cells to form the floor of the neural tube.

Closure of the neural tube proceeds bidirectionally, ending with closure of the cranial and caudal openings (neuropores). The cranial neuropore finally closes on day 24 and the caudal neuropore closes on day 26 of development. Closure of the neural tube is susceptible and a common cause of birth defects.

The neural crest, a migratory cell population, begins to emigrate from the dorsal half of the neural tube around the time of neural tube closure. They have a diverse and complex fate that include cartilage in the head, melanocytes, the medullary cells of the adrenal gland, glial Schwann cells, and neurones of both the peripheral and autonomic nervous systems. Aberrant neural crest migration may result in Hirschsprung's disease of the bowel (congenital megacolon or aganglionosis), but not neural tube defects.

A variety of malformations result from failure of part of the neural tube and overlying skeleton to close, usually at the cranial or caudal end of the nervous system. Such neural tube defects originate during the third week of development and are the commonest group of neurological malformations encountered in humans, occurring in 1 in 300 to 1 in 5000 births, depending on the geographical region. In spina bifida, the vertebral arch is defective dorsally, usually caudally in the lumbrosacral region (spina bifida occulta), and in severe cases the meninges protrudes from the vertebral canal (meningocele), sometimes including neural tissue (myelomeningocele) with associated neural impairment. Rarely, failure of cranial neural tube closure results in anencephaly where the forebrain is in contact with the amniotic fluid and degenerates (it is fatal). Approximately 50 per cent of neural tube defects may be prevented by women taking folic acid, even in the babies of mothers who have previously given birth to infants with neural tube defects. However, it must be taken during the first few weeks of pregnancy since this is when the neural tube is closing and hence susceptible to perturbations.

163A: Excitation depends more on the influx of extracellular calcium than release from internal stores

In smooth muscle, actin and myosin filaments occur but are less obvious on microscopy, giving it a non-striated appearance. Most smooth muscle has extensive electrically conducting gap junctions between cells which allows propagation of waves of electrical excitation through the tissue. Smooth muscle is usually under autonomic (involuntary nervous) or hormonal control, unlike skeletal muscle which is under somatic control. Unlike skeletal muscle, smooth muscle can generate active tension in the absence of any neural activity (latch bridge mechanism).

There is a vesicular sarcoplasmic reticulum close to the membrane (caveolae), but no T-tubular system. This is because the slow speed of smooth muscle does not require an elaborate mechanism for intracellular calcium release. For this reason, and because of the higher surface area to volume ratio of smooth muscle cells, excitation depends more on the influx of extracellular calcium than release from internal stores, since smooth muscle has a less well-developed sarcoplasmic reticulum.

The intrinsic myogenic response in smooth muscle opposes stretch. The result is that contraction may be generated by mechanical stretch of muscle fibres, for example in blood vessel walls. This is partly the basis for autoregulation of blood flow in the cerebral, coronary and renal vascular beds. It also plays a role in the peristaltic movements of material in the intestine.

164E: Cranial nerve VIII as it enters the internal acoustic meatus

The internal acoustic meatus (IAM) is contained in the posterior cranial fossa. It transmits cranial nerves VII and VIII. The abducens nerve in the cavernous sinus lies in the middle cranial fossa, along the body of the sphenoid bone. The mandibular division of the trigeminal nerve (Vc) exits the middle cranial fossa through the formamen ovale, the temporal lobe occupies the middle cranial fossa, and the temporomandibular joint (TMJ) is a joint between the head of the mandible and the mandibular fossa of the squamous part of the temporal bone.

165B: 15–40 days

Hepatitis A has a short incubation period of between 15 and 40 days. The infection is transmitted by the faecal–oral route and takes hold very quickly. The virus replicates in the gastrointestinal tract and is shed in the faeces during both the incubation and acute phases of the disease.

166C: β_2-adrenoceptor agonism

Asthma is an inflammatory (reactive) disorder of the airways characterized by reversible airway obstruction (or bronchospasm). It results from a type I hypersensitivity reaction, where the IgE-mediated degranulation of mast cells and release of inflammatory mediators is central to the pathogenesis.

Bronchial smooth muscle contains β_2-adrenoceptors. Throughout the body, β_2-adrenoceptors act to relax smooth muscle. Salbutamol stimulates these receptors (i.e. it is a selective β_2-adrenoceptor agonist), thereby relaxing the smooth muscle in the airways and increasing their calibre. Longer-acting β_2-adrenoceptor agonists (such as salmeterol) play a role in more severe asthma.

Bronchial smooth muscle also contains muscarinic receptors. Stimulating these receptors causes smooth muscle contraction. Therefore muscarinic antagonists (such as ipratropium) are useful adjuncts in the management of asthma.

Other drugs used in the management of asthma include steroids (oral or inhaled), leukotriene receptor antagonists (e.g. montelukast), xanthines (e.g. theophylline) and sodium cromoglycate.

167E: May contain ectopic tissue

A Meckel's diverticulum is the anatomical remnant of the vitello-intestinal duct. In the developing fetus the vitello-intestinal duct connects the primitive midgut to the yolk sac and also plays a part in intestinal rotation. The urachus (a derivative of the allantois) is different and connects the bladder to the umbilicus in the fetus. After birth the urachus becomes known as the median umbilical ligament.

The vitello-intestinal duct normally regresses between the fifth and eighth weeks of development, but in 2 per cent of individuals it persists as a remnant of variable length and location, known as a Meckel's diverticulum – in honour of J. F. Meckel who first discussed the embryological basis of this anomaly in the nineteenth century. Most often it is observed as a 2-inch (5 cm) intestinal diverticulum projecting from the antimesenteric wall of the ileum, about 2 feet (60 cm) from the ileocaecal valve. It is about twice as common in males as in females. However, this useful mnemonic ('the rule of 2s') holds true in only two-thirds of cases; the length of the diverticulum is variable and its site may be more proximal.

It is estimated that 15–30 per cent of individuals with a Meckel's diverticulum develop symptoms from intestinal obstruction, gastrointestinal bleeding, acute inflammation (diverticulitis) or perforation. Its blind end may contain ectopic tissue, namely gastric mucosa (in 10 per cent of cases), liver, pancreatic tissue, carcinoid or lymphoid tissue. This is important because gastric mucosa bears HCl-secreting parietal cells and can therefore ulcerate within the diverticulum (like a stomach ulcer) causing bleeding. Bowel obstruction may be caused by the trapping of part of the small bowel by a fibrous band (that represents a remnant of the vitelline vessels) connecting the diverticulum to the umbilicus. Symptoms may closely mimic appendicitis. Therefore if a normal-looking appendix is found at laparoscopy, or during an open appendicectomy, it is important to exclude a Meckel's diverticulum as a cause of the patient's symptoms. Mortality in untreated cases is estimated to be 2.5–15 per cent.

168D: Specialized intercellular junctions exist between myocytes

The structure of cardiac muscle correlates beautifully with its function. Certain features concerning cardiac myocytes are worth remembering:

- They are shorter than skeletal muscle cells.
- They are branched.
- Cardiac myocytes typically contain a single, centrally placed nucleus (unlike skeletal muscle fibres that are multinucleate, with peripherally located nuclei).
- Intercalated discs with gap junctions results in a syncytium where adjacent cardiac cells are mechanically and electrically coupled to one another, optimizing cardiac contractility.
- They are rich in mitochondria.
- There is sarcoplasmic reticulum.
- There are transverse tubules at the Z-line. Note that in skeletal muscle the T-tubules are located at the junction of the A and I bands.
- There are unstable resting membrane potentials of pacemaker cells.
- Cardiac muscle contracts spontaneously (myogenic).

A property shared by skeletal and cardiac muscle is their striated microscopic appearance from the highly organized arrangement of actin and myosin filaments.

169A: Bacterial endotoxin induces the acute-phase response

The acute-phase response is part of the innate (natural) immune system. Macrophages are exquisitely sensitive to the lipopolysaccharide (LPS) present in certain bacteria. They respond by producing cytokines, notably TNFα, IL-1 and IL-6 (but not IL-10 which can generally be thought of as an inhibitory cytokine). The aforementioned cytokines act on the liver to increase the concentration of many key serum proteins to aid the host defence response (such as C-reactive protein, serum amyloid protein, mannose binding protein, fibrinogen, complement). C-reactive protein (CRP) concentrations form a useful marker for detecting the presence (or confirming the absence) of inflammation or infection; this is a readily available laboratory test in the hospital setting. In addition, monitoring the trend in CRP values (as opposed to one-off values) provides the clinician with extremely valuable information as to whether the patient is getting better or worse.

Activation of the acute-phase response is responsible for a number of different effects. First, it is responsible for the fever that may accompany a variety of different inflammatory and infectious states, through the action of IL-1 on the thermosensory centres in the anterior hypothalamus. Second, hepatic protein synthesis is diminished and the level of serum albumin decreases. This is an attempt by the body to conserve protein and is responsible for the hypoalbuminaemia that often accompanies many disease states. Third, TNFα (cachectin) and IL-1 have catabolic effects and are responsible for the cachexia and anorexia seen in a variety of chronic inflammatory and infectious conditions. TNFα is also believed to be responsible for the cachexia seen in malignancy (cancer cachexia). In the latter, TNFα is produced by macrophages in response to the tumour, or by the tumour cells themselves. Finally, activation of the acute-phase response is central to the pathogenesis of septic shock where excessive activation of the acute-phase response leads to an overproduction of cytotoxic cytokines, resulting in a massive inflammatory reaction that may culminate in multiple organ failure and death.

170B: Limbic system

The limbic system is concerned with unconscious biological drives and emotions. It is considered the limbic lobe, hippocampus, anterior thalamic nucleus, hypothalamus and amygdala.

171C: Mitochondria can multiply independently

Smooth endoplasmic reticulum (ER) is involved in steroid hormone synthesis, whereas rough ER makes polypeptides. Mitochondria are the key organelles in aerobic respiration. Mitochondria are able to multiply independently. They are thought to have evolved millions of years ago from primitive bacteria (endosymbiotic theory), and therefore contain everything that is required to be self-sufficient, including DNA and ribosomes. Prokaryotic cells have no membrane-bound organelles; it is eukaryotic cells which have internal compartmentalization of organelles, hence division of labour (specialization). The Golgi apparatus has a role in the transportation and modification of proteins, such as the glycosylation to proteins. It is the lysosomes and proteasomes that are involved in the degradation of proteins.

172D: III

There are 12 pairs of cranial nerves that, together with the 31 pairs of spinal nerves, constitute the peripheral nervous system. The central nervous system comprises the brain and spinal cord. A peripheral nerve is a mixed nerve containing motor, sensory and autonomic (parasympathetic, sympathetic) elements. Parasympathetic outflow arises from the 'craniosacral' region; i.e. from certain cranial nerves and sacral roots S2–4. Cranial nerves III (occulomotor), VII (facial), IX (glossopharyngeal) and X (vagus) carry parasympathetic fibres whose function is primarily secretomotor (e.g. salivary secretions in the case of cranial nerve VII), ciliary motor (pupillary reflexes and accommodation in the case of cranial nerve III), while cranial nerves IX and X play an integral role in blood pressure regulation. Sympathetic outflow is principally 'thoracolumbar' (i.e. from spinal segments T1 through to L2). The sympathetic nervous system serves vasomotor (vascular tone), sudomotor (sweating) and pilomotor functions, in addition to controlling smooth muscle and sphincter tone and playing a key role in cardiovascular homeostasis.

Understanding the above makes it easy to predict the outcome of particular lesions in certain clinical settings. Take an occulomotor (3rd) cranial nerve palsy, for instance. Interruption of the parasympathetic fibres to the constrictor pupillae muscle results in a unilaterally dilated pupil (mydriasis) as an important hallmark of a 3rd-nerve palsy. This can thus easily be distinguished from a Horner's syndrome (sympathetic chain disruption), which causes a unilaterally constricted pupil (miosis).

173C: Excitation–contraction coupling requires calcium-induced calcium release

The most important source of activator calcium in cardiac muscle remains its release from the sarcoplasmic reticulum. Calcium, however, also enters from the extracellular space during the plateau phase of the action potential. This calcium entry provides the stimulus that induces calcium release from the sarcoplasmic reticulum (calcium-induced calcium release). The result is that tension generated in cardiac, but not in skeletal, muscle is profoundly influenced both by extracellular calcium levels and factors that affect the magnitude of the inward calcium current. This is of practical value in two key clinical situations: in heart failure where digoxin is used to increase cardiac contractility (by increasing the intracellular calcium concentration), and in hyperkalaemia where calcium gluconate is used to stabilize the myocardium.

The force of contraction of cardiac muscle is heavily dependent on its stretched fibre length. This is the basis of the Frank–Starling mechanism that adjusts the energy of cardiac contraction in response to diastolic stretch (filling). This autoregulatory mechanism makes the heart a self-regulating pump with respect both to demands from the peripheral circulation and in balancing the pumping by the right and left sides of the heart.

The plateau phase of the action potential in cardiac muscle (principally due to calcium influx) maintains the membrane at a depolarized potential for as long as 500 ms. The result is that the cell membrane is refractory throughout most of the mechanical response, largely due to the inactivation of fast sodium channels. This prevents tetany upon repetitive stimulation which would be detrimental to cardiac output. Furthermore, the prolonged refractory period in cardiac muscle allows the impulse that originates in the sinoatrial node to propagate throughout the entire myocardium just once, thereby preventing re-entry arrhythmias.

174B: It depends on the action of prostaglandins within the hypothalamus

Fever is brought about by toxins from microorganisms which act on cells of the immune system to produce cytokines (including IL-1, IL-6 and TNFα). It is the body's immune response to the invading microorganism, rather than a direct result of the microorganism *per se* that results in fever. The cytokines produced by the immune system act as endogenous pyrogens and act on the hypothalamus to generate fever, via the production of prostaglandins. Aspirin works as an antipyretic by blocking the enzyme (cyclo-oxygenase) that generates prostaglandins.

Fever also results from a variety of non-infectious causes, in addition to the infectious ones. Examples are various inflammatory conditions, connective tissue diseases, drug reactions and malignancies.

Fever is evolutionary advantageous; it inhibits the growth of some microorganisms (most organisms only grow well in narrow temperature range), increases the rate of production of antibodies, improves the efficiency of leukocyte killing, and decreases the mobility of the host (thereby aiding recovery of the host and preventing spread of infection to other individuals). However, in some situations fever becomes maladaptive resulting in hyperpyrexia, dehydration and death.

175D: Abnormal passive abduction of the extended knee

The medial collateral ligament of the knee prevents abduction of the leg at the knee. It extends from the medial femoral epicondyle to the shaft of the tibia. The oblique popliteal ligament resists lateral rotation during the final degree of extension. The posterior cruciate ligament prevents posterior displacement of the tibia. The anterior ligament helps lock the knee joint on full extension.

176B: Southern blotting

The polymerase chain reaction (PCR) is an amplification process used to amplify small amounts of DNA in order to perform analysis. It does not identify specific sequences. The DNA can then be analysed using Southern blotting. PCR involves synthesizing two oligonucleotide primers, that is short segments of RNA, that will bind to the DNA and when added to denatured DNA will bind to the DNA and amplify the DNA. The cycle is continually repeated 20–30 times, resulting in an exponential increase in the quantity of DNA. Reverse transcription PCR uses RNA. RNA is too unstable to be used for PCR, so it must be converted to a complementary copy of DNA using reverse transcriptase. PCR is then performed.

Southern blotting involves digestion of DNA and are denatured in alkali making them single-stranded. A permanent copy of the single strands is made by placing the DNA on a nitrocellulose filter – i.e. the Southern blot. A target radioactively labelled DNA fragment is then added and will bind to its homologous DNA fragment (if present). The DNA is then washed to remove any unbound DNA. The hybridized DNA can then be visualized as a band using autoradiography.

Northern blotting is similar to Southern blotting but uses mRNA as the target nucleic acid, rather than DNA. The mRNA can be hybridized to a radiolabelled DNA probe.

Western blotting is used to analyse proteins that are separated by electrophoresis, transferred to nitrocellulose, and reacted with antibody for detection.

177A: The posterior crico-arytenoids are the only muscles that separate the vocal cords

The posterior crico-arytenoid muscles are perhaps the most important muscles in the body as they are the only intrinsic muscles of the larynx that open up the airway by separating the vocal cords. Without them asphyxiation would quickly ensue.

All the intrinsic muscles of the larynx are supplied by the recurrent laryngeal nerve of the vagus, with the exception of the important cricothyroid muscle, which is supplied by the external branch of the superior laryngeal nerve. Cricothyroid is the muscle which is principally concerned with altering voice pitch by altering the length of the vocal cords. Damage to the superior laryngeal or recurrent laryngeal nerves can occur during thyroid, oesophageal or aortic arch surgery, leading to changes in the character of the voice and even airway compromise (Semon's law).

The true vocal cords form the superior border of the cricothyroid membrane and are lined by stratified squamous mucosa, not the typical respiratory epithelium that lines the rest of the respiratory tract. This confers protective properties on the vocal cords, which are subject to 'wear and tear' from vocalization. The same is true of the epiglottis which is also lined by 'protective' stratified squamous epithelium. The epiglottis is largely composed of elastic cartilage, rather than hyaline cartilage.

The cricoid cartilage is the only complete ring of cartilage within the human body, in contrast to the tracheal rings which are C-shaped rings of hyaline cartilage which provide support to the trachea but are deficient posteriorly.

178D: The nucleus accumbens and substantia nigra are rich in dopamine

The nervous system can be arbitrarily divided into the somatic (or 'voluntary') and autonomic (or 'involuntary') parts. The autonomic nervous system consists of two arms, namely the sympathetic and parasympathetic nervous system. Both sympathetic and parasympathetic fibres consist of two neurones (first-order or preganglionic, and second-order or postganglionic, neurones) and two synapses (the synaptic cleft between the first- and second-order neurones and the synaptic cleft between the second-order neurone and the organ or effector). There are key differences between both the neurones and the synapses of the sympathetic and parasympathetic nervous systems.

First-order (preganglionic) sympathetic and parasympathetic neurones are myelinated, whereas second-order (postganglionic) sympathetic and parasympathetic neurones are small, unmyelinated fibres. In both the sympathetic and parasympathetic nervous system, preganglionic neurones release acetylcholine which acts on postsynaptic nicotinic cholinergic receptors. However, they differ at the second synapse (between second-order neurones and the effector) where noradrenaline is the principal chemical neurotransmitter used within the sympathetic nervous system (although this is not entirely true because the postganglionic sympathetic nerve fibres to the sweat glands, the piloerector muscles and a few blood vessels are cholinergic), but acetylcholine is the principal neurotransmitter used within the parasympathetic nervous system (but this time acting on muscarinic cholinergic receptors).

The neuromuscular junction (the synapse between somatic motor neurones and skeletal muscle) operates by way of acetylcholine acting through nicotinic acetylcholine receptors. The substantia nigra is a dense area of dopaminergic neurones which forms part of the basal ganglia; degeneration leads to Parkinson's disease. The periaqueductal grey is a region rich in endogenous opioids which is believed to play a pivotal role in attenuation of painful stimuli through descending inhibition from higher centres. The noradrenergic-rich locus coeruleus is believed to play a key role in attention. The nucleus accumbens is dopamine-rich and plays an important role in addiction and reward. The adrenal medulla is an endocrine gland, but is effectively a specialized second-order (postganglionic) sympathetic nerve terminal that secretes approximately 70 per cent adrenaline, 30 per cent noradrenaline. Excess catecholamines are secreted by the adrenal medulla in a condition known as a phaeochromocytoma, which is a rare tumour of the adrenal gland. A thorough grounding of the aforementioned chemical neurotransmitters is imperative if one is to understand certain disease states and how particular drugs act within the nervous system.

179B: Skin

Immunologically privileged sites are anatomical sites that are normally segregated from the immune system. Immunological privilege results from the effects of both physical barriers to cell and antigen migration and soluble immunosuppressive mediators such as certain cytokines. Such sites include:

- central nervous system
- eyes
- testes
- uterus (fetus)
- interior of red blood cells (one mechanism by which malaria evades the immune system).

Note that the skin is not an immunologically privileged site and is rich in Langerhans' dendritic cells.

By definition, immunologically privileged sites are sites in which immunocompetent hosts can maintain allogenic tissues without eliciting rejection. Thus HLA matching is not required for corneal transplants and the rarity with which such transplants reject has contributed to the considerable success rate of corneal transplants. In addition, the immunologically privileged environment of the uterus may help to explain the mysterious lack of rejection of the fetus which has puzzled generations of reproductive immunologists, but is obviously of compelling importance for the propagation of the species.

Damage to an immunologically privileged site can induce an autoimmune response, presumably because the adult immune system has never been exposed to the antigens sequestered in such sites. In other words, the immune system has not had the opportunity to become tolerant to such antigens. Thus a breakdown in the blood–brain barrier may lead to multiple sclerosis (a chronic inflammatory, demyelinating condition of the central nervous system, resulting in multifocal white matter lesions separated in time and space), damage to the blood–testis barrier may result in infertility (an autoimmune reaction to one's own spermatozoa) and a trauma to the eye may result in sympathetic ophthalmia (where rupturing one eye results in the release of antigens, which triggers an autoimmune attack on both eyes).

180D: Borrelia burgorferi – athropod vector-borne entry

Borrelia burgorferi is spread by ticks and is caused by Lyme disease. *Rickettsia rickettsii* also is usually spread by ticks. *Clostridium tetani* enters the body through wounds. *Neisseria meningitidis* and *Corynebacterium diphtheriae* both enter via the respiratory tract.

181D: RNA polymerase II gives rise to protein encoding mRNA

In prokaryotes, both transcription and translation occur in the cytoplasm; whereas in eukaryotes, transcription occurs in the nucleus and translation in the cytoplasm. Transcription is the process of synthesizing messenger RNA (mRNA) from DNA; it is catalysed by the enzyme RNA polymerase II. RNA and DNA is always synthesized in a 5′ → 3′ direction.

The production of mature mRNA is a result of gene splicing. The introns which are non-coding sequences of DNA are removed and intervening exons are joined together. The exons are then coded into proteins during translation.

Amino acids are coded for by groups of three bases and these three bases together make up a codon. As there are four types of base, there is a potential for 4^3 (or 64) amino acids. Only 20 amino acids are used in protein synthesis, so in fact 44 codons are considered redundant.

182B: Embryologically starts out at the foramen caecum of the tongue

The thyroid gland is an endocrine gland that sits as the base of the neck like a bow-tie. It consists of two lateral lobes and an isthmus which is attached via Berry's ligament to the second to fourth tracheal rings (it is not attached to the thyroid cartilage, but sits lower down in the neck). The fact that the thyroid gland is attached to the trachea by Berry's ligament and also the fact that it is invested within pretracheal fascia explains why the thyroid gland moves up with swallowing. This is important clinically as it defines a swelling within the neck as being of thyroid origin.

The embryology is important. The thyroid gland descends from the foramen caecum between the anterior two-thirds and posterior one-third of the tongue via the thyroglossal duct. If the embryology is faulty it can lead to problems in later adult life. An incompletely descended thyroid gland may persist in adult life as a lingual thyroid or a thyroglossal cyst.

The blood supply to the thyroid is by way of the superior thyroid artery (which is a branch of the external thyroid artery), the inferior thyroid artery (which is a branch of the thyrocervical trunk of the first part of the subclavian artery) and, rarely, the small thyroidea ima which arises from the aorta to supply the isthmus. Venous drainage is through the superior and middle thyroid veins to the internal jugular veins and via the inferior thyroid veins to the brachiocephalic veins (usually on the left). The arterial supply and venous drainage is important to know about when considering thyroid surgery.

The thyroid gland is stimulated by TSH (which is produced from the anterior lobe of the pituitary gland) to produce T3 and T4 – hormones that play an important role in basal metabolic rate.

183D: Lead to tolerance

Opioids are mainly used in the hospital setting for their analgesic properties. They are now believed to act both peripherally (outside the central nervous system) and within the CNS itself. Unfortunately opioids exert most of their beneficial effects and side effects through the same opioid receptor (μ-receptors). It is therefore unlikely that we will ever be able to develop a synthetic opioid agent that has the analgesic properties of other opioids without their unpleasant side effects.

Opioids induce side effects through both excitatory and inhibitory mechanisms. Excitatory effects are:

- pinpoint pupils (direct effect of opioids on the Edinger–Westphal nucleus)
- nausea and vomiting (direct effect on the area postrema)
- pruritus (due to mast-cell degranulation and histamine release)
- dysphoria and euphoria (direct effect on the CNS).

Inhibitory effects are:

- cardiorespiratory depression
- sedation
- relaxation of smooth muscles – constipation, urinary retention.

Constipation and nausea/vomiting are common side effects of opioids. It is therefore always a good idea to co-prescribe laxatives and antiemetics whenever an opioid is prescribed.

Opioids cause tolerance, dependence and withdrawal with increasing use. Tolerance means increasing dosages of the drug need to be used in order to obtain the same effect.

It is important to know how to reverse the effects of opioids because opioid overdose may be fatal. Specific opioid antagonists include naloxone and naltrexone. Flumazenil antagonizes the effects of benzodiazepines.

184B: Results in mast-cell degranulation

Hypersensitivity is a condition in which undesirable tissue damage follows the development of humoral or cell-mediated immunity. Gell and Coombs classified hypersensitivity reactions into four types. However, some also include a fifth type, as shown below.

Gell and Coombs' classification of hypersensitivity reactions

- *Type I*. Mast-cell degranulation mediated by pre-formed IgE bound to mast cells. Immediate (within minutes). Anaphylaxis, atopic allergies.
- *Type II*. Antibodies directed towards antigens present on the surface of cells or tissue components. Humoral antibodies participate directly in injuring cells by predisposing them to phagocytosis or lysis. Good examples are transfusion reactions, autoimmune haemolytic anaemia and Goodpasture's syndrome. Initiates within several hours.
- *Type III*. Formation of antibody–antigen complexes (immune complex mediated). Good examples are the Arthus reaction, serum sickness, and SLE. Initiates in several hours.
- *Type IV*. Delayed type of hypersensitivity. Cell-mediated. T-lymphocytes involved. Granulomatous conditions. Contact dermatitis. Initiation time is 24–72 hours.
- *Type V*. Due to the formation of stimulatory autoantibodies in autoimmune conditions such as Graves' disease.

185A: Pain from the transverse colon is usually referred to the midline area below the umbilicus

Referred pain is not well understood. Somatic referred pain is very well localized and intense. Visceral pain is the opposite and conveyed by automatic fibres. Diaphragmatic pain is usually referred to the shoulder. Appendix pain is usually referred to the umbilicus.

186B: Mitosis always produces genetically identical daughter cells

Mitosis is the process of cell division in somatic cells and produces two genetically identical diploid cells. Meiosis occurs in gamete formation and differs from mitosis in two important respects: each daughter cell contains half the genetic information (haploid) and the resultant cells differ in their genetic material. There are two separate phases (or divisions) in meiosis. In the first division, two genetically different haploid cells are formed, and in the second each of the haploid cells divides.

The exchange of genetic material occurs in Prophase I. The cell cycle is controlled internally by gene products called cyclins which vary in concentration throughout the cell cycle. Cyclin-dependent kinases control the activity of cyclins by switching on cyclins through phosphorylation. p53 is an example of a tumour suppressor gene. It normally functions to inhibit the cell cycle. p53 is the most common mutated gene in cancers. It encodes a transcription factor which downregulates the cell cycle preventing the cell from undergoing mitosis. Oncogenes control cell growth and differentiation, examples of which include growth factors, growth factor receptors and nuclear transcription factors.

187D: Genioglossus muscle protrudes the tongue

Call it what you will, but the tongue is composed of striated, voluntary or skeletal muscle, not smooth muscle. The tongue assists in the formation of a food bolus and propagation towards the back of the mouth and thence into the oesophagus. The tongue also plays a key role in the suckling reflex in neonates, in the articulation of speech and the special sense of taste. Its epithelium is composed of stratified squamous (protective) epithelium as, like the skin, it is subject to 'wear and tear'. Tumours arising from the tongue are therefore typically squamous cell carcinomas.

Special taste sensation is by way of the chorda tympani division of the facial nerve for the anterior two-thirds of the tongue and the glossopharyngeal nerve for the posterior one-third. Taste sensation on the anterior two-thirds of the tongue is therefore commonly lost in a facial nerve (or Bell's) palsy. Somatic sensation is by way of the mandibular division of the trigeminal nerve for the anterior two-thirds of the tongue (lingual nerve) and the glossopharyngeal nerve for the posterior one-third.

All the muscles of the tongue are supplied by the hypoglossal, or 12th cranial nerve, with the exception of the palatoglossus muscle which is supplied by the pharyngeal plexus of nerves (IX, X and sympathetics). The hypoglossal nerve may be injured in a carotid endarterectomy or submandibular gland procedures. The most important muscle to know about is the genioglossus muscle which serves to protrude the tongue. When genioglossal muscle tone is lost, as in someone with a decreased level of consciousness, or a fractured mandible (where the genioglossus muscle arises), the tongue falls back and obstructs the airway, rapidly resulting in hypoxia and death if basic life support measures are not quickly instigated.

188C: The Q-T interval gives a rough indication of the duration of ventricular systole

The nature of the electrocardiogram (ECG) is important to understand. As a junior doctor you will reading and interpreting ECGs every day at work.

- P-wave = atrial depolarization
- QRS complex = ventricular depolarization
- T-wave = ventricular repolarization.

(Electrical activity resulting from atrial repolarization is 'hidden' within the QRS complex.)

The Q-T interval gives a rough indication of the duration of ventricular systole. The first heart sound results from closure of the atrioventricular valves and occurs as the ventricles contract. It therefore coincides with the QRS complex. The second heart sound is due to closure of the aortic and pulmonary valves, respectively, and occurs at about the same time as the T-wave.

189D: May occur in systemic lupus erythematosus

Type III hypersensitivity reactions are mediated by antibodies. Type IV reactions are cell-mediated through specifically sensitized T-lymphocytes. Nickel sensitivity is a type IV hypersensitivity reaction.

Allergic rhinitis is a type I hypersensitivity reaction. Systemic lupus erythematosus (SLE) is a type III hypersensitivity reaction where large amounts of immune complexes form between nuclear antigens and antibodies.

Latex allergies can be one of three types:

- irritant contact dermatitis (non-immune)
- allergic contact dermatitis (type IV hypersensitivity reaction)
- immediate hypersensitivity (type I hypersensitivity reaction or anaphylaxis) – what everyone worries about!

190D: Transpeptidase

Antibiotics act by specifically binding to macromolecules only found in the parasite. Transpeptidase is the only penicillin-binding protein listed; it is inactivated when binding occurs.

191B: Cytosine always pairs with guanine

DNA consists of a right-handed double helix with 10 bases per turn. Adenine and guanine are purine bases; cytosine, thymine (and uracil) are pyrimidine bases (remembered by the 'y' in pyrimidine, thymine, cytosine). Adenine pairs with thymine in DNA via two hydrogen bonds. Adenine pairs with uracil in RNA. Guanine pairs with cytosine in DNA via three hydrogen bonds.

192D:They are all supplied by the inferior thyroid artery

The parathyroid glands are pinkish/brown glands usually found on the posterior aspect of the thyroid gland. There are usually four, two on each side (in 90 per cent of subjects), but this varies from two to six. Each weighs about 50 mg and measures 6 × 3 × 2 mm. The superior parathyroid glands arise from the fourth branchial pouch, whereas the inferior parathyroids are third branchial pouch derivatives. The thymus gland, however, also derives from the third branchial pouch. Therefore, the inferior parathyroid glands may get dragged down with the thymus into the mediastinum, making the position of the inferior parathyroid glands highly variable. The superior glands are more constant in position.

The parathyroid glands are all usually supplied by the inferior thyroid artery. A consequence of this is that the inferior thyroid artery should always be preserved during a total thyroidectomy to prevent ischaemia of the parathyroid glands, which would render the patient hypocalcaemic and necessitate lifelong calcium supplementation.

The parathyroid glands secrete parathyroid hormone from chief (or principal) cells. Parathyroid hormone plays an essential role in calcium homeostasis. Calcitonin, however, is secreted by the parafollicular cells of the thyroid gland. A parathyroid adenoma is a benign tumour of usually one (but sometimes more than one) parathyroid gland that leads to the overproduction of parathyroid hormone and hypercalcaemia. Treatment consists of neck exploration and removal of the problematic parathyroid adenoma (parathyroidectomy). Care must be taken to avoid damaging the recurrent laryngeal nerves. Exposure of the thymus through a median sternotomy may rarely be necessary, given the liability of the inferior parathyroid glands to end up in unusual positions.

193A: In terminally differentiated squamous cells

Warts, caused by papilloma virus, are non-malignant tumours of squamous cells. Infectious papilloma viruses are most likely to be found in terminally differentiated squamous cells, and are not found in either the basal cells, in the surface layers of warts, in transformed cancer cells, or throughout the warts.

194E: May be minimized by blood-group matching

Hyperacute rejection is due to the formation of preformed antibodies against the donor organ. It occurs within minutes of transplantation so the surgeon can usually see the changes taking place as the anastomoses are completed.

The antibodies are usually directed against blood group antigens and it can therefore be minimized by blood-group matching. The blood groups and HLA antigens of autografts (tissue from the same individual) will be identical, so hyperacute rejection will never occur in such circumstances.

No drug treatment can reverse hyperacute rejection; the main treatment is removal of the transplanted organ.

Transplant rejections can be classified into the following types:

- *hyperacute* – preformed antibodies (minutes–hours)
- *accelerated acute* – reactivation of sensitized T-cells and secondary antibody response (days)
- *acute* – cytotoxic T-cell mediated with primary activation of T-cells (days to weeks)
- *chronic* – antibody-mediated vascular damage (months to years, controversial).

195B: Paired t-test

A paired *t*-test allows a comparison of mean potassium values before and after treatment by comparing each patient's initial serum level with his or her repeat value.

196B: Promoters

Transcription of genes is initiated by promoters. Enhancers and silencers are proteins that bind to the promoter region on the DNA and will influence gene transcription. Exons carry the coding sequences of DNA.

197D: Lateral rectus is supplied by the abducens nerve

The extra-ocular muscles are innervated by the 3rd (occulomotor), 4th (trochlear) and 6th (abducens) cranial nerves. The trochlear nerve supplies only one muscle and that is the superior oblique muscle. The abducens nerve also supplies only one muscle and that is the lateral rectus muscle. This may be remembered by 'S04, LR6'. All the remaining muscles are supplied by the occulomotor nerve – that is, the superior rectus, inferior rectus, inferior oblique and medial rectus are all supplied by the occulomotor, or 3rd, cranial nerve. Injury to any of these cranial nerves (3rd, 4th or 6th) may result in ophthalmoplegia and double vision (diplopia).

The recti muscles are easily understood as they move the eyeball in the respective directions indicated by their name. The superior and inferior obliques are more difficult to understand. The superior oblique muscle moves the cornea downwards and outwards, whereas the inferior oblique muscle moves the cornea upwards and inwards. The reason for this is that the oblique muscles pass posteriorly to attach behind the axis of movement and therefore impart movement opposite to their suggested names. Weakness of the extra-ocular muscles may occur in the autoimmune condition, myasthenia gravis.

The levator palpebrae superioris is the exception to the above. It elevates the eyelid but has a dual innervation from both the occulomotor nerve and sympathetic fibres. The latter innervate a small smooth muscle portion of the levator muscle known as Muller's muscle. The clinical significance of this dual innervation is that a 3rd cranial nerve (occulomotor) palsy, or sympathetic interruption (Horner's syndrome), may result in a droopy eyelid (ptosis). To distinguish the two it is essential to lift up the eyelid and inspect the pupil to see if it is enlarged (mydriasis, in an occulomotor nerve palsy) or constricted (miosis, in a Horner's syndrome). Furthermore, in an occulomotor palsy the eyeball points downwards and outwards from the unopposed action of superior oblique and lateral rectus, supplied by the 4th and 6th cranial nerves. Horner's syndrome is associated with hemifacial anhidrosis (absent sweating of the ipsilateral face), flushing symptoms (the so-called Harlequin syndrome or effect) and enophthalmos (a sunken eyeball), in addition to ptosis and miosis.

198B: Nitric oxide

The importance of endothelium in vascular responses was first noted when it was discovered that removing the endothelium from perfused arteries prevented the vasodilator action of acetylcholine on those vessels. The endothelium-derived relaxing factor has since been recognized as nitric oxide (a vasodilator). Vasopressin, angiotensin II, thromboxane A2 and noradrenaline are all vasoconstrictors.

Since its discovery, nitric oxide has been implicated in a diverse array of different biological processes, both physiological and pathological, besides vasodilatation, including:

- acting as a neurotransmitter
- the killing of microorganisms by phagocytes
- long-term potentiation (memory)
- male erection (Viagra enhances the effect of nitric oxide)
- sepsis
- excitotoxicity.

In addition, nitric oxide explains how glyceryl trinitrate exerts its beneficial effect in angina. More and more is being discovered about nitric oxide all the time.

199D: Result from a breakdown in immunological tolerance

Autoimmune diseases result from the direct attack by the host immune system against its own, or self, antigens (autoantigens), usually as a result of a breakdown in immunological tolerance. They are normally acquired, rather than congenital, and for some unknown reason they are more common in women than men. The female preponderance is often taken to imply that sex hormones are involved in the pathogenesis.

It is still unclear as to the exact nature of the stimulus that triggers an autoimmune reaction. The most plausible explanation is that certain exogenous agents (such as a dietary factors, drugs or microbial agents), that share epitopes with self-antigens, stimulate an immune response against both themselves and the host tissues, producing tissue-damaging reactions. This is known as 'molecular mimicry'. However, genetic factors undoubtedly also play a role. For instance, autoimmune diseases are often associated with specific HLA types.

Although in many cases the precise combination of pathogenic mechanisms is not understood, either antibody or T-cells can cause tissue damage in autoimmune disease.

200A: Reed–Sternberg cells

Reed–Sternberg cells are diagnostic for Hodgkin's lymphoma. The Philadelphia chromosome and decreased quantities of leucocytes alkaline phosphatase are commonly observed in chronic myelogenous leukaemia. Auer rods are most often seen in increased numbers in acute myelogenous or myelonocytic leukaemia. Pappenheimer bodies are abnormal iron granules found inside red blood cells. They are associated with sideroblastic anaemia, haemolytic anaemia, and sickle cell disease.

201C: Affects males and females equally

Autosomal dominant disorders affect males and females equally since there is no involvement of the sex chromosomes and autosomes are similar for males and females. Only one of the parents need carry the abnormality for it to be classified as an autosomal dominant disorder; if both parents were required to carry the abnormality it would be an autosomal recessive disorder.

Only half the children of an affected adult would inherit the condition since half would receive the normal autosome. Carriers of an autosomal dominant trait do not exist; carriers of a dominant character exhibit the disease.

Autosomal dominant conditions are commonly transmitted from one generation to the next, either because of their late onset (e.g. Huntington's disease), or because reproduction occurs before death ensues.

202D: Inflammation may cause referred pain to the ear

The palatine tonsils ('tonsils') are a large collection of lymphoid tissue that project into the oropharynx from the tonsillar fossa, between the palatoglossal arch (in front) and the palatopharyngeal arch (behind). They are most prominent in early life and regress in later years as the lymphoid tissue atrophies. The surface marking is medial to the lower masseter. The palatine, lingual, pharyngeal ('adenoids') and tubal tonsils collectively form an interrupted circle of protective lymphoid tissue at the upper end of the respiratory and alimentary tracts known as Waldeyer's ring. This area has a role in the priming of lymphocytes for antigens during the early years of life.

The floor of the tonsillar fossa (lateral wall) is the lower part of the superior constrictor, with styloglossus on its lateral side. The luminal surface of the tonsil is covered by non-keratinized stratified squamous epithelium which deeply invaginates the tonsil forming blind-ended tonsillar crypts. The tonsillar branch of the facial artery (in turn a branch of the external carotid artery) forms the main arterial supply. It enters the tonsil by piercing the superior constrictor.

The main function of the tonsils is immunological, especially within the early years of life. Since they harbour microbes, this makes them vulnerable to infection and inflammation (tonsillitis). Lymphatic channels pierce the superior constrictor to reach the deep cervical nodes, especially the jugulodigastric (or tonsillar) node below the angle of the mandible. This is the lymph node that is most commonly enlarged in tonsillitis (jugulodigastric lymphadenopathy). The mucous membrane overlying the tonsil is supplied mainly by the tonsillar branch of the glossopharyngeal nerve. The glossopharyngeal nerve also supplies the middle ear through its tympanic branch. This explains why tonsillitis commonly causes referred pain to the middle ear. Ear pain may also feature in the early postoperative period after tonsillectomy.

Tonsillectomy (removal of the tonsils) is indicated for recurrent episodes of tonsillitis or obstructive sleep apnoea. Removal does not appear to compromise immune function. The main complication after tonsillectomy is haemorrhage and the usual cause is venous, rather than arterial bleeding, from the external palatine, or paratonsillar, vein. The close proximity of the internal carotid artery (which lies 2.5 cm posterolateral) to the palatine tonsil must be borne in mind at tonsillectomy in order to prevent inadvertent injury.

203B: Local metabolic activity is the chief factor determining rate of blood flow to the heart

Given that there is a high myocardial oxygen demand at rest (around 20 times that of skeletal muscle), certain functional adaptations ensure that supply adequately meets demand.

- The heart receives 4–5 per cent of the cardiac output.
- There is a high capillary density.
- There is a high oxygen extraction ratio. The myocardium extracts around 70 per cent of the oxygen that is delivered to it from the coronary blood. In contrast, the body average is only 25 per cent.
- There is efficient metabolic hyperaemia, where local metabolism is the dominant controller of coronary flow. The extra oxygen required at high work rates is supplied chiefly by an increase in blood flow rather than an increase in the oxygen extraction ratio.

Unlike other vascular beds, the coronary flow to the left ventricle is greatest in diastole. This occurs because of the mechanical compression of the coronary vessels during systole, such that there is reversal of the transmural pressure gradient across the vessel wall, leading to momentary occlusion. Coronary perfusion is reduced in aortic stenosis (narrowing) because the coronary ostia lie distal to the aortic valve. This is why patients with aortic stenosis get angina.

In hypothermia there is a fall in metabolic rate and cardiac output. This reduces cardiac work, resulting in a decrease in the rate of production of vasodilator metabolites (adenosine, carbon dioxide etc.). The reduction in coronary artery perfusion pressure explains why angina is commonly triggered by exposure to the cold.

204B: Gram-positive bacteria retain an iodine purple dye complex

Microorganisms can be classified into bacteria, viruses, fungi, protozoa and parasites. Bacteria can be classified according to their:

- staining properties – Gram-positive, Gram-negative, acid-fast etc.
- morphology – round (cocci), rods (bacilli), spiral (spirochaetes), comma-shaped (vibrio), flagellated, possession of a capsule etc.
- oxygen requirements – aerobic or anaerobic; obligate or facultative
- ability to form spores – spore-forming or non-spore forming.

In Gram-positive bacteria, the peptidoglycan forms a thick (20–80 nm) layer external to the cell membrane. In Gram-negative species the peptidoglycan layer is thinner (only 5–10 nm) but is overlaid by an outer membrane. The principal molecules in the outer membrane of Gram-negative bacteria are lipopolysaccharides.

These structural differences form the basis of the Gram stain. Gram-positive bacteria are able to retain an iodine purple dye complex when exposed to a brief alcohol wash. Gram-negative bacteria have a smaller cell wall but a higher lipid content and as a result the alcohol washes away the purple dye. Gram-positive bacteria appear blue and Gram-negative bacteria are counter-stained with a pink dye.

As a general rule:

- all cocci are Gram-positive (except *Neisseria* which causes meningitis and gonorrhoea)
- all bacilli are Gram-negative (except *Clostridia*, Mycobacteria and the organisms that cause anthrax, listeria, diphtheria and actinomycosis).

The lipopolysaccharide (LPS) in the outer membrane of Gram-negative bacteria is a complex molecule found nowhere else in nature and is an important factor in bacterial survival in the mammalian host. It consists of three portions:

- A lipid portion (lipid A) embedded in the outer membrane (the damaging endotoxin). As it is embedded in the outer membrane it exerts its effects only when bacteria lyse.
- A conserved core polysaccharide.
- The highly variable O-polysaccharide (O-antigen), responsible for antigenic diversity. It has been hypothesized that such structural variability is an attempt by the bacterium to evade host defences.

Endotoxins are not in themselves toxic (unlike exotoxins) but they can induce toxic effects due to their potent activation of the complement cascade, coagulation cascade and stimulating the release of powerful cytokines (such as TNFα, IL-1 etc.) from leucocytes. In overwhelming infections, the patient is said to suffer from endotoxic shock.

205C: Inferior mesenteric artery

The artery to the hindgut and its derivatives is the inferior mesenteric artery. The coeliac artery supplies structures derived from the caudal foregut. In the fetus, the ductus arteriosus shunts blood from the pulmonary trunk to the aorta to bypass the lungs. The superior mesenteric artery supplies the structures derived from the midgut. In the fetus, the umbilical artery delivers blood to the placental circulation.

206E: Marfan's syndrome

As a general rule, disorders that affect metabolic pathways/enzymes are autosomal recessive, whereas diseases that affect structural proteins are autosomal dominant. Thus Marfan's syndrome, Huntington's disease and neurofibromatosis (Von Recklinghausen's disease) are examples of autosomal dominant conditions as they affect structural proteins. Cystic fibrosis and phenylketonuria are autosomal recessive since they affect metabolic pathways.

Haemophilia A, haemophilia B (or Christmas disease) and red/green colour-blindness are examples of sex-linked conditions.

207C: Trapezius

The spinal accessory nerve is a branch of the 11th cranial nerve. It has been given the name spinal accessory since it originates from the upper end of the spinal cord (spinal roots, C1–C5). It passes through the foramen magnum and 'hitches a ride' with the cranial accessory nerve originating from the nucleus ambiguus. It passes out of the skull again by way of the jugular foramen. Its function is to supply only two muscles in the neck – the sternocleidomastoid and trapezius muscles.

Stylopharyngeus is innervated by the glossopharyngeal nerve and palatoglossus is supplied by the pharyngeal plexus (IX, X, sympathetics). Buccinator, on the other hand, is regarded as a muscle of facial expression and is therefore innervated by the facial nerve. Consequently, in a facial nerve (Bell's) palsy, food may collect in the vestibule of the mouth.

The surface marking of the spinal accessory nerve is important. It traverses the posterior triangle of the neck from one-third of the way down the posterior border of the sternocleidomastoid muscle to one-third of the way up the anterior border of trapezius where it terminates (the 'rule of thirds'). It is vulnerable to iatrogenic injury in procedures that necessitate dissection within the posterior triangle of the neck, such as excision biopsy of a lymph node. In a radical en-bloc lymph node dissection of the neck for malignant disease, the spinal accessory nerve may have to be sacrificed deliberately in order to obtain satisfactory clearance.

Damage to the spinal accessory nerve in the posterior triangle of the neck leads to a predictive weakness of the trapezius muscle. This results in an inability to shrug the shoulder on the side in which the spinal accessory nerve is affected. The sternocleidomastoid muscle is typically spared as the branch to sternocleidomastoid is given off prior to the spinal accessory nerve entering the posterior triangle of the neck. The trapezius muscle also plays a role in hyperabduction of the arm and so activities such as combing one's hair would become more difficult. In the long term, a trapezius palsy (with dropping of the shoulder) may result in a chronic, disabling neuralgia. This may occur as a result of pain from neurological dennervation, adhesive capsulitis of the shoulder joint, traction radiculitis of the brachial plexus or, more commonly, from fatigue.

208A: Purkinje fibres lead to contraction of the apex before the base of the heart

The group of cells that show the highest automaticity (that is, the cells with which the resting membrane potential drifts towards the threshold fastest) dictates the overall heart rate and is accordingly called the primary intrinsic pacemaker of the heart. These are normally the pacemaker cells from the sinoatrial (SA) node which discharge at about 60–80 times/min. The SA node is found in the right atrium near its junction with the superior vena cava. The SA node receives a rich innervation from both arms of the autonomic nervous system (sympathetic and parasympathetic). By this means they can exert a powerful extrinsic influence on the heart.

Atrial fibres conduct impulses from the SA node to the atrioventricular (AV) node. The AV node provides the only communication in the normal heart between the atria and ventricles. Conduction through this node is slower than the remaining myocardium; this synchronizes the sequential atrial and ventricular contraction. Purkinje fibres are confined to the ventricles.

Impulse generation is due to spontaneous diastolic depolarization of the cells. The SA node has intrinsic rhythmicity and can generate impulses independently, even when completely dennervated.

Purkinje fibres are larger than ventricular myocardial cells and this facilitates the rapid spread of depolarization over the entire ventricular myocardium. Purkinje fibres travel to the apex before proceeding to the base of the heart. This arrangement enables the activation wave to spread from the apex to the base of the ventricles. The resulting pattern of activation leads to a ventricular contraction from apex to base which optimizes the extrusion of blood from the chambers.

Problems with cardiac conduction are commonly encountered in clinical practice. Arrhythmias are the commonest cause of death following a myocardial infarction. In the event that the SA node function is abnormal, as in sick sinus syndrome, or following myocardial ischaemia, other sites with a slower intrinsic rate can substitute the role of the pacemaker, resulting in an escape rhythm.

209D: Neisseria meningitidis

The spleen plays an important role in the removal of dead and dying erythrocytes and in the defence against microbes. Removal of the spleen (splenectomy) leaves the host susceptible to a wide array of pathogens but especially to encapsulated organisms.

Certain bacteria have evolved ways of evading the human immune system. One way is through the production of a 'slimy' capsule on the outside of the bacterial cell wall. Such a capsule resists phagocytosis and ingestion by macrophages and neutrophils. This allows them not only to escape direct destruction by phagocytes but also to avoid stimulating T-cell responses through the presentation of bacterial peptides by macrophages. The only way that such organisms can be defeated is by making them more palatable by coating their capsular polysaccharide surfaces in opsonizing antibody.

The production of antibody against capsular polysaccharide primarily occurs through T-cell independent mechanisms. The spleen plays a central role in both the initiation of the antibody response and the phagocytosis of opsonized encapsulated bacteria from the bloodstream. This helps to explain why following a splenectomy the host is most susceptible to infection by encapsulated organisms, notably *Streptococcus pneumoniae* (Pneumococcus), *Neisseria meningitidis* (Meningococcus) and *Haemophilus influenzae*.

Understanding the above, one can quickly envisage what preventative strategies must be employed post-splenectomy. Patients are given relevant vaccinations and are advised to take prophylactic penicillin, in most cases for the rest of their lives. In addition, they are advised to wear a Medic Alert bracelet to warn other healthcare professionals of their condition.

210C: Right hepatic artery

The cystic artery most commonly arises form the right hepatic artery. In decreasing order of occurrence, it can also arise from the left hepatic artery, gastro-duodenal artery, or hepatic artery proper. The superior pancreatico-duodenal artery is located too inferiorly to contribute to the blood supply to the gall bladder.

211C: Fifty per cent

The key to this question is to understand that, in order to have a child with an autosomal recessive disease, both parents must carry the gene; so although the mother may have the disease, the father has to be a carrier. The question fails to inform you that he has the disease, so you can safely assume that he carries only one abnormal gene. To be a carrier for an autosomal recessive disease, you will have one normal and one abnormal copy of the gene. As his mother carries both abnormal genes, and his father carries one abnormal gene and one normal gene, there is a 50 per cent chance that the teenager has the disease and a 50 per cent chance that he is a carrier.

Phenylketonuria (PKU) is an inborn error of metabolism. As a result of a specific enzyme deficiency, phenylalanine accumulates. The enzyme block leads to a deficiency of tyrosine, leading to a reduction in melanin; thus children often have blue eyes and blonde hair. Pigmented areas of the brain are affected, such as the substantia nigra. PKU is tested for at birth in children using the Guthrie test. PKU can be treated by removing phenylalanine from the diet. If PKU is detected early enough in childhood, mental retardation can be prevented.

212C: Secreto-motor innervation is via the glossopharyngeal and auriculotemporal nerves

The parotid gland is the largest of the major salivary glands. It is mainly a serous gland, with only a few scattered mucinous acini. This in part explains why salivary stones (calculi) are rarely encountered in the parotid gland and are found more often in the submandibular gland, where the secretion is more mucinous and where the gland lies below the opening of the duct (which impedes drainage and encourages stasis).

Anteriorly, the gland overlaps the masseter. The parotid duct (of Stensen), not to be confused with Wharton's duct (which is the submandibular duct), passes forward over the masseter and turns around its anterior border to pierce the buccinator (not masseter) muscle. The buccinator muscle acts like a sphincter at this point and plays an extremely important role in preventing the reflux of air into the parotid (and hence its insufflation) when the intraoral pressure is raised, as when playing a trumpet. The duct opens on the mucous membrane of the cheek opposite the second upper molar tooth.

The parotid gland consists of two lobes, superficial and deep. Hence the importance of looking in the mouth in cases where a parotid swelling is present, to look for, or exclude, involvement of the deep lobe. There is no middle lobe, although there may be an accessory lobe. The parotid is surrounded by a tough fascial capsule, derived from the investing layer of deep cervical fascia, that is richly innervated. It is the acute swelling of this fibrous envelope that produces the pain of mumps parotitis, a virus infection of the gland.

From superficial to the deep within the parotid lie the following:

- five terminal branches of the facial nerve (also known as the pes anserinus, or 'goose's foot')
- retromandibular vein
- external carotid artery.

The branches of the facial nerve lie most superficially within the parotid gland and hence are extremely vulnerable to damage in parotid surgery. Thus, if the retromandibular vein comes into view, it is too late; the facial nerve has already been severed! It is important to identify and protect the various branches of the facial nerve, which may be remembered by the mnemonic 'ten Zulus baited my cat' (from top to bottom):

- ten = **t**emporal branch
- Zulus = **z**ygomatic branch
- baited = **b**uccal branch
- my = **m**arginal mandibular branch
- cat = **c**ervical branch.

The branches of the facial nerve are also likely to be injured by a malignant tumour of the parotid which is usually highly invasive and quickly involves the facial nerve, causing a facial paralysis.

The secreto-motor supply to the parotid (for secretion of saliva) is by way of parasympathetic fibres of the glossopharyngeal nerve, synapsing in the otic ganglion and relaying onwards to the parotid gland through the auriculotemporal nerve. The importance of knowing this lies in a phenomenon known as Frey's syndrome which may occur, not infrequently, following parotid surgery, or penetrating trauma to the parotid gland. It is caused by misdirected reinnervation of the auriculotemporal nerve fibres to the sweat glands in the facial skin following its injury. The patient may complain of gustatory sweating (i.e. a stimulus intended for saliva production produces sweating instead).

213D: They lack nuclei and mitochondria

Erythrocytes do not contain nuclei (they are anucleate) or mitochondria. This maximizes the haemoglobin-carrying capacity of red cells. The absence of mitochondria precludes aerobic energy production; hence they are very efficient oxygen transporters because they do not consume any O_2 directly. Erythrocytes are thus totally dependent on the anaerobic metabolism of glucose to generate the energy needed to maintain electrochemical gradients across their cell membranes.

Without nuclei, erythrocytes are unable to replace deteriorating enzymes and membrane proteins; this shortens their life expectancy. The average lifespan of a normal erythrocyte is 120 days (or 16–18 weeks). Lifespan may be reduced further as a result of the premature destruction of red cells. This is a feature of haemolysis. Aged red cells are removed from the circulation by the spleen and liver.

Erythrocytes contain the enzyme carbonic anhydrase that catalyses the reaction $CO_2 + H_2O = H^+ + HCO^{3-}$ and requires zinc as a cofactor. This plays an important role in carbon dioxide transport and in the buffering of pH.

Erythrocytes do not burst when placed in 0.9% (normal) saline, since this is isotonic with their contents.

214B: It is a known carcinogen

Helicobacter pylori is a Gram-negative, micro-aerophilic, motile, spiral-shaped bacterium which selectively colonizes the mucous layer of the stomach and duodenum. Around 50 per cent of all humans worldwide are infected with the organism. However, it seems to cause disease only in a small proportion of all those infected. It is still unclear at present as to why this is the case but it probably reflects differences in virulence among different strains, along with differences in the background genetics of the host that affects their susceptibility to the organism.

It is now firmly established that *H. pylori* causes more than 90 per cent of duodenal ulcers and up to 80 per cent of gastric ulcers. The link between *H. pylori* infection and subsequent gastritis and peptic ulcer disease has been established through studies of human volunteers, antibiotic treatment studies and epidemiological studies. *H. pylori* is also a known risk factor for gastric adenocarcinoma and lymphoma. Indeed, *H. pylori* has been classified as a class 1 (definite) carcinogen for malignancy.

H. pylori is unique among bacteria in being able to survive within the acidic environment of the stomach. It achieves this by producing a urease enzyme which produces ammonia from endogenous urea, thereby buffering gastric acid in the immediate vicinity of the organism. The elaboration of urease by *H. pylori* forms the basis of the urea breath test that may be used in the diagnosis of *H. pylori* infection.

H. pylori is treated with antibiotic therapy. *H. pylori* eradication therapy (also known as triple therapy) usually consists of a proton pump inhibitor in conjunction with two antibiotics. At present, there is no known vaccination against *H. pylori*. However, development of a vaccine against *H. pylori* would have the potential to prevent peptic ulcer disease and perhaps even gastric carcinoma.

215A: A- and B-cells

In the pancreas, A- and B-cells of the Islets of Langerhans secrete glucagons and insulin, respectively. Pancreatic D1 cells release a product similar to vasoactive intestinal polypeptide (VIP). Pancreatic polypeptide cells secrete pancreatic polypeptide and D-cells secrete somatostatin. Acinar cells are part of the exocrine, not endocrine, pancreas and are involved in the release of enzymes and digestive juices, rather than hormones.

216A: 45XO

This is Turner's syndrome. It is a chromosome disorder caused by the lack of the Y chromosome (45XO). Features include widely spaced nipples, short stature, webbed neck, a kinked aorta (coarctation of aorta), primary amenorrhoea, high arched palate. 47XXY is Klinefelter's syndrome which is associated with tall stature.

217C: The pituitary and sphenoidal air sinus lie in its medial wall

The cavernous sinus is one of those tricky areas that is difficult to get one's head around. It consists of a plexus of veins that lies alongside the sphenoid in the middle cranial fossa. Blood can flow in either direction in the cavernous sinus, depending on local venous pressures. In addition, there are no valves in the cavernous sinus or its connected veins.

The function of the cavernous sinus is unclear. However, since it surrounds the internal carotid artery, which forms the main blood supply to the brain, some have suggested that the cavernous sinus may have evolved to act as a cooling system for the brain. A sort of counter-current mechanism is set up whereby the venous blood contained within the cavernous sinus may actually draw out heat from the internal carotid artery at its centre. However, rupture of the internal carotid artery within the cavernous sinus (usually a result of an internal carotid artery aneurysm, or following trauma) may result in a carotico-cavernous fistula.

The walls of the cavernous sinus may be summarized as follows:

- Roof – anterior and posterior clinoid processes with uncus of temporal lobe and internal carotid artery on it, cranial nerves III and IV
- Floor – greater wing of sphenoid
- Anterior wall (narrow) – medial end of superior orbital fissure, ophthalmic veins, orbit
- Posterior wall (narrow) – dura of posterior fossa, superior and inferior petrosal sinuses, peduncle of brain
- Medial wall – dura over sphenoid, sella turica, pituitary, sphenoidal air sinus
- Lateral wall – dura, temporal lobe, cranial nerves III, IV, Va, Vb in wall (from top to bottom)
- Contents – internal carotid artery (with its associated sympathetic plexus), cranial nerve VI, blood.

Note that the optic nerve is not contained within the cavernous sinus.

The area of facial skin bounded by the upper lip, nose, medial part of cheek and the eye is a potentially dangerous area to have an infection (the so-called 'danger area of the face'). An infection in this area may result in thrombosis of the facial vein, with spread of organisms through the inferior ophthalmic vein to the cavernous sinus. This may result in a cavernous sinus thrombosis. By the superficial middle cerebral vein, such thrombosis may spread to the cerebral hemisphere, which may be fatal unless adequately treated with antibiotics.

218E: They deform as they pass through the capillaries

Unstressed erythrocytes normally appear as biconcave discs. This provides a 20–30 per cent greater surface area than a sphere relative to cell volume, thus significantly enhancing gaseous exchange. This shape, with the fluidity of the plasma membrane, allows the erythrocyte to deform easily thus making them able to pass through the smallest capillaries. Erythrocytes appear spherical in a genetic condition known as hereditary spherocytosis.

Normal red blood cells are around 7 microns in diameter, whereas the diameter of capillaries is only around 5 microns. Red cells possess deformable walls and therefore become bullet-shaped as they pass through capillaries. This enables 'bolus flow' or 'plug flow' which eliminates some of the internal friction associated with lamina sliding over one another (Fahraeus–Lindqvist effect). The reduction in apparent viscosity means that capillaries have a lower resistance to flow than they would do if the blood were a uniform fluid containing the same amounts of protein without the red cell membrane to parcel it up. The efficiency of bolus flow depends critically on the deformability of the red cell, and this is impaired in many clinical conditions. The most dramatic of these is sickle cell anaemia.

Erythrocytes make a major contribution to the buffering capacity of the blood through the action of carbonic anhydrase and haemoglobin contained within the red cells. Indeed, red cells are responsible for most of the buffering power of whole blood.

Erythropoiesis (the production of red cells) is stimulated by the hormone erythropoietin, but the main source of erythropoietin is the kidney, not erythrocytes.

The capillary bed has a greater cross-sectional area than the venular bed. Blood therefore travels more slowly in capillaries compared to venules. This prolongs the time available for gaseous exchange. Red cells are not evenly distributed across the bloodstream in large blood vessels, but form an axial stream away from the vessel wall, leaving a cell-deficient layer of plasma at the margins. This marginal layer helps to ease the blood along.

219D: Is caused by a toxin which increases adenylate cyclase activity

Cholera is caused by *Vibrio cholerae*, a Gram negative, comma-shaped, flagellated bacterium. It is usually transmitted by contaminated water supplies, as deduced from the famous epidemiological work of John Snow in the 1850s, who was able to trace a cholera outbreak in London to a single water pump that had become contaminated with sewage. Removing the handle of the water pump led to a dramatic reduction in the number of new cases of cholera.

The diarrhoea of cholera is caused by the action of an exotoxin or enterotoxin (not endotoxin) called cholera toxin. The toxin increases the activity of adenylate cyclase resulting in the massive secretion of chloride, sodium and water (so-called 'rice-water diarrhoea'). The watery diarrhoea may be so extreme that death may occur from dehydration and electrolyte imbalance. The mucosa is not invaded by the bacteria (in contrast to *Salmonella*, *Shigella* and *Campylobacter*) so that mucosal inflammation is only slight and there is no ulceration.

Overall absorption from the gut remains intact so that oral rehydration therapy can replace massive fluid and electrolyte losses, reducing the mortality from 50 per cent to less than 1 per cent. Antibiotics (such as tetracyclines) are used as an adjunct to fluid therapy. Antibiotics diminish the duration and volume of the fluid loss and hasten clearance of the organism from the stool.

220C: Parotid salivary gland

The glossopharyngeal nerve provides parasympathetic innervation for the parotid salivary gland, via the auriculotemporal nerve. The facial nerve supplies the parasympathetic innervation of the lacrimal, nasal, sublingual and submandibular glands.

221D: The risk of having a child with Down's syndrome is approximately 1 in 1000 if the mother is 30 years old

Down's syndrome is trisomy 21. It arises in approximately 1 in 700 births, but there is a strong association between the incidence and advancing maternal age. When the mother is 30 years old, her risk of having a child with Down's syndrome is 1 in 1000. Affected children have a lower intelligence quotient (IQ). Classical features include epicanthic folds, a protruding tongue, a single palmar crease, a wide gap between the first and second toe, cardiac anomalies including atrial and ventricular septal defects. Early death occurs in 15–20 per cent of cases and is usually cardiac-related.

A large proportion of (but not all) individuals will develop Alzheimer's disease in later life. This is believed to occur through a gene dosage effect and the accumulation of amyloid precursor protein (APP, the protein linked to Alzheimer's) which is coded for by chromosome 21.

The extra chromosome arises in 94 per cent of cases from non-dysjunction at maternal Meiosis I. Robertsonian translocations account for 5 per cent of cases. One per cent of cases occur due to mosaicism.

222B: Buccinator

There are four muscles of mastication: temporalis, masseter, medial pterygoid and lateral pterygoid. They are all first branchial arch derivatives and are therefore all innervated by the same nerve (mandibular division of trigeminal, or Vc).

The buccinator muscle is regarded as a muscle of facial expression and is therefore a second branchial arch derivative innervated by the facial, or 7th, cranial nerve. This is one of many situations in which a good knowledge of embryology and especially the branchial arches may help to predict the anatomy.

223D: It is reversed by plasmin (fibrinolysin)

One of the drawbacks of having a high-pressure circulation is that even slight damage to blood vessels, especially on the arterial side, can lead to a rapid loss of circulatory blood volume. To prevent bleeding we have developed quite complicated responses to vessel damage designed to stop bleeding. Three key physiological events occur upon the onset of bleeding:

- vasoconstriction
- platelet aggregation to form the primary haemostatic plug
- activation of the clotting cascade to form a fibrin plug (secondary or stable haemostatic plug).

The balance of all components – vessel wall, platelets, adhesive and coagulation proteins and regulatory mechanisms – determines the effectiveness of the haemostatic plug in maintaining the structural and functional integrity of the circulatory system.

Blood platelets are formed from megakaryocytes in the bone marrow. They are anucleate, but the cytoplasm contains electron-dense granules, lysosomes and mitochondria. Each megakaryocyte is responsible for the production of around 4000 platelets. The half-life of platelets in the blood is about 8–12 days.

The clotting cascade involves a series of several highly specific serine proteases which activate each other in a stepwise manner. In this way a rapid response is achieved because at each step the signal is amplified. Clotting factors are produced in the liver so that liver failure results in a tendency to bleed (anticoagulant state). The final stage of the clotting cascade involves the conversion of fibrinogen to fibrin; this is catalysed by thrombin, not prothrombin, which is the inactive precursor of thrombin.

Plasmin acts as a regulatory mechanism to keep the clotting cascade in check and to prevent the over-clotting of blood which could have disastrous consequences (such as the occlusion of blood vessels). It degrades both fibrin and fibrinogen to products that can inhibit thrombin. Fibrinolytic agents are widely used in clinical practice, a good example being the use of thrombolytics in acute myocardial infarction.

224C: It is the second commonest human carcinogen worldwide

A third of the world's population are currently infected with the hepatitis B virus. Hepatitis B is a double-stranded DNA virus, usually transmitted haematogenously, by sexual intercourse, or vertically from mother to baby. Hepatitis A (not hepatitis B) is acquired by the faeco-oral route.

Infection during childhood leads to a high rate of chronic carriage of the virus, with only 10 per cent of children clearing the virus. This chronic carrier state is associated with long-term complications in later life. Ninety per cent of adults, on the other hand, clear the virus, with only 10 per cent of adults becoming chronic carriers of the virus.

Hepatic complications of hepatitis B infections include:

- acute viral hepatitis
- fulminant hepatic failure
- chronic active and chronic persistent viral hepatitis
- cirrhosis
- hepatocellular carcinoma.

Chronic carriage of the virus is facilitated by the ability of the hepatitis B virus to integrate into the DNA and to infect hepatocytes which normally express low levels of MHC class I on their cell surface. Both these strategies help the virus to evade the host's defence mechanisms. Damage to the liver usually results from the host's immune response in an attempt to clear the virus (so-called immune pathology).

It is now well recognized that hepatitis B is a risk factor for the development of primary liver cancer (hepatocellular carcinoma). Indeed, after tobacco smoking, hepatitis B is the second most common human carcinogen worldwide.

Hepatitis B is effectively prevented (not treated) by hepatitis B vaccination. Vaccination is mandatory for all healthcare professionals who regularly come into contact with blood products. Hepatitis B is treated with serum immunoglobulin and antiviral agents (α-interferon, lamivudine).

225E: 23 years of age

Fusion of the ilium, ischium and pubis at the acetabulum is usually complete by the age of 23. From birth to the early twenties, the three bones are held together by Y-shaped cartilage.

226E. Exhibits a genetic phenomenon known as 'anticipation'

Huntington's disease is a late-onset, autosomal dominant disorder characterized by CAG trinucleotide repeat sequences within the *huntingtin* gene on chromosome 4 (myotonic dystrophy is a CTG trinucleotide repeat disorder). This translates into poly-glutamine repeats within the huntingtin protein (not the fibrillin protein which forms the basis of Marfan's syndrome).

Huntington's disease is characterized clinically by a triad of choreiform (dance-like) movements, cognitive changes and psychiatric disturbances. It is Parkinson's disease that is characterized clinically by a triad of bradykinesia, rigidity (which may be of the lead-pipe or cog-wheel variety) and resting tremor. Histologically, Huntington's disease is characterized by atrophy and loss of neurones in the caudate nucleus and putamen.

It is also important to appreciate that Huntington's disease exhibits a genetic phenomenon known as 'anticipation'. This simply means that both the age of onset and severity of the disease phenotype alters with successive generations as a result of the unstable trinucleotide repeat sequence.

227B: The anterior communicating artery joins the two anterior cerebral arteries

The internal carotid and vertebral systems anastomose with each other around the optic chiasm and infundibulum of the pituitary stalk at the base of the brain, forming the arterial Circle of Willis. The circle is formed in the following way:

- *Posteriorly*. At the lower border of the pons, two vertebral arteries combine to form the basilar artery. At the upper border of the pons, the basilar artery terminates as right and left posterior cerebral arteries.
- *Anteriorly*. Each internal carotid artery gives off an anterior and middle cerebral artery.

The circle is completed anteriorly by the single, anterior communicating artery which connects the two anterior cerebral arteries. The circle is completed posteriorly by the two posterior communicating arteries that connect the posterior cerebral arteries with the internal carotid arteries.

The communicating vessels allow equalization of blood flow between the two sides of the brain and can allow anastomotic compensation if parts are occluded. However, compensation is not always effective owing to the small size of the blood vessels and a stroke (or cerebrovascular accident) may result.

Congenital berry aneurysms are abnormal dilatations of blood vessels, usually located around the Circle of Willis (because here the tunica media is weakest). Rupture of an aneurysm of the arterial circle accounts for 90 per cent of subarachnoid haemorrhages.

228D: Interstitial fluid hydrostatic pressure is normally negative

Four primary forces determine the movement of fluid across the capillary membrane (Starling's forces):

- capillary hydrostatic pressure – 'forces fluid out'
- plasma colloid osmotic pressure – 'pulls fluid in'
- interstitial fluid hydrostatic pressure – 'pushes fluid in'
- interstitial fluid colloid osmotic pressure – 'pulls fluid out'.

At the arterial end of the capillary, the capillary hydrostatic pressure exceeds the plasma colloid osmotic pressure and fluid is drawn out of the capillary into the interstitium. By this means transport of nutrients to the tissues occurs. However, as one moves along the capillary the capillary hydrostatic pressure falls such that, at the venous end of the capillary, the plasma colloid osmotic pressure exceeds the capillary hydrostatic pressure and fluid moves back into the capillary, removing cellular excreta. In this way, about 90 per cent of the fluid that has filtered out of the arterial ends of capillaries is reabsorbed at the venous ends. Only the remainder flows into the lymph vessels.

Interstitial fluid hydrostatic pressure is normally subatmospheric (negative). This results from the suction effect of the lymphatics returning fluid to the circulation. This maintains the structural integrity of the tissues, keeps the interstitial spaces small and reduces distances for diffusion.

Movement of lymph in one direction along the lymphatics depends on:

- filtration pressure from capillaries
- action of local muscles
- action of local arterial pulsation
- respiratory movement (thoraco-abdominal pump) with intermittent negative pressures in the brachiocephalic veins
- smooth muscle in the walls of larger lymphatics (sympathetically controlled)
- valves within.

Oedema (excess fluid accumulation in the extracellular spaces) results from:

- elevated capillary pressure
- decreased plasma colloid osmotic pressure
- increased interstitial fluid protein
- increased capillary permeability
- blockage of lymph return (lymphoedema).

Diffusion distances are greatly increased as a result of oedema and this can interfere with cell nutrition.

229D: Establishes persistence through antigenic variation

HIV is an enveloped RNA retrovirus containing two copies of genomic RNA and three viral enzymes (reverse transcriptase, protease and integrase). HIV RNA is transcribed by viral reverse transcriptase into DNA that integrates into the host-cell genome. HIV is transmitted by three routes: sexual contact, blood-borne transmission (transfusions or contaminated needles), or vertically from mother to baby (transplacental or via breast milk).

The CD4 antigen on helper T-cells is the receptor for the gp120 viral envelope protein, allowing HIV to infect CD4 T-cells (helper T-cells). The destruction of CD4 cells is central to the pathogenesis of HIV infection. CD4 cells play a pivotal role in the orchestration of both humoral and cell-mediated immune responses. Therefore, by directly infecting and eliminating CD4 cells, the HIV virus leads to a slow and progressive decline in immune function. The end result is AIDS (acquired immunodeficiency syndrome) where the body opens up a whole range of opportunistic infections, the consequences of which are often fatal.

There are several ways in which the HIV evades the host immune system and establishes persistence. For example:

- by directly infecting cells of the immune system, thereby enabling the virus to 'hide' from the immune system
- by infecting macrophages and dendritic cells in addition to CD4 cells, thereby establishing an important reservoir of infection in lymphoid tissues and forming a site for continued viral replication
- by directly integrating into the host cell DNA
- by constantly mutating in a process known as antigenic variation.

The generation of new antigenic variants is primarily a function of the high intrinsic error rate present in the reverse transcriptase enzyme (1 in 1000 base-pair error rate). The huge number of variants of HIV in a single infected patient during the course of infection eventually swamps the immune system, leading to its collapse.

230E: Tremor

Hyperthyroidism is associated with tremor, tachycardia, low serum cholesterol and hyperreflexia. All the other options are classical findings of hypothyroidism.

231C: It is the most common inherited disease in Caucasians

Cystic fibrosis (also known as mucoviscidosis) is an autosomal recessive condition, caused by a genetic mutation in the cystic fibrosis transmembrane regulator (CFTR) on chromosome 7. It is the most common inherited disease in Caucasians, affecting 1 in 2500 children. Cystic fibrosis carriers are believed to offer a selective advantage to the population by being relatively more resistant to cholera. This may explain the fact that, on the basis of the frequency of affected homozygotes in the white population, 2–4 per cent must be heterozygote carriers (using the Hardy–Weinberg equation).

Clinical manifestations relate mainly to the lungs (chronic lung infections, especially caused by *Pseudomonas aeruginosa*, bronchiectasis) and the digestive system (meconium ileus, pancreatic insufficiency, failure to thrive). There is no cure for cystic fibrosis. Treatment is mainly supportive, through a multidisciplinary approach, consisting of vigorous chest physiotherapy, mucolytics, antibiotics to treat chest infections, pancreatic enzyme replacement (Creon), and in some cases heart–lung transplantation may be an option in the final stages of the disease. Life expectancy is markedly reduced with a median survival of around 35 years. End-stage lung disease is the principal cause of death.

Gene therapy is not a well-established treatment option and is still best confined to clinical trials. The main problems that have been encountered in the application of gene therapy to clinical practice concern the targeting of vectors to specific sites and integration into the genome.

232C: A subdural haematoma lies in the plane between the dura and arachnoid mater

The pia mater is to brain as periosteum is to bone. The pia mater is therefore the innermost layer of the meninges and invests the central nervous system to the depths of the deepest fissures and sulci.

The dura mater is the outermost layer of the meninges closest to the bone. It consists of two layers, an outer endosteal layer and inner meningeal layer. The two layers separate to enclose the venous sinuses and folds of the inner layer project into the cranial cavity and are responsible for the formation of the four fibrous flanges, or septa, that minimize rotatory displacement of the brain (the falx cerebri, the falx cerebelli, tentorium cerebelli, diaphragma sellae). The dura mater is richly innervated and therefore dural stretch causes pain that is commonly experienced as a headache. Two good examples are the headache of meningitis which is caused by inflammation of the meninges, and a post-lumbar puncture headache where a headache results from the stimulation of sensory nerve endings in the dura after removal of cerebrospinal fluid.

The arachnoid mater is a delicate membrane that sits in between the dura and pia mater. It is connected to the pia mater by many fine filamentous processes (hence the name arachnoid, or spider-like). The region between the pia and arachnoid mater is the subarachnoid space, filled with cerebrospinal fluid. The term 'leptomeninges' refers to the arachnoid and pia mater.
A good understanding of the various meningeal layers is necessary in order to understand the various types of intracranial haemorrhage that may occur.

An extradural haematoma occurs between the endosteal layer of the dura mater and the skull. It is commonly the result of trauma with bleeding from the middle meningeal artery. It is often associated with an underlying fracture (commonly in the region of the pterion which is the surface marking for the anterior branch of the middle meningeal artery that is commonly implicated). Containment of the arterial bleed may lead to a lucid interval until the pressure builds up to such a point that compression of the brain occurs with resulting coma.

A subdural haematoma is often a result of venous bleeding in the space between the dura and arachnoid mater. It commonly occurs in the elderly, demented, or alcoholics where shrinkage of the brain occurs. This stretches the bridging veins that run across the surface of the brain and makes them vulnerable to tearing. Since the bleed is venous rather than arterial, lower pressures result in a more gradual accumulation of blood than an arterial bleed. The result is a gradual deterioration in cognitive function and patients often present with confusion (chronic subdural haematoma).

A subarachnoid haematoma is an arterial bleed that occurs in the subarachnoid space, between the pia and arachnoid layers. This usually follows rupture of a berry aneurysm in the region of the Circle of Willis. This causes blood to contaminate the cerebrospinal fluid, which is visible at lumbar puncture.

Finally, an intracerebral bleed occurs within the brain parenchyma itself and is therefore unrelated to the cranial meninges.

233B: Cerebral blood flow is very sensitive to changes in the pCO_2 of the perfusing blood

The cerebral circulation does not consist of functional end-arteries. Rather, a rich vascular anastomosis known as the Circle of Willis surrounds the base of the brain, into which all the main arteries to the brain connect so that if one artery should block, the brain can still be supplied by the other arteries in this anastomotic arrangement.

Cerebral blood flow is little affected by cardiovascular reflexes (i.e. the autonomic nervous system). Carbon dioxide is the most important determinant of cerebral blood flow, via its local vasodilator action (in underperfused areas carbon dioxide accumulates and this leads to vasodilatation and restoration of normal cerebral perfusion). Hyperventilation leads to washout of carbon dioxide from the blood and constriction of cerebral blood vessels. This may result in syncope following a panic attack. In addition, it explains why hyperventilating prior to diving into water can result in syncope underwater and drowning. The local effect of carbon dioxide on the cerebral vasculature is deliberately utilized in the management of head injury where hyperventilation is used to reduce raised intracranial pressure.

The rate of cerebral blood flow remains essentially stable, up to a point, with changing blood pressure owing to local autoregulation of flow. Autoregulation is very well developed in the brain;

a fall in blood pressure causes the resistance vessels to dilate and thereby maintain flow. Cerebral autoregulation seems to involve both myogenic and metabolic mechanisms.

The important relationship between the cerebral perfusion, mean arterial blood pressure and intracranial pressure is as follows:

CPP = MABP – ICP

where CPP is cerebral perfusion pressure, MABP is mean arterial blood pressure and ICP is intracranial pressure. It stems from the fact that the adult brain is enclosed in a rigid, incompressible box, with the result that the volume inside it must remain constant (Monro–Kelly doctrine). A rise in intracranial pressure therefore decreases cerebral perfusion pressure (and hence cerebral blood flow). In raised intracranial pressure, as the brainstem becomes compressed, local neuronal activity causes a rise in sympathetic vasomotor drive and thus a rise in blood pressure. This is known as the Cushing's reflex. This elevated blood pressure evokes a bradycardia via the baroreceptor reflex. The Cushing's reflex helps to maintain cerebral blood flow and protect the vital centres of the brain from loss of nutrition if the intracranial pressure rises high enough to compress the cerebral arteries.

234D: Mutations in the haemagglutinin molecule are responsible for antigenic drift

Viruses can be classified according to:

- particle structure (i.e. virus family)
- genomic type – RNA or DNA, single-stranded or double-stranded.

In addition, single-stranded RNA viruses can be divided into positive-stranded (coding) and negative-stranded (non-coding) RNA.

Influenza is a member of the Orthomyxoviridae family of viruses and has a negative single-stranded RNA genome. The spherical surface of the virus is a lipid bilayer (envelope) containing the viral haemagglutinin (HA) and neuramidase (NA) which determine the subtype of the virus. The HA molecule mediates the entry of the virus into host cells. The NA molecule may be important in the release of viruses from host cells.

Epidemics of influenza occur through mutations, resulting in amino acid substitutions of the HA and NA that allow the virus to escape most host antibodies (antigenic drift). Pandemics, which tend to be longer and more widespread then epidemics, may occur when both the HA and NA are replaced through recombination of RNA segments with those of animal viruses, making all individuals susceptible to the new influenza virus (antigenic shift). The most notable influenza pandemics occurred in 1918, 1957 and 1968, resulting in millions of deaths worldwide. The virus that caused the last pandemic (H3N2) has been drifting ever since and we have no idea when the next pandemic will occur.

Transmission of influenza occurs by droplet inhalation. The initial symptoms of influenza are due to direct viral damage and associated inflammatory responses. Life-threatening influenza is often due to secondary bacterial infection as a result of the destruction of the respiratory epithelium by the influenza virus.

Influenza may be prevented by a vaccine that consists of inactivated preparations of the virus. It provides protection in up to 70 per cent of individuals for about one year. It is recommended for those only at high risk of acquiring the virus. The vaccines in use contain the HA and NA components in relation to the prevalent strain or strains of influenza circulating the previous year. Each year the World Health Organization recommends which strains should be included.

235B: Low calcium intake

High dietary intake of calcium promotes calcium absorption, suppresses PTH release and bone dissolution and thus protects against osteoporosis. Excess alcohol intake, sedentary lifestyle, early menopause and a thin body habitus all promote bone loss.

236E: Affects the intrinsic, rather than the extrinsic, pathway for blood coagulation

Haemophilia A is a sex-linked (X-linked recessive) disorder that results in a reduction in the amount or activity of the clotting factor, factor VIII, a member of the intrinsic pathway. Since the inheritance pattern is X-linked the disorder primarily affects males, since female individuals who carry the affected gene usually do not have bleeding manifestations. Clinically there is a tendency toward easy bruising and haemorrhage after trauma or operative procedures. In addition, spontaneous haemorrhages are frequently encountered in regions of the body normally subject to trauma, particularly the joints (haemarthroses).

Factor IX deficiency is known as haemophilia B (or Christmas disease) and is clinically indistinguishable from haemophilia A. Treatment of haemophilia A includes clotting factor replacement with recombinant factor VIII. The continued presence of this devastating disease throughout history may be explained by the protective effect against ischaemic heart disease in haemophilia carriers (by reducing the 'stickiness' of the blood; a similar effect to aspirin).

237C: It is secreto-motor to the lacrimal gland

The facial, or 7th cranial, nerve has a variety of different functions and is important clinically. Its functions may be summarized as follows:

- is associated developmentally with the second branchial arch
- supplies the muscles of facial expression
- gives special taste sensation to the anterior two-thirds of the tongue via the chorda tympani nerve
- carries secreto-motor fibres to the lacrimal gland through the greater petrosal nerve
- is secreto-motor to the submandibular and sublingual glands
- gives somatic sensation to the external auditory meatus.

Special taste from the posterior third of the tongue is carried by the glossopharyngeal nerve. The levator palpebrae superioris muscle, responsible for elevating the eyelid, is not a muscle of facial expression – it is innervated by the occulomotor nerve and sympathetics. The orbicularis oculi muscle, responsible for blinking and for screwing the eye tight, is regarded as a muscle of facial expression and is supplied by the facial nerve.

The four principal muscles of mastication (temporalis, medial and lateral pterygoids, masseter) are all supplied by the mandibular division of the trigeminal nerve. Note buccinator is not a muscle of mastication and is innervated by the facial nerve.

Understanding the above helps to explain what happens when things go wrong. A facial nerve (Bell's) palsy results in weakness of the muscles of facial expression down one side of the face, leading to a droop. Note that this is a lower motor neurone palsy and that all the muscles down the side of the face are affected including the forehead muscles. This is in sharp contrast to a cerebrovascular accident, or upper motor neurone facial palsy, where the upper (forehead) muscles are spared since they are bilaterally innervated from both cerebral cortices.

Beside a droopy face, however, a Bell's palsy also results in loss of sensation to the anterior two-thirds of the tongue and hyperacusis (sensitivity to sounds) as a result of denervation of the stapedius muscle, which normally serves to dampen down sounds in the middle ear. Dry eyes occur as a result of the loss of the secreto-motor supply to the lacrimal gland (and hence the need to protect the eye to prevent keratitis and corneal ulceration in a facial nerve palsy). This is exacerbated by the denervation of the orbicularis oculi muscle which normally functions to spread the tear film over the surface of the cornea with the blinking reflex.

Although it may not seem very important, the small somatic sensory branch of the facial nerve (that supplies the external auditory meatus) may explain why in Ramsey–Hunt syndrome (herpes zoster infection of the geniculate ganglion) herpes vesicles are found around the external auditory meatus.

This question illustrates nicely how a good understanding of anatomy may help the student in future clinical practice.

238B: The vital capacity is the sum of the inspiratory reserve volume, the expiratory reserve volume and the tidal volume

Spirometry traces are easy to understand if you remember the following two rules:

- There are four lung volumes and five capacities that you need to remember.
- A capacity is made up of two or more lung volumes.

The *four lung volumes* are:

- *Tidal volume* = volume of air inspired or expired with each normal breath in quiet breathing – approximately 500 mL
- *Residual volume* = the volume of air that remains in the lung after forced expiration
- *Inspiratory reserve volume* = extra volume of air that can be inspired over and above the normal tidal volume
- *Expiratory reserve volume* = extra volume of air that can be expired by forceful expiration after the end of a normal tidal expiration.

The *five lung capacities* are:

- *Functional residual capacity* = the volume of air that remains in the lung at the end of quiet expiration – equal to the sum of the residual volume and the expiratory reserve volume
- *Inspiratory capacity* = inspiratory reserve volume + tidal volume
- *Expiratory capacity* = expiratory reserve volume + tidal volume
- *Vital capacity* = inspiratory reserve volume + tidal volume + expiratory reserve volume (or total lung capacity minus residual volume)
- *Total lung capacity* = vital capacity + residual volume.

The residual volume (and therefore functional residual capacity and total lung capacity) cannot be measured directly by spirometry. They are measured by either whole-body plethysmography, or by using the helium dilution or nitrogen washout techniques.

239B: Delayed hypersensitivity reaction against the bacteria

Mycobacteria stimulate a specific T-cell response of cell-mediated immunity resulting in granuloma formation. While this is effective in reducing the infection, the delayed hypersensitivity (type IV) reaction also damages the host tissues. Damage therefore primarily results from the host's immune response in an attempt to clear the body of infection – so-called immune pathology. The formation of granulomas is the host's attempt to wall off the mycobacteria from the rest of the body, thereby preventing dissemination. When an individual is immunosuppressed (in HIV for example), dissemination therefore occurs more readily with disastrous consequences.

The tubercle bacilli can survive within macrophages and this may account for latent infections and reactivation of tuberculosis in later life. There is no significant humoral response to mycobacteria. Necrosis does occur in tuberculosis, but it is usually within the granuloma (caseous necrosis). *M. tuberculosis* causes little or no direct or toxin-mediated damage.

240D: Ptosis of the left eye

This patient has Horner's syndrome. Unilateral loss of sympathetic innervation of the face results in ptosis, pupil constriction (miosis), anhidrosis, facial flushing and enophthalmos. Lateral deviation of the eye would suggest damage to the 3rd cranial nerve.

241D: It is more common in regions of the world in which malaria is endemic

Sickle cell anaemia is an autosomal recessive condition, caused by a single base change in the DNA coding for the amino acid in the 6th position of the beta-haemoglobin chain (adenine is replaced by thymine). This leads to an amino acid change from glutamic acid to valine. The resultant haemoglobin, HbS, has abnormal physiochemical properties that leads to sickling of red bloods cells and sickle cell disease. Homozygosity at the sickle cell locus is known as sickle cell anaemia, while heterozygosity at the same locus is known as the sickle cell trait. Where malaria is endemic, as many as 30 per cent of black Africans are heterozygous. This frequency may be related in part to the slight protection against *Plasmodium falciparum* afforded by HbS.

Clinical manifestations do not occur until around 3–6 months after birth when the main switch from fetal to adult haemoglobin occurs (fetal haemoglobin does not contain β-haemoglobin chains). Clinical manifestations relate to the sickling of red blood cells as a result of the production of a structurally abnormal haemoglobin. This includes haemolysis (the average red cell survival is shortened from the normal 120 days to approximately 20 days) and occlusion of small blood vessels resulting in ischaemic tissue damage (so-called painful vaso-occlusive crises). The latter crises are precipitated by factors such as infection, acidosis, dehydration or hypoxia. Homozygotes sickle at Po_2 levels of 5–6 kPa (i.e. normal venous blood) and thus sickling takes place all the time. Heterozygotes sickle at Po_2 levels of 2.5–4 kPa and therefore only sickle at extremely low oxygen tensions.

The spleen is enlarged in infancy and childhood, as a result of extramedullary haematopoiesis, but later is often reduced in size (autosplenectomy) as a result of erythrostasis within the spleen leading to thrombosis, autoinfarction or at least to marked tissue hypoxia. Therefore one should not expect to find a palpable spleen on examining an adult with sickle cell anaemia.

242B: The intervertebral joints are secondary cartilaginous joints

The spinal cord terminates at the level of L1/L2. Below this only nerve roots exist within the vertebral canal (cauda equina). It is therefore safe to perform a lumbar puncture at the level of L3/4 or L4/5. Fortunately for the purpose of a lumbar puncture, the dural sac containing the cerebrospinal fluid does not terminate until the level of S2.

The intervertebral joints are secondary cartilaginous joints. Between each vertebral body lies an intervertebral disc which is predominantly created from an annulus fibrosus of fibrocartilage with an internal nucleus pulposus, a bubble of semiliquid gelatinous substance derived from the embryonic notochord. With age the fibrocartilaginous annulus does deteriorate and may weaken, often in the lower lumbar region, giving rise to a slipped, or prolapsed, disc. In such cases the nucleus pulposus is typically extruded posterolaterally.

The relationship of the nerve roots to intervertebral discs is of great importance. At the level of the L4/5 disc, the 4th lumbar nerve roots within their dural sheath have already emerged from the intervertebral foramen and so are not lying low enough to come into contact with the disc. The roots that lie behind the posterolateral part of this disc are those of the 5th lumbar nerve and these are the ones likely to be irritated by the prolapse. Thus the general rule throughout the vertebral column is that when a disc herniates (usually posterolaterally, rather than in the midline) it may irritate the nerve roots numbered one below the disc.

The spinal cord is supplied by the single, anterior spinal artery and two (right and left) posterior spinal arteries. Since there is only one anterior spinal artery, the spinal cord is vulnerable to anterior ischaemia (the anterior spinal artery syndrome). The posterior columns (mediating light touch and proprioception) remain intact, but most of the rest of the cord below the level of the lesion is affected, leading to weakness (corticospinal tract involvement) and loss of pain/temperature sensation (anterolateral, or spinothalamic, tract involvement).

The richly supplied red marrow of the vertebral body drains through its posterior surface by large basivertebral veins into Batson's internal vertebral venous plexus, which lies inside the vertebral canal, but outside the dura (in the extradural space). It drains into the external vertebral venous plexus and thence into regional segmental veins. These veins are valveless and often act as a subsidiary route for blood flow when the inferior vena cava cannot cope with a sudden flush of blood resulting from a sudden increase of intra-abdominal pressure (e.g. straining, coughing, sneezing). A rise in pressure on the abdominal and pelvic veins would tend to force the blood backward out of the abdominal and pelvic cavities into the valveless veins within the vertebral canal. This existence of this venous plexus may explain how carcinoma of the prostate, kidney, breast, bronchus and thyroid may metastasize to the vertebral column.

243E: It helps to prevent the formation of pulmonary oedema

Surfactant is formed in and secreted by type II pneumocytes. The active ingredient is dipalmitoyl phosphatidylcholine. It helps prevent alveolar collapse by lowering the surface tension between water molecules in the surface layer. In this way it helps to reduce the work of breathing (makes the lungs more compliant) and permits the lung to be more easily inflated.

Since the surfactant remains at the water-air interface, the space between surfactant molecules decreases as the surface area is reduced; this is equivalent to raising its concentration which lowers surface tension. This prevents alveolar collapse. Likewise, the decreasing effect of surfactant as the lungs inflate helps to prevent overinflation. This unique property of surfactant helps to stabilize different sizes of alveoli (otherwise the smaller alveoli would empty into the larger alveoli by LaPlace's law).

Surfactant is not produced in any significant quantity until the 32nd week of gestation and it then builds up to a high concentration by the 35th week (the normal gestation period is 39 weeks). Premature delivery may therefore result in inadequate surfactant production and respiratory distress syndrome of the newborn (hyaline membrane disease).

Surfactant also plays an important role in keeping the alveoli dry. Just as the surface tension forces tend to collapse alveoli, they also tend to suck fluid into the alveolar spaces from the capillaries. By reducing these surface forces, surfactant prevents the transudation of fluid. In this way surfactant acts as an important safety mechanism against the formation of pulmonary oedema.

244C: Typically affects the apical lung in post-primary TB

One-third of the world's population are infected with *Mycobacterium tuberculosis*. It is a major cause of death worldwide and is rapidly increasing in prevalence, in part because of the sharp increase in the number of individuals infected with HIV and because of the recent emergence of multi-drug resistant TB. Mycobacteria are obligate aerobic, rod-shaped, non-spore forming, non-motile bacilli with a waxy coat that causes them to retain certain stains after being treated with acid and alcohol; they are therefore known as acid–alcohol-fast bacilli (AAFB). Mycobacteria do not readily take up the Gram stain but they would be Gram-positive if the Gram stain could penetrate their waxy walls. The Ziehl–Neelsen stain is used instead to visualize the organisms, which stain pinkish red.

The pattern of host response depends on whether the infection represents a primary first exposure to the organism (primary TB) or secondary reactivation or reinfection (post-primary or secondary TB). Primary TB is most often subpleural, most often in the periphery of one lung, in the mid-zone. The residuum of the primary infection is a calcified scar in the lung parenchyma (Ghon focus) along with hilar lymph node enlargement, together referred to as the Ghon complex. Secondary TB most often occurs at the lung apex (Assman lesion) of one or both lungs which may cavitate and heal by dense fibrosis. The apex of the lung is more highly oxygenated, allowing the aerobic mycobacteria to multiply more rapidly. Involvement of extrapulmonary sites (kidney, meninges, bone etc.) is not uncommon.

M. tuberculosis is resistant to penicillin and requires multimodal antibiotic therapy (which may be remembered by RIPE) to prevent the emergence of resistance:

- rifampicin (main side-effect, liver toxicity)
- isoniazid (main side-effect, peripheral neuropathy)
- pyrazinamide (main side-effect, liver toxicity)
- ethambutol (main side-effect, optic neuropathy with visual disturbances).

Several months of combination treatment are required to treat *M. tuberculosis*. Pyridoxine (vitamin B_6) should be given with isoniazid to prevent isoniazid neuropathy.

M. tuberculosis can be prevented by immunization with BCG, a vaccine made from non-virulent tubercle bacilli. However, the protective efficacy of the vaccine is variable, ranging from 0 to 80 per cent depending on the part of the world in which it is administered.

245C: 500–1000 mL

Fluid balance is maintained by water intake that is equal to losses in urine, stool, sweat and insensible losses (through skin and lungs).

246C: Defective haem synthesis results in porphyria

- Sickle cell disease is due to the production of abnormal globin.
- Thalassaemia is due to the decreased production of normal globin.

Both sickle cell and thalassaemia seemingly developed as a form of carrier resistance against malaria, and as such are widespread in areas profoundly affected by malaria, predominantly Africa, South East Asia, the Mediterranean, and the Middle East.

The porphyrias are a group of genetic diseases resulting from errors in the pathway of haem biosynthesis, resulting in the toxic accumulation of porphyrin precursors. Interestingly, porphyria has been suggested as an explanation for the origin of vampire and werewolf legends and is believed to have accounted for the insanity exhibited by King George III that may have cost Britain the American War of Independence.

Carbon monoxide binds 250 times more avidly to haemoglobin than oxygen, resulting in the formation of carboxyhaemoglobin. The result is a decrease in the oxygen-carrying capacity of the blood. Carbon monoxide is a colourless, odourless and tasteless gas, so poisoning often occurs unnoticed. Levels of carboxyhaemoglobin >50–60 per cent result in death. The treatment is 100% oxygen which competitively displaces carbon monoxide from the haemoglobin, thereby decreasing the half-life of carboxyhaemoglobin from around 4 hours to 30 minutes.

Cyanide binds more strongly than oxygen to the iron atom present in the enzyme, cytochrome oxidase. This deactivates the enzyme and the final transport of electrons from cytochrome oxidase to oxygen cannot be completed. As a result, oxidative phosphorylation is disrupted, meaning that the cell can no longer produce ATP for energy. Tissues that mainly depend on aerobic respiration, such as the central nervous system and heart, are particularly affected, rapidly resulting in death.

247D: Lymphatics of the breast have connections with those of the opposite breast

The base of the breast is fairly constant. From the sternal edge to the midaxillary line and from the 2nd to 6th ribs, two-thirds of its base overlies pectoralis major and one-third overlaps on to serratus anterior. Contraction of the underlying pectoralis major muscle (by putting one's hands on their hips and pushing in) exacerbates any asymmetry between the breasts (e.g. as a result of a breast cancer) and is a clinically useful manoeuvre.

The breast's main purpose is lactation. The organ enlarges in pregnancy in preparation for lactation. After the menopause, involution (atrophy) occurs. Hence mammograms are less useful in the young (when the breast tissue is dense and cancers do not show up as well), but are more useful at the time of the menopause and beyond, when the breast tissue is composed of mainly fat (less dense on mammography) enabling cancers to show up more clearly.

Blood supply to the breast is mainly derived from the lateral thoracic artery (a branch of the second part of the axillary artery). However, the internal thoracic, thoracoacromial and posterior intercostal arteries also send branches to the breast.

The lymph drainage is of considerable anatomical and clinical importance because of the frequent development of cancer in the gland and the subsequent dissemination of malignant cells along the lymphatics to the lymph nodes. Around 75 per cent of the lymphatic drainage of the breast passes to 20–30, or so, axillary lymph nodes. They are usually described as lying in the following groups, which can be remembered by the mnemonic, APICAL:

- A = **a**nterior (or pectoral) group
- P = **p**osterior (or subscapular) group
- I = **i**nfraclavicular (or deltopectoral) group
- C = **c**entral group
- A = **a**pical group
- L = **l**ateral (or brachial) group.

The medial quadrants of the breast (where fortunately cancer is less common) enter the thorax to drain into the internal mammary lymph nodes alongside the internal thoracic artery. Thoracic lymph nodes are difficult or impossible to treat, but lymph nodes of the axilla can be removed surgically.

The superficial lymphatics of the breast have connections with those of the opposite breast, anterior abdominal wall and supraclavicular lymph nodes. These tend to convey lymph from the breast when the other channels are obstructed by malignant disease, or following their destruction after radiotherapy or surgery.

248C: During exercise, blood flow to the upper portion of the lung increases

Systolic and diastolic pressures in the pulmonary artery are about one-sixth those in the aorta and so is the pulse pressure. This is because the pulmonary vascular resistance is about one-sixth of the systemic vascular resistance. The blood flow is the same in both circulations, otherwise blood would accumulate in one or other bed.

In a standing subject, blood flow is less in the upper parts of the lung than the lower regions, but this is not matched by the differences in ventilation, so that the ventilation/perfusion ratio is not the same in all parts of the lung. A standing subject has a higher ventilation/perfusion ratio at the apex than the base.

During exercise, recruitment of the apical vessels occurs to accommodate the increase in cardiac output and pulmonary blood flow that occurs with exercise. This has the effect of increasing the area of capillaries available for gas exchange.

The pulmonary vasculature exhibits a peculiar property found nowhere else in the circulation, known as hypoxic pulmonary vasoconstriction. It consists of contraction of smooth muscle in the walls of the small arterioles in response to hypoxia – the opposite effect to that normally observed in the systemic circulation. The mechanism remains obscure. It has the effect of directing blood flow away from hypoxic regions of the lung (e.g. poorly ventilated areas of the diseased lung in adults) and in this way helps to optimize the local ventilation/perfusion ratios.

249C: It results from the secretion of exotoxin

All members of the *Clostridia* group of organisms have the following properties:

- Gram-positive bacilli
- obligate anaerobes
- spore-forming
- saprophytic (i.e. live in the soil)
- motile (but non-invasive)
- exotoxin-producing.

Clostridia are responsible for causing several diseases in man: *C. tetani* (tetanus), *C. botulinum* (botulism), *C. perfringens*, formerly known as *C. welchii* (gas gangrene and food poisoning) and *C. difficile* (pseudomembranous colitis).

Tetanus is typically a disease of soldiers, farmers or gardeners. It is caused by deep penetrating wounds caused by objects contaminated with soil, which introduces spores into the tissue. As soon as the wound becomes anaerobic, the tetanus spores germinate to produce vegetative cells, which then multiply and release a potent neurotoxin called tetanospasmin. Only the tiniest quantities of exotoxin are required for the disease to develop. The bacteria producing the exotoxin are entirely non-invasive and lack all other virulence factors apart from the capacity to produce toxin. The exotoxin binds to local nerve endings, travels up the axon to the spinal cord, traverses a synpatic junction and finally gains entry to the cytoplasm of inhibitory neurones. Within these cells the toxin exerts a highly specific proteolytic activity on one of the proteins (synpatobrevin) present in the vesicles that is responsible for the normal trafficking of inhibitory neurotransmitter to the synaptic junction. As a result the inhibitory neurone cannot transmit its impulse and there is unopposed stimulation of skeletal muscles by motor neurones. Death is normally due to muscular spasm (spastic paralysis) extending to involve the muscles of the chest so that the patient is unable to breathe.

As in other diseases caused entirely by an exotoxin, tetanus can be treated by passive immunization with antitoxin, and prevented by vaccination with toxoid. However, antitoxin cannot neutralize any toxin that has already entered neurones. Antibiotics are of limited value against anaerobic bacteria like *Clostridia* because they cannot penetrate the necrotic infected area in sufficient concentrations to be effective; surgical debridement of wounds is far superior.

250E : Arginine

Nitric oxide (NO) is generated from arginine in a reaction catalysed by NO synthase. The other product of the reaction is citrulline.

251D: Blood group O is recessive to A and B

ABO blood groups are inherited in the following manner. Blood group O is recessive to both A and B, but A and B exhibit co-dominance. Thus AO or AA = blood group A; BO or BB = blood group B; OO = blood group O; AB = blood group AB. Blood group O is the most common blood group in the UK population. There is no known evolutionary advantage of being one ABO blood group over another, although people with blood group O are more susceptible to duodenal ulceration than other blood groups, and patients with blood group A are at higher risk of developing gastric carcinoma. Duffy blood-group–negative individuals are resistant to *Plasmodium vivax*, since the Duffy antigen acts as a receptor for invasion by the human parasite.

Since individuals with blood group AB have no antibodies present in their serum it follows that they are universal recipients. However, they can only donate to other AB individuals. Individuals of blood group O have antibodies present in their serum against blood groups A and B. It follows that they can only receive from other group O individuals. However, they are universal donors since the antibodies are rapidly diluted in the recipient's blood. Since blood group O is the universal donor it is used in emergency situations where there is not enough time to determine the exact blood grouping of the patient.

252B: The direction of fibres of the external intercostal muscle is downwards and medial

The intercostal neurovascular bundle lies in a groove on the undersurface of each rib, running in the plane between the internal and innermost intercostal muscles.

The vein, artery and nerve lie in that order, from above downwards, under cover of the lower border of the rib. This may be remembered by VAN:

- V = **v**ein
- A = **a**rtery
- N = **n**erve.

Thus, a needle or trocar for drainage, or aspiration, of fluid from the pleural cavity is inserted just above the rib in order to avoid the main vessels and nerves.

The fibres of the external intercostal muscle pass obliquely downwards and forwards from the sharp lower border of the rib above to the smooth upper border of the rib below. This may be remembered because it follows the same direction as having one's hands in pockets. Although important for the mechanics of respiration, the diaphragm is the main muscle of respiration.

253D: Carotid bodies primarily respond to hypoxia

A chemoreceptor is a receptor that responds to a change in the chemical composition of the blood. They are the most important receptors involved in the minute-to-minute control of ventilation. There are both central and peripheral chemoreceptors.

Central chemoreceptors lie within the medulla of the brainstem. They primarily respond to hypercapnia by increasing the ventilatory rate and depth of ventilation.

Peripheral chemoreceptors lie in the carotid bodies (at the origin of the internal carotid artery) and in the aortic arch. Carotid bodies are not to be confused with the nearby carotid sinus baroreceptors which comprise stretch receptors in the wall of internal carotid arteries. Carotid bodies primarily respond to hypoxia by increasing the ventilatory rate and depth of ventilation.

Eighty per cent of the hypercapnic response driving ventilation arises from the central chemoreceptors; 20 per cent arises from the peripheral chemoreceptors. The response of the central chemoreceptors to arterial $P\text{CO}_2$ is therefore more important than that of the peripheral chemoreceptors. The hypoxic response driving ventilation almost all comes from the peripheral chemoreceptors.

Each carotid body is only a few millimetres in size and has the distinction of having the highest blood flow per tissue weight of any organ in the body (20 mL/g per minute). This high flow is consistent with the prompt physiological reflex functions of the carotid body. Carotid bodies sample the partial pressure of oxygen in the blood, not its oxygen content. Anaemia, when the oxygen content is low but the $P\text{CO}_2$ is normal, does not stimulate them.

254D: It may cause blackwater fever

Malaria is a worldwide infection that affects 500 million people and kills 3 million people (mostly children) per year; it is therefore the major parasitic cause of death and is the most deadly vector-borne disease in the world. Malaria is caused by protozoan parasites of the genus *Plasmodium*. There are four main strains that infect humans: *P. falciparum*, *vivax*, *malariae* and *ovale*.

Of these, *P. falciparum* is the most virulent, most widespread, most drug-resistant and causes the most morbidity and mortality through its ability to cause cerebral malaria, severe anaemia, hypoglycaemia, lactic acidosis, renal failure, pulmonary oedema and shock ('algid malaria'). Blackwater fever is characterized by intravascular haemolysis, haemoglobinuria and kidney failure.

P. falciparum is the most pathogenic strain for two principal reasons:

- It can develop in red cells of all ages; the other less pathogenic species are limited to growing in subpopulations of cells – either very young or very mature cells. *P. falciparum* can therefore cause higher levels of parasitaemia.
- The distinctive behaviour of *P. falciparum*-infected red cells – namely cytoadherence to vascular endothelium and sequestration – minimizes removal of infected erythrocytes by the spleen.

Plasmodia is transmitted to humans by more than a dozen species of female *Anopheles* mosquito which require a blood meal before they can breed (the *Aedes* mosquito acts as a vector for yellow fever and Dengue fever, not malaria). The male mosquitoes feed harmlessly on plant sap. The *Anopheles* mosquito vector is also the definitive host in which sexual reproduction occurs; thus fertilization occurs in the insect, not in the human!

Malaria is treated with supportive management and chemotherapy. Preventative strategies include chemoprophylaxis (which is by no means 100 per cent effective!), vector control (such as insecticides) and bite prevention (insect repellents, mosquito nets, covering up exposed areas especially at dawn and dusk). Unfortunately, at present no effective vaccination exists for the prevention of malaria. The quest to develop a malaria vaccine is currently an active area of research.

255A: Tyrosine

Tyrosine is the precursor of each of these neurotransmitters. Tyrosine hydroxylase converts tyrosine to DOPA, which is in turn converted to dopamine, then to noradrenaline and finally adrenaline.

256C: Is associated with berry aneurysms of the Circle of Willis

Adult polycystic kidney disease is one of the most common inherited disorders in humans, affecting approximately 1 in 1000 individuals and accounting for 10 per cent of cases of end-stage renal failure. It is inherited as an autosomal dominant condition with a late-onset mode of presentation. Eighty-five per cent of cases have been localized to a gene on the short arm of chromosome 16 (*PKD1* gene). A second gene (*PKD2*), responsible for around 15 per cent of cases, has been localized to the long arm of chromosome 4. The corresponding gene products have been named polycystin-1 and polycystin-2, although their exact function is unknown.

Both kidneys are progressively replaced by enlarging cysts which compress and replace the functioning renal parenchyma, leading to renal failure. The condition usually presents in adult life (typically around 40 years of age). When renal failure occurs it usually progresses to end-stage renal failure at between 40–60 years of age.

Adult polycystic kidney disease is associated with cerebral berry aneurysms (so that death may occur due to subarachnoid haemorrhage). Other extrarenal manifestations include liver, pancreatic and splenic cysts.

257D: It lacks a true serosal surface

The oesophagus is a segmental muscular tube running from the cricoid ring, at the level of C6, to the cardia of the stomach. It is 25 cm long (with the distance from the upper incisor teeth to the lower oesophageal sphincter being approximately 40 cm). These distances are useful to learn for the purposes of endoscopy. The upper third of the oesophagus consists of skeletal muscle (voluntary muscle which initiates swallowing) but then there is a progressive change to smooth muscle, such that the lower third of the oesophagus consists only of smooth muscle.

Blood supply and lymphatic drainage is segmental. The upper third of the oesophagus is supplied by the inferior thyroid artery and lymphatics drain to the deep cervical group of lymph nodes. The middle third of the oesophagus is supplied directly by branches from the descending thoracic aorta and lymphatics drain to the pre-aortic and para-aortic lymph nodes. The lower third of the oesophagus is supplied by the left gastric artery and lymphatics drain to the coeliac group of lymph nodes. However, within the oesophageal walls there are lymphatic channels which enable lymph to pass for long distances within the viscus so that drainage from any given area does not strictly follow the above pattern.

The surface epithelium is largely non-keratinizing stratified squamous epithelium. This is normally replaced by columnar epithelium at the gastro-oesophageal junction, but columnar epithelium may line the lower oesophagus. An oesophagus that has the squamocolumnar junction 3 cm or more above the gastro-oesophageal junction is abnormal and called Barrett's oesophagus. This is a metaplastic change taking place in response to acid reflux and is a premalignant condition.

Except for the short intra-abdominal segment of the oesophagus there is no serosal surface. This is important to know about for two reasons. First, it makes the oesophagus vulnerable to anastomotic leakage in the postoperative period. Second, because the oesophagus lacks a serosal covering, oesophageal carcinoma encounters few anatomic barriers to local invasion.

258C: The Haldane effect describes changes in the affinity of the blood for CO_2 with variations in the PaO_2

Carbon dioxide is transported in the blood in three ways:

- bicarbonate accounts for about 80–90 per cent of the total CO_2 in the blood
- carbamino compounds (5–10 per cent)
- physically dissolved in solution (only 5 per cent).

Carbon dioxide is carried on the haemoglobin molecule as carbamino-haemoglobin; carboxyhaemoglobin is the combination of haemoglobin with carbon monoxide.

Venous blood contains a higher pCO_2 than arterial blood and is therefore more acidic (through the formation of carbonic acid), with a lower pH.

Carbon dioxide is approximately 20 times more soluble in plasma than is O_2. This means that CO_2 diffuses about 20 times more rapidly than does O_2. This rapid diffusion of CO_2 through aqueous solutions means that the elimination of CO_2 is much less of a problem than is O_2 delivery, so O_2 is likely to be the factor affected first in disorders of respiration.

Binding of oxygen with haemoglobin tends to displace carbon dioxide from the blood; this is known as the Haldane effect. In the capillaries, the Haldane effect causes increased pick up of CO_2 because of O_2 removed from the haemoglobin, while in the lungs it causes increased release of CO_2 because of O_2 pick up by the haemoglobin.

259B: Parasites may remain dormant in the liver as hypnozoites

The malaria parasite has a complex life cycle. In their definitive host (the mosquito), the parasites undergo a cycle of sexual and asexual development. In their intermediate host (the human), the parasites undergo two cycles of asexual development (in the liver and in red blood cells). In addition there are alternating and extracellular stages. The genetic recombination allowed by the sexual stage is one element in the remarkable antigenic diversity seen within malaria parasite populations that enables it to evade the immune response. The malaria life cycle is easiest to understand if it is broken down into three stages.

The intermediate host (humans) – hepatic stage

Human infection begins when sporozoites are introduced into an individual's bloodstream as an infected mosquito takes a blood meal. Within 30 minutes, they disappear from the blood as they infect hepatocytes. Here they undergo the first round of asexual reproduction (exoerythrocytic shizogeny) and develop into exoerythrocytic schizonts. These exoerythrocytic schizonts may contain many thousands of merozoites. On invasion of the hepatocyte by *Plasmodium vivax* and *P. ovale*, the development of the schizont is retarded, and a 'dormant' stage of the parasite, the hypnozoite, is formed. This is responsible for disease relapse months to years after supposed chemotherapeutic cure and clearance of bloodstream forms of the parasite.

The intermediate host (humans) – erythrocytic stage

The released merozoites infect red cells where they undergo another round of asexual reproduction (erythocytic schizogeny) changing from merozoite, to trophozoite (feeding stage), to schizont. Eventually the cell ruptures and releases new merozoites (usually between 8 and 32), which go on to infect more red cells. Generally the parasite's life cycle stages are highly synchronized, such that at any one time all the parasites are at the trophozoite stage, or all are at the schizont stage. Fever in malaria is either tertian (every 48 hours in *Plasmodium falciparum*, *vivax* and *ovale*) or quartan (every 72 hours in *P. malariae*) and is due to the synchronized release of merozoites from red cells. Malignant tertian fever is due to P. falciparum. In addition, on infection of new blood cells, instead of forming trophozoites the parasites may grow into the immature gametocytes. These are not released from the red cell until taken up by a feeding mosquito.

The determinate host (mosquito)

The female *Anopheles* mosquitoes ingest blood as part of their life cycle. Here the normal asexually dividing bloodstream forms die, but the gametocytes are stimulated to mature to microgametes (male) and macrogametes (female). Fertilization occurs in the mosquito midgut resulting in the formation of a zygote. This then goes on to produce a wormlike form, the ookinete, which penetrates the midgut wall of the mosquito, forming an oocyst, located between the epithelium and the basement membrane. Note that the zygote is the sole diploid stage of malaria parasites; the only meiosis event during this life cycle occurs within a few hours of zygote formation. Within the oocyst a cycle of asexual reproduction (sporogeny) then takes place, with the formation of numerous sporozoites. When mature, the oocyst bursts open releasing these sporozoites, which then migrate to the insect's salivary glands. From here they may enter the bloodstream of a new host, thus completing the parasite's life cycle.

260C: Decrease in serum IgM

A deficiency in the production of J-chains for immunoglobulins could result in a decrease in serum IgA and IgM levels. These antibodies are dimers and pentamers of the basic immunoglobulin molecule and require a J-chain to join the immunoglobulin chains.

261A: Better sanitation

The reduced incidence of serious infections (e.g. typhoid, cholera, tuberculosis, smallpox) is mainly the result of improved sanitation. Indeed, sanitation, particularly sewage systems and the provision of fresh water supplies, has had a much greater impact on the incidence of these diseases than have advances in medical science. Thus for tuberculosis most of the decline in mortality came before the introduction of chemotherapy and the BCG vaccination. Having said that, mortality from bacterial infections had been much reduced by the advent of antibiotics and vaccinations have led to a considerable reduction in incidence of many viral infections. One such success story has been the worldwide eradication of smallpox through a mass vaccination programme. After successful vaccination campaigns the World Health Organization officially declared the total eradication of smallpox in 1979.

262C: The narrowest part of the oesophagus is at the level of cricopharyngeus

There are four classical points along the oesophagus where constrictions take place:

- Point 1 – cricopharyngeus sphincter, 15 cm from the incisor teeth, which is the narrowest part of the oesophagus. Its function is to prevent air entering the oesophagus and stomach. The cricopharyngeus sphincter relaxes with the swallowing reflex.
- Point 2 – where the oesophagus is crossed by the aortic arch, 22 cm from the incisor teeth.
- Point 3 – where the oesophagus is crossed by the left principal bronchus, 27 cm from the incisor teeth.
- Point 4 – where the oesophagus passes through the opening in the diaphragm, 38 cm from the incisor teeth.

Although the left atrium is in front of the lower part of the oesophagus below the left bronchus, it is only when enlarged (e.g. in mitral valve disease) that the left atrium causes an indentation in the oesophagus, resulting in difficulty swallowing, or dysphagia.

These constrictions are of considerable clinical importance since they are sites where swallowed foreign bodies can lodge, or through which it may be difficult to pass an oesophagoscope. Since a slight delay in the passage of food or fluid occurs at these levels, strictures commonly develop here following the drinking of caustic fluids. These constrictions are also common sites of carcinoma of the oesophagus.

The lower oesophageal sphincter is not a true anatomical sphincter, but rather a functional one. Maintenance of the lower oesophageal sphincter is largely brought about through the following features:

- the effect of the right crus of the diaphragm forming a 'sling' around the lower oesophagus
- the oblique angle the oesophagus takes on entering the gastric cardia (Angle of His) acting as a flap-valve mechanism
- greater intra-abdominal pressure than intra-gastric pressure acting to compress the abdominal part of the oesophagus
- mucosal rosette (prominent folds at the gastro-oesophageal junction)
- phrenico-oesophageal ligament (fold of connective tissue)
- the effect of gastrin in increasing lower oesophageal sphincter tone
- unidirectional peristalsis.

A problematic lower oesophageal sphincter may lead to problems, such as gastro-oesophageal reflux disease, hiatus hernia, or a condition known as achalasia.

263E: The shape of the curve is explained by the physico-chemical properties of haemoglobin

The haemoglobin oxygen dissociation curve is sigmoidal in shape. The sigmoid response reflects the underlying biochemical properties of haemoglobin and results from cooperativity. That is, the protein cannot be considered in terms of four independently oxygen-binding subunits. As haemoglobin binds successive oxygens, the oxygen affinity of the subunits increases. Hyperbolic curves are exhibited by monomeric molecules such as myoglobin. The significance of the sigmoidal curve is that it means that haemoglobin becomes highly saturated at high oxygen partial pressures (and is therefore highly efficient at collecting oxygen), and releases a significant amount of oxygen at pressures which are fairly low, but not extremely so (with the result that haemoglobin is highly effective at supplying oxygen where it is needed).

The effect of things that shift the curve to the right (raised CO_2, lowered pH, increased temperature, increase in 2,3-DPG) is to increase oxygen availability in the tissues. The effect of CO_2/H^+ on O_2 carriage is known as the Bohr shift or effect. This is exactly what is needed in metabolizing tissues; release of acids or CO_2 thus liberates O_2 to fulfil the metabolic needs of the tissue. Do not confuse this with the effect of changes in O_2 on CO_2 carriage, which is called the Haldane effect.

A shift of the oxygen dissociation curve to the left is characteristic of fetal haemoglobin. When compared with adult haemoglobin, it is composed of two alpha and two gamma chains, instead of the usual two alpha and two beta chains of adult haemoglobin. This arrangement assists in the transfer of oxygen across the placenta from the maternal to the fetal circulation. The corollary of this is that fetal tissue oxygen levels have to be low to permit the release of oxygen from the haemoglobin.

264D: Disease results from the immune response to schistosome eggs

Parasitic infections may be caused by protozoa or metazoa. Parasitic protozoa (e.g. *Plasmodium falciparum*) are single-celled nucleate organisms that possess all processes necessary for reproduction. A metazoon is a multicellular organism. Examples of infective metazoa include helminths (parasitic worms) which can be subdivided into three classes: nematodes (roundworms), cestodes (flatworms) and trematodes (flukes). Schistosomiasis is the most important helminth disease infecting 200 million people worldwide. Three major species of schistosome parasite can infect humans: *Schistosoma mansoni*, *japonicum* and *haematobium*. All are trematodes (flukes).

The life cycle of the flatworms that cause human schistosomiasis involves a sexual stage in the human (the definitive host) and an asexual stage in the freshwater snail host, which acts as a vector or intermediate host. Schistosome eggs excreted in the faeces or urine hatch out in fresh water and release miracidia that invade snails; free-swimming cercaria are released from the snail and invade human skin, losing their tails and becoming known as schistosomulae. The larvae migrate through the bloodstream via the lungs and liver to the veins of the bladder (*Schistosoma haematobium*) or bowel (*Schistosoma mansoni* and *japonicum*) where they develop into adult males and females. The adults lay eggs, which are excreted by the host, thus completing the cycle.

The pathophysiology of schistosomiasis is mainly due to the immune response against the schistosome eggs. In the liver this may result in granuloma formation, extensive fibrosis (pipe-stem portal fibrosis) and portal hypertension (hepatosplenic schistosomiasis). *Schistosoma haematobium* is responsible for urinary schistosomiasis, where granulomatous inflammation and fibrosis in the bladder may result in haematuria, obstructive uropathy, and squamous cell carcinoma of the bladder.

Schistosomiasis is treated with praziquantel which removes the flukes, but in advanced cases the pathology is irreversible. Intense inflammatory reactions are provoked when the worms killed by treatment are carried back into the liver.

265E: Coxsackie B

Myocarditis is most commonly caused by Coxsackie group B virus and may be preceded by gastrointestinal or respiratory symptoms. Rhinoviruses, coronaviruses and adenoviruses are associated with the common cold, influenza-like illnesses and gastrointestinal disturbances. Mumps causes orchitis and parotitis/parotidomegaly.

266E: The death rate from gastric carcinoma has fallen

The death rate from lung cancer in women has shown a steep rise since 1955 with no decline in the rate of increase. This may be attributable to the increasing smoking habits of women in modern society. In males the death rate from lung cancer peaked in the mid-1980s and has shown a slight fall since then. Suicide rates in all countries fall during wartime and was low in the 1950s. Since then it has shown a steady increase in both sexes.

In 1980 the terms HIV and AIDS did not even exist. However, as of January 2006, just over 25 years after its recognition, the World Health Organization has estimated that 38.6 million people worldwide are HIV-positive and more than 25 million people have died of AIDS-related deaths since its recognition, making it one of the most destructive pandemics in recorded history.

Much more mysterious is the downward trend in deaths from stomach carcinoma over the past 50 years. Such trends provide us with valuable information regarding the aetiology of stomach cancer. This downward trend may be due to a decrease in some dietary carcinogens. However, the more recent decline may in part be due to *Helicobacter pylori* eradication therapy since it is now believed that *H. pylori* plays a pivotal role in the development of gastric carcinoma.

267C: It forms the main muscle of respiration at rest

The diaphragm is a musculo-tendinous structure composed of outer skeletal muscle fibres and a central tendinous region. It partitions the thoracic from the abdominal cavity and is the main muscle of respiration at rest (accounting for 70 per cent of inspiration at rest). Upon inspiration, the diaphragm contracts, which lowers the diaphragm. This decreases pressure within the thoracic cavity and air moves into the lungs, resulting in lung inflation. Upon expiration, the diaphragm relaxes and the diaphragm moves up.

The diaphragm receives motor innervation from the phrenic nerve (C3, C4, C5). ('C3, C4, C5, keeps the diaphragm alive!'). The diaphragm has no other motor supply other than the phrenic nerve. This is why cervical spine injuries with injury to the cervical spinal cord can be so disastrous – and hence the importance of proper cervical spine immobilization in trauma victims.

The phrenic nerve is two-thirds motor and one-third sensory. The sensory nerve supply to the diaphragmatic parietal pleura and diaphragmatic peritoneum covering the central surfaces of the diaphragm is from the phrenic nerve. The sensory supply to the periphery of the diaphragm is from the lower six intercostal nerves.

268E: Increased blood viscosity

At high altitude, a decreased atmospheric pressure results in decreased ambient oxygen concentrations and therefore a decrease in arterial $P\text{O}_2$. In the short term, an increase in pulmonary ventilation occurs due to stimulation of peripheral chemoreceptors by an oxygen lack. Hyperventilation causes a respiratory alkalosis (rise in arterial pH) by blowing off CO_2. This inhibits the central chemoreceptors and thereby opposes the effect of low $P\text{O}_2$ to stimulate the peripheral chemoreceptors (braking effect). Hypoxia leads to pulmonary vasoconstriction and pulmonary hypertension.

Acclimatization (i.e. adaptive responses to sustained and gradually increasing hypoxia) occurs in the longer term through a variety of different mechanisms:

- Removal of the braking effect – by changes in the composition of the cerebrospinal fluid (a reduction in the bicarbonate concentration of the cerebrospinal fluid) and increasing the renal excretion of bicarbonate – results in increased pulmonary ventilation.

- Erythropoiesis – through the effect of hypoxia stimulating erythropoietin secretion from the kidney – increases the oxygen carrying capacity of the blood, but in doing so raises blood haematocrit and blood viscosity, the effects of which can be deleterious.
- There is increased cardiac output.
- There is increased capillarity (increased number of capillaries in tissues).
- An increase in the concentration of 2,3-DPG causes a rightward shift of the oxygen dissociation curve that results in better unloading of oxygen.
- There is cellular acclimatization – changes occur in the mitochondria and oxidative enzymes inside cells.

If a person ascends to a high altitude too quickly (without giving enough time for these acclimatization mechanisms to develop), or remains at high altitude for too long, high-altitude or mountain sickness may result. There is only one treatment for high-altitude sickness and that is immediate descent from the mountain.

269E: Are responsible for causing Kuru in humans

Prions are a novel, infectious agent composed of protein only. They differ from all known pathogens. They lack nucleic acid and cannot be considered microorganisms. They are highly resistant to decontamination methods such as standard autoclaving (heat), disinfectants (chemicals) and ionizing radiation.

If abnormal prion protein is inoculated into a normal host, conformational changes are induced in the normal host prions resulting in their conversion to abnormal host prions. These abnormal host proteins then induce further conformational changes in remaining normal host prions. Thus, the original inoculated protein is able to catalyse a chain reaction in which host proteins become conformationally abnormal. This is unaccompanied by inflammation, immune reaction or cytokine release.

Well-known prion diseases include Kuru, scrapie, bovine spongiform encephalopathy (BSE) and Creutzfeldt–Jakob disease (CJD). Kuru is probably one of the most fascinating stories to have emerged from any epidemiological investigation. It occurred in villages occupied by the Fore tribes in the highlands of New Guinea who practised ritual cannibalism as a rite of mourning for their dead. The first cases occurred in the 1950s and involved progressive loss of voluntary control, followed by death within a year of the onset of symptoms. Interestingly, Kuru occurred only in individuals who participated in cannibalistic feasts. Such cannibalism was believed to be responsible for the transmission of prions in Kuru.

There is still much work to be done in determining the exact modes of transmission of prions and in enhancing our understanding of the molecular biology of prions. In addition the exact interrelations between the different prion-related diseases (e.g. BSE and new-variant CJD) needs to be clarified.

270A: C5a

C5a is a component of complement. Activation of complement by endotoxin or antigen-antibody complexes produces C5a, which is a neutrophil and macrophage chemotactant. *HLA-A* and *HLA-B* are genes for the human leucocyte antigens and they control the synthesis of class I major histocompatibility complex. The J-chain of IgM and IgA does not possess chemotactant properties. The variable region of the heavy chain of IgG is not known as a best neutrophil or macrophage chemotactant.

271C: Lung cancer

Currently lung cancer is the most common cause of death from cancer in women, followed by breast cancer and then colorectal cancer. Breast cancer is the commonest cancer (in terms of incidence) in women, followed by lung cancer and then colorectal cancer.

The most common cause of death from cancer in men is lung cancer followed by prostate cancer and then colorectal cancer. In men the commonest cancer (in terms of incidence) is prostate cancer, followed by lung and then colorectal cancer.

272E: The sympathetic trunks pass posterior to the medial arcuate ligament.
See Table 4. The left phrenic nerve pierces the muscle of the left dome of the diaphragm.

Table 4

Vena cava opening (T8)	Inferior vena cava Right phrenic nerve
Oesophageal opening (T10)	Oesophagus Left and right vagus nerves (RIP = right is posterior) Oesophageal branches of left gastric vessels Lymphatics from lower 1/3 oesophagus
Aortic opening (T12)	Aorta Azygous and hemiazygous veins Thoracic duct
Crura (T12)	Greater, lesser and least splanchnic nerves
Behind medial arcuate ligament	Sympathetic trunks
Behind lateral arcuate ligament	Subcostal (T12) neurovascular bundle

The inferior vena cava passes through the central tendinous portion of the diaphragm and not the muscular portion of the diaphragm at the T8 level. The reason for this is clear: if the vena cava passed through the muscular part of the diaphragm, each time the diaphragm contracted with respiration it would obstruct venous return causing syncope.

273B: Under resting conditions, equilibration between alveoli $P\text{O}_2$ and red blood cell Po_2 occurs one-third of the way along the pulmonary capillary
Gas exchange within the lung takes place at the level of the alveoli. It obeys Fick's law, which states that the rate of transfer of a gas through a sheet of tissue is directly proportional to the tissue surface area and the difference in partial pressure between the two sides and inversely proportional to the tissue thickness. The area of the blood gas barrier in the lung is enormous (50–100 m^2, about the size of a tennis court) and the thickness is only 0.3 μm in some places, so the dimensions of the barrier are ideal for diffusion.

Any disruption to the factors that affect the rate of gas transfer through the respiratory membrane may result in disease states. For example, the thickness of the respiratory membrane increases significantly in interstitial fibrosis, pulmonary oedema and pneumonia interfering with the normal respiratory exchange of gases. Likewise, the surface area may be greatly decreased in emphysema, to name just a few examples.

The capillaries form a dense network in the walls of the alveoli. The diameter of a capillary is just large enough for a red blood cell; this further increases the efficacy of gaseous exchange by reducing the distance required for diffusion to take place. At rest, each red blood cell spends, on average, about 0.75 s in the capillary network, and during this time probably traverses two or three alveoli. Under typical resting conditions, the capillary $P\text{O}_2$ virtually reaches that of the alveolar gas (i.e. equilibration occurs) when the red cell is about one-third of the way along the capillary. This acts as a safety factor so that, during exercise, when the time spent in the capillary by the red cell decreases, it does not compromise oxygenation.

Carbon monoxide (rather than chlorine gas), is the gas of choice for measuring the transfer factor (i.e. the effectiveness of the diffusing surface). Carbon monoxide is used in the test because its great avidity for haemoglobin means that its concentration in the blood can be assumed zero and does not need to be measured.

274D: Anaplasia is almost a complete lack of differentiation

There are certain definitions regarding tumours that need to be remembered and understood:

- *Tumour* simply means 'swelling', which can be benign or malignant.
- *Neoplasm* simply means a 'new growth'. It is synonymous with tumour and can be benign or malignant. Malignant neoplasms can be primary or secondary. The latter are also known as metastases.
- *Hypertrophy* is an increase in tissue growth through an increase in cell size.
- *Hyperplasia* is an increase in tissue growth through an increase in cell numbers.
- *Metaplasia* is an adaptive response resulting in the replacement of one differentiated cell type with another.
- *Dysplasia* literally means 'disordered growth'. It is the disordered development of cells resulting in an alteration in their size, shape and organization.
- *Carcinoma-in-situ* is an epithelial tumour with features of malignancy but it has not invaded through the basement membrane.
- *Carcinoma* is a malignant tumour of epithelial derivation. By definition, because it is malignant, the basement membrane has been breached.
- *Anaplasia* is the almost complete lack of differentiation (i.e. poorly differentiated).

A more formal definition of a neoplasm is 'an abnormal mass of tissue, the growth of which exceeds and is uncoordinated with that of the normal tissues and persists in the same excessive manner after cessation of the stimuli which evoked the change'. The latter part of this definition is to distinguish a true neoplasm from the endometrial growth that normally accompanies the menstrual cycle; endometrial tissue is normally responsive to sex hormones and regresses upon its cessation; a true neoplasm would persist.

275D: Leucocytes, erythrocytes and fibrin filling of the alveolar spaces

Lobar pneumonia may progress through four stages:

- congestion (in the first 24 hours) – inflammatory exudate
- red hepatization
- grey hepatization
- resolution (complete recovery).

Red hepatization is characterized by a firm consistency to the lung due to filling of the alveolar spaces by extravasated erythrocytes, fibrin and leucocytes. A fibrin meshwork and degenerating erythrocytes defines grey hepatization.

276B: Cholera

Infections, in general, can be transmitted horizontally or vertically, through direct contact or indirect contact. Vertical transmission occurs when the mother is the source of infection for the fetus.

Examples of horizontal routes of transmission are:

- air-borne diseases (e.g. tuberculosis), via droplet inhalation/aerosol
- water-borne diseases (e.g. cholera)
- food-borne diseases (e.g. dysentery) – also known as faecal–oral spread
- blood-borne (e.g. hepatitis C)
- sexual contact (e.g. HIV)
- oral contact/salivary transfer (e.g. Epstein–Barr virus)
- vector-borne diseases carried, for example, by rats or mosquitoes (e.g. plague, malaria)
- infected/contaminated inert objects, or fomites (e.g. tetanus).

Vertical routes of transmission include:

- transplacental (e.g. rubella)
- parturition/puerperal (e.g. ophthalmia neonatorum)
- breast milk (e.g. CMV).

277C: It crosses the midline at the level of T5

The thoracic duct is 45 cm long and commences at T12 from the cisterna chyli which lies to the right of the aorta. It drains all lymph below the diaphragm, left thorax and left head and neck regions. Valves are present along the duct and encourage the propagation of chyle along the duct.

It ascends behind the right crus and to the right of the aorta and oesophagus. It crosses the midline to the left, posterior to the oesophagus, at the level of T5. It passes over the dome of the left pleura, anterior to the left vertebral and subclavian arteries and enters the confluence of the left subclavian and internal jugular veins.

The equivalent to the thoracic duct on the right is the right lymphatic trunk. This drains on the right into the confluence of the right subclavian and internal jugular veins.

Injury to the thoracic duct may occur following trauma, or during insertion of a central venous catheter on the left-hand side. This may result in a chylothorax (a collection of lymph within the thoracic cavity). A haemothorax is a collection of blood.

278E: Emphysema results in increased lung compliance

Compliance is expressed as volume change per unit change in pressure. Elastance is the reciprocal of compliance. Compliance is extremely small in infants compared to adults. The pressure/volume curve of the lung is nonlinear with the lungs becoming stiffer at high volumes. The curves that the lungs follow in inflation and deflation are different. This behaviour is known as 'hysteresis'. The lung volume at any given pressure during deflation is larger than during inflation. This behaviour depends on structural proteins (collagen, elastin), surface tension and the properties of surfactant.

A sigh or yawn is a reflexly generated single deep breath which occurs after a period of quiet breathing. The purpose of the lung inflation, which stretches and unfolds the alveolar surface area, is to spread out the surfactant molecules, returning the alveolar surface tension to its normal value.

Various disease states are associated with either a decrease or increase in the lung compliance. Fibrosis, atelectasis and pulmonary oedema all result in a decrease in lung compliance (stiffer lungs). An increased lung compliance occurs in emphysema where an alteration in elastic tissue is probably responsible (secondary to the long-term effects of smoking). The lung effectively behaves like a 'soggy bag' so that a given pressure change results in a large change in volume (i.e. the lungs are more compliant). However, during expiration the airways are less readily supported and collapse at higher lung volumes resulting in gas trapping and hyperinflation. Reduced gas transfer results from a loss of interstitial tissue causing loss of available active alveolar area.

279E: Liposarcoma is a malignant tumour of adipose tissue

In general, benign tumours are designated by attaching a suffix – oma – to the cell of origin. Thus an adenoma is a benign tumour of glandular epithelial cells. However, there are exceptions to this rule. For example a lymphoma is a malignant lymphoreticular tumour.

Malignant tumours arising from connective tissue are called sarcomas. Thus a liposarcoma is a malignant tumour of adipose tissue, leiomyosarcoma is a malignant tumour of smooth muscle, and rhabdomyosarcoma is a malignant tumour of skeletal muscle. Malignant tumours of epithelial origin are called carcinomas. Thus an adenocarcinoma is a malignant neoplasm of glandular epithelium, and squamous cell carcinomas are malignant neoplasms arising from squamous epithelium.

280D: Occlusion of the hepatic venous drainage

Budd–Chiari syndrome is due to extensive occlusive fibrosis of the hepatic venous drainage. Patients present with ascites, hepatomegaly and portal hypertension.

281B: Prospective studies allow direct determination of incidence rates

In a prospective (or cohort) study, exposed and non-exposed individuals are identified and followed up over time to determine the incidence of a specific clinical disease, or event. For example, a population of smokers and non-smokers are followed up to provide comparison rates for lung cancer or heart disease. The incidence of a disease is the number of new cases per unit population per unit time.

Cross-sectional studies are like a snapshot in time and measure both exposure and outcome at one time point. They provide information on disease prevalence in a population. Prevalence of a disease is the proportion of a population that exhibits the disease at any one time.

Retrospective (or case–control) studies compare individuals with and without a disease to determine possible associations or risk factors for the disease in question. However, bias may influence the recall of exposure in these studies, especially if possible associations are known (recall bias). In addition, selection bias may impact on the study. A case–control study, on the other hand, is relatively easy and inexpensive to conduct because long-term follow up is not required and this type of study is therefore suitable for studying rare diseases.

282E: The lungs receive a dual blood supply

The right and left lungs are not mirror images of each other. While the right lung is composed of three lobes, the left lung possesses only two. Each of the lobes, in turn, are separated by fissures or interlobar clefts. Thus, on the right, there must be two fissures separating three separate lobes (these are the oblique and the horizontal fissures, respectively). On the left there is only one fissure separating the two lobes and that is the oblique fissure. Thus the horizontal fissure exists only on the right.

There are typically ten anatomically definable bronchopulmonary segments within each lung, each containing a segmental (tertiary) bronchus, a segmental artery, a segmental vein, lymphatics and autonomic nerves and separated from their adjacent segments by connective tissue. Each is pyramidal in shape with its apex towards the lung root and its base towards the surface of the lung, and each is anatomically and functionally separate from the rest. The importance of understanding bronchopulmonary segments is that diseased segments, since they are structural units, can be selectively removed surgically (segmentectomy). Nowadays this can be performed by video-assisted thoracoscopic surgery (VATS).

The right bronchus is shorter, wider and more vertical than the left bronchus so that foreign bodies that fall down the trachea are more likely to enter the right bronchus. Furthermore, material aspirated by a supine, comatose or anaesthetised patient would tend to gravitate into the apical segment of the right lower lobe, which is consequently a common site for aspiration pneumonia and abscess formation.

The lungs receive a dual blood supply by way of the pulmonary artery and the bronchial arteries. Thus obstruction of a small pulmonary arteriole by a pulmonary embolus has no effect in an otherwise healthy individual with an intact bronchial circulation. In such circumstances, pulmonary embolism usually results in infarction only when the circulation is already inadequate, as in patients with heart or lung disease. A large embolus that impacts in the main pulmonary artery, or that lodges at the bifurcation (as a saddle embolus), results in sudden death.

283C: Each haemoglobimolecule combines with eight oxygen atoms

The formation of haemoglobin is:

- four pyrrole rings ⟶ protoporphyrin IX
- protoporphyrin IX + Fe^{2+} ⟶ haem
- haem + polypeptide (globin) ⟶ haemoglobin chain (alpha or beta)
- two alpha chains + two beta chains ⟶ haemoglobin A (normal adult Hb).

In normal adult haemoglobin, iron exists in the reduced, or ferrous (Fe^{2+}) state, rather than the ferric (Fe^{3+}) state. Oxygen combines with the ferrous iron that is present within the haem molecules and not with the globin chains. The globin molecules that surround the haem molecule serve two key functions; they form a microenvironment in which the Fe^{2+} is protected from oxidation and also contribute to the unique oxygen binding properties of haemoglobin (allosterism and cooperativity). When iron exists in the ferric state, instead of the normal ferrous state, the haemoglobin is known as methaemoglobin. This is abnormal and has a reduced oxygen-carrying capacity, resulting in cyanosis.

Haemoglobin consisting of two alpha and two gamma chains is fetal haemoglobin. Normal adult haemoglobin contains two alpha and two beta chains. Since each haemoglobin chain has a haem prosthetic group, there are four iron atoms in each haemoglobin molecule. Each of these can bind with one molecule of oxygen, making a total of four molecules of oxygen (or eight oxygen atoms) that can be transported by each haemoglobin molecule.

Why do we have red blood cells?

- Primarily for the transport of haemoglobin and oxygen. If haemoglobin molecules were free in the plasma (and not wrapped up inside red cells) they would get filtered through the capillary membrane into the tissue spaces, or through the glomerular membrane and would escape into the urine. For haemoglobin to remain in the bloodstream, it must exist inside red blood cells.
- There are enzyme systems in the red cell that help to prevent haemoglobin breakdown. For example, methaemoglobin reductase converts ferric (Fe^{3+}) methaemoglobin back to ferrous (Fe^{2+}) haemoglobin.
- Carbonic anhydrase is restricted to the red cells and is crucial in CO_2 transport.
- The chemical environment in the cell, especially the presence of DPG, displaces the dissociation curve to the right so that oxygen unloads readily in active tissues.
- If haemoglobin were free in plasma, the viscosity of blood would rise to intolerable levels and colloid osmotic pressure would increase considerably. The viscosity effect is especially important in capillaries where the presence of red cells in blood gives it an anomalously low viscosity (Fahraeus–Lindqvist effect).

284C: Metaplasia in the bronchus involves a change from columnar to stratified squamous epithelium

Metaplasia is the reversible change of one fully differentiated cell type into another fully differentiated cell type, in response to injury. It often represents an adaptive response to environmental stress. Squamous metaplasia is by far the commonest. Its significance lies in the fact that it can become dysplastic if the agent that caused the metaplasia persists and is capable of inducing dysplasia.

Important sites of metaplasia

- *Lower end of the oesophagus* – in response to acid reflux (Barrett's oesophagus). The normal stratified squamous epithelium is replaced by gastric-type columnar epithelium which is able to produce mucus and protect the epithelium from acid reflux.
- *Bronchi* – where the normal respiratory (ciliated columnar) epithelium is replaced by stratified squamous epithelium under the influence of chronic irritation by cigarette smoke (squamous metaplasia).
- *Transformation zone of the cervix* – in response to environmental changes during the reproductive cycle and in response to human papilloma virus. The normal columnar endocervical epithelium is replaced by stratified squamous epithelium.
- *Bladder* – squamous metaplasia in response to chronic inflammation, infection and irritation (schistosomiasis, calculi etc.).

285C: Phaeochromocytoma

Phaeochromocytoma is a neoplasm of the adrenal medulla. It presents with a triad of hypertension, adrenal mass and elevated catecholamines.

286D: Randomized controlled trial

Randomized controlled trials form the gold standard in epidemiological research. They resemble cohort studies in many respects, but include the randomization of participants to exposures. Randomization is an important part of the study design because it eliminates the effects of selection and confounding biases. Double-blinding (keeping trial participants and investigators oblivious to the assigned intervention) adds to the value of a randomized controlled trial by eliminating the effects of information bias.

Case reports are unreliable as they represent only single cases and do not have a comparison group to allow assessment of associations. However, they are often the first foray into a new disease or area of enquiry. Case–control studies are prone to bias. Cross-sectional studies measure both exposure and outcome simultaneously, so the temporal relationship between the two may be unclear.

287B: It extends above the clavicle superiorly

The pleura clothes each lung and lines the thoracic cavity. It is composed of two layers. The visceral layer on the lung surface is in contact with parietal pleura that lines the thoracic wall (rib cage, vertebra, diaphragm), the surfaces being lubricated by a thin film of fluid. The space in between the two layers is known as the pleural space, or cavity.

The parietal pleura (along with the apex of the lung) projects 2.5 cm above the medial third of the clavicle superiorly. A penetrating wound above the medial end of the clavicle may therefore involve the apex of the lung, resulting in a pneumothorax or a collapsed lung. This is most commonly seen as an iatrogenic complication during the insertion of a subclavian (central) venous line. Owing to the obliquity of the thoracic inlet, the pleura does not extend above the neck of the first rib, which lies well above the clavicle.

It is also important to remember that the lower limit of the pleural reflection, as seen from the back, lies below the medial border of the 12th rib, behind the upper border of the kidney. It is vulnerable to damage here during removal of the kidney (nephrectomy) through an incision in the loin. Proper identification of the 12th rib is essential to avoid entering the pleural cavity.

The visceral pleura is poorly innervated, has an autonomic nerve supply and is insensitive to ordinary stimuli. The parietal pleura, on the other hand, receives a rich innervation from the intercostal nerves and the phrenic nerve and is sensitive to pain. Thus, in tuberculosis or pneumonia pain may never be experienced. However, once lung disease crosses the visceral pleura to involve the parietal pleura, pain becomes a prominent feature. Lobar pneumonia with pleurisy is a good example. Since the lower part of the costal parietal pleura receives its innervation from the lower five intercostal nerves, which also innervate the skin of the lower anterior abdominal wall, pleurisy in this area commonly produces pain that is referred to the abdomen. This has sometimes resulted in a mistaken diagnosis of an acute abdominal lesion. In a similar manner, pleurisy of the central part of the diaphragmatic pleura, which receives sensory innervation from the phrenic nerve (C3, 4, 5), can lead to referred pain over the shoulder, since the skin of this region is supplied by the supraclavicular nerves (C3, 4).

The reflections (and therefore the surface anatomy) of the pleural linings and lungs may be remembered by the '2, 4, 6, 8, 10, 12 rule':

Pleura

- Starts 2.5 cm above the mid-point of the medial third of clavicle
- Meet in midline at rib **2**
- Left side diverges at rib **4** (to make room for the heart)

- Right side continues parasternally to rib **6**
- Both cross rib **8** in mid-clavicular line
- Both cross rib **10** in mid-axillary line
- Both reach posterior chest just below rib **12**

Lung

- Below rib **6**, the lungs extend to **2** rib spaces less than pleura (i.e. opposite rib **6** mid-clavicular line, rib **8** mid-axillary line and rib **10** posteriorly).
- The parietal pleura extends a further **2** rib spaces inferiorly than the inferior lung edge to allow space for lung expansion.

Note how the right and left reflections are not identical to one another. On the left it is displaced by the central position of the heart.

288D: It acts via a secondary messenger

Erythropoietin is a glycoprotein hormone, produced mainly by the juxtaglomerular apparatus of the kidney in adults. In the fetus, it is almost solely produced by the liver.

Once released, it acts on specific receptors which leads to activation of tyrosine kinase, which in turn promotes transcription towards the manufacture of more red cells from bone marrow.

The major factor causing erythropoietin release is local hypoxia in the kidney which may be derived from anaemia or systemic hypoxia. Erythropoietin secretion is a prominent feature of acclimatization to high altitude. A deficiency of erythropoietin partly explains the anaemia seen in individuals with chronic renal failure. Recombinant erythropoietin is now available, revolutionizing their treatment.

289D: Invasion beyond the basement membrane

The defining and most reliable characteristic differentiating a benign from a malignant tumour is the ability of the latter to invade through the basement membrane into the surrounding tissues and metastasize to distant sites.

Both benign and malignant tumours increase in size with time. However, malignant tumours tend to grow more rapidly and aggressively than benign tumours. The result is that malignant tumours tend to outstrip their blood supply, leading to necrosis. Haemorrhage occurs as a result of the fragile new vasculature that forms in an attempt to increase blood supply to the tumour.

Chromosomal abnormalities do not define a tumour as malignant as this may be a feature of both benign and malignant tumours. The presence of a pseudo-capsule is typically a feature of benign lesions and results from the neoplasm expanding symmetrically and compressing the surrounding stroma. Such encapsulation tends to contain the benign neoplasm as a discrete, readily palpable and easily movable mass that can be surgically enucleated since a well-defined cleavage plane exists around the tumour.

In general, benign tumours are well-differentiated, meaning the tumour cells resemble the normal mature cells of the tissue of origin of the neoplasm and display well-ordered maturation. Malignant tumours, in contrast, range from well-differentiated to undifferentiated, or poorly differentiated. Malignant tumours composed of undifferentiated cells are said to be anaplastic.

290B: Liver necrosis

Overdoses of paracetamol overwhelm the liver's glutathione reductase capacity. The toxic metabolites accumulate and produce hepatic necrosis.

291C: Ninety-five per cent of the subjects will have a blood glucose between 6.7 and 12.3

The blood glucose values follow a normal (Gaussian) distribution since the mean and median values are equal. Ninety-five per cent fall between two standard deviations (and not two standard errors!) of the mean, that is between 6.7 and 12.3. Another 2.5 per cent of subjects will have a blood glucose greater than 12.3, and 2.5 per cent will have a blood glucose of less than 6.7. It is sometimes easier to physically draw the bell-shaped distribution and mark out the values on it: 68 per cent of values lie one standard deviation away from the mean. 99 per cent of values lie within 2.6 standard deviations away from the mean.

292C: It is responsible for the formation of the transverse and oblique sinuses

The pericardium refers to the sac that encloses the heart. It comprises three layers: an outer fibrous pericardium and an inner serous pericardium (which comprises both an outer parietal layer and an inner visceral layer). There is a small amount of pericardial fluid between the visceral and parietal layers of the serous pericardium. This allows the heart to move freely within the pericardial sac.

The pericardium serves two main functions. First, it protects and lubricates the heart. Second, it contributes to diastolic coupling of the left and right ventricles. However, cardiac contractility functions normally (although maybe not optimally) in the absence of a pericardium. Indeed, after coronary artery bypass grafting surgery the pericardium is often left open (pericardiotomy) to prevent the build-up of fluid in the postoperative period causing a tamponade effect.

Between the parietal and visceral layers there are two pericardial sinuses. The transverse sinus lies in between the pulmonary artery and aorta in front and the pulmonary veins and superior vena cava behind. The oblique sinus is a space behind the heart between the left atrium in front and the fibrous pericardium behind, posterior to which lies the oesophagus. The transverse sinus is especially important in cardiac surgery. A digit and ligature can be passed through the transverse sinus and, by tightening the ligature, the surgeon can stop the blood flow through the aorta or pulmonary trunk while cardiac surgery is performed.

The fibrous pericardium and the parietal layer of the serous pericardium receive a rich innervation from the phrenic nerve. However, the visceral layer is insensitive. The pain of pericardial inflammation (pericarditis) is pronounced, originates in the parietal layer and is transmitted by way of the phrenic nerve.

If extensive fluid collects within the pericardial cavity it interferes with the action of the heart since the fibrous pericardium is inelastic. The pericardial cavity, in this way, behaves like a rigid box with only a finite amount of space. Thus, if the pressure builds up within the compartment, something else has to give and this usually results in compression of the heart. Such a situation is most commonly encountered in the case of penetrating trauma where the build-up of blood within the pericardial space often results in a cardiac tamponade, manifesting as a precipitous fall in cardiac output. Pericardiocentesis (removal, by needle, of pericardial fluid) may be a life-saving manoeuvre in such circumstances.

293B: Production is decreased by angiotensin-converting enzyme inhibitors

Aldosterone is a steroid hormone secreted by the zona glomerulosa layer of the adrenal cortex. Secretion continues following the removal of the kidneys and their juxtaglomerular cells because other factors other than the renin–angiotensin system result in the secretion of aldosterone (e.g. hyperkalaemia).

Angiotensin-converting enzyme (ACE) inhibitors tend to reduce the level of angiotensin II which normally stimulates the adrenal cortex to produce aldosterone. The reduction of angiotensin II and aldosterone, in part, explains the antihypertensive effect of angiotensin-converting enzyme inhibitors.

Aldosterone increases the excretion of both potassium and hydrogen ions from the distal convoluted tubule and collecting ducts. This results in a potassium diuresis and an acidic urine of low pH.

294A: Hyperchromatism

Both cytology and histology involve the study of cells at the microscopic level. Cytology studies individual cells and cell morphology. Histology studies cells within the context of tissues and provides information about tissue architecture. Only histology can provide definitive diagnosis of invasion.

The cytological features of malignancy include:

- increased nuclear to cytoplasmic ratio
- hyperchromatism (darkly staining nuclei due to increased amounts of DNA)
- prominent nucleoli
- variability in cellular and nuclear size and shape (cellular and nuclear pleomorphism)
- high mitotic index (increased mitotic rate)
- abnormal mitotic figures
- lack of differentiation (anaplasia).

The histological features of malignancy include all of the above, plus:

- loss of normal tissue architecture
- infiltrative borders, with a disordered growth pattern
- invasion beyond the basement membrane
- lymphovascular involvement
- excessive necrosis and haemorrhage
- loss of cell-to-cell cohesion, resulting in shedding.

Pyknosis, karyorrhexis and karyolysis are cytological features of cell death (necrosis and apoptosis), rather than malignancy.

295E: Amyloid

Amyloid is an acellular material that is eosinophilic. After Congo red staining, there is apple-green birefringence under plane polarized light. Calcium salts tend to be deeply basophilic, not eosinophilic with routine stains. Cholesterol deposits tend to dissolve out of tissues with routine processing agents and only empty outlines are seen of where the crystals were once present. Myocyte fibrinoid necrosis would be moderately cellular and eosinophilic.

296E: The mean and standard deviation of a random sample will generally be different from the mean and standard deviation of the true population

The standard error of the mean (SE) measures the variability of a sample statistic (i.e. mean or proportion) in relation to the true population characteristic (i.e. how accurate the sample mean is an estimate of the true population mean). The standard deviation (SD) is a measure of the variability of observations around the mean.

The SE is equal to the SD divided by the square-root of the sample size. The SE is therefore generally smaller than the SD. In addition, the SE is smaller when the sample size is larger.

- The mean is the arithmetic average.
- The median is the middle value when the values are ranked.
- The mode is the value that occurs most often.

In a normal (Gaussian) distribution, the mean = median = mode. In skewed distributions the following three rules apply:

- The median always lies between the mean and the mode.
- The mode occurs at the maximum point in a frequency distribution curve.
- The mean is affected by outliers.

Thus:

- In a positively skewed distribution: mean>median>mode.
- In a negatively skewed distribution: mode>median>mean.

297D: Occlusion of the anterior interventricular artery (left anterior descending artery) results in an anterior myocardial infarction

The heart is composed of cardiac muscle. This cardiac muscle receives the oxygen and nutrients that it requires to pump effectively through the coronary arteries. There are two principal coronary arteries, the right and the left. The right coronary originates from the anterior aortic sinus, whereas the left coronary artery originates from the left posterior aortic sinus. The left coronary artery divides into an anterior interventricular (or left anterior descending) artery and circumflex branches. The right coronary gives off the posterior interventricular (posterior descending) artery. The right coronary supplies the right atrium and part of the left atrium, the sinoatrial node in 60 per cent of cases, the right ventricle, the posterior part of the interventricular septum and the atrioventricular node in 80 per cent of cases. The left coronary artery supplies the left atrium, left ventricle, anterior interventricular septum, sinoatrial node in 40 per cent of cases and the atrioventricular node in 20 per cent of cases.

Understanding the above, one is able to predict the consequences of a blockage within a particular coronary artery. Thus a lesion within the anterior interventricular artery (of the left coronary artery) leads to an anterior myocardial infarct and death of the left ventricular muscle, resulting in congestive cardiac failure. A lesion within the right coronary artery would be expected to produce arrhythmias since the dominant arterial supply to the sinoatrial and atrioventricular nodes is through the right coronary artery.

Angina pectoris originates in the muscle or the vessels and is transmitted by sympathetic nerves. The pain of angina is often referred to the left arm and shoulder, but also frequently to the neck, throat and even to the side of the face. The reason for this is that the heart originates during embryonic life in the neck, as do the arms. Therefore both these structures receive pain fibres from the same spinal segments. Angina is usually a result of the laying down of fatty deposits within the coronary arteries (atherosclerosis). However, angina may also occur in the absence of atherosclerosis, in cases such as aortic stenosis, cocaine misuse, vasculitis, and variant (Prinzmetal's) angina; the latter being due to vasospasm of the coronary arteries.

298C: Activation results in the stimulation of aldosterone release

Angiotensinogen is synthesized by the liver. Renin catalyses the production of angiotensin I (a decapeptide) from angiotensinogen. Angiotensin I is further cleaved to an octapeptide, angiotensin II, by ACE found mainly in the capillaries of the lungs. Collectively, this is known as the renin–angiotensin system:

angiotensinogen → (renin) → angiotensin I → (ACE in lungs) → angiotensin II

The effects of activation of the renin–angiotensin system are several:

- stimulation of aldosterone release from the adrenal cortex; this increases sodium and water retention, helping to maintain the arterial pressure
- enhanced NaCl and water reabsorption from the proximal convoluted tubule
- angiotensin causing widespread vasoconstriction, increasing the systemic vascular resistance and so the arterial pressure (the resulting vasoconstriction also reduces the GFR at a time when water has to be conserved)
- stimulation of ADH secretion from the posterior pituitary, leading to an increased solute-free water reabsorption
- stimulation of thirst (dipsogenic effect).

299B: Lymphatics

Metastasis is the seeding of tumour cells to sites distant and detached from the primary tumour. This is different from invasion which is spread in continuity.

As a general rule, carcinomas (malignant tumours of epithelial origin) most often metastasize via the lymph; sarcomas (malignant tumours of connective tissue origin) most often metastasize via the bloodstream.

Thus, breast carcinomas often spread to local lymph nodes (axillary and internal mammary), whereas osteosarcomas typically spread via the bloodstream, forming cannonball metastases in the lungs. However, this rule is slightly misleading because ultimately there are numerous interconnections between the vascular and lymphatic systems. In addition, every rule has exceptions (e.g. follicular carcinoma of the thyroid spreads by the haematogenous route).

Neoplasms, in general, may metastasize by several routes:

- local invasion (direct spread)
- via the bloodstream (haematogenous route)
- via the lymphatics
- trans-coelomic spread (e.g. across the peritoneal or pleural cavities)
- via the cerebrospinal fluid (for central nervous system tumours)
- peri-neural spread (e.g. adenoid cystic carcinoma of the parotid)
- implantation/accidental seeding during surgery – iatrogenic.

300C: Hepatic angiosarcoma

Environmental exposure to vinyl chloride is associated with the later development of hepatic angiosarcoma. Focal nodular hyperplasia and hepatic fibroma are not linked to any defined underlying carcinogen exposure. Hepatic adenomas occur sporadically in the setting of exogenous steroid hormone use. Hepatocellular carcinoma is associated with cirrhosis, chronic viral hepatitis and aflatoxin exposure.

301B: This difference would have arisen by chance alone less than one time in 200

Do not confuse the terms standard error and standard deviation. The standard deviation gives a measure of the spread of the distribution. The smaller the standard deviation (or variance), the more tightly grouped the values are. If the values are normally distributed, approximately 95 per cent of values lie within two standard deviations of the mean (not standard errors!).

The standard error is a measure of how precisely the sample mean reflects the population mean. The standard error can be used to construct confidence intervals. Typically a 95 per cent confidence interval is quoted, which means that we are 95 per cent certain that the true population mean lies within the interval given by mean ± 1.96 standard errors. In this case the 95 per cent confidence interval is approximately 0.5 ± 0.4, or 0.1–0.9. There is therefore a 5 per cent chance that the true population mean lies outside the range 0.1–0.9.

The *p*-value is a probability that derives from statistical significance tests. It takes a value between 0 and 1. Values close to zero suggest that the null hypothesis is unlikely to be true. The smaller the *p*-value, the more significant the result. A significant result is normally taken as a *p*-value <0.05 (or 5 per cent), meaning that the difference would have arisen by chance alone in less than 1 time in 20. A *p*-value <0.005 (or 0.5 per cent) is highly significant, meaning that the difference would have arisen by chance alone less than 1 time in 200.

302D: The posterior wall of the canal is bounded by transversalis fascia and the conjoint tendon medially

Many students are troubled by the anatomy and significance of the inguinal canal. Its boundaries are:

- *Anterior wall:* skin, superficial fascia, external oblique (for whole length), internal oblique for lateral one-third
- *Posterior wall:* transversalis fascia (for whole length), conjoint tendon and pectineal (Cooper's) ligament medially
- *Floor:* inguinal ligament (Poupart's ligament)

- *Roof:* arching fibres of internal oblique and transversus abdominus which fuse to form the conjoint tendon on the posteromedial aspect of the canal.

The inguinal canal is an oblique passage that runs from the deep to the superficial inguinal rings and serves to transmit the testis (in the developing male) and spermatic cord in adulthood. It therefore functions to exteriorize the testis so that an optimal temperature can be obtained in order for spermatogenesis to proceed. In the female the inguinal canal transmits the round ligament of the uterus and by this means helps to maintain and support the uterus in its typical anteverted, anteflexed position.

The deep inguinal ring is a hole in the transversalis fascia and lies a finger-breadth above the mid-point of the inguinal ligament (i.e. half way between the anterior superior iliac spine and pubic tubercle). The superficial inguinal ring is a hole in the external oblique aponeurosis. The key to understanding the inguinal canal is to concentrate on the internal oblique layer which laterally forms the anterior wall of the inguinal canal. The internal oblique then arches over the top of the canal forming its roof and then blends with the transversus abdominus layer posteriorly and medially to form the conjoint tendon.

A hernia is simply a protrusion of a viscus, or part of a viscus, outwith its normal position. A femoral hernia can be distinguished from an inguinal hernia by its position. An inguinal hernia lies above and medial to the pubic tubercle, while a femoral hernia lies below and lateral to the pubic tubercle. The pubic tubercle is thus an important landmark in differentiating a femoral from an inguinal hernia. In addition, an inguinal hernia may be either direct or indirect. A direct hernia passes straight through a weakness in the anterior abdominal wall and passes through the superficial ring only. An indirect hernia, in contrast, passes through both the deep and superficial inguinal rings and thereby passes along the entire length of the inguinal canal.

303D: A fall in pressure in the afferent arteriole promotes renin secretion

The juxtaglomerular apparatus is a specialization of the glomerular afferent arteriole and the distal convoluted tubule of the corresponding nephron and is involved in the regulation of extracellular volume and blood pressure via the renin–angiotensin system.

The juxtaglomerular apparatus has three components:

- macula densa – specialized epithelial cells lining the distal convoluted tubule
- juxtaglomerular cells (also known as granular cells) of the afferent arterioles – modified smooth muscle cells that are renin-secreting
- extraglomerular mesangial cells (also known as Lacis cells or Goormaghtigh cells) – their function remains obscure.

The extraglomerular mesangial cells contain contractile proteins that are instrumental in the fine tuning of glomerular filtration. They have phagocytic properties and may act as antigen-presenting cells. They may also be the site of secretion of the hormone erythropoietin.

The renin–angiotensin system is triggered to release renin under three circumstances:

- fall in the renal perfusion pressure detected by baroreceptors in the afferent arterioles
- activation of the sympathetic nervous system – this occurs when there is a fall in arterial blood pressure
- reduced sodium delivery to the macula densa (as detected by osmoreceptors) – this occurs when there is also a fall in renal perfusion pressure.

An unknown paracrine factor is believed to act between the macula densa and juxtaglomerular cells to stimulate renin release (a prostaglandin or nitric oxide has been postulated).

The renin–angiotensin system is strongly implicated in the pathogenesis of hypertension secondary to renal artery stenosis. The juxtaglomerular apparatus of the affected kidney responds to decreased perfusion pressure by increasing renin secretion (Goldblatt hypertension).

304C: Astrocytomas

It is estimated that 50 per cent of bronchial carcinomas have metastasized by the time of clinical presentation. Breast carcinoma metastasizes readily to sites such as the lung, bone and brain. Melanoma is an aggressive tumour that can metastasize to virtually any site within the body. It therefore carries an extremely poor prognosis. Renal cell carcinomas characteristically invade the renal veins and extend into the inferior vena cava (sometimes reaching as far up as the right atrium), so that blood-borne metastases are common, especially to the lungs, liver and bone.

Astrocytomas (and even the poorly differentiated form, glioblastoma multiforme), rarely metastasize to sites outside of the central nervous system since they are contained by the blood–brain barrier. They usually metastasize outside the central nervous system *only* if there is a breach in the blood–brain barrier, or if there is an artificial connection (such as a ventriculoperitoneal shunt) connecting the central nervous system with another part of the body.

305C: Neuroendocrine cells

Small-cell undifferentiated pulmonary carcinoma (oat-cell carcinoma) is closely linked to smoking. This malignancy is thought to arise from neuroendocrine cells of the bronchial mucosa. Clara cells may give rise to certain pulmonary adenocarcinomas, and metaplastic bronchial epithelium is a likely source of squamous cell carcinomas. Alveolar pneumocytes rarely undergo malignant transformation.

306D: The negative predictive value is 0.99

The *sensitivity* indicates how sensitive the test is at picking up those people who have the disease. It is equal to the number of people who are both disease-positive and test-positive divided by the number who are disease-positive. In this example, it is 4/5. The *specificity* indicates how good the test is at picking up those people who do not have the disease. It is equal to the number of people who are both disease-negative and test-negative divided by the number of people who are disease-negative. In this example it is 90/95.

The *positive predictive value* estimates the probability that a subject, who has a positive test, truly has the disease. In this example, it is 4/9. The *negative predictive value* estimates the probability that a subject who has a negative test truly does not have the disease. Here it is 90/91. The sensitivity and specificity are independent of disease prevalence.

307E: It forms the entrance to the lesser sac

The greater and lesser sacs of the peritoneal cavity communicate with each other by way of the epiploic foramen (of Winslow). This is therefore a key landmark within the abdomen both anatomically and clinically. The boundaries of the epiploic foramen are as follows:

- anteriorly – the lesser omentum with the common bile duct, portal vein and common hepatic artery in its free edge
- posteriorly – inferior vena cava
- superiorly – the caudate (not quadrate) lobe of the liver
- inferiorly – first part of duodenum
- medially – lesser sac (posterior to stomach)
- laterally – greater sac.

From a clinical standpoint, the epiploic foramen is important for two reasons. First, it may be the site of internal herniation of bowel. Second, compression of the common hepatic artery in the free edge of the lesser omentum by a carefully placed hand in the epiploic foramen may be a life-saving manoeuvre at laparotomy to control bleeding from the liver (Pringle's manoeuvre).

308A: It increases in response to a loss of circulating volume of at least 10 per cent

ADH synthesis occurs in the cell bodies of the magnocellular neurones in the supraoptic (5/6) and paraventricular nuclei (1/6) of the hypothalamus. From there, ADH is transported down the axons of these neurones to their endings in the posterior pituitary (neurohypophysis or pars nervosa) where they are stored as secretory granules prior to release. Release is controlled directly by nerve impulses passing down the axons from the hypothalamus; this process is known as neurosecretion.

Increased secretion of ADH occurs in response to two main stimuli: an increase in plasma osmolality and a decrease in effective circulating volume. Significant changes in secretion occur when osmolality is changed as little as 1 per cent. Such a change is detected by osmoreceptors that lie outside the blood–brain barrier and appear to be located in the circumventricular organs, particularly the organum vasculosum of the lamina terminalis. In this way, the osmoreceptors rapidly respond to changes in plasma osmolality and in normal individuals plasma osmolality is maintained very close to 285 mOsm/L. ADH secretion is considerably more sensitive to small changes in osmolality than to similar changes in blood volume. Plasma ADH levels do not increase appreciably until blood volume is reduced by about 10 per cent, when ADH plays a significant role in the response to haemorrhage.

ADH has two main actions: it increases free-water absorption from the collecting ducts of the kidney (thereby conserving water), and it is a potent vasoconstrictor. The mechanism by which ADH exerts its antidiuretic effect is through the action on V2 receptors and insertion of protein water channels (aquaporins) in the luminal membranes of collecting-duct cells. Aquaporins are stored in endosomes inside cells and ADH causes their translocation to the cell membrane via a cyclic AMP pathway. In this way, the urine becomes concentrated and its volume decreases in response to an increase in plasma osmolality and a rise in ADH; this osmoregulatory action of ADH is a good example of a homeostatic mechanism. Vasoconstriction is mediated via V1 receptors (and the phosphoinositol pathway). The latter effect has an important role in maintaining arterial blood pressure in haemorrhagic shock.

Hypersecretion of ADH occurs in the syndrome of inappropriate ADH release (SIADH). Diabetes insipidus is the syndrome that results when there is ADH deficiency (cranial form), or when the kidney fails to respond to the hormone (nephrogenic form). It should not be confused with diabetes mellitus; the term 'diabetes' is derived from the Greek meaning 'siphon', and simply reflects the excessive passing of urine in both conditions.

309C: Have a peak incidence in those less than 50 years of age

Carcinomas are much more common than sarcomas. The former are malignant neoplasms derived from epithelium, whereas sarcomas are malignant neoplasms derived from connective tissue. Sarcomas have a peak incidence in those under 50 years of age. The preferred route of metastasis for sarcomas is via the bloodstream; this contrasts with carcinomas, which usually metastasize by the lymphatics. Understandably the liver and lungs are most frequently involved secondarily in such haematogenous dissemination since all portal drainage flows to the liver and all caval blood flows to the lungs.

No in-situ phase has been identified for sarcomas, unlike in carcinomas where there is often an in-situ phase. As a result sarcomas generally carry a poor prognosis.

310D: Elevated serum gamma-glutamyl transpeptidase

Elevated serum gamma-glutamyl transpeptidase (GGT) may be the only laboratory abnormality in patients who are dependent on alcohol. Heavy drinkers may also have an increased MCV.

311A: Valvulae conniventes

The following distinguish large bowel from small bowel in the cadaver, at laparotomy and on imaging. Large bowel has the following three characteristic features:

- haustra (synonymous with sacculations)
- appendices epiploicae
- taeniae coli.

Valvulae conniventes (synonymous with plica circulares) are a feature of small bowel rather than large bowel.

312D: The kidney is able to generate new bicarbonate from glutamine

The precision with which hydrogen ion concentration is regulated emphasizes its importance to the various cell functions. The normal pH of the blood is held remarkably constant in the range 7.35–7.45. It is essential that the pH be kept within these stringent limits to prevent the denaturing of body proteins and enzymes. This is yet another example of homeostasis, whereby the constancy of the 'internal milieu' is essential to life.

There are three primary systems that regulate the pH in the body:

- the chemical buffer systems of the body fluids
- the respiratory system (which regulates the removal of CO_2 and therefore carbonic acid from the blood)
- the kidneys.

The bone and liver also play a small role in the regulation of pH. When there is a change in pH, the buffer systems work fastest (within a fraction of a second) to minimize the change in pH. Of these, the bicarbonate buffer system is the most important extracellular buffer. The second line of defence is the respiratory system which acts within a few minutes. These first two lines of defence keep the pH constant until the more slowly responding third line of defence, the kidneys, can eliminate the excess acid or base from the body. Although the kidneys are relatively slow to respond compared with the other defences (taking hours to days), they are the most powerful of the acid–base regulatory systems.

The renal tubule actively secretes hydrogen ions and reabsorbs bicarbonate ions. Acute renal failure therefore results in an inability to excrete acid and metabolic acidosis. There are three main methods by which the kidney absorbs bicarbonate:

- replacement of filtered bicarbonate with bicarbonate that is generated in tubular cells
- generation of new bicarbonate by the phosphate buffer system which carries excess hydrogen ions into the urine
- generation of new bicarbonate from glutamine molecules that are absorbed by the tubular cell (the ammonia buffer system).

313B: Tumour growth obeys Gompertzian kinetics

Consider the growth of a tumour. A cell divides to form two cells, these divide to form four cells, and so on. Assuming no cell losses, the tumour will double in cell numbers every few days (a typical cell cycle in a mammalian cell is about 24 hours). Cells continue to multiply because there is loss of the normal regulatory mechanisms that restrict tissue growth (such as contact inhibition). It is unusual for a tumour to become clinically obvious until there are about 10^9 cells (30 divisions), or one gram of tumour cells (corresponding to a tumour diameter of approximately 1 cm).

However, as the tumour continues to grow it begins to outstrip its own blood supply so that an increasing number of cells are lost by apoptosis. Also, as the tumour expands, more and more cells are shed through exfoliation, hypoxia, non-viability, metastasis and host defences. The result of this is two-fold. First, the rate of tumour growth begins to slow down from the initial exponential pattern. The tumour growth curve therefore tends to assume a sigmoidal shape (Gompertzian kinetics).

Second, it means the growth fraction (the proportion of cells within the tumour population that are in the proliferative pool) of smaller tumours is greater than that of larger tumours. As tumours continue to grow, cells leave the replicative pool in ever-increasing numbers, owing to shedding or lack of nutrients, by differentiating and by reversion to the resting phase of the cell cycle, G_0. Thus, by the time the tumour is clinically detectable, most cells are not in the replicative pool (and so are relatively resistant to the effects of chemoradiotherapy). The growth fraction is usually 4 per cent to 80 per cent, with an average of less than 20 per cent. Even in some rapidly growing tumours, the growth fraction is only approximately 20 per cent. Indeed, some normal tissues, such as bone marrow and alimentary mucosa, have larger growth fractions and shorter mitotic cycle times than many cancers, even cancers of those tissues. Ultimately the progressive growth of tumours and the rate at which they grow are determined by the excess of cell production over cell loss.

It is very important to recognize that the clinical phase of a tumour – that is, the time from it becoming clinically apparent until it causing the death of the patient (assuming no treatment) – is short in comparison to the preclinical phase. Thus, by the time a solid tumour is detected, it has already completed a major portion of its life cycle. During the long preclinical phase there is time for invasion and metastasis to occur. In addition there is time for cell heterogeneity to develop within the tumour. This means that over and above the initial mutations, further genetic events occur in sub-populations of the tumour, leading to variation and the outgrowth of sub-populations with different patterns of differentiation and properties (a form of Darwinian evolution).

314E: Locus coeruleus

The locus coeruleus is located in the pons and produces most of the noradrenergic output to the brain. It has receptors for opiates and autoreceptors for noradrenaline and GABA. The locus coeruleus is involved in alertness (reticular activating system) and the anxiety response.

315D: It is stimulated to contract by cholecystokinin

The gall bladder has three main functions: it stores bile, concentrates bile (5- to 20-fold), and adds mucus to the bile secreted by the liver. It has a capacity of about 50 mL. Its mucous membrane is a lax areolar tissue lined with simple columnar epithelium. Under the epithelium there is a layer of connective tissue, followed by a muscular wall that contracts in response to cholecystokinin, a peptide hormone secreted by the duodenal mucosa in response to the entry of fatty foods into the duodenum.

The gall bladder is supplied by the cystic artery, usually a branch of the right hepatic artery. It runs across the triangle formed by the liver, common hepatic duct and cystic duct to reach the gall bladder (Calot's triangle). Calot's triangle reliably contains the cystic artery, the cystic lymph node (of Lund), connective tissue and lymphatics. It is important to dissect out this triangle at laparoscopic cholecystectomy in order to successfully identify and ligate the cystic artery prior to removal of the gall bladder.

The gall bladder is not essential for life. Indeed rats and horses manage perfectly well without gall bladders. Patients who have had their gall bladder removed lead a normal life and can expect a normal life expectancy. Removal of the gall bladder (cholecystectomy) is a common operation. Indications usually relate to gallstone disease, but rarely it may be performed for conditions such as carcinoma of the gall bladder. It may be performed open, but is mostly performed nowadays by the laparoscopic (keyhole) route.

316D: The low blood flow in the vasa recta assists in the formation of concentrated urine

In a normal adult human the combined blood flow through both kidneys is about 1200 mL/min, or about 20 per cent of the cardiac output. Considering that the kidneys constitute only about 0.4 per cent of the total body weight, they receive an extremely high blood flow compared with other tissues. The high flow to the kidneys greatly exceeds their metabolic demands (the kidneys account for only 6 per cent of total oxygen consumption). The purpose of this additional flow is to supply enough plasma for the high rates of glomerular filtration that are necessary for precise regulation of body fluid volumes and solute concentrations. Organic para-aminohippuric acid has traditionally been used to measure renal blood flow.

The kidneys have effective mechanisms for maintaining the constancy of renal blood flow and GFR over an arterial pressure range between 70 and 170 mmHg, a process called autoregulation. This helps to maintain a normal excretion of metabolic waste products, such as urea and creatinine, that depend on GFR for their excretion. Autoregulation is an intrinsic property of the kidney; therefore transplanted kidneys will autoregulate. There are two main theories to explain how renal autoregulation of blood flow occurs: tubuloglomerular feedback and the myogenic mechanism.

Angiotensin II preferentially constricts the efferent more than the afferent arteriole. This has the effect of raising glomerular filtration pressure, while reducing renal blood flow. Under the circumstances of decreased arterial blood pressure (when angiotensin II is released) this helps to prevent decreases in GFR (tubuloglomerular feedback method of autoregulation); at the same time by reducing renal blood flow it causes increased reabsorption of sodium and water. In cases of renal artery stenosis, maintenance of the glomerular filtration pressure is dependent on the angiotensin II-dependent vasoconstriction of the efferent arteriole. Administration of ACE inhibitors abolishes the vasoconstriction of the efferent arteriole, resulting in an abrupt fall in the glomerular filtration rate. This explains why ACE inhibitors are contraindicated in renal artery stenosis.

Flow to the renal medulla is supplied by long capillary loops called the vasa recta. These descend into the medulla in parallel with the Loops of Henle. The blood flow in them is very low compared with flow in the renal cortex. This helps to maintain the hyperosmotic medullary interstitial gradient, thereby assisting in the formation of a concentrated urine.

317B: It is highly dependent on VEGF

As soon as tumours grow to more than about 1–2 mm^3 they require the development of new blood vessels to sustain them, a process called angiogenesis (not to be confused with apoptosis which is programmed cell death). This is because the 1–2 mm zone represents the maximum distance across which oxygen and nutrients can diffuse from blood vessels. Beyond 1–2 mm the tumour fails to enlarge without blood vascularization because hypoxia induces apoptosis by activation of p53. Neovascularization has a dual effect on tumour growth: perfusion supplies nutrients and oxygen to the growing tumour, and newly formed endothelial cells stimulate the growth of adjacent tumour cells through the secretion of cytokines.

Tumour cells elaborate angiogenic factors that induce new blood vessel formation. Of the dozen or so tumour-associated angiogenic factors that have been discovered, the two most important are vascular endothelial growth factor (VEGF) and basic fibroblast growth factor (bFGF). Much attention has focused on the use of angiogenesis inhibitors to cure cancer since angiogenesis is critical for the growth and metastasis of tumours. Whether this theoretical benefit translates into clinical practice is another matter and clinical trials are currently in progress.

Angiogenesis is also a hallmark of granulation tissue. It plays an important physiological role in wound healing by assisting in the delivery of oxygen and nutrients to healing tissue, where it is required for growth and repair. Granulation tissue produces a rich 'cytokine soup', including secretion of VEGF and bFGF which stimulates angiogenesis.

318B: Delirium

Hypernatraemia and hyperkalaemia indicate dehydration which is the most common cause of delirium.

319B: It may refer pain to the right shoulder tip

The surface marking of the gall bladder is opposite the tip of the right ninth costal cartilage; that is, where the lateral edge of the right rectus sheath crosses the costal margin. This is an important landmark as it is the site of maximal abdominal tenderness in gall bladder disease.

Gallstone disease may refer pain to the right shoulder tip (Kehr's sign). There is an important anatomical explanation underlying this phenomenon. An inflamed or distended gall bladder may irritate the diaphragm which is supplied by the phrenic nerve ('C3, C4, C5, keeps the diaphragm alive!'). These very same nerve roots also provide sensation to the right shoulder tip by way of the supraclavicular nerves (C3, 4, 5). The body misinterprets the signals that it receives and interprets the pain signals as coming from the right shoulder tip. This is the concept of referred pain (pain felt remote from the site of tissue damage). The very same phenomenon may occur in a ruptured ectopic pregnancy, or splenic rupture, but in this instance the diaphragmatic irritant is free blood within the peritoneal cavity. Indeed, anything that irritates the diaphragm may cause referred pain to the right shoulder tip.

Courvoisier's law states that, in the presence of obstructive jaundice, a palpable gall bladder is unlikely to be due to gallstones. The reason is that gallstones cause chronic inflammation, fibrosis and a shrunken gall bladder. Rather, the law implies that a palpable gall bladder is more likely to be caused by carcinoma of the head of pancreas causing an obstruction to biliary outflow. Note, however, that the law is not true the other way round (i.e. in the presence of obstructive jaundice an impalpable gall bladder is always due to gallstones) as 50 per cent of dilated gall bladders cannot be palpated on clinical examination, due to either the patient's obesity or because of overlap of the liver.

Cholelithiasis (the presence of gallstones) is a common condition. Often they are picked up incidentally on ultrasound scan. The stones are of two types: calcium bilirubinate and cholesterol. In Europe and the United States, 85 per cent are cholesterol stones. Three factors seem to be involved in the formation of cholesterol stones: bile stasis, supersaturation of bile with cholesterol (lithogenic bile) and nucleation factors. Crucially, however, 80 per cent of patients with gallstones remain asymptomatic throughout their life. Therefore in a patient with proven gallstones on ultrasound scan a good history is imperative in order to assess whether, or not, the patient's symptoms are really due to the gallstones. If not, they are unlikely to benefit from having the gall bladder removed.

320D: The glomerular filtration barrier comprises three layers

In the normal adult human the GFR (or normal renal clearance) averages 125 mL/min, or 180 litres a day. The entire plasma volume (about 3 L) can therefore be filtered and processed by the kidney approximately 60 times each day. The rate of urine production in humans is dominated by tubular function and not by GFR. The GFR remains relatively constant through autoregulation.

After 35 years of age, GFR falls at about 1 mL/min each year. By the age of 80, GFR has fallen to about 50 per cent of its youthful level. GFR can decrease by as much as 50 per cent before plasma creatinine rises beyond the normal range. Consequently, a normal creatinine does not necessarily imply normal renal function, although a raised creatinine does usually indicate impaired renal function.

A substance used to measure the GFR must be freely filtered at the glomerulus, not be secreted by the tubules, not be reabsorbed, not be metabolized or synthesized in the body, not alter the renal function/GFR, be non-toxic and be soluble in plasma. Such a substance is the polyfructose molecule, inulin. However, it is too cumbersome to use in routine clinical practice. Instead, GFR is more commonly quantified by measuring the 24-hour urinary creatinine excretion. Para-aminohippuric acid is used to measure renal blood flow and not GFR.

The glomerular filtration barrier comprises three layers:

- the capillary endothelium
- basement membrane
- a layer of epithelial cells (podocytes).

From the anatomy of the glomerulus, it is clear that the 'actual filter' (and the primary restriction point for proteins) is the basement membrane layer.

321D: Hepatocellular carcinoma and polyvinyl chloride exposure

A carcinogen is a substance, form of energy or organism capable of inducing a cancer. The following carcinogens have been strongly associated with the workplace:

- scrotal cancer (Pott's cancer) in chimney sweeps
- mesotheliomas in people exposed to asbestos (workers in the building industry, ship construction and demolition)
- transitional cell bladder carcinoma in rubber and dye workers, due to exposure to β-naphthylamine
- angiosarcomas in workers exposed to polyvinyl chloride
- skin carcinoma in workers exposed to ultraviolet radiation (principally outdoor occupations, e.g. farmers).

322B: Exercise

Exercise promotes glucose utilization and increased insulin sensitivity. All other options tend to exacerbate insulin resistance.

323E: The right subhepatic space or hepatorenal pouch (of Rutherford–Morison) is the most dependent part of the peritoneal cavity

The liver capsule is composed of two adherent layers: a thick fibrous inner layer called Glisson's capsule (note Gerota's fascia surrounds the kidney) and an outer serous layer that is derived from the peritoneum. Glisson's capsule covers the entire surface of the liver and the serous layer covers most of the liver surface, excluding the 'bare' area of the liver near the diaphragm, the porta hepatis, and the area where the gall bladder is attached to the liver. So tough is Glisson's capsule that a subcapsular haematoma occurring as a result of liver parenchymal injury may be effectively contained by the capsule. The capsule is richly innervated by autonomic fibres, so capsular stretching as a result of malignancy, for example, may be intensely painful.

The liver receives a dual blood supply, from the hepatic artery and the portal vein. The portal vein provides 75 per cent of the total hepatic blood flow, the hepatic artery 25 per cent. The portal vein contains blood from the gut, rich in products of digestion, but is only approximately 85 per cent saturated with oxygen. The hepatic artery oxygen concentration, however, is approximately 99 per cent. Each vessel therefore supplies approximately equal amounts of oxygen to the liver.

The ligamentum venosum is a remnant of the ductus venosus (a channel that shunts blood from the left umbilical vein directly into the inferior vena cava, during gestation, thereby bypassing the liver and preserving oxygenated blood for the head and neck region). The ligamentum teres (or round ligament), in the free edge of the falciform ligament, is a remnant of the left umbilical vein.

Within the peritoneal cavity proper there are various spaces that are potential sites in which pus may collect (forming an abscess). The most important spaces to recognize are the right and left subphrenic (subdiaphragmatic) spaces, the pelvis, the right and left paracolic gutters and the right subhepatic space (also known as the hepatorenal pouch of Rutherford–Morison). When lying supine, the latter space is the most dependent part of the peritoneal cavity and hence is an area where intraperitoneal fluid is likely to accumulate in the form of an abscess (or 'collection'). The left subhepatic space is the lesser sac.

324E: The maximum concentrating ability of the human kidney is 1200 mOsm/L

The filtered load of glucose normally undergoes complete reabsorption in the proximal convoluted tubule (remember the most important substances for survival are generally absorbed first). Therefore, no glucose is usually found in the urine. However, when the filtered load exceeds the capacity of the tubules to reabsorb glucose (as in uncontrolled diabetes mellitus), urinary excretion of glucose occurs (glycosuria).

Seventy per cent of sodium reabsorption takes place in the proximal convoluted tubule, 20 per cent takes place in the ascending limb of the Loop of Henle, and only 10 per cent takes place in the distal convoluted tubule and collecting ducts. It is only the latter which is aldosterone-dependent.

The maximum concentration of urine that can be excreted by the human kidney is 1200 mOsm/L, four times the osmolality of plasma. This is primarily a function of the length of the Loop of Henle, the hyperosmotic medullary interstitial gradient and the concentration of ADH. A counter-current multiplication system sets up an osmotic gradient in the renal medulla which allows an efficient way for urine to be concentrated over a relatively short distance along the nephron with minimal energy expenditure. The descending limb of the Loop of Henle is permeable to water (but only slightly permeable to salt and urea). Therefore water is progressively absorbed down the limb, becoming more concentrated (up to 1200 mOsm/L). The ascending limb is impermeable to water but permeable to sodium chloride. The tubular fluid is therefore hypotonic by the time it reaches the distal convoluted tubule and collecting ducts. In the presence of a high concentration of ADH, by the time the urine is excreted it has a high osmolality (up to 1200 mOsm/L).

The limited ability of the human kidney to concentrate urine to a maximal concentration of 1200 mOsm/L helps to explain why severe dehydration occurs on drinking seawater. The osmolality of seawater averages 2400 mOsm/L, so drinking one litre of seawater would give a total solute concentration of 2400 mOsm. If the maximal urine concentrating ability of the human kidney is 1200 mOsm/L, two litres is required to rid the body of these solutes. This would result in a net loss of one litre for every litre of seawater drunk, explaining the rapid dehydration that occurs in shipwreck victims who drink seawater. In short, if lost at sea, you are better off drinking nothing than drinking seawater.

325C: Burkitt's lymphoma

Oncogenic microorganisms are capable of producing tumours. Most are viral. However, *Helicobacter pylori* is a good example of a bacterium that has been associated with gastric carcinoma and gastric lymphoma, while *Schistosoma haematobium* is a good example of a parasitic infection that is capable of producing squamous cell carcinoma of the bladder.

Viruses are obligate intracellular parasites that rely on the host cell's replicative machinery to reproduce themselves. Oncogenic viruses have therefore evolved to induce host-cell replication by activating genes for cell growth. This confers a survival advantage on the virus. However, it is when proliferation becomes uncoordinated and excessive that carcinoma results.
The Epstein–Barr (DNA) virus has been implicated in the pathogenesis of three human cancers:

- Burkitt's lymphoma
- nasopharyngeal carcinoma
- Hodgkin's disease.

Other well-described oncogenic viruses, besides EBV, include two RNA viruses

- human T-cell leukaemia virus (HTLV-1)
- hepatitis C virus, leading to hepatocellular carcinoma

and three DNA viruses

- hepatitis B virus, leading to hepatocellular carcinoma
- human herpes virus type 8 (HHV-8), leading to Kaposi's sarcoma in HIV individuals
- human papilloma virus, leading to cervical carcinoma or anal carcinoma.

There are several *mechanisms* by which viruses can induce malignancy:

- directly, by becoming integrated into a cell's genome and by activation of cellular oncogenes
- indirectly, through processes (e.g. chronic inflammation) which predispose to malignancy – the mitotically active tissue presumably provides a fertile soil for mutations
- by the production of proteins that inactivate tumour suppressor proteins, such as p53.

326C: Papillary thyroid cancer

In the UK the most common primary thyroid cancer seen is the papillary variant which typically affects young women. Risk factors include previous radiation exposure (e.g. Chernobyl) and previous radiotherapy. Secondary thyroid cancers (metastases) are rare but can arise secondary to renal cell carcinomas. In the developing world, the follicular variant is most common and is associated with iodine deficiency and longstanding goitres. Medullary thyroid tumours (associated with multiple endocrine neoplasia type 2) and lymphomas are less common.

327B: They feature at the lower end of the oesophagus

Portosystemic anastomoses are important sites in the body at which the portal venous circulation meets the systemic venous circulation. There are five principal sites where this takes place:

- lower end of the oesophagus
- upper end of the anal canal
- periumbilical region of the anterior abdominal wall
- bare area of the liver
- retroperitoneum.

In liver failure (cirrhosis), fibrosis of the liver takes place with obliteration of the blood vessels within it. Blood from the portal vein is then unable to drain through the liver into the inferior vena cava. As a result, 80 per cent of the portal blood flow is shunted into collateral channels, so that only 20 per cent reaches the liver. The portosystemic anastomoses open up in liver failure (but not in renal failure) and act as collateral channels, allowing an alternative path for blood to flow. Nevertheless, the opening up of the collaterals does not decrease the level of pressure within the portal system and portal hypertension ensues. The consequence of this is splenomegaly as a result of portal hypertension. However, the spleen *per se* is not a site of portosystemic anastomosis.

The most important area to remember as a site of portosystemic anastomosis is the lower end of the oesophagus, because of its clinical significance. The veins from the lower third of the oesophagus drain downwards to the left gastric vein (portal system) and above this level oesophageal veins drain into the azygous and hemiazygous systems (systemic system). Subsequently in portal hypertension, dilatations of the veins within the lower end of the oesophagus may take place. These are known as oesophageal varices. The same effect also takes place at the other sites of portosystemic anastomosis. However, there is one key difference between the lower oesophagus and these other sites – that is, oesophageal varices have thin walls and are prone to rupture, as predicted by LaPlace's law. Rupture of oesophageal varices may result in a catastrophic upper gastrointestinal bleed that is often fatal.

Dilatations of veins within the anterior abdominal wall (also a site of portosystemic anastomosis) are known as caput medusae, because of their resemblance to the hair of the Greek mythological character, Medusa. Venous dilatations within the upper end of the anal canal in portal hypertension may lead to the formation of haemorrhoids. However, in practice, they rarely lead to problems and the presence of oesophageal varices is far more significant.

328D: It is richer in potassium than any other gastrointestinal secretion

The salivary glands can be divided into the major (parotid, submandibular and sublingual) glands and minor glands.

- Parotid secretion is mainly serous.
- Submandibular secretion is mainly mixed (mucinous and serous).
- Sublingual secretion is mainly mucinous.

In humans, about 1–1.5 litres of saliva are secreted each day. In the unstimulated state, most of the saliva originates from the submandibular gland, but when active most of the saliva arises from the parotid gland. Secretion is an active process. The two-stage hypothesis of salivation states that a primary secretion is first formed by secretory end-pieces (that resembles an ultrafiltrate of plasma), which is then modified as it flows along the duct system. Na^+ and Cl^- are absorbed, and

K^+ and HCO_3^- are secreted, as saliva flows along the ductal system. In addition, the ducts have a low water permeability. The final saliva is hypotonic with respect to plasma and contains a higher potassium concentration than any other gastrointestinal secretion of the body.

Saliva contains principally water, mucus, enzymes (principally salivary amylase, lingual lipase and the antibacterial enzyme, lysozyme), antibodies and inorganic ions. It does not contain trypsin which is secreted by the exocrine pancreas.

Sialolithiasis (stone formation) may occur in any major salivary gland but is most common in the submandibular gland. There are two reasons for this phenomenon. The submandibular saliva is rich in mucus and is, thus, more viscous than parotid saliva. In addition the submandibular duct ascends against gravity when the body is upright, bends at the posterior edge of the mouth, and takes a long and tortuous course. This means there is a particular tendency in this gland to secretory congestion and calculus formation.

329A: They behave in a dominant fashion

Cancer is a genetic disease. Oncogenes are growth-promoting genes that are expressed in normal cells (the correct name for its normal precursor is proto-oncogene). They encode for oncoproteins (growth factors, growth receptor molecules, signal transducing molecules, nuclear transcription factors, regulators of the cell cycle) that positively regulate growth and are involved in the growth and differentiation of normal cells. Transcription of oncogenes is tightly regulated in normal cells.

Over-expression of oncoproteins, or mutations of oncogenes resulting in the inappropriate activation of oncoproteins, leads to abnormal cell growth and survival (i.e. tumourigenesis). Mutations in oncogenes that result in tumours are generally gain-of-function mutations, so oncogenes behave in a dominant manner to promote cell transformation; that is, only one copy of the defective gene is sufficient to cause cancer.

Proto-oncogenes are converted into oncogenes through a variety of mechanisms that include:

- point mutations
- chromosomal rearrangements
- gene amplification
- incorporation of a new promoter (by viruses)
- incorporation of enhancer sequences (by viruses).

The last two mechanisms are also referred to as insertional mutagenesis.

BRCA-1 is a tumour suppressor gene that accounts for a small proportion of breast cancers.

330B: GABA

Axons of the Purkinje neurones have GABA as the neurotransmitter, which is inhibitory in nature.

331E: Splenectomized patients are at high risk of post-splenectomy sepsis

The spleen, the largest of the lymphoid organs, lies under the diaphragm on the left side of the abdomen. It may be summarized by 1, 3, 5, 7, 9, 11. That is, it measures $1 \times 3 \times 5$ inches, weighs 7 ounces (200 g) and lies beneath the 9th to 11th ribs. The spleen lies at the far left margin of the lesser sac below the diaphragm. Thus, if one's hand is placed in the lesser sac (via the epiploic Foramen of Winslow) the spleen is the most laterally placed structure palpable.

Accessory spleen (splenunculi) represent congenital ectopic splenic tissue and are found in up to 20 per cent of individuals. One or several may be found, usually along the splenic vessels or in the peritoneal attachments. They are rarely larger than 2 cm in diameter.

Two 'pedicles', the gastrosplenic and lienorenal ligaments, connect the hilum of the spleen to the greater curvature of the stomach and the anterior surface of the left kidney, respectively. The splenic vessels and pancreatic tail lie in the lienorenal ligament. The short gastric and left gastro-epiploic vessels run in the gastrosplenic ligament.

The functions of the spleen may be summarized by FISH:

- **F**iltration and removal of old blood cells and encapsulated microorganisms
- **I**mmunological functions (production of IgM and opsonins)
- **S**torage function (30 per cent of the total platelets within the spleen)
- **H**aematopoiesis (in the developing fetus).

It has recently been evoked that the spleen has an endocrine function through the production of an immuno-potentiating peptide called tuftsin. The kidney, rather than the spleen, is the major site of erythropoietin secretion. Note that the spleen only acts as a site of haematopoiesis in the adult in diseased states where extramedullary haematopoiesis is a feature, such as thalassaemia.

Splenectomy (i.e. removal of the spleen) may be performed as an emergency procedure when the spleen has ruptured through trauma, or as an elective (i.e. scheduled) procedure, usually for haematological disorders where hypersplenism has caused an abnormality in one or more blood parameters. It is essential to understand the anatomical relations of the spleen (e.g. the pancreatic tail, stomach, splenic flexure of the colon, left kidney, diaphragm) in order to prevent inadvertent injury to these at splenectomy. Splenectomized patients are at high risk of post-splenectomy sepsis, especially from encapsulated organisms such as *Haemophilus*, *Meningococcus* and *Streptococcus*. Prophylaxis consists of the relevant vaccinations and lifelong penicillin.

332E: Parietal cells

Goblet cells are mucus-secreting cells widely distributed in epithelial surfaces, but especially dense in the gastrointestinal and respiratory tracts.

Kupffer cells have phagocytic properties and are found in the liver. They participate in the removal of ageing erythrocytes and other particulate debris.

The gastric mucosa contains many cell subtypes including acid-secreting cells (also known as parietal or oxyntic cells), pepsin-secreting cells (also known as peptic, chief or zymogenic cells) and G-cells (gastrin-secreting cells). Peptic cells synthesize and secrete the proteolytic enzyme, pepsin. Parietal cells actively secrete hydrochloric acid into the gastric lumen accounting for the acidic environment encountered in the stomach. However, parietal cells are also involved in the secretion of the glycoprotein, intrinsic factor.

Intrinsic factor plays a pivotal role in the absorption of vitamin B_{12} from the terminal ileum. Autoimmune attack against parietal cells leads to a lack of intrinsic factor and hydrochloric acid, leading to vitamin B_{12} deficiency and achlorhydria. This is known as pernicious anaemia.

333D: p53 and Rb-1 are tumour suppressor genes

Tumour suppressor genes encode proteins that negatively regulate cell proliferation and thus suppress tumour growth. p53 and Rb-1 are good examples located on chromosomes 17 and 13 respectively. Normal p53 is the so-called 'guardian of the genome' and triggers apoptosis and cell-cycle arrest in genetically damaged cells (i.e. it is pro-apoptotic). Mutations in p53 therefore result in the propagation of genetically damaged cells and tumourigenesis. Indeed, approximately 50 per cent of human tumours contain mutations in the p53 gene. p53-related cancers are more aggressive and have a poorer prognosis.

In contrast to oncogenes, tumours caused by tumour suppressor genes are generally caused by mutations that result in a loss of function of the gene product; neoplastic growth resulting from the loss of the protective role of tumour suppressor genes. Loss of tumour suppressor function usually requires the inactivation of both alleles of the gene, so that all of the protective effect of tumour suppressor genes is lost. That is, tumour suppressor genes are generally deemed to behave in a recessive manner.

Cellular proliferation is therefore tightly regulated by two sets of opposing functioning genes: the growth-promoting genes (proto-oncogenes) and the negative cell-cycle regulators (tumour suppressor genes). Abnormal activation of proto-oncogenes and/or loss of function of tumour suppressor genes leads to the transformation of a normal cell into a cancer cell.

334C: Buccinator

Buccinator is a muscle of facial expression and is therefore innervated by the facial nerve. The lateral pterygoid, masseter, anterior belly of digastric and temporalis are all muscles of mastication and therefore innervated by the mandibular division of the trigeminal nerve (Vc).

335D: It lies level with the hilum of the kidneys

The transpyloric plane (of Addison) is an important landmark. It lies halfway between the suprasternal notch and the symphysis pubis at the level of L1. It coincides with the following:

- L1 vertebra
- fundus of gall bladder
- hilum of kidneys
- hilum of spleen
- pylorus of the stomach (hence the name transpyloric)
- termination of the spinal cord in adults
- neck of pancreas
- origin of the portal vein
- origin of the superior (not inferior) mesenteric artery
- duodenojejunal flexure
- attachment of transverse mesocolon
- tip of ninth costal cartilage.

The aorta bifurcates at the level of L4, not L1.

336B: It is potentiated by histamine

There are three classic phases of gastric acid secretion:

- *Cephalic* (preparatory) phase [significant]. This results in the production of gastric acid before food actually enters the stomach. It is triggered by the sight, smell, thought and taste of food acting via the vagus nerve.
- *Gastric* phase [most significant]. This is initiated by the presence of food in the stomach, particularly protein-rich food.
- *Intestinal* phase [least significant]. The presence of amino acids and food in the duodenum stimulate acid production.

Gastric acid is *stimulated* by three factors:

- acetylcholine – from parasympathetic neurones of the vagus nerve that innervate parietal cells directly
- gastrin – produced by pyloric G-cells
- histamine – produced by mast cells.

Histamine stimulates the parietal cells directly and also potentiates parietal cell stimulation by gastrin and neuronal stimulation. H_2 blockers such as ranitidine are therefore an effective way of reducing acid secretion.

Gastric acid is *inhibited* by three factors:

- somatostatin
- secretin
- cholecystokinin.

337E: Results from loss of heterozygosity of the normal Rb gene

Retinoblastoma is a fascinating condition and important to know about. Much is known about retinoblastoma because the gene responsible for the condition was the first tumour suppressor gene to be discovered. In addition, studying the tumour has provided us with valuable information into how tumour suppressor genes function. Retinoblastoma is caused by a mutation in Rb-1 (a tumour suppressor gene) on the long arm of chromosome 13. Approximately 60 per cent of cases are sporadic and 40 per cent are inherited, being transmitted as an autosomal dominant trait. Although inherited as an autosomal dominant trait, cancer results only when both copies of the normal gene are lost. This apparent paradox is explained by Knudson's two-hit hypothesis.

Knudson suggested that, in inherited cases, one genetic change (first hit) is inherited from an affected parent (i.e. the condition is inherited in an autosomal dominant manner) and is therefore present in all somatic cells of the body, whereas the second mutation (second hit) occurs after birth through some form of somatic mutation in one of the many retinal cells (which already carry the first mutation). In other words, loss of heterozygosity of the normal Rb gene results in cancer.

The mutation rate for the gene is thought to be 1 per 10 million, about the same as the number of divisions that are needed to form the adult retina; thus the chance of a somatic mutation occurring in a subject with only one functioning gene is very high. In sporadic cases, however, both mutations (hits) occur somatically within a single retinal cell. Patients with familial forms of retinoblastomas are at increased risk of developing extraretinal cancers (such as osteosarcomas) because the newborn child carries an inherited mutant Rb allele in all somatic cells of the body.

338C: Third branchial pouch

The following structures arise from each branchial pouch:

- first pouch – Eustachian tube, middle ear, mastoid, and inner layer of the tympanic membrane
- second pouch – middle ear, palatine tonsils
- third pouch – inferior parathyroid glands, thymus
- fourth pouch – superior parathyroid glands, ultimobranchial body which forms the parafollicular C-cells of the thyroid gland, musculature and cartilage of larynx (along with the sixth pharyngeal pouch)
- fifth pouch – rudimentary structure
- sixth pouch – along with the fourth pouch, contributes to the formation of the musculature and cartilage of the larynx.

339D: The anterior surface of the right adrenal gland is overlapped by the inferior vena cava

The adrenal glands lie anterosuperior to the upper part of each kidney. They weigh approximately 5 g each and measure 50 mm vertically, 30 mm across and 10 mm thick. They are somewhat asymmetrical, with the right adrenal being pyramidal in shape and left adrenal being crescentic, and lie within their own compartment of (Gerota's) renal fascia. A fascial septum separates the adrenal gland from the kidney, which explains why in nephrectomy (removal of the kidney) the latter gland is not usually displaced (or even seen).

Each gland, although only weighing a few grams, has three arteries supplying it: a direct branch from the aorta, a branch from the renal artery and a branch from the inferior phrenic artery. This reflects the high metabolic demands of the tissue. The single main suprarenal vein drains into the nearest available vessel: on the right it drains into the inferior vena cava and on the left directly into the renal vein. The right adrenal gland is tucked medially behind the inferior vena cava. In addition, the right suprarenal vein is particularly short and stubby. Both these features make the inferior vena cava vulnerable to damage in a right adrenalectomy.

The adrenal gland comprises an outer cortex and an inner medulla, which represent two developmentally and functionally independent endocrine glands within the same anatomical structure. The medulla is derived from the neural crest (ectoderm). It receives preganglionic sympathetic fibres from the greater splanchnic nerve and secretes adrenaline (70 per cent) and noradrenaline (30 per cent). The cortex is derived from mesoderm and consists of three layers, or zones. The layers from the surface inwards may be remembered by the mnemonic GFR (which also stands for glomerular filtration rate):

- G = zona **g**lomerulosa (secretes aldosterone)
- F = zona **f**asciculata (secretes cortisol and sex steroids)
- R = zona **r**eticularis (secretes cortisol and sex steroids).

340C: It stimulates gastric acid production

Gastrin is secreted by gastrin-secreting cells (G-cells) found in two locations: the pyloric region of the stomach and the upper half of the small intestine. Gastrin is released by:

- vagal stimulation
- distension of the pyloric antrum
- proteins (especially partially digested proteins) in the food.

Gastrin is inhibited by:

- a low pH in the lumen of the pyloric antrum (negative feedback loop)
- somatostatin.

Gastrin has three main actions:

- it stimulates gastric acid secretion
- it stimulates gastric motility
- it stimulates exocrine pancreatic secretions.

Overproduction of gastrin leads to excessive gastric acid secretion and the formation of multiple peptic ulcers. This is known as the Zollinger–Ellison syndrome and is often due to a gastrin-secreting tumour (gastrinoma).

341C: May produce paraneoplastic syndromes

Currently lung cancer is the most common cause of death from cancer in both men and women. It is estimated that some 50 per cent of bronchial carcinomas have metastasized by the time of clinical presentation. Lung carcinoma is most commonly due to squamous cell carcinoma as a result of squamous cell metaplasia from smoking. Tobacco smoking is believed to account for 80–90 per cent cases of lung carcinoma; the remainder are associated with radon gas and asbestos exposure.

The pathological effects of any tumour may be local or distant; distant effects may be metastatic or non-metastatic (paraneoplastic). Applying this to lung carcinoma we have:

Local effects

- *Pulmonary involvement* – cough (infection distal to airway blocked by tumour caused by disruption of the mucociliary escalator), haemoptysis (ulceration/necrosis of tumour), breathlessness (local extension of tumour), chest pain (involvement of pleura and/or chest wall), wheeze (narrowing of airways).
- *Local invasion* – hoarseness (recurrent laryngeal nerve infiltration), Horner's syndrome (infiltration of the ipsilateral sympathetic chain), wasting of the intrinsic hand muscles (brachial plexus infiltration), diaphragmatic paralysis (phrenic nerve invasion), pleural effusions (tumour spread into pleura), pericarditis (pericardial involvement), superior vena cava obstruction (direct compression by tumour).

Distant effects

- *Metastatic* – pathological fractures (bone metastases), neurological symptoms (brain metastases), hepatomegaly or jaundice (liver metastases).
- *Non-metastatic* (paraneoplastic) effects – ectopic hormone production (ADH, ACTH, PTHrP, serotonin etc.), common generalized symptoms (weight loss, anorexia, lassitude) from the acute-phase response (IL-1, IL-6, TNFα).

Paraneoplastic syndromes are symptoms and signs associated with a malignant tumour that are not due to direct local effects of the tumour or the development of metastases.

342A: Peptidoglycan

Prokaryotes have peptidoglycan in their cell walls which makes them susceptible to penicillin. Sterol and endoplasmic reticulum are features of eukaryotic cells. Bacteria generally contain single, circular chromosomes (plasmids). Prokaryotes contain 70S, rather than 80S ribosomes which are characteristic of eukaryotes.

343D: It is unimportant in humans

The vermiform (worm-shaped) appendix is a blind-ending tube varying in length (commonly 6–9 cm) which opens into the posteromedial wall of the caecum, where the taeniae coli converge. The appendix is an intraperitoneal structure and therefore has its own short mesentery, the mesoappendix. Within the mesentery lies the appendicular artery, a branch of the ileocolic artery which arises from the superior mesenteric artery.

The surface marking of the base of the appendix is situated one-third of the way up the line joining the anterior superior iliac spine to the umbilicus (McBurney's point). This is an important landmark when making an appendicectomy (McBurney's or Gridiron) incision. The position of the free end of the appendix, however, is very variable. The most common, as found at operation, is the retrocaecal or retrocolic position (75 per cent of cases), with the subcaecal or pelvic position next in order of frequency (20 per cent of cases). Less commonly, in 5 per cent of cases it lies in the pre-ileal or retro-ileal positions, or lies in front of the caecum, or in the right paracolic gutter.

The appendix has no known physiological function in man and can therefore be removed without any consequences. It probably represents a degenerated portion of the caecum that, in ancestral forms, aided in cellulose digestion. In the other animals, the appendix is much larger and provides a pouch off the main intestinal tract, in which cellulose can be trapped and be subjected to prolonged digestion. The abundance of lymphoid tissue within the submucosa of the appendix has prompted the concept that the appendix is the human equivalent of the avian bursa of Fabricius as a site of maturation of thymus-independent lymphocytes. While no discernible change in immune function results from appendicectomy, the prominence of lymphatic tissue in the appendix of young adults seems important in the aetiology of appendicitis.

344D: The main stimulation for secretion occurs during the intestinal phase

The pancreas is a mixed endocrine (ductless) and exocrine gland that forms embryologically from the fusion of separate dorsal and ventral pancreatic buds (endodermal outgrowths from the primitive foregut). The embryology helps to explain how aberrations of development lead to the formation of an annular pancreas, or pancreas divisum, either of which may lead to problems in later life.

The exocrine component of the pancreas consists of closely packed secretory acini which drain into a highly branched duct system. Approximately 1500 mL of pancreatic juice is secreted each day into the duodenum via the pancreatic duct. The alkaline pH of the pancreatic secretion (approximately 8.0) is due to a high content of bicarbonate ions and serves to neutralize the acidic chyme as it enters the duodenum from the stomach.

With regard to the secretion of gastric acid, it is possible to distinguish cephalic, gastric and intestinal phases in the pattern of secretion. The weak cephalic phase contributes only 15 per cent of the total response, an enzyme-rich secretion caused by vagal efferents. The weak gastric phase also contributes only 15 per cent of the total response and is again enzyme-rich, caused by vaso-vagal reflexes originating in the stomach and gastrin secretion. The main stimulation (70 per cent of the total response) is the intestinal phase caused by food entering the duodenum from the stomach. Secretin, a hormone released by endocrine cells scattered in the duodenal mucosa, promotes the secretion of copious watery fluid rich in bicarbonate. The major stimulus for the release of secretin is acid. Cholecystokinin, also derived from duodenal endocrine cells, stimulates the secretion of enzyme-rich pancreatic fluid. Secretin and cholecystokinin act synergistically.

345E: Secondary carcinoma

Tumours or neoplasms may be benign or malignant. Malignant tumours may be primary or secondary. The commonest intracerebral neoplasms are secondaries, accounting for approximately 50 per cent of all intracerebral tumours. The five most common primary sites are the lung, breast, skin (melanoma), kidney and gastrointestinal tract.

Ninety per cent of normal brain tissue is composed of glial (supporting) cells, while the remaining 10 per cent is composed of neurones. That is, there are about 10 times as many glia as there are neurones in normal brain parenchyma. Primary intracerebral neoplasms therefore predominantly arise from the glial cells, rather than the neurones. Astrocytoma is the commonest type of glioma. Meningiomas originate from the arachnoid granulations and press into the brain tissue from outside.

346D: Liver

After metastasing to the pericolonal lymph nodes, colonic tumour cells are then usually drained by the mesenteric lymphatics into blood vessels, the portal vein and finally into the liver. The other choices are less likely sites of initial distant tumour spread.

347B: It may result in thrombosis of the appendicular artery (endarteritis obliterans)

Acute appendicitis is the most common acute surgical condition of the abdomen. Approximately 7 per cent of the population will have appendicitis in their lifetime, with the peak incidence occurring between the ages of 10 and 30 years. Appendicitis is relatively uncommon at the two extremes of life since obstruction of the lumen is the usual cause of appendicitis and the lumen of the appendix is relatively wide in the infant and is frequently completely obliterated in the elderly.

Afferent nerve fibres concerned with the conduction of visceral pain from the appendix accompany the sympathetic nerves and enter the spinal cord at the level of T10. Consequently, the appendix refers visceral pain to the T10 dermatome which lies at the level of the umbilicus. Only later, when the parietal peritoneum overlying the appendix becomes inflamed, does the pain become more intense and localize to the right iliac fossa in the region of McBurney's point.

The following three factors contribute to why the appendix is prone to infection:

- It is a long, narrow blind-ended tube which encourages stasis of large bowel contents.
- It has a large amount of lymphoid tissue in its wall (submucosa).
- The lumen has a tendency to become obstructed by hardened intestinal contents (enteroliths or faecoliths) which leads to further stagnation of its contents.

The sequence of events underlying acute appendicitis is worth understanding. The initial event is probably related to obstruction of the mouth of the appendix. The most common cause of obstruction is a faecolith. This leads to formation of a closed system and the build-up of mucinous secretions (appendiceal mucocele). The distended appendix can become secondarily infected and inflamed (appendicitis). This may subsequently lead to formation of an appendix mass, or abscess. Alternatively, the pressure within this closed system may begin to rise until the point is reached that it begins to compress the superficial veins in the wall of the appendix. Obstruction to venous outflow leads to oedema and a further increase in pressure. The pressure continues to rise until eventually the appendiceal artery is compressed and thromboses (endarteritis obliterans). Since the appendiceal artery is an end-artery and does not anastomose with any other artery, it therefore represents the entire vascular supply of the appendix. The appendix subsequently undergoes ischaemic necrosis and gangrene, that may eventually result in a perforated appendix.

Acute appendicitis almost always requires surgical intervention. This may be performed by open or laparoscopic techniques. It rarely resolves with conservative management and 'watchful waiting' risks progression to perforation and generalized peritonitis, which carries with it a high mortality. There is only one situation in which conservative management is a feasible alternative to surgery, and that is when an appendix mass (or abscess) is present and the patient is not compromised. Even then, however, it is advisable to remove the appendix later after an interval of 6–8 weeks.

348A: Trypsin is a powerful activator of other pancreatic proteolytic enzymes

The pancreatic enzymes degrade proteins, carbohydrates, lipids and nucleic acids. The pancreatic proteolytic enzymes, trypsin and chymotrypsin, are secreted as inactive proenzymes that require activation in the small intestine. Enterokinase (enteropeptidase), an enzyme secreted by the duodenal mucosa, activates trypsinogen to form trypsin; trypsin then activates chymotrypsinogen to form chymotrypsin and other proenzymes into active enzymes. Trypsin can also activate trypsinogen; therefore once some trypsin is formed, there is an autocatalytic chain reaction. By releasing the enzymes as inactive zymogens that become activated far from their site of origin, this mechanism prevents autodigestion of the pancreas.

However, the powerful nature of these proteolytic enzymes necessitates another mechanism to prevent digestion of the pancreas. The same cells that secrete the proteolytic enzymes also secrete another substance called trypsin inhibitor (not a trypsin activator which would be disastrous!). Trypsin inhibitor surrounds the enzyme granules and prevents activation of trypsin both inside the secretory cells and in the acini and ducts of the pancreas. It therefore acts as an additional safeguard should some of the trypsinogen be activated to trypsin. Following exocytosis this inhibitor is diluted out and becomes ineffective. Since trypsin activates the other pancreatic proteolytic enzymes too, trypsin inhibitor therefore also prevents the subsequent activation of the others.

When the pancreas becomes severely damaged or when the duct becomes blocked, large quantities of pancreatic secretion become pooled in the damaged areas of the pancreas. Under these circumstances, the effect of trypsin inhibitor is overwhelmed, in which case the pancreatic secretions rapidly become activated and literally digest the entire pancreas, giving rise to a condition known as acute pancreatitis. This can be lethal; even if not fatal, it may lead to a lifetime of pancreatic insufficiency.

349E: Secondary carcinoma

Tumours or neoplasms may be benign or malignant. Malignant tumours may be primary or secondary. Secondary bone tumours (i.e. metastases) are the commonest malignant tumour of bone, occurring in 70 per cent of patients with disseminated malignant disease. They are more common than all the primary malignant tumours put together. After the liver and lung, the bone is the third most common site for metastatic spread. The commonest primary malignant tumour of bone is the osteosarcoma.

The six most common tumours that spread to bone are:

- multiple myeloma
- breast
- bronchus (lung)
- prostate
- kidney
- thyroid (follicular subtype).

Secondary bone tumours may be associated with an osteolytic (bone-dissolving) or osteoblastic (bone-forming) reaction within the bone. Interestingly both prostate and breast carcinoma have a propensity to form osteoblastic lesions within the bone. The direct effect of metastatic tumours on the bone is one explanation for the hypercalcaemia that is commonly seen in malignancy. Other factors seem to play a role, however, such as the release of parathyroid hormone-related protein (PTHrP) by tumour cells.

350D: Autoclaving

Bacillus anthracis is a Gram-positive, spore-forming microbe. Autoclaving is the best option for killing vegetative cells and spores.

351D: It provides a route of access to the lesser sac

The greater omentum (or gastrocolic omentum) is a double sheet of peritoneum, fused and folded on itself to form an integral structure comprising four layers. It contains adipose tissue of variable amount, depending on the nutritional status of the patient, and hangs down like an apron overlying loops of intestine. The anterior two layers descend from the greater curvature of the stomach (the lesser omentum, not the greater omentum, arises from the lesser curvature of the stomach) where they are continuous with the peritoneum on the anterior and posterior surfaces of the stomach. Posteriorly, they ascend to the transverse colon where they loosely blend with the peritoneum on the anterior and posterior surfaces of the transverse colon and the transverse mesocolon above it.

The right and left gastroepiploic arteries run between the layers of the greater omentum and supply it, close to the greater curvature of the stomach. The greater omentum may undergo torsion, and if this is extensive the blood supply to part of it may be cut off causing necrosis. The lesser sac may be accessed through the greater omentum (by incising between the greater curvature of the stomach and the transverse colon and lifting the stomach up).

The greater omentum is of paramount surgical importance. Surgeons sometimes use the omentum to buttress an intestinal anastomosis, or in the closure of a perforated gastric or duodenal ulcer ('omental patch repair'). One important function of the greater omentum is to attempt to limit the spread of intraperitoneal infections. Indeed, the greater omentum is often referred to by surgeons as the 'great policeman of the abdomen'. The lower, right and left margins are free and it moves about the peritoneal cavity in response to peristaltic movements of the neighbouring gut. In an acutely inflamed appendix, for example, the inflammatory exudate causes the omentum to adhere to the appendix and wrap itself around the infected organ. By this means, the infection is often localized to a small area of the peritoneal cavity, thus saving the patient from a serious generalized peritonitis. The greater omentum is also commonly found plugging the neck of a hernial sac, thereby preventing the entry of coils of small intestine and strangulation of bowel. In the first two years of life, the greater omentum is poorly developed and thus is less protective in a young child.

352C: Islets of Langerhans make up only 2 per cent of the volume of the gland

The endocrine tissue of the pancreas forms Islets of Langerhans. They make up about 2 per cent of the volume of the pancreas, whereas the exocrine portion makes up 80 per cent and ducts and blood vessels make up the rest. Pancreatic endocrine tissue, like all endocrine tissue, is ductless.

There are several different types of islet cell, each producing a different hormone:

- α-islet cells secrete glucagon
- β-islet cells secrete insulin
- δ-islet cells secrete somatostatin
- F-islet cells secrete pancreatic polypeptide.

Each of these hormones passes directly into the bloodstream.

Glucagon has a reciprocal action to that of insulin. It is glycogenolytic, gluconeogenic, lipolytic and ketogenic.

353D: May be seen in histological section

Apoptosis (from the Greek meaning 'to fall off', as the leaves from a tree) is programmed cell death. It acts to eliminate unwanted cells or damaged cells with abnormal DNA. It involves the death of individual cells, rather than large groups of adjacent cells (which is usually the case in necrosis). Apoptosis is usually unaccompanied by inflammation (as is the case in necrosis). A key feature of apoptosis is that cells can be eliminated with minimal disruption to adjacent cells.

Apoptosis may be physiological (as a normal part of growth and development), as well as pathological, where balancing the production of new cells enables a stable cell population. A good example of physiological apoptosis is the shaping of the hands in embryogenesis. Under normal conditions, apoptosis is precisely regulated by pro-apoptotic (p53, c-myc, Bax, Bad) and anti-apoptotic (Bcl-2, Bcl-XL) factors. Alteration in the fine balance of pro-apoptotic and anti-apoptotic factors may result in neoplasia (e.g. loss of p53 is found in many tumours).

Apoptosis is clearly visible in histological sections; apoptotic cells are seen as rounded membrane-bound bodies ('apoptotic bodies'). These bodies are eventually phagocytosed and digested by adjacent cells so that no clump of cellular debris is left permanently behind. The key differences between necrosis and apoptosis are summarized in Table 5.

Table 5 Apoptosis and necrosis compared

Apoptosis	Necrosis
Energy dependent (active process)	Energy independent
Internally programmed or 'suicide'	Response to external injury
Affects single cells	Affects groups of cells
No accompanying inflammation	Accompanied by inflammation
Physiological or pathological	Always pathological
Plasma membrane remains intact	Loss of plasma membrane integrity
Cell shrinkage, fragmentation and formation of apoptotic bodies	Cell swelling and lysis

354E: Destroys CD4 T-lymphocytes

HIV is the virus responsible for causing AIDS. It multiplies in CD4 lymphocytes and this multiplication leads to severe lymphopenia due to the lysis of the CD4 cells. HIV is a member of the retrivirus group and contains single-stranded RNA and an enzyme that synthesizes DNA from RNA (reverse transcriptase). It also has an envelope.

355B: They enter the bladder obliquely forming a flap valve

The ureters are segmental muscular tubes, 25 cm long, composed of smooth (involuntary) muscle throughout their entire length. They are lined by transitional epithelium (urothelium) throughout their length. Indeed the whole urinary tract, including the renal pelvis and bladder, with the exception of the terminal urethra, is lined by transitional epithelium. The clinical significance of this is that the whole urinary tract epithelium is susceptible to widespread malignant change in response to carcinogens and, as a result, tumours of the urothelium are more often multifocal compared to other sites (the so-called 'field effect'). Only the terminal (glandular part of the urethra) is lined by stratified squamous epithelium.

It is important to recognize and distinguish the ureter from surrounding vessels and nerves in the living body during surgery in order to prevent inadvertent damage. The ureter is characteristically a whitish, non-pulsatile cord, which shows peristaltic activity when gently pinched with forceps (i.e. it vermiculates). There is no situation where it is more important to recognize and preserve the ureters than at hysterectomy where the ureters lie in close proximity to the uterine vessels and ligaments. Incorrect ligation of the ureters instead of the uterine vessels may be prevented by correctly identifying the ureters (by assessing for vermiculation) and by remembering the mnemonic 'water under the bridge' (i.e. the ureters are crossed above by the uterine arteries).

Blood supply to the ureters, like the oesophagus, is segmental. The upper third is supplied by the renal arteries, the middle third from branches given off from the descending abdominal aorta, and the lower third by the superior and inferior vesical arteries. Blood supply to the middle third is the most tenuous. Consequently, the middle third of the ureter is most vulnerable to postoperative ischaemia and stricture formation if blood supply to it is endangered by stripping the ureter clean of its surrounding tissue at surgery.

Along the course of the ureter are three constrictions worth remembering as they are often the site of hold-up for ureteric calculi (stones):

- the pelviureteric junction
- where the ureter crosses the pelvic brim in the region of the bifurcation of the common iliac artery
- the vesicoureteric junction.

The last is the point of narrowest calibre.

In both sexes the ureters run obliquely through the bladder wall for 1–2 cm before reaching their orifices at the upper lateral angles of the trigone. This forms a flap valve preventing reflux of urine retrogradely back up the ureters. If this flap valve is congenitally deficient, vesicoureteric reflux results.

356B: It is actively concentrated in the gall bladder

The liver secretes approximately 500 mL of alkaline bile daily. It is composed of 97 per cent water, 0.7 per cent bile salts (sodium and potassium salts of bile acids), 0.2 per cent bile pigments (bilirubin and biliverdin) and 2 per cent of other substances (bicarbonate, fatty acids, cholesterol, lecithin). Bile salts are derived from cholesterol – do not confuse them with bile pigments which are the breakdown products of the haem component of haemoglobin. In addition it is the accumulation of bile pigments (bilirubin) that leads to jaundice.

Bile salts are responsible for the emulsification of fat in the chyme, by the formation of micelles. This aids in their absorption. Bile contains no digestive enzymes.

Between 90 and 95 per cent of the bile salts are absorbed from the small intestine and then excreted again from the liver; most are absorbed from the terminal ileum. This is known as the enterohepatic circulation. The entire pool recycles twice per meal and approximately 6–8 times a day. Disruption of the enterohepatic circulation, either by terminal ileal resection or through a diseased terminal ileum (e.g. Crohn's disease), results in decreased fat absorption and cholesterol gallstone formation. The latter is believed to result because bile salts normally make cholesterol more water-soluble through the formation of cholesterol micelles.

Between meals the Sphincter of Oddi which guards the opening of the bile duct into the duodenum is constricted and bile passes into the gall bladder. The gall bladder serves three main functions. It concentrates bile (5- to 20-fold) by the active reabsorption of salt and water through the gall bladder epithelium. It also stores bile and secretes mucus into the bile. The periodic discharge of bile from the gall bladder aids digestion but is not essential for it.

357D: Inflammation is intimately connected with the clotting system

Acute inflammation is a stereotyped, non-specific response to tissue injury. It occurs in response to a variety of different tissue insults (both exogenous or endogenous) and not just from infection. For example, it also occurs after ischaemia (hypoxic injury), physical trauma, or in response to noxious chemicals, such as insect bites. Inflammation is fundamentally a protective response, the ultimate goal of which is to rid the organism of both the initial cause of cell injury (e.g. microbes, toxins) and the consequences of such injury (e.g. necrotic tissues). In some situations, however, inflammation may be harmful to the host (a good example is meningitis).

The four cardinal features of acute inflammation are redness (rubor), swelling (tumour), heat (calor) and pain (dolor). Some also add a fifth, such as loss of function (functio laesa), or increased secretion (fluor). Acute inflammation is part of the innate immune response occurring prior to the development of any adaptive immune response that may later occur. In this way acute inflammation acts as a 'danger signal' augmenting the adaptive immune response. The inflammatory response is immediate, but non-specific, whereas the adaptive immune response is slower to develop but is highly specific and acquires memory.

Acute inflammation is initiated by a variety of chemical mediators, all of which interact in a synergistic manner to produce inflammation. These include bacterial-derived products, histamine, serotonin, arachidonic acid metabolites, cytokines and members of the complement, kinin, clotting and fibrinolytic systems. The clotting system and inflammation are intimately connected. Therefore bleeding at the site of injury can initiate acute inflammation.

There are three main phases of acute inflammation:

- widespread vasodilatation (hyperaemia)
- increased vascular permeability
- leucocyte extravasation and phagocytosis.

The predominant cell type in acute inflammation is the neutrophil (the macrophage predominates in chronic inflammation). Acute inflammation is of relatively short duration, lasting for minutes, several hours or a few days. If it persists for longer then it is generally regarded as chronic inflammation.

358E: Sixth cervical vertebra

C6 is the critical boundary of the root of the neck. To enter the neck from the chest, the vascular structures pass through a ring-like opening bounded by the scalene muscles laterally, the sternum and 1st rib anteriorly and the vertebra (C6).

359D: It contains the pampiniform plexus

The contents of the spermatic cord are easily remembered using the 'rule of 3's':

- '3 constituents' – vas deferens (the round ligament is the female equivalent), lymphatics, obliterated processus vaginalis
- '3 nerves' – genital branch of the genitofemoral nerve (motor to cremaster, sensory to cord), ilioinguinal nerve (within the inguinal canal but outside the spermatic cord), autonomics
- '3 arteries' – testicular artery, artery to the vas (from the superior or inferior vesical artery), cremasteric artery (from the inferior epigastric artery)
- '3 veins' – pampiniform plexus, vein from the vas, cremasteric vein
- '3 fascial coverings' – internal spermatic fascia, external spermatic fascia, cremasteric muscle & fascia (not dartos muscle which is contained within the wall of the scrotum).

360B: Gastric acid assists in the absorption of iron

Every day 7–10 litres of water enter the alimentary canal. Most of this is absorbed by the end of the small intestine so that only 500–600 mL enters the colon. Further reabsorption occurs in the colon so that only about 100 mL are lost from the body in the faeces.

Glucose absorption is dependent on sodium absorption, via a sodium (secondary active) cotransport mechanism. Conversely, the presence of glucose in the intestinal lumen facilitates the absorption of sodium. Water follows by osmosis. This is the physiological basis for the treatment of sodium and water loss in diarrhoea by oral administration of solutions containing sodium chloride and glucose (oral rehydration therapy). Most of the ingested sodium is reabsorbed (normally less than 0.5 per cent of intestinal sodium is lost in the faeces) because of its rapid absorption through the intestinal mucosa. If absorption is greater than the body requirements, the excess is excreted by the kidneys.

A good way to think about the order of absorption of substances throughout the gastrointestinal tract is to remember that the most important substances for survival are generally absorbed first, followed by the less important ones. Thus, glucose takes place mainly in the upper small intestine (duodenum and jejunum), but vitamin B_{12} is absorbed further down, in the terminal ileum (since bodily stores of vitamin B_{12} can last up to 2 years in the complete absence of vitamin B_{12} intake).

Iron is absorbed more readily in the ferrous state (Fe^{2+}), but most of the dietary iron is in the ferric (Fe^{3+}) form. Gastric acidity releases iron from the food and favours the ferrous form which is absorbed more easily. The importance of this function in humans is indicated by the fact that iron deficiency anaemia is a troublesome and relatively frequent complication of partial gastrectomy.

361D: Amyloidosis

The four possible outcomes of acute inflammation are:

- resolution (with the complete restoration of normal tissue architecture and function)
- abscess formation (a localized collection of pus surrounded by granulation tissue; pus is a collection of neutrophils in association with dead and dying organisms)
- progression to chronic inflammation
- death (a good example being meningitis).

Amyloidosis follows chronic inflammation, rather than acute inflammation.

362B: Lunate

The lunate is the most commonly dislocated carpal bone; it usually displaces anteriorly by rotation on its proximal, convex surface which articulates with the radius. The displaced bone may compress the median nerve in the carpal tunnel. The scaphoid bone is the most commonly fractured carpal bone and has an increased risk of avascular necrosis.

363D: It is supplied by T10 sympathetic nerves

The testis is supplied by the testicular artery which arises directly from the descending abdominal aorta at the level of approximately L2. Although at first glance this may seem illogical, when the testis is in closer proximity to other blood vessels such as the internal iliac, the explanation lies in the fact that the testis develops high up on the posterior abdominal wall early in embryonic life. As it descends into the scrotum during development, the testis carries with it the same blood supply that it received whence it was positioned on the posterior abdominal wall (i.e. from the aorta).

The testis drains by way of the pampiniform plexus into the inferior vena cava on the right side, but into the left renal vein on the left side. This may account for the fact that varicoceles (varicosities of the pampiniform plexus secondary to incompetent venous valves) are more common of the left compared with the right. The accumulation of serous fluid around the testis is known as a hydrocele.

As a general rule regarding lymphatic drainage, superficial lymphatics (i.e. in subcutaneous tissues) tend to run with superficial veins, whereas deep lymphatics run with arteries. The testis thus drains lymph to the para-aortic set of lymph nodes, since the testicular artery arises from the aorta. The testis never drains to the inguinal group of lymph nodes, although the scrotum may. The clinical consequence of this is that a testicular carcinoma never results in inguinal lymphadenopathy, unless the scrotum is also involved. A scrotal carcinoma, on the other hand, would be expected to produce inguinal lymphadenopathy and this holds true in clinical practice.

The testis is supplied by T10 sympathetic nerves. The consequences of this are two-fold. First, it results in testicular pain (trauma, testicular torsion etc.) being referred to the umbilicus (T10 dermatome). Second, the ureters are also supplied by T10 sympathetics. Thus a renal calculus may refer pain down to the testis, as is seen in classical renal colic.

364D: Protein is spared until relatively late

Starvation is a chronic state resulting from inadequate intake of energy. Four main metabolic processes occur during starvation: glycogenolysis, gluconeogenesis, lipolysis and ketogenesis. No significant hypoglycaemic episodes occur until the end stage of starvation is entered.

During the immediate phase of starvation (0–24 hours), reserves of glycogen from liver and skeletal muscle are utilized. Glucose produced from glycogen lasts only 24 hours. The blood glucose is maintained after glycogen is depleted by gluconeogenesis for which the main substrates are amino acids, lactic acid and glycerol.

In general, fats spare nitrogen so that protein is preserved until relatively late in starvation. During prolonged starvation, ketone bodies (acetone, acetoacetate, β-hydroxybutyrate) derived from fats are used by the brain and other tissues (such as heart muscle). Although the brain is usually heavily dependent on glucose as its energy source, during starvation it adapts to using ketones.

When fat stores are finally used up, protein catabolism increases and death follows from proteolysis of vital muscles (cardiac muscle, diaphragm). The average time to death is about 60 days.

365B: It usually heals by organization and repair

Chronic inflammation is inflammation of prolonged duration (weeks or months) in which active inflammation, tissue destruction and attempts at repair are occurring simultaneously. It may follow acute inflammation (secondary chronic), or it may occur *de novo* in the absence of a preceding acute inflammatory phase (primary chronic).

Chronic inflammation arises in situations where the injurious stimulus persists, as when:

- the injurious agent is endogenous (e.g. acid in stomach and peptic ulceration)
- the injurious agent is non-degradable (e.g. dust particles in pneumoconiosis)
- the injurious agent evades host defence mechanisms (e.g. many intracellular organisms such as tuberculosis)
- the host attacks components of self (e.g. autoimmunity)
- host resistance (immunity) is suppressed (e.g. malnutrition, HIV).

Neutrophils are a feature of acute, rather than chronic, inflammation. Chronic inflammation is characterized by more extensive tissue destruction than acute inflammation owing to the lengthy nature of the process and the greater lysosomal rupture with the release of numerous lytic enzymes. The destroyed tissue is replaced by granulation tissue. Healing occurs by organization and repair (with fibrosis leaving a scar), rather than through resolution (which is typical of acute inflammation).

The pathological consequences of chronic inflammation include:

- tissue destruction and scarring
- development of cancer – the mitotically active tissue provides a fertile ground for the accumulation of mutations
- amyloidosis –the extracellular deposition of abnormal and insoluble, β-pleated proteinaceous deposits.

Amyloid causes its pathological effects by accumulating in body tissues.

366A: Proximal convoluted tubule

The concentration of glucose is highest in the proximal convoluted tubule and therefore most reabsorption takes place here. The concentration of glucose in the other portion of the nephron is close to zero.

367B: It lies medial to the obturator nerve and anterior to the ureter

The ovary is ovoid in shape, measuring about 3 cm long, 2 cm wide and 1 cm thick (smaller than the testis), being smaller before menarche and postmenopausally. The anterior border of the ovary is attached to the posterior leaf of the broad ligament by a double fold of peritoneum, the mesovarium. The ovary is thus an intraperitoneal structure and the surface of the ovary, covered with cuboidal epithelium faces the peritoneal cavity. Therefore ova extruded from the ovary actually pass into the peritoneal cavity. One consequence of this is that an ectopic pregnancy may occur within the peritoneal cavity, in addition to occurring within the fallopian tube.

The ovary flops laterally to lie in the ovarian fossa on the lateral pelvic wall. Immediately behind the fossa is the ureter which may be damaged while operating on the ovary and lateral to the ovary is the obturator neurovascular bundle. A diseased ovary may therefore cause referred pain along the cutaneous distribution of the obturator nerve on the inner side of the thigh. Nerve supply to the ovary is sympathetic originating at T10 and therefore ovarian pain may also be referred to the peri-umbilical region.

The suspensory ligament of the ovary transmits the ovarian artery, vein and lymphatics. As a general rule regarding lymphatic drainage, superficial lymphatics (i.e. in subcutaneous tissues) tend to run with superficial veins, whereas deep lymphatics run with arteries. As the artery starts from the aorta, lymph drainage therefore passes to the para-aortic lymph nodes. The same applies with the testis in the male.

368C: TSH

The pituitary gland (hypophysis) is the conductor of the endocrine orchestra. It is divided into an anterior part and a posterior part. The anterior pituitary (adenohypophysis or pars distalis) secretes six hormones:

- FSH and LH – reproduction
- ACTH – stress response
- TSH – basal metabolic rate
- GH – growth
- prolactin – lactation.

The posterior pituitary (neurohypophysis or pars nervosa) secretes only two hormones:

- ADH (vasopressin) – osmotic regulation
- oxytocin – milk ejection and labour.

Testosterone is produced from Leydig cells in the testis and from the adrenal glands. CRH is produced by the median eminence of the hypothalamus.

369C: Tuberculosis

Granulomatous inflammation is a distinctive pattern of chronic inflammation characterized by granuloma formation. It usually occurs in response to the presence of indigestible matter within macrophages. Histologically, a granuloma consists of a microscopic aggregation of activated macrophages that are transformed into epithelium-like cells (epithelioid macrophages), surrounded by a collar of mononuclear leucocytes, principally lymphocytes and occasionally plasma cells. Epithelioid cells may coalesce to form multinucleate giant cells. Their nuclei are often arranged around the periphery of the cell – Langhans' giant cells. Do not confuse the term granuloma with granulation tissue; the latter is a wound-healing phenomenon and does not contain granulomas.

Tuberculosis is the archetypal granulomatous disease, but it can also occur in other disease states such as other infections (e.g. leprosy, schistosomiasis), foreign bodies, which may be endogenous (bone, adipose tissue, uric acid crystals) or exogenous (e.g. silica, suture materials). Some causes are idiopathic, such as Crohn's disease and sarcoidosis. Note that Crohn's disease, but not ulcerative colitis, is associated with the presence of granulomas. Lobar pneumonia and bronchopneumonia do not characteristically form granulomas.

If the granuloma is large it may outstrip its own blood supply, resulting in central necrosis. Tuberculosis is characteristically associated with caseating granulomas, with central caseous necrosis. Other conditions such as Crohn's disease and sarcoidosis are associated with non-caseating granulomas.

370D: Tricuspid

Clinically this patient has bacterial endocarditis. In drug abusers, it usually affects the tricuspid valve because contamination from dirty needles drains into the right side of the heart. It is usually caused by *Staphylococcus aureus*.

371A: It is drained by tributaries of both the inferior mesenteric and internal iliac veins

The rectum is 12 cm long, starting at the level of S3 and ending at the puborectalis (levator ani-pelvic floor). It is lined by typical columnar intestinal epithelium with many mucous secreting cells (transitional epithelium is almost exclusively confined to the urinary tract of mammals where it is highly specialized to accommodate a great deal of stretch and to withstand the toxicity of the urine).

The rectum has no mesentery and is therefore regarded as retroperitoneal. It is covered by peritoneum on its front and sides in its upper third, only on its front in its middle third and the rectum lies below the peritoneal reflection in its lower third. Do not be confused; although the rectum has no mesentery, the visceral pelvic fascia around the rectum is often referred to by surgeons as the mesorectum. The pararectal lymph nodes are found within the mesorectum, which is removed together with the rectum as a package during rectal excision for carcinoma.

Blood supply is by way of the superior rectal (inferior mesenteric), middle rectal (internal iliac) and inferior rectal (internal pudendal) arteries. The importance of understanding the blood supply of the rectum lies in its vulnerability during the resection of a rectal carcinoma and the formation of a join (anastomosis) from the two remaining ends of the bowel. If blood supply to the anastomosis is tenuous, then the anastomosis may break down in the postoperative period with disastrous consequences. The venous drainage is as for the arteries. Note, however, that there is a portosystemic anastomosis in the lower rectal and upper anal canal walls, as branches of the superior rectal (portal) and inferior/middle rectal veins (systemic) meet in the external and internal venous plexuses. This poses a site where haemorrhoids may form in portal hypertension.

The rectum receives parasympathetic fibres from the pelvic splanchnic nerves, or nervi erigentes, originating from S2 to S4. It functions to relax the internal sphincter, contract the bowel and transmit a sense of fullness. Note that the vagus nerve only supplies the bowel up to two-thirds along the transverse colon. The whole of the rest of the bowel inferior to this level (the so-called hindgut) receives parasympathetic fibres by way of the pelvic splanchnic nerves. Remember parasympathetic outflow from the spinal cord is craniosacral, whereas sympathetic outflow is thoracolumbar. Sympathetic supply to the rectum is through the lumbar splanchnics and superior hypogastric plexus. Sympathetics contract the internal sphincter, relax the bowel and transmit pain.

372D: Identical twins show 90 per cent concordance

In type 1 diabetes mellitus identical twins have 50 per cent concordance, whereas in type 2 there is 90 per cent concordance. Type 1 is associated with HLA DR 3/4, whereas type 2 has no HLA association. Type 1 is a disorder of insulin deficiency and therefore presentation is with weight loss and ketone production, usually early in life in the teenage years. Type 2, which commonly presents after the age of 40, is associated with obesity and insulin resistance rather than insulin deficiency *per se*.

373A: Granulation tissue actively contracts

The stages of wound healing are as follows:

- coagulation/haemostasis (immediate)
- inflammation (0–4 days) – initially neutrophils and then macrophages which remove tissue debris
- fibroplasia and epithelialization (4 days to 3 weeks) – neovascularized tissue is known as granulation tissue
- contraction, maturation and remodelling (3 weeks to 18 months) – fibroblasts differentiate into myofibroblasts which are responsible for active wound contraction.

Maximal wound tensile strength is achieved at about day 60, when it is 80 per cent of normal.

Resolution is the most favourable outcome of the healing process because it refers to the complete restitution of normal tissue architecture and function. It can occur only if tissue damage is slight, followed by rapid removal of debris. No scar tissue forms in pure resolution.

Repair, on the other hand, is the replacement of damaged tissue by fibrosis or gliosis, which fills or bridges the defect, but has no intrinsic specialized function relevant to the organ in which repair occurs. It occurs when there is substantial damage to the specialized connective tissue framework and/or the tissue lacks the ability to regenerate specialized cells. The result of repair is a scar.

Tissue repair occurs through the formation of granulation tissue. It derives its name from the granular appearance seen by early military surgeons in the bases of wounds that were about to heal, hence the association with a favourable outcome. The granules are caused by the sprouting of endothelial buds as a result of angiogenesis. Granulation tissue replaces a disorganized mess with orderly new fibrous tissue, a process called organization. Granulation tissue should not be confused with granulomas (aggregates of activated macrophages), which are not an integral part of granulation tissue.

Granulation tissue is defined by the presence of three cell types:

- macrophages – responsible for removing tissue debris
- fibroblasts – responsible for laying down the collagen in fibrous tissue that aids wound contraction
- endothelial cells – responsible for the formation of new blood vessels (angiogenesis).

Lymphocytes and plasma cells may also be present.

Healing by primary intention refers to incised wounds where the edges can be apposed. *Healing by secondary intention* is where there has been tissue loss and the edges cannot be suitably apposed. Healing by secondary intention is slower since granulation tissue has to form from the base of the wound and re-epithelialization has to occur from the edges to cover this. The granulation tissue eventually contracts, resulting in scar formation.

374E: Transitional cell carcinoma

Ninety per cent of bladder cancers are transitional cell carcinomas derived from the bladder urothelium. Risk factors include industrial chemicals, smoking and infection. Schistosomiasis and bladder stones predispose to the squamous cell variety.

375E: The ureter is closely related to the lateral fornix of the cervix

The supports of the uterus are extremely important. The lateral (or transverse) cervical ligaments condense around the uterine artery and run to the lateral pelvic wall. The uterosacral ligaments are primarily condensations of fascia running backwards from the cervix of the uterus past the rectum and attaching to the sacrum. The round ligament of the uterus is the female remnant of the embryonic gubernaculum which guides the testis to the scrotum in the male. It is a continuation of the ovarian ligament which is in the broad ligament attaching the ovary to the uterus. The round ligament then continues from the wall of the uterus in the anterior leaf of the broad ligament to the pelvic wall and then through the deep inguinal ring and inguinal canal to fade out into the labium majorum. It is important only in helping to hold the uterus in its usual anteverted, anteflexed position (i.e. the uterus tends to lie tipped forwards over the female bladder).

Some support is also offered by the anterior pubocervical ligaments. Similarly the broad ligament holds the uterus in that position but it does not contribute a great deal to preventing uterine prolapse (procidentia). The latter is a condition where the pelvic floor is so weakened, usually following multiple childbirth, that the uterus tends to prolapse through the vagina. This can adversely affect the base of the bladder or even obstruct the ureters and therefore may lead to urinary infections, incontinence or renal failure.

The blood supply comes mainly from the uterine artery, which takes a very tortuous course up the uterus (to allow for expansion in uterine hypertrophy, e.g. pregnancy). It is a branch of the internal iliac. In so reaching the uterus, the uterine artery must pass across and above the ureter which is heading past the uterus to the bladder. During hysterectomy this relationship is enormously important as the uterine arteries must be ligated and cut. Clearly one must recognize the difference and realize the close proximity of the ureter and uterine artery.

The ureters lie adjacent to the lateral fornix of the cervix. Consequently a ureteric calculus may be felt in the lateral fornix on vaginal examination. The posterior fornix actually has overlying it the peritoneum of the recto-uterine Pouch of Douglas, which is normally occupied by coils of small intestine or sigmoid colon and lies between the uterus anteriorly and the rectum posteriorly. The Pouch of Douglas is the most dependent part of the pelvis. Consequently, blood may collect here in a ruptured ectopic pregnancy. A needle may be passed into this space (in an attempt to aspirate blood) in order to diagnose the condition (culdocentesis). Furthermore, the instrument used in illegal abortions, if missing the cavity of the uterus, could actually penetrate the posterior fornix and subsequently the peritoneal cavity, often leading to fatal peritonitis and sepsis.

376C: A fasting glucose of 7.5 mM on two occasions is consistent with a diagnosis

It is vital to be aware of the diagnostic criteria for diabetes. A fasting glucose of >7 mM, or a glucose of >11.1 mM two hours after a 75 g glucose load, is diagnostic. A random glucose of >11.1 mM is also consistent with a diagnosis. One abnormal laboratory value is diagnostic in symptomatic individuals; two abnormal values are needed in asymptomatic individuals. Impaired glucose tolerance is defined as a glucose level of 7.8–11.1 mM two hours after 75 g glucose, and impaired fasting glucose is defined as a fasting glucose level above 6 but less than 7 mM.

377B: Peripheral neurones

The cells of the body are divided into three groups on the basis of their proliferative capacity:

- Continuously dividing cells (self-renewing or labile cells) continue to proliferate throughout life. This includes surface epithelia and cells of the bone marrow. Bone has excellent properties of regeneration, and remodelling of a fractured callus can produce complete restoration of a fractured bone.
- Quiescent (or stable) cells normally demonstrate a low level of replication. However, they can undergo rapid division in response to stimuli and are thus capable of reconstituting the tissue of origin. They are considered to be in G0 of the cell cycle but can be stimulated into G1. In this category are the parenchymal cells of virtually all the glandular organs of the body. This is best exemplified by the ability of the liver to regenerate after hepatectomy and after toxic, viral or chemical injury. However, regeneration does not necessarily mean restoration of normal structure. Thus if damage to the liver continues while replication occurs, there may not be a complete return to original architecture, and if the damage is severe then cirrhosis may result.
- Non-dividing (or permanent) cells have left the cell cycle and cannot replicate so that regeneration is not possible. Neurones of the central nervous system (brain and spinal cord) and skeletal and cardiac myocytes belong to this group. That these cells cannot regenerate probably reflects the fact the spatial organization of these tissues is so specific that regeneration would result in functional chaos. The result is that damaged areas of cardiac muscle are replaced by fibrous scar tissue following a myocardial infarction.

The absence of regeneration within the central nervous system reflects not only the intrinsic properties of the neurones themselves, which are incapable of dividing, but also the inhibitory environment present within the central nervous system. Under normal circumstances, the physiological purpose of the inhibitory environment present within the CNS is to prevent the formation of unwanted connections and to help to maintain the structural integrity of white matter tracts. However, this is detrimental in the setting of injury. Thus, gliosis is the only reaction that the brain and spinal cord can make following injury, and the inability of central neurones to regenerate may result in permanent loss of function (e.g. permanent paralysis in the case of spinal cord trauma).

Peripheral nerves, on the other hand, unlike their central nervous system counterparts, are able to regenerate following injury, with axonal growth occurring at a rate of around 1 mm per day. A better understanding of why regenerative capacity is so much greater in the peripheral than in the CNS may open up new therapeutic windows for repairing the damaged CNS in patients for whom there is currently little hope.

378E: Factor XII

Deficiency of factor XII (Hageman factor) results in thrombosis rather than bleeding. The mechanism appears to be deficient activation of fibrinolysis and both thrombophlebitis and myocardial infarction have occurred in severe cases. It is inherited in an autosomal recessive manner. Deficiencies of the other factors listed are associated with bleeding.

379D: The gastroduodenal artery is a branch of the common hepatic artery

The blood supply of the stomach is initially quite confusing, easily forgotten and commonly asked about, but a few key rules make this a simple area of anatomy that will never be forgotten.

Rule 1

The coeliac trunk divides into three main branches, which can be easily remembered by the mnemonic left-hand side (LHS):

- left gastric artery (L)
- common hepatic artery (H)
- splenic artery (S).

Rule 2

For the purposes of remembering the blood supply to the stomach, the stomach can be divided into three main areas:

- lesser curvature
- greater curvature
- fundus.

Rule 3

The lesser curvature is supplied by the left and right gastric arteries. The left gastric, as already mentioned, comes directly off the coeliac trunk. The right gastric is a branch of the common hepatic artery.

Rule 4

The greater curvature is supplied by the right and left gastroepiploic arteries. The right gastroepiploic artery comes off the gastroduodenal artery. The left gastroepiploic artery comes off the splenic artery.

Rule 5

The fundus is supplied by the six, or so, short gastric arteries which arise from the splenic artery.

Rule 6

The gastroduodenal artery is an important artery to remember for clinical purposes. It arises from the common hepatic artery and lies posterior to the first part of the duodenum. A posteriorly situated duodenal ulcer may erode through the duodenal wall into the blood vessel causing catastrophic, life-threatening haemorrhage. Urgent endoscopy or laparotomy may be required to stop the bleeding.

380D: It is an anabolic hormone

Insulin acts via cell membrane spanning receptors which have intrinsic receptor tyrosine kinase activity. When insulin binds to the receptor, the tyrosine kinase is phosphorylated, resulting in a cascade of intracellular signalling mechanisms which results in glucose uptake into the cell. It is secreted by beta cells of the pancreas. Somatostatin is secreted by delta cells. Secretion is inhibited by somatostatin, which is always considered an inhibitory hormone. Insulin is considered an anabolic hormone; i.e. it takes up glucose into the cell and converts it to larger 'building blocks' such as proteins and fats. Release of insulin is stimulated not only by the ingestion of glucose but also amino acids which it will convert into larger proteins.

381C: Liquefactive necrosis classically occurs in the brain

Necrosis is abnormal tissue death during life. Necrosis is always pathological and is accompanied by inflammation. Groups of cells are involved and undergo swelling and lysis. Necrotic cells are phagocytosed by inflammatory cells. There are several different types of necrosis:

- *Coagulative* (structured) necrosis is the most common form. It results from interruption of blood supply. Tissue architecture is preserved. It is seen in organs supplied by end-arteries, such as the kidneys, heart, liver and spleen.
- *Liquefactive* (colliquative) necrosis occurs in tissues rich in lipid where lysosomal enzymes denature the fat and cause liquefaction of the tissue. It characteristically occurs in the brain.
- *Caseous* (unstructured) necrosis has a gross appearance of soft, cheesy, friable material. Tissue architecture is destroyed. It is commonly seen in tuberculosis.
- *Fat* necrosis can occur following direct trauma (e.g. breast) or enzymatic lipolysis (e.g. pancreatitis).
- *Fibrinoid* necrosis is seen in the walls of arteries that are subjected to high pressures, as in malignant hypertension. The muscular wall undergoes necrosis and is associated with deposition of fibrin.
- *Gangrenous* necrosis is irreversible tissue death characterized by putrefaction. It may be wet, dry or gaseous. The tissues appear green or black because of breakdown of haemoglobin.

382B: Left atrium

Pressure in the left atrium can be approximated by wedging an arterial catheter in the small branch of the pulmonary artery. The pulmonary vascular tree abuts the left atrium anatomically. The pulmonary artery carries deoxygenated blood from the right ventricle into the pulmonary circulation where it is oxygenated and then returned into the left atrium via the pulmonary veins.

383E: Cloquet's node lies most medially within the femoral canal

The boundaries of the femoral triangle are the inguinal ligament superiorly, the medial border of adductor longus medially and the medial border of sartorius laterally.

The contents of the femoral triangle from lateral to medial may be easily remembered by the mnemonic NAVY:

- **N** = nerve (femoral) outside the femoral sheath
- **A** = artery (femoral) within the femoral sheath
- **V** = vein (femoral) within the femoral sheath
- **Y** = Y-fronts (most medially).

Within the femoral sheath lies the femoral artery, vein and a space most medially known as the femoral canal. The purpose of the femoral canal is to allow the laterally placed femoral vein to expand into it thereby encouraging venous return. However, a piece of bowel or omentum may extend down into the femoral space, causing a femoral hernia. Within the space of the femoral canal normally lies extraperitoneal fat and a lymph node which is often given its eponymous name, Cloquet's lymph node. Cloquet's lymph node drains the lower limb, perineum and anterior abdominal wall inferior to the umbilicus. It may be enlarged (as inguinal lymphadenopathy) in cases of carcinoma and infection at these sites.

The femoral artery lies at the mid-inguinal point (half-way between the anterior superior iliac spine and symphysis pubis), as opposed to mid-point of the inguinal ligament (half-way between the anterior superior iliac spine and the pubic tubercle) which is the surface marking of the deep inguinal ring. The surface marking of the femoral artery is imperative to understand as, not only does it provide a site for the clinician to assess the femoral pulse, but it also provides the clinician with a surface landmark for gaining access to the femoral artery for procedures such as coronary angioplasty and lower limb angiography and embolectomy.

384B: Prolactin is under dominant inhibitory regulation

Oxytocin and ADH are synthesized in the paraventricular and supraoptic nuclei of the hypothalamus. They are transported from the hypothalamus down into the posterior pituitary gland (or neurohypophysis) via magnocellular neurones and are stored in the posterior pituitary as vesicles prior to release into the bloodstream.

GH, ACTH, TSH, prolactin and LH/FSH are released from the anterior pituitary gland. Prolactin is under inhibitory control by dopamine but can also be stimulated by TRH/TSH. Catecholamines, serotonin and thyroxine are amine hormones, whereas cortisol, aldosterone, androgens, oestrogens, progesterone and vitamin D are steroid hormones. All other hormones are peptide hormones.

Insulin, growth hormone and prolactin act via tyrosine kinase receptors. Adrenaline, ACTH, TSH, LH/FSH, glucagon and somatostatin act via G-protein receptors coupled to cAMP. The G-protein coupled receptor activates adenylate cyclase which in turn generates cAMP in an amplification process. GnRH and TRH act via G-protein receptors coupled to intracellular calcium as a second messenger. This is undertaken through activation of phospholipase C. It is the steroid hormones which bind to intracellular receptors.

385B: Digestion of dead tissue by saprophytic bacteria

In gangrene, tissue that is dead is digested by bacteria which are incapable of invading and multiplying in living tissue (saprophytes), a process known as putrefaction. Gas production may be present in some forms of gangrene (e.g. gas gangrene from clostridial anaerobic infection), but not others.

Necrosis of tissue is an essential prerequisite for gangrene. Necrosis, however, may be caused by ischaemia (secondary gangrene, or dry gangrene), or by bacterial toxins (primary gangrene, or moist gangrene).

386D: Cholecystokinin

Cholecystokinin (CCK) is responsible for stimulation of gall bladder contraction. The release of CCK is stimulated by dietary fat. It is produced in the I-cells of the duodenum and jejunum. Moreover, CCK also stimulates the release of pancreatic enzyme secretion and decreases the rate of gastric emptying.

387B: It has high mobility at the expense of stability

The shoulder joint, like the hip joint, is a synovial joint of the ball and socket variety. The joint cavity, as is the case with all synovial joints, is lined by articular hyaline cartilage and not fibrocartilage. As with all joints, stability is brought about by the way the various bones articulate with one another (through their incongruous surfaces) and through the various ligaments, tendons and muscles that surround the joint. Clearly, it is impossible to have a joint that is both highly mobile and perfectly stable, as a highly mobile joint requires a wide range of movement, in all possible degrees of freedom, which is in itself intrinsically unstable. In contrast to the hip joint where stability is of paramount importance, in the shoulder joint, mobility comes at the expense of stability.

The rotator cuff muscles are the most important factor in maintaining the stability of the shoulder joint and preventing dislocation. The ligaments and bones are less important in the case of the shoulder joint. There are only four muscles of the rotator cuff, and these may be remembered by the mnemonic SITS:

- **s**upraspinatus
- **i**nfraspinatus
- **t**eres minor
- **s**ubscapularis.

Note that teres major is not a rotator cuff muscle. Note also that the first three muscles are placed posteriorly, behind the shoulder joint, while only one of the rotator cuff muscles (subscapularis) is positioned anteriorly. This may in part explain why the shoulder more commonly dislocates anteriorly, rather than posteriorly. An alternative explanation may relate to the deficiency of the joint capsule inferiorly, which makes the shoulder susceptible to antero-inferior dislocation when in the abducted, externally rotated position. The above two explanations are not mutually exclusive.

It should never be forgotten that the axillary nerve lies in close proximity to the shoulder joint and the surgical neck of the humerus. Consequently, it is vulnerable to injury at the time of a shoulder dislocation, or while attempting to reduce the shoulder back into its normal position following a dislocation. It is therefore imperative (from both clinical and medicolegal points of view) that the integrity of the axillary nerve be documented, both after seeing the patient who has a dislocated shoulder, but also following successful reduction.

388E: It has a peak hormonal concentration in the morning

Cortisol is a steroid hormone that is released in stress to cause an increase in blood glucose. It is a catabolic hormone. It is stimulated by ACTH released from the anterior pituitary. ACTH is stimulated by CRH released from the median eminence of the hypothalamus. It has a diurnal variation and peaks on waking up in the morning. Its lowest level is around midnight and this is why a 'midnight cortisol' is used to detect excess cortisol production in Cushing's syndrome.

389A: Immobility

A thrombus is solid material formed from the constituents of blood in flowing blood. Three primary influences predispose to thrombus formation, the so-called Virchow's triad:

- damaged vessel wall – denuded endothelium
- changes in blood flow – turbulence, stasis
- alterations in blood constituents – platelets, clotting factors, blood, hyperlipidaemia, hyperviscosity etc.

The normal, intact endothelium is anti-thrombotic. This prevents the clotting of blood within the normal circulation. When the endothelium is injured, thrombosis occurs. Under physiological circumstances this prevents haemorrhage, as part of the normal haemostatic response to injury. Only when the formation of thrombus becomes excessive does it become pathological, resulting in vascular obstruction or migration of the thrombus to a distant site (embolization).

Heparin and warfarin both reduce the risk of thrombosis by their action on the clotting cascade. Thrombocytopenia means a low platelet count which also reduces the risk of thrombosis. Increased blood viscosity increases the risk of thrombosis ('thicker blood clots more easily'). Immobility increases the risk of thrombosis by stasis.

390D: Second rib

The palpable space immediately inferior to the clavicle is the first intercostal space, and below is the 2nd rib.

391B: It may refer pain to knee

The hip joint, like the shoulder joint, is a synovial joint of the ball and socket variety. In general it can be said that in all joints stability and range of movement are inversely proportional to one another. The shoulder joint is the most commonly dislocated joint in the body because it has adapted for a high degree of mobility at the expense of stability. The hip joint is an exception to the rule and provides a remarkable example of a joint that has a high degree of both mobility and stability. Its stability is largely a result of the adaptation of the acetabulum and femoral head to one another, with a snug fit of the femoral head into the acetabulum, deepened by the labrum and further reinforced by three ligaments on the outside of the capsule (the iliofemoral, ischiofemoral and pubofemoral ligaments). The iliofemoral ligament (of Bigelow) is the strongest of the three ligaments. The short muscles of the gluteal region are important muscular stabilizers. Since the hip is such a stable joint, it requires considerable force to become dislocated. When it does occur, it usually dislocates in the setting of a road traffic accident, where typically the hip joint dislocates posteriorly. The hip's great range of mobility results from the femur having a long neck that is much narrower than its head.

The hip joint lies deep to the pulsation of the femoral artery at the mid-inguinal point (half-way between the anterior superior iliac spine and the symphysis pubis, in contrast to the middle of the inguinal ligament which is half-way between the anterior superior iliac spine and the pubic tubercle, which marks the site of the deep inguinal ring). The mid-inguinal point is the surface marking of the hip joint and pain at this point may indicate pathology originating in the hip joint. Posterior to the hip lies the important sciatic nerve. Consequently, the sciatic nerve is at risk in a posterior surgical approach to the hip, or in a posterior dislocation.

The hip joint is innervated by the sciatic, femoral and obturator nerves (Hilton's law). The knee joint is also innervated by the same nerves. This may explain why hip pathology commonly refers pain to the knee. In a child who presents with a painful knee, examination should always consist of examination of the ipsilateral hip joint, in addition to examination of the knee, so as not to miss a diseased hip.

The blood supply to the femoral head originates from three important sources.

- The most important is via retinacular vessels that run up from the trochanteric anastomosis and then along the neck of the femur to supply the major part of the head. The trochanteric anastomosis is formed by an anastomosis of the medial and lateral circumflex femoral arteries and the superior and inferior gluteal arteries.
- The second supply is from the obturator artery in the ligamentum teres (round ligament). This is usually more important in the young child.
- A third supply is via the nutrient, or diaphyseal, artery of the femur, originating from the profunda femoris artery.

A fractured neck of femur may disrupt these vessels and consequently disrupt the blood flow to the femoral head, resulting in avascular necrosis. This condition frequently occurs in osteoporotic elderly women following a fall. The femoral head must be taken out and replaced with a prosthesis quickly so that mobility may be regained.

392D: PTH acts directly on osteoblasts in bone

Four hormones are primarily concerned with the regulation of calcium metabolism:

- parathyroid hormone (PTH)
- activated vitamin D (1,25-dihydroxycholecalciferol)
- calcitonin (secreted from the parafollicular cells – also known as the clear or C-cells – of the thyroid gland, and relatively unimportant in humans)
- parathyroid hormone-related protein (PTHrP), important in the hypercalcaemia of malignancy.

The main regulatory tissues are bone, kidney and intestine.

Activated vitamin D

The 25-hydroxylation step of vitamin D activation occurs in the liver, whereas the 1-hydroxylation step occurs in the kidneys. Activation of vitamin D requires both activation steps and PTH.

- *Intestine*. 1,25-dihydroxycholecalciferol promotes the intestinal absorption of calcium and phosphate. Absence leads to rickets in children and osteomalacia in adults.
- *Kidneys*. Increased tubular reabsorption of calcium and phosphate.
- *Bone*. Mobilization of calcium and phosphate.

Effects of PTH

PTH is secreted from the chief cells (also known as principal cells) of the parathyroid glands. The major regulator of PTH secretion is extracellular calcium. Circulating ionized calcium acts directly on the parathyroid glands in a negative-feedback fashion to regulate the secretion of PTH. The pituitary gland does not play a role in the secretion of PTH.

- *Bone*. Resorption with calcium and phosphate release into the bloodstream. PTH acts directly on osteoblasts and osteocytes that contain membrane receptors for PTH. Osteoclasts do not themselves have membrane receptors for PTH. Instead, it is believed that the activated osteoblasts and osteocytes send a secondary but "unknown" paracrine signal to the osteoclasts causing them to resorb bone.
- *Kidney*. PTH acts on the kidneys to increase calcium reabsorption and increase phosphate excretion (phosphaturic effect). There is one caveat to this; although PTH enhances renal calcium reabsorption, in hyperparathyroidism urinary calcium excretion is paradoxically increased because the reabsorbing mechanism is saturated. This increases the tendency to renal stone formation in hyperparathyroidism.
- *Intestine*. PTH increases the formation of activated vitamin D and this increases calcium absorption from the gut.

393E: **It generally has a worse outcome than thrombus**

- A thrombus is an organized mass of blood constituents that forms in flowing blood (i.e. in the living body).
- A clot is a solid mass of blood constituents formed in stationary blood when blood is allowed to coagulate outside the body or post-mortem.
- An embolus is an abnormal mass of undissolved material (of solid, liquid or gaseous origin) that is carried in the bloodstream from one place to another.

Thrombus and clot can be readily distinguished from one another at post-mortem (Table 6).

Table 6 Distinguishing thrombus and post-mortem clot

Thrombus	Post-mortem clot
Grey	Dark purple-red
Organized structure forming lines of Zahn (the pale lines are platelet aggregates enmeshed in fibrin, whilst the intervening dark lines are composed of red blood cells)	Separation of red blood cells and plasma producing a 'chicken fat' appearance since red cells often gravitate to the bottom of post-mortem clot
Dull surface and firm consistency	Shiny surface and gelatinous consistency ('redcurrant jelly')
Adherent to vessel wall	Peels away easily from the vessel wall
Dry, granular and friable	Moist and rubbery
Conforms to shape of vessel	Does not conform to shape of vessel
May show features of recanalization	

Veins, rather than arteries, are the most common source of emboli. Emboli most commonly arise from thrombosis formed within the deep veins of the lower limb and pelvis; thrombus formed here is known as a deep vein thrombosis. Anatomy ensures that emboli of venous origin lodge in pulmonary arteries. The size of the pulmonary artery blocked depends on the size of the thrombo-embolus. Usually they are small and lodge in small pulmonary arteries, but sometimes an extensive thrombus from the deep veins ends up as a saddle embolus blocking the main pulmonary artery. This massive pulmonary embolus is the commonest preventable cause of death in hospitalized, bed-bound patients.

An embolus is not always due to thrombus, although about 95 per cent of all emboli are thrombotic. Other emboli include:

- solid material – fat, tumour cells, atheromatous material, foreign matter
- liquid material – amniotic fluid
- gaseous material – air, nitrogen bubbles.

The ischaemia resulting from an embolus tends to be worse than that due to thrombosis because the blockage is so sudden. Thrombi tend to slowly occlude the vessel lumen. Thrombi are therefore less likely to cause infarction since they provide time for the development of alternative perfusion pathways by way of collaterals.

394B: Left suprarenal vein

The left suprarenal vein empties into the left renal vein which crosses the vertebral column to reach the inferior vena cava. The left renal vein also receives the left gonadal vein.

395E: The pulsation of the radial artery may be felt at its base

The contents and boundaries of the anatomical snuffbox are shown in Table 7.

Table 7

Base	From proximal to distal – radial styloid, scaphoid, trapezium, base of 1st metacarpal
Roof	Skin Fascia
Medially (ulnar side)	Extensor pollicis longus tendon
Laterally (radial side)	Extensor pollicis brevis tendon Abductor pollicis longus tendon
Contents	Cephalic vein (beginning in its roof) Terminal branches of radial nerve (supplying the overlying skin) Radial artery (on its floor)

The anatomical snuffbox is an important region clinically for three reasons. First, tenderness within the anatomical snuffbox may indicate a fractured scaphoid bone. This is important to recognize since X-rays are often unremarkable in the early stages and, if left untreated, there is a risk of avascular necrosis of the scaphoid (in fact, the proximal scaphoid segment necroses since it receives its blood supply from distal to proximal). Second, tendonitis of the abductor pollicis longus and extensor pollicis brevis tendons may occur; this is known as DeQuervain's tenovaginitis stenosans. Third, the cephalic vein is almost invariably found in the region of the anatomical snuffbox. The anatomical snuffbox therefore forms a useful landmark for the purpose of gaining intravenous access.

396C: Thyroxine promotes the growth and development of the brain

The thyroid gland primarily produces T4 which is converted to T3 (the more active form) in the periphery. Thyroxine is released when TSH, produced from the anterior pituitary, binds to cell surface receptors on the thyroid gland. TRH is a hypothalamic hormone which causes TSH secretion. TSH release is under inhibitory control by dopamine. Thyroxine increases basal metabolic rate. Protein, carbohydrate and fat metabolism is increased. Thyroxine, although not a steroid, does not act on cell surface receptors, but acts on intracellular receptors bound to promoters of genes. It directly affects gene transcription in this way. Thyroxine plays an extremely important role in the myelination of axons during brain development. Neonatal deficiency leads to reduced axonal conduction velocities at the critical time in development when the brain is growing and maturing, resulting in developmental delay and mental retardation. This is known as cretinism or congenital hypothyroidism. Thyroid replacement therapy must be initiated soon after birth if mental retardation is to be prevented. Affected infants should be identified on neonatal biochemical screening (Guthrie test).

397C: It is an abnormal reduction of the blood supply to, or drainage from, an organ or tissue

- *Ischaemia* is an abnormal reduction of the blood supply to, or drainage from, an organ or tissue.
- *Infarction* is the death of tissues specifically caused by ischaemia or loss of blood supply.
- *Necrosis* refers to generalized tissue death due to toxins, trauma or vascular occlusion.

Ischaemia is most commonly due to vascular narrowing or occlusion from atherosclerosis. However, blood supply to tissues may be inadequate for a variety of reasons, besides vascular occlusion. Thus ischaemia may also result from states of shock (i.e. circulatory collapse with low arterial blood pressure). The commonest causes of shock are insufficient blood volume (hypovolaemia), sepsis and heart failure. In all cases there is a low blood pressure. All tissues may therefore become ischaemic and any organ may fail as a result.

The outcome of ischaemia is determined by a variety of factors:

- The nature of the vascular supply (the most important factor). The presence of collaterals is protective against the effects of ischaemia. Conversely, blockage of an end-artery will almost always cause infarction.
- The tissue involved. The brain and heart are more susceptible to the effects of hypoxia.
- The speed of onset. Slowly developing occlusions are less likely to cause infarction since they provide time for the development of alternative perfusion pathways.
- The degree of obstruction and the calibre of the vessel occluded.
- The oxygen content of the blood supplying the ischaemic tissue.
- The presence of concomitant heart failure.
- The state of the microcirculation, as in diabetes mellitus.

398E: The submucosa of the duodenum

The Brunner glands are located in the submucosa of the duodenum. These glands are connected to the interstitial lumen by ducts that open into certain crypts. They secrete an alkaline product that protects the duodenal mucosa from the acidic chyme and helps achieve an optimal pH for the enzymes.

399C: The suprapatellar bursa (pouch) communicates with the knee joint

The knee joint is a synovial joint (the largest in the body), of the modified hinge variety. The bony contours contribute little to the stability of the joint. Nevertheless, the ligaments and muscles make it a very stable joint which rarely dislocates.

The cruciate ligaments are two very strong ligaments that cross each other within the joint cavity, but are excluded from the synovial cavity by a covering of synovial membrane (they are therefore described as being intracapsular, but extrasynovial). They are crucial in the sense that they are essential for stability of the knee. They are named anterior and posterior according to their tibial attachments. Thus the anterior cruciate ligament is attached to the anterior intercondylar area of the tibia and runs upwards, backwards and laterally to attach itself to the medial surface of the lateral femoral condyle. The anterior cruciate prevents anterior displacement of the tibia on the femur. Backward displacement of the tibia on the femur is prevented by the stronger posterior cruciate ligament. The integrity of the latter is therefore important when walking down stairs or downhill. Tears of the anterior cruciate ligament are common in sports injuries, whereas tears of the posterior cruciate ligament are rare since it is much stronger than the anterior cruciate.

Bursae are lubricating devices found wherever skin, muscle or tendon rubs against bone. There are approximately a dozen bursae related to the knee joint. The details are not important, only the salient points. For instance, it would be important to remember that the suprapatellar bursa communicates with the knee joint. An effusion of the knee may therefore extend some 3–4 finger-breadths above the patella into the suprapatellar pouch. The prepatellar and infrapatellar bursae do not communicate with the knee joint, but may become inflamed causing a painful bursitis. Inflammation of the prepatellar bursa is known as housemaid's knee, whereas that of the infrapatellar bursa is called clergyman's knee.

The menisci, or semilunar cartilages, are cresent-shaped laminae of fibrocartilage, the medial being larger and less curved than the lateral. They have an important role in:

- distributing the load by increasing the congruity of the articulation
- contributing to stability of the knee by their physical presence and by acting as providers of proprioceptive feedback
- acting as shock absorbers through a 'cushioning' effect
- probably assisting in lubrication.

However, the menisci do not play a role in the locking/unlocking mechanism of the knee joint. This is primarily the responsibility of the popliteus muscle.

The menisci are liable to injury from twisting strains applied to a flexed weight-bearing knee. The medial meniscus is much less mobile than the lateral meniscus (because of its strong attachment to the medial collateral ligament of the knee joint) and it cannot as easily accommodate abnormal stresses placed on it. This, in part, explains why meniscal lesions are more much common on the medial side than on the lateral.

The menisci are so effective that if they are removed, the force taken by the articular hyaline cartilage during peak loading increases by about 5-fold. Meniscectomy (removal of the menisci), or damage to the menisci, therefore exposes the articular hyaline cartilage to much greater forces than normal and evidence of degenerative osteoarthritis is seen in 75 per cent of patients 10 years after meniscectomy.

400C: Hyperkalaemia occurs

Diabetic ketoacidosis results from insulin deficiency. Insulin is normally responsible for the uptake of glucose by cells in the body. Most of the pathological features can be attributed to one of the following effects of insulin lack:

- hyperglycaemia in the blood, or
- intracellular glucose deficiency.

A good way of thinking about diabetic ketoacidosis is therefore 'starvation in the midst of plenty'.

Insulin deficiency results in lipolysis, glycogenolysis, gluconeogenesis and ketogenesis, in an analogous way to starvation. The production of ketone bodies results in an acetone breath and a metabolic acidosis with a fall in blood pH. The resulting acidosis stimulates the respiratory centre. This leads to a characteristic breathing pattern seen in diabetic ketoacidosis known as Kussmaul's breathing. Glucose spills over into the urine (glyosuria) when glucose levels exceed the capacity of the kidneys to reabsorb glucose. This produces an osmotic diuresis (with consequent polyuria and polydipsia). The overall effect is a massive loss of fluid in the urine causing dehydration and circulatory collapse. Dehydration is worsened by the vomiting and hyperventilation that may also occur. Circulatory failure in itself worsens the metabolic acidosis (through lactic acidosis, acute renal failure etc.) and leads to uraemia. A vicious circle is set up leading to coma and death.

Insulin is normally responsible for driving potassium into cells. Insulin deficiency therefore results in hyperkalaemia. This is worsened by any dehydration, metabolic acidosis, or renal impairment from circulatory failure, that may also be present. Despite the hyperkalaemia, total body potassium content is actually low (secondary to vomiting, renal losses etc.).

The aims of treatment in diabetic ketoacidosis are three-fold: insulin replacement, rehydration with intravenous fluids and potassium replacement. The latter requires special attention; although potassium is initially high, when insulin is given potassium is rapidly driven into cells resulting in hypokalaemia. Potassium therefore needs to be cautiously and judiciously replaced during the treatment of ketoacidosis.

401C: It induces acute inflammatory changes, maximal at 1–3 days post-infarct

Myocardial infarction is infarction of the myocardium as a result of severe ischaemia leading to necrosis of the myocardium. It is usually due to coronary artery occlusion secondary to atherosclerosis, with or without superimposed thrombosis or plaque haemorrhage. Only rarely is a myocardial infarct due to an embolic event. In at least 10 per cent of patients myocardial infarction is painless or 'silent'; this is particularly true in diabetics and elderly patients because of the accompanying autonomic neuropathy.

If a patient survives an acute infarction, the infarct heals through the formation of scar tissue. The infarcted tissue is not replaced by new cardiac muscle because cardiac myocytes are permanent (non-dividing) cells and cardiac muscle is therefore unable to regenerate. Scar tissue does not possess the usual contractile properties of normal cardiac muscle; the result is contractile dysfunction or congestive cardiac failure.

The macroscopic and microscopic changes of myocardial infarcts follow a predictable sequence of events. The chief features are coagulative necrosis, inflammatory cell infiltration, followed by organization and repair where granulation tissue replaces dead muscle and is gradually converted into scar tissue. The entire process from coagulative necrosis to the formation of well-formed scar tissue takes 6–8 weeks (Table 8).

Table 8 Macroscopic and microscopic changes

Time	Macroscopic changes	Microscopic changes
0–12 hours	None	None
12–24 hours	Infarcted area appears pale with blotchy discolouration	Infarcted muscle brightly eosinophilic with intercellular oedema; beginning of neutrophilic infiltrate
24–72 hours	Infarcted area appears soft and pale; mottling with a yellow-tan infarct centre	Coagulation necrosis and acute inflammatory response most prominent; loss of nuclei and striations; marked infiltration by neutrophils
3–10 days	Hyperaemic border develops around yellow dead muscle	Organization of infarcted area and replacement with granulation tissue; dying neutrophils with macrophages predominating; disintegration and phagocytosis of dead myofibres
Weeks to months	Tough grey-white scar	Progressive collagen deposition; infarct replaced by dense acellular scar

402D: Calcaneo-fibular ligament

The most common ankle sprain is lateral which occurs as a result of excessive inversion of the foot and dorsiflexion of the ankle. The deltoid ligament, also known as the medial ligament of the ankle, is very strong and located at the medial malleolus. Excessive eversion would be the most likely mechanism of injury.

403E: Roots lie in the neck between the scalenus anterior and medius muscles

There are two principal enlargements of the spinal cord, the cervical and lumbar enlargements, that give rise to the brachial and lumbrosacral plexuses respectively, that innervate the upper and lower limbs. Both enlargements are due to the greatly increased mass of motor cells in the anterior horns of grey matter in these situations.

The brachial plexus has root values C5–8 and T1. In 10 per cent of cases the brachial plexus may be either pre-fixed (C4–8) or post-fixed (C6–T2) as an anatomical variant. The anatomical relations of the different parts of the brachial plexus are important:

- *roots* – exit their respective intervertebral foraminae between the scalenus anterior and medius muscles (interscalene space)
- *trunks* – at the base of the posterior triangle of the neck, lying on the 1st rib posterior to the third part of the subclavian artery
- *divisions* – behind the middle third of the clavicle
- *cords* – in the axilla, in intimate relation to the second part of the axillary artery
- *terminal branches* – in relation to the third part of the axillary artery.

The relationships of the roots, trunks and divisions of the brachial plexus to the scalene muscles, 1st rib and clavicle are important. Compression within a fixed space (the thoracic outlet) may lead to symptoms resulting from compression of the brachial plexus and/or nearby vascular structures (subclavian artery and vein). This is known as the thoracic outlet syndrome.

The serratus anterior muscle is innervated by the long thoracic nerve of Bell (C5, 6, 7). This may be remembered by the old aphorism 'C5, 6, 7 – Bell's of heaven'. Denervation of the serratus muscle may result in winging of the scapula.

There are two recognized types of brachial plexus palsy; both usually occur as a result of trauma or obstetric injury. The first type follows injury to the upper roots of the brachial plexus (typically C5–7) and is known as the Erb–Duchenne palsy. The arm typically lies in a waiter's tip position. The second type follows injury to the lower roots of the brachial plexus (typically C8, T1) and is known as Klumpke's palsy. The hand in this case typically takes on the position of a 'claw'.

404E: Congenital adrenal hyperplasia (adrenogenital syndrome) results in virilization and salt wasting

Disorders of the adrenal gland may relate to the adrenal cortex, medulla, or both. There is only one disorder worth mentioning that selectively affects the adrenal medulla. That is a phaeochromocytoma – a tumour of the adrenal medulla that results in the overproduction of catecholamines (such as adrenaline and noradrenaline). This leads to hypertension, headaches, palpitations and sweating (all known effects of adrenaline).

Conditions of the adrenal cortex may result from an overproduction or an underproduction of hormones. An overproduction of cortisol is known as Cushing's syndrome. There are several causes of Cushing's syndrome, the most common being iatrogenic (the use of exogenous steroids). However, the term Cushing's disease is strictly used to describe Cushing's syndrome as a result of an ACTH-producing pituitary tumour, or adenoma.

An overproduction of aldosterone from the zona glomerulosa of the adrenal cortex, as a result of a functioning adenoma, is known as Conn's syndrome. The overproduction of aldosterone leads to increased excretion of potassium and hydrogen ions from the distal convoluted tubule and collecting ducts of the kidney resulting in a hypokalaemic metabolic alkalosis.

Adrenal insufficiency (also known as Addison's disease) results in decreased production of glucocorticoids and mineralocorticoids from the adrenal cortex. It is most commonly a result of destruction of the adrenal cortex by autoimmune adrenalitis. Decreased mineralocorticoid activity results in sodium loss and decreased potassium excretion, with consequent hyperkalaemia, hyponatraemia, volume depletion and hypotension. Hypoglycaemia may occasionally occur as a result of glucocorticoid deficiency and impaired gluconeogenesis. Stresses such as infections, trauma or surgery may precipitate a life-threatening adrenal crisis, which may prove fatal unless corticosteroid therapy is begun immediately.

Congenital adrenal hyperplasia (or adrenogenital syndrome) represents a group of autosomal recessive, inherited metabolic disorders characterized by a deficiency in a particular enzyme involved in the biosynthesis of cortical steroids, particularly cortisol and aldosterone. 21-hydroxylase deficiency accounts for 90 per cent of cases. Steroidogenesis is then channelled into other pathways leading to increased production of androgens, leading to virilization in females and genital enlargement and/or precocious puberty in males. Simultaneously, the deficiency of cortisol results in increased secretion of ACTH, resulting in adrenal hyperplasia. Impaired aldosterone secretion leads to salt wasting. Patients are treated with exogenous steroids which, in addition to providing adequate levels of glucocorticoids, suppress ACTH levels and thus decrease the synthesis of the steroid hormones responsible for many of the clinical abnormalities.

405B: Most commonly occurs at branching points within the circulation

Atherosclerosis is a focal disease of the tunica intima of large and medium-sized arteries and consists of the gradual accumulation of focal raised patches (plaques) on the arterial lining in response to arterial wall injury. Its complications are the main cause of death in urbanized societies.

The anatomical sites of atherosclerosis are somewhat predictable. Plaques generally occur at branching points and bends in arteries exposed to high pressure, pulmonary arteries being relatively spared, veins completely so. The turbulence and eddy currents set up at branching points exposes the intimal surface to haemodynamic injury and encourages the uptake of circulating lipoproteins and macrophages into the vessel wall. Thus atherosclerotic plaques are common at sites of bifurcation such as:

- the entrance to the coronary ostia (causing a myocardial infarction)
- close to where the descending abdominal aorta bifurcates into the common iliac arteries (resulting in an abdominal aortic aneurysm)
- in the internal carotid artery close to where the common carotid bifurcates into internal and external branches (resulting in a cerebrovascular accident)
- close to where the renal arteries break off the aorta (resulting in renal artery stenosis)
- in the ileo-femoral arteries of the lower limb (causing lower limb ischaemia).

The lesions are essentially foci of chronic inflammation in which the macrophages seem to be doing harm. The basic lesion consists of a raised focal plaque within the intima with a core of lipid (mainly cholesterol) and a covering fibrous cap.

The four most important risk factors for atherosclerosis to remember are those that are potentially controllable, namely high cholesterol, diabetes mellitus, smoking and hypertension. All are associated with intimal injury and accelerate atherosclerosis. Atherosclerosis is a reversible disease process so that risk-factor modification ameliorates the size of atherosclerotic plaques. Risk-factor modification forms an essential part of the management of patients with known atherosclerotic disease.

406E: Tibial nerve

Tarsal tunnel syndrome results from entrapment of the tibial nerve as it passes deep to the flexor retinaculum between the medial malleolus and calcaneus.

407C: The musculocutaneous nerve arises from the lateral cord

This is a common question! The three cords of the brachial plexus lie in close relation to the second part of the axillary artery. Thus the posterior, lateral and medial cords lie posteriorly, laterally and medially to the second part of the axillary artery, respectively, in the axilla. There is no anterior cord:

- lateral cord – musculocutaneous nerve
- medial cord – ulnar nerve
- posterior cord – radial nerve, axillary nerve
- medial and lateral cords – median nerve.

408D: It is essential for spermatogenesis

Testosterone is a steroid hormone, secreted by the interstitial cells (of Leydig) within the mature testis. It is essential for the growth and division of the germinal cells in forming sperm and in the development of the secondary sexual characteristics. Sertoli cells, on the other hand, are postulated to act as 'nurse' cells, providing structural and metabolic support for the developing spermatogenic cells.

Whereas follicle stimulating hormone (FSH) is trophic to Sertoli cells, luteinizing hormone (LH) is trophic to the Leydig cells. LH, secreted by the anterior pituitary, stimulates the Leydig cells to secrete testosterone through the formation of cyclic AMP via the G-protein coupled serpentine LH receptor. The secretion of LH in turn depends on the pulsatile release of gonadotrophin-releasing hormone (GnRH) from the hypothalamus. Androgen production from the adrenal cortex (and to a lesser extent from the ovaries) of females is normal and is responsible for the growth of pubic and axillary hair.

409C: One of the first signs of toxicity is perioral paraesthesia

Two separate classes of local anaesthetics exist: amides and esters. Amides account for the majority of local anaesthetics in clinical use, although cocaine is an ester. Local anaesthetics work by blocking sodium channels. This prevents depolarization and thereby propagation of pain impulses along the nerve.

Local anaesthetics tend to block the smaller fibres before the larger ones; that is the smaller pain fibres are blocked first (Aδ and C fibres) with sparing of the larger neurones such as the motor fibres

The addition of adrenaline to local anaesthetic has three effects. First, it prevents bleeding by a direct effect of adrenaline on the local vasculature causing vasoconstriction. Second, by way of vasoconstriction it prevents systemic absorption of the local anaesthetic thereby preventing toxicity/side effects and increasing the local duration of action. Third, by preventing systemic absorption it allows larger doses to be used than would otherwise be allowed in the absence of adrenaline. However, because of this 'vasoconstrictive effect', adrenaline must never be used on pedicles that contain an end-artery (e.g. digits, nose tips, ear lobe, penis) where ischaemic necrosis may result.

It is important that the maximum dose of local anaesthetic not be exceeded, otherwise the consequences may be lethal. This is because local anaesthetics are cardiotoxic by way of blocking sodium channels and interfering with cardiac conduction. One of the earliest and reliable signs of systemic toxicity is perioral tingling. This may be followed by cardiovascular collapse and death.

410E: Caudate lobe of the liver

The greater sac communicates with the lesser sac through the epiploic Foramen of Winslow. The superior boundary is the caudate lobe of the liver. The common bile duct lies in the free edge of the lesser omentum, that forms the anterior boundary. The first part of the duodenum is the inferior boundary. The posterior boundary is the inferior vena cava.

411D: It contains ten tendons within it

The carpal tunnel is a fibro-osseous tunnel situated on the flexor aspect of the proximal part of the hand and lying between the flexor retinaculum and the carpal bones. It contains the median nerve and ten flexor tendons that include:

- four tendons of flexor digitorum superficialis
- four tendons of flexor digitorum profundus

- flexor carpi radialis tendon
- flexor pollicis longus tendon.

The flexor retinaculum is attached to the tubercle of the scaphoid and pisiform proximally and the hook of the hamate and trapezium distally. Its function is to prevent bow-stringing of the flexor tendons at the wrist.

Since the carpal tunnel exists as a confined space, entrapment of the median nerve may occur within it. This is commonly due to a build-up of fluid within the carpal tunnel, or because of hypertrophy of the bones/ligaments/tendons that surround, or are contained within, the carpal tunnel. Compression of the median nerve within the carpal tunnel is known as carpal tunnel syndrome. Note this is different to cubital tunnel syndrome which refers to compression of the ulnar nerve behind the medial epicondyle at the elbow. The ulnar artery and nerve do not pass through the carpal tunnel, but instead pass superficial to the carpal tunnel in their own fibro-osseous tunnel commonly given the name Guyon's canal. The ulnar nerve and artery are therefore unaffected in carpal tunnel syndrome.

The clinical features of carpal tunnel syndrome relate to loss of function of the median nerve. There are both motor and sensory components. The median nerve supplies four muscles in the hand, given by the mnemonic LOAF:

- **l**ateral two lumbricals
- **o**pponens pollicis
- **a**bductor pollicis brevis
- **f**lexor pollicis brevis.

All four muscles are weak in someone with carpal tunnel syndrome. In addition, there is loss of sensation over the lateral three and a half digits, which is median nerve territory. However, since the palmar cutaneous branch of the median nerve passes superficial to the carpal tunnel, there is no loss of sensation over the thenar eminence in someone with carpal tunnel syndrome.

412A: The menopause is associated with an increase in follicle stimulating hormone

Oestrogen production during the menstrual cycle is principally 17β-oestradiol. It increases steadily during the follicular phase to reach a peak prior to ovulation (when it has a positive feedback effect on the anterior pituitary initiating the FSH and LH surges). Both FSH and LH are needed in order for ovulation to take place.

Fertilization of the human ovum normally takes place in the outer third of the fallopian tubes. Over the next 5–7 days the fertilized ovum travels along the uterine tube and spends several days free in the uterus prior to implantation. This involves a complex series of events. A defect in any of the processes leading up to implantation may result in an abnormal extrauterine (ectopic) pregnancy.

At the menopause, follicles disappear and are replaced by fibrous tissue. The decreased production of oestrogens from the ovaries results in loss of the negative-feedback effect of oestrogens on the anterior pituitary and a rise in FSH. This rise in FSH can be measured and used to verify commencement of the menopause.

Oestrogen production is mainly confined to ovarian tissue, but both the adrenal cortex and adipose tissue contribute to oestrogen production. Adipose tissue contains an aromatase enzyme that converts androgens to oestrogens. Oestrogen continues to be produced therefore after the menopause and provides an ongoing stimulus for the formation of breast cancer. Tamoxifen blocks the action of oestrogen on breast tissue and is used in the treatment of breast cancer. Newer aromatase inhibitors block the peripheral conversion of androgens to progesterone. They are used to treat breast cancer in postmenopausal patients when oestrogen production from the ovaries ceases and where the peripheral conversion of androgens to oestrogens becomes more important.

413C: Inhibits platelet aggregation

Aspirin irreversibly blocks the action of the cyclo-oxygenase enzyme that is involved in arachidonic acid metabolism, leading to prostaglandin and thromboxane A2 production. It does this by acetylating a serine residue at the active site, thereby excluding arachidonic acid. Aspirin has anti-inflammatory, analgesic, antipyretic and antiplatelet actions. All four actions result from the decreased production of prostaglandins and thromboxane A2. Aspirin has no effect on the coagulation cascade. The antiplatelet effect of aspirin deserves special mention and is widely used therapeutically in the primary and secondary prevention of cardiovascular and cerebrovascular disease. Aspirin has also recently been shown to have a protective effect against colorectal carcinoma.

The antiplatelet effect of aspirin largely arises through the opposing effects of thromboxane A2 (produced by platelets) in promoting platelet aggregation and prostaglandin I2 (produced by endothelial cells) inhibiting platelet aggregation. Aspirin, by inhibiting the cyclo-oxygenase enzyme, results in decreased production of thromboxane A2 from platelets (thus inhibiting platelet aggregation) and prostaglandin I2 from endothelial cells (thus promoting platelet aggregation). However, the thromboxane A2 effect outweighs the prostaglandin I2 effect for two reasons:

- Aspirin is taken orally, high concentrations of aspirin are found within the portal vein which results in platelets being exposed to a high concentration of aspirin. This is contrary to endothelial cells that are in contact with lower concentrations of aspirin once it has been diluted throughout the body and because of presystemic metabolism of aspirin to salicylate by esterases in the liver.
- Platelets have no nuclei. This means once cyclo-oxygenase is inhibited, production is abolished for the rest of the platelet's lifespan. Thromboxane A2 synthesis does not therefore recover until the affected cohort of platelets is replaced in 7–10 days. Endothelial cells, on the other hand, are nucleated so are able to resynthesize new cyclo-oxygenase enzyme (and therefore prostaglandin I2).

414A: Aortic

The lymphatic drainage of an organ is related to its blood supply. The lymphatic drainage of the testis drains along the testicular artery to reach the lymph nodes along the aorta.

415E: The dorsalis pedis pulse is lateral to the extensor hallucis longus tendon

The arterial supply to the lower limb is important since atherosclerosis within the arteries can lead to peripheral vascular disease and symptoms of intermittent claudication. Determining the level of arterial obstruction requires being able to palpate the pulses of the various parts of the arterial tree. This requires a precise knowledge of anatomy.

The aorta bifurcates into the common iliac vessels at the level of L4. The common iliac bifurcates into the external and internal iliac vessels. As the external iliac artery passes under the inguinal ligament it changes its name to the common femoral artery. Thus the femoral artery is a direct continuation of the external iliac artery. The pulsation of the femoral artery may be palpated at the mid-inguinal point (at a point half-way between the anterior superior iliac spine and the symphysis pubis). This is different from the mid-point of the inguinal ligament which corresponds to a point half-way along the inguinal ligament (between the anterior superior iliac spine and the pubic tubercle) which marks the site of the deep inguinal ring.

Between 3 and 4 cm below the inguinal ligament the common femoral artery divides into superficial femoral and deep femoral (profunda femoris) branches. The superficial femoral artery is the commonest site for peripheral vascular disease in the lower limb. The superficial femoral artery continues through the adductor canal (also known as the subsartorial or Hunter's canal) and after passing through the adductor hiatus becomes known as the popliteal artery. Within the popliteal fossa, the popliteal artery lies deep to the tibial nerve and the popliteal vein. This explains why a normal popliteal artery is so difficult to feel. A palpable popliteal artery normally implies it is aneurysmal (abnormally dilated).

The popliteal artery bifurcates into anterior and posterior tibial arteries. The posterior tibial artery is easily palpated posterior to the medial malleolus at the level of the ankle. A useful mnemonic for remembering the order of structures behind the medial malleolus (from anterior to posterior) is 'Tom, Dick and Harry':

- Tom = **t**ibialis posterior tendon (most anteriorly)
- Dick = flexor **d**igitorum longus tendon
- and = **a**rtery (posterior tibial), **n**erve (tibial nerve)
- Harry = flexor **h**allucis longus tendon (most posteriorly).

The anterior tibial artery continues down into the foot as the dorsalis pedis artery. However, in 10 per cent of subjects this is absent. The pulsation of dorsalis pedis may be felt lateral to the extensor hallucis longus tendon, between the first and second metatarsals. A useful mnemonic for remembering the order of structures in the anterior compartment of the leg (from medial to lateral) is 'Tim hath a very nasty disease, parathyroid':

- Tim = **t**ibialis anterior tendon (most medially)
- hath = extensor **h**allucis longus tendon
- a very nasty = neurovascular bundle consisting of **a**rtery (dorsalis pedis), **v**eins (venae comitantes of anterior tibial) and **n**erve (deep peroneal nerve)
- disease = extensor **d**igitorum longus tendon
- parathyroid = **p**eroneus tertius tendon (most laterally).

416A: Acclimatization of the sweating mechanism occurs in response to heat

Thermoregulation is one of the principal functions of the hypothalamus (not thalamus). The central thermodetectors are located primarily within the preoptic area of the hypothalamus and to a lesser extent the adjacent areas of the anterior hypothalamus.

The apocrine sweat glands of the axilla, perineum and breast areolae play little role in thermoregulation. They are analogous to the odiferous glands of many mammals, but their biological significance in humans is unknown. It is the eccrine sweat glands that play an important role in heat loss by evaporation.

Non-shivering thermogenesis in brown fat is particularly important in keeping human infants and hibernating mammals warm. This process involves the uncoupling of oxidative phosphorylation within mitochondria via a specialized protein in the inner mitochondrial membrane called thermogenin. In adults, however, the importance of brown adipose tissue in heat generation is relatively small.

Humans are one of only a few animals who acclimatize actively to heat. When exposed to hot weather for a period of 1–6 weeks, a person sweats progressively more profusely. This increased effectiveness of the sweating mechanism is caused by a direct increase in the sweating capability of the sweat glands themselves. Also associated with acclimatization is a decrease in the concentration of sodium chloride in the sweat, which allows the conservation of body salt. Most of this effect is caused by increased secretion of aldosterone.

417A: Reduced surface mucus secretion

Within the normal gastric epithelium there is a fine balance between the normal damaging forces (such as gastric acidity and peptic enzymes) and various protective mechanisms (such as surface mucus production, bicarbonate secretion, mucosal blood flow, elaboration of prostaglandins, tight junctions between cells, epithelial regenerative capacity etc.). Any disruption to this fine balance, either as a result of increased damaging forces, or through impaired defences, may result in epithelial damage and formation of a peptic ulcer. One of the main drawbacks of aspirin is the risk of gastric erosions and peptic ulcer disease that is associated with its use. This is principally brought about through the following mechanisms:

- a direct irritant effect of aspirin
- a reduction in PGE2 (that normally serves to increase local mucus and bicarbonate secretion thereby protecting the gastric mucosal lining)
- a reduction in PGI2 (thereby resulting in reduced blood flow to the gastric lining, mucosal ischaemia and preventing the elimination of acid that has diffused into the submucosa)
- increased acid production from gastric parietal cells (prostaglandins normally inhibit acid secretion)
- the anti-platelet effect of aspirin which propagates any bleeding that may result from an already injured gastric mucosal surface.

Aspirin has no effect on gastric motility. Patients over 65 years old, or those with a history of a previous peptic ulcer, should have a proton pump inhibitor (such as omeprazole) co-administered with aspirin. This has been shown to reduce the risk of gastrointestinal bleeding and peptic ulceration.

418A: Superior rectal vein

Internal haemorrhoids are formed by varicosities of the branches of the superior rectal vein. External haemorrhoids are formed by varicosities of the branches of the inferior rectal vein.

419A: The cephalic vein lies within the deltopectoral groove

The superficial venous drainage of the upper and lower extremities forms an important piece of applied anatomy. There are four veins that the student should know well: the cephalic and basilic veins in the upper limb and the long and short saphenous veins of the lower limb. All run from superficial to deep and contain valves within their lumen. Both these factors prevent the reflux of blood and encourage venous return to the heart.

The cephalic vein of the upper limb commences in the roof of the anatomical snuffbox and runs up the lateral border of the arm. It lies within the groove between the deltoid and pectoralis major muscle (the deltopectoral groove) and ends by piercing the clavipectoral fascia to enter the axillary vein.

The basilic vein runs up the medial border of the upper limb. It perforates the deep fascia in the middle of the arm, half-way between the elbow and axilla, and becomes the axillary vein at the lower border of teres major.

The long (great) saphenous vein, the longest vein in the body, begins as the upward continuation of the medial marginal vein of the foot. It courses upwards in front of the medial malleolus, in close proximity to the saphenous nerve, and runs up to lie a hand's breadth behind the medial border of the patella. It ends by passing through the cribriform fascia that covers the saphenous opening of the fascia lata. Here it joins the femoral vein at the saphenofemoral junction.

The long saphenous vein is important clinically for three reasons. First, incompetence of the valves within it may lead to the formation of superficial venous dilatations in the distribution of the long saphenous vein. These are known as varicose veins. Second, because the anatomy of the long saphenous vein is so reliable (more so than any other vein in the body), it makes the long saphenous vein a good choice for a venous cut-down, if emergency venous access is required. Third, because of its remarkably constant anatomy and because the long saphenous vein is the longest vein in the body, the long saphenous vein is often harvested in vascular surgery and used to bypass arterial obstructions, a good example being in the case of coronary artery bypass grafting procedures where the long saphenous vein is one of many grafts that may be used to bypass blocked coronary arteries.

The short (small) saphenous vein drains the lateral margin of the foot and lies with the sural nerve behind the lateral malleolus. It passes upwards in the subcutaneous fat to the midline of the calf and pierces the deep fascia to enter the popliteal vein at the saphenopopliteal junction. Like the long saphenous vein, the short saphenous vein is vulnerable to the formation of varicosities.

A number of tributaries join the great saphenous vein in the region of the saphenous opening. This is important for two reasons. First, they may form a site for recurrence following varicose vein surgery. Second, the fact that the upper end of the long saphenous vein has these tributaries converging upon it easily distinguishes it from the femoral vein, which at this level only receives the long saphenous vein itself. It is imperative that the long saphenous vein is distinguished from the femoral vein at the saphenofemoral junction, during varicose vein surgery, in order to prevent inadvertent ligation of the femoral vein, which one hears about from time to time in medicolegal reports.

If surgery is performed for varicose veins (a high ligation tie and stripping of the vein), the saphenous nerve (a branch of the femoral nerve) is vulnerable to injury when stripping the long saphenous vein because of its close proximity to the long saphenous vein. Likewise, the sural nerve is at risk of being injured in stripping of the short saphenous vein.

420A: Cyclizine acts on the histaminergic system

Antiemetics are drugs that are used clinically to suppress the vomiting reflex. This is mediated primarily through their suppressive effect at specialized sites within the central nervous system wherein the vomiting reflex is mediated, namely the vomiting centre, chemoreceptor trigger zone in the area postrema (an area of the brain which is devoid of blood–brain barrier and thereby in direct contact with emetogenic chemicals within the bloodstream) and the vestibular system (the latter site explains motion sickness).

A vast array of drugs are used within the clinical setting, all of which act at different sites within the nervous system and upon different neurochemical systems, yet all result in a similar desired effect (i.e. suppression of vomiting). The clinical importance of this is pharmacological synergy, namely the additive effect of two different antiemetics used in combination being greater than the sum of the two separate effects because of the different mechanisms of action. It also allows the astute clinician to pick and choose an antiemetic (and thereby a mode of action) that conforms well to a specified clinical scenario (Table 9).

Table 9

Chemical neurotransmitter	Examples of drugs
Acetylcholine	Anticholinergics (e.g. hyoscine)
Histamine	Antihistamines (e.g. cyclizine)
5-hydroxytryptamine (serotonin)	5-HT3 receptor antagonists (e.g. ondansetron, granisetron)
Dopamine	Dopamine antagonists (e.g. metoclopramide, domperidone, prochlorperazine)

A good example is motion sickness which seems to depend on the influential effect of the environment on the vestibular system, the effects of which in turn are mediated through the cholinergic system. It is thus easy to see why hyoscine is the most efficacious drug in the setting of motion sickness, but is less efficacious in other situations. Dopamine antagonists, such as metoclopramide, and 5-HT3 antagonists are ineffective in the treatment or prevention of motion sickness. Similarly, domperidone is the drug of choice in Parkinson's disease since it is a dopamine antagonist that does not cross the blood–brain barrier; if metoclopramide were to be used instead (similarly a dopamine antagonist but does cross the blood–brain barrier) symptoms of Parkinson's disease would be exacerbated.

421E: Ulnar nerve

A 'claw hand' is associated with injury to the ulnar nerve at the wrist affecting the interossei, lumbricals and hypothenar muscles of the hand. It is characterized by hypothenar eminence wasting, hyperextended metacarpophalangeal joints and flexed interphalangeal joints.

422B: All the interossei are supplied by the ulnar nerve

The basic action of the interossei and lumbrical muscles is to cause extension at the interphalangeal joints and flexion at the metacarpophalangeal joints. In addition, the palmar interossei adduct the fingers (PAD), while the dorsal interossei abduct the fingers (DAB). The lateral two lumbricals are supplied by the median nerve and the medial two lumbricals by the ulnar nerve. However, all the interossei are supplied by the ulnar nerve. As a general rule all the intrinsic muscles of the hand are supplied by the ulnar nerve (T1), except for the LOAF muscles (lateral two lumbricals, opponens pollicis, abductor pollicis brevis and flexor pollicis brevis muscles).

The hand receives a rich arterial supply from both the radial and ulnar arteries. In the palm they anastomose to form two palmar arterial arcades, the superficial and deep palmar arches. The superficial palmar arch is formed by a direct continuation of the ulnar artery meeting the superficial palmar branch of the radial artery. The deep palmar arch is an arterial arcade formed by the terminal branch of the radial artery anastomosing with the deep branch of the ulnar artery. For a visual assessment of the contribution of the radial and ulnar arteries to the blood supply of the hand, Allen's test may be performed. Make a clenched fist and occlude the radial and ulnar arteries. When the fist is released the skin of the palm is seen to be pale, but colour should return rapidly on the release of either one of the arteries. If there is an obvious delay after releasing the ulnar artery compared with the radial, it suggests that the radial supply is dominant and that procedures that might damage the radial artery (such as cannulation) should be avoided.

The deep fascia of the palm is known as the palmar aponeurosis. It is continuous proximally with the flexor retinaculum and widens distally in the hand by dividing into four slips, one for each finger. The palmar aponeurosis is firmly attached to the skin of the palm and assists the latter in gripping an object. Also by virtue of its toughness, it protects the underlying tendons and synovial sheaths. Contracture of the palmar aponeurosis and its digital slips may occur, resulting in fixed flexion deformities of the fingers concerned (usually the ring and little fingers). This is known as Dupuytren's contracture. Dupuytren's contracture is a phenomenon of the palmar aponeurosis and has nothing to do with the underlying muscles or tendons. Ischaemic contracture of muscle is known instead as Volkmann's ischaemic contracture. The latter usually results from an arterial injury, as a complication of a fracture, or following compartment syndrome. It results from the replacement of muscle by fibrous tissue, which contracts to produce a deformity.

423D: Streptokinase

Thrombolytics are substances that break down fibrin (fibrinolytics). Streptokinase is used as a therapeutic fibrinolytic agent in the management of acute myocardial infarction. Warfarin prevents the formation of thrombus by decreasing the amount of vitamin K-dependent clotting factors, but it does not possess fibrinolytic activity. Heparin potentiates the action of antithrombin and also prevents the formation of thrombus, but has no fibrinolytic activity. Aspirin is an antiplatelet agent that acts by reducing the aggregation of platelets. Fibrinogen is a precursor of fibrin, which is involved in the formation of thrombus.

Section 2
Principles of Surgery-in-General

Extended matching questions

1. Blood transfusions

A Group A RhD-negative
B Group B RhD-positive
C Group O RhD-positive
D Group O RhD-negative
E Anti-D immunoglobulin
F Iron sulphate tablets

For each of the patients described below, select the single best treatment from the options listed above. Each option may be used once, more than once or not at all.

1 A 35-year-old woman with blood group B RhD-negative following a left-sided nephrectomy is found to have a haemoglobin level of 6.5.
2 A 66-year-old man with prostate carcinoma and blood group A RhD-positive is found to have a haemoglobin level of 7.1.
3 A patient with blood group B RhD-positive following a right-sided hemicolectomy is found to have a haemoglobin level of 9.4.
4 A 75-year-old man with metastatic colorectal carcinoma and blood group O RhD negative is found to have a haemoglobin level of 7.3.
5 A woman with blood group B RhD-negative and thyroid disease is found to have a haemoglobin level of 11.0 having just given birth to a baby with blood group B RhD-positive.

2. Lumps in the groin

A Testicular cancer
B Testicular torsion
C Direct inguinal hernia
D Indirect inguinal hernia
E Varicocele
F Hydrocele
G Sebaceous cyst
H Epididymal cyst
I Epididymo-orchitis

For each of the patients described below, select the single most likely diagnosis from the options listed above. Each option may be used once, more than once or not at all.

6 A 27-year-old man presents with a soft lump in the right scrotum. On examination there is a positive cough impulse and the doctor is unable to get above the lump. The patient is able to push the lump back, and when the doctor places his fingers over the right groin the lump does not reappear even when the patient coughs.
7 A 26-year-old man presents with a 3-day history of pain in the left scrotum. On examination the scrotum is hot, swollen and tender.

8 A 22-year-old man presents with a painless swelling in the right scrotum. On examination the swelling is non-tender but contains a firm mass which does not seem separate from the testicle. The scrotal swelling brightly transilluminates.

9 A 32-year-old man presents complaining of a 'dragging' sensation in the left scrotum. On examination, the doctor can palpate a soft mass which feels like a 'bag of worms' but only when the patient is standing.

10 A 21-year-old man presents with sudden onset of left testicular pain which came on 2 hours ago. When the doctor tries to examine him, he almost jumps off the bed.

3. Lumps in the neck

A Lymph node
B Branchial cyst
C Thyroglossal cyst
D Cystic hygroma
E Epidermal cyst
F Salivary gland calculus
G Warthin's tumour
H Pleomorphic adenoma
I Multinodular goitre

For each of the patients described below, select the single most likely diagnosis from the options listed above. Each option may be used once, more than once or not at all.

11 A 34-year-old man presents with a firm lump in the right side of his neck just below the mandible. The lump measures 3 cm. The skin appears attached to the lump and there is a small punctum visible.

12 A 25-year-old man has a small lump in the midline of his neck. The lump is non-tender and rises on protruding the tongue.

13 A 33-year-old woman is referred by her GP with a 3 cm firm lump on the right side of her neck. The lump moves on swallowing but does not move on protruding the tongue. Her mother had thyroid cancer.

14 A 14-year-old girl presents with a 2 cm soft, fluctuant lump on the right side of her neck adjacent to the angle of the mandible. The lump transilluminates and is cystic on ultrasound.

15 A 45-year-old man complains of an intermittent swelling that is sometimes painful on the left side of his face and upper jaw. He has linked it to meal times and tried different foods but there has been no improvement.

4. Diseases of the hepatobiliary system

A Plain abdominal X-ray
B Pelvic X-ray
C Ultrasound scan
D Non-contrast-enhanced CT
E Contrast-enhanced CT
F Endoscopic retrograde cholangiopancreatogram (ERCP)
G Magnetic resonance cholangiopancreatogram (MRCP)
H Percutaneous transhepatic cholangiopancreatogram (PTC)

For each of the patients described below, select the single best investigation from the options listed above. Each option may be used once, more than once or not at all.

16 A 65-year-old woman is referred with a 4-month history of weight loss and progressive jaundice. Her CA19-9 is raised and her ultrasound reveals dilated hepatic ducts. ERCP was attempted but was abandoned due to failure of passage of the scope beyond the distal common bile duct stricture.

17 A 43-year-old woman who is rather overweight presents with a 3-day history of right upper quadrant pain, fevers and vomiting. Her liver biochemistry is within normal limits but she does demonstrate a neutrophilia.

18 A 60-year-old woman with a previous history of gallstones presents with colicky abdominal pain and vomiting. Her abdomen is distended and bowel sounds are increased. She is often constipated but feels that this is different.

19 A 35-year-old man with a history of alcohol abuse presents to A&E with a 2-day history of epigastric pain. His amylase on admission is 1200 and he is pyrexial. His liver biochemistry demonstrates an obstructive picture.

20 A 45-year-old woman presents with right upper quadrant pain and vomiting. Her bilirubin and alkaline phosphatase are raised. A stone is seen in the common bile duct on ultrasound and measures 1.2 cm. The common bile duct itself measures 1.3 cm.

5. Fractures of the hip

A Traction
B Dynamic hip screw
C Cannulated screws
D Intramedullary hip screw
E Uncemented hemiarthroplasty
F Cemented hemiarthroplasty
G Total hip replacement

For each of the patients described below, select the single best treatment from the options listed above. Each option may be used once, more than once or not at all.

21 A 67-year-old woman suffers from rheumatoid arthritis which affects both hips. She falls when walking back from town. Her plain X-ray reveals an intracapsular fracture of the femoral neck.

22 A 62-year-old man is knocked off his bike and has an intertrochanteric fracture of the left femur which extends down the shaft.

23 A 35-year-old woman is hit by a car. The plain X-ray shows an intracapsular fracture of the right femoral neck.

24 An 80-year-old woman trips on the pavement and falls. Her plain X-ray reveals an intracapsular femoral neck fracture.

25 An 80-year-old man slips in the bathroom and presents to A&E with a shortened left leg. The plain X-ray demonstrates an extracapsular fracture of the femoral neck.

6. Arterial blood gases

A Metabolic acidosis
B Metabolic acidosis with compensation
C Metabolic alkalosis
D Metabolic alkalosis with compensation
E Respiratory acidosis
F Respiratory acidosis with compensation
G Respiratory alkalosis
H Respiratory alkalosis with compensation

For each of the combination of test results below, select the single most likely diagnosis from the options listed above. Each option may be used once, more than once or not at all.

26 pH = 6.95, Po_2 = 10 kPa, Pco_2 = 4.1 kPa, BE = –8.5
27 pH = 7.26, Po_2 = 10 kPa, Pco_2 = 4.0 kPa, BE = –5.2
28 pH = 7.69, Po_2 = 10 kPa, Pco_2 = 6.1 kPa, BE = +1.3
29 pH = 7.59, Po_2 = 10 kPa, Pco_2 = 2.3 kPa, BE = –5.5

7. ATLS classification of haemorrhagic shock

A Class I
B Class II
C Class III
D Class IV

For each of the patients described below, select the single most likely classification from the options listed above. Each option may be used once, more than once or not at all.

30 A 35-year-old woman suffers from endometriosis and bleeds heavily every month. Her heart rate is 105/min and all other parameters are normal.
31 A 13-year-old boy has a nasal angiofibroma and loses 2 per cent of his circulating volume following a nosebleed. His pulse is 120/min.
32 A 25-year-old man is hit by a car and has multiple fractures. His pulse is 133/min, BP is 110/85 mmHg, respiratory rate is 24/min, and urine output is 35 mL/min.
33 An 85 kg man has had a handlebar injury and lacerated his liver. It is estimated that he has bled approximately 2 L into his abdomen.
34 A 45-year-old man is brought in from a road traffic accident. His pulse is 160/min, BP is 75/50 mmHg, and he is unresponsive.

8. Burns

A 1 per cent
B 9 per cent
C 18 per cent
D 27 per cent
E 36 per cent
F 45 per cent
G 54 per cent

For each of the patients described below, select the single best assessment of burns extent from the options listed above. Each option may be used once, more than once or not at all.

35 A man suffers full-thickness burns to his perineum.
36 A man suffers full-thickness burns to the whole of his left arm.
37 A woman suffers full-thickness burns to her face and head.
38 A woman suffers full-thickness burns to the whole of her left leg.
39 A man suffers full-thickness burns to his back.

9. Jaundice

A Biliary colic
B Prehepatic jaundice
C Hepatocellular jaundice

D Gallstone in common bile duct
E Sclerosing cholangitis
F Carcinoma of head of pancreas
G Cholangiocarcinoma
H Pancreatitis
I Gallstone ileus
J Mirizzi syndrome

For each of the patients described below, select the single most likely diagnosis from the options listed above. Each option may be used once, more than once or not at all.

40 A 45-year-old woman presents to A&E with epigastric pain, jaundice, vomiting and fever. Her bilirubin is 125 μmol/L, ALT 135 iu/L, alkaline phosphatase 700 iu/L, WBC 21×10^9/L and amylase 115 U/mL. On ultrasound the gall bladder wall measures 5 mm and gallstones are seen. The common bile duct measures 9 mm in diameter and the intrahepatic ducts are prominent.

41 A 65-year-old woman presents to her GP with general malaise and grumbling abdominal pain. Her daughter thinks she is looking a little yellow. Her GP refers her for a specialist opinion and on examination there is a mass in the right upper quadrant.

42 An obese 40-year-old woman presents to A&E complaining of a 5-day history of epigastric pain, jaundice and vomiting. She has upper abdominal tenderness and deranged liver biochemistry. An ultrasound reveals a common bile duct diameter of 8 mm, no intrahepatic duct dilatation, and a thin-walled gall bladder containing sludge but no gallstones are seen.

43 A 23-year-old man returns from a holiday in the Far East. He presents to A&E with fever and jaundice. His bilirubin and ALT are raised but the rest of his liver biochemistry is within normal limits.

44 A 45-year-old woman presents with epigastric tenderness and jaundice. She has deranged liver biochemistry and a long history of inflammatory bowel disease.

45 A 15-year-old boy of African origin presents with splenomegaly and jaundice. He is complaining of abdominal pain and his bilirubin is 100 μmol/L.

10. Paediatric abdomen

A Gastro-oesophageal reflux disease
B Pyloric stenosis
C Duodenal atresia
D Malrotation
E Volvulus
F Intussusception
G Meconium ileus
H Hirschsprung's disease
I Meckel's diverticulum

For each of the patients described below, select the single most likely diagnosis from the options listed above. Each option may be used once, more than once or not at all.

46 An 8-month-old boy presents with vomiting and rectal bleeding. There is a sausage-shaped mass palpable in the left side of the abdomen.

47 A 3-day-old boy with Down's syndrome presents with vomiting and dehydration. A plain abdominal X-ray demonstrates two bubbles of gas in the upper abdomen.

48 A 7-week-old boy is brought into A&E. He presents with non-bilious vomiting and dehydration, and on examination there is an olive-sized mass in the right upper quadrant.

49 A 4-year-old girl presents with dark-red rectal bleeding. She is anaemic but haemodynamically stable. On examination there are no significant findings.

50 A 3-day-old girl with cystic fibrosis has a palpable mass in the right lower quadrant. A plain abdominal X-ray reveals dilated small bowel loops.

11. Swollen painful joints

A Osteoarthritis
B Gout
C Rheumatoid arthritis
D Tuberculosis arthritis
E Neuropathic joint disease

For each of the patients described below, select the single most likely diagnosis from the options listed above. Each option may be used once, more than once or not at all.

51 A 35-year-old woman develops pain, swelling and stiffness of her hands. On examination, 2 years after the onset of her joint complaints, she is found to have swelling and tenderness in relation to the metacarpo-phalangeal joints. X-rays of the affected joints show diminution of joint space, osteoporosis and marginal erosions of the articulating bones.

52 A 60-year-old woman complains of pain and swelling in both her knees of gradual onset over a duration of 2 years. On examination, there is evidence of excess synovial fluid and synovial thickening in both knee joints and local tenderness. Standing X-rays of her knees show diminution of joint space, sclerosis and cysts in the adjacent bones. Osteophytes are also seen at the articular margins.

12. Pathological fractures

A Osteosarcoma
B Osteomalacia
C Metastatic carcinoma
D Osteoblastoma
E Ewing's sarcoma

For each of the patients described below, select the single most likely diagnosis from the options listed above. Each option may be used once, more than once or not at all.

53 A 14-year-old boy has suffered with left knee pain, which has been gradually increasing in severity over the last month. It is constant in nature and keeps him awake at night. On examination, the overlying skin is warm and shiny. A radiograph of the knee joint demonstrates bone destruction in the metaphysis of the left femur with areas of new bone formation and periosteal elevation.

54 A 16-year-old boy presents with pain in his right upper arm. There is no history of trauma. On examination, he is well with a hot, hard swelling in the middle of his right arm. X-rays demonstrate an onion skin-shaped bone lesion in the medulla of the humerus.

13. Nerve root/nerve injuries

A Forth lumbar nerve root
B Fifth lumbar nerve root
C First sacral nerve root
D Sciatic nerve
E Tibial nerve
F Common peroneal nerve
G Deep peroneal nerve
H Superficial peroneal nerve

For each of the patients described below, select the nerve root or nerve that is the most likely diagnosis from the options listed above. Each option may be used once, more than once or not at all.

55 A wholesale market producer has been experiencing pain in the lower back for 3 months. During the last 3 weeks he has noticed that the pain radiates down the back of his left leg and now he has difficulty walking. On examination, elevating his left lower limb aggravates the pain. There is diminished sensation on his left heel and along the lateral border of his left foot. The ankle jerk is absent on this side.

56 A construction worker presents with loss of sensation over the front and lateral side of his leg and foot. There is no foot drop, but he is unable to evert his foot.

14. Skin conditions

A Basal cell carcinoma
B Malignant melanoma
C Squamous cell carcinoma
D Solar keratosis
E Keratocanthoma

For each of the patients described below, select the single most likely pathological condition from the options listed above. Each option may be used once, more than once or not at all.

57 An 80-year-old retired builder presents with a chronic and slowly enlarging skin lesion over his left cheek. On examination, this lesion is pearly white with an associated telangiectasia.

58 An 82-year-old retired woman presents with a 2-month history of a facial skin lesion. The lesion has now disappeared.

59 A 34-year-old lawyer presents with an itchy brown pigmented lesion on her right lower limb. She states it occasionally bleeds.

15. Trauma patient

A Tension pneumothorax
B Cardiac tamponade
C Flail segment
D Ruptured spleen
E Haemothorax

For each of the patients described below, select the single most likely diagnosis from the options listed above. Each option may be used once, more than once or not at all.

60 A 39-year-old woman was a pedestrian hit by a car while crossing the road. She complains of chest and abdominal pains. On examination, her GCS score is 14/15 (E4, V4, M6). Her vital observations are as follows: BP 86/32 mmHg; pulse 145/min. She has bruising and tenderness over her lower left 9th and 10th ribs. She has rebound tenderness and guarding over the left upper quadrant of her abdomen. Her chest X-ray demonstrates left rib fractures affecting ribs 8–10.

61 A 44-year-old man is involved in a road traffic accident. He was a driver of a delivery truck, travelling at 50 miles/h and was hit from the side. On arrival at A&E he is unstable. His vital observations are as follows: BP 90/32 mmHg; pulse 160/min; respirator rate 45 breaths/min. On examination, his neck veins are engorged and distended. His trachea is central with quiet heart sounds.

16. Lower leg ulceration

A Chronic obliterative arterial disease
B Venous ulcer
C Traumatic ulcer
D Rheumatoid arthritis
E Squamous cell carcinoma

For each of the patients described below, select the single most likely diagnosis from the options listed above. Each option may be used once, more than once or not at all.

62 A 72-year-old woman presents with an ulcer over the anteromedial aspect of the lower limb. It is flat, with edges sloping towards the centre, and has seropurulent discharge. She does not recall any trauma. She has suffered 'for years' with an aching pain over the leg due to her varicose veins. Over the last 2 months she has noted that this area is now brown in colour.

63 An 80-year-old retired cook has noticed that the edge of an ulcer situated above the medial malleolus for 17 years has recently become 'heaped up' and bleeds easily on contact.

17. Aneurysms

A Immediate ultrasound
B Insert intravenous lines, cross-match blood and transfer to theatre
C Immediate CT head scan
D Immediate CT chest scan
E Immediate endovascular stenting

For each of the patients described below, select the single most appropriate initial line of management from the options listed above. Each option may be used once, more than once or not at all.

64 A 67-year-old man is admitted as an emergency with back pain. He is found to be shocked with a blood pressure of 90/40 mmHg. An epigastric mass is palpable and tender.

65 A 67-year-old man is admitted with a palpable expansive epigastric mass and thoracic back pain. His blood pressure is normal and there is gross widening of the mediastinum on chest X-ray.

66 A 26-year-old man is admitted following a sudden onset of severe headache coupled with photophobia and neck stiffness.

18. Metabolic disorders of adrenal dysfunction

A Cushing's disease
B Cushing's syndrome
C Conn's syndrome
D Addison's disease
E Multiple endocrine neoplasia type 1 (Werner's syndrome)
F Multiple endocrine neoplasia type 2a

For each of the patients described below, select the single most appropriate diagnosis from the options listed above. Each option may be used once, more than once or not at all.

67 A 30-year-old woman with known pernicious anaemia suffers with dizzy spells, fatigue and lethargy. Her investigations reveal a low blood pressure and high serum potassium concentration.

68 A 42-year-old woman presents with epigastric pain. Her past medical history includes: peptic ulcers and hirsutism. She is under investigations for bilateral lower limb oedema. Her recent blood tests demonstrate hypercalcaemia and hypoglycemia.

19. Paediatric urogenital conditions

A Inguinal hernia
B Epispadias
C Hypospadias
D Non-communicating hydrocele
E Communicating hydrocele
F Posterior urethral valves

For each child described below, select the single most appropriate diagnosis from the options listed above. Each option may be used once, more than once or not at all.

69 A newborn is referred, as his mother is concerned that he does not appear to urinate from the end of his penis. His urinary stream points downwards. On examination, his external urethral meatus is located on the ventral aspect of the penile shaft.

70 A 2-year-old boy is referred with a scrotal swelling during the day. At night, it resolves. On examination, there is a fluctuant transilluminable swelling in the right scrotum. It is not possible to get above the swelling. No bowel sounds are auscultated in the swelling.

20. Vomiting

A Gastric volvulus
B Oesophageal varices
C Caecal carcinoma
D Strangulated hernia
E Achalasia

For each of the patients described below, select the single most likely diagnosis from the options listed above. Each option may be used once, more than once or not at all.

71 A 30-year-old woman presents with acute abdominal pain localized to her umbilicus. She also presents with vomiting. She underwent a diagnostic laparoscopy 5 days earlier, which was negative.

72 A 55-year-old writer presents to A&E with abdominal pain and haematemesis. On examination, he is ethanolic with hepatomegaly. He is also noted to have spider naevi and palmar erythema.

21. Paediatric gastrointestinal disorders

A Hypertrophic pyloric stenosis
B Intussusception
C Gastro-oesophageal reflux
D Mesenteric adenitis
E Meckel's diverticulum
F Appendicitis

For each of the patients described below, select the single most likely diagnosis from the options listed above. Each option may be used once, more than once or not at all.

73 A 6-month-old boy presents with colicky abdominal pain, two episodes of bilious vomiting and rectal bleeding. On examination, the abdomen is tender in the right hypochondrium and there is a sausage-shaped palpable mass.

74 A 6-year-old boy presents with two episodes of vomiting, coupled with central abdominal pain. He has a 2-day history of a sore throat and enlarged tonsils. On examination, he is apyrexial (but his mother reports a temperature of 38°C yesterday) with a pulse rate of

100/min. His mucosa membranes are dry with increased skin turgor. His tonsils are enlarged with obvious pus. His abdomen is soft, but tender to palpation.

75 A 2-year-old boy presents with dark-red rectal bleeding and general pallor. There has been no vomiting and abdominal examination is unremarkable.

76 A 4-week-old boy presents with non-bilious vomiting after feeding for 1 week. He has lost weight and is clinically dehydrated.

22. Rectal pain

A Rectal prolapse
B Solitary rectal ulcer syndrome
C Carcinoma of the rectum
D Fissure-in-ano
E Proctalgia fugax
F First-degree haemorrhoids

For each of the patients described below, select the single most likely diagnosis from the options listed above. Each option may be used once, more than once or not at all.

77 An 18-year-old girl presents with a 3-week history of severe pain at defecation, with bleeding. Digit examination is not possible because of the pain.

78 A 23-year-old male university student presents with a 3-month history of severe fleeting rectal pain, which occurs about three times a week. There are no aggravating or relieving factors. He denies any other gastrointestinal symptoms. Digital rectal examination and sigmoidoscopy are normal.

23. Diarrhoea

A Non-bacterial food poisoning
B Carcinoma of the anus
C Typhoid fever
D Acute appendicitis
E Amoebic dysentery
F Ulcerative colitis

For each of the patients described below, select the single most likely diagnosis from the options listed above. Each option may be used once, more than once or not at all.

79 A 25-year-old woman is admitted to hospital with anorexia, abdominal pain and diarrhoea over the previous 24 hours. She has vomited and has a low-grade pyrexia. She is tender in the lower abdomen and on rectal examination.

80 A 70-year-old man recently returned from Bangladesh is admitted with a high temperature and persistent bloody diarrhoea with a grossly abnormal rectal mucosa on sigmoidoscopy.

81 A 64-year-old man is admitted with a 3-month history of intermittent diarrhoea, anorexia and weight loss. He has a recent 1 week history of passing painless motions with dark-red blood mixed within the stool.

24. Dysphagia

A Achalasia
B Oesophageal carcinoma
C Pharyngeal pouch
D Inflammatory stricture
E Plummer–Vinson syndrome
F Retrosternal palsy

For each of the patients described below, select the single most likely diagnosis from the options listed above. Each option may be used once, more than once or not at all.

82 A 75-year-old women presents with a 4-month history of difficulty swallowing. She is now having difficulty swallowing fluids. Of note, she is a regular smoker.

83 A previously fit 32-year-old woman presents with a productive cough and pyrexia. At night, her coughing is worse. Moreover, she has difficulty swallowing fluids and complains of retrosternal pain.

84 A 73-year-old homeless man has a history of recurrent sore throats for which he has completed a course of antibiotics, but there has been no improvement. He presents to A&E with a lump on the left side of his neck.

25. Testicular conditions

A Seminoma
B Teratoma
C Torsion of testis
D Torsion of hydatid of Morgagni
E Inguinal hernia

For each of the patients described below, select the single most likely diagnosis from the options listed above. Each option may be used once, more than once or not at all.

85 A 25-year-old man discovers a hard lump on his left testicle. His GP has arranged a blood test (β-hCG) which is positive.

86 An 18-year-old man, an avid football player, develops a sudden onset of acute pain in his right testicle. There is no history of trauma. On examination, he is apyrexial and there is a small and very tender lump on the superior pole of the right testicle. The testicle is located in a normal anatomical position.

26. Jaundice

A Gilbert's syndrome
B Common bile duct stone
C Acute alcoholic hepatitis
D Carcinoma of head of pancreas
E Primary biliary cirrhosis
F Ascending cholangitis
G Hepatic metastases
H Cholangiocarcinoma
I Primary sclerosing cholangitis

For each of the patients described below, select the single most likely diagnosis from the options listed above. Each option may be used once, more than once or not at all.

87 A 30-year-old man, with a 7-year history of ulcerative colitis, complains of fluctuating jaundice, right upper quadrant pain and weight loss for the previous 6 months. Plasma alkaline phosphatase is 20 U/L (normal range 30–130 U/L).

88 A 25-year-old man has noticed mild intermittent jaundice for the past 6 years. His blood tests demonstrate a moderate unconjugated hyperbilirubaemia with otherwise normal liver function tests and hepatic histology.

89 A 57-year-old woman presents with a 5-week history of jaundice, anorexia and weight loss. She has a pyrexia of 37.8°C. She has tender enlarged liver (12 cm), mild ascites, widespread spider naevi and palmar erythema. Laboratory studies demonstrate a leucocytosis of

20×10^9/L, plasma alanine transaminase 280 U/L (normal range 2–50 U/L), plasma albumin 24 g/L (normal range 35–50 g/L), and prothrombin time of 20 seconds (control 13 s).

90 A 62-year-old man presents with a 3-month history of weight loss, increasing jaundice and nocturnal epigastric pain. Five years ago he underwent an anterior resection of the rectum. On examination, there is a right upper quadrant mass that moves on respiration. Laboratory studies show plasma alkaline phosphatase of 752 U/L (normal range 30–130 U/L).

27. Haematuria

A Transitional cell carcinoma
B Pelvi-ureteric junction obstruction
C Renal cell carcinoma
D Pyelonephritis
E March haemaglobinuria

For each of the patients described below, select the single most likely diagnosis from the options listed above. Each option may be used once, more than once or not at all.

91 A 45-year-old man presents with loin pain and haematuria. He has a palpable mass in his loin.

92 A 24-year-old runner presents after passing blood in his urine after a training session for a marathon race. His physical examination and radiological images are normal.

93 A 68-year-old man presents with acute painless frank haematuria. He had a similar episode several months ago. Moreover, he has noticed recent clots in his urine. On examination, his abdomen is soft and non-tender.

28. Prostate cancer

A Open prostatectomy and radiotherapy
B Hormonal manipulation
C Cytotoxic chemotherapy
D Palliative radiotherapy
E Watchful waiting

For each of the patients described below, select the single most appropriate primary therapy from the options listed above. Each option may be used once, more than once or not at all.

94 An 85-year-old man presents with established carcinoma of the prostate and is noted to have a non-tender fracture of the fourth lumbar vertebra on routine investigations. He earlier underwent a bilateral orchidectomy.

95 A 52-year-old man presents with nocturia. On rectal examination, a hard lump is noted. Biopsy demonstrates a prostatic adenocarcinoma, which is intracapsular and surrounded by normal prostate.

96 A 75-year-old man presents with back pain. Medical treatment has not improved his symptoms. Formal investigations demonstrate a carcinoma of the prostate with metastatic spread to the lumbar spine.

29. Wound infections

A Clean
B Clean contaminated
C Contaminated
D Dirty

For each of the patients described below, select the single most appropriate category from the options listed above. Each option may be used once, more than once or not at all.

97 A 15-year-old man underwent an emergency appendicectomy for a perforated appendix.
98 A 62-year-old man underwent an elective right-sided hemicolectomy for bowel cancer.
99 A 31-year-old man underwent an elective inguinal hernia repair.
100 A 42-year-old woman underwent an open cholecystectomy.

30. Endocrine

A Addison's disease
B Cushing's syndrome
C Diabetes insipidus
D Diabetes mellitus
E Graves' disease
F Hashimoto's thyroiditis
G Hypercalcaemia of malignancy
H Pituitary failure
I Phaeochromocytoma
J Primary hyperparathyroidism
K Primary hypothyroidism
L Secondary hyperparathyroidism

For each patient described below, choose the single most likely diagnosis from the above list of options. Each option may be used once, more than once or not at all.

Normal ranges are: sodium 135–145 mmol/L; potassium 3.4–5.0 mmol/L; calcium 2.20–2.65 mmol/L; phosphate 0.8–1.4 mmol/L; PTH 1.1–6.8 pmol/L.

101 A 30-year-old man complains of polyuria and polydipsia. His fasting blood glucose is 4.7 mmol/L. Biochemical investigations reveal: Na 140 mmol/L; K 4.2 mmol/L; Ca 2.85 mmol/L; phosphate 0.4 mmol/L; PTH 4.2 pmol/L.

102 A 50-year-old Asian woman complains of tingling in her hands and feet. On checking her blood pressure, her hands reveal carpal spasm. Her fasting blood glucose is 4.9 mmol/L. Biochemical investigations reveal: Na 141 mmol/L; K 4.1 mmol/L; Ca 1.85 mmol/L; phosphate 1.4 mmol/L; PTH 80 pmol/L.

103 A 50-year-old Asian woman complains of nocturia and dizziness. Her fasting blood glucose is 3.9 mmol/L. Biochemical investigations reveal: Na 131 mmol/L; K 6.1 mmol/L; Ca 2.75 mmol/L; phosphate 1.0 mmol/L; PTH 1.3 pmol/L.

31. Rheumatology

A Acute gout
B Ankylosing spondylitis
C Enteropathic arthritis
D Haemarthrosis
E Osteoarthritis
F Pseudogout
G Psoriatic arthropathy
H Reactive arthritis
I Reiter's syndrome
J Rheumatoid arthritis
K Septic arthritis
L Systemic lupus erythematosus

For each patient described below, choose the single most likely diagnosis from the above list of options. Each option may be used once, more than once or not at all.

104 A 60-year-old man complains of knee pain and examination reveals a moderate effusion. Withdrawal of fluid and microscopy reveals crystals, which on viewing under polarized light are positively birefringent.

105 A 19-year-old man returns from holiday in Tenerife. Four weeks later he develops a swollen, hot, painful, red knee joint, with an effusion. The knee is tapped and 20 mL of turbid yellow fluid is withdrawn. Microbiology reveals Gram-negative intracellular diplococci.

32. Hepatology

A Autoimmune hepatitis
B Carcinoma of the head of pancreas
C Cholangiocarcinoma
D Crigler–Najjar syndrome
E Dubin–Johnson syndrome
F Gallstones
G Gilbert's syndrome
H Hepatitis A
I Hepatitis B
J Hepatitis C
K Malaria
L Primary biliary cirrhosis
M Primary sclerosing cholangitis

For each patient described below, choose the single most likely diagnosis from the above list of options. Each option may be used once, more than once or not at all.
Normal ranges are: bilirubin 3–17 μmol/L; ALT 3–35 iu/L; ALP 30–300 iu/L.

106 An 18-year-old presents with jaundice. On questioning he admits that the last time he had a cold he went a slightly yellow colour. His brother has had a past episode of jaundice. Liver function tests reveal: bilirubin 80 μmol/L; ALT 25 iu/L; ALP 150 iu/L.

107 A 55-year-old woman presents with painless jaundice and pruritus. On direct questioning she admits to having dark urine and pale stools. On examination, she is noted to have xanthelasma and moderate hepatomegaly. Liver function tests reveal: bilirubin 200 μmol/L; ALT 67 iu/L; ALP 723 iu/L. Antimitochondrial antibodies are positive.

108 A 22-year-old student has just returned from an uneventful holiday in Africa. He is jaundiced and has moderate hepatomegaly. Liver function tests reveal: bilirubin 110 μmol/L; ALT 250 iu/L; ALP 350 iu/L. Also detected are specific IgM antibodies.

33. Abdominal trauma

A Emergency laparotomy
B Diagnostic peritoneal lavage (DPL)
C Wound exploration under local anaesthetic
D Abdominal ultrasound (FAST scan)
E CT abdomen
F Angiography
G Observation

For each of the patients described below, select the single most likely diagnosis from the options listed above. Each option may be used once, more than once or not at all.

109 An 18-year-old man sustains a low-energy gunshot wound from close range to his hypogastric area. His blood pressure is 100/65 mmHg and his pulse is 130 beats/min.

110 A 42-year-old female is involved in a motorcycle accident with a Glasgow Coma Score (GCS) of 7 following a severe head injury. A left-sided pneumothorax was treated with a chest drain insertion and her pulse is now 150 beats/min and blood pressure 120/75 mmHg after two litres of crystalloid. Her abdomen is soft but difficult to assess.

111 A 24-year-old male is brought into hospital with an abdominal stab wound which appears superficial and the abdomen is soft. His pulse is 110 beats per minute and blood pressure is 130/80 mmHg.

34. Lumps

A Neurofibroma
B Lipoma
C Ganglion
D Histiocytoma
E Sebaceous (epidermoid) cyst
F Dermoid cyst
G Ivory osteoma

For each of the patients described below, select the single most likely diagnosis from the options listed above. Each option may be used once, more than once or not at all.

112 A 42-year-old woman has a 1.5 cm swelling above the outer canthus of the eye. On examination, it is soft, deep to the skin, with no deep attachments.

113 A 52-year-old man has a 1 cm cutaneous lump on the anterior aspect of the lower limb which followed an insect bite one year earlier.

114 A 37-year-old man presents with a 3 cm lump on his forehead that has been present for many years. On examination, the lump is hard and deep to the skin.

35. Intestinal polyps

A Anterior resection
B Subtotal colectomy
C Panproctocolectomy
D Regular endoscopic surveillance
E Abdominoperineal excision
F Endoscopic excision
G Restorative proctocolectomy
H No treatment required

For each of the patients described below, select the single most likely treatment option from the list above. Each option may be used once, more than once or not at all.

115 A 45-year-old patient with familial adenomatous polyposis presents with severely dysplastic changes in the sigmoid colon.

116 An elderly patient presents with per-rectal bleeding. She is known to have haemorrhoids but on rigid sigmoidoscopy demonstrates a small polyp 14 cm from the anal verge. Barium enema is normal and histology reveals a metaplastic polyp.

117 A 19-year-old female has longstanding ulcerative colitis affecting the whole colon. She is found to have a malignancy on a biopsy taken 5 cm from the anal verge and severe dysplasia on other biopsies from the colon.

36. Cancer staging

A Dukes' A
B Dukes' B
C Dukes' C
D Dukes' D
E Clarke's level I
F Clarke's level II
G Clarke's level III
H Clarke's level IV
I Clarke's level V

For each of the patients described below, select the single most likely diagnosis from the options listed above. Each option may be used once, more than once or not at all.

118 A melanoma invading the papillary dermis.
119 A melanoma invading the subcutaneous tissue.
120 A sigmoid colon tumour involving the circumferential margins, but no lymph node deposits.
121 A rectal tumour with liver metastases

37. Anaemia

A Iron-deficiency anaemia
B Hereditary spherocytosis
C Vitamin B_{12} deficiency anaemia
D Sickle cell disease
E Beta-thalassaemia
F Pernicious anaemia
G Glucose-6-phosphate dehydrogenase deficiency
H Sideroblastic anaemia

For each of the patients described below, select the single most likely diagnosis from the options listed above. Each option may be used once, more than once or not at all.

122 A 42-year-old African male has recently been diagnosed with malaria and is taking quinine. He presents with fatigue, dark urine and shortness of breath.
123 An 11-year-old Scottish, Caucasian girl presents with mild anaemia and jaundice. Her blood tests reveal a normal MCV, but her red cell osmotic fragility test is increased.
124 A 25-year-old African man presents with severe lumbar back pain and jaundice. His blood tests demonstrate a normocytic, normochromic anaemia, high reticulocyte count. His ESR is low.

38. Complications of blood transfusions

A Immediate haemolytic reaction
B Febrile reaction
C Allergic reaction
D Hypothermia
E Viral hepatitis
F Septicaemia
G Delayed haemolytic reaction

For each of the patients described below, select the single most likely diagnosis from the options listed above. Each option may be used once, more than once or not at all.

125 A 72-year-old male is transfused with blood for an acute gastrointestinal bleed. Thirty minutes later he develops a temperature of 39.5°C, tachycardia and hypotension. There is no evidence of haemolysis on blood film.

126 An 82-year-old woman develops a temperature of 38°C and a moderate headache three hours after her blood transfusion is administered.

127 A 65-year-old woman presents one week post-transfusion with anaemia, jaundice and fever.

39. Fractures

A Transverse
B Spiral
C Stress
D Pathological
E Open
F Comminuted
G Incomplete

For each of the patients described below, select the single most likely diagnosis from the options listed above. Each option may be used once, more than once or not at all.

128 A marathon runner presents with a fractured metatarsal bone. There is no history of trauma.

129 A 13-year-old boy falls while playing football. He has an abrasion over the site of tenderness and an X-ray shows a fracture through one of the cortices.

130 An 84-year-old woman presents with a painful right tibia. Her X-ray shows abnormal cortical thickening, a visible fracture and thickening in a bowed tibia.

40. Acid–base balance

A Metabolic alkalosis
B Metabolic acidosis
C Uncompensated respiratory alkalosis
D Uncompensated respiratory acidosis
E Compensated respiratory alkalosis
F Compensated respiratory acidosis

For each of the case scenarios described below, select the single most likely diagnosis from the options listed above. Each option may be used once, more than once or not at all.

131 pH 7.3, Pao_2 8.5 kPa, $Paco_2$ 9.8 kPa, HCO_3 33 mmol/L.

132 pH 7.55, Pao_2 10 kPa, $Paco_2$ 7.3 kPa, HCO_3 43 mmol/L.

133 pH 7.3, Pao_2 8.5 kPa, $Paco_2$ 8.0 kPa, HCO_3 27 mmol/L.

41. Informed consent

A Patient
B Partner
C Parents
D Surgeon
E Psychiatrist
F Judge
G Hospital management

For each of the case scenarios described below, select the single most likely person from the options listed above from whom to take consent. Each option may be used once, more than once or not at all.

134 A 15-year-old girl refuses to have an appendicectomy.
135 An unconscious stabbed patient needs an emergency thoracotomy.
136 A diabetic patient with chronic, stable schizophrenia presents with a gangrenous toe which requires an amputation. He understands the implications but refuses surgery.

42. Neck anatomy

A Phrenic nerve
B Stellate ganglion
C Thoracic duct
D Parathyroid glands
E Recurrent laryngeal nerve
F External laryngeal nerve

For each of the case scenarios described below, select the single most likely structure from the options listed above that is likely to have been injured. Each option may be used once, more than once or not at all.

137 The patient is complaining of tingling in the tips of their fingers.
138 An opera singer complains that her voice is becoming weak after singing for a short period of time.
139 A smoker presents with unilateral ptosis and a small pupil.

43. Innervation of lower limb muscles

A Obturator nerve
B Saphenous nerve
C Femoral nerve
D Tibial nerve
E Superficial peroneal nerve
F Deep peroneal nerve
G Sural nerve

For each of the muscles below, select the single most likely nerve from the options listed above. Each option may be used once, more than once or not at all.

140 Tibilis anterior
141 Quadratus femoris
142 Adductor magnus

44. Brachial plexus injuries

A C5
B C5–6
C C5–7
D C7–8, T1
E C8, T1
F C6–8
G C5–8, T1

For each of the case scenarios described below, select the single most likely diagnosis from the options listed above. Each option may be used once, more than once or not at all.

143 A healthy full-term baby was born 5 hours ago after a prolonged labour. The child's right arm is medially rotated with the palm of the hand facing backwards.

144 While the patient is holding on to the overhead railing, the bus suddenly stops. The patient presents with weakness of the small muscles of the hand and sensory loss over the medial aspect of the hand and forearm.

145 A motorcyclist is involved in an accident. His right upper limb is paralysed and insensate.

45. Herniae

A Direct inguinal
B Indirect inguinal
C Obturator
D Femoral
E Epigastric
F Para-umbilical
G Umbilical
H Pantaloon

For each of the anatomical locations described below, select the single most likely diagnosis from the options listed above. Each option may be used once, more than once or not at all.

146 Arising in the upper, inner thigh.
147 Arising from the umbilicus in the adult.
148 Arising below and lateral to the pubic tubercle.

46. Tumour markers

A CA-125
B Ca19-9
C PSA
D CEA
E LDH
F Alpha-fetoprotein
G Thyroglobulin

For each of the neoplasms below, select the single most likely diagnosis from the options listed above. Each option may be used once, more than once or not at all.

149 Ovarian carcinoma
150 Hepatocellular carcinoma
151 Colorectal cancer

47. Adrenal pathology

A Cushing's syndrome
B Phaeochromocytoma
C Conn's syndrome
D Addison's disease
E Multiple endocrine neoplasia 1
F Multiple endocrine neoplasia 2a
G Multiple endocrine neoplasia 2b

For each of the case scenarios below, select the single most likely diagnosis from the options listed above. Each option may be used once, more than once or not at all.

152 A 42-year-old woman presents with epigastric pain. Her past medical history includes duodenal ulcers, hirsutism and bilateral pitting leg oedema. Investigations reveal hypercalcaemia.

153 A 72-year-old smoker presents with polydipsia and polyuria. On clinical examination he has a moon face, buffalo hump, abdominal striae and hypertension.

154 A 42-year-old woman (with known pernicious anaemia) faints. She is hypotensive and her blood tests demonstrate hyperkalaemia.

48. Chest pain

A Myocardial infarction
B Pneumonia
C Pulmonary embolus
D Pneumothorax
E Tietze's syndrome (costochondritis)
F Oesophageal spasm
G Dissecting aortic aneurysm

For each of the case scenarios below, select the single most likely diagnosis from the options listed above. Each option may be used once, more than once or not at all.

155 A 16-year-old girl presents with a history of asthma and epilepsy with anterior chest pain and shortness of breath. On percussion her anterior chest wall is tender.

156 A 63-year-old man presents with crushing, retrosternal chest pain which radiates to his jaw. A coronary angiogram 3 months previously was normal.

157 A 32-year-old woman presents 3 weeks post-partum with pleuritic chest pain, breathlessness and haemoptysis.

49. Metabolic abnormalities

A Hypokalaemia
B Hyperkalaemia
C Hyponatraemia
D Hypernatraemia
E Hypophosphataemia
F Hyperphosphataemia
G Hyperglycaemia

For each of the case scenarios below, select the single most likely diagnosis from the options listed above. Each option may be used once, more than once or not at all.

158 A 63-year-old woman with congestive cardiac failure is commenced on oral steroids for an acute exacerbation of COPD. She takes regular furosemide and aspirin.

159 A 51-year-old alcoholic man with Boerhaave's syndrome receives a feeding jejunostomy.

160 A 25-year-old man sustains a partial-thickness burn in his left arm. He has proteinuria and his creatine kinase is elevated.

50. Lung volumes

A Inspiratory reserve volume
B Tidal volume
C Functional residual capacity
D Total lung capacity
E Vital capacity
F Residual volume
G Expiratory reserve volume

For each of the equations described below, select the single most likely option from those listed above. Each option may be used once, more than once or not at all.

161 Residual volume + expiratory reserve volume = ?
162 Total lung capacity –vital capacity = ?
163 Vital capacity – (expiratory reserve volume + inspiratory reserve volume) = ?

EMQ answers and explanations

1. Blood transfusions

B&L **For further reading, see *Bailey and Love*, Chapter 2, 'Shock and blood transfusions'.**

1 D

A patient with group B blood has anti-A antibodies and therefore cannot receive group A blood. This patient is also RhD-negative and so cannot receive RhD-positive blood. The patient could take iron sulphate tablets but, with a haemoglobin level of 6.0, a blood transfusion is a better option.

2 A

A patient with group A blood has anti-B antibodies and therefore cannot receive group B blood. This patient is also RhD-positive and so can receive RhD-positive or negative blood. The patient could take iron sulphate tablets but, with a haemoglobin level of 6.0, a blood transfusion is a better option.

3 F

The haemoglobin level is not very low and so a gradual normalization with iron sulphate tablets is a better option compared with the risks associated with blood transfusion. Blood transfusion is usually considered when the haemoglobin level drops below 8 g/dL.

4 D

A patient with group O blood has anti-A and anti-B antibodies and can only therefore receive group O blood. This patient is also RhD-negative and so cannot receive RhD-positive blood.

5 E

A woman who is RhD-negative but exposed to the RhD-antigen via childbirth or transfusion will go on to develop antibodies that would attack a subsequent RhD-positive baby *in utero*. Anti-D immunoglobulin will reduce her immune response and therefore reduce the risk of developing antibodies.

2. Lumps in the groin

B&L **For further reading, see *Bailey and Love*, Chapter 75, 'Testis and scrotum'.**

6 D

There is a positive cough impulse suggestive of bowel herniation. The doctor cannot get above the lump, suggesting that it arises from the inguinal canal. The hernia can be reduced back along the inguinal canal from the scrotum and upon occlusion of the deep inguinal ring the hernia is controlled. This is pathognomonic for an indirect inguinal hernia.

7 I

Epididymo-orchitis is an infection of the epididymis and testis and can be mistaken for torsion. The clue here is the prolonged history.

8 A

Any firm scrotal mass is cancer until proven otherwise. Testicular cancer may often be associated with a hydrocele.

9 E

This is a classic description of a varicocele. These are more common on the left as the left testicular vein drains into the left renal vein whereas the right testicular vein drains directly into the IVC.

10 B
A history of sudden onset of severe testicular pain with such a short duration must be presumed to be testicular torsion until proven otherwise. This is a surgical emergency.

3. Lumps in the neck

B&L **For further reading, see *Bailey and Love*, Chapter 45, 'Pharynx, larynx and neck'.**

11 E
Epidermal cysts originate in the skin and have a characteristic punctum. They commonly occur in the head and neck region.

12 C
This is the classic description of a thyroglossal cyst and forms from a persistent thyroglossal duct.

13 I
Lumps that move on swallowing must be attached to the larynx or trachea and are most commonly thyroid lumps. Multinodular goitres are the most common thyroid lumps.

14 D
A cystic hygroma is a lymphangioma which usually presents in childhood. Cystic hygromas typically occur in the neck and transilluminate.

15 F
Stones can form in the salivary glands, especially in the submandibular glands. Obstruction of the salivary gland duct can cause pain and swelling.

4. Diseases of the hepatobiliary system

B&L **For further reading, see *Bailey and Love*, Chapter 63, 'The gallbladder and bile ducts', and Chapter 64, 'The pancreas'.**

16 H
This woman has a tumour at the head of the pancreas. If retrograde stenting via ERCP is not possible, then anterograde stenting via a percutaneous approach (PTC) is the next step to relieve jaundice.

17 C
This is a classic story of acute cholecystitis which can be diagnosed on ultrasound, which can also detect gallstones.

18 A
This is a story of bowel obstruction which may be due to gallstone ileus. Dilated loops of bowel may be seen and perhaps the gallstone itself.

19 B
This man has acute pancreatitis. The most common causes include alcohol excess and gallstones. There is an obstructive picture, so ultrasound can confirm and may detect the obstructing gallstone. CT is used to detect pancreatic necrosis several days later.

20 F
There is a gallstone obstructing the common bile duct. It can be removed by ERCP.

5. Fractures of the hip

B&L **For further reading, see *Bailey and Love*, Chapter 35, 'Hip and knee'.**

21 G
In elderly patients, hemiarthroplasty is indicated for intracapsular fractures unless there is a diseased acetabulum, when a total hip replacement is preferred.

22 D
An intramedullary screw is indicated in intertrochanteric fractures with extension into the shaft. This is because there is a nail for the shaft and a screw for the head.

23 C
Cannulated screws are preferred in younger patients with intracapsular fractures and thereby preserving the head of the femur. This is because femoral head prostheses have a limited lifespan.

24 E
In elderly patients with an intracapsular fracture, uncemented hemiarthroplasty is preferred to cemented hemiarthroplasty, to decrease the risk of fat embolism.

25 B
Dynamic hip screws are preferred for extracapsular femoral fractures.

6. Arterial blood gases

B&L **For further reading, see *Bailey and Love*, Chapter 13, 'Perioperative care'.**

26 A
The pH is low = acidosis; the PCO_2 is normal = not a respiratory cause; the base excess is negative = metabolic acidosis.

27 A
The pH is low = acidosis; the PCO_2 is normal = not a respiratory cause; the base excess is negative = metabolic acidosis.

28 C
The pH is high = alkalosis; the PCO_2 is high = respiratory compensation; the base excess is normal.

29 H
The pH is high = alkalosis; the PCO_2 is low = respiratory cause; the base excess is negative = metabolic compensation.

7. ATLS classification of haemorrhagic shock

B&L **For further reading, see *Bailey and Love*, Chapter 2, 'Shock and blood transfusions'.**

30 A
Class I shock = 0–15 per cent of circulatory volume blood loss. There is only tachycardia.

31 A
Class I shock = 0–15 per cent of circulatory volume blood loss. There is only tachycardia.

32 B
Class II shock = 15–30 per cent of circulatory volume blood loss. There is tachycardia, tachypnoea, narrowing of pulse pressure, slight drop in urine output (normal is 0.5 mL/kg/h), slight confusion.

33 C
Class III shock = 30–40 per cent of circulatory volume blood loss. There is tachycardia, tachypnoea, drop in systolic blood pressure, oliguria, agitated/drowsy.

34 D
Class IV shock = >40 per cent of circulatory volume blood loss. There is extreme tachycardia, tachypnoea, often undetectable, anuria, unconscious.

8. Burns

B&L **For further reading, see *Bailey and Love*, Chapter 28, 'Burns'.**

Apply Wallace's rule of 9s:

35 A – 1 per cent for perineum
36 B – 9 per cent for each arm
37 B – 9 per cent for face and head
38 C – 18 per cent for each leg
39 C – 18 per cent for the back of trunk

9. Jaundice

B&L **For further reading, see *Bailey and Love*, Chapter 63, 'The gallbladder and bile ducts', and Chapter 65, 'The small and large intestines'.**

40 J
Mirizzi syndrome occurs when a gallstone in the gall bladder causes compression on the common bile duct resulting in obstructive jaundice. There is gallstone cholecystitis here as well.

41 F
This obeys Courvoisier's law which states that a palpable gall bladder in the presence of jaundice is more likely to be malignancy than gallstones.

42 D
This is a classic story of gallstone obstruction of the common bile duct.

43 C
This is most likely to be infective hepatitis.

44 E
This woman has ulcerative colitis which is associated with sclerosing cholangitis.

45 A
This boy is in sickle cell crisis with haemolytic jaundice. Sickle cell anaemia almost exclusively occurs in black Americans and black Africans.

10. Paediatric abdomen

B&L **For further reading, see *Bailey and Love*, Chapter 6, 'Principles of paediatric surgery, Part II: Abdominal'.**

46 F
This is the classic story of intussusception which occurs in young children and is most often idiopathic. There is redcurrant jelly stool due to bleeding.

47 C
This is the double-bubble sign seen on plain X-ray and represents dilated proximal duodenum and stomach due to duodenal atresia. It is associated with Down's syndrome.

48 B
This is the classic story of pyloric stenosis and most commonly affects males in the first few months of life. They usually present with non-bilious projectile vomiting.

49 I
This girl has a Meckel's diverticulum which most likely contains gastric mucosa causing rectal bleeding.

50 G
Most patients with meconium ileus have cystic fibrosis. Meconium is fetal stool and in this case is impacted in the ileum and can be felt as a mass. The obstructing meconium leads to dilatation of small bowel loops more proximally.

11. Swollen painful joints

B&L **For further reading, see *Bailey and Love*, Chapter 37, 'Inflammation and infection and musculoskeletal tumours'.**

51 C
The patient has rheumatoid arthritis. In this chronic inflammatory disorder, patients present with bilateral and symmetrical polyarthropathy affecting the small joints of the hand with sparing of the distal interphalangeal (DIP) joints and involvement of the metacarpophalangeal (MCP) and proximal interphalangeal (PIP) joints. X-ray findings include narrowing of joint space, periarticular osteopenia, juxta-articular bony erosions (non-cartilage protected bone), subluxation with gross deformity and periarticular soft tissue swelling.

52 A
The patient has osteoarthritis (OA). In degenerative joint disease, patients present with joint pain, tenderness and stiffness due to the process of progressive deterioration of articular cartilage and formation of new bone (osteophytes) at the joint surface. While osteoarthritis can affect any joint in the body, the disorder commonly affects the hands, hips, knees, neck and lumbar spine. In the hands, OA typically targets the PIP, DIP, scaphotrapeziotrapezoid and the first carpometacarpal joints. X-ray shows that the affected joint spaces are narrowed with reactive subchondral sclerosis (eburnation). Bony erosions are centrally located (in contrast to the marginal erosions in rheumatoid arthritis). Other classic radiographic findings include osteophytes and subchondral cysts. Heberden's nodes at the DIP joints and Bouchard's nodes at the PIP joints of the hands are areas of osteophyte formation. Moreover, periarticular soft tissue swelling, intra-articular loose bodies and osseous fusion can also be seen.

12. Pathological fractures

B&L **For further reading, see *Bailey and Love*, Chapter 37, 'Inflammation and infection and musculoskeletal tumours'.**

53 A
The patient has osteosarcoma of the left femur. These highly malignant lesions appear in two age groups: between 10 and 20 years, and those aged over 50 (secondary to Paget's disease). Osteosarcoma usually occurs at the metaphysis of long bones and presents with pain, associated with a history of trauma. X-ray findings include periosteal new bone formation, which produces a speckled triangle (Codman's triangle) with a 'sun-ray speculation'. Resectable tumours are now treated with cytotoxic therapy, followed by surgical resection. The 5-year survival rate is 50 per cent.

54 E
Ewing's sarcoma is a rare malignant bone tumour. The common areas in which it occurs are the pelvis, ribs, humerus and femur (in the long bone medullary cavity). It is more common in males and usually presents in childhood or early adulthood, with a peak between 10 and 20 years of age. Patients usually present with bone pain. Radiological findings are a permeative lytic

lesion with periosteal reaction. The classic description of lamellated or 'onion skin' type periosteal reaction is often associated with this lesion.

13. Nerve root/nerve injuries

B&L **For further reading, see *Bailey and Love*, Chapter 27, 'Extremity trauma'.**

55 C

Compression of the first sacral nerve root results in pain in the posterior leg and ankle, reduced plantar flexion, reduced sensation in the lateral aspect of the foot and loss of the ankle reflex.

Table 10 Lumbar radiculopathy secondary to lumbar disc protrusions

	L4/L4	L4/L5	L5/S1
Disc	5%	45%	50%
Root	L4	L5	S1
Reflex	Knee	–	Ankle
Motor	Knee extension	Extensor hallucis longus Tibialis anterior	Plantar flexion
Sensory	Medial calf	Lateral calf	Lateral foot
Pain	Anterior thigh	Posterior leg	Posterior leg Ankle

56 H

The superficial peroneal nerve supplies the peroneal muscles, hence the loss of ankle eversion. It should be differentiated from the common peroneal nerve injury, which involves loss of function in both superficial and deep peroneal nerves. The deep peroneal nerve supplies the anterior compartment of the leg; injury causes inability to dorsiflex the foot.

14. Skin conditions

B&L **For further reading, see *Bailey and Love*, Chapter 39, 'Skin and subcutaneous tissue'.**

57 A

Basal cell carcinoma is the most common type of skin cancer. It is considered malignant because it can cause significant local destruction by invading into the surrounding tissues. Most lesions are located on the patient's head and neck (80 per cent). It occurs more often in men than in women. Most basal cell carcinomas are seen in patients over the age of 40 years. Patients present with a shiny and pearly white nodule on sun-exposed areas.

58 E

Keratocanthoma is a benign lesion that originates in the pilosebaceous glands and closely resembles squamous cell carcinoma. In most cases, a keratocanthoma is characterized by rapid growth over a few weeks to months, followed by spontaneous resolution over 4–6 months. It usually appears as a volcano-like bump on the sun-exposed skin of middle-aged and elderly individuals. Most lesions cause minimal skin destruction, but a few behave more aggressively and can spread to regional lymph nodes.

59 B

Malignant melanoma is a tumour of melanocytes. The cells are found in the skin, bowel and eye. There are five types of malignant melanoma of the skin:

- superficial spreading (most common) – usually palpable with an irregular edge
- lentigo maligna (least common) – least malignant, usually located on the face of the elderly (Hutchinson's freckle)

- nodular – most malignant, affects the young and may ulcerate and bleed
- acral – affects palms and soles (includes subungual tumours) and has poor overall prognosis
- amelanotic – pink in colour but usually pigmented at base; poor prognosis.

Patients present with changes to the shape or colour of existing moles or appearance of new skin lesions. They cause pruritus, ulceration or bleeding. Urgent excisional biopsy is recommended.

Resection on a malignant melanoma is based on Breslow staging (Table 11).

Table 11 Breslow staging of melanoma

Depth of lesion (mm)	Recommended width of excision (mm)
< 0.75	2
0.76–1.5	20
1.6–3.0	50
> 3.0	50

15. Trauma patient

B&L **For further reading, see *Bailey and Love*, Chapter 22, 'Early assessment and management of trauma'.**

60 D

This patient is presenting with a ruptured spleen (left lower rib fractures with associated hypotension) secondary to trauma. Patients present with abdominal pain, left shoulder tip pain (Kehr's sign), hypotension and tachycardia. Bruising may present over the left upper abdomen, left chest, or left lower back and is associated with underlying haemorrhage.

61 B

The patient has a cardiac (pericardial) tamponade. The clinical syndrome is caused by accumulation of fluid in the pericardial space, which results in reduced ventricular filling and subsequent haemodynamic compromise. Cardiac tamponade presents with Beck's triad: quiet and muffled heart sounds, hypotension and distended neck vein (jugular venous distention). An emergency pericardiocentesis is the life-saving treatment of choice.

16. Lower leg ulceration

B&L **For further reading, see *Bailey and Love*, Chapter 54, 'Venous disorders'.**

62 B

Venous ulcers are commonly secondary to venous stasis from varicose veins and/or deep vein thrombosis. They invariably begin after the skin of the leg has been injured. However, the patient may not recall the initial insult. Chronic venous insufficiency may occur secondary to longstanding high pressure in the veins. This high venous pressure results in reflux (reverse flow) in the veins. Characteristic changes occur at the medial gaiter area of the leg. The classical changes include ulceration, haemosiderin deposition, thrombophlebitis, venous eczema and scars, lipodermatosclerosis,'inverted champagne bottle leg', pitting oedema, healed ulceration (atrophie blanche), ankle flare (corona phlebectatica), and loss of hair.

63 E

A chronic venous ulcer may rarely undergo metaplasia to form an ulcerating squamous cell carcinoma, which is called a Marjolin's ulcer. In 1828, Dr Jean Nicolas Marjolin first described the occurrence of ulcerating lesions within scar tissue. Marjolin's ulcer is the term given to these aggressive epidermoid tumours that arise from areas of chronic injury (burn injuries, osteomyelitis, post-radiotherapy).

17. Aneurysms

B&L **For further reading, see *Bailey and Love*, Chapter 54, 'Venous disorders'.**

64 B

An aneurysm is an abnormal, permanent dilation of a blood vessel, to 1.5–2 times its normal diameter. Patients who present with back pain and shock should be managed as a high index of suspicion as having a leaking abdominal aortic aneurysm (AAA). They need immediate resuscitation and reconstruction surgery, as 50 per cent of patients die before reaching hospital, and of those who arrive, 50 per cent die either of shock before theatre and renal failure after surgery. An elective operation has under 6 per cent mortality rate. Thus, asymptomatic aneurysms are regularly followed up with ultrasound or CT scan. This is because an AAA with a diameter of more than 6 cm has a high chance of rupture within 1 year. The immediate management of this patient is to insert intravenous lines, cross-match and transfer to theatre.

65 D

A patient with a widened mediastinum on chest X-ray needs to have the diagnosis of a thoracic aortic aneurysm excluded. The gold standard investigation to detect this abnormality is an angiogram. However, a CT scan is easier, time-efficient and non-invasive. Both investigations will demonstrate whether the aneurysm is secondary to an aortic dissection. As this patient is cardiovascularly stable, there is time to undergo formal investigations.

66 C

The patient's history is suggestive of a subarachnoid haemorrhage secondary to an aneurysmal bleed. In general, patients present with a sudden onset of a severe headache coupled with neck pain, vomiting and photophobia. The diagnosis of a subarachnoid haemorrhage is confirmed with a CT head scan. The Fisher grade classifies the appearance of the subarachnoid haemorrhage on a CT head scan (Table 12).

Table 12 Fisher grading for subarachnoid haemorrhage

Grade	Appearance
1	None evident
2	Less than 1 mm thick
3	More than 1 mm thick
4	Any thickness with intraventricular haemorrhage or parenchymal extension

The World Federation of Neurosurgeons (WFNS) classification uses the Glasgow Coma Scale (GCS) score and focal neurological deficit to classify the severity of symptoms (Table 13). A cerebral angiogram will identify the underlying aneurysm.

Table 13 World Federation of Neurosurgeons (WFNS) classification

Grade	GCS score	Focal neurological deficit
1	15	Absent
2	13–14	Absent
3	13–14	Present
4	7–12	Present or absent
5	< 7	Present or absent

18. Metabolic disorders of adrenal dysfunction

B&L **For further reading, see *Bailey and Love*, Chapter 49, 'Adrenal gland and other endocrine disorders'.**

67 D

In 60 per cent of cases, Addison's disease, an adrenocortical insufficiency, is caused by an autoimmune disorder. There is an association with other autoimmune conditions (i.e. chronic thyroiditis, Graves' disease, hypoparathyroidism, hypopituitarism, myasthenia gravis or pernicious anaemia). Other causes include tuberculosis, metastases (lung cancer), amyloidosis and bleeding. Patients present with muscle weakness, fatigue, loss of appetite, weight loss, dizzy spells (low blood pressure), nausea, diarrhoea, vomiting, irritability and depression. Routine investigations may reveal hypercalcaemia, hypoglycaemia, hyponatraemia, hyperkalaemia, eosinophilia, lymphocytosis and metabolic acidosis.

68 E

Multiple endocrine neoplasia is due to neoplasia of APUD cells (amine precursor uptake and decarboxylation). Inheritance may be sporadic or autosomal dominant. They are classified into three types:

- MEN 1 – parathyroid gland, pancreatic islet cells and pituitary gland (common), thyroid and adrenal cortex (rare)
- MEN 2a – parathyroid hyperplasia, medullary thyroid carcinoma and phaeochromocytoma
- MEN 2b – MEN 2a and neurofibromatosis.

This patient is suffering from MEN1. Her signs and symptoms can be classified by organ system.

- *Parathyroid*. Hyperparathyroidism is present in 90 per cent or more of patients.
- *Pancreas*. Pancreatic islet cell tumours occur in 60–70 per cent of patients. Approximately 40 per cent of islet tumours originate from beta-cells, secrete insulin (insulinoma) and cause hypoglycaemia. Most islet tumour cells secrete pancreatic polypeptides. Gastrin is secreted by many non-B-cell tumours (increased gastrin secretion is linked to the duodenum). Increased gastrin secretion increases gastric acid production, which may inactivate pancreatic lipase leading to diarrhoea and steatorrhoea. Increased gastrin secretion also leads to peptic ulcer formation in more than 50 per cent of MEN 1 patients.
- *Pituitary*. Pituitary tumours can occur In MEN 1. The majority are prolactinomas, followed by tumours that secrete growth hormone and prolactin, and ACTH. Excess hormones may lead to other clinical syndromes (i.e. excess prolactin: galactorrhoea; excess growth hormone: acromegaly; excess ACTH: Cushing's disease).

Overall, this patient's symptoms may be associated with the following:

- hypercalcaemia from hyperparathyroidism
- excess steroid production from Cushing's disease
- Zollinger–Ellison syndrome.

19. Paediatric urogenital conditions

B&L **For further reading, see *Bailey and Love*, Chapter 6, 'Principles of paediatric surgery, Part 12: Genetourinary'.**

69 C

Hypospadias is a common congenital abnormality in which the external urethral meatus is located on the ventral aspect of the penis. Epispadias occurs when the meatus is located on the dorsal aspect of the penis. Chordee is a condition in which the head of the penis curves downward or upward at the junction of the head and shaft of the penis.

70 E

The testis descends from the posterior wall of the abdomen into the scrotum via the inguinal canal. It carries a pouch of peritoneum called the processus vaginalis. In a child's first year, the processus vaginalis becomes obliterated, leaving the tunica vaginalis surrounding the testis. If this does not occur, the scrotal sac fills with peritoneal fluid via a communicating hydrocele. Owing to the continuity with the peritoneal cavity, the swelling will increase in size during standing and resolve when lying down. If the sac fills with bowel contents, an inguinal hernia will be present. A non-communicating hydrocele occurs when the processus vaginalis has closed, but the reabsorption of fluid from the tunica vaginalis is incomplete. This condition is present at birth and does not change in size.

20. Vomiting

B&L **For further reading, see *Bailey and Love*, Chapter 57, 'Hernias, umbilicus and abdominal wall', and Chapter 60, 'Stomach and duodenum'.**

71 D

A hernia is a protrusion of an organ or the fascia through the wall of the cavity that normally contains it. An incisional hernia occurs when the defect is the result of an incompletely healed surgical wound. The small bowel has herniated through a defect in the linea alba, which was not closed adequately during her diagnostic laparoscopy. A strangulated hernia occurs when pressure on the hernial contents may compromise blood and may cause ischaemia, and later necrosis and gangrene. Clinically, strangulated hernias are painful. The pain is coupled with abdominal tenderness. Nausea, vomiting and a fever may also be noted.

72 B

This patient has haematemesis (vomiting blood) secondary to oesophageal varices. Oesophageal varices are dilated submucosal veins in the lower oesophagus. They are often a consequence of portal hypertension. Cirrhosis is a common cause of portal hypertension. The patient's history of alcohol use, hepatomegaly, and peripheral stigmata of liver disease (spider naevi and palmar erythema) is in keeping with this underlying diagnosis. His portal hypertension is a result of enlarged collateral channels between the portal and systematic circulation (at points of portal systemic anastomosis: Table 14).

Table 14 Sites of portosystemic anastomosis

Site	Portal circulation	Systemic circulation
Oesophagus	Left gastric vein	Azygous vein
Paraumbilical	Paraumbilical vein	Superior epigastric vein
Retroperitoneal	Right, left and middle colic veins	Renal, suprarenal, paravertebral and gonadal veins
Patent ductus venosus	Left branch of portal vein	Inferior vena cava
Rectal	Superior rectal vein	Middle and inferior rectal veins

21. Paediatric gastrointestinal disorders

B&L **For further reading, see *Bailey and Love*, Chapter 6, 'Principles of paediatric surgery, Part II: Abdominal'.**

73 B

Intussusception is an invagination of one segment of bowel into another segment of bowel. Peristalsis lengthens the invaginated portion and each peristaltic wave results in a bout of colic. A viral illness is thought to enlarge Peyer's patches, resulting in an intussusception. In the adult population, this may also be associated with intestinal polyps or tumours. Early symptoms are nausea, vomiting and abdominal pain. Later, rectal bleeding ('redcurrant stool') and a sausage-shaped mass may be palpable in the abdominal examination. An ileocaecal intussusception is the most common type. The investigations of choice are an ultrasound and barium enema. A barium enema can be diagnostic and therapeutic (inflation of air). Further treatment includes an urgent laparotomy for reduction with or without bowel resection.

74 D

This child is presenting with mesenteric adenitis. This condition is a self-limiting inflammatory process that affects the mesenteric lymph nodes in the right lower quadrant of the abdomen. It is frequently caused by a viral pathogen. The patient has a history of fever, enlarged lymph nodes and generalized abdominal pain. The abdominal pain and tenderness are often centred in the right lower quadrant, but they may be more diffuse than appendicitis. The site of tenderness may shift when the position of the patient changes. The clinical presentation of mesenteric adenitis may mimic appendicitis. With appendicitis, children often present with pyrexia, facial flushing and localized abdominal pain.

75 E

Meckel's diverticulum is the most common congenital abnormality of the small intestine. It is caused by an incomplete obliteration of the vitelline duct. It is present in approximately 2 per cent of the population, with a male predominance. The rule of 2s may be applied:

- 2 per cent of the population
- 2 types of ectopic tissue (gastric and pancreatic)
- 2 years of age at time of presentation
- 2 times more common in males to be affected.

The most common presenting symptom is painless rectal bleeding followed by intestinal obstruction, volvulus and intussusception.

76 A

Hypertrophic pyloric stenosis is an obstruction of the pyloric lumen due to pyloric muscular hypertrophy. It affects 1 in 250 infants, is more common in firstborn males and occurs at age 2–6 weeks. The typical infant presents with non-bilious projectile vomiting and dehydration. On examination, gastric peristaltic waves may be present and a discrete 2–3 cm firm movable 'olive-like' mass may be palpable. The classic laboratory finding is a hypochloraemic, hypokalaemic metabolic alkalosis. Repeated vomiting results in a loss of HCl, causing the hypochloraemic metabolic alkalosis. The patient is likely to be dehydrated from repeated gastrointestinal loss and poor oral intake. The diagnosis is confirmed by abdominal ultrasound. Initial treatment is correction of the dehydration and electrolyte abnormality. Definitive treatment is a longitudinal pyloromyotomy.

22. Rectal pain

B&L **For further reading, see *Bailey and Love*, Chapter 68, 'The rectum'.**

77 D

A fissure-in-ano is a split or tear in the mucosa lining the lower rectum (anus). Common causes include Crohn's disease, iatrogenic (post-haemorrhoidectomy) and chronic constipation (passing dry hard stools). Patients suffer from pain during bowel movement, spasm of the anal sphincter coupled with bright-red rectal bleeding.

78 E

Proctalgia fugax is a sudden, severe and episodic pain in the rectum lasting several seconds to minutes. It is associated with cramps in the pubococcygeus or levator ani muscles. It often presents in the middle of the night and lasts less than 20 minutes. Of note, levator ani syndrome presents with pain and lasts longer than 20 minutes.

23. Diarrhoea

B&L **For further reading, see *Bailey and Love*, Chapter 67, 'The vermiform appendix', Chapter 65, 'The small and large intestines', and Chapter 69, 'The anus and anal canal'.**

79 D

Appendicitis is a result of acute inflammation of the appendix. The main symptom is abdominal pain. The pain is generalized and then localizes to the right lower quadrant (McBurney's point). On clinical examination, rebound tenderness is noted. Rectal examination may also illicit tenderness. Patients also present with loss of appetite, which can progress to nausea and vomiting. Other symptoms include constipation or diarrhoea, low-grade fever and abdominal swelling. The diagnosis is based on patient history and physical examination supported by an elevated neutrophilic white cell count.

80 E

Amoebic dysentery is transmitted through contaminated food and water sources and is caused by the amoeba *Entamoeba histolytica*. Patients can present with frequent, loose and bloodstained stools, weight loss, dehydration, indigestion, colic abdominal pain and rectal bleeding. The most frequent sites of infection are the caecum, ascending colon and sigmoid colon. The amoebae affect the underlying mucosa causing inflammation and ulceration.

81 B

Anal carcinoma, typically a squamous cell carcinoma, arises near the squamocolumnar junction. The adult population is most commonly affected (average age of presentation is 60 years). Right-sided colon cancer commonly presents with anaemia and weight loss, whereas transverse and left-sided colon cancer presents with change in bowel habit, blood mixed with stool, and weight loss. Risk factors for this condition include human papillomavirus, smoking, immunosuppression, benign anal lesions (inflammatory bowel disease, haemorrhoids, fistulae) and sexual activity (multiple sexual partners and anal intercourse).

24. Dysphagia

B&L **For further reading, see *Bailey and Love*, Chapter 59, 'The oesophagus'.**

82 B

Oesophageal cancer can be divided into various subtypes based on anatomical location. In general, a cancer in the upper two-thirds is a squamous cell carcinoma and one in the lower third is an adenocarcinoma. In cases of squamous cell carcinoma, which are similar to head and neck cancers, there is an association with tobacco and alcohol excess. Cases of adenocarcinoma are often associated with gastro-oesophageal reflux disease and Barrett's oesophagus. Patients present with dysphasia, odynophagia and weight loss. Initially, patients have difficulty with swallowing hard and bulky substances, but will progress to having difficulty with soft foods and liquids.

83 A

Achalasia is an oesophageal motility disorder involving the smooth muscle layer of the oesophagus and the lower oesophageal sphincter. The oesophageal sphincter fails to relax owing to a defect of the parasympathetic Auerbach's myenteric plexus. Patients present with difficulty swallowing fluids and solids. The patient will eat slowly and may employ the Valsalva manoeuvre to force food boluses from the oesophagus into the stomach. Regurgitation may lead to aspiration pneumonia.

84 C

Pharyngeal pouches occur most commonly in patients aged over 70 years. Typical symptoms include dysphagia, regurgitation, chronic cough, aspiration and weight loss. The aetiology remains unknown, but many theories centre upon a structural or physiological abnormality of the oesophageal muscles. The pharyngeal pouch is thought to be due to a mucosal out-pouching between the two parts of the inferior constrictor: thyropharyngeus above and cricopharyngeus below. The potential gap is called Killian's dehiscence. Food is propelled from the pharynx to the oesophagus by a series of sequential contractions of the superior, middle and thyropharyngeus constrictors. Then the cricopharyngeus, which as a sphincter, relaxes to allow food to enter the oesophagus. If it fails to relax, the pressure above will produce a posterior out-pouching through the weak Killian's dehiscence. It cannot expand posteriorly because of the adjacent vertebrae, so it descends down the back of the oesophagus to present as a lump in the posterior triangle of the neck. This is usually on the left as the oesophagus lies in the left side of the vertebral bodies. The diagnosis is confirmed on barium studies.

25. Testicular conditions

B&L **For further reading, see *Bailey and Love*, Chapter 75, 'Testis and scrotum'.**

85 B

Teratomas are germ cell tumours commonly composed of multiple cell types derived from one or more of three germ layers. They belong to a class known as non-seminomatous germ cell tumours (NSGCTs). All of this class are the result of abnormal development of pluripotent cells: germ cells and embryonic cells. Histologically, teratomas have contained hair, teeth and bone. The age of onset is 20–30 years. Formal investigations include blood tests (α-fetoprotein and β-hCG) and radiological imaging (ultrasound and CT scan of abdomen and pelvis). Surgical treatment is the mainstay, but teratomas are also chemosensitive.

86 D

A cyst of the hydatid of Morgagni is also known as an 'appendix testis'. It is a remnant of the Mullerian duct and located at the top of the testis. It is comparable to the fimbriated end of the fallopian tube in females. It may become twisted upon itself, causing a painful lump, which remains in a similar anatomical position. In cases of testicular torsion, the testicle will reside in a higher position and may be rotated.

26. Jaundice

B&L **For further reading, see *Bailey and Love*, Chapter 61, 'The liver'.**

87 I

Primary sclerosing cholangitis (PSC) is a chronic liver disease caused by progressive inflammation and scarring of the bile ducts of the liver. The inflammation impedes the flow of bile to the gut, which can ultimately lead to liver cirrhosis, liver failure and liver cancer. The underlying cause of the inflammation is believed to be autoimmunity. Patients present with fatigue, lethargy, jaundice, malabsorption, steatorrhoea, cirrhosis and dark urine. There is an association of PSC with ulcerative colitis: as many as 5 per cent of patients with ulcerative colitis may progress to develop primary sclerosing cholangitis, and about 70 per cent of people with primary sclerosing cholangitis have ulcerative colitis. The following blood studies may suggest the diagnosis of primary sclerosing cholangitis:

- elevated alkaline phosphatase or γ-glutamyltransferase (GGT)
- elevated serum transaminase level (but may be normal)
- elevated serum bilirubin level (in advanced stages)
- serum albumin and prothrombin time abnormal (with advanced disease)

- immunoglobulin IgG and IgM levels elevated in 48 and 80 per cent of cases, respectively
- the presence of perinuclear antineutrophil cytoplasmic autoantibodies (p-ANCAs) in 60–82 per cent of patients.

Radiological imaging can aid diagnosis: endoscopic retrograde cholangiopancreatography (ERCP) and magnetic resonance cholangiopancreatography (MRCP).

88 A

Gilberts' syndrome is a common hereditary cause of increased unconjugated bilirubin in the bloodstream. Mild jaundice may appear with exertion, stress, fasting and infections (but there may be no symptoms). It has an autosomal dominant pattern of inheritance.

89 C

Acute alcoholic hepatitis is an acute inflammation of the liver secondary to alcohol excess. Symptoms include jaundice, hepatomegaly, ascites, fatigue and hepatic encephalopathy. Peripheral stigmata of cirrhosis also include spider naevi, scleral icterus, palmar erythema, gynaecomastia and asterixis. The diagnosis is made by taking a full medical history, physical examination, ultrasound, and bloods tests (abnormal liver and clotting function tests: aspartate aminotransferase (AST) and alanine aminotransferase (ALT), prothrombin time (PT)).

90 G

Hepatic metastases is a malignant neoplasm that has spread to the liver from a primary site. Colon cancer can spread to other organs in the body including the lungs and liver (stage III disease). Between 20 and 25 per cent of patients with colorectal cancer have liver metastases at the time of their diagnosis. Patients present with jaundice, anorexia, nausea, fevers, pain in the upper right part of the abdomen, and weight loss. Blood tests demonstrate elevated plasma alkaline phosphatase and carcinoembryonic antigen. An ultrasound and CT scan of the abdomen will confirm the diagnosis.

27. Haematuria

B&L **For further reading, see *Bailey and Love*, Chapter 71, 'The kidneys and ureter' and Chapter 72, 'The urinary bladder'.**

91 C

Renal cell carcinoma is also known as hypernephroma, Grawitz tumour or clear cell carcinoma. The classical triad of presentation occurs in 10–15 per cent of patients: haematuria, flank pain and a loin mass. Patients can also present with malaise, weight loss, anorexia, polycythaemia (secondary to excess erythropoietin production), anaemia (secondary to depression of erythropoietin), varicocele (secondary to obstruction of the testicular vein), hypertension (secondary to renin secretion by the tumour), hypercalcaemia (secondary to ectopic parathormone production by the tumour), cannonball metastases (which may disappear after nephrectomy), pyrexia of unknown origin and nephritic syndrome.

92 E

March haemaglobinuria occurs when blood (haemogloblin from red cells) is seen in the urine after strenuous exercise. The repetitive nature of severe exercise caused by mechanical trauma may result in haemolysis. Free haemoglobin released from lysed red blood cells is filtered into the urine. Defects in red blood cell membrane have been identified in selected patients.

93 A

Transitional cell carcinoma of the bladder is the most common cause of painless haematuria. Transitional epithelium lines the entire urinary tact, so these tumours may arise from the renal pelvis to the end of the urethra in females and to the end of the prostatic urethra in males.

Patients commonly present with haematuria, dysuria, polyuria and nocturia. If left untreated, local invasion of the bladder neck may lead to incontinence. Obstructive hydronephrosis and clot retention are also recognized complications. There are recognized *risk factors*:

- *Cigarette smoking*. Smoking increases the risk of developing bladder cancer nearly 5-fold. As many as 50 per cent of all bladder cancers in men and 30 per cent in women are linked to cigarette smoke.
- *Chemical exposure at work*. About one in four cases of bladder cancer are caused by exposure to carcinogens. Dye workers, rubber workers, aluminium workers, leather workers, truck drivers and pesticide applicators are at the highest risk. Arylamines are the chemicals most responsible.
- *Radiation and chemotherapy*. Women who received radiation therapy for the treatment of cervical cancer have an increased risk of developing transitional cell bladder cancer. Some patients who have received chemotherapy with cyclophosphamide (Cytoxan) are also at an increased risk.
- *Parasite infection*. In developing countries, infection with schistosomiasis has been linked to bladder cancer.

28. Prostate cancer

B&L **For further reading, see *Bailey and Love*, Chapter 73, 'The prostate and seminal vesicles'.**

94 E

Staging is one of the most important factors in determining the best way to treat prostate cancer. This patient has stage T4 disease. The cancer has spread to the bladder, rectum, lymph nodes, or distant organs (bone). This cancer is not curable, but treatment is directed at improving the patient's quality of life. Treatment options may include:

- hormone therapy
- external-beam radiation (in selected cases: radiotherapy for pain from bone metastases)
- surgery (TURP) to relieve symptoms such as bleeding or urinary obstruction
- watchful waiting – for older men whose cancer causes no symptoms or for those who have another serious illness.

95 A

This patient has stage T1 disease (intracapsular tumour surrounded by a normal prostate). This patient is well. Surgery coupled with radiotherapy offers the best chance for a cure. Treatment options include the following.

- For elderly men without any symptoms and/or having other serious health problems, watchful waiting and radiation therapy (external beam or brachytherapy) are reasonable options.
- Men who are younger and healthy may consider watchful waiting, surgery to remove the prostate (radical prostatectomy), or radiation therapy (external-beam or brachytherapy).

96 D

This patient has stage T4 disease. The cancer has spread to the bladder, rectum, lymph nodes, or distant organs (bone). This cancer is not curable, but treatment is directed at improving the patient's quality of life. The patient is suffering from lumbar back pain, which is not responding to medical treatment. Treatment options include:

- hormone therapy
- external-beam radiation (in selected cases: radiotherapy for pain from bone metastases)
- surgery (TURP) to relieve symptoms such as bleeding or urinary obstruction
- watchful waiting for older men whose cancer is causing no symptoms or for those who have other serious illness.

29. Wound infections

B&L **For further reading, see *Bailey and Love*, Chapter 3, 'Wounds, tissue repair and scars'.**

See Table 15.

97 D

This patient has a dirty wound. Examples are wounds made in the presence of pus, a perforated viscus or traumatic wounds. The infection rate is 40 per cent.

98 C

This patient has a contaminated wound. Examples are incisions contaminated by opening the colon, open fractures or animal bites. The infection rate is 20 per cent.

99 A

This patient has a clean wound. Examples are incisions through uninfected skin that do not breach any hollow viscus (inguinal hernia repair). The infection rate is 2 per cent.

100 B

This patient has a clean contaminated wound. Examples are incisions that breach a hollow viscus other than the colon (open cholecystectomy). The infection rate is below 10 per cent.

Table 15 Classification of wounds

Classification	Description	Infective risk (%)
Clean (class I)	Uninfected operative wound No acute inflammation Closed primarily Respiratory, gastrointestinal, biliary and urinary tracts not entered No break in aseptic technique Closed drainage used if necessary	< 2
Clean contaminated (class II)	Elective entry into respiratory, biliary, gastrointestinal, urinary tracts and with minimal spillage No evidence of infection or major break in aseptic technique Example: appendectomy	< 10
Contaminated (class III)	Non-purulent inflammation present Gross spillage from gastrointestinal tract Penetrating traumatic wounds <4 hours Major break in aseptic technique	About 20
Dirty (class IV)	Purulent inflammation present Preoperative perforation of viscera Penetrating traumatic wounds >4 hours	About 40

30. Endocrine

B&L **For further reading, see *Bailey and Love*, Chapter 49, 'Adrenal glands and other endocrine disorders'.**

101 J

The diagnosis is primary hyperparathyroidism. This patient has symptomatic hypercalcaemia with polyuria and polydipsia. The high calcium fails to suppress PTH secretion, making a parathyroid adenoma most likely. This is an important point – a normal PTH in this instance is *abnormal*, since in normal individuals a high calcium would suppress PTH secretion and one should expect in such instances a *low* PTH. The low phosphate fits with primary hyperparathyroidism since PTH has a phosphaturic effect at the level of the renal tubules.

Other symptoms of hypercalcaemia may be remembered by 'bones, stones, abdominal moans and psychotic groans' (i.e. bony pains, renal stones, constipation, abdominal pains and psychiatric disturbances).

Management consists of control of calcium with fluids, furosemide and bisphosphonates. An ultrasound and/or Sestamibi scan may be used to localize the parathyroid adenoma. Definitive treatment is surgical: neck exploration and parathyroidectomy.

102 L

The diagnosis is secondary hyperparathyroidism. This patient demonstrates symptomatic hypocalcaemia with acroparasthesia (pins and needles in the peripheries) and an elevated PTH. Chvostek's sign (gentle tapping over the facial nerve causing twitching of the facial muscles) and Trousseau's sign (carpopedal spasm) would be expected to be positive.

Secondary hyperparathyroidism is physiological compensatory hypertrophy of all parathyroid glands because of hypocalcaemia, such as occurs in renal failure or vitamin D deficiency. PTH levels are raised due to loss of the inhibitory feedback effect of calcium on the parathyroid glands. PTH levels fall to normal on correction of the cause of hypocalcaemia where this is possible.

103 A

This patient has Addison's disease (primary hypoadrenalism), as manifested by hypotension, hypoglycaemia, hyponatraemia and hyperkalaemia, as a result of mineralocorticoid and glucocorticoid deficiency. Diagnosis is confirmed by a short synACTHen (synthetic ACTH) test, whereby the endocrine response of the adrenal gland (cortisol production) is measured in response to a given bolus of synthetic ACTH. An absent or impaired cortisol response in seen in Addison's disease.

31. Rheumatology

B&L **For further reading, see *Bailey and Love*, Chapter 37, 'Inflammation and infection and musculoskeletal tumours'.**

104 F

Crystal-related arthropathy defines a syndrome of synovitis in response to crystal deposition/formation in the joint. There are two main forms: gout and pseudogout. Gout is the more common entity. The main distinguishing features are given in Table 16.

Table 16 Gout and pseudogout

Gout	Pseudogout
Affects smaller joints	Affects large joints
Pain intense	Pain moderate
Joint inflamed	Joint swollen
Hyperuricaemia	Chondrocalcinosis
Uric acid (monosodium urate) crystals: • Needle-like • 5–20 μm long • Exhibit strongly negative birefringence under plane polarized light • Often associated with increased polymorphs	Calcium pyrophosphate crystals: • Rhomboid • Slightly smaller than urate crystals (<10 μm) • Show positive birefringence under plane polarized light
Treatment is analgesia and prophylaxis	Treatment is analgesia; no prophylaxis available

105 K
The diagnosis is septic arthritis until proven otherwise. The organism responsible in this particular instance is *Neisseria gonorrhoeae* (gonococcal arthritis), although the most common organism implicated in septic arthritis over all age groups is *Staphyloccoccus aureus*. Gonococcal arthritis may cause a septic arthritis (as illustrated here with the presence of organisms within joint aspirate), or a reactive arthritis with sterile joint fluid. The treatment consists of oral penicillin, ciprofloxacin or doxycycline for 2 weeks, and joint rest.

32. Hepatology

B&L **For further reading, see *Bailey and Love*, Chapter 61, 'The liver'.**

106 G
The diagnosis is Gilbert's syndrome, which affects some 2–3 per cent of the population. The clinical features are mild, fluctuant unconjugated hyperbilirubinaemia.

The jaundice is typically mild and presents only intermittently, often noticed after an infection or a period of fasting. This is possibly because fasting increases plasma concentrations of free fatty acids which compete with bilirubin for transport by albumin and uptake into liver cells. Bilirubin rarely exceeds 100 μmol/L. There may be mild malaise and hepatic tenderness, but there are no other abnormal physical signs. The liver is histologically normal and individuals have a normal lifespan.

The hyperbilirubinaemia is due to a defect in the regulatory part of the gene coding for bilirubin UDP-glucuronyl transferase; in some cases there is also decreased hepatic uptake of bilirubin. In cases where there is a family history, the pattern of inheritance is autosomal dominant.

107 L
The symptoms, signs and liver function tests are consistent with a mixed cholestatic/obstructive and hepatocellular picture. A high titre of antimitochondrial antibodies is characteristic of primary biliary cirrhosis, which is an autoimmune condition that typically affects middle-aged women.

Antimitochondrial antibodies are found in the serum of over 95 per cent of patients with primary biliary cirrhosis, and of the mitochondrial proteins involved, the antigen M2 is specific to the condition. Diagnosis can be confirmed by liver biopsy.

The course and prognosis is very variable, although the median survival is only 7–10 years. Once jaundice develops, survival is below 2 years. Liver transplantation should therefore be offered when the serum bilirubin reaches 100 μmol/L. Post-transplantation 5-year survival is above 75 per cent.

108 H
The history and liver function tests are characteristic of acute hepatitis, with a predominantly raised ALT reflecting hepatocellular damage ('transaminitis'). The travel history and the timing of the events make viral hepatitis A the most likely cause in this particular case.

Serum transaminases rise 22–40 days after exposure, IgM rises from day 25 and signifies recent infection; IgG remains detectable for life. Infection with hepatitis A virus never progresses to chronic liver disease and only rarely causes fulminant hepatitis, so the mortality rate associated with hepatitis A infection is about 0.1 per cent.

33. Abdominal trauma

B&L **For further reading, see *Bailey and Love*, Chapter 26, 'Chest and abdomen'.**

109 A
Gunshot wounds are a clear indication for laparotomy even if the patient is not clinically shocked. The trajectory and projectile of a bullet is unpredictable and the damage is difficult to assess from inspection.

110 B
The patient is stable enough to undergo DPL, but not to be transferred to the radiology department for a CT scan ('doughnut of death').

111 C
This patient appears stable and if his peritoneum is intact he may be a suitable candidate for conservative management (routine observations).

34. Lumps

B&L **For further reading, see *Bailey and Love*, Chapter 45, 'Pharynx, larynx and neck', Chapter 25, 'Trauma to the face and mouth', Chapter 36, 'Foot and ankle', Chapter 27, 'Extremity trauma' and Chapter 37, 'Inflammation and infection and musculoskeletal disorders'.**

112 F
A dermoid cyst is a subcutaneous lump that develops mostly in the midline along the lines of fusion in the face and neck. It is a result of the inclusion of epidermal cells deep to the skin, which can be congenital or secondary to trauma.

113 D
This is also known as a dermatofibroma. They often occur on the lower limbs and like implantation dermoid cysts, often follow trauma. They are skin-coloured in appearance and woody-hard in consistency.

114 G
This is an ivory osteoma, a benign swelling which results from an osteoma (benign bone tumour) of the outer table of the skull.

35. Intestinal polyps

B&L **For further reading, see *Bailey and Love*, Chapter 65, 'The small and large intestines', Chapter 68, 'The rectum' and Chapter 69, 'The anus and anal canal'.**

115 G
This operation involves excision of the entire colon and rectum, with an ileo-anal anastomosis. It is a complex operation but aims to preserve continence.

116 H
These polyps do not have a malignant potential and can be left alone.

117 C
It is not possible to establish adequate clearance distally and preserve the anal sphincter. The whole of the colon is required to be excised to avoid potential future malignancy.

36. Cancer staging

B&L **For further reading, see *Bailey and Love*, Chapter 68, 'The rectum'.**

118 F

119 I
Clarke's levels are defined as:

- I – confined to the epidermis
- II – extends to the papillary dermis
- III – extends to the papillary-reticular junction

- IV – extends to the reticular dermis
- V – invades the subcutaneous tissue.

120 B

121 D

- Dukes' A – limited to the colonic wall
- Dukes' B – extends through the muscularis propria (muscle layer of wall)
- Dukes' C – mesenteric lymph node involvement
- Dukes' D – spread beyond regional lymph nodes, or involvement of adjacent structures.

37. Anaemia

B&L **For further reading, see *Bailey and Love*, Chapter 13, 'Perioperative care'.**

122 G
Glucose-6-phosphate dehydrogenase deficiency is a hereditary condition in which red blood cells break down, or haemolyse, when the body is exposed to certain drugs, stress, or infection. Risk factors include aspirin, antimalarials, non-steroidal anti-inflammatory drugs; and it is more common in patients of African American, or Middle Eastern descent, with a male predominance.

123 B
This condition is inherited in an autosomal dominant pattern, mostly seen in northern Europeans. The defect in the cell membrane leads to premature cell destruction.

124 D
The diagnosis is sickle cell crisis. The definitive diagnosis is made through haemoglobin electrophoresis.

38. Complications of blood transfusions

B&L **For further reading, see *Bailey and Love*, Chapter 2, 'Shock and blood transfusion'.**

125 F
The risk is highest in blood maintained in suboptimal conditions where the blood is not stored properly prior to transfusion.

126 B
This occurs secondary to a leucocyte antigen and may be treated with anti-pyretics and antihistamines.

127 G
The patient is usually immunized to the antigen at previous transfusion, but the concentration of the antibodies are too low to produce an immediate reaction. Production of a further IgG usually one week later leads to delayed haemolysis.

39. Fractures

B&L **For further reading, see *Bailey and Love*, Chapter 27, 'Extremity trauma'.**

128 C
This is also known as a 'march' fracture.

129 G
This is an incomplete, or 'greenstick', fracture because it involves one of the cortices.

130 D
The patient has Paget's disease as evidenced by thickening of the bone and a bowed tibia. It is associated with an isolated elevated alkaline phosphatase, in the presence of normal calcium, phosphate and aminotransferases. A bone scan is useful for determining the activity and extent of this condition.

40. Acid–base balance

B&L **For further reading, see *Bailey and Love*, Chapter 13, 'Perioperative care'.**

131 F
The pH reveals acidosis which must be respiratory in origin in view of the elevated carbon dioxide. The elevated bicarbonate indicates a metabolic alkalosis in an attempt to correct the abnormality. This scenario occurs in chronic respiratory disease.

132 A
Respiratory compensation occurs within minutes. The carbon dioxide rises in an attempt to compensate for a metabolic alkalosis, as in pyloric stenosis.

133 D
This is an uncompensatory respiratory acidosis as the bicarbonate is within normal limits. This occurs in acute ventilatory compromise, as in a flail chest.

41. Informed consent

B&L **For further reading, see *Bailey and Love*, Chapter 9, 'Surgical ethics'.**

134 C
An adolescent has the right to accept surgery, but those under 18 cannot refuse life-saving surgery and the parents can consent for this procedure.

135 D
The surgeon has a legal and moral duty to treat the patient in an emergency under these circumstances.

136 A
Even those 'under section' to receive psychiatric treatment cannot be forced to have a surgical procedure for a physical condition if they are deemed to be competent.

42. Neck anatomy

B&L **For further reading, see *Bailey and Love*, Chapter 45, 'Pharynx, larynx and neck'.**

137 D
Acral parasthesia is a common manifestation of hypocalcaemia secondary to damage to the parathyroid glands.

138 F
Injury to the external laryngeal nerve, which supplies the important cricothyroid muscle (that controls voice pitch), produces this deficit.

139 B
These are the manifestations of Horner's syndrome.

43. Innervation of lower limb muscles

140 F
The deep peroneal nerve is also known as the anterior tibial nerve. It supplies the muscles of the anterior compartment of the leg, extensor hallucis longus, extensor digitorum longus, extensor digitorum brevis, peroneus tertius and, most importantly, tibialis anterior.

141 C
Quadratorus femoris is composed of three vastus muscles and rectus femoris. The femoral nerve also innervates iliacus, pectineus and sartorius.

142 A
The obturator nerve supplies the muscles of the medial compartment of the thigh.

44. Brachial plexus injuries

B&L **For further reading, see *Bailey and Love*, Chapter 24, 'Neck and spine' and Chapter 33, 'The spine'.**

143 B
This is an Erb's palsy, caused by injury to the upper trunk of the brachial plexus (C5–6). The hand takes on the 'waiter's-tip' position.

144 E
This is Dejerine–Klumpke palsy, caused by injury to the lower roots of the brachial plexus (C8, T1). It gives the typical appearance of a 'claw-hand'.

145 G
The patient has lost all innervation to his right upper limb.

45 Herniae

B&L **For further reading, see *Bailey and Love*, Chapter 57, 'Hernias, umbilicus and abdominal wall'.**

146 C
Obturator hernias protrude through the obturator foramen which is bounded by the superior pubic ramus, anterior acetabular wall and ischio-pubic ramus. Irritating the obturator nerve can lead to referred knee pain, or parasthesia in the inner thigh.

147 F
Umbilical hernias in the adult population are rare. They are secondary to increased intra-abdominal pressure. A para-umbilical hernia is seen more commonly.

148 D
Femoral hernias pass through the femoral canal which is below and lateral to the pubic tubercle. The femoral canal is medial to the femoral vein and contains fat and lymphatics ('Cloquet's lymph node').

46 Tumour markers

B&L **For further reading, see *Bailey and Love*, Chapter 76, 'Gynaecology', Chapter 61, 'The liver' and Chapter 68, 'The rectum'.**

149 A
CA-125 is used for the diagnosis, response to treatment and follow-up for recurrence in ovarian tumours.

150 F
Alpha-fetoprotein is often raised in hepatocellular carcinoma. It is the most widely used tumour marker for the condition and is an independent prognostic indicator.

151 D
CEA (carcino-embryonic antigen) is the tumour marker of choice for patients with colorectal cancer.

47 Adrenal pathology

B&L **For further reading, see *Bailey and Love*, Chapter 49, 'Adrenal glands and other endocrine disorders'.**

152 E
MEN 1:

- parathyroid gland adenomas
- pancreatic islet cell tumours
- pituitary gland adenomas.

MEN 1 patients can have duodenal ulcers secondary to:

- Hypercalcaemia secondary to hyperparathyroidism
- Excess steroid production from Cushing's disease
- Zollinger–Ellison syndrome (gastrinoma)

153 A
An ACTH-secreting lung tumour produces adrenal cortical hyperplasia and Cushing's syndrome. This is separate from Cushing's disease which is produced from hypersecretion of ACTH from the anterior pituitary gland.

154 D
Addison's disease is adrenocortical insufficiency. Sixty per cent are autoimmune in aetiology (pernicious anaemia and Hashimoto's thyroiditis). Other causes include TB, lung metastases and amyloidosis.

48. Chest pain

B&L **For further reading, see *Bailey and Love*, Chapter 50, 'The breast' and Chapter 51, 'Cardiac surgery'.**

155 E
Tietze's syndrome, or costochondritis, presents with pain and swelling over the sternocostal junction. It is usually evident on palpation and perceived pain is exacerbated with respiration.

156 F
The condition should be suspected in the absence of cardiac pathology. Oesophageal manometry is used to make the diagnosis.

157 C
The symptoms of a pulmonary embolus include sudden-onset dyspnoea, tachypnoea, pleuritic chest pain, cough and haemoptysis. On clinical examination, a pleural friction rub may be auscultated. Risk factors are attributed to Virchow's triad. Her risk factors include recent pregnancy which changes blood flow dynamics and increases the risk of a pulmonary embolus developing.

49. Metabolic abnormalities

158 A

Both loop diuretics and corticosteroids cause hypokalaemia.

159 E

Hypophosphataemia occurs during acute alcohol withdrawal. It is also a risk when giving carbohydrates after fasting ('refeeding syndrome').

160 B

Burns cause the release of myoglobin secondary to rhabdomyolysis. This blocks the renal tubules, resulting in acute renal failure and consequently hyperkalaemia.

50. Lung volumes

B&L **For further reading, see *Bailey and Love*, Chapter 52, 'The thorax'.**

See Figure 6.

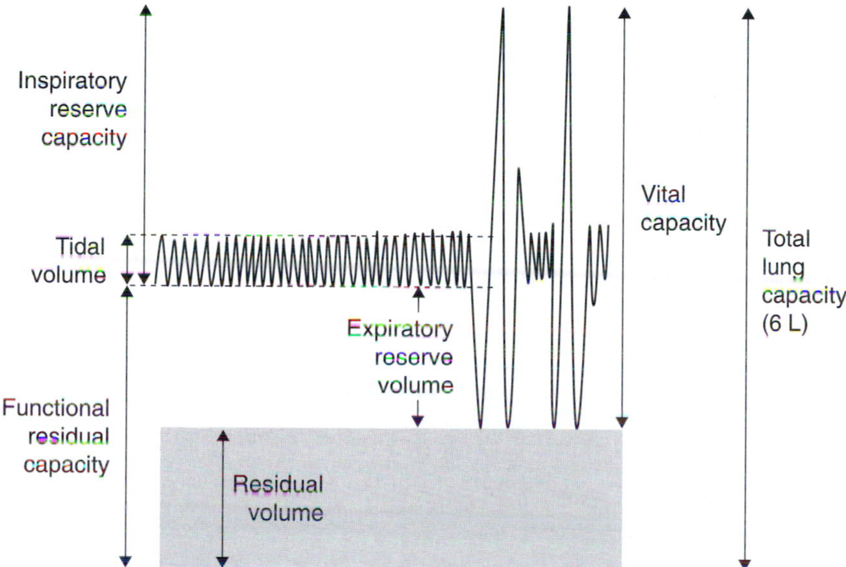

Figure 6 Lung spirometry.

161 C

- Functional residual capacity.

162 F

- Residual volume.

163 B

- Tidal volume.

Index

Numbers in italics refer to figures; those in bold type refer to tables